Drawing from LINE to LIFE

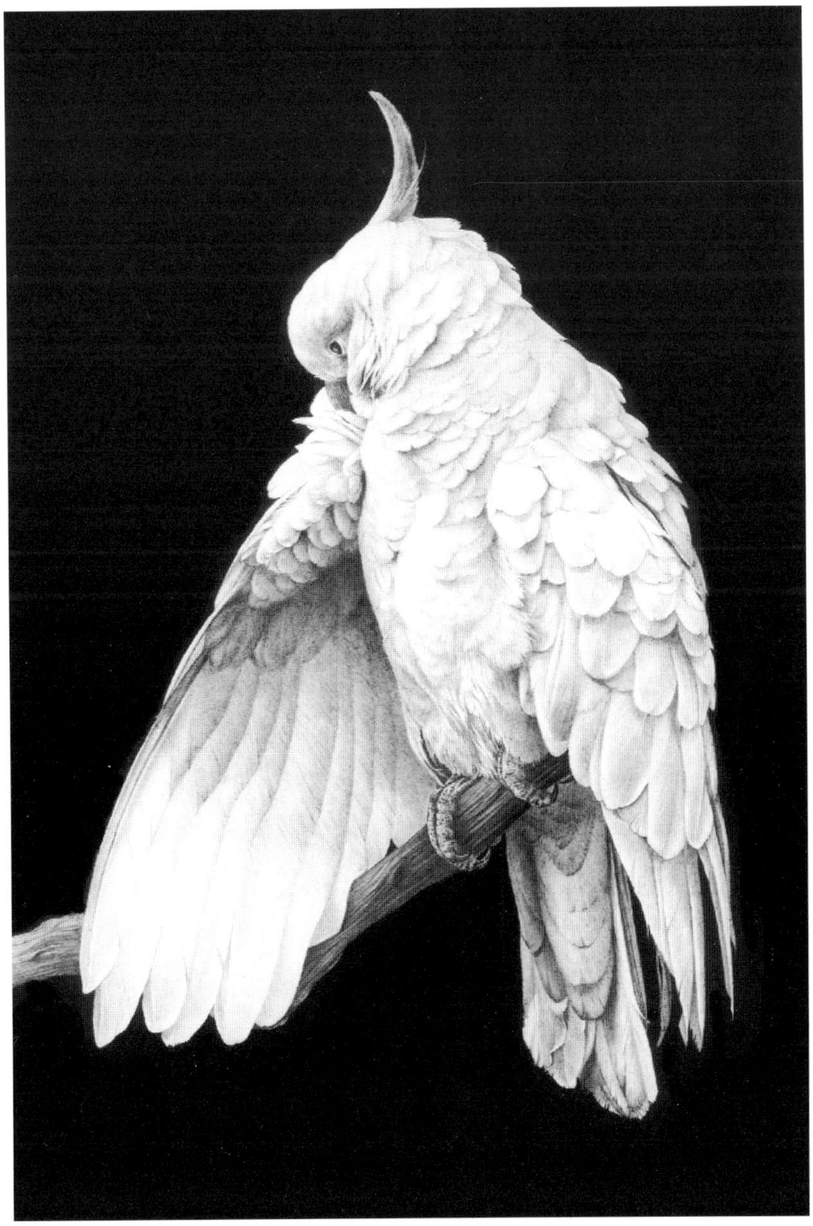

| MIKE SIBLEY DIP.A.D. |

Dedicated to my wife Jenny, for her support and putting up with many months of being an artist's and writer's widow, and who might remember who I am.

ISBN 978-0-9551578-0-6

First edition 2006
Reprinted 2007
Reprinted 2013

Published by MSFA Publishing
Greenfields House, Sessay, Thirsk,
North Yorkshire, YO7 3ND, England

www.ThePencilPoint.com

www.SibleyFineArt.com

QUACKS The Printers
Jackson House, 7 Grape Lane, Petergate
York, YO1 7HU, England

Book Design by L.M.Weil Graphic Design
email: lindaweil@exemail.com.au

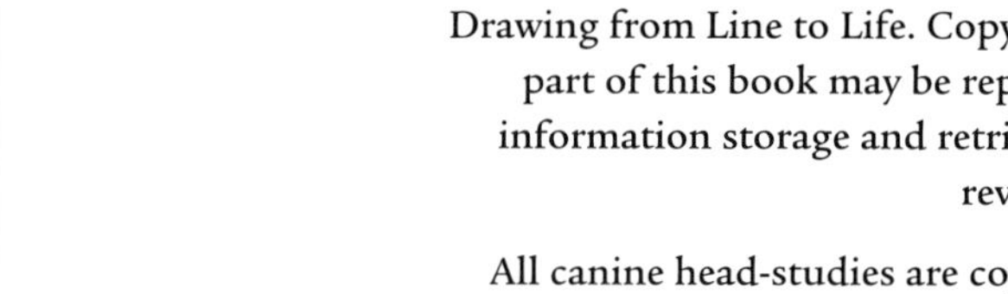

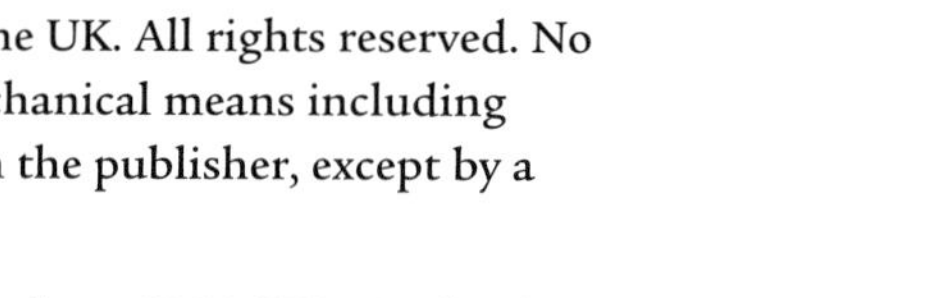

Foreword

by

David Shepherd OBE, FRSA, FRGS

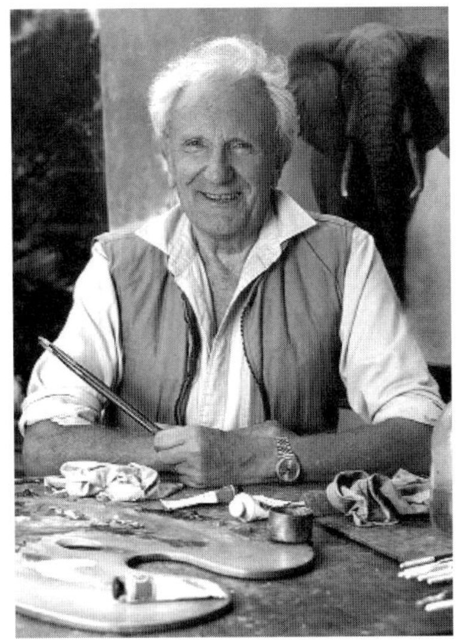

I was delighted when I received a request from Mike Sibley to write a brief foreword to the reprint of this book because, for many years, I have admired his incredible work. Moreover, some years ago, my wife and I purchased a gorgeous black and white landscape, illustrated on page 227, *Done Balin'*, which encapsulates all that I love to paint in oils; a long distant past when bees were buzzing and there was no pollution and everyone seemed to take life at a more leisurely pace. We bought the print to remind us of Cookie and Willow, our two bearded collies who we adore and who rule our lives.

Looking through this magnificent volume, I am absolutely amazed at Mike's talent and what he achieves with a pencil. It is more than a book of lovely illustrations. It is a mine of information, demonstrating his technique in the minutest detail and it is a source of inspiration and information for those who work in this difficult medium. In short, Mike's book is unique and surely a work to treasure for anyone who is interested in English landscapes, portraits, and, in my view, dogs as well! So read it, enjoy it and learn from it. Thank you Mike for producing such a master work.

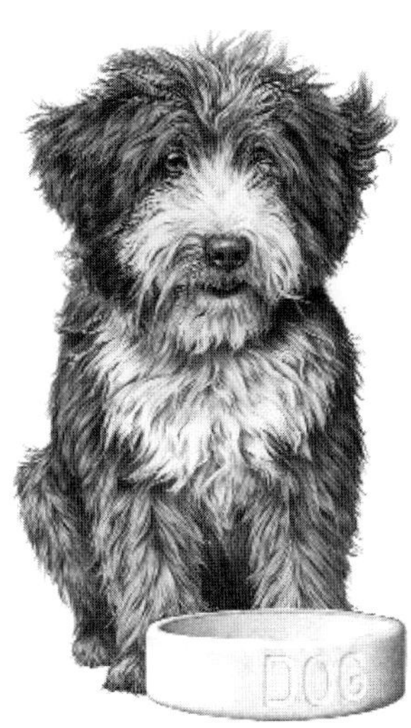

Introduction

'I pray every day that God makes me like a child, that is to say that He will let me see nature and interpret it as a child does, without prejudice.'

Jean Baptiste Camille Corot

We are all born with the ability to draw. As soon as a baby learns to hold a crayon or pencil it begins to create. It doesn't paint, it doesn't engrave or carve - it draws. It is not my intention in this book to teach you to draw but rather to help you along the more pleasurable path of self-discovery. To re-discover the innate drawing ability that you were born with - to see with the clarity of the child that you once were.

All you need is a few basic tools - pencils, an eraser, and paper. You don't even need a studio. I drew all the small illustrations and demonstrations in this book sitting not at my drawing board but on a bar stool at my workbench, working by the light of a desklamp.

The pencil itself, humble, unassuming, and often derided, is, in my view, the most efficient, accurate and controllable medium available to any artist. It's a living tool, an extension of the hand and mind.

Somewhere in between a rapid sketch, a line drawing and photo-realism, you'll discover your natural inclination. Only practice will lead you to where you feel most comfortable, and your individual style, as intimate and personal as your handwriting, will develop. Over time, practiced techniques will become ingrained in your brain until you no longer need to give them conscious thought. At that point your mind has control of your pencil, and the real journey of discovery begins.

Be proud of what you produce, and don't deprecate pencil. In the seventeenth century, the French Royal Academy's view was that drawing held the higher regard over painting, because drawing appealed to the mind, while colour appealed only to the senses.

'Every child is an artist. The problem is how to remain an artist once he grows up.'

Pablo Picasso

Times have changed, and opinions have altered. So let's begin, and between us help to restore drawing to its rightful place - an art medium that commands respect as a true creative art form.

Mike Sibley

Acknowledgements

I am indebted to a wonderful support team, without whose assistance this book would never have seen the light of day. This has been a truly international endeavour, made possible only by the Internet and Adobe, whose PDF files have been circling the globe.

First and foremost, I have to thank my tireless Australian graphic designer Linda Weil, for the many long hours spent on layout design, and for her professional guidance in all aspects of publishing. My sincere thanks also go to my editor Monica Burnette in America, for kerbing my wilder flights of fancy, correcting my wayward grammar, and shaping the individual chapters into a cohesive book. And not forgetting my intrepid 'test pilots' and proof readers Edith Harris (UK) and Phill Bearden (USA) for telling me when I was complicating the simple, or not explaining in a lucid manner; to my father Philip, for his continuing support and assistance; to my fellow forum members at ArtPapa.com; and to Toby Levin (and everyone in the DrawingTogether2 group at Yahoo!) for her constant nagging, until I cracked under the strain and began to write.

My grateful thanks also go to the following contributors; in no particular order, except for Diane at the top of the list because, alphabetically, she's nearly always last:

Diane Wright - *www.dianewrightfineart.com*
Jim Hicks
Bethany Kerr - *www.sketchesbybethany.net*
Rosalie Ferry
Carol Rosinski - *www.toadhollowstudio.com*
Rose Baggs
Edith Harris - *www.eyshasfineart.co.uk*
Lucy T Conway
Margaret Dent - *www.margaretdentfineart.com*
Geary Wootten - *www.gearywootten.com*
Rebekah Lynn - *www.rebekahlynn.com*

And for permission to reproduce their copyrighted images and products:
Berjaya, my open-edition art publisher
Burns Pet Nutrition - *www.burns-pet-nutrition.co.uk*
Kopykake (Kobra K5000) - *www.kopykake.com*

Biography

'Drawing is not what one sees but what one can make others see.'
Edgar Degas

Mike Sibley was born in 1948 in the small country village of Orsett in Essex, England. After moving to Cheshire, he attended Sale Grammar School, where he showed an early talent for monochrome work, often illustrating his essays with ballpoint pen drawings. He graduated in nine subjects including Art and Pottery.

Aged eighteen years, Mike attended the Manchester College of Art and Design and, from 1967-70, the Leeds College of Art and Design, where he was awarded his Diploma in Art and Design in Fine Art (Dip.A.D.), which is now the BA honours degree.

Mike met his wife Jenny in 1977, and she encouraged him to draw her dogs as a logo design for her Kennel Club pedigree forms. Jenny never got those drawings, but it was the start of Mike's successful transition to the professional art world. Drawing commissions by day, and working as a taxi driver at night, the demand for commission work soon meant that he could give up cab driving and concentrate on art alone.

Prints of Mike's work soon followed, and in 1980 he became one of the World's few professional graphite artists. His highly successful range of canine head studies became the UK's best selling series of prints in the 1980's. Achieving worldwide acceptance, this range is still in print today. His first limited edition print, an edition of 50 Irish Water Spaniel prints, sold out at its Crufts 1990 release in just three and a half hours.

'MIKE, WHO USES ONLY GRAPHITE PENCIL FOR HIS WORK, WILL OFTEN SPEND OVER TWO HUNDRED HOURS ON A SINGLE DRAWING, AND HE IS RENOWNED FOR HIS FINE DETAIL AND CAREFUL OBSERVATION.'

Mike, who uses only graphite pencil for his work, will often spend over two hundred hours on a single drawing, and he is renowned for his fine detail and careful observation.

In 1991 Mike and Jenny returned to the countryside, buying a four-acre smallholding in Yorkshire, where they still reside. Here they are surrounded by their horses, cats, chickens, sheep, goats, and, of course, dogs. When Mike's not drawing he's usually to be found working with his tractor, welding in his workshop, or exploring Nature along the two-mile farm track on which they live. The beauty of the Yorkshire countryside and his many farmyard animals make a regular appearance in his work.

Mike designed and built his well known website (*www.SibleyFineArt.com*) in 2001 and the Starving-Artists.net site, where artists can showcase their work. He also hosts his own drawing forum at ArtPapa.com. He continues to write the well-known artists tutorials for SibleyFineArt.com, and it was from these tutorials that this book began its life.

Contents

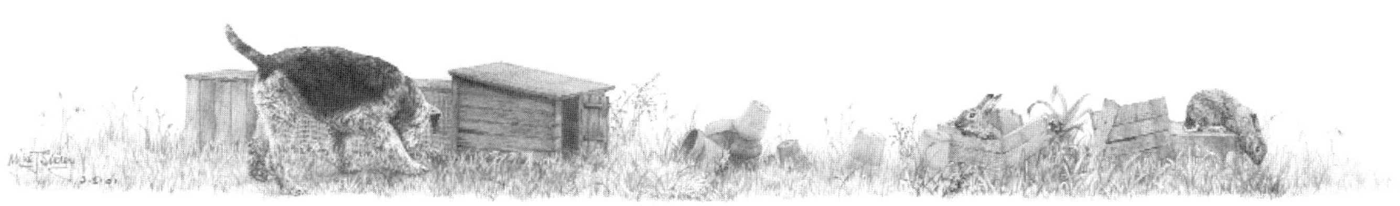

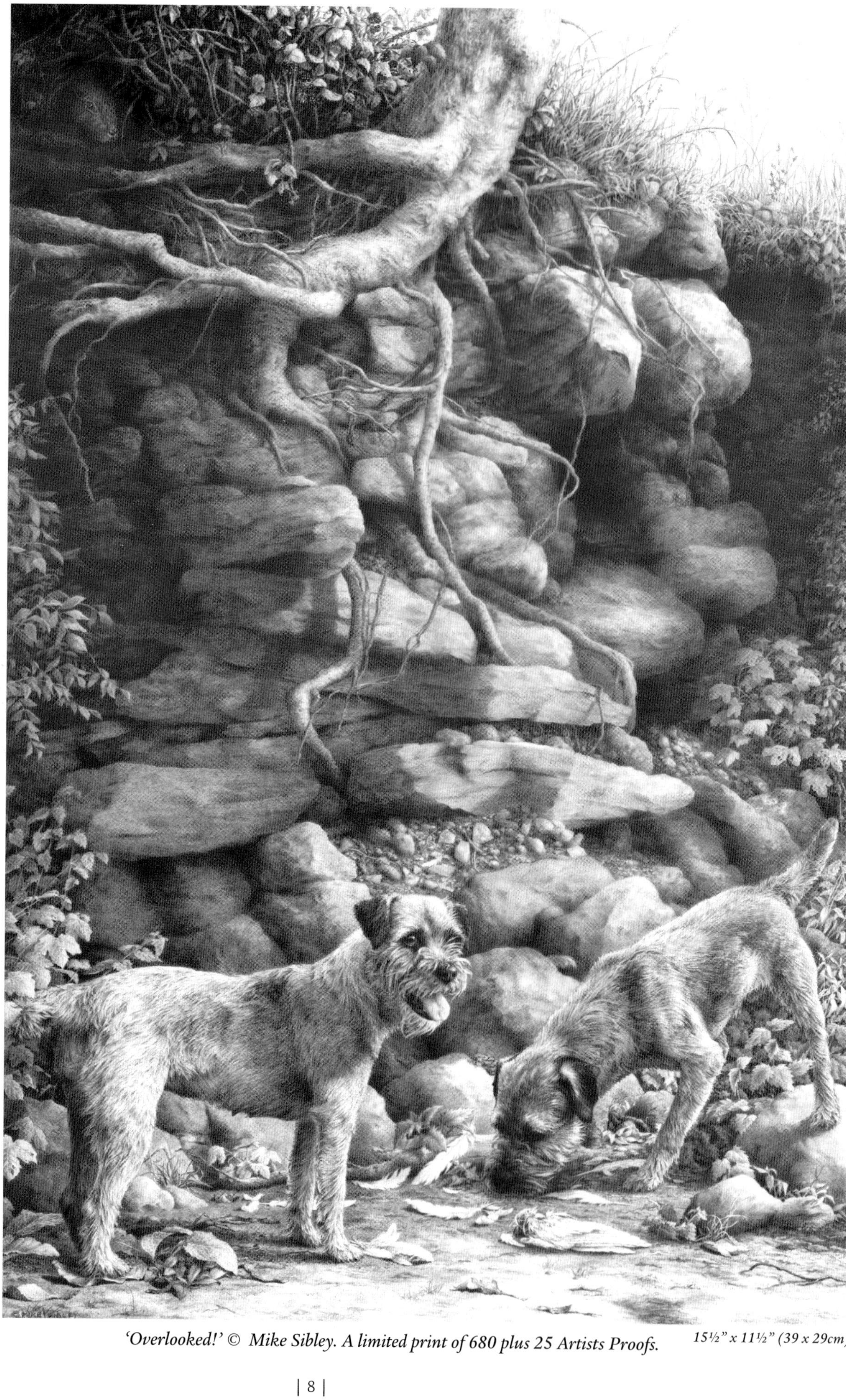

'Overlooked!' © Mike Sibley. A limited print of 680 plus 25 Artists Proofs. *15½" x 11½" (39 x 29cm)*

From Line to Life
explained...

There are, in my opinion, three styles of drawing - Line drawing, representational drawing incorporating tone and form, and a style attempting a reality that echoes Life.

No one is better or worse than another, just different. But in terms of techniques they do present a natural course of learning. I say 'learning' and not 'improvement' because technical prowess and artistic ability are not the same thing. You will learn many techniques throughout this journey but your masterpiece may well be a beautifully executed line drawing.

A simple line drawing may elicit a quick glance in passing. A drawing that includes basic shading and three-dimensional shaping may hold the brain for a moment while it looks a little deeper. But a fully-fledged, realistic, three-dimensional drawing that takes detailing to a new level should hold the brain's attention and not release it until it has analysed it in full. The first brings quick recognition. The second adds little to the experience. But the third is absorbed and possibly educates.

I am not in any way belittling simpler forms of drawing. The greatest joy is drawing simply for fun; seeing what you are capable of, exploring an image, attempting a likeness, recreating a texture. All these things amount to a worthy enterprise. No message; nothing more than a personal journey of exploration. It all depends, I suppose, on your goal as an artist. Drawing for fun is a wonderful exercise. But sooner or later you will begin to test your own abilities to see if you can exceed your previous standard. No-one likes to take a step backwards so your drawing will inevitably improve step by step.

With continuing practice, the day will dawn when you find that testing yourself no longer holds much interest. You no longer need to think about which technique to employ to achieve a particular look. Your pencils have become extensions to your hand, which is itself an extension of your mind. You think; you draw. Now you will wish to extend your boundaries and show the world not your personal drawing prowess but the message behind it, the very essence of what you are trying to convey with your drawing. Excuse me for a moment while I

'THERE IS SO MUCH TO LEARN. BUT IT ALL STARTS WITH A SIMPLE LINE DRAWING.'

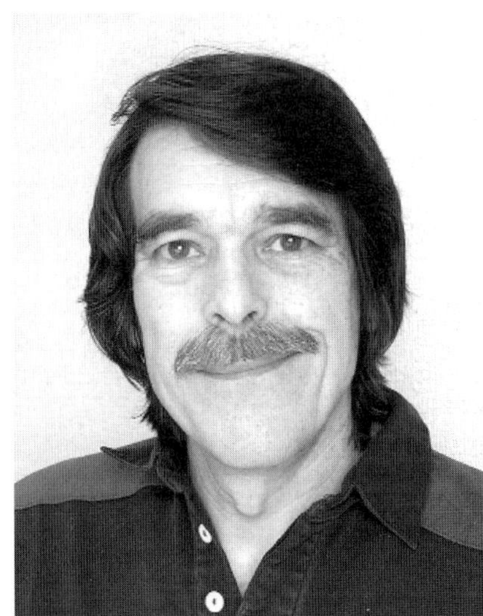

slip into dog-talk – it's where my experience lies. For many years I saw each canine portrait as a technical challenge and strove to achieve the goal presented to me. Now I look at source photographs of a dog and see past the physical drawing to the underlying challenge of, for example, character or movement. I know I can draw it. It is no longer a question of displaying the physical body for my viewer to enthuse over but a project that is centred on the story that I wish to tell or the emotion I want to arouse.

Analysis shifts focus to other aspects of the subject. The work may become more detailed if it is the minutia that contains the message. In my case I have a love of natural forms so I pay as much attention to a foreground leaf as I do to the central character. Or it may become ever simpler as the analysis homes in on the essential element within the drawing. As with the drawing that powers its way into the mind with exaggeration or abundant detail, so simplicity too can be a powerful tool. Many years ago I saw a drawing of a Cheetah that consisted of just a few sinuous lines. The liquid movement and sheer strength depicted by those lines has stayed with me to this day. The coat texture, the eye, the facial features... none were important. Analysis by the artist of his personal feelings for that animal (whether studied or instinctive) had reduced that drawing to its absolute essence with an incredibly powerful result.

Line to Life then follows a natural progression and any stage can be developed into an art form in its own right.

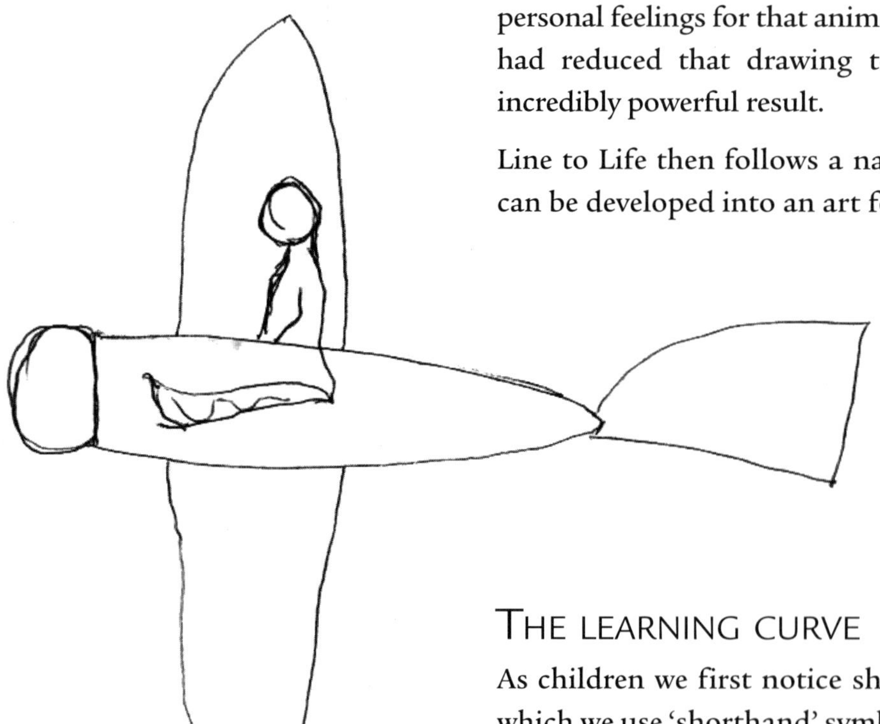

The learning curve

As children we first notice shape - outlines and features - for which we use 'shorthand' symbols and line. A house is typically a square box with four square windows, a central door and a pointed roof. Whatever the variations may be one thing remains constant – it is always drawn as seen square on to the viewer and therefore in two-dimensions.

A face is a circle. Inside, an arc represents the mouth and two opposing arcs form eyes. The nose may be omitted entirely – possibly because it has no definable sharp outline. The Airplane shown here illustrates much of our early learning. I discovered this drawing beneath the wallpaper of our guest bedroom. You will notice that it makes no attempt to depict solid form and is pure, two-dimensional drawing. Everything is drawn as though it was facing the viewer and everything is in its rightful place. It has two wings that are, well, wing-shaped and protrude from the body of the plane. The tail is at the rear. The circle at the front is the propeller as seen, quite logically, from the front. And the pilot sits inside the fuselage.

'Painting is easy when you don't know how, but very difficult when you do!
Edgar Degas

Strange that this is a propeller-driven monoplane. We have them fly regularly overhead from a nearby RAF training school but jet fighters and helicopters overfly us also. Why not draw one of those? I strongly suspect that what we have here is a collection of symbols. All aircraft are propeller-driven. Just as all trains are steam powered. And all houses are square with four windows.

I believe these symbols, or vestiges of them, are retained throughout our life and are the brain's storage and naming system – much in the way that your computer uses icons to signify functions. We all recognise the 'Print' button even though our printer looks nothing like the one on the icon.

In later life our brains continue to use outline to quickly distinguish one object from another, to name it, pigeonhole it and move quickly on. It's an efficient system based on easily stored symbols – the same symbols we possessed as children. But it teaches us little or even nothing as no specific information is retained. But, as you will read throughout this book, we can turn this symbol system to our own advantage and control the brain of our viewers.

Moving on

I'm sure that many people go through life using just this basic recognition system but we, as budding artists, will begin to notice more. Initially, perhaps, we notice the rounded form of the things we are drawing. We begin to add experimental tone to line drawings – maybe just a suggestion of shadow to differentiate one plane from another. We may include the shadow beneath the chin, for example, to show that the face is nearer the viewer than the neck. With this and similar discoveries comes learning. The young artist's brain begins to look a little deeper - to categorise then pause to analyse the subject in three as well as two dimensions.

Inevitably this leads the Artist to enquire ever deeper. Analysis of the subject now stores information not only of outline and three-dimensional shape but also of the lighting and other environmental influences. These are the factors that produce the image the way we see it. Here also begins the discovery of real texture.

Representation to 'reality'

In the representational, tonal drawing stage, surfaces and their textures will probably have been suggested. I am often asked to critique work where tonal drawings attempt to portray hair by the addition of an over-layer of 'hairy' lines. The result succeeds in part - the viewer knows the object is hair-covered - but fails to provide the information that translates into near-reality.

In reality, tonal shaping of an animal's body does not exist as an entity. What we see as three-dimensional shape is solely the result of reflections of light from the hair. It seems more appropriate then to draw the hair and not the tone. Observation has shifted the essential basic approach. Not hair texture added over tone but the hair itself relaying the underlying three-dimensional form by virtue of its shadows and highlights.

Oh to be an Artist

One of the wonderful benefits of being an artist is the growing ability to see what is around you; not to just note it in passing but to really see it. The more detailed your work becomes the more you will search subconsciously for information to store. Have you ever been stung by a plant? A stinging Nettle perhaps? Seen in passing they are quickly identified and seen merely as objects to be avoided.

I know people who can walk the full length of the two-mile farm track on which I live and see nothing at all except, possibly, the Hambleton Hills four miles distant. I, on the other hand, can find enough to interest me for hours right at my feet. Realism in drawing brings out the Sherlock Holmes in you. You'll not only notice those nettles, you'll appreciate the hairy stalks, the ridges and valleys of their leaves and the insect life that lives upon them. You'll wonder at the infinite variation of leaf curl and store it away for future use and see too the way that shadows cast by upper leaves separate them visually from the leaves below.

There is so much to learn. But it all starts with a simple line drawing.

'Why does it make our hearts fill with such excitement when we are working on something that we consider beautiful?

Maybe it is the feeling that some lost time will never be remembered again, or that something beautiful will remain unnoticed...'

Bethany Kerr, Artist

Learning the language

I have a love for the minute things in life. The little spots of beauty that many people fail to see attract me. It's what drives me; my love of the subject and a real desire to say 'Hey, look at this. Isn't it beautiful!'. Of course it's no use we artists just drawing something quickly in a sort of shorthand that only we recognise - to remind us of what we saw - that will say little to anyone else. The act of drawing itself is enjoyable but of no real importance if it isn't saying something. It's the result that counts. I feel the need to reproduce everything in all its glory so the viewer can properly appreciate the beauty of what I am displaying before them and to do that I had to learn the 'language'. Unlike other languages, however, we are allowed the freedom to each invent our own. What matters is not the language itself but the content. Writers, for example, fall into many camps – the Hack, the Novelist, the Author, the Ghostwriter – each producing a certain quality of work. Where one might use suggestion another will write fully fleshed descriptions. Each employs different styles but all carry a specific message. I consider my own work to be descriptive – usually exposing every element to view and taking my time to do so.

'When I saw your work I could feel what you were saying so clearly ... and it was not rushed ... and I did not want it to be! I wanted to let my eyes move into the drawing and live there a while. There is no part of your drawings that do not invite careful consideration. This is a rare thing and I think it is why you are such a success. People want to be invited to slow down and see the beauty you have found for them.'

Artist Carol Rosinski talking about my drawings.

Practice and more practice

Practice is half of the battle. Couple practice with a knowledge of techniques and the ability to see, to really experience your subject, and you cannot fail to progress. Each drawing will set a standard for the next and, as no one likes to regress, you cannot fail to improve.

Occasionally you will greatly exceed your own expectations and produce a milestone drawing – one that you will look back on in years to come with great affection, recognising the great leap forward. It's as though you were allowed a glimpse into a secret garden full of new ways of thinking. You can only gain permanent access to this garden by constant practice; to pause is to revert to old ways. Only once you have made it your home will you realise there is a gate at the far end. The life of an artist is one continuous journey so let's get started!

The tools I use - and others...

'THE TOOLS WE USE AND THE PAPER WE DRAW ON, COUPLED WITH PERSONAL VISION AND PREFFERED TECHNIQUES, ALL COMBINE TO PRODUCE OUR OWN UNIQUE STYLES. THIS CHAPTER DETAILS MY PERSONAL FAVOURITES TO ASSIST YOU IN MAKING YOUR INITIAL CHOICES BUT ULTIMATELY YOU MUST USE WHATEVER YOU FEEL COMFORTABLE WITH.'

I am often asked about the tools I use to create my drawings. Do I use traditional wood-cased pencils or mechanical ones? What type of eraser do I use? What paper do I draw on? Do I work at a desk or a table? The simple answer to these questions is that I use the tools I feel most comfortable with.

Pencils

The development of 'lead' pencils began with the discovery of natural deposits of graphite (thought to be lead) in the English Lake District. Brand names such as Cumberland and Derwent still allude to the area. Later Conti in France mixed powdered graphite with clay and fired the result in a kiln to give different grades, much as we use today.

It's the proportion of graphite to clay that determines the grade - the softer grades contain more graphite and the harder grades incorporate greater amounts of clay. Today the graphite is synthetically produced, which is of real benefit as the grades can be precisely reproduced from batch to batch. In the U.S.A. Alfred Berol (founder of the Eagle Pencil Company in 1856) set up a scientific system using special testing machines to produce seventeen equally spaced degrees of hardness. Despite this, subtle differences between manufacturers may lead you to prefer one brand to another. My own preference is for Staedtler.

Pencil grades

Various grading methods exist but in the most common system the grades generally range from 9B to 9H. The soft grades are B, 2B, 3B and on to 9B. The hard grades range from H to 9H. In between lies the neutral HB and, just to confuse us, the black sheep of the range is called F and slots in between HB and H. I use F quite extensively.

In general I would suggest limiting your initial arsenal to 2B as your softest grade and adding HB and 2H. There is little to be gained by extending this range, although you might add a 6B and 4H. For example, grades softer than 6B begin to show their granular structure, which can be visually distracting if you are attempting to produce a flat, believable area of tone.

Why this selection? Well, I find that 2B, HB and 2H have sufficient spread and overlap to do almost anything. In reality I actually use 2B, F and 2H the most.

I do not, for example, see the point of including a B grade in your collection as a heavy hand with HB will overlap a light hand with 2B. This overlap extends to most grades. My personal exception is the use of HB and F, which are next to each other in hardness and the difference is slight. I use both but I prefer F to HB as I find it easier to control. Likewise H can be dispensed with. Next to F in hardness, its tones are easily covered by the overlap of F to 2H. I also use 4H and sometimes 6H, which I use for adding very light tones over previous drawing where I want to dull the white content.

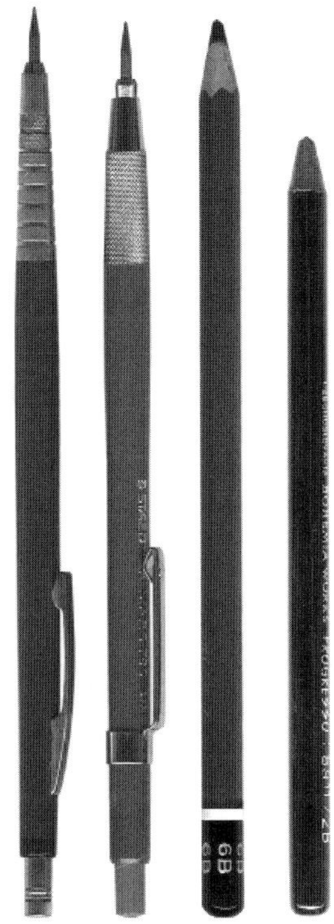

Left to right:
Faber clutch pencil, Staedtler clutch pencil, Wood-cased pencil, Progresso solid graphite stick.

Pencil types

There are three basic types of graphite pencil available - wood-cased, solid graphite, and mechanical pencils. You might also like to try experimenting with carbon and charcoal pencils. Although I use carbon pencils for sketching they are outside the scope of this book, as I don't include their use, or charcoal, in my work.

Since its invention, the traditional wood-cased pencil has served artists well and is the preferred choice of many. Usually cased in Cedar, these pencils possess a lightness that can aid subtle shading techniques but they also suffer from a number of disadvantages. For instance, a variety of points can be achieved but very fine points tend to require the use of an emery board or other abrasive surface. Sharpening, in my opinion, should be accomplished simply and effectively in the shortest time possible so the artist's concentration is not broken.

For bold styles of drawing, solid graphite pencils, such as Progresso, hark back to the early days of the square-section graphite sticks from the English Lake District. They are very useful, although care must be taken not to break the body in use. Available grades tend to be in the softer range. Although I keep both 2B and 6B I rarely use them except for outdoor sketching and for lightly washing tone over an indented area (see Indenting tool).

Mechanical pencils come in two forms - the 'automatic' pencil with a thin .5mm or .7mm lead that doesn't need sharpening (akin to the propelling pencil) and the more robust clutch

A LITTLE HISTORY...

The Borrowdale graphite deposit discovered in 1564, in the English Lake District, remains the purest ever found.

Its value was such that it was mined for only six weeks a year and the loaded wagons, bound for London, were escorted by armed guards. In 1830, when lead cost £15 a ton, a similar weight of graphite was worth £3600!

During the time of its production the export of graphite was prohibited so the English Guild of Pencilmakers, who handcrafted wooden cases for the writing sticks, enjoyed a worldwide exclusivity of the finished product.

pencil, also known as the drafting pencil or lead holder. This type takes a 2mm lead (similar to a wood-cased pencil) that is held in place by a three-pronged clutch at the drawing end. Depressing the top cap opens the clutch around the lead at the base allowing it to be extended or adjusted in length to suit the current application.

Almost since the day I started drawing in earnest (way back in the 1970s) I have eschewed the use of conventional, cedar-cased pencils. They have their place and many artists use nothing else but I use only one, a 6B, and then infrequently. Why? Well, in my opinion there's little worse than using a tool that continually shifts its length and weight and I don't see any advantage in drawing with a tool that has to be constantly relearned. On the other hand the clutch pencils that I use possess none of these faults and many advantages.

The clutch pencil remains a known constant at all times. Neither length nor weight change. Balance remains true, affording very precise control. Sharpening involves only the enclosed lead and not the outer casing, allowing needle-sharp points to be easily achieved when required. The only thing you can't do with a clutch pencil that you can with its wood-cased cousin is to tuck it behind your ear. Some makes of clutch pencil even include a built in sharpener that, although rarely used, can be a lifesaver during outdoor drawing trips.

But, I hear you say, if the leads are interchangeable how do I know which grade I've put in which holder? Well, the good folks at Staedtler have thought of that. Every time you buy a pack of a dozen leads, you'll find inside a replacement, colour-coded end cap for the pencil. Green, for example, denotes grade F, purple denotes 2B, red 2H and so on. I suggest you keep the original chrome cap on the HB in case you need to use the integral sharpener, which the plastic colour-coded ones dispense with.

If you decide to try clutch pencils I recommend you purchase just three and load them with 2B, HB and 2H - these will achieve almost all the effects you might need. There are various minority manufacturers of clutch pencils but the brand leaders tend to survive longer. My 2H and 4H leads are loaded into Faber Castell clutch pencils but the majority are by Staedtler who produce the widest range of graphite grades and dedicated tools. When buying Staedtler pencils I prefer the pencil-like slim barrel of the Mars Technico lead holders (*Reference #780*) rather than the fatter 'economy' ones (*Reference #782 and #788*).

Sharpeners

For mechanical pencils

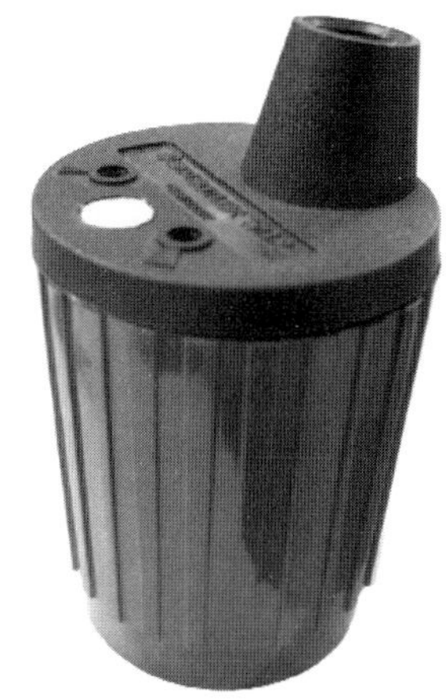

Staedtler sharpener

If you are drawing with clutch pencils the Staedtler sharpener (Reference #502), shown right, is a 'must have' item. Purpose made to sharpen the leads inside these pencils; it is capable of producing needle-sharp points if required. On top is a lead cleaner (a fibrous insert into which the sharpened pencil point is pushed to clean it of loose graphite powder) and, to either side of this, are two small holes - extend the lead into either to obtain a set length - one gives a sharp point, the other a standardised blunt tip. You can also save the waste graphite and use it with a brush for gently adding tonal values - a method you'll meet later in Basic Techniques.

For wood-cased pencils

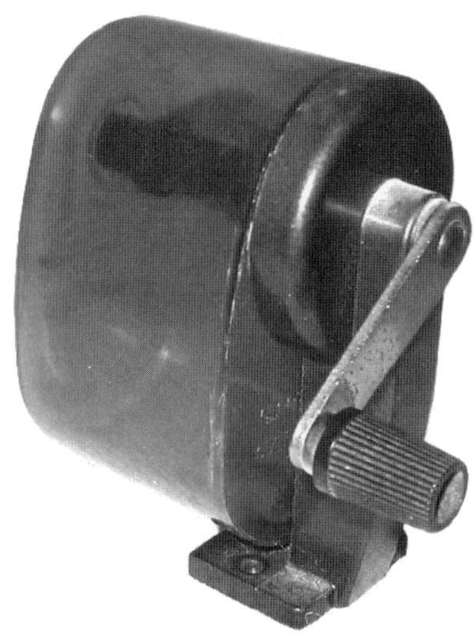

Mechanical sharpener for wood cased pencils

The conventional sharpener (see below) is used not only for sharpening wood-cased pencils but also to obtain very usable points on stick erasers. For speed of use and consistency of point you may also wish to purchase a hand-cranked or electric desktop sharpener. Buy the finest quality you can afford in order to obtain the best results.

Other sharpening tools include emery boards for fine finishing of points and a sharp craft knife or scalpel for shaping custom points. Personally I work with a rounded, chisel point that rarely requires sharpening and can, as you will learn later, make almost any mark desired with a simple turn of the body of the pencil.

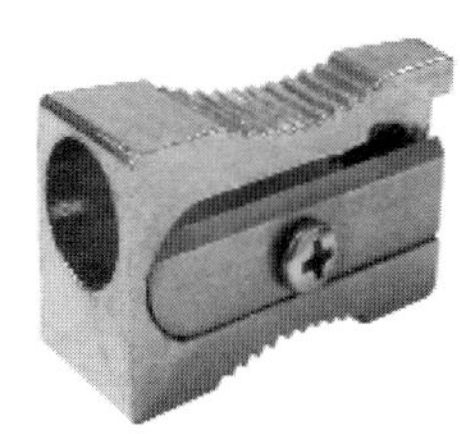

Conventional sharpener for wood cased pencils

Erasers

Conventional types

A wide variety of conventional erasers exist but many may cause more harm than good. Beware! Throwing away an eraser that has just caused a hole to appear in your paper is a hard way to learn.

The main requirement is for a soft eraser that can gently remove graphite and not grind it ever deeper into the paper's surface. It is for this reason that I no longer use typewriter or ink erasers. Apart from the block eraser (which I only use for cleaning the margin around a drawing on completion) I make most use of Staedtler's stick erasers because of their versatility. Variants of the Staedtler 'click' model are available under the 'Alvin' and 'Pentel Clic' brand names and are readily obtainable from many stationery suppliers. The refills will

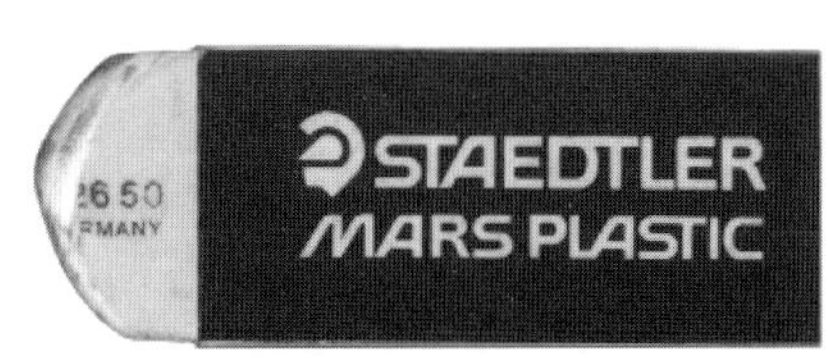

Recommended Staedtler eraser

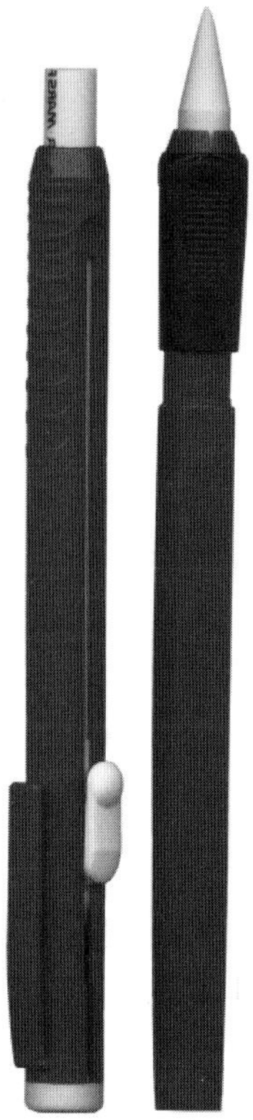

Staedtler stick erasers

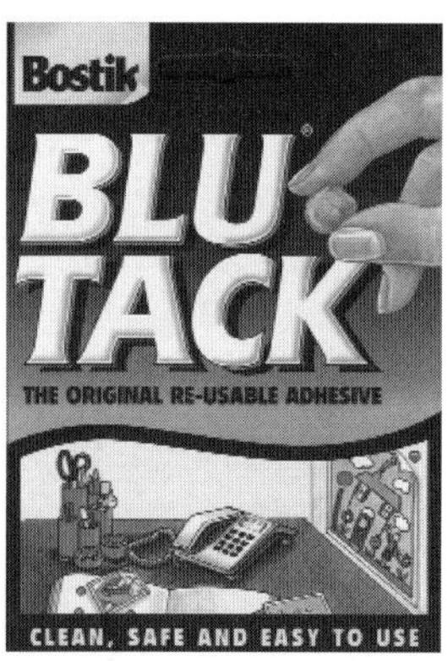

Blu Tack - the wonder product for graphite artists

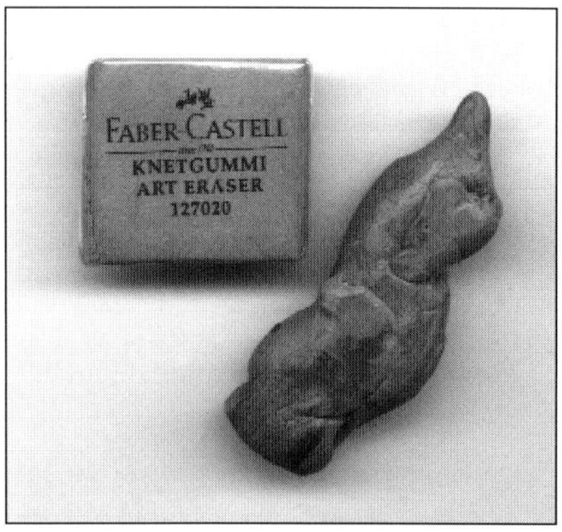

The kneadable eraser - also known as putty rubber.

equally fit all stick erasers. The soft art eraser core can be formed to a very fine point using a conventional pencil sharpener. Alternatively, a scalpel or craft knife can be used to cut a chisel point, which can be used to cut fine lines into softly applied graphite. The same effect can be achieved with a fine point but the chisel point adds a useful stiffness that helps steer the eraser with more accuracy.

Unconventional Types

There is only one in this category and I cannot praise it enough. Bostik's Blu-Tack has allowed my drawing to develop like no other product ever has. Perhaps its greatest strength lies in its unparalleled ability to remove already applied graphite and to 'draw' light or white shapes within it. The lightest touch lifts graphite straight from the paper and, with practice, whole areas can be gradually faded. In pre-applied graphite, it leaves a clear, sharp-edged impression of easily preformed shapes so it is exceptional at suggesting background foliage, hairs in areas of deep shadow, or anywhere that a suggestion is to be preferred over sharp focus. For making additions at a late stage it is unsurpassed - a determined series of touches of Blu-Tack can take 6B almost back to white before finishing with a conventional soft art eraser.

There are similar products on the market but they are not as effective as Blu-Tack, which works because of its inherent stickiness. Don't use it like a standard eraser or rub with it. Just touch it on graphite and it lifts the top layer off. With practice you can achieve remarkable graduations and subtleties of tone. You'll be reading much more about this product throughout the book as my own drawing style relies heavily on its use.

Blu-Tack is a UK product and is readily available only in Australia, the UK and Scandinavia. For this reason I have set up a facility on my website (www.SibleyFineArt.com) where Blu-Tack may be purchased.

Kneadable Eraser

The kneadable eraser (also known as the putty rubber) is, as its name suggests, malleable and may be formed into any desired shape. It is an excellent and versatile eraser and many artists use it extensively. I used one myself until I purchased a batch that crumbled in use. It was that event that led me to the discovery of the benefits of Blu-Tack, which I tried out of desperation and necessity.

Kneadable erasers will pick up graphite with just a touch but, not being sticky in nature, this action requires a little force.

The working edge can of course be pinched, rolled and pressed into any shape that you desire from a fine point to a knife-edge or flat stump and, being dense in nature, the shape will hold true for some considerable time.

However in many applications kneadable erasers may require a rubbing action to work efficiently. This action is not recommended, as any mechanical movement may have the effect of forcing graphite further into the grain of the paper rather than removing it. Try the kneadable eraser for yourself, experiment and make your own decisions about its use. It may be the eraser for you.

Hand-guards

A VARIETY OF METHODS TO PROTECT YOUR DRAWING

You may think these aren't necessary; that they get in the way of your work; that you cannot see all of your drawing all of the time. But the first time you use one you'll fully appreciate the benefits. A 'hand-guard' is not a single tool as it encompasses many methods but they all share the same goal - to keep the artist's hand off the drawing surface. The villain here is the natural oil that keeps your skin supple and waterproof. Make no mistake; if you do not use a hand-guard, the oil from your skin will irrevocably alter your drawing surface. You will find this particularly noticeable (and almost impossible to repair) in areas of flat tone. Your hand or finger, wherever it touches your paper, will leave an oily film that will attract graphite. That area will behave differently from those surrounding it and will inevitably show as a darker tone.

My own hand-guard in use. Note the twin clips to prevent rotation and movement.

I have seen many methods described over the years - including hand-rests formed by flat, wooden bridges, raised by blocks at each end to keep them clear of the drawing surface. Have you ever studied a workman digging a hole? As he digs he stands in the hole, not on the surrounding, higher surface. As with the workman, I prefer my hand to be on the same level as my paper, not poised above it.

I once tried using light cotton gloves but didn't like the loss of feeling of the pencil between my fingers. Some artists I know use cotton gloves regularly; sometimes with the finger ends cut off. Others wear latex gloves. Personally, I would advise against using these methods, as the secondary benefit of a hand-guard is lost - the prevention of smudging caused by the hand resting and dragging on previously applied graphite. Gloves have the disadvantage of collecting graphite as you work and may smear it across your drawing surface.

A better method is to use a sacrificial strip as a hand-guard. I know artists who use strips of drafting paper and clear polyacetate sheet. Be aware that this last contains static electricity that will attract stray graphite granules to it, and any movement of the strip may grind them into your drawing surface.

The minimum requirement for a guard should be one that cannot physically move and keeps your hand off your drawing surface. Your drawing is thus protected from the oil in your skin and the movement of your hand as you work. The sacrificial strip remains inert and takes all the punishment and damage that your drawing would otherwise suffer.

A useful method, similar to my own, involves using a long piece of scrap matboard (which you can probably obtain free of charge from your local picture framer) and taping it to your drawing table, covering the part of your drawing that you would be resting your hand on. You can easily move it when necessary and it is stiff enough not to move at all.

Personally, I use a strip of the same card that I draw on and measuring about six inches wide and eighteen inches long (15cm x 46cm). Not being as thick as matboard, I feel as though I am working directly on the drawing surface and the tone of the strip exactly reflects the tone of my paper so I don't find it distracting. Not one but two drawing board clips, about two inches (5cm) apart, clip the bottom end to my drawing board. One clip would allow the strip to rotate; two keep it completely immobile. Every few days I turn the strip over and roll a cylinder of Blu-Tack over it to pick up any stray graphite.

'A reminder to 'Put rice pudding in bottom oven at 3pm' has saved me on more than one occasion from incurring the wrath of a hungry wife on her return home!'

The strip has other advantages too. Being flexible I can curve it back and away from my drawing, without unclipping it, at any time to check on the overall progress of my work. I use it to shape my pencil point - a quick scribble soon forms it into the flat, chisel end that I prefer. I can check a tone before I apply it to my drawing. And I can practice drawing shapes such as leaves and keep these as handy references as I invent an area of foliage.

If the telephone rings (I keep a cordless phone on top of my drawing board) I can quickly jot down the order for ten copies of my latest print without disturbing my train of thought. Similarly I can make notes and thumbnail sketches of ideas that spring into my mind as I work. I use it as a memo pad. A reminder to 'Put rice pudding in bottom oven at 3pm' has saved me on more than one occasion from incurring the wrath of a hungry wife on her return home!

Because I use the sheet for all of these purposes I keep the same sheet in use for the entire time span of each drawing. As a drawing often takes over 150 hours to complete, the strip becomes very grubby indeed. You only need to look once at the oil-stained area where your hand has rested to fully appreciate the potential damage that your drawing would otherwise have suffered! Once used you will never again wish to work with your hand on your drawing surface.

And finally, the strip has one other use - I use it as a time sheet - something I find to be of such importance that I'm elevating it to a tool in its own right.

The Time Sheet

The Time Waster's Salvation

In the early days when I drew commissions to generate my income I charged by the hour. Rather than guess or just estimate each day's work span I kept a time sheet. I would 'clock-on' when I first picked up my pencil and clock-off whenever I stopped, even if for just few a few minutes. A typical day might look like this:

10:30/1:05	*2:35*
1:25/2:00	*:35 (stopped for lunch)*
2:44/3:50	*1:06*
3:58/5.45	*1:47*

Total: 6 hours 3 minutes

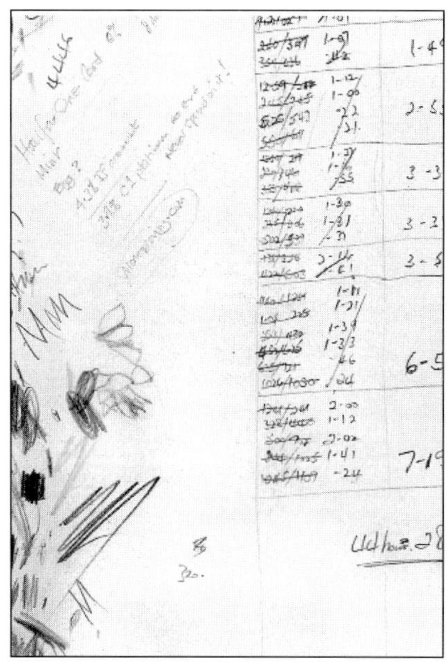

A section of my hand-guard in use showing time sheet.

This taught me a valuable lesson. You'll see that my lunch break was 44 minutes long. It should have been just 30 minutes but I went to check on the ducks and topped up their pond. Then, as I was passing, I stopped to give the goats some more hay and drifted into the vegetable garden and pulled up a few weeds. None of this was necessary and it cost me 14 minutes of lost drawing time. And this is a mild case of time wasting!

I continue this practice today, even though I no longer need to know the completion time. It's a very forceful reminder of time wasted when I thought I'd had a long and productive day only to find, when I totalled the time as I left my studio, that I had only been drawing for three and half hours and not the five hours that I was expecting. I can recommend this system to anyone who works in an environment that is surrounded by distractions.

Work surfaces

OK, we've made our choices and purchases and now, apart

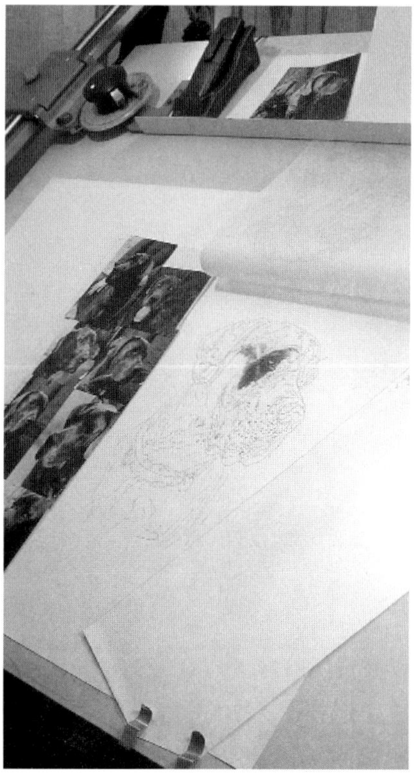

My modified A0 drawing board.

from paper, have our basic tool kit ready for action. So, on what do we work? Space restrictions obviously play a part, as do budgets and personal preferences but some things stay constant.

Main requirements

First and foremost, whether you choose to draw on a board on your lap, a table top, a drawing table or board or sitting at an easel, the surface must be perfectly smooth. You want to stay in control of your drawing and not have flaws or surface indentations from your drawing board randomly appear. There may be times that you choose to use a technique (in the manner of brass rubbings) that relies on laying a particular surface beneath your drawing paper - wood or linen perhaps - in order to reproduce that texture into your drawing. But this should be your choice, not one imposed upon you by your drawing board's surface.

To 'smooth' I will also add 'hard'. I know some artists who prefer a soft surface to work on - achieved by laying additional sheets of paper beneath the sheet they intend to draw on. Try it. Experiment. If it works well for you then use it. Personally, I detest any degree of movement in my paper. Whenever my pencil point touches the paper I want to know that the pressure I'm applying is going to remain a constant factor. Sometimes I'll draw with force to achieve a dark, sharp line; at others I'll draw with the graphite tip barely stroking the surface. It is imperative that the paper remains static and doesn't behave as though I'm trying to write with a marker pen on the top of a waterbed! There's such a subtle difference of line or tone depending on the pressure you apply that having the paper sink beneath your pencil point can severely affect your control. The more constants you can introduce into your drawing technique the better your control becomes.

With these thoughts in mind, your choice of work surface can vary widely while still conforming to the most important requirements. I made my first drawing board from a cupboard door, which I covered with a sheet of Formica plastic laminate. Beneath, I hinged two wooden wedged-shaped legs so they could be folded flat to the board for storage. I used this at home and at art shows for about five years before I progressed to a second-hand professional-style drawing board. The A0 size (48 x 36 inch or 1.2 x 1 metre) surface was a luxury that I had not previously known. Acres of empty board, which I soon learned to fill with source and reference photos surrounding my drawing.

Studio setup

I still use an A0 drawing board but my current one is a draughtsman's board - with modifications. Attached to a massively heavy pedestal with integral spring-assisted height adjustment, it also has a lockable board angle adjustment by means of a handle handily placed just below the front edge. Its main advantages are its completely stable nature and hard, smooth Melamine surface. The personalisation extends to removing the parallel rulers and bolting a metal shelf in their place. This holds a mini-easel that displays my trial drawing (if I produced one before beginning the drawing itself), my reference and source photos, the remote control for my music centre and a cordless phone sitting in its charger. Mounted on the board itself are a digital clock and cups in which I keep balls of Blu-Tack and a selection of blending stumps. Below these, in the bottom right corner, is a lump of old, retired Blu-Tack into which I push freshly sharpened pencil points to clean them of graphite dust.

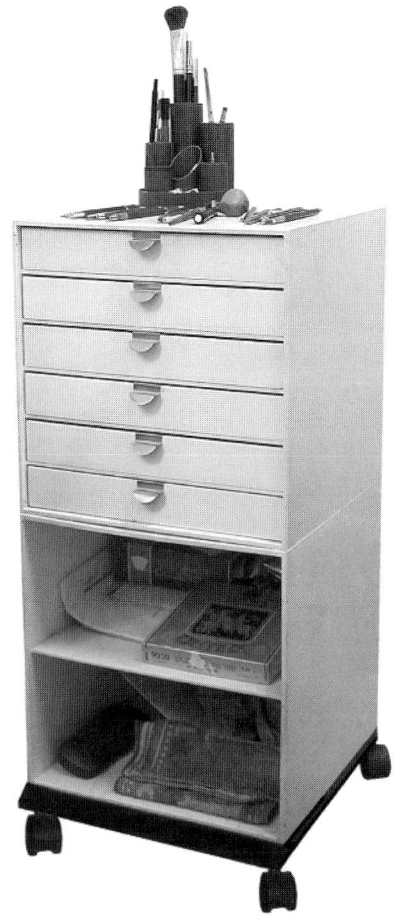

My purpose-made, mobile unit for materials

By the side of my draughtsman's chair is a purpose-made, mobile unit that contains shallow drawers for pencils, packs of leads and Blu-tack and even refills for the coffee machine. In short, it is a work area as self-contained as I can make it. Disruptions are cut to the minimum.

Do you need to go to these extremes? Almost certainly not. One friend and fellow artist produces very creditable commissioned portraits as she curls up on the family sofa with her drawing board lying in her lap. Other friends produce wonderful work from their kitchen tables or spare rooms. It is, as I have mentioned before, all down to personal preference.

Blenders

Tortillons and Stumps

Unfortunately the names of these two blending tools are often ascribed to each other or even described as being interchangeable for a single product. For the record, a tortillon is a small, hollow, rolled paper blender with a single point. A stump (also known as a torchon) is the puny tortillon's big and beefy brother - a solid cylinder of rolled paper with a point at either end. They each have their uses, which you will best discover in practise. I often use old, graphite-laden tortillons as 'pencils' to spontaneously draw far-distant elements in misty scenes, to add subtle texture to old whitewashed walls or to add gentle tone to white areas that I wish to diminish in importance in favour of others - thus ensuring that the eye highlight is the brightest point on the paper.

Colour shapers

These are, as their names suggest, tools intended for oil and acrylic painters. But they are also a useful reminder that any tool may be of use no matter what its original intention may have been.

Colour shapers come in two shapes, two grades and a number of sizes. The chisel-ended shape can at times be used to blend areas of flat tone and the pointed, conical version works as a very creditable blender in tight or awkward situations. Both are mounted into the ferules of paintbrush handles.

One artist I know uses the hard version of these shapers to great effect but I much prefer the soft, flexible type. The effect in use is akin to painting with graphite. Very subtle ranges of blending can be achieved in a way not offered by tortillons, which tend to pick up or absorb a generous quantity of graphite as they blend an area. The flexible colour shaper, while receiving an outer coating of graphite, absorbs virtually none at all. The consequence is that where tortillons tend to lighten an area being blended, the colour shapers merely redistribute the available graphite with a less noticeable change in overall tone. Rolling the point in a ball of versatile Blu-Tack will soon clean the business end.

Experimentation is the key to such tools. I find the pointed version invaluable for blending when drawing remarques - tiny, two-inch (5cm) high drawings in the bottom margins of prints - where no other tool has room to work. You'll find instructions for making your own tortillons in Chapter six.

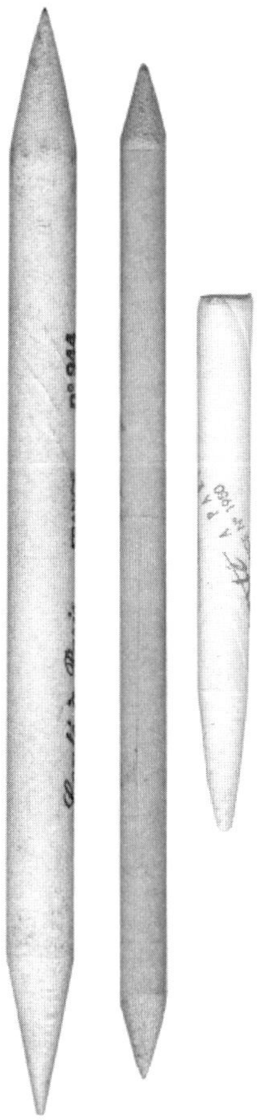

Left: Stumps (Torchons)
Right: Tortillon

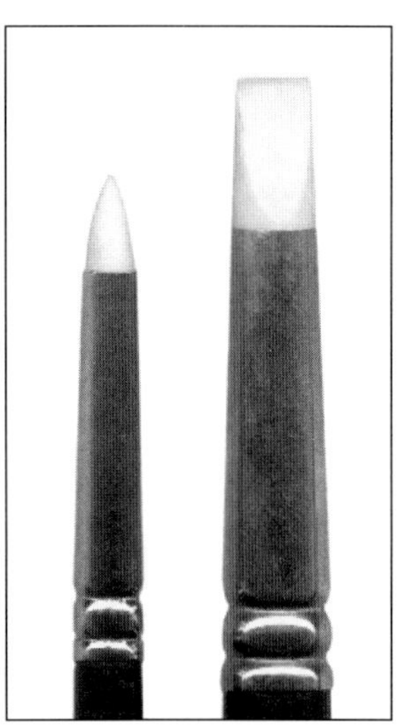

Colour Shapers:
Taper and Flat Chisel points

Other blenders

First, a blender you must never use - your finger. However tempting it may be, never bring your fingers into contact with your paper. As I explained earlier, the hand-guard is used to prevent this very action so don't undo its admirable work.

If you wish to use your finger, first wrap it in something that will protect your drawing from your skin's natural oil. The list of available coverings is endless but you may as well choose a covering suited to the job in hand. My two favourites are kitchen paper towels and soft toilet tissue. The first blends without the graphite absorption of the second whereas the second offers a more subtle blending action. If you use facial tissues make certain they do not contain oily moisturiser.

Chamois leather is a popular (and more professional) alternative. Some artists stress that the leather must be natural chamois; others find that synthetic chamois leathers work just as well. We're back to personal preference again. I suggest, initially at least, that you don't buy chamois from art stores - the prices can be very high. Buy instead large pieces of synthetic chamois leather at an automotive or hardware store. Soak them in washing-up liquid and warm water overnight and then throw them in the washing machine with your laundry. That gets rid of the troublesome oils before you cut them into usable pieces.

Unlike my throwaway tissues, chamois does need to be cared for. If, for instance, it dries out and cracks put a few drops of mineral oil onto your hands and use them to work the oil into the chamois (always use animal-based oils on leather). Then, after a wash in warm soapy water, it will be almost as new.

Don't be blinkered by convention and assume, for example, that because chamois is generally used on the finger that no other method exists. Try slipping a wood-cased pencil into thin chamois and use the tip of the pencil to blend with. An artist friend of mine blends with a felt pad to great effect. Experiment with whatever you find because the tool you didn't know you were looking for may be within your reach right now.

Indenting tools

I thought I'd discovered this technique until someone said "Oh, indenting. I haven't used that for years!". Oh, well. But I did discover what I believe to be the best tool for the job. The tool itself is used to create clean white lines, such as whiskers and similar features, in areas of darker tone or even complex detailing. The lines are pressed into the paper then later drawing is applied across the top to expose them. I know artists who use a variety of tools for indenting ranging from plastic knitting needles to dentists' tools. My own tool consists of a large sewing-up needle mounted in an old clutch pencil. You'll read all about this technique and how to make a tool like mine in a later chapter. In the meantime try a simple tool such as an empty, fine-tipped, ballpoint pen. Make sure it's totally free of ink; pull the ink tube off for safety and experiment on spare scraps of card. When you understand the principle and have exhausted the possibilities of its uses it's time to make your own custom-built tool.

'I THOUGHT I'D DISCOVERED THIS TECHNIQUE UNTIL SOMEONE SAID "OH, INDENTING. I HAVEN'T USED THAT FOR YEARS!"

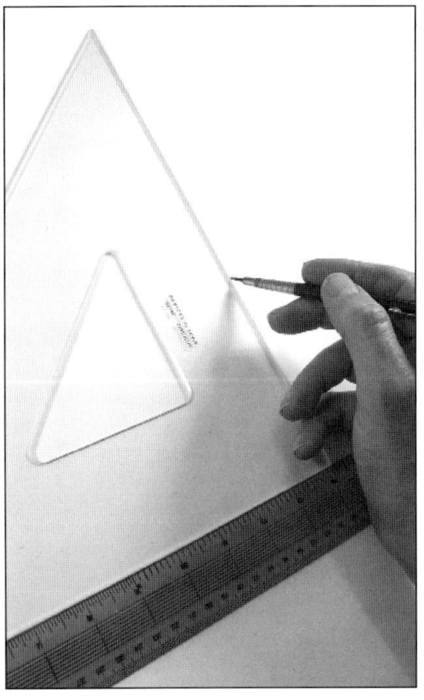

A setsquare (triangle) and ruler are essential for defining the border of your drawing.

Other tools

Setsquares and Rulers

Defining a border for your composition will help you keep control of your drawing as you work. It's also essential if you want to fit your drawing into a standard size of frame or mat. But even more essential is that the border is accurate with parallel opposing sides and square corners. A ruler and 30 /60 /90 triangle (setsquare) will greatly assist you with this task especially if you buy the biggest setsquare available - the bigger it is, the more accurate will be your marking out.

Personally, I draw the border very lightly with a 2H pencil - just heavy enough to see but light enough to completely erase if I need to. If you draw it with too heavy a hand you will indent the paper, which will show if you later decide to extend the drawing area.

A useful tip is to mark the edges of your paper at the top and bottom of both vertical lines and both ends of the horizontal ones. If you later accidentally erase one of your border lines you can use these markers to accurately draw it in again. This assumes that your paper is larger than the image that you are about to draw. It should be! Avoid the terrible discovery that you left insufficient margin if, at a late stage, you need to extend your drawing in order for it to succeed.

A ruler is often essential for perspective drawing. However good you are at drawing by eye, nothing compares to a ruler for drawing straight lines. This is especially true if you are producing an architectural drawing or any study that includes man-made structures or objects that the eye expects to be straight. There's no 'cheating' involved, just common sense. Having said that, I'm not advocating that you draw your finished lines with a ruler. I prefer, at times when I've used a ruler, to treat them as guidelines only. I rule faint lines to guide my later hand drawn lines, as I believe this ensures the necessary accuracy while not inviting a conflict between mechanical and hand-drawn elements.

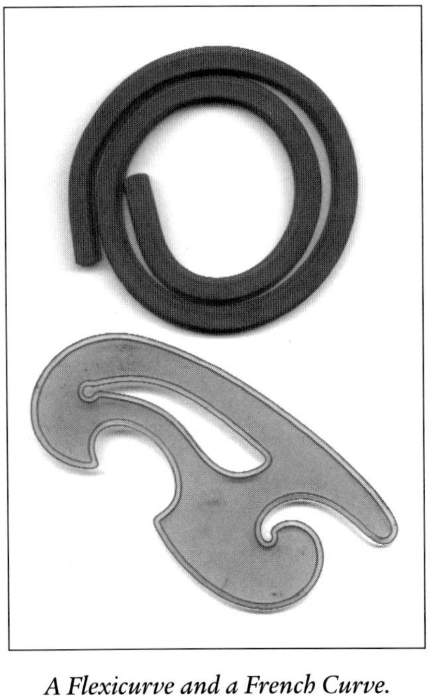

A Flexicurve and a French Curve.

Templates, French and Flexible Curves

There are all manner of shape templates available, produced mainly for technical drawing, which may be of use to you. I don't use any, preferring to construct my own ellipses and curves by eye but if you have difficulty with these then consider buying suitable templates. I include French Curves here - those sinuous plastic shapes that allow you to draw progressively unwinding curves. Again, I don't use or own one, preferring the greater flexibility offered by constructing curved shapes myself. The eye is extremely adept at seeing errors in such shapes and you can use this to your advantage, visual feedback constantly telling you what to alter. When it looks right, it is right. I go into this in more depth in a later chapter.

A more versatile partner of the French Curve is the Flexicurve. This is a flat-bottomed, square-section length of plastic, which you can bend into any desired shape. It can be very useful for creating smooth curves, especially when drawing man-made objects that need to be perfectly drawn. It's possibly a purchase worth considering. Although I have one, I can't recall the last time I used it or even where it is. *(Though my Graphic Designer Linda has kindly supplied us a photo of hers.)*

'BE AWARE THAT THE TOOTH OF MANY GENERAL WATERCOLOUR PAPERS WILL NOT HOLD UP WELL TO ERASING SO BE CAREFUL WITH YOUR CHOICE.'

Paper types

There is only one definite requirement for a drawing paper - the possession of enough tooth (roughness) to hold graphite particles. That's the easy part. Unfortunately from here on it gets more complicated because, unlike other art media where the tools take precedence over the support, in graphite drawing the paper is of paramount importance. A quality drawing paper must be durable enough to take repeated erasure without serious damage to the surface and have sufficient tooth to hold soft grades of graphite while being smooth enough to allow the blending of perfectly graduated tones. Ultimately, experimentation and personal preference will rule your final choice because so many variables exist. Even similar types, such as Bristol, can vary between manufacturers.

Unless you are familiar with technical terms used for papers, I suggest you turn the page and read the glossary before you proceed. Here are a few suggestions:

Recommended Drawing Papers

These can vary widely from cheap notepads to wonderful, hand-made papers. Always use the best paper that you can afford. Cheap papers may drastically reduce the range of available tones and may indeed destroy themselves in time due to their lignin content. Stable rag papers will outlive you and carry your work on through successive generations. Degas used Canson Mi-Teintes; Michelangelo is believed to have used Fabriano Roma papers. The more-affordable paper is machine-

> 'You can choose to work with one or a number of papers; the choice is yours. Personally I usually use Mellotex and prefer to work with one known surface. Other artists often choose their paper surfaces to best match the most prominent texture or technique in their work.'

made, usually lightly compressed and sized, and the surface has a moderate but practical durability. Many possess a medium to coarse vellum finish with a relatively rough tooth.

Bristol board

Without a doubt this is the most durable, all-purpose drawing paper available. The surface is very hard (more heavily compressed than general drawing papers), heavily sized, polished and compressed. It comes in plate and vellum finishes and in several thicknesses. Plate finish denotes a very smooth surface suitable for harder grades of graphite, offering only a modicum of tooth for soft graphite. The Vellum is an excellent finish for graphite pencil, coloured pencil and charcoal use offering ample tooth for the softest grades and, as a result, deep blacks. The use of a hand-guard is a must with this finish.

Mellotex (formerly Ivorex)

I draw on Mellotex, which is a UK product. It is primarily an uncoated, smooth both sides, archival paper (7.5 pH) commonly used by printers but also available in UK art shops. The weight varies between 185 to 385gsm. I use the 290 and 340gsm varieties, which approximates to a 22" x 30" sheet of 140lb watercolour paper. It has a very smooth ivory plate finish (almost devoid of any noticeable surface texture and similar to Bristol smooth) so it takes light tones and detail well but still possesses enough tooth to accept 2B (and 6B, which I rarely use). Mellotex can withstand an amazing amount of punishment without a single fibre lifting so I can (and often do) repeatedly draw over-strength then reduce with Blu-Tack until I achieve the correct appearance.

Strathmore

Probably the most popular range of drawing papers. The Strathmore Bristol Vellum Series 300 has a definite texture to it. Strathmore Bristol Smooth Series 300 is much smoother but seems to have a tiny bit more tooth than any other Bristol. Strathmore Drawing (smooth) 80lb 400 Series is another popular choice from the range with a very pleasant drawing surface.

Canson

Canson Bristol Vellum Acid Free has an obvious pattern and your drawing will lose clarity. However, Canson Bristol smooth is great for smooth skin tones and erases repeatedly and well but you have to work pretty hard to get really dark values. Canson Mi-teintes, as used by Degas, is a pastel drawing paper but I know at least one graphite artist who loves it.

Fabriano

Fabriano of Italy makes some superb hand-made papers. Fabriano hotpressed watercolour 300gsm paper, for example, will take a lot of punishment from Blu-Tack erasing (I know one artist who completely erased an entire stone wall from behind her subject) and indents perfectly if you need to produce clean-sided white lines such as whiskers. It has a relatively hard surface and you are able to build up textures and erase easily. A variety of Fabriano papers exist including Artistico (has a little more tooth than some others) and Uno. They're not cheap but worth the premium.

Illustration boards

I find boards, such as Crescent Illustration Board, too soft to work on and the tooth is not suitable for holding deep blacks. Also take the ultimate use of your artwork into consideration. If it's for printing then this is not, as I explain later, a good choice.

Other papers

- Arches Watercolour Paper Hot Press Smooth is preferred by some, but the paper is really creamy in colour.
- Goldline Bristol Board can expand your available tonal range, as it is a lot whiter than the Strathmore equivalent. It is also smoother.
- Strathmore Pastel Paper 400 series has a good tooth and erases well but has an obvious laid texture.
- Strathmore 100% Cotton Patent Office Paper has an extremely smooth surface, which makes deep blacks difficult to achieve but it's good for fine, hard-grade graphite work.
- Strathmore Bristol Board Smooth 500 series is useful but has an extremely smooth surface making true darks difficult to render.
- Strathmore Drawing Paper 500 series is another good choice but has a little too much tooth for some applications.
- Rising Stonehenge is, I believe, generally a poor choice, possessing little tooth.
- Arches 140 lb hot press is another good choice but erasing tends to lift fibres.
- Other quality brands you may discover include Waterford and Saunders.

If you chat to the salesperson in the shop they may give you offcuts to sample in the hope of future sales. You may also find

Glossary

Bristol: Drawing paper that has two or more sheets pasted together to form plies - 2-ply, 3-ply sheets etc.

Lignin: A constituent of wood pulp that, exposed to heat or sunlight, forms acids which over a period of time destroy the structure of the paper.

Rag: Made from cotton rag fibres. it has no wood pulp content and none of the related disadvantages.

pH: A measure of acidity versus alkalinity. 7pH is neutral; a lower number indicates acidity and a higher number alkalinity.

Acid-free: A stable alkaline paper buffered with calcium carbonate to neutralise acid compounds either atmospheric or as a result of aging.

Archival: The ultimate in non-aging paper with a 7.5 pH minimum and devoid of unbleached wood pulp.

gsm: Indicates Grams per Square Metre in the metric paper weight system - the weight of one square metre. A 22" x 30" sheet of 140lb paper is equivalent to 300gsm (sometimes written as g/m^2).

'I have been trying to figure out which paper I like the best. The last couple of drawings have been on the Bristol Smooth paper. I switched back to the Bristol Vellum recently for comparison. It's amazing the difference the paper really makes. It seems that I have to 'work harder' to get the smoothness I desire. Which means - I have to really push on my tortillon to get the graphite to smooth out and then lift the excess off with my Blu-Tack eraser. Whereas on the Bristol smooth or even the Arches - just a light touch of the tortillon is all I need. But I like the 'feel' and texture of the Vellum paper. It seems to take the darker, softer pencil grades better (2B) and offers an easier texture build up. These are subtle quality differences and I like both papers but I am trying to figure out when to use which paper for the best result.'

Diane Wright, Artist

sketchpads of the same papers, which are excellent for experimentation.

If you wish to print from your drawing

There are a number of considerations to take into account if your drawing is ultimately destined for print production.

Use a flexible paper or board. Flatbed scanners are greatly improved but I still have my work scanned by a laser drum scanner - the industry standard procedure. To do this the artwork has to be taped around a revolving drum. If you draw on illustration board or a similar, thick, non-flexible support you will have three options:

1. To use a process camera (not a good idea - I've never had anything but poor-quality results)
2. To use a flatbed scanner (much better than they used to be) but your paper may have to be trimmed to the size of the scanner bed. The glass bed is often below the level of the surrounding case so correct contact cannot be achieved with over-sized artwork.
3. To have the outer skin of your illustration board stripped from the backing. This can be done but it is not a pleasant job and much better that you use a flexible support in the first place.

Use a white paper if the white will be used as your final highlights. I have had two experiences of a drum scanner picking up the slight off-white of my paper as an actual tone and I know other artists who have experienced the same problem. This causes the printing plate to have a dot pattern within a highlighted area where I actually intended the virgin white to show through. I print in monochrome (actually twin-plate Duotone) and the result is a dull, lifeless print. The problem is exacerbated when printing in colour as the whites can reproduce as pale yellows. I now use a super-white version of Mellotex.... and have the same problem in reverse - I find myself printing on paper that is not quite as white as the paper I draw on. Sometimes you just can't win.

Fixatives

A commonly held belief is that you can use hairspray to fix your drawing. Trained chemists have spent years developing and refining artists' fixatives so don't use a cheap alternative designed purely for sticking hair together. You don't know how stable it is or if it will damage your paper or drawing over time. Respect your own work, use only the best materials and treat your paper to the benefit of a fixative's built-in ultraviolet filter.

A variety of fixatives exist such as the workable types that allow you to erase fixed graphite. Most are aerosol types and use chemicals that will have you struggling from the studio for air. Efficient ventilation is a must - or a gas mask and good pair of running shoes! Personally I prefer to use Winsor & Newton's 'Fixative for Pastel, Charcoal and Pencil'. Spray in a number of light coats while holding your breath. I've used it on really thin 40gsm bank paper with no ill effects. The idea is not to soak the paper, just to lay a thin coat of lacquer on top so it binds the graphite. I've smelled worse brands but you'll need those running shoes to get away while your studio returns to a normal Earth atmosphere! It dries with a matte finish, which offers a number of advantages - one being the formation of a synthetic 'tooth' that permits the addition of further layers of graphite and another is the removal of glare from graphite. With the glare removed, it's often the first time I really get to see my drawing properly. It can be quite magical!

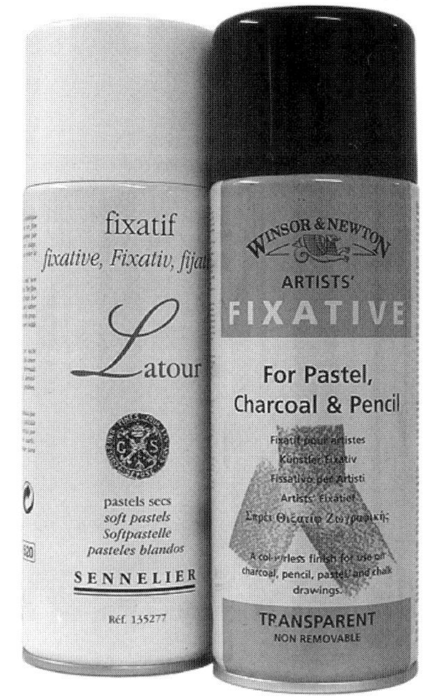

I stopped using one excellent make of fixative when the spray head was redesigned and it developed a tendency to spit. As a result I now always spray onto scrap card at one side of the drawing then, if the spray is even, I'll pass it across the drawing and back. This is repeated until I feel everything is glued into place. When you've used your fixative be sure to invert the can and spray until only propellant can be seen. This will keep the spray head clear and prevent spitting next time.

Learning patience

Patience. The final, and arguably most important, tool. Easier preached than done, I agree, but a job worth doing is worth doing well. So often I have seen an animal portrait ruined by a hastily drawn neck because the artist, having completed the face, had lost interest in the more mundane sections. In doing so they destroyed any sense of reality. It's important to remember that it only takes one hurried area to drag the rest of the drawing down to its level. Never let time become a factor in your drawing. It will take as long as it takes. If given the time it demands the result will be well worth the effort and, as you'll learn in a later chapter, time spent in proper preparation pays ten-fold in time saved later on.

A TIP ON PATIENCE ...

If time concerns you then try this strategy. If you're right handed, start top left and work across and down always with the rest of the drawing covered up. Now treat every little area as a full drawing in its own right. This may not be a method of drawing you're used to but I can recommend it. Now instead of your project being, let's say, a 40-hour drawing, it has become a collection of 80 half-hour drawings. Not only is this far more manageable, you also get to congratulate yourself for successfully completing a drawing 80 times instead of just once!

That's my personal approach. At no time do I consider the overall layout to be a complete drawing in itself. The 'drawing' is the area I'm working on. When it's completed (or as near complete as I can manage without reference to everything yet to be drawn around it) I move on to the next 'drawing'. My separation from the overall study is such that one day I make that move yet again but find there's nowhere left to work. I put it away for a day or two, come back to it with fresh eyes and make any adjustments required. That's often the first time, except in my mind, that I really get to see the drawing as one complete entity.

Basic techniques
Drawing the line...

'LINE IS A MAN-MADE DEVICE - A VERY USEFUL ONE, BUT TOTALLY DIVORCED FROM NATURE. NOTHING IN LIFE HAS A LINE AROUND IT.'

Whether your interest lies in pure line drawing, tone rendering or near-realism one thing is of paramount importance - that you acquaint yourself with the basic techniques. With continuing practice and the basics firmly embedded in your mind it will be only a matter of time before they become second nature.

Let's begin with Line and Tone (often referred to as Value). Line is all a pencil can draw. But that line can be narrow and hard to broad and soft and it can be used for simple outlining or the building up of complex tones. To complicate the distinctions between the two, tones themselves can be produced by pure line or by flat shading. However, it is important you understand that Line drawing, or 'outlining', and Tone drawing are two separate disciplines. I would recommend that you never mix the two. Tone added to a line drawing may suggest form but rarely reality. Line used in a tone drawing will almost always destroy reality. Line is a man-made device - a very useful one, but totally divorced from Nature. Nothing in life has a line around it.

Using Line

Drawing is not necessarily about representing something in a realistic way and sometimes it can just be a 'shorthand' memo to yourself that no one else can fully understand. Line is a great sketching tool and an ideal way of quickly capturing the shape of things, as it breaks the subject down into its simplest components. In essence line drawing is about identifying and indicating edges without regard to surface textures, shaping or lighting. An edge may be the external outline or the shape of an internal structural feature. It may also be a boundary between light and strong shadow, if making note of that edge aids understanding or helps to recall the lighting conditions at a later date - perhaps back in the studio when you decide to incorporate the subject into a composition.

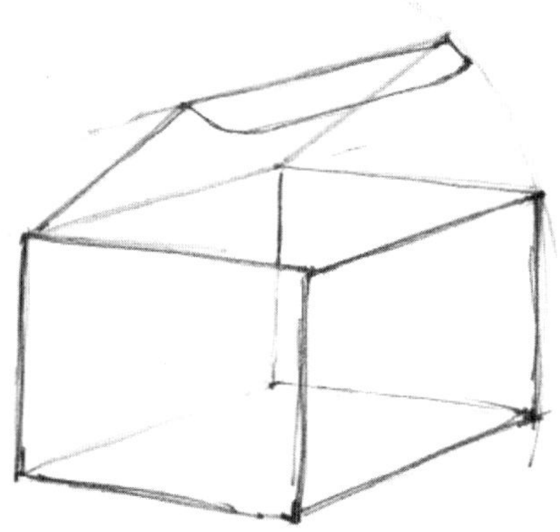

Line drawing of a box. The internal structure has been included to explore and construct it as a three dimensional form.

One of the supreme advantages of using line is that it takes away the need to recreate a true reality. Instead it allows experimentation and unnatural ways of exploring the subject.

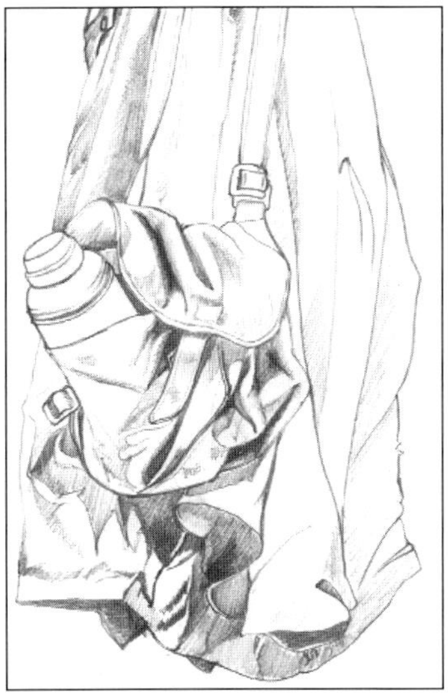

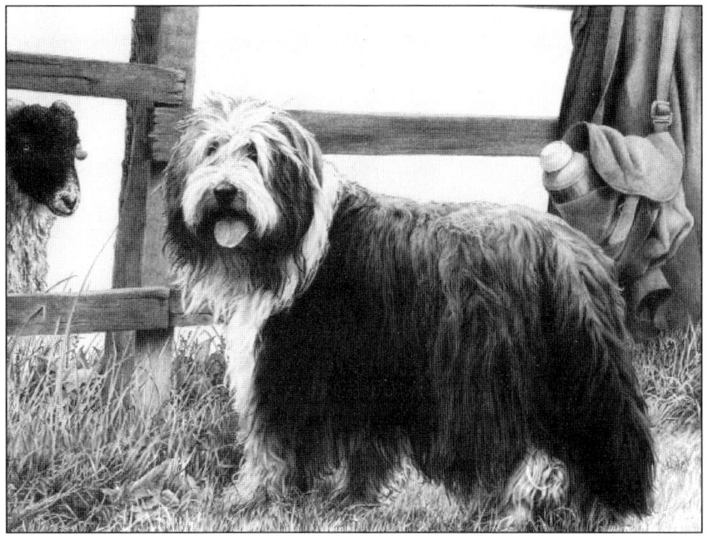

Far Left: My waxed jacket, a bag and vacuum flask hanging on the back of my studio door.

Left: The sketch translated in the final study.

Although I usually work with photographs, if I need something at short notice I'll sketch it instead. Line produces nearly all the information I require and even the tone in this drawing of my coat is produced by line.

A simple box, for example, can be viewed inside and out at the same time - we can depict edges and sides that would usually be invisible. This is a great way of discovering true three-dimensional form and exploring perspective. I learnt a lot from such exercises at Art College - in constructing objects, such as a three-pin plug, I began to gain a true understanding of volume, form and space. I also learnt that almost everything could be broken down into simple shapes and manageable elements.

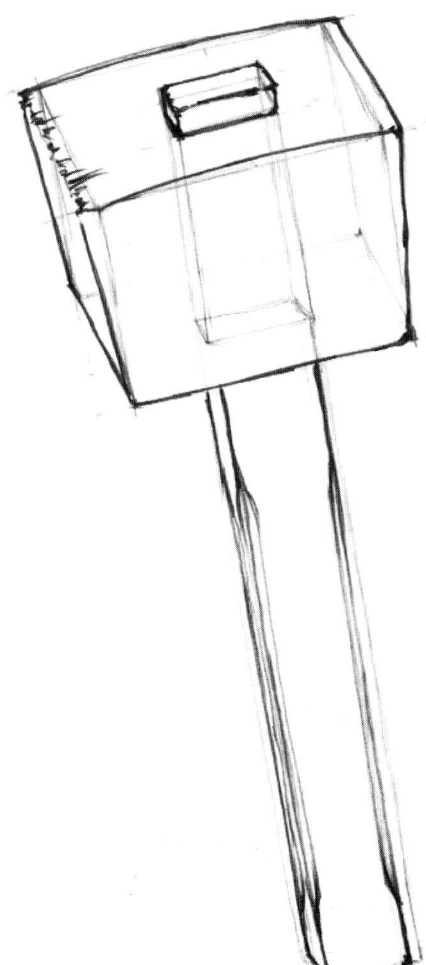

This drawing of a carpenter's mallet, for example, is based around two boxes - one for the head and another for the handle. I drew this freehand but use a ruler if it helps you to draw the construction lines. Draw the two boxes so that one fits through the other and don't worry about the way it should look at this early stage. As you draw, make a note of size relationships by comparing each line and its angle to those around it. This is often known a Sight Sizing. I spanned the head with my finger and thumb then used this as a measurement of the handle - it turned out to be three and a half heads long. If you're drawing a large object - imagine this mallet is ten feet high - hold your pencil vertically at arm's length, slide your thumb up the barrel until the remaining length exactly spans the side of the head that's facing you. Now use this to measure all the other edges. You can also check angles by holding your pencil vertically, visually butting it up to an edge, and then tilting it until it lines up. By moving it to other angled edges, comparisons can easily be made between them.

This simple exercise contains the basics of perspective. Don't concern yourself with recession, this is too close for it to

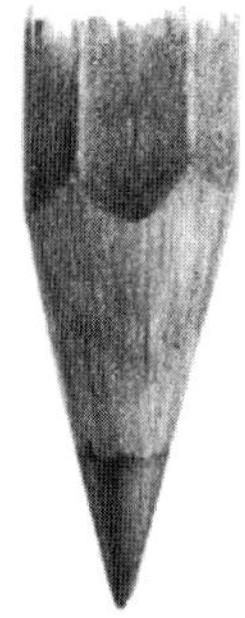

Conventional point

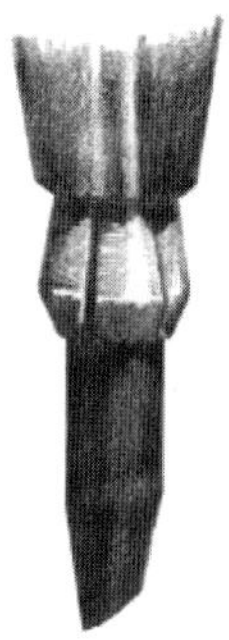

Chisel-point

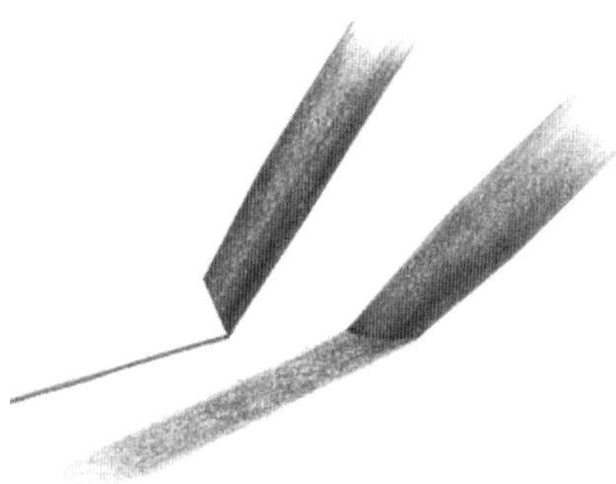

Both fine and broad lines being drawn with a Chisel point.

'Do all your work as though you have 1000 years to live'
Shaker saying

matter, just concentrate on making opposite sides parallel to each other. Further observation shows that the head has angled striking faces, the top is slightly curved and the gently tapering handle is designed to stop the head flying off - much to my wife's relief, as it's my mallet! Now we can begin to modify the original boxes and gradually, one step at a time, construct a true likeness. Learning to see the basic building blocks inside objects will greatly simplify your ability to depict them. Suddenly even complex objects become manageable and far easier to draw.

So far we've not been concerned with the type of line we've been drawing. But line possesses three variables - width, weight and sharpness. In practice the width of the line you produce, the weight or pressure that you apply to the tip, and the quality of the edges of the line are dependent on each other.

Width

The width of any line you draw depends on a number of factors but the principle one is the shape of your pencil point. Many artists use a sharp point and many tutoring books tell you that a sharp point is the ideal. Personally, the first thing I do when I've sharpened my pencil is rub off the sharp tip. Why? Well, a number of reasons. First, any amount of pressure will crumble and probably break the tip and I don't want a splinter of graphite firmly embedded in my drawing. Second, it will wear rapidly and within a few strokes your point will probably be similar to mine. Finally, I dislike breaking my concentration to sharpen my lead so I use an oblique chisel point. This allows me to produce a wide variety of line with a simple turn of my pencil and, by slightly and constantly turning it as I work, I can maintain a sharp edge for some considerable time. With practise you begin to gain a feel for the point in use - it can involve sound as well as the feedback travelling up your pencil - a sharp point or edge travelling over your paper feels nothing like a flat face skating over it. Learn to be aware of this and use your hand-guard to test your point before making a crucial mark.

If a sharp point is your preference or you require one for a particular quality of line (as I do at times) then use a good quality pencil sharpener. Personally, I use clutch pencils so I have only the lead to sharpen and not the wood casing too. Using the purpose-made sharpener, clutch pencil leads can possess extremely fine points. In the case of wood-cased pencils consider using a scalpel for initial sharpening then finish with an emery board, fine glasspaper or even a strip of coarse drawing paper to form the point. Always be aware of the shape of the lead point when drawing - I regularly look at the silhouette of mine against the paper's surface as I work - turning the chisel-point to the angle I require for the next line.

Weight

The weight, or pressure, that you apply to your drawing tip dictates both the tonal strength of your line and its width. Decreasing the pressure will result in a lightly toned, fine line and, conversely, increasing the weight increases the density of the line. Be careful when using excessive weight with a hard grade of graphite; if you later need to erase the line you may find that a groove in your paper remains. Subsequent drawing over this area is likely to make it reappear as a distracting, light line, which is very difficult to remove. Drawing the same tone into the groove often works but it requires a great deal of care to obtain a precise match. Better to have not caused the mark in the first place by switching to a softer grade.

Weight can also be used to produce a variety of effects. For example, try varying the weight of the line as you begin or end to form tapers that fade to white. Using a light pressure when applying a broad, soft grade point will cause it to deposit graphite only on the tops of the paper's tooth giving a soft-edged, misty line. Applying a medium to heavy pressure to the same soft grade, such as 2B, will fill the tooth of the paper, producing deep, rich tones, and successive applications will build up the graphite until you achieve dense blacks. At the other extreme, drawing lightly with a hard grade, perhaps a 2H or 4H, using just the weight of the pencil, will give you a line that is barely detectable but it is a great way of applying tone with repeated cross-hatching or the close placing of parallel lines.

Drawing with a 2B chisel-edge point:

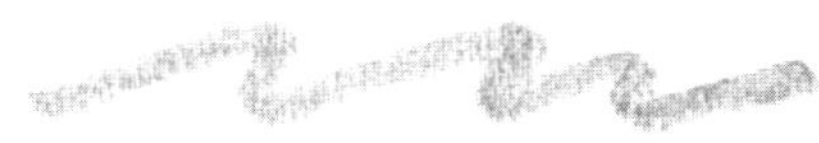

Lightly applied with flat face

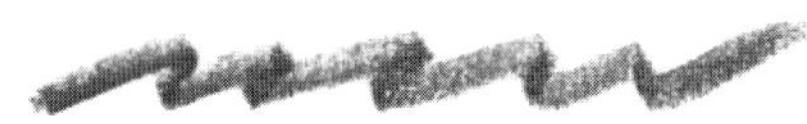

Medium weight with flat face

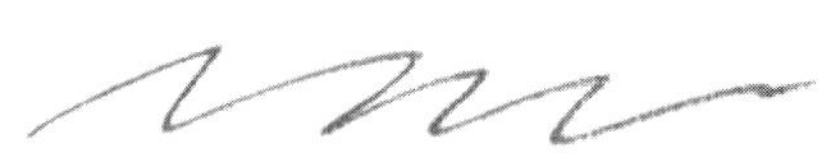

Medium weight with sharp edge

Weights and Line Gradations

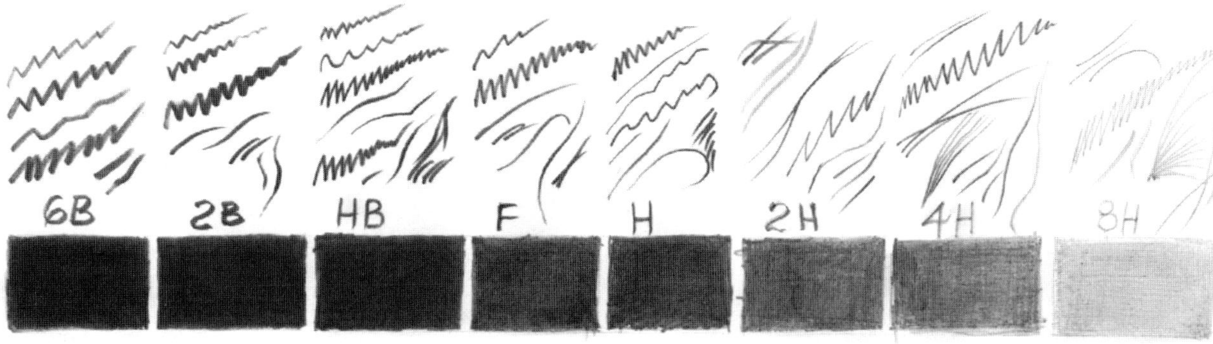

Experimenting with weights and graduations of line. The boxes are shaded with maximum weight.

'ONLY EXPERIENCE WILL TELL YOU WHICH GRADE MAKES WHICH MARK ON ANY PARTICULAR PAPER SURFACE.'

If you experiment with different grades, varying the weight of each, you'll soon see that the lines produced by adjacent grades overlap in intensity. This becomes self-evident if you shade in adjacent shapes of each tone.

Edge quality

Different grades of graphite produce differing qualities of line. A soft grade (B to 8B) draws a line with a soft edge. Drawn with a light pressure, the coarse graphite grains tend to sit on top of the paper's tooth. Applying additional weight forces the graphite into the depths of the tooth but the grains will begin to crumble as you draw. In the first case the texture of the paper will be evident along the edges of your line (or even break across it if the line is thin) and in the second instance, the crumbling grains will give the edge a ragged appearance. Both can be used to your advantage at times if they suit the particular texture you are recreating.

For really sharp lines with clean-cut edges use a hard grade (H to 8H). These grades have increasingly finer grain structures with no detectable irregularities along their edges. The disadvantage is that you may not be able to create the depth of tone that you desire but using a combination of grades can overcome this problem.

In practice two things will determine the kind of mark you make - your paper's texture and the graphite grades of your pencils. Unfortunately there are no hard and fast rules. Only experience will tell you which grade makes which mark on any particular paper surface. Drawing realistically in great detail, for example, requires a smooth paper. Individual pencil marks will be barely discernable, if at all, graduated areas of tone will possess smooth transitions and the minimal surface texture of the paper will not visually distract the eye. The disadvantage is that smooth paper possesses less tooth so you will need softer pencils to create dark shades. Softer grades, of course, draw lines with less-sharp edges, which is not welcome in realistic drawing, so it becomes a compromise. Rough paper, on the other hand, holds more graphite and allows your drawings to have deeper shadows, and more contrast - but the grainy texture makes realistic drawing difficult.

Choosing which grade to use for a particular subject is more important than you might at first appreciate. Just because you customarily use an HB is no good reason for using it for everything. Instead, tailor your grades to suit the job in hand.

This boat, for example, has a hard, varnished surface. The dog has soft, thick hair. There are no comparable similarities so why use the same pencil for both? The boat was drawn by building up layers of tone with 2H and 4H pencils. The hard, light grey tones produced by these leads were ideal; the fine grain structure left no distracting blemishes and permitted smooth, graduated toning with a suggestion of woodgrain.

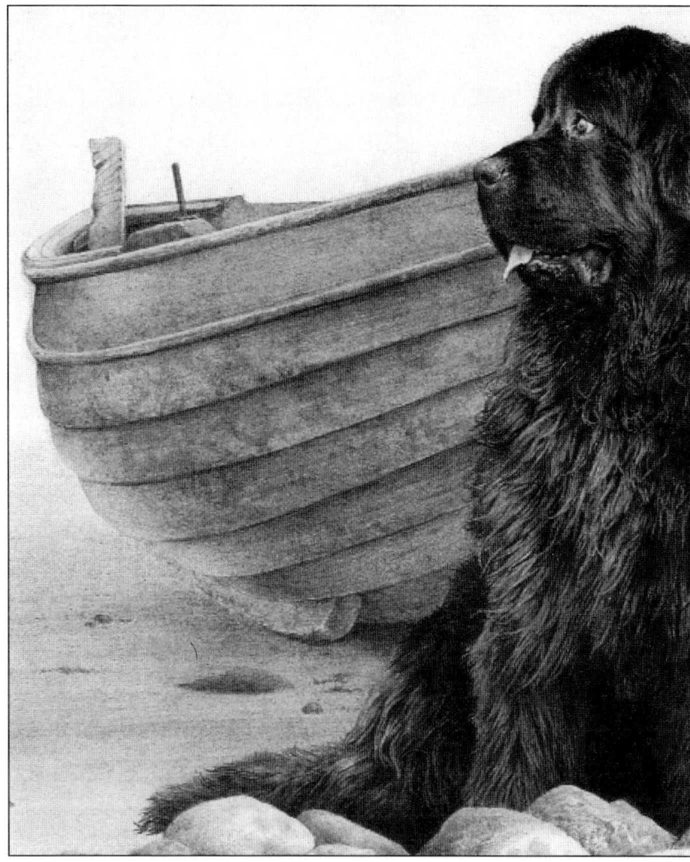

Few, if any, of the qualities of the leads required for the drawing of the boat are of use for depicting the dog. In this case I've used a mixture of HB and 2B grades with a little 6B between the legs. The softer grades produce softer lines and are ideal for suggesting soft surfaces.

Remember too that the tonal range of each pencil grade overlaps those to either side. To draw a hard edge within the dog, around the eye for example, I use an HB lead applied with some weight. The resulting line possesses the sharpness that I need. Drawing is then commenced with 2B, working over and away from the outer edge of the HB line. With correct weighting the two grades will be indistinguishable but you have the advantage of the harder grade's ability to produce a crisper line.

Line is an extremely useful servant. If you generally use a guideline drawing as an armature around which you build a finished drawing, the line drawing effectively removes all lighting and three-dimensional form, allowing you, the artist, to dictate your own conditions and requirements rather than having a photograph or model dictate them to you. It also permits the reduction of anything to its constituent parts and inner building blocks, greatly simplifying a complex subject. Line can produce quick sketches as memory aids or finished, expressive artwork.

'LINE IS AN EXTREMELY USEFUL SERVANT... LINE CAN PRODUCE QUICK SKETCHES AS MEMORY AIDS OR FINISHED, EXPRESSIVE ARTWORK.'

What line can't do, in my opinion, is invoke a sense and depth of reality. Line is not what the brain expects to see in a real situation so we need to resort to other means - in this case tone or value drawing, which is what we'll explore in the next chapter.

Tone drawing
The shady side of drawing...

'UNLIKE LINE DRAWING, WHICH CAN BE TACKLED WITH LITTLE OR NO PREPARATION, TONE DRAWING DEMANDS SOME PRIOR THOUGHT.'

Tone (or Value) drawing is, to all intents, opposite in almost all respects to line drawing. The edges that we drew with line, to describe the outline and the position and shape of internal parts, are now merely junctions between textures or tonal values. Line plays no part at all. We are concerned solely with the content of the areas that line previously drew around. Instead of two parallel lines showing us the top and bottom edges of a belt around a man's waist, now we draw the belt itself. In doing so we can convey much more information about it - we can show its curve, texture, highlights and shadows - all previously impossible with pure line. As we don't have the use of line to show where the belt stops and the shirt begins, we let the eye know where the boundary is by using the differences in texture and reflection. Our concentration is on lighting, form and textures - using or opposing each to identify the others.

At first, it can often seem strange to not draw a line. Where the edge of a light area meets the white of your paper you can almost feel a compulsion to do so. However, even if outlining is your only solution to a problem, the line should be broken or otherwise engineered to appear not to be a line at all. In all other cases draw as though line does not exist and concentrate entirely on the uses of texture and tonal values in your drawing.

When you compare the work of different artists it often elicits the feeling that the work of one, although highly detailed, is flat and lifeless where the work of another has a presence that grabs your attention. The simple answer often lies in the wider range of tonal contrasts used. As you will learn, it pays to widen your tonal range as far as you can so that your darkest darks really offset your brightest whites. Both will benefit your drawing by working against each other to produce that attention-grabbing contrast.

Unlike line drawing, which can be tackled with little or no preparation, tone drawing demands some prior thought. Before you begin, stand back and think about what you are about to draw. Identify in your mind the area of darkest tone and the brightest highlights; consider the different textures and how the treatment of each might help you describe how they relate to each other and the overall form and shape; and study the lighting to see how it affects the tones in describing the three-dimensional form - and how you might engineer a possible improvement

Tonal values can be applied in a number of ways - using a brush and powdered graphite, cross-hatching, circular marks, random scribblings, zigzag shading, and the drawing of adjacent parallel lines. My main preference is for the last of these.

Tone: the zigzag method

This is probably the most generally used method. However, a very common fault arising from zigzag shading is the drawing of a uniform set of lines, each beginning and ending below the one before. Coupled with this is a second fault - the change in direction begins at the stopping point so it is inevitable that an overlap of graphite occurs. A tapering area is shaded twice until the lines completely diverge. Both faults compound to produce a band of darker tone working its way down the paper. If you later extend this area by joining more shading onto it you will never rid yourself of that dark band. Worse still, if your second area overlaps the first to even the minutest degree you will simply reinforce the banding. The problem is best tackled by discarding this method.

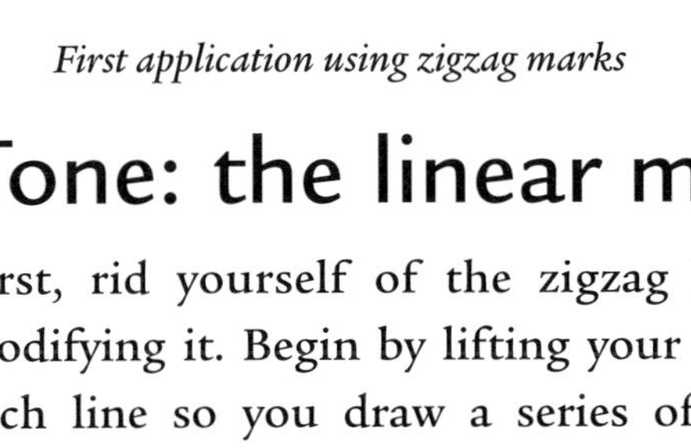

First application using zigzag marks

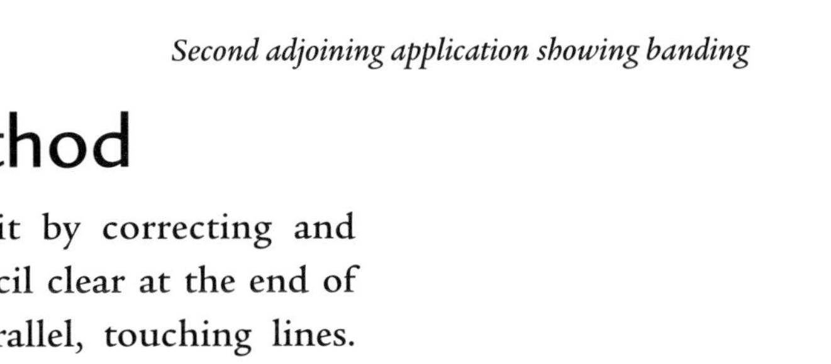

Second adjoining application showing banding

Tone: the linear method

First, rid yourself of the zigzag habit by correcting and modifying it. Begin by lifting your pencil clear at the end of each line so you draw a series of parallel, touching lines. Known as hatching, this will prevent the darker tone as you change direction.

Second, learn to decrease pressure at the end of the line and apply it gradually at the beginning. The fading out of the ends will greatly simplify the grafting on of later shading. Literally

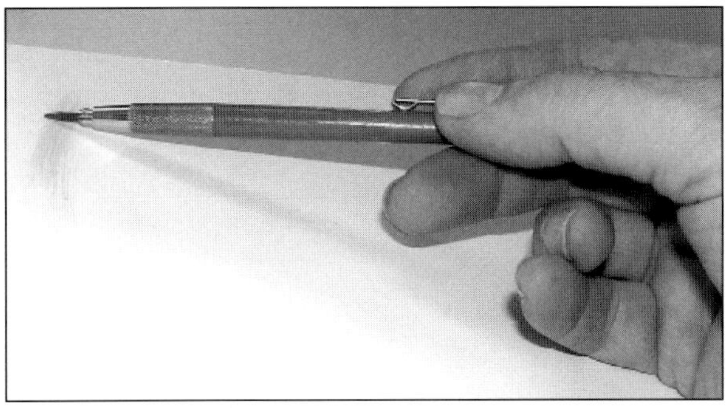

Fig 1

'stroke' the lines onto your paper; swinging your point in a flat arc. I often rest my little finger on my hand-guard whilst doing this to perfectly control the height of my pencil's tip above the paper (*fig 1*). The aim is to deposit graphite on the tops of the paper's tooth for subsequent blending although dark tones may benefit from being drawn directly into the depths of the tooth for maximum coverage.

For light tones in particular, I hold my pencil as near to the top as I can and use it almost flat to the paper in wide sweeping arcs. Draw from your elbow, not your wrist - you will achieve a greater control and a wider and flatter arc. If you try this, beware of letting the body of your clutch pencil come into contact with your paper - a model with a milled, metal ferrule may leave metallic marks where it touches.

When attempting to draw lightly, especially where accuracy is vitally important, mental stress can transmit itself to your hand. Your grip on the pencil will increase and cause over-dark tones. If this begins to happen, consciously relax your grip and the improvement will be immediate and noticeable.

Because the linear technique doesn't permit the weight of line of the zigzag method, shade the area downwards then back up

First application of parallel lines

Second adjoining application with no banding

and repeat the operation, layering as many times as necessary to obtain the density of tone required. If light gaps appear between lines, fill them on the way back up. Looking at the gap and not at the lines you are drawing will guide your eye to where the extra tone needs to be applied.

And finally, vary the length of the lines. The greater the variation, the better you avoid any repetitive series of darker tones that the eye can detect. In the example above I've deliberately left the additional shading lighter across the join to help you understand what's going on. In practice I would strengthen the second area until it exactly matched the tone of the original application. I would probably also blend the graphite at that stage but we'll return to that subject later.

Improved results are achieved by laying down the adjacent lines as above then slightly shifting their angle by just a degree or two as they are worked back up. This prevents later lines perfectly following previous ones and over-darkening the tone as a result. It also fills in any lighter spaces and partially blurs any detectable lines.

Graduated tones follow a similar method but employ additional layers, applied as required. However, a degree of planning is involved before drawing commences. Why? Because filling the tooth with a light tone compromises your ability to add dark tone. Artists who sketch in 'trial' tones before the true drawing begins employ a practice I commonly encounter. Usually this is localised to a particular area and is used as a way of sorting out comparative tonal strengths. But successive drawing then has to be carried out on a surface with only partial tooth remaining. It is very difficult, and sometimes impossible, to add a dark tone over a light one - 6B needs the full depth of the paper's tooth and will not adhere to an area partially filled with a hard grade. Sort this problem out in your mind first or draw your trial tones on a separate piece of similar paper. Preserve your paper's pristine tooth.

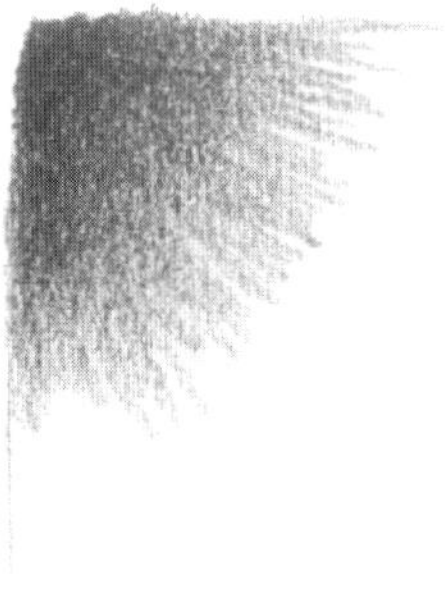

Initial 6B application

HB extension applied over 6B

2H extension applied over 6B and HB. Note the smoothed structure of the 6B

If the gradation is severe, whenever possible begin by laying down your darkest tone, fading it out so you can graft on the mid-tone section. Fade that section out in turn to accept the lightest tone. This strategy correctly places your harder grades over the softer ones. I recommend it, as the harder grades will burnish and smooth the coarse grains of the dark tone and increase its perceived depth.

For gently graduated, lightly toned areas you can work in reverse if you restrict your shading to just one or two similar graphite grades, building up your tones by a combination of repeated layering and additional weight.

Circular shading with 2B on rough watercolour paper using progressively less pressure

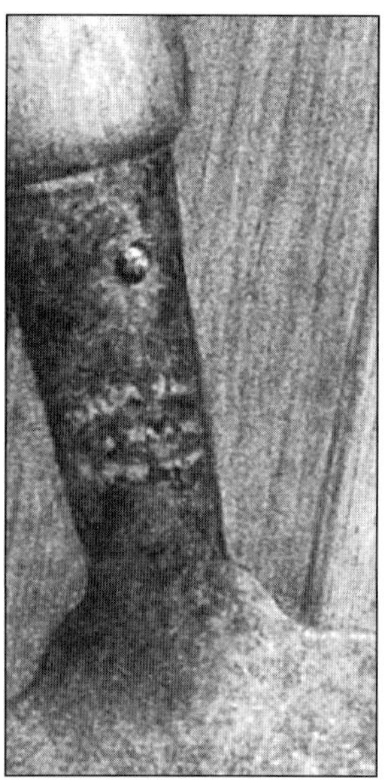

Circular marks used to 'sculpt' a worn, rusty surface - producing three-dimensional shaping, rust pitting and illegible writing in one continuous process. The pencil tip rarely left the surface.

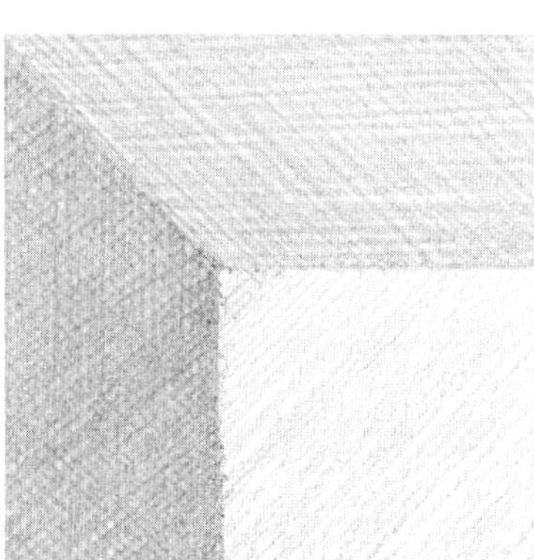

Freehand cross-hatching with HB in three directions

Tone: the circular method

Where it is of paramount importance that no line structure shows in your shading the circular technique offers fine control. Personally, I rarely use this method for areas of flat or graduated tone. It isn't as effective on my plate-finish Mellotex as it is on vellum or coarse surfaces, but it is a good tool to have at my disposal. The technique involves the application of graphite with small circular movements. It works well for dark shadows, forcing soft grains deep into the paper and, if pressure is kept constant, with no obvious flaws. The granular structure of 6B and softer grades can, as is often the case, be visually intrusive so a final burnishing with the rounded tip of a 2B pencil will smooth and deepen the area. It is certainly true that this method deposits graphite deeper into the tooth whatever the grade of graphite, as it approaches every small indentation from all angles.

In the circular shading example shown here, I've used the indentations of the paper to help me reduce the intensity of the tone. I began in the top left corner with a very sharp point and extended the area in arcs towards the bottom right. By gradually using less pressure and allowing a flat face to wear on the point, the graphite deposits ranged from deeply embedded to just grazing the top of the tooth.

My personal use of the circular method more often involves drawing an area in its entirety in one pass. It helps me to 'feel' the texture I'm drawing, to 'sculpt' the surface, such as in the ferule of this old hand fork. Here it was ideal for exploring and creating the rusty pits and illegible writing, the indentation around the rivet, the overall conical shaping and the highlight around the top edge. The whole area was drawn in one sitting with a chisel-pointed 2B pencil and, for the greater part, without lifting the pencil point from the paper. A final light layer of 2H was used to dim all the highlights except the key highlight on the rivet.

Tone: the cross-hatch method

This well-known method echoes that used by pen and ink artists and, being capable of spontaneity in execution, it's an ideal sketching tool. Drawing from life, which I thoroughly recommend, is a good way to learn this technique. Aim to quickly capture form, not detail, and cross-hatching will soon become instinctive. It can also, with repeated and careful application, produce very realistic textures and graduated tone. Its very nature encourages the awareness of three-dimensional form, as the drawn lines can follow contours, and localised changes to tonal values are quickly accomplished. If later blending is planned, line direction does not affect the eventual appearance, as they will disappear. With great care and time the cross-hatching method can, even without blending, produce wonderfully realistic tones. It's a method I often use myself, usually to boost or fine-tune hatched, linear-drawn tone. By crossing the previous lines obliquely or at right angles the resulting tone is quite markedly increased in value.

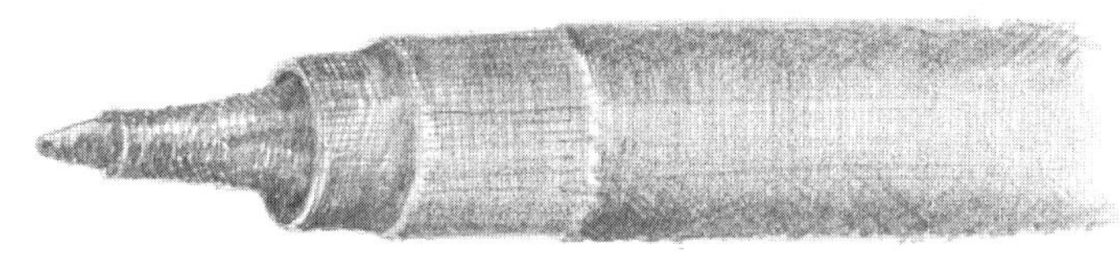

Quick sketch using only cross-hatching

Tone: the brush method

Although I don't use this method (and probably never will) I am fully aware of its use and uses. It's particularly effective for toning down white expanses. Either purchase powdered graphite or take a 2B lead and grind some on fine sandpaper. Canadian Artist Margaret Dent described her method of working to me, "Take a very soft brush (a make-up blusher brush is ideal), dip it in the graphite, tap it to dislodge the largest chunks and then very gently smooth it on the paper. It's actually a lot of fun to do and comes out very nice and even, perfect for the sky." You can also work in reverse with this method - drawing light into dark with Blu-Tack, electric, conventional, and kneadable erasers.

Tone: other methods

At times I use a graphite-impregnated tortillon or stump to apply small areas of tone; other artists use yet different methods. British artist Edith Harris used the following techniques to reproduce the textures of a felt hat - "I use Staedtler clutch pencils and a sharpener. Instead of wasting the powdered graphite I use it on a paper towel to blend in and get darker darks. I fold my towel into different shapes; chisel, point, diagonals etc. First I put a very little of the graphite onto a white plate and dip in the towel gently, I then rub the towel on the plate to take off the excess. Finally I rub in a circular motion in the area I want to apply it. Then I do another layer if I want it darker." I'm not endorsing this method or any other but suggesting that experimentation is the key to finding what best works for you. Don't be limited by 'standard' or 'accepted' practices. I have a sheet of card from thirty years ago that

'I use a soft brush to put the powdered graphite on my paper then use a chamois or felt to rub in or lighten. I use Blu-Tack to fine tune then believe it or not what's left on the paper doesn't smear or rub off. I can draw on top and add details or erase and it's not messy at all. I get various shades by rubbing with a chamois or paper towel but I can also use my pencils to draw over it and all the layers give a lot of depth.

I get the powder from a couple of art stores. You have to go to the model car and train section - they use the powdered graphite as a lubricant on the wheels.'

Lucy T. Conway, artist

'DON'T BE LIMITED BY STANDARD OR ACCEPTED PRACTICES...'

In the 1920s, a professor, recognised as the world's leading electronics authority, proved mathematically that a radio tuning coil could not work unless it was 2" in diameter and shielded in a can 5" wide. The dictum was accepted as a law of electronics. Ignorant of both the professor and his law, Bill Lear, of Lear Jet fame, built a coil one half of the 'minimum' size enclosed within a 2" can which worked to perfection enabling him to produce the first car radios on which his fortune was based.

contains some of my own experiments. One in particular involved applying model aircraft dope* with a brush to areas of dense 6B - I found I could 'paint' with graphite. It's a technique I abandoned but others remain.

Tone in use

However you apply your graphite (brush, tissue or pencil) there may be a need for a final burnishing with tissue to force the graphite 'wash' into the fibre of the paper. Use a circular motion for this, as it will guarantee that you cross any lines and drag the graphite into adjacent light gaps. Small, tight circles work best with no more than a medium pressure. If the blending or burnishing is carried out lightly you may have the advantage of being able to add subsequent layers, building up the tone until you reach the desired value.

In practice it is better for your applied tone to be a little darker than required, as your blending tool will absorb some graphite as you work, subtly lightening the tone. When drawing graduated tone in small areas I render the darkest tones a degree or two darker than is required, correctly draw the mid tones and omit the light tones, leaving the area white. Then taking up a stump or tortillon I very lightly blend the area, working from dark to light. This gently reduces the over-dark tones in value, leaves the mid tones alone (if I use H or harder - usually 2H) and creates the light tones by dragging graphite over the white of my paper.

It takes both time and practice to make these techniques become second nature - and still longer to devise your own. You will make many mistakes along the way but each one will teach you more. Welcome mistakes as positive experiences. As a graphite artist it is imperative that you learn these value application and manipulation techniques, or at least appreciate the need for them, as your 'colours' are simply texture and tone. Nothing else exists so don't remove half the weapons from your arsenal.

Widening your range of tones as much as you can will increase the contrasts and greatly add to your drawing's attention grabbing 'punch'. Never be afraid of going too dark. It often seems easier to begin lightly and then build up to darker tones but, as I explained, really dark values result from the full use of the available tooth. Before you begin, take a long look at what you are about to draw and identify in your mind the area of darkest tone and the brightest highlights. If you can't find

**Dope - a material-stiffening varnish used on old aeroplanes built with wood and fabric.*

anything with any real tonal depth then stamp your authority on the piece and invent something. The increased breadth of contrast will add greater depth to your drawing. You don't need to draw these dark areas first, just keep them in mind as you work and all your other tones will adjust themselves to it.

However, if you can establish the deepest shadows early in the drawing you'll have both the highlight (paper surface) and darkest tones to refer to for all the intermediate tones. To use darker values at first is undeniably daunting. No doubt you will be afraid of not being able to erase them and ruining your work. But Blu-Tack will allow you to return almost back to white if you need to. You can banish your fears now you have the means to fade your blacks by controllable degrees.

At the other extreme, never underestimate the importance of white space in a drawing. Since graphite can only decrease the tonal value of the paper, the surrounding white space remains the area of greatest brightness. Don't crowd your paper with the image but maintain a good balance. By allowing the eye to register the white space it will visually increase the intensity of your blacks and so give added impact to your key highlights. I am, of course, talking about subjects such as portraiture with no background or setting. However, if your drawing is a landscape or includes a setting of some kind then stay in control - adding light tone to the sky, for example, will leave only the true highlights white and considerably boost their effectiveness. The brush and graphite powder method may serve you well with this.

Many of my early 'dog in landscape' drawings have a white sky but as soon as I learnt the great advantages of adding even the slightest amount of tone I've never repeated that mistake. Indeed I usually tone down the sky before I begin work on any other element.

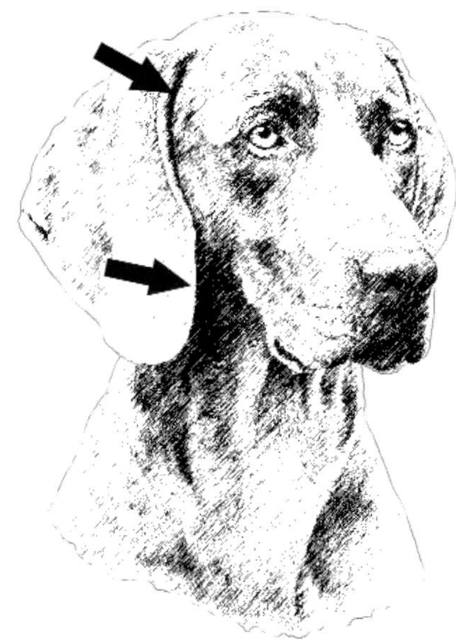

Identifying the darkest tonal values in the preparatory stage. Here they will be used to visually throw the lighter ear forwards.

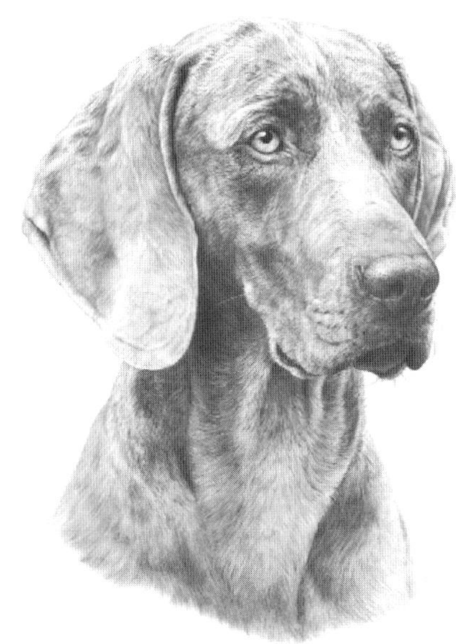

The completed drawing

Putting it all together

If your drawing doesn't include a background you need to carefully consider the lighting before you begin. A halo of tone surrounding your subject, known as a vignette, is quite unnatural and rarely a successful solution. No matter how realistic your drawing, the halo will immediately denote it as being a drawing. Look for potential problem areas before you begin and adjust your lighting to overcome them or consider toning down the entire background to define the outline of your subject. Better still, exaggerate the shadows around the

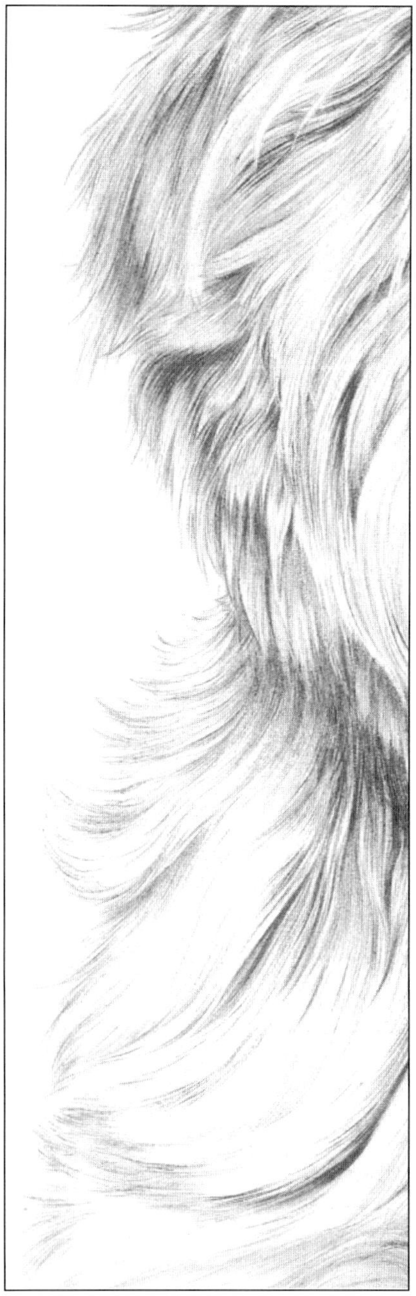

Edge shadows used to define the outline

edges, inventing shadows beneath individual hairs on the lighted side. This will give the eye an outline to follow and increase the sense of three-dimensional form.

With practice it's really not too difficult to invent a little shadow around the edges where no shadow should exist. Use the tiny shadows cast by individual stray hairs around the edge to discretely display the outline. And you can suggest that the edge recedes away from the viewer by using a little light toning - even though in reality that edge should be in full light. The brain is a very lazy animal and if you send it the right signals (or even the wrong ones, as in this case) it will just assume that what it's seeing is correct and make excuses or find reasons to

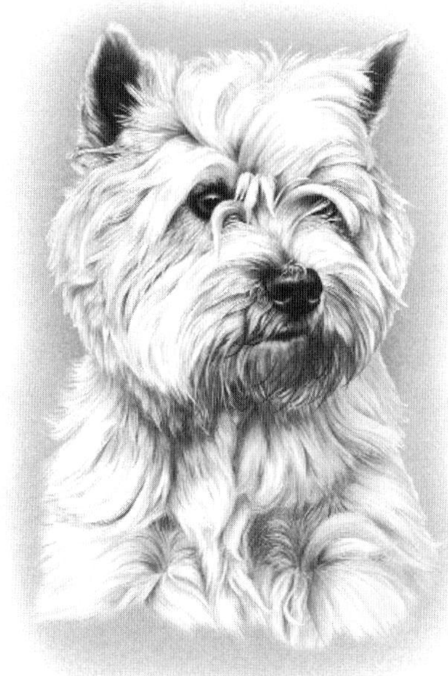

White dog on white paper with a typical vignette used to define the outline, which damages the sense of reality by isolating the truncated portrait.

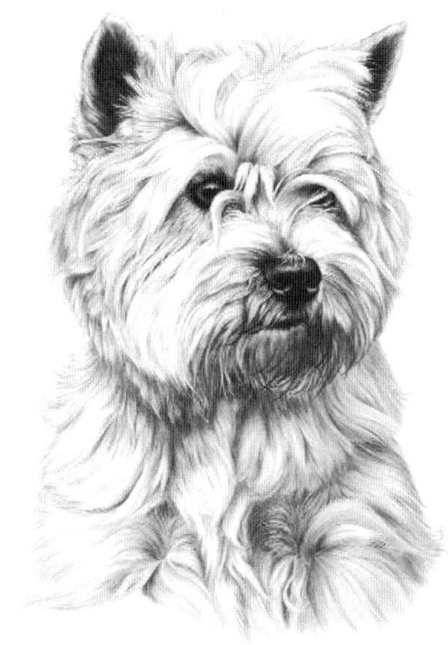

Using edge shadowing to define the outline and depict a sense of reality even though the shadows don't necessarily conform to the rules of reality.

justify its decision. You can also add a little shadowing in broken sections - suggest a line, leave a break, suggest a continuation. If you get it right the brain will just follow through and see an edge where no edge actually exists.

When employing only tone, a graphite artist works in a similar way to a painter. The actual mechanics are different but you need to think in identical terms - areas rather than lines, and using adjacent areas of contrasting tone and texture to define edges. We differ from painters only in our lack of colour so we have to engineer our tones to compensate. A painter, for example, can apply green lettering to a red package where the tonal values of the two colours are identical. We cannot show that either are green or red but we need to be aware before commencing that the tones must be made to differ. Failure to do so will render the text invisible. This is one reason why I always work with colour photographs!

In the example shown here, the preparatory line drawing defines all edges without the use of tone. Conversely the finished drawing (a detail from my Done Balin' study) uses only opposing tones to describe three-dimensional shape and delineate the various surfaces and their edges. Not having the use of line can at first present a problem but you will soon learn to use the background to your advantage. For example,

'FIND BEAUTY NOT ONLY IN THE THING ITSELF BUT IN THE PATTERN OF THE SHADOWS, THE LIGHT AND DARK WHICH THAT THING PROVIDES.'
Junichiro Tanizaki

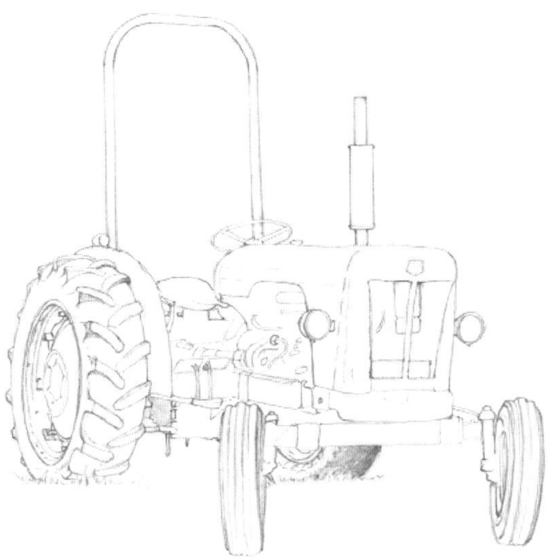

Pure line drawing

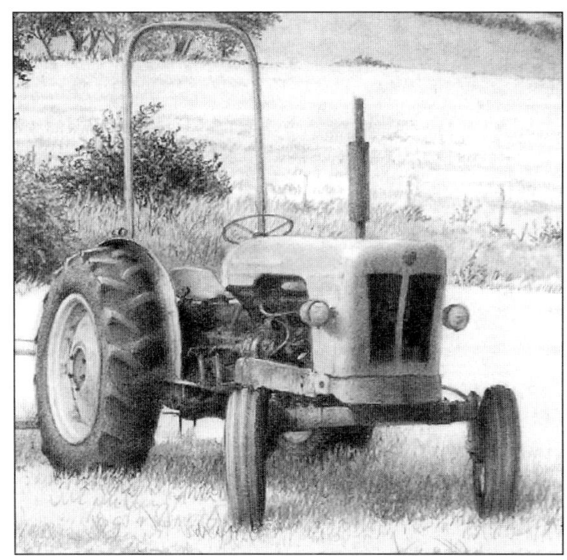

Tone drawing employing no line

Both drawings are shown actual size

only the dark foliage behind the rollbar's left-hand upright describes its light edge. Higher up, this edge virtually disappears against the lighter field - but this is entirely natural and conforms to reality. The brain receives sufficient clues to visually continue the line through. Learn to trust your eyes and draw what you see (even in a make-believe world such as mine). More crucially, don't draw what you can't see, and you will achieve a realistic drawing.

Erasing Techniques

Now you see it - now you don't

THE PENCIL APPLIES GRAPHITE; THE ERASER REMOVES IT - TWO TOOLS THAT PERFECTLY COMPLEMENT EACH OTHER.

Erasing is an integral part of the drawing process, not just a means of correcting errors. Perhaps the appearance of one third of every image that I produce is as a result of erasing techniques. Think of erasing not as a means of removing unwanted drawing but of removing graphite. This extends its use to the removal of deliberately over-applied graphite.

The pencil applies graphite; the eraser removes it - two tools that perfectly complement each other.

For example, instead of trying to create a section of drawing that consists of delicate and subtle tonal variations, it is often easier to broaden your range of available tones (to draw over-strong) and then to progressively remove the top-most layer of graphite until the desired look is achieved. Often it's not possible to determine the final look until you see it so this method allows you to 'fade' an area by degrees until it looks correct.

Yet another example of this would be to lightly draw in sections of grey tone through which you later want to 'draw' white lines using a sharpened eraser.

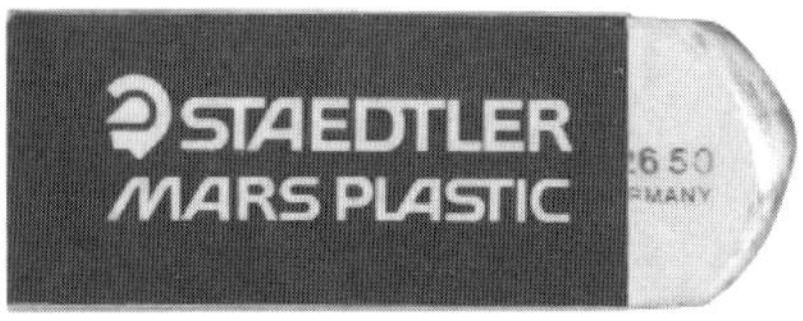

Soft art erasers

Conventional vinyl soft art erasers are a good choice for reasons of safety. If you own typewriter or ink erasers, now is the time to throw them away. I can sum up the difference between these and a soft art eraser in two words - safety and effectiveness. The harder and harsher the eraser, the more likely it is to push graphite grains ever deeper into your paper.

All solid erasers will do this, it's their nature, but the softer the erasing material the more delicate will be the removal. I've learned the hard way - from bitter experience. I still own an early drawing in which the highlight in the eye has a greenish tint - from the typewriter correction fluid that I attempted to fill the hole with!

Whenever the use of a solid eraser, as opposed to malleable

putty or kneadable erasers, is required I perform it with a Staedtler stick eraser. This versatile, pencil-shaped eraser contains a cylindrical core that can be formed into a very fine point using a conventional pencil sharpener. This leaves a flexible tip that assists in very precise and delicate erasing. Of course, other tips may also be formed with the aid of a craft knife or scalpel - from wide chisel ends (useful both across the width and as a narrow knife edge) to narrow chiselled, bevelled or custom tips cut after the point has been sharpened. I find these erasers a delight to use.

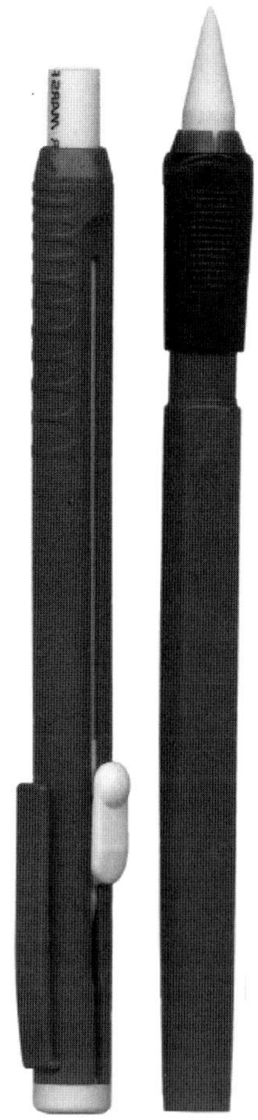

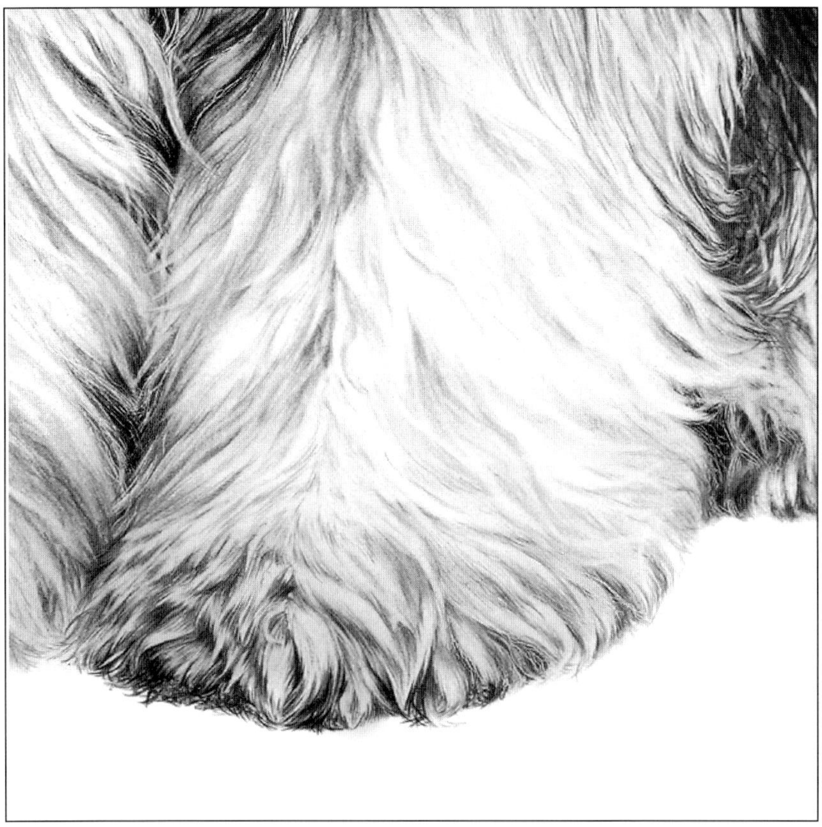

This Old English Sheepdog's paw shows multiple uses of a conventional eraser. Drawn in 1983, this is a large drawing approximately 24" x 18" (61 x 45cm) and the paw measures 4" (10cm) across.

In all areas except the toes, where a different technique was used, the darker shadows were first established then the shadows cast by the locks of soft hair were lightly applied with a soft 6B pencil. The curved ends of the locks and 'stray' white hairs (those that apparently cross other hair) were drawn with a stick eraser cut to a wide chisel point with a craft knife. The width offers additional stiffness and longevity to the erasing point. This technique works well on drawings of this scale and on lightly applied graphite.

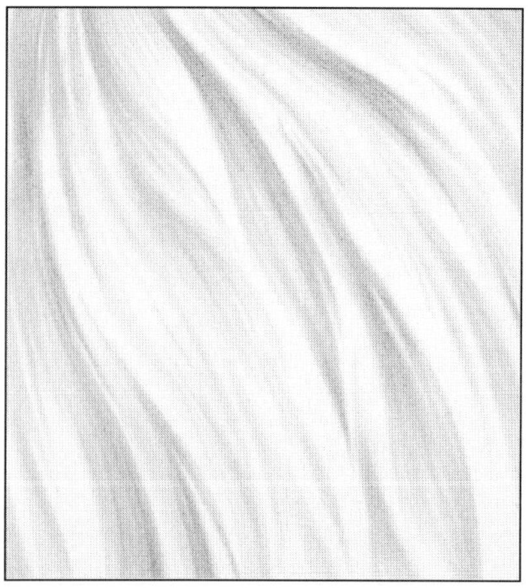

Lightly applied 6B pencil

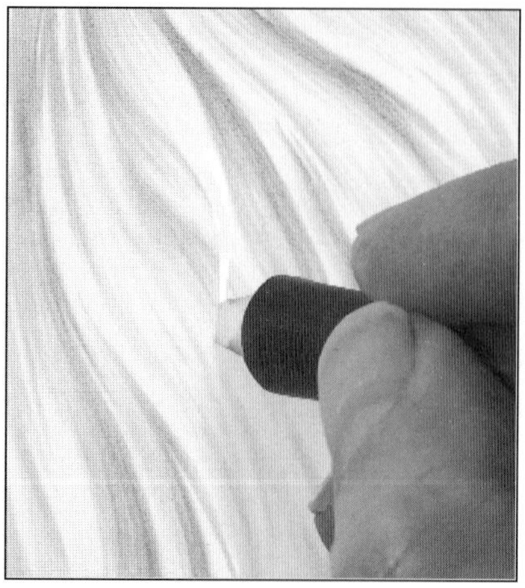

Drawing hairs with a chisel-ended stick eraser.

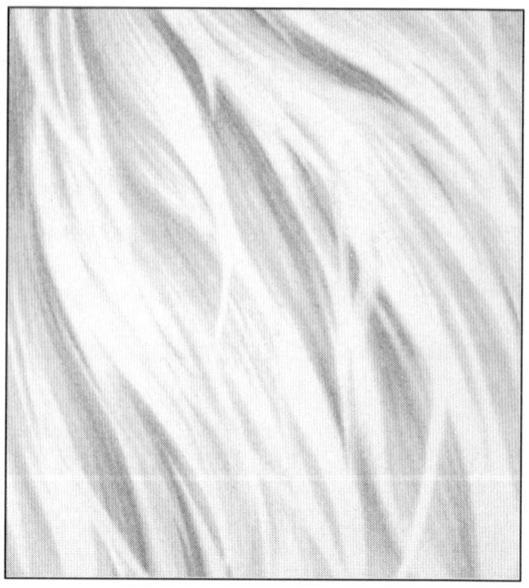

The final result

Electric erasers

I don't own or use one but many artists I know do have one and can't live without it. A good battery powered electric eraser is particularly effective at lifting out tiny highlight dots in eyes - or so I'm told. If you are really brave and you know exactly where you want the highlights to be, you could hold the eraser in one spot until it actually digs down into the surface of your paper just past the graphite layer to get down to pure white again. This can be an effective cure for a late change of design but, in my opinion, this is a case of poor planning or a last-ditch rescue attempt. I certainly wouldn't recommend this procedure. So many times have I heard of a drawing ruined by an eraser digging too deeply into the paper surface and leaving an irreparable mark - or even a hole! The removal of surface graphite with Blu-Tack or a kneadable eraser, coupled with time and care and the final use of a pointed, stick eraser, will more safely achieve the same effect.

If you want to add a battery eraser to your armoury you should be able to buy a small, lightweight one that fits the hand for about £28 ($50). I'm told you will never regret buying one ... but I remain to be convinced.

Eraser shields

There may be occasions when very precise erasing is required and the use of a shield, such as a plastic ruler, may be the answer. I sometimes use this method to clean the margin of my drawing on completion. Being able to see through a transparent ruler allows you to exactly line up its edge with the edge of your drawing. Now you can erase in safety and, if you cut a chisel end on your eraser, you can erase right up to the line. This method is particularly useful if you want to reduce the size of your drawing at a late stage - not that I recommend that practice but it does work.

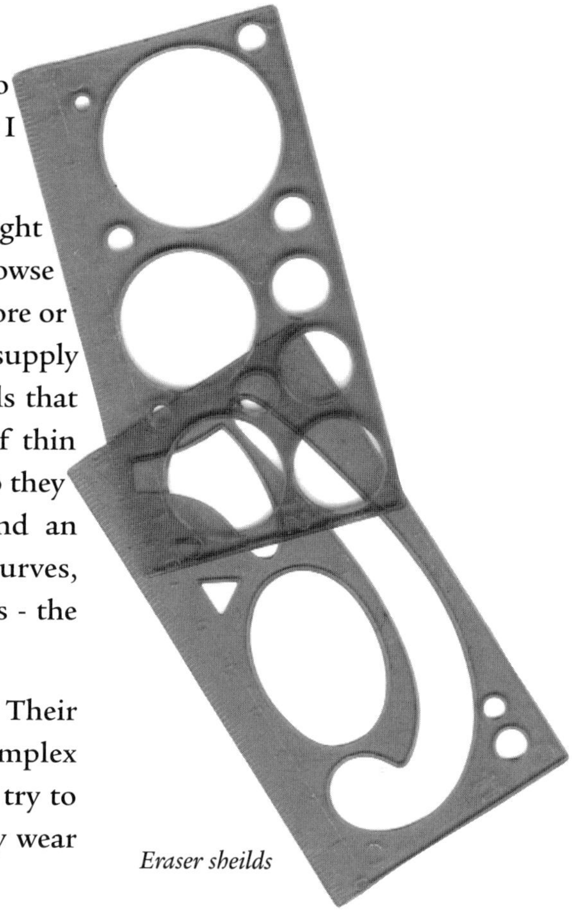

Eraser sheilds

Just as the plastic ruler allows you to erase perfectly straight lines there are other eraser shields available. Have a browse through the architects drawing products area in an art store or use your imagination when looking through office supply catalogues. The latter often sell all sorts of creative tools that you can use to control your eraser. Some are made of thin aluminium but buy see-through plastic ones if you can so they can be lined up as perfectly as my ruler. You'll find an abundance of curved shapes, progressive French curves, protractors, circle and ellipse templates, lettering stencils - the list and variety of shapes is endless.

Eraser shields work very efficiently with electric erasers. Their relatively fine points can easily follow the most complex contours. However, when buying templates or shields, try to obtain the thinner variety. Thick templates can rapidly wear the sides of the points of electric erasers.

Kneadable erasers

Kneadable Erasers (putty rubbers) are excellent tools and I've had very good results in the past. I was introduced to them at Art College - perfect for bored students; they bounce well off walls - particularly effective, I recall, at frightening life models with multiple near misses!

As the name suggests, these erasers can be kneaded into a ball and pinched and pulled into any shape desired. They are firm enough not to collapse in use - pinched to an edge or pulled to a point, the shape will survive short sessions of erasing without needing to be reformed. They will also erase by the conventional rubbing action or, to some extent, by being pressed onto the graphite surface. Personal experimentation is the best teacher.

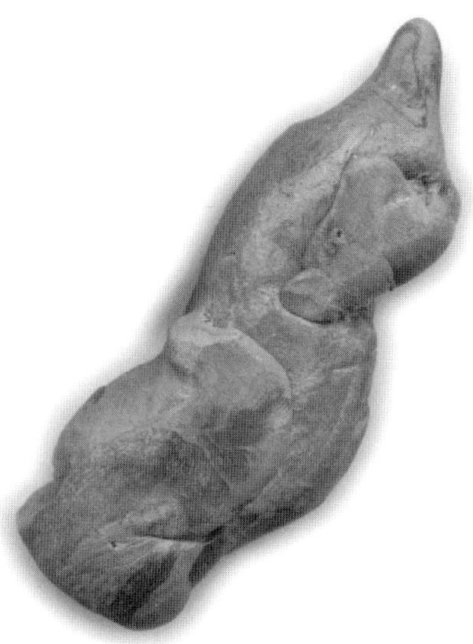

The designer's kneadable eraser - which she affectionately calls her 'wombat poo'

When the surface of the eraser gets dirty you can pull and fold it to a clean surface. Use a large piece for large areas, tear off smaller pieces for erasing in tight spots or form it into a point and apply with a twist to erase small highlights and spots. Note that 'twist' - kneadable erasers often require a mechanical movement to work effectively - I'll return to that subject shortly. I used these erasers happily for a number of years then I bought a batch that crumbled and broke up in use. In desperation, I grabbed a piece of the nearest equivalent - Blu-Tack - and I've used virtually nothing else since.

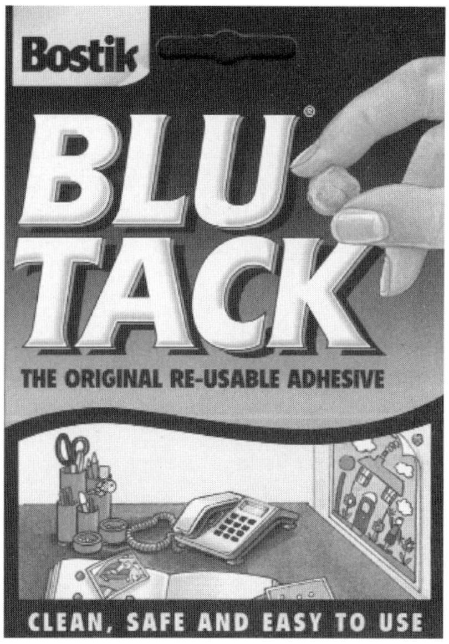

The magical eraser

It looks like a kneadable eraser; handles like a kneadable eraser but is a tool of unsurpassed excellence! Blu-Tack - the non-toxic, non-sticky putty that is used for fixing posters to walls. This stuff is God's own gift to graphite artists. I still haven't exhausted the range of uses offered by this versatile eraser. Before you ask, I don't own shares in Blu-Tack, but I do use it extensively. I've tried similar products, generically known as Wall Putty, but only Blu-Tack possesses all the qualities we need - an enhanced ability to be readily formed into any shape and an all-important inherent tackiness.

Kneaded Erasers are good tools to have but they lack the stickiness of Blu-Tack. If you form a point in both then touch the point of the kneaded eraser onto an area of graphite and lift it straight up, you will see very little difference. Repeat the exercise with Blu-Tack and you will see that a round area of graphite has been removed.

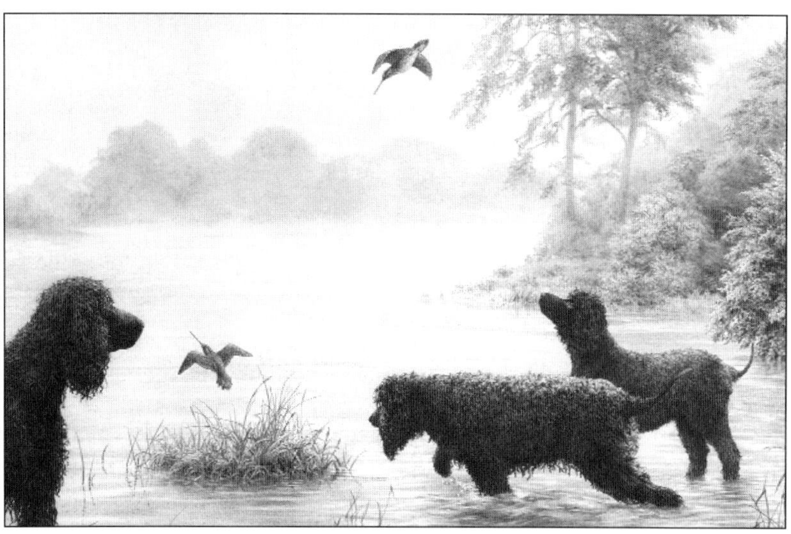

'...(Blu-tack) is the only product known to me that can fade an area of graphite drawing while maintaining the detail.'

I stated earlier that all solid erasers need some degree of mechanical action to work. This twisting or rubbing action will most probably force some graphite deeper into the grain of the paper - the reverse of the desired result - or it might damage the paper's fibre structure. Blu-Tack requires no mechanical action at all to work - no rubbing, no twisting - a touch is all that is required. As a result it is the only product known to me that can fade an area of graphite drawing while maintaining the detail.

I should stress that although Blu-Tack is tacky it is not so sticky that it will leave remnants of itself on your drawing. This just doesn't happen. It's this slight stickiness that you turn to your advantage. To progressively fade a small area, for example, dab or roll a piece of Blu-Tack over the area then repeat using the same face. The face will become progressively dirtier as it lifts the graphite so the fading of the area of your drawing will become more and more subtle. Blu-tack really gives infinite control.

Don't regularly throw Blu-Tack away. Older Blu-Tack possesses different qualities from new. It will be years, rather than months, before you need to throw it out. To clean it, simply stretch a ball into a long rope (or just pull pieces off) then squash it all back into a ball again.

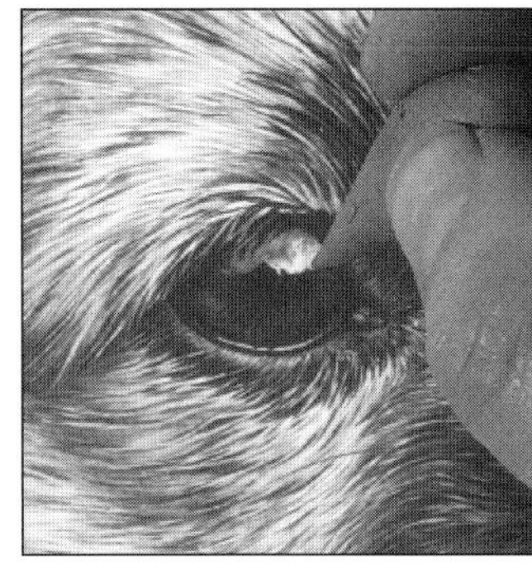

Cleaning the eye highlight - spot erasing with Blu-Tack

I rarely erase for effect except for the constant use of Blu-Tack. Many subtle effects are gained by drawing in an exaggerated way (deeper tones, for example) then incrementally removing graphite to adjust the area until it is sufficiently faded. Often I redraw and partially remove an area many times until I feel the 'reality' is correct.

Once you own Blu-Tack you need never again feel afraid of over-darkening an area of your drawing. You can load an area with as much graphite as you want because you now have the means to remove it. The following technique can be applied to any area of tone that you require being a little (or a lot) lighter. This is where conventional and kneadable erasers will let you down - neither can gently remove half a layer of graphite without disturbing the remainder beneath. This eraser can!

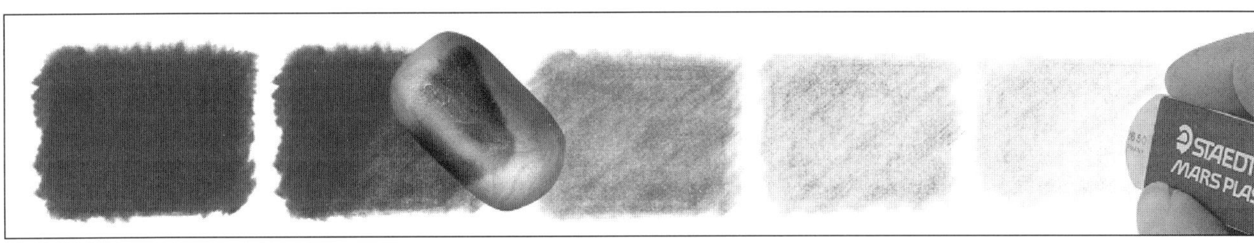

With Blu-Tack, care and the final use of a soft vinyl art eraser, areas of dark tone can be returned almost to white without destroying the surface of the paper.

For large areas roll the putty into a cylinder with as smooth a face as possible (try rolling it on your drawing board). Now gently roll the cylinder over the area to be lightened and repeat as required. With a little practice you will soon become proficient and experimentation will find other methods to suit differing requirements.

For smaller areas try rocking or pressing your eraser on your drawing board to form a flat surface then rock that in turn on your drawing. A light dragging or stroking action can also be very effective.

'ONCE YOU OWN BLU-TACK YOU NEED NEVER AGAIN FEEL AFRAID OF OVER-DARKENING AN AREA OF YOUR DRAWING.'

For spot erasing or lightening tone in very confined spaces, pinch and roll a small piece into a point between your fingers. A repeated series of dabs will remove graphite by degrees until the desired translucency is achieved.

The ability of Blu-Tack to lift graphite clear of the surface without causing smearing, impaction or smudging makes it ideal for drawing light into dark. Very subtle shapes within

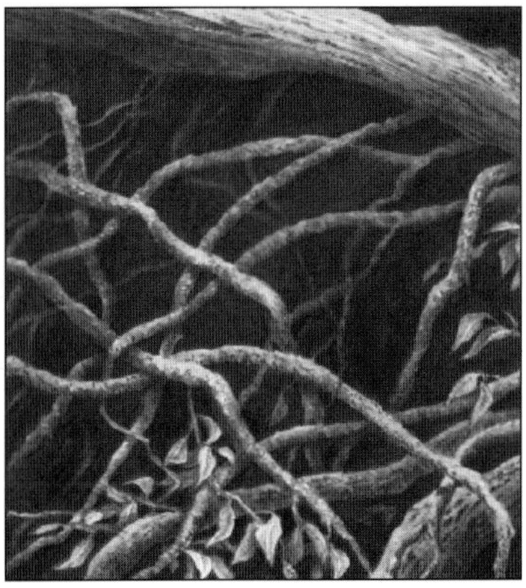

Original drawing with 2B background

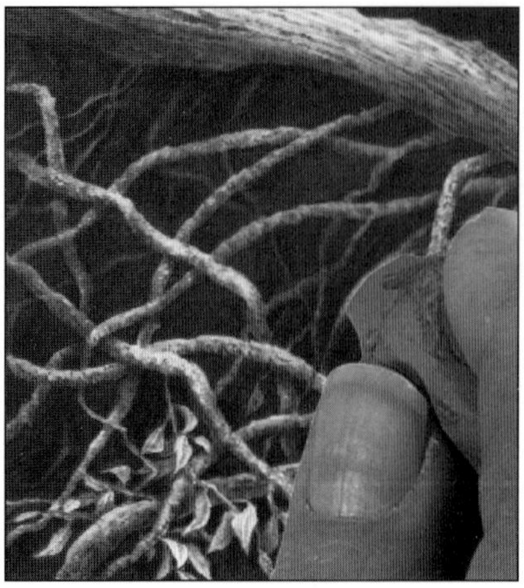

Cutting in an additional branch with a knife edge of Blu-Tack

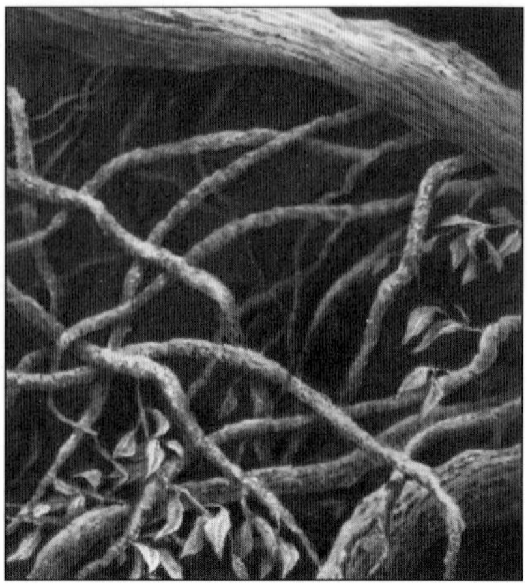

Apparent shaping is the result of repeated and localised erasing

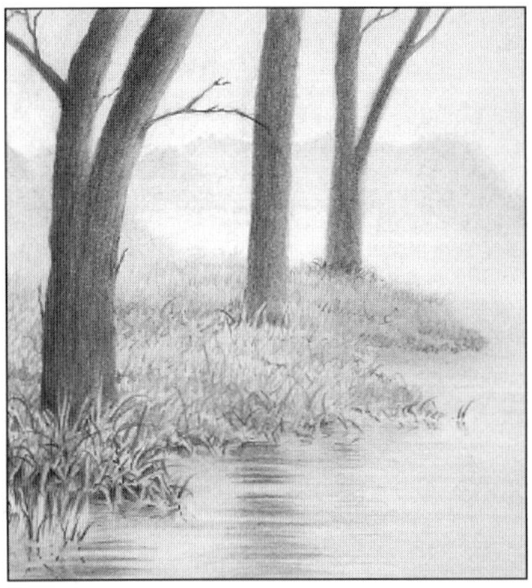

Using strong tones to more easily establish the detail

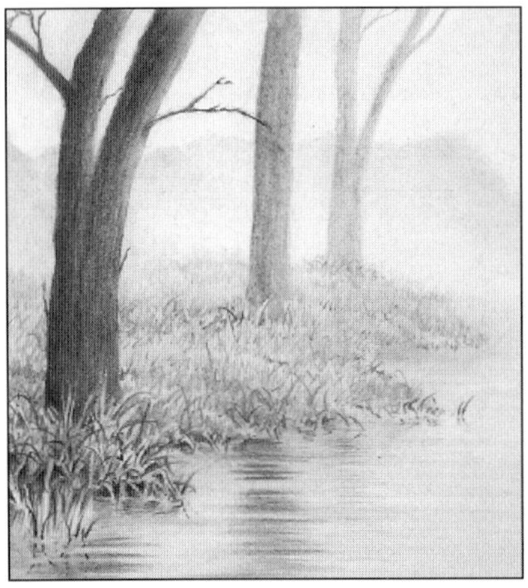

Fading with Blu-Tack while maintaining the detail

areas of shadow can be established or spot highlights created with a series of touches with an appropriately formed point or edge. Leaf shapes, highlights, vague amorphous shapes in shadows, a suggestion of hair inside of a dog's ear - the list is endless. This technique will suit anything that doesn't need to be pure paper-white, whether pre-planned or an afterthought.

These Blu-Tack techniques allow total control over aerial perspective - the apparent and gradual loss of contrast, tonal strength and detail as objects recede into the distance. And it allows full control too over the subtlety of, for example, a misty scene. You can draw textures and detail with ease by first using a greater strength and a wider range of contrasts than usual, then using your Blu-Tack eraser to progressively 'fade' as required - and without affecting the detail!

The same technique was used to achieve the very subtle shading required by the white coats of these Clumber Spaniels. The graphite was first applied using stronger tones than those desired then Blu-Tack was used at each stage to progressively reduce the intensity of the overall tones without disturbing the detail. This method allows very subtle changes of tone and barely discernable but visually important detail to be produced - an effect that is almost impossible to produce by drawing alone, even with the lightest touch.

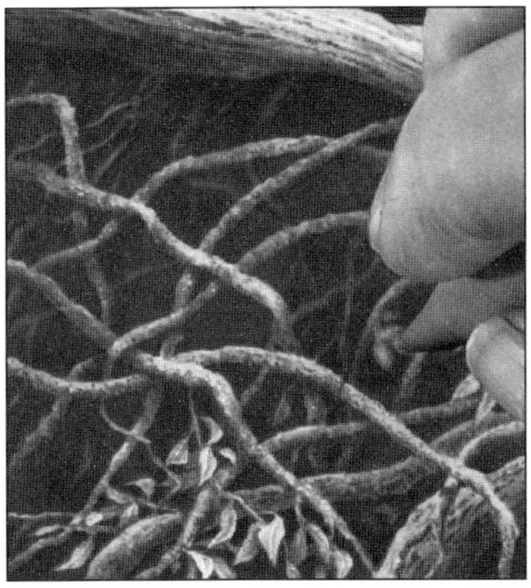

Cutting in additional leaves with pointed Blu-Tack

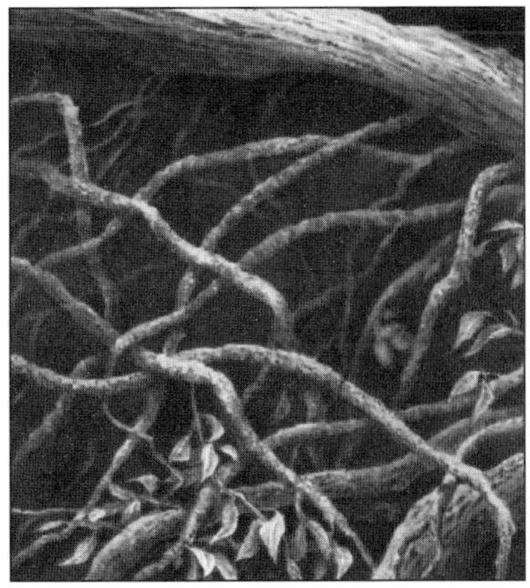

Erased shapes ready for shaping and toning

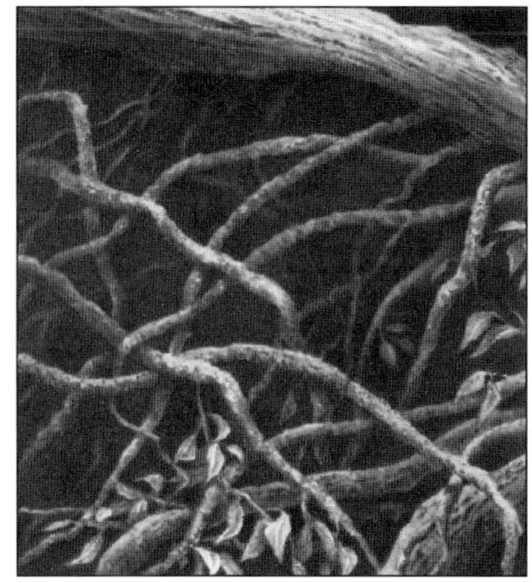

The final result

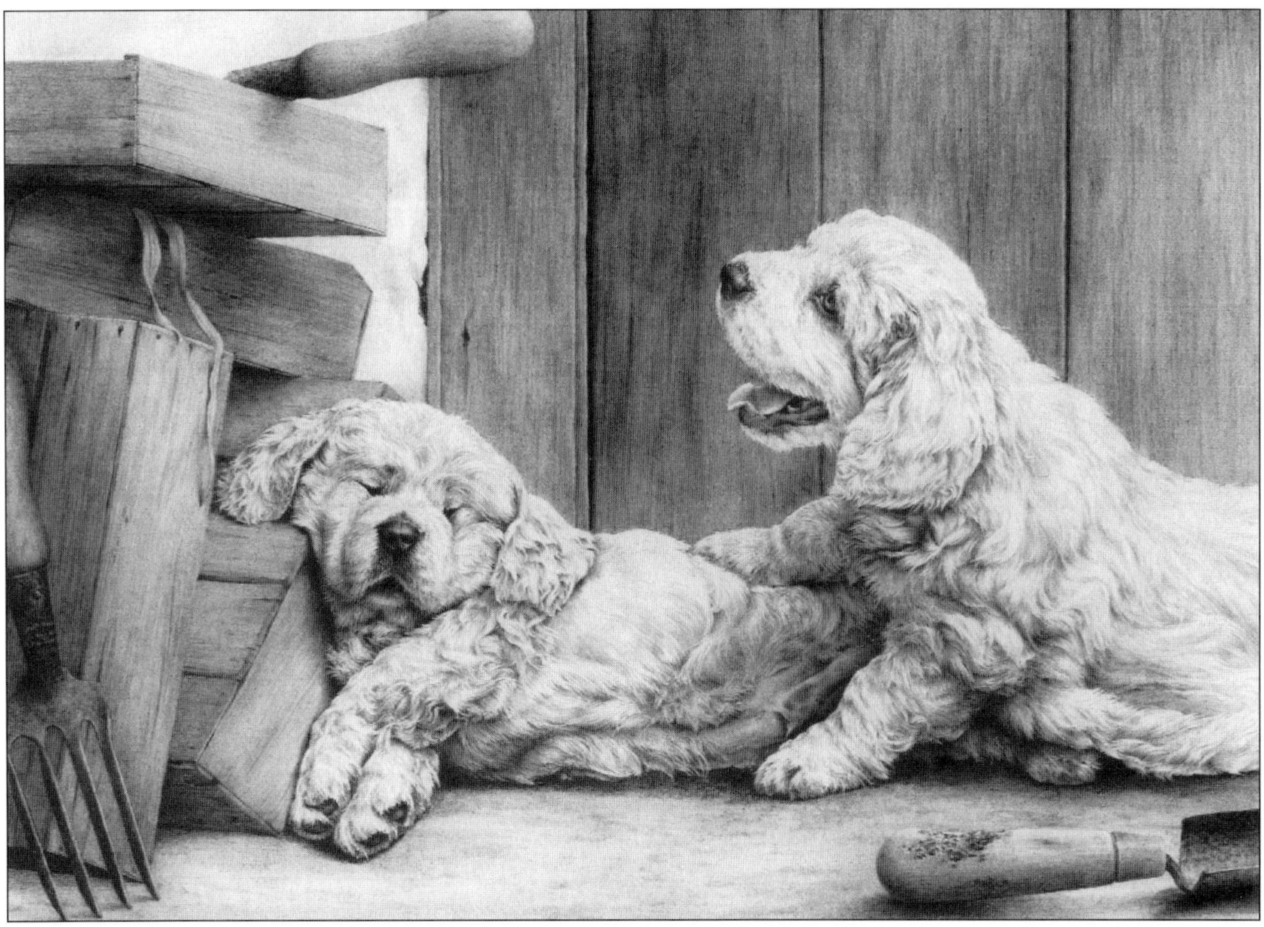

11" x 8" (28 x 20cm)

The Gardeners
featuring Clumber Spaniels. A limited edition print of 850 plus 25 Artist's Proofs.

Blending & Layering

Blurring the vision...

'CAREFUL PREPARATION IS THE KEY TO SUCCESS... YOUR AIM MUST BE TO LAY DOWN AN EVEN LAYER OF GRAPHITE - IT'S YOUR PENCIL THAT PRODUCES THE GRADUATED OR EVENLY TONED AREA AND NOT YOUR BLENDER...'

Blending, the art of smudging graphite, infers a direct blurring of detail or texture. This chapter also includes layering, as the technique overlaps the boundaries of blending and can produce similar results. Essentially, blending involves the redistribution of previously applied graphite to eliminate any sign of linear shading or unevenness of application. The area being blended may be a gradation of tones from dark to light, where the purpose is to make them flow seamlessly from one extreme to the other, or there may be areas of flat tone, where a continuity of surface is essential. Where the eye expects the surface to be completely smooth and free of blemishes, blending provides a solution to achieving a sense of reality.

Layering, on the other hand, involves successive layers of graphite that build up tone and, by altering the spacing or angle of the lines of the shading, fill in any irregularities in the previous layer. It's a more painstaking process but, in my opinion, provides a greater degree of control and an overall enhanced reality to textures. A layer, that performs a similar function to blending but without the blurred result, usually involves a single top layer of a hard grade such as 4H. This serves purely to reduce contrast and physically smooth out the graphite grains of the layer beneath.

Think of it as a layer that dulls highlights and polishes the previous layers to an even sheen. I prefer layering to blending in almost all cases as it maintains detail where detail is required and simply mutes it. I've also found that you can't take short cuts and miss out the 'detail' stage. The results are worth the effort of supplying a degree of detail that later blending or lightening will partially remove. Often a mere suggestion is all that remains but that is sufficient to boost the perceived reality of the area.

Personally, I recommend that you avoid blending until you have discovered everything that a pencil is capable of. When you reach the point that you no longer have to think about how to achieve a particular effect then add blending to your stock of tools. I've been drawing professionally for over twenty-five years and it's only in the last year or two that I have begun to use blending in any way at all.

Blending does, of course, have definite uses, in human portrait work, for example, where it can be invaluable in producing smooth graduated shading. But I suggest that you first learn to achieve tonal gradations using just your pencil with careful hatching and crosshatching and the choice of appropriate grades of graphite. Blending then serves only to add a final polish, and to fuse and obliterate distracting lines into a more believable reality.

Take your development one stage at a time. I believe there is a time in realistic drawing where detail is king - you can become fixated by its production but it's a necessary learning phase. Later you'll see that detail only supports the overall message and you'll learn to be more objective - using detail to provide visual keys where they are required and removing them by blending in areas of distraction. It's an apprenticeship - in the same way that a seemingly simple clown on the high wire has first to be a master of his craft.

I would not habitually blend anything - particularly hair, which I know some artists do - I blend only when the technique produces the actual desired appearance. Hair, for example, needs crisp detailing to look realistic and I prefer to let the pencil produce the look I'm after. If I've spent time achieving sharp highlights in a curving lock of hair I don't want to blend it into a blurred image of its former self. One specific exception is the soft hair of many puppies that doesn't throw deep or sharp shadows. I draw such textures lightly, following the direction of the hair, and then very gently blend with a tortillon to blur the edges. But I do not (and will never) blend where the detail counts, such as the mouth, eyes, and muzzle detail (*fig 1*). Any areas I do blend serve only to emphasise the unblended, sharply drawn features, which contain the character and emotional content.

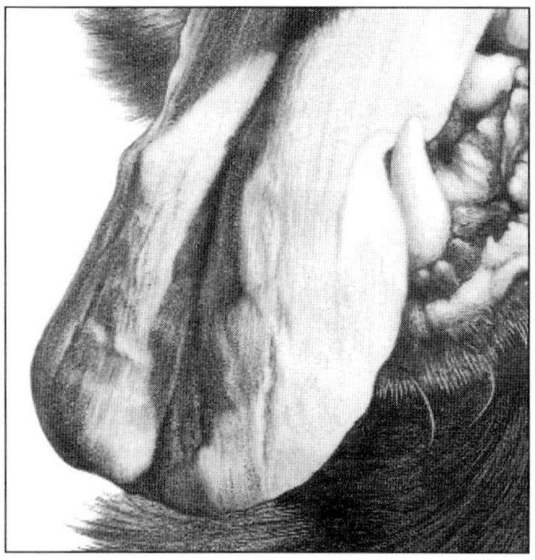

Fig 1. This German Shepherd's tongue contains no blending at all. Purely layering different grades of pencil produces the subtle gradations of tone. Blending would have inevitably destroyed the detail.

How not to blend

Ultimately it doesn't matter what technique is used as long as the result is what you want but I will add a word of caution. There is a tendency, particularly in the work of the inexperienced artist, to see blending as a shortcut - either as a way of speeding up the coverage of an area of little interest or as a way of suggesting form in an area that is not understood. This thinking is to be avoided at all cost. Blending is a delicate

'BLENDING IS A DELICATE OPERATION, SHOULD ONLY BE CARRIED OUT TO PRODUCE A PARTICULAR EFFECT, AND REQUIRES PROPER CARE IN THE PREPARATORY STAGES.'

operation, should only be carried out to produce a particular effect, and requires proper care in the preparatory stages.

Blending is all too often over-worked, and appears to be lacking in definition and intensity. Graphite is a very fine medium and requires a delicate touch at all times. There are times when a tissue-covered finger or a torchon can heavily blend an area but only with experience and if additional graphite is to be layered on top. I've seen too many over-blended graphite drawings and even when an artist succeeds in blending the graphite smoothly, the drawing sometimes lacks depth, vigour and reality. With the possible exception of skin in portraiture, keep blending to a minimum and use its lack of definition as a means of forcing the viewer's attention onto the sharply defined elements. In reality, smoothly rendered drawings with a lot of depth and detail are produced only by delicate, carefully constructed hatched, crosshatched or circular shading applied to a smooth surface.

Graphite has a very fine structure and behaves just like forensic fingerprint powder. It will adhere to areas of your paper wherever you have touched it - attracted by the natural oils from your skin. Achieving smooth, consistent blends in these areas is almost impossible. All of your best efforts will be in vain if you don't heed this warning. Use a hand-guard at all times and never use your fingers to directly blend graphite!

Blending basics

Careful preparation is the key to success. Hurried or careless application of shading will always produce poor results (*fig 2*). Blending has its limitations - it will lighten dark tone and darken light tone by redistributing graphite from one to the

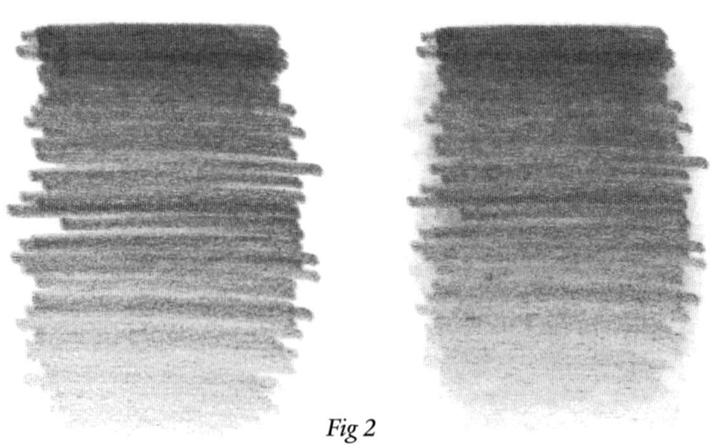

Fig 2

Unblended Blended

The wrong method - 2B on watercolour paper. Blended with tortillon.

Fig 3

Unblended Blended

The correct method - 2B on watercolour paper. Blended with tortillon.

Fig 4

Unblended layers of 2B, HB, 2H and 8H on watercolour paper.

other but it cannot obliterate a hard edge or seamlessly blend dark to light if an area of white intervenes. Your aim must be to lay down an even layer of graphite - it's your pencil that produces the graduated or evenly toned area and not your blender, which serves only to smooth out irregularities. When the preparation is carried out with care, and due attention is given to the application of the required tones, blending will correctly perform its function (*fig 3*).

Compare the two blended areas above with this purely layered area (*fig 4*). Layering is a prolonged process but offers much greater control and flexibility. Here the darkest band at the top was established with 2B and then extended downward to just below the halfway point using progressively less pressure. Next a layer of HB was applied over the 2B and drawn down to the three-quarter point. Then a layer of 2H was applied over the previous two layers and almost down to the bottom. Finally a layer of 8H was drawn over the entire area. These successive layers not only permit fine control over the overall tonal gradation, they also blend the graphite granules of the softer grades, giving them a smooth, polished appearance.

Leaving some texture in a drawing often gives a lively quality that can be drowned by over-blending so, before you blend, think about its necessity and where in your drawing the blending will appear. Don't blend unless it will produce a positive enhancement to your drawing. Logically, blending works best for the mid or background - it's where the eye expects to find a blurring of detail and soft-focus textures and will even accept purely randomised and blurred, abstract backgrounds as conforming to reality. However, there may be times that foreground blending is required. A smooth counter

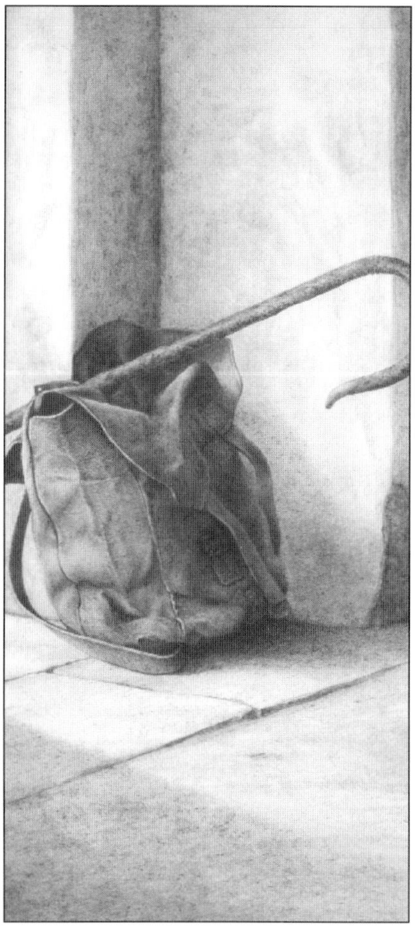

Fig 5. detail from 'Ready and waiting'.

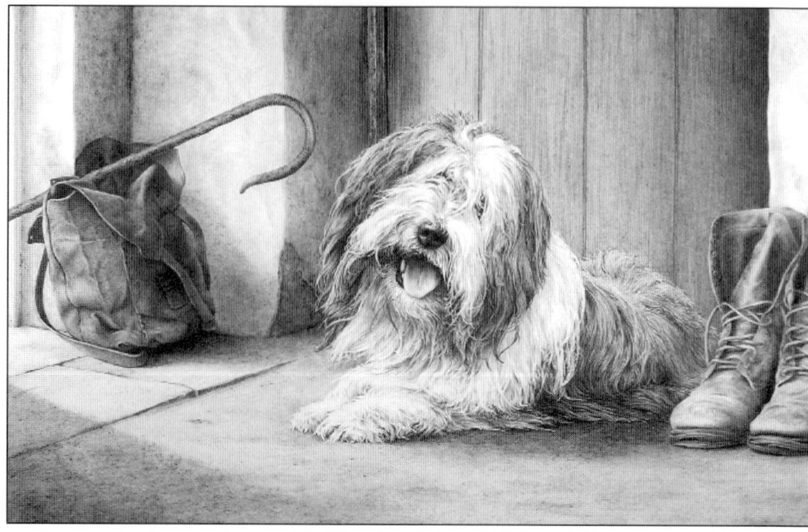

Fig 5. Ready and waiting.

top, for example, upon which your subject sits may require the smoothing out of irregularities.

Personally I wouldn't entertain the use of foreground blending except in circumstances where the texture produced is exactly the one I wish to depict. Such exceptions include muddy or dusty floors, uneven plastered walls, anywhere that doesn't include sharp edges or hard shadows. The slab floor and walls in this Bearded Collie study (*fig 5*) are totally blended - in fact much of the 'detail' was drawn with an old graphite-coated tortillon. Graphite, mainly 2B and F in this case, was repeatedly applied to the floor and blended until I achieved the desired appearance. The initial blending was carried out with a piece of toilet tissue wrapped around my finger. As I am very familiar with the properties of my paper I blended some areas with excessive pressure, knowing that it would cause 'clumping' of graphite grains and raised fibres, which I used to suggest the broken, uneven surfaces.

The blending tool I use depends on the size and value of the

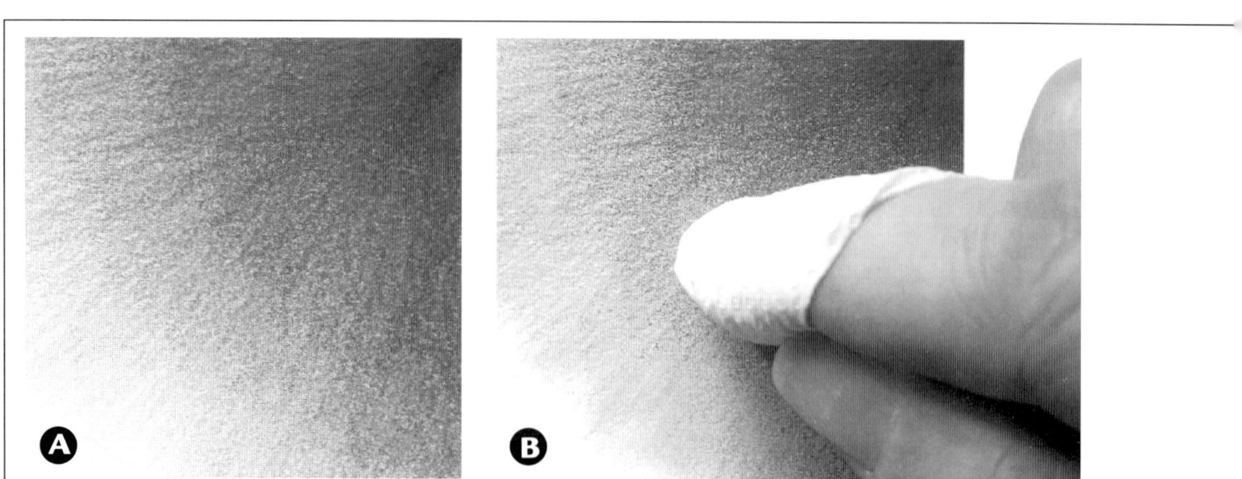

area to be blended. I have stumps (torchons), which I rarely use, and tortillons. Stumps, being solid-bodied, have a harder point so they absorb less graphite. Torillons tend to absorb more, which means they can deposit more too - even where not required. My greater use of the softer tortillons occurs because I generally employ used, graphite-saturated tortillons. In other words - I don't clean them, other than to press their points into Blu-Tack to remove surface graphite. For tight spots and where a clean point is necessary I prefer to use a Colour Shaper. This absorbs very little graphite and is easily cleaned by twisting the point into a kneadable eraser or Blu-Tack.

The right tool for the right job really depends on your requirements. There isn't a rule you can apply for stating which tool is the one ideally suited to the job - testing and experience usually serve to suggest the most appropriate. I use graphite-laden tortillons to draw faint, distant trees and other features. For large areas I wrap a kitchen paper towel or toilet tissue around my finger and use that. Other artists prefer cotton fabric or felt pads and Q-tips or cotton buds. Facial tissues are another alternative but take care that they are not medicated or contain moisturisers - oily content of any kind is to be avoided. A square of thin leather chamois wrapped around your index finger affords very controllable blending and you can fold or roll it and use the points for blending smaller areas. Experimentation is the key - use whatever best fits your immediate requirements, and your particular style and way of working.

Remember that blending redistributes graphite so the direction of your blending dictates the final result. The example below (*fig 6*) shows blending from dark to light where the intention was to produce a small gradation of tone. Blending was carried out with

'My chamois are really thin and very soft. I keep a new one on hand at all times and I have two used ones going - one really dirty, one partially dirty.

When it comes to cleaning, I hand wash them in dish soap then give them a good rinse. Place them in the dryer for about 15 minutes on medium. Then I add a couple drops of linseed oil on my hands and rub it evenly all over the chamois. Put it back in the dryer for the remaining time (about 15 minutes) and....voila! Nice supple pieces to start all over again with.'

Geary Wooten, Artist

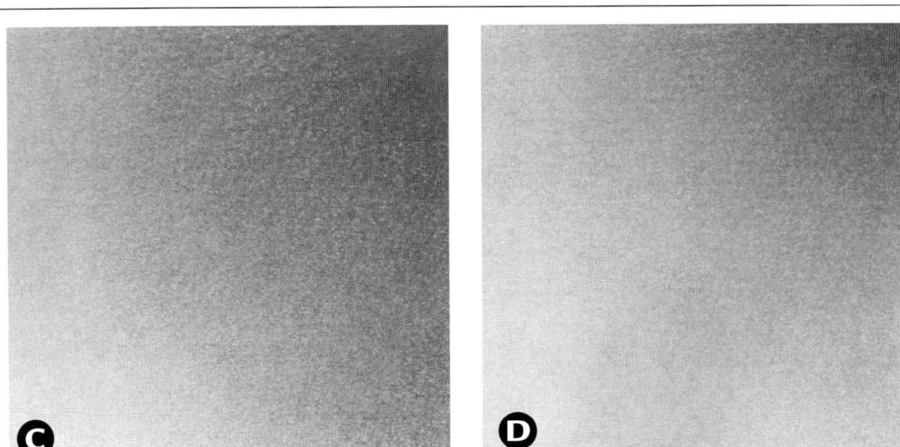

Fig.6

A. Radial hatching with 2B, HB and 2H on coarse watercolour paper prior to blending.

B. Blending with kitchen paper towel from dark to light.

C. Completed blending.

D. Note fingerprint at bottom - nothing will remove it. Do not touch paper before blending!

lightly applied, circular movements of the towel, working in overlapping arcs down towards the lightest area. Before this was reached the weight of the blending was considerably reduced then finally altered from circular to radiating lines so the light area received little redistributed graphite. The towel picked up soft graphite from the darkest corner then, having mixed it with the central HB, picked up HB graphite and spread that over and into the 2H. Finally, having picked up 2H, the resulting graphite mix was spread evenly over the rest of the area. A clean towel was then used to blend in the reverse direction, working towards, but not reaching, the darkest corner. This brightened the lighter area by removing graphite.

To achieve a greater gradation, blend from light to dark to prevent the softer graphite being dragged over the light area. It is also possible to lighten over-blended tone by removing graphite with Blu-Tack. Use other methods first, such as a pad of clean chamois or soft toilet tissue, to remove as much graphite as possible and only then resort to Blu-Tack.

Pull a finger of Blu-Tack out from the ball and form it into a perfectly smooth, curved surface with rounded edges. Now stroke it very lightly, barely touching the paper, outwards from the lightest tone. This method is for rescue use only and I don't recommend it except in desperate circumstances. If you try it, never stop your Blu-Tack without gradually lifting it clear as you stroke. Lifting it directly will leave a visible edge that blending will not eliminate.

In the previous example the application of the graphite was

Fig 7

Vertical hatching and, following the contours, crosshatching on smooth Mellotex.

Dark tones first blended with tortillon. Central tone gently blended with toilet tissue. Finally the entire area was blended light to dark with toilet tissue.

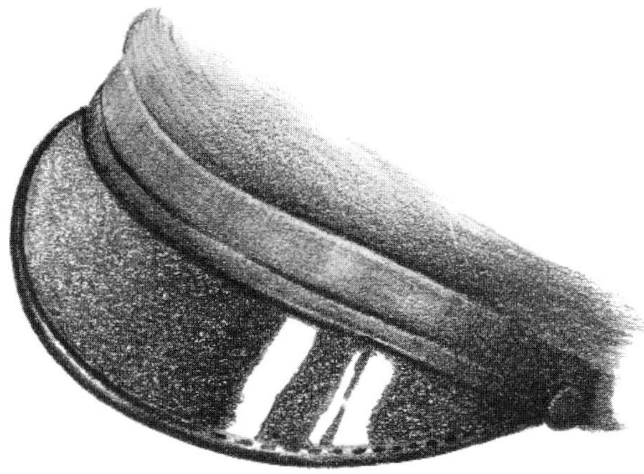

Fig 8

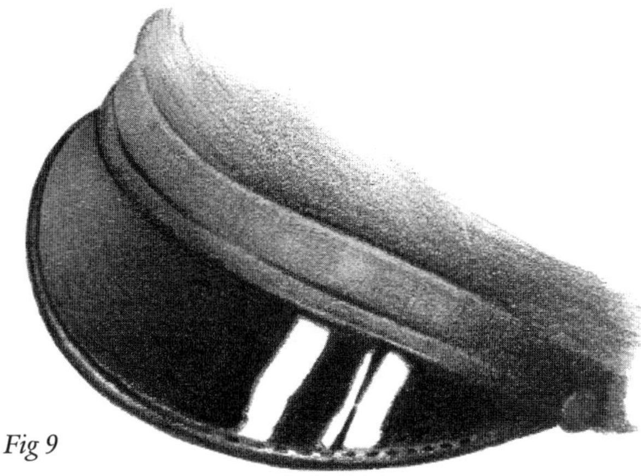

Fig 9

deliberately coarse so you could see the direction and position of the various grades. In use, hatching and cross-hatching, and building up the tones by layering will obtain much better results (*fig 7*). Although blending will, theoretically, eliminate all signs of linear shading it is still preferable that your hatching follows the contours of the surface. It will at least be a constant reminder of the three-dimensional shape under your pencil and allow you to 'sculpt' the object.

If blending is carried out with a light touch, preserving the tooth of the paper as much as possible, further layers can be added as required to subtly fine-tune the tonal shaping.

Burnishing

Before you decide to blend always bear in mind that it will partially flatten the tooth of your paper. If additional drawing needs to be carried out in that area, blending with medium to heavy pressure may make further layers difficult, or even impossible, to apply.

Layering, however, doesn't suffer from this limitation. As long as the order of application is correct - always hard over soft - additional layers will be possible. This can be of great benefit when drawing a hard, shiny surface such as the celluloid peak of a military-style cap. Allowing too much of the texture of your paper to show will prevent it from looking really flat and shiny (*fig 8*).

One certainty with such surfaces is that they contain absolutely featureless, graduated tone. Employing a hard grade of graphite to heavily blend or 'burnish' the dark-toned areas often gets rid of the intrusive grain structure of the softer grade beneath it and helps to fill every indentation in the paper (*fig 9*). I drew this cap on textured watercolour paper, using 2B for the darkest tones. The burnishing layer predominantly consisted of HB with 2H over the lighter tones and 8H over the

'Said Hamlet to Ophelia,
I'll draw a sketch of thee,
What kind of pencil
shall I use? 2B or not 2B?'

Spike Milligan

lightest. Working in small circles achieves the best results, as it ensures every indentation is approached from all angles. However, where the circles might show or not offer proper tonal management, usually over the lightest tones, light hatching from dark to light gives better control. For general use or as a starting point, try burnishing 6B with 2B, and 2B with HB or even 2H. Depending on the choice of burnishing grade, the actual tonal value may remain much the same (although the perceived tone will darken owing to the removal of the white content) but the area will gain a more even appearance. Where surface texture indentations are a major distraction, it will be necessary to first layer with the same or a slightly harder grade of graphite until the white content has been eliminated. You can then burnish the result with a harder grade. To burnish a soft grade on a smooth or plate surface with the minimum of tonal alteration, choose a much harder grade as your burnishing point - try 2H, for example, to burnish 2B.

Handmade tortillon

Making tortillons

Tortillons are relatively cheap to buy but you can easily make your own if you prefer - with a bit of practice. Simply take a bought one apart and you'll soon understand their construction. Instead of using the soft blotting-paper material used for the commercial varieties experiment with different paper types. The degree of softness or hardness of the point is determined by the type of paper you choose to make it out of. You may find the perfect type to suit you.

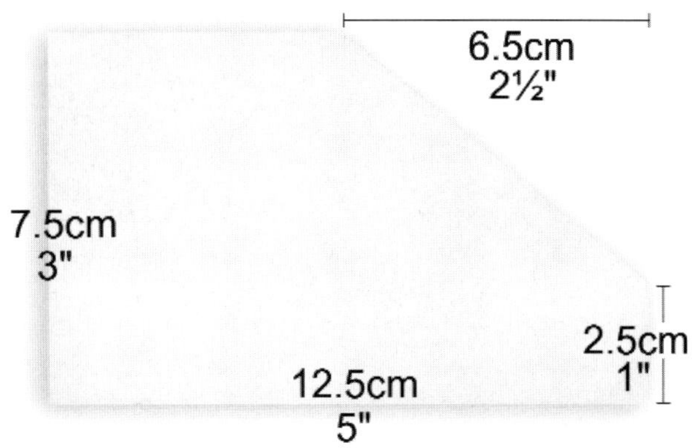

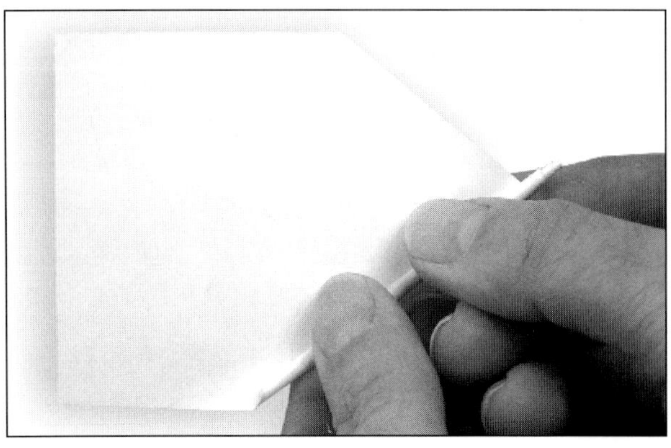

How to make a handmade tortillon.

I find thinner paper is easier to roll so I use 80gsm fan-fold or copier paper. Take your piece of paper and a big wastepaper basket (you'll need it for the failures!), now fold over the bottom corner two or three times or, as I do, use a very thin knitting needle to start the roll then pull it out. The angle is critical - too steep and you'll have a long, weak point, not steep enough and a point will not form on the end.

When you've rolled the entire sheet, wrap a small length of masking tape around it then cut off the excess length with a pair of scissors. I find it helps if you then hold the tapered section and twist the body in an anti-clockwise direction to tighten up the roll and firm the point. A second piece of

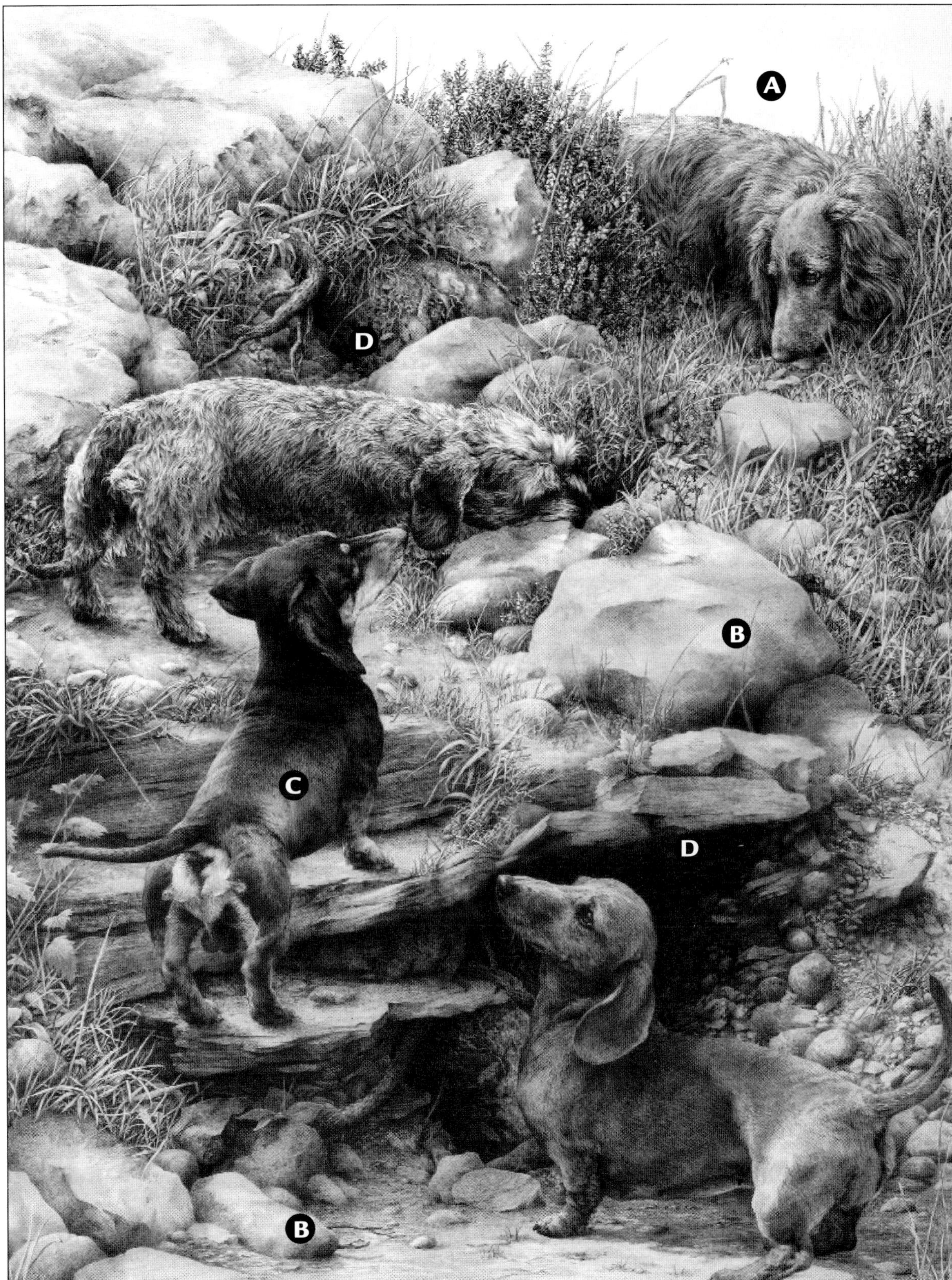

'The Warreners' © Mike Sibley. A limited edition print of 550 copies. 15½" x 11½" (40 x 30 cm)

masking tape just above the top of the taper keeps the roll held tight. A better alternative to masking tape is Scotch 810 Magic Mending Tape as the adhesive is more permanent and doesn't squeeze out around the edges with use.

Here is how all these various methods of blending are combined in the above example 'The Warreners'.
A - Sky: paper towel blending
B - Boulders/Ground: tortillon blending
C - Dogs: layering only
D - Rabbit Holes: burnishing

Indenting
The pointed approach...

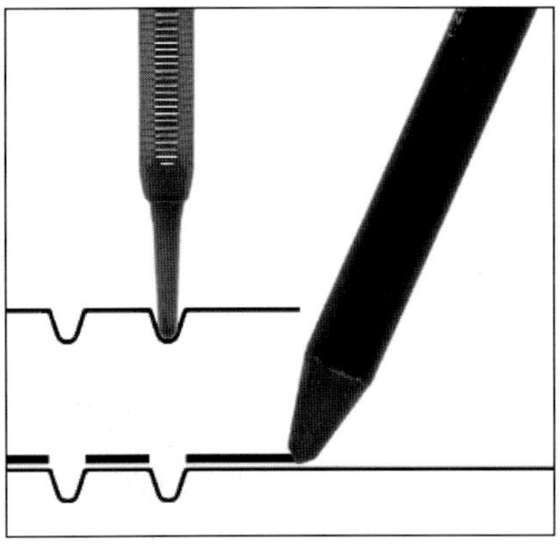

Fig 1

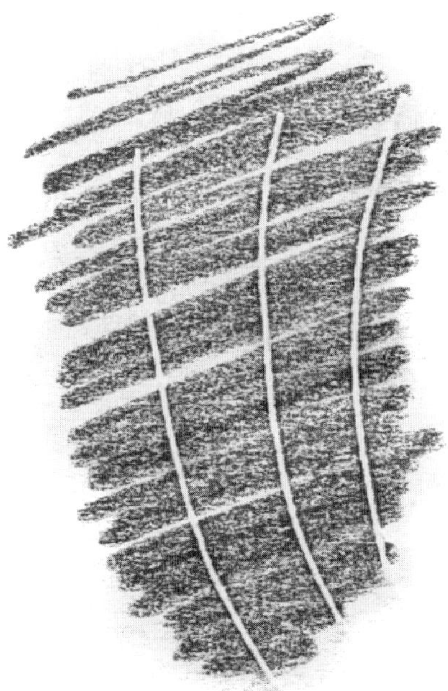

Fig 2. Indented lines appearing as 6B is applied with a Progresso pencil.

This range of techniques is properly termed 'indenting' or 'impressing' but you may also know it as 'incising' - I used that term a long time ago and it stuck. Strictly speaking, of course, incising involves the act of cutting, which is not what we want at all. No, our goal is to produce a smooth-edged indentation in the paper that later drawing will skip over (*fig 1*).

As a child did you ever play with one of those 'magic painting' books? The ones where you painted clear water over the page and a coloured picture miraculously appeared! The technique of indenting is similar, and as magical, but in reverse. Here you apply graphite to the page and pure white lines appear (*fig 2*). The method relies on the prior pressing, or indenting, of carefully positioned lines into the surface of your paper. Be aware that it works on some surfaces better than others. If the fibre structure is too loose you may produce lines with irregular or fuzzy edges. Your paper must possess enough weight, or thickness, to accept the impression but you may have problems with paper that is too thick or soft. And speaking of softness, you will achieve the best results by having a really hard surface beneath your paper. A Melamine or other plastic laminate surface, as found on most quality drawing boards, is ideal or you could try a sheet of safety glass. If your paper sinks beneath the pressure of your indenting stylus then control of direction will be difficult, the lines are less likely to possess sharp, clean edges and your stylus may actually tear the fibres. Experimentation is the key. What works for me may not work for you so you need to find your own solution.

The Tools

In my early days I experimented with the use of my thumbnail, a blunt carpenter's bradawl, a raffia needle, a boxwood pottery tool, an empty ballpoint pen and other various points but I now use a custom-made stylus. I know other artists who use knitting needles quite effectively.

Let's get right down to basics. What we want to achieve is a controlled indentation, or valley, in the surface of the paper over which succeeding layers of graphite will expose and leave as a white line. There is only one requirement - a point that will indent but not tear the paper's surface. In short, a rounded, smooth tip, not a sharp point.

My own tool consists of a large darning or sewing-up needle mounted in an old clutch pencil or lead holder. These needles suit perfectly as they are designed to pass between sewn threads and not split them, which they achieve by having the blunt, rounded tip that we require. To make this indenting tool you will need to remove the eye from the needle because it may be too wide to fit the internal tube. Simply hold the eye of the needle in a pair of pliers and the body in another pair alongside them. Now bend the needle away from you (to avoid any flying steel splinters) by twisting the pliers in opposing directions until the eye of the needle snaps off. Open the clutch of the pencil and insert the broken needle to check for size. If it's a loose fit wrap tape around the needle until the clutch holds it firmly in place. You now have a purpose-made indenting stylus that by its very nature is as comfortable to hold and as controllable as your pencils.

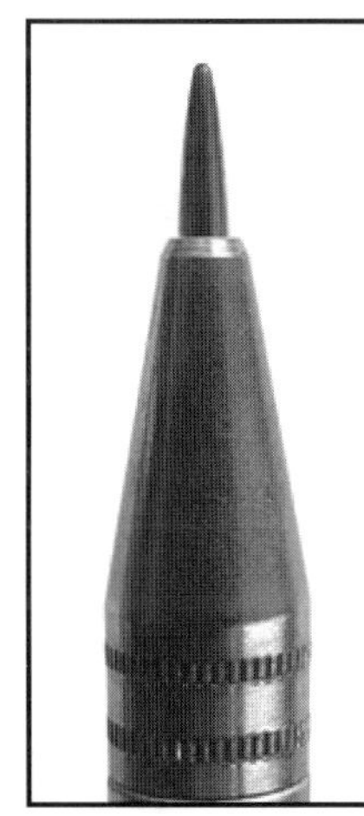

I actually use two of these, the one shown here and a version with a thinner tip. In the second case I took a lighter needle and slightly rounded its sharp point with an oilstone. Even so, it has to be used with care and never vertically, as the tip is still capable of catching and tearing paper fibres.

Uses

You've made your stylus or found a suitable tool, tested it, experimented and it produces good, clean lines. So... what can you use it for? Well, my main use, as you may have guessed, is to produce white hairs in dark areas. Other uses include cats' whiskers, especially the long brow-whiskers that cut across the direction of surrounding hair. Now you may begin to understand why I am so insistent on these indented lines being sharp-edged. Used properly and after some practice, you should be able to indent a line that has perfectly parallel sides. The secret to this is maintaining the same pressure throughout the length of the hair. If you increase pressure the point will sink deeper and widen the line. Conversely slackening pressure will narrow it so any inconsistency of pressure will cause the line to look unnatural. Keeping the pressure constant is made much easier by following my earlier advice - a hard surface below and paper not too thick or thin - preferably with a smooth, tight-fibre surface.

'WHAT WE WANT TO ACHIEVE IS A CONTROLLED INDENTATION, OR VALLEY, IN THE SURFACE OF THE PAPER OVER WHICH SUCCEEDING LAYERS OF GRAPHITE WILL EXPOSE AND LEAVE AS A WHITE LINE.'

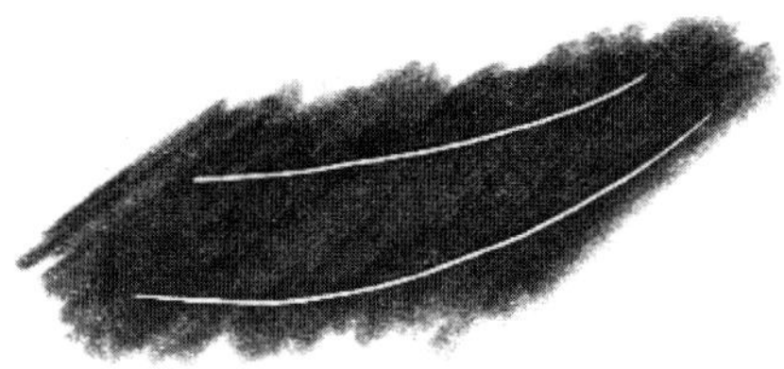

Top line: showing from left to right how a constant decrease of pressure produces a tapering point.

Below line: Tapers at both ends resulting from a constant increase then decrease of pressure.

You can, of course, use the properties of decreasing pressure to control the termination of the line. In the case of dogs' hairs and, in particular, cats' whiskers, you need to produce a constant-width line ending in a fine taper - easily produced by a steady decrease in pressure aimed at applying no pressure at all at the terminal point.

Before you get carried away with enthusiasm for your newfound technique - a word of caution. An indented line cannot be erased so you must get it right first time. The first key to this is observation - making quite certain that you know where the line is to be positioned, its start and end points, its curvature and width and its final taper. The second is practice - dry runs. It often helps to draw a very faint guideline following the desired path of the indent. If you do this, draw it with a single movement of your wrist so you know you can recreate the arc with your stylus. It is important that you draw it slightly to one side of the required path because if you incorporate any of the guideline into the indent the graphite will be difficult or even impossible to remove - the pressure used for the indentation will deeply embed any existing graphite that it crosses. Better to follow the golfer's method of practice swings - get yourself balanced and take repeated 'swings' with the point of your stylus just clear of the paper. When you feel your hand is following the correct arc and everything else is as it should be, commit the line to paper.

If you make a mistake all is not lost - but you cannot re-route the hair, position a new hair that crosses the old one obliquely or alter the existing indent. What you can do, however, is draw it out - drawing into and carefully filling the indent until its internal and external values match. It's time-consuming and a pains-taking process but it can be done. Better still to get it right first time!

Let the magic begin...

OK, we have our indented line but how do we see it, protect it, work around it and make it appear as though it is a white whisker positioned on top of the graphite layers 'beneath' it?

You'll soon discover just how hard you can draw across this indent without graphite dropping into it. In fact, you'll find that the harder you apply pressure to lines or tone that cross it, the more defined it will appear.

First it will help if you mark its presence, which is simply achieved by taking a soft grade pencil and lightly shading across it. You'll find that crossing it at an angle works best. If you attempt to draw directly across it at right angles you run the risk of your pencil point dropping into it. The same applies to shading along its length. As you can see from the top illustration a bonus of the indent, when applied to a plate finish paper, is that the pressure of the stylus raises the edges. The burr produced here produces a darker line along both edges and also helps prevent the pencil dropping into the indentation. I prefer to use a 6B Progresso solid graphite pencil for this stage - its physical lightness aids delicacy and a wide, smooth tip also assists. Keep this shading light. It does not conform to, or even take into consideration, the correct tonal value of the area and may need to be removed later. For now it is simply a marking device.

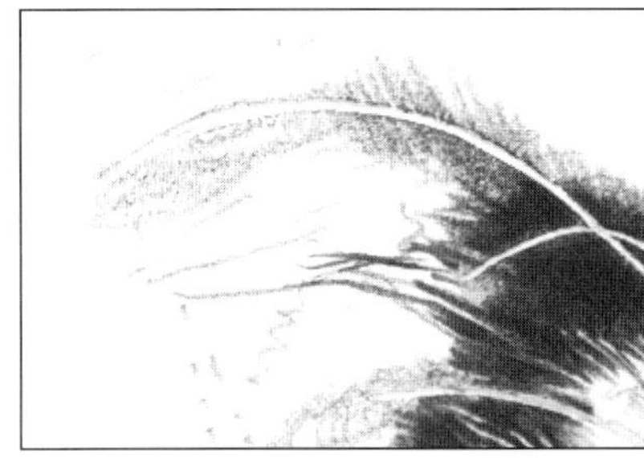

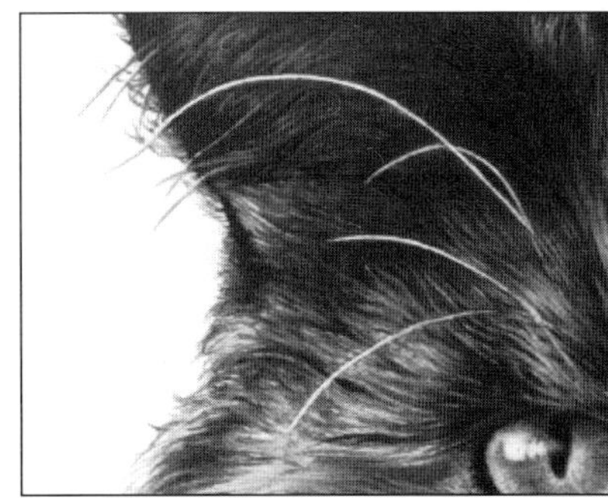

Protecting the virginity of the line is of paramount importance. You can lift out graphite dust with a knife-edge of Blu-Tack or kneadable eraser but if you physically draw into the indent, removing the graphite will be both difficult and necessary. The eye expects to see a sharp-edged, parallel-sided, pure white whisker and any deviation from this will destroy the apparent reality you are seeking to achieve. Using a fixed hand-guard to prevent graphite being smudged into the indent is a great help.

Having lightly marked the position of your line you can now safely forget it. Just be aware of it as you work around it, stopping at one edge and continuing at the other. If the indent crosses an area of deep, dark tone use the wide, flat tip of a soft pencil, such as 6B, to draw over and across it with ever-increasing pressure. If you're using a card such as Mellotex or Bristol board, don't worry, no amount of pressure will obliterate the line, instead it will simply define the edges more and more clearly.

As the drawing progresses to either side of the indent you'll begin to see it appear as an entity in its own right. Now is the time to exaggerate, to fool the brain into thinking the line is a whisker lying on a plane above the surrounding drawing. You need to send the right signals, to build in clues to help the brain decipher the area the way you want to have it deciphered. How? By being forceful. By including clues with such obvious solutions that no brain can fail to recognise a whisker when it sees one.

We use the 'status', or out-of-place, hairs that I will describe fully in chapter 14. I deliberately cross these whiskers with strong images such as exaggerated shadows between locks of

'Wherever possible, engineer strong elements that cross the line of travel of the indented hair to emphasise its presence, delineate its edges and throw it forwards.'

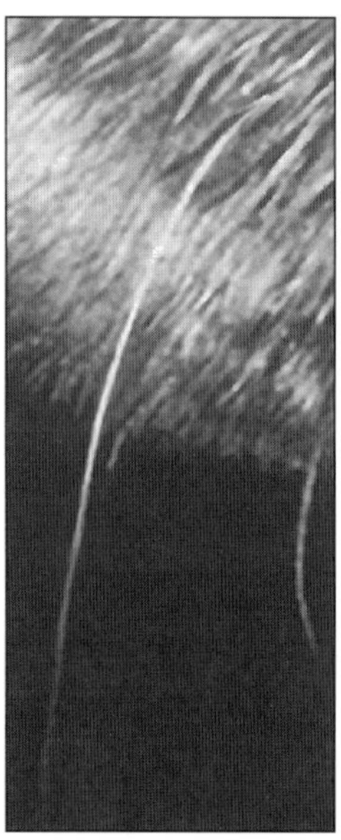

Tuck the whisker's root behind other hair, and tone the tapering end so the central white purity reads as a highlight.

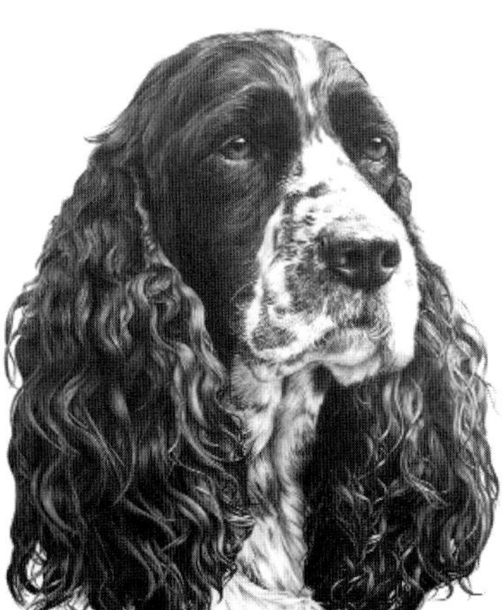

hair or individual lighter hairs. These dark shadows and strong lines visually reinforce their continuity to either side of the white indent. They are used to force the eye into taking notice of the way the white line breaks them as it crosses over. There, I've said it - 'crosses over' - the only visual conclusion that the brain can arrive at. Not under or through but over. Finally, the exaggerated shadows of the dark hair beneath gives them an enhanced three-dimensionality that the indent, deliberately, does not echo. These signals can be read in no other way than a white whisker lying on a separate plane, which is exactly the aim. Wherever possible, engineer strong elements that cross the line of travel of the indented hair to emphasise its presence, delineate its edges and throw it forwards.

Now that we have the whisker on a plane in front of the hair we have to find a way of joining the two at one end. No whisker ever just begins - it has a root from which it must spring. This may sound obvious but it should be made obvious. The actual root is probably rarely seen but it must be suggested in order to preserve a look of reality. In practice, you need only tuck the base of the whisker behind other hair but you must then be aware that it should contain the shadow of that hair. Again we can use this to our advantage - even if the shadow does not exist in reality, including it will send the right signals and move the end of the whisker from the front plane back into the plane containing the hair. All of this is achieved with a little subtle shadowing drawn directly into the terminus of the indentation with a 2H or similar grade. This device is double-edged for not only does this shadow tell the brain that the whisker springs from the hair, it also reinforces that the rest of it is on a plane nearer to us. As a further refinement, adding just a touch of light tone to the other, tapering, end will give the whisker a true curvature, as its central white purity will be read as a highlight.

Incidental uses

So far we have been studying the use of indenting for a major element but its uses extend to more mundane, but equally important, areas. Personally, I don't often use indenting preferring, where possible, to draw positively rather than negatively - drawing two tapering converging lines to suggest a tapering white hair between them. With experience I can draw very fine negative lines but there are times when the complexity required or accuracy necessitates the use of indenting.

Here, on the top lip of this Springer Spaniel, I've used my indenting tool to produce a fringe of 'random' hairs. Indenting often works best in these situations - where the impressed hairs have a dark or black background. Once the lines are impressed, you have the freedom to concentrate on the underlying area in the knowledge that the hairs above are already established. Note too that the areas above and below the fringe employ only negative drawing. Indenting does not feature here at all and is, in my opinion, best kept for occasional use where necessary. Although the casual observer may not (and hopefully never will) detect the technique it does produce a unique line. I drew this in 1990 and I can still tell where I did and did not employ the method.

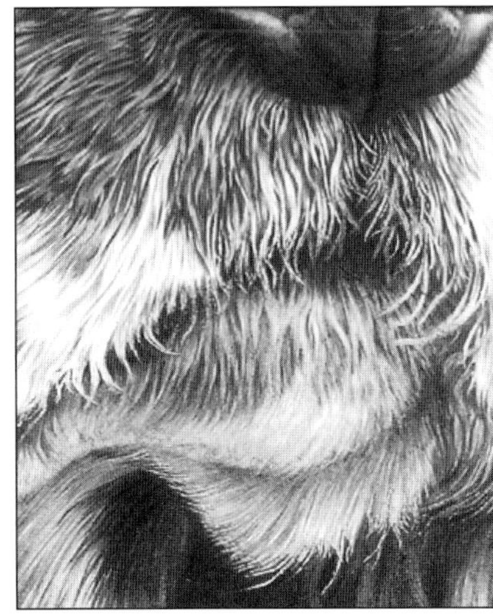

How is this achieved? The process begins soon after the lightly applied guidelines are in place. Starting at one end of the lip, the position of each major hair is determined. By this I mean those hairs that are out of place or for any other reason attract the eye - the status hairs. The line drawing (*fig 1*) is cut with an eraser and the lines impressed. Intermediate hairs, between status hairs, are indented spontaneously with an eye to the prevention of repetition. On completion the lower halves of the hairs are revealed (*fig 2*) by a light application of 6B. The lower jaw is drawn up close to the hairs but not into them (*fig 3*). I work dark to light wherever possible so the dark tone behind the hairs is now established. This area of shadow is now drawn back down to merge with the drawing of the chin below (*fig 4*). Working again from dark to light (fig 5), the dark band above the lip fringe is established and extended into the hairs above and down into the fringe below. Finally (*fig 6*) the roots of the fringe are blended into the drawing above and the indented lines themselves are toned down to give them form.

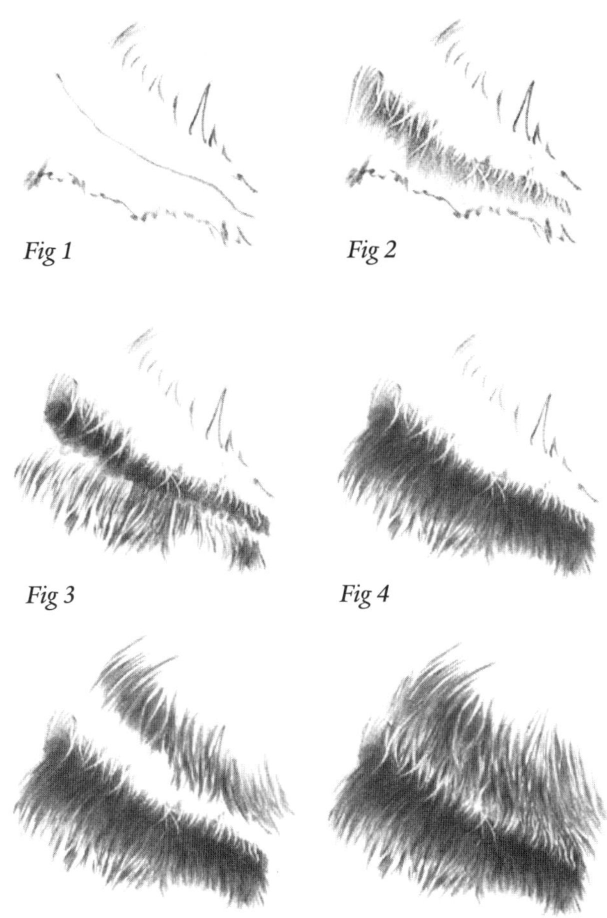

Fig 1 *Fig 2* *Fig 3* *Fig 4* *Fig 5* *Fig 6*

In the following example spontaneous applications of indented lines lead the brain to deduce wiry or harsh hair.

Remember that this technique produces fine white or light lines with certain clarity. Don't therefore employ the method in situations where no such clarity would naturally exist. For example, I've used indenting between the shoulders of this dog but not on his rear

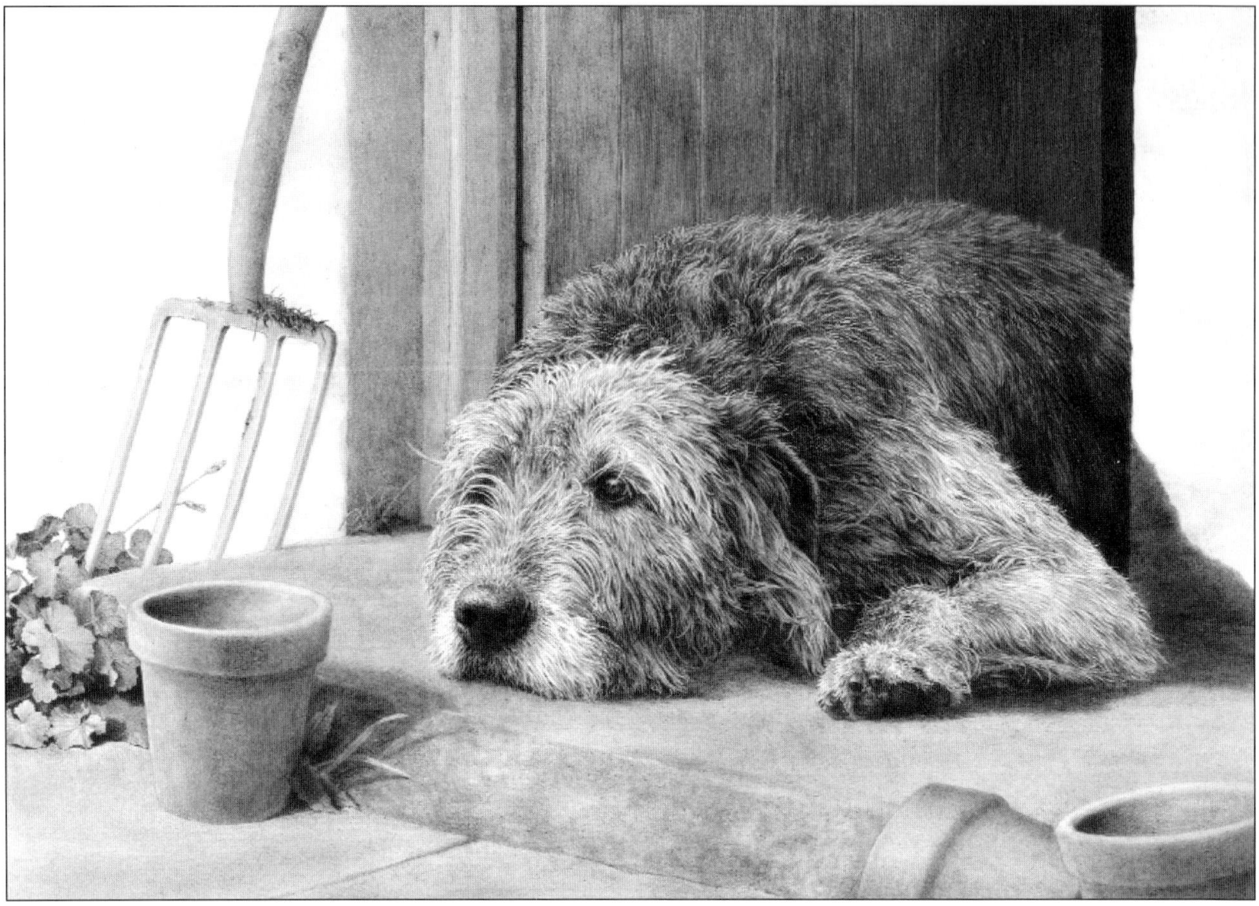

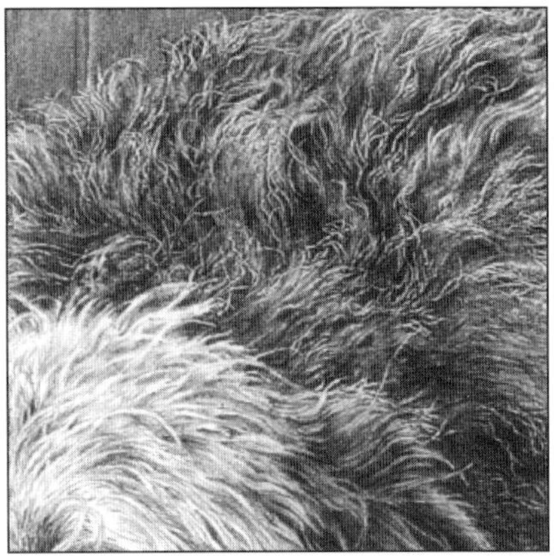

hindquarters. Employ the technique for foreground use, tentatively for the mid-ground but never for background situations where the eye does not expect to see such sharp detail. In this drawing I deliberately moved the rear end of the dog out of sharp focus to emphasise the head, neck and shoulders and to suggest recession. Any use of indenting behind the shoulders would have damaged or even destroyed the effect I was attempting to create.

Indenting indirectly

With this method, instead of indenting directly into your paper's surface, you use an intermediary sheet of tracing paper. It's a technique of which I have some experience but subsequently discarded. However, you may find it useful when indenting soft or coarse paper surfaces. It guarantees that no fibres will be torn and, if you're new to the techniques of indenting, it offers safety leading to confidence. However, as with all the methods described here, lines indented in error still cannot be removed.

Among the definite advantages are having full sight of your drawing beneath at all times and the ability to draw the

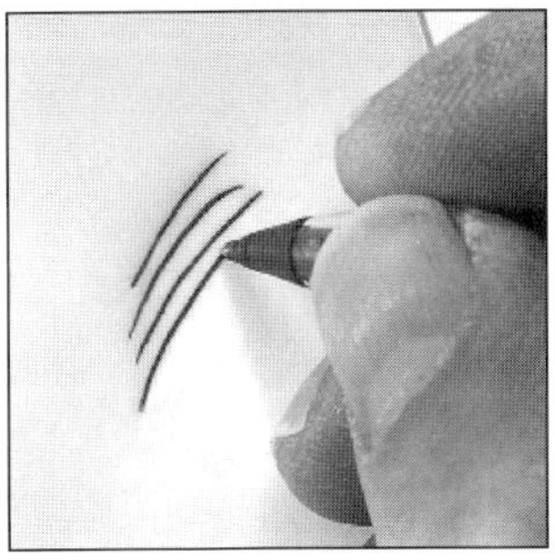

Indenting with a ballpoint pen onto Mellotex through tracing paper.

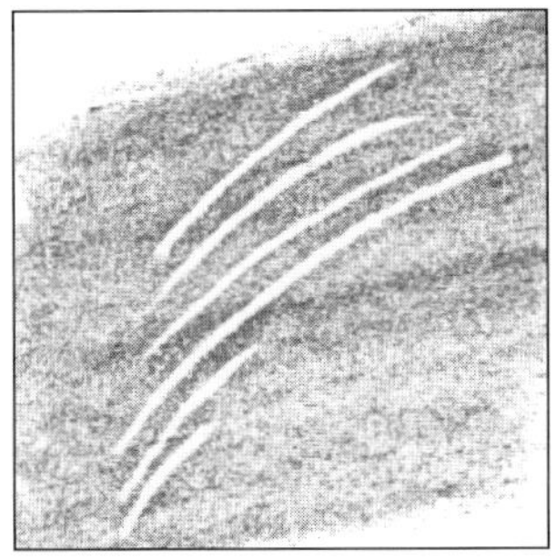

Indents exposed with 6B Progresso pencil.

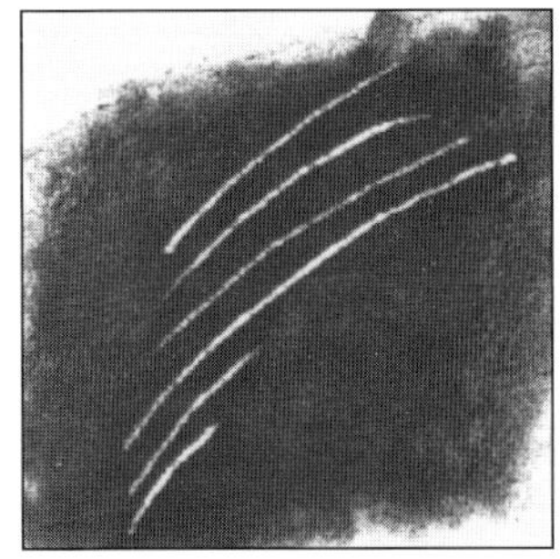

With two additional layers of 6B at maximum weight.

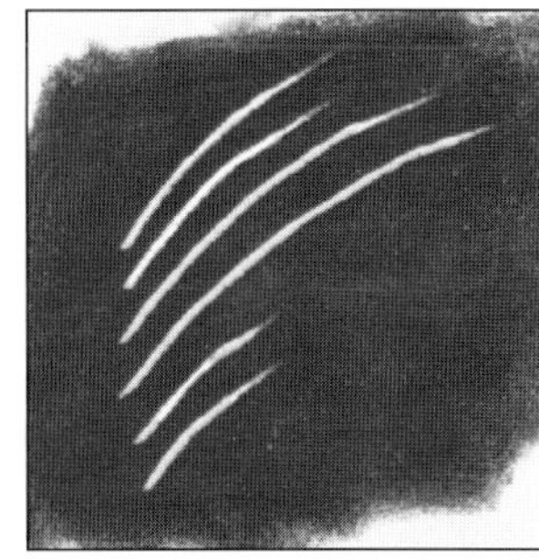

Stylus direct-to-surface indents for comparison.

indentations without physically touching the paper's surface. This allows you to draw with a hard-grade pencil or pen, as I have done here, leaving visible evidence of the lines drawn. Use of this method permits you to plan ahead. You can for instance plot all the indentations by drawing them onto the tracing paper first and then re-tracing them to indent your paper.

The reasons I no longer use this method are evident above. After applying a light layer of 6B graphite the results at first look promising. However, you will notice the marks have distinctly soft edges and further applications of 6B, applied with maximum pressure, show the edges collapsing.

Compare them to the marks shown above right. These were indented directly into the paper's surface with a stylus and have the customary sharp and burred edges. They remain more sharply defined despite identical treatment.

Texture and detail indenting

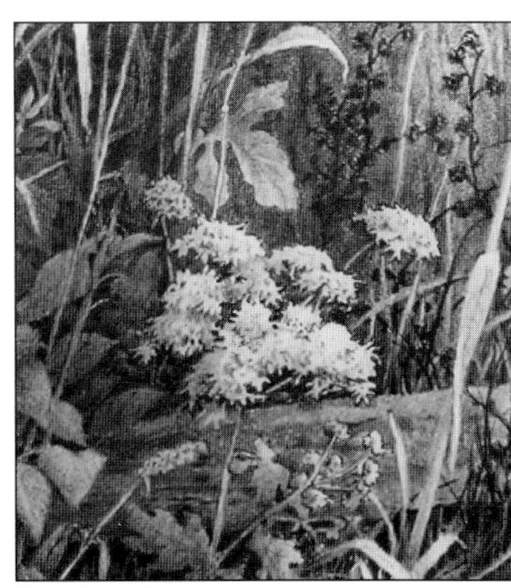

So far I have implied that indenting only involves line. Not true. Dot indenting is just as valuable. I use this infrequently but there are times when I have a key element in which I need to preserve the virgin white of the paper. I could use liquid frisket to mask it but I dislike the lack of spontaneity that applying it involves. In the case of the detail from 'Spinney Lane End' illustrated here, I had the intention right at the outset of the design stage of including shaded flower heads of white Cow Parsley. The weeds around and behind it were drawn spontaneously - designed as I drew - so I needed to protect the Cow Parsley and remind myself of where it was to appear. Dot indenting the principal flower heads solved this problem as surrounding drawing merely skipped over the marked position. A final light layer of 2H added the desired tone to signal that these flowers were in shade.

Indenting with graphite

So far I've covered indenting using only our custom-made tool but another method also exists - and one I use more frequently. Of the methods and means discussed so far this one is probably the most surface dependant. In other words, it works for me on Mellotex but may not work for you if your paper possesses a softer surface, a looser fibre or more tooth.

As I've mentioned before, I don't employ any form of underdrawing and carefully guard the available tooth of my paper. These days if I want to explore and define tonal relationships within an area I do it on a separate, small preparatory trial drawing. Adding exploratory graphite values directly to your drawing presents a real problem as it partially fills the tooth and limits the subsequent graphite-holding property of the paper. A light, trial application of HB, for example, will severely limit the later application of 6B that may have been a better choice.

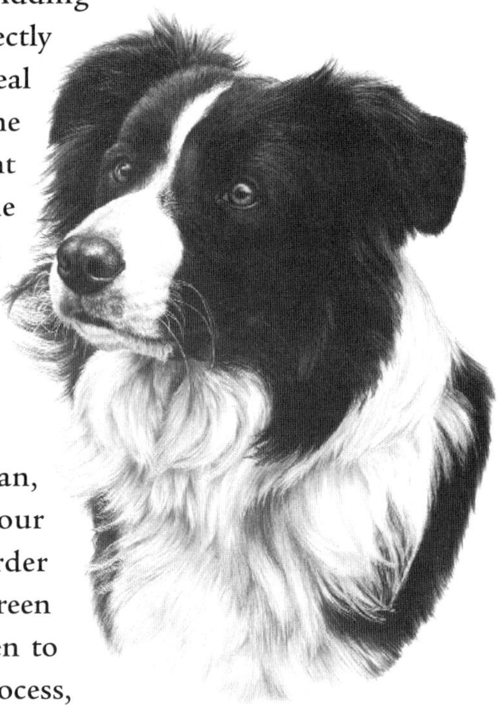

This potential problem can, however, be turned to our advantage. Think of the harder grade as a resist. Where a silkscreen printer applies wax to the screen to resist ink during the printing process, we can use a hard grade of graphite to resist a softer grade. As a rule the greater the difference between grades the greater the resist. I usually use 2H or harder to resist 6B or 4H to resist 2B. This is particularly true when drawing on coated card - a subject I'll return to in a moment.

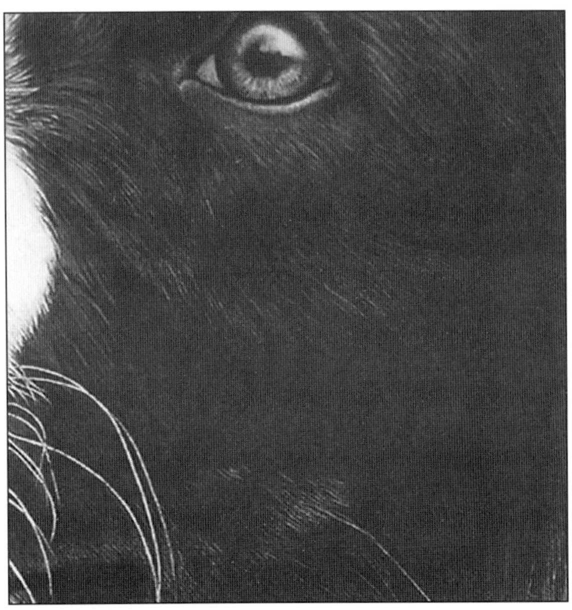

This area of my Border Collie drawing was produced using this method.

The white whiskers were produced with the use of my indenting tool but the less obvious highlighted detail was first drawn in with 2H and 4H in the knowledge that 6B would have insufficient tooth remaining to adhere. The 6B was then applied in

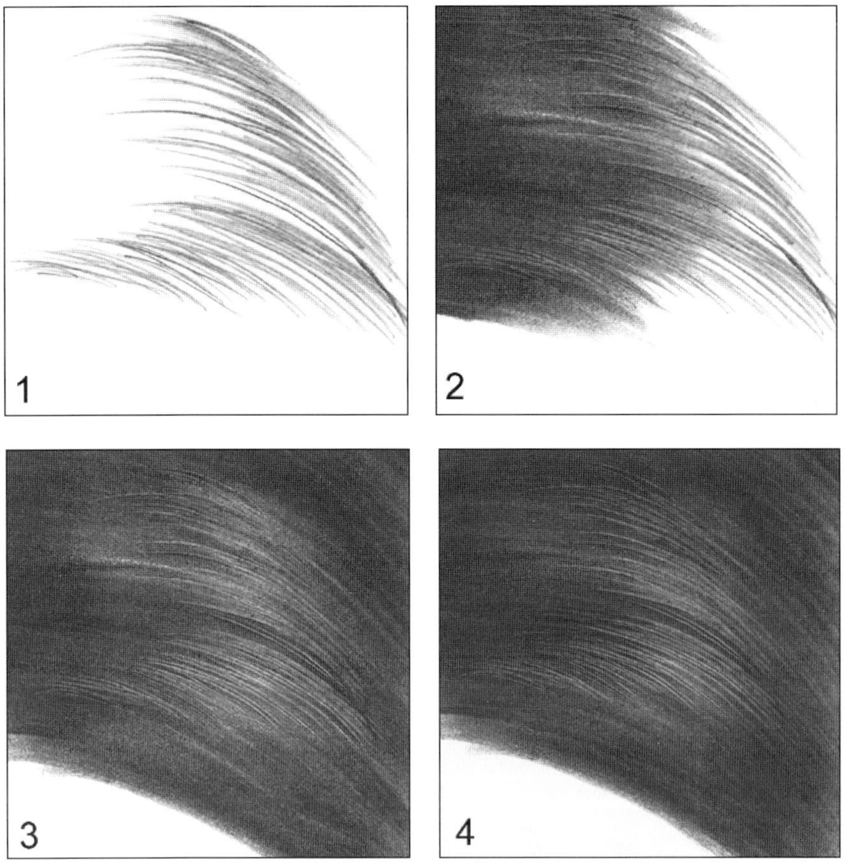

1. Area indented with a sharp 4H, drawing 'random' hair highlights.

2. Drawing with 6B into the 4H area following the hair direction.

3. 6B drawn back in from the other direction with reduced weight as it overlaps the 4H indenting.

4. Value increased and detail enhanced with 2B. Finally 2H was used to merge the ends of the indented 4H into the 2B/6B.

The result is the simulation of hair with natural random highlights as it curves over the body. Although this method requires a lot of practice it is surprisingly effective. Unlike stylus indenting it is preferable to layer the dark values in the same direction as the indents. In this case drawing across the shallow indents can render them almost invisible.

the direction of the hair, with sufficient force to embed grains into the virgin tooth, with no allowances being made for the previously drawn areas, which my pencil just skated over. A final burnish with 2B consolidated and smoothed the grains of the 6B without altering the appearance of the H areas, other than to fill in between the lines where I'd left gaps to denote shadows.

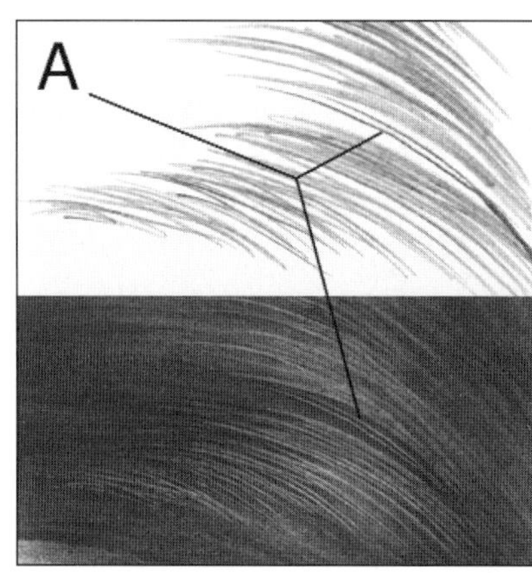

Follow the area 'A' (*right*) - easily detected throughout the process above - and you'll see that it begins as a pair of positive marks that finish as negative highlights. You need to bear this 'negative' factor in mind when you apply the 4H. Strange though it may at first seem, you are drawing highlights, not hairs or shadows. Shadows are produced by not drawing line - the negative spaces. These deliberate, virgin spaces left either side of the two lines that constitute 'A' were destined from the outset to be intense shadows. The closely spaced lines to either side translate as a mass of highlights, which contrast with and emphasise the shadows between them.

Coated-card techniques

If you are unfortunate enough to have to draw on coated card (and I am!) then the graphite indenting technique is

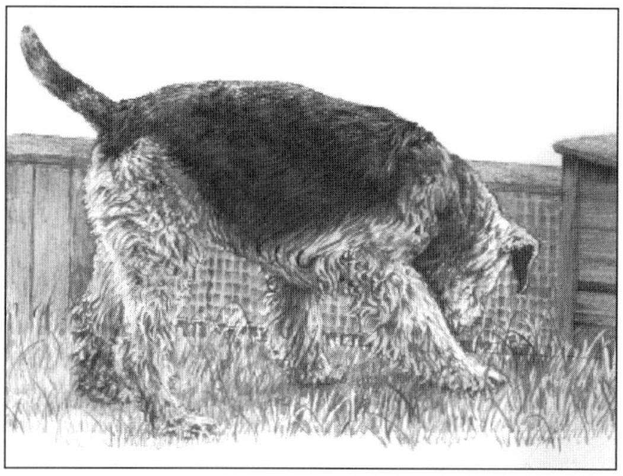

Part of a remarque from 'Visiting Aunt Maud' Approx size: 1½ " (38 mm) high

invaluable. I am regularly commissioned to add remarques (1½" high drawings in the bottom margin) to copies of my limited edition prints. These prints, for best results, are printed on thick paper coated with a calcium carbonate buffer. The printing quality is where the advantages cease, as it is one of the worst surfaces to draw on. Erasing is absolutely impossible. Blu-Tack will lighten values to some extent but any mechanical rubbing action outside of the image area immediately results in a distracting, shiny patch - and any inside the area renders it incapable of accepting graphite. Dark values are incredibly difficult to attain - I have to almost carve them into the coating. Yet if I break through the coating the instant dark value that results renders the drawing useless, as its rough texture is completely foreign to the rest of the image.

OK, so that's what I can't do. But what I can do is use graphite indenting. Whatever you remember from my description above, multiply it by ten. If 2H is applied to coated-card, 2B will never layer on top of it. Incidentally, 6B won't adhere to anything and just polishes the coating. So, I can produce light to medium detail with 2H and dark values with 2B. Using the technique I described above I can leave gaps between the 2H knowing that 2B will adhere and form shadows. Halftones and gradations are formed partly by grade F but blending provides the complete answer. I drag and blend the darkest values over to the lightest to create the mid-tones.

Indenting in general is a very useful tool but one to be treated with caution. I suggest you always question the need for its use before employing it. Essentially, it is a tool for producing a certain quality of line; it is not a negative drawing shortcut. Treat it with respect and it will produce some astounding results for you.

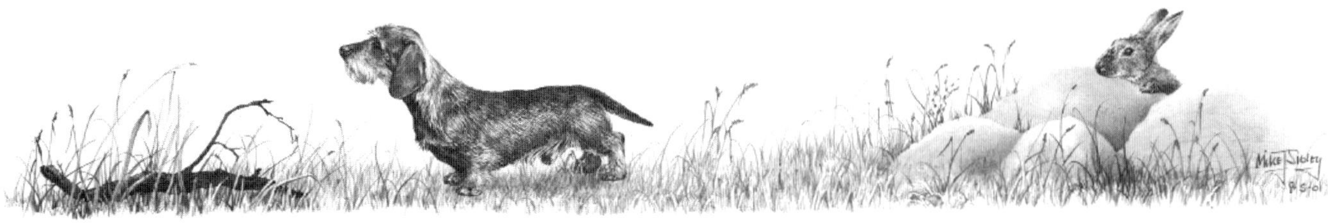

Panoramic remarque from 'The Warreners'

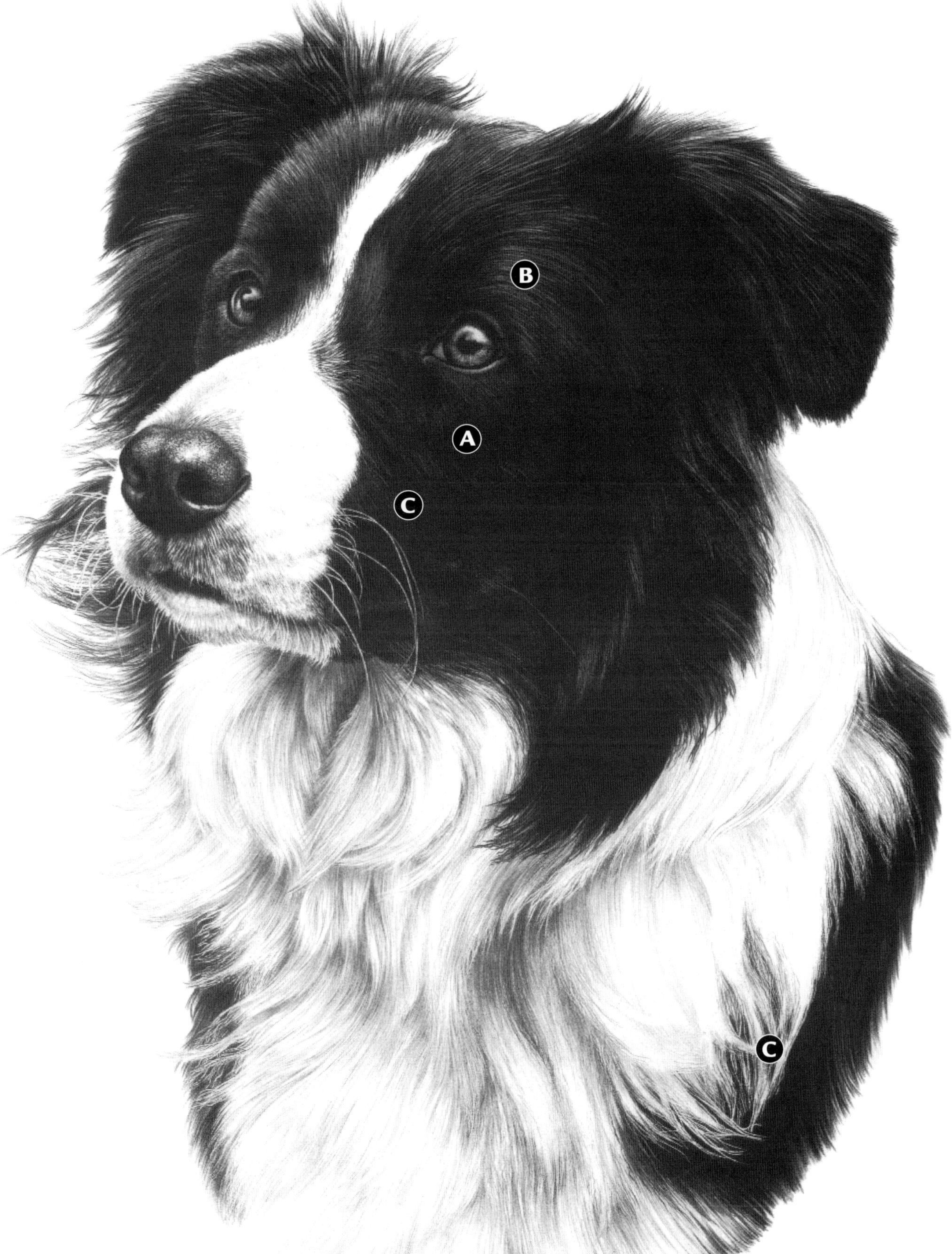

How indenting was used in the Border Collie
A: 2H indenting: side of face
B: 4H indenting: eye 'striations'
C: Stylus indenting: Whiskers; hair fringe on top lip and beneath bottom jaw, overlap of white/black at right hand side of body - etc

Live demonstration

Charlotte, my granddaughter...

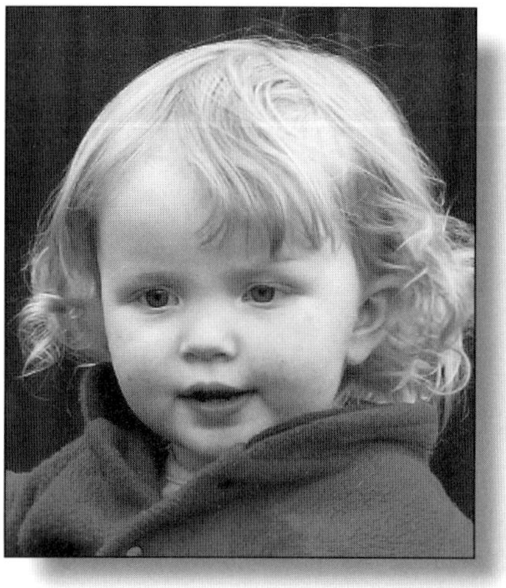

Later in this book you'll hear me say 'don't be afraid of attempting anything new' so I thought I should put myself in that position too. I have an interest in human portraiture but I've never before attempted it.

I considered a number of papers before deciding on my favourite Mellotex. Although its smooth surface permits delicate shading, it's too smooth for some techniques, such as blocking in tone and then blending it into adjacent areas. Mellotex, similar to 500 series Strathmore plate finish, lacks sufficient tooth to take a wide spread of smudged graphite, as the original block is soon depleted. However, the surface is ideal for very fine, light hair. I've decided to accept the extra work involved in cross-hatching the facial shaping in return for subtler detailing in the hair.

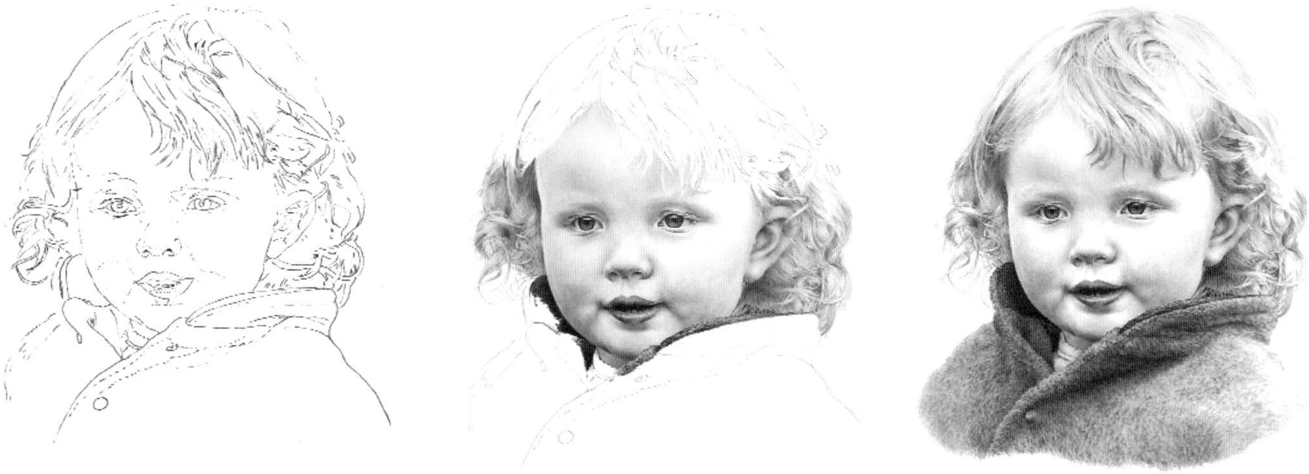

I've also been giving a lot of thought to the background. A dark background would undeniably simplify the drawing of the hair, but I've decided a white background will best complement Charlotte's delicate colouring. Perhaps unusually for a portrait, she is not looking at us and involving us in the composition. I think this physical separation combined with delicate tones will work here. By not making everything superficially obvious I plan to make the viewer actively participate in order to gain a better understanding.

I'll pause between each stage to write the notes that follow.

STAGE 1:

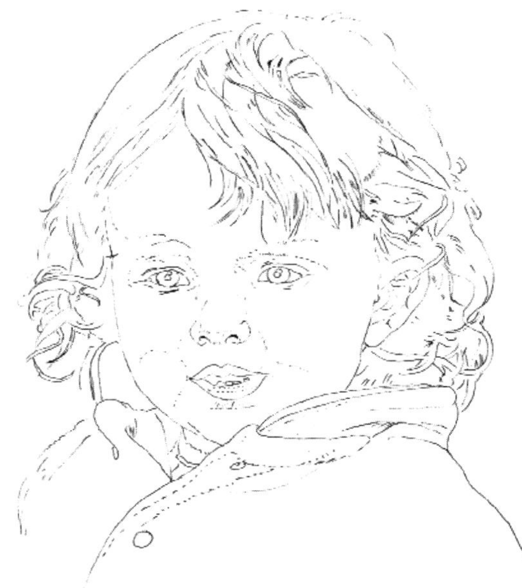

The guidelines, very lightly drawn with 2B, have been digitally enhanced throughout. For speed the original photo was projected and traced onto copy paper. Here it was reworked and refined. Problem areas were identified and resolved, and then the result was projected onto the final drawing surface as shown here.

STAGE 2:

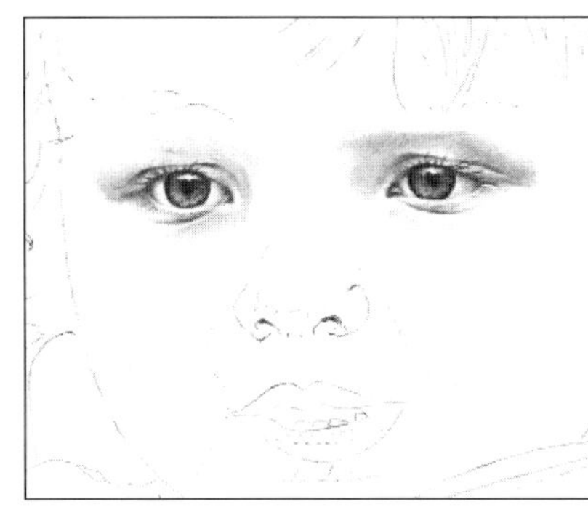

I'm going to begin with the eyes because, by first defining an area of sharp-edged clarity, I will have something against which I can balance the more delicate shading of the face. The paper represents my lightest tone and the pupils of the eyes contain the darkest so, with both established, all other tones will more easily fall into place.

I'm attempting to pull Charlotte's eyes out of the shadow of her brow for added emphasis but I won't describe in detail the drawing of her eyes as you can read about this in much more detail in chapter 23. However, I know I must resist the temptation to keep working on them before I have completed the surrounding facial structures. Only then will I be able to correctly fine-tune them.

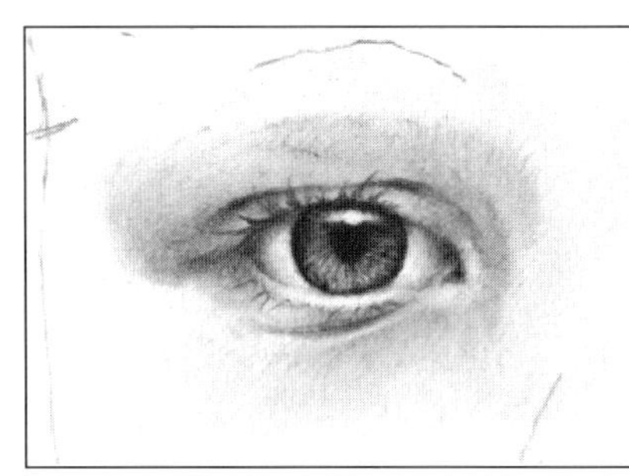

Close-up of left eye with more shading established.

STAGE 3:

I intended to draw the nose next but instead I've decided to complete the mouth. The plan is to first finish the lips and teeth and then build up the surrounding tones of the cheeks to give me a better idea of the tonal values I require to build the nose.

The lips are being built up with layers of hatched 2B, F and 2H lines, which are then blended with a colour-shaper. I'm paying particular attention to the highlight as this tells us the lips are moist and rounded, and the highlight itself describes the bottom lip's shaping and fullness. I'm also gradually pushing the teeth into shade, to the point where they are understandable but not visually distracting.

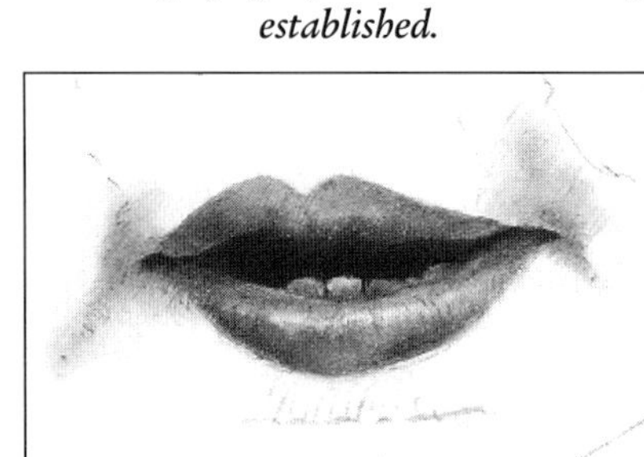

The mouth is nearing completion. The teeth are still too visually conspicuous and need further shading at this stage.

Because the tonal gradations in the chin and cheek areas are so fluid and delicate, I'm experiencing an unexpected problem. I'm tending to begin too lightly and with too hard a grade. It's not easy, and sometimes impossible to layer a soft grade over a harder one, so building up tone by hatching and blending is being made more difficult that it need be. Sooner or later I'll find the right combination of grades, and the sooner the better!

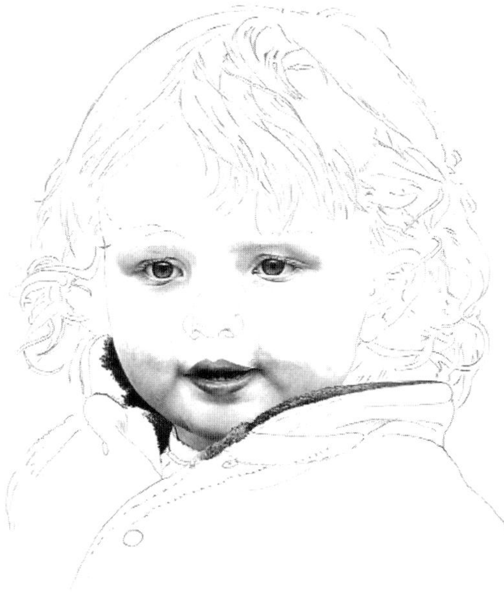

The tonal values used for the shaping of the cheeks and chin should assist with determining the tones required for the nose.

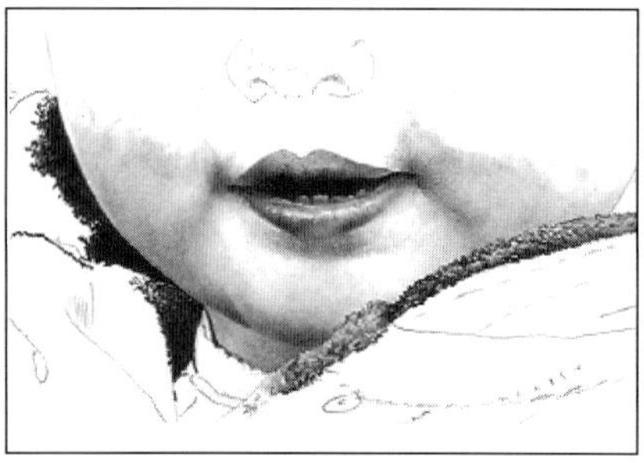

Stage 4:

The combination of grades that seems to be working is F and 2H, with the occasional very light prior application of 2B, all applied by hatching and cross-hatching with gentle strokes of a flat tip. Indentations caused by heavy-handed lines are to be avoided at all cost, as blending will not eradicate them.

After blending with a tortillon, further applications of 2H gradually build up and smooth the gradations. The tortillon, now graphite-coated, is also often employed like a soft pencil for fine-tuning areas. Where I want to blend and lighten in one step I'm using a clean colour-shaper instead. All other blending is being carried out with a homemade copy-paper tortillon. This suits the job perfectly, as it absorbs little graphite; the tip suffers minimal wear even under pressure; and the slim but rigid body aids accuracy.

I find that squinting through half-closed eyes at my reference photographs sufficiently reduces the detail to allow me to correctly see the differing blocks of tone. Establishing the darker blocks first, carefully avoiding the creation of hard edges, gives me a good feel for the correct shaping. These blocks are then extended with lighter tone, and the very lightest tones are left white. Blending from dark to light then produces smooth gradations and drags graphite lightly into the white areas.

I've also drawn the coat adjacent to her face so I can properly judge the tones required for her cheek. The coat is important to me, as my intention from the start has been to use its texture to contrast with, and thus emphasise, the smoothness of Charlotte's skin. To increase that contrast, I'm interpreting the shadows within the coat's texture as small angular shapes, understating its softness rather than attempting to faithfully copy it.

Tip

Remember, nothing in life has a line around it. So erase all your guidelines to faint shadows before starting a new area.

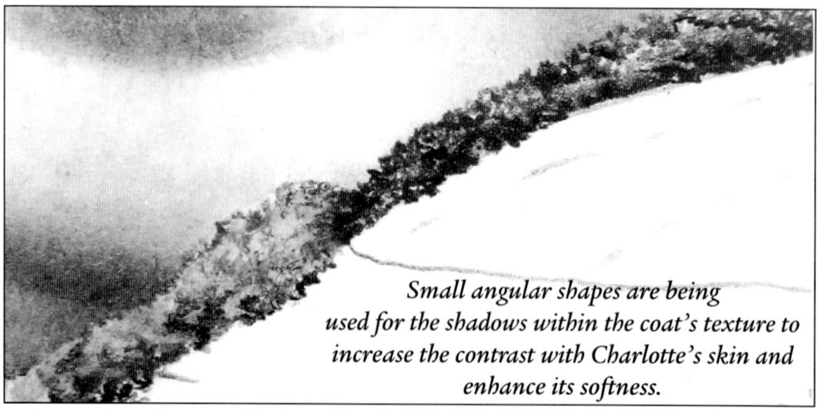

Small angular shapes are being used for the shadows within the coat's texture to increase the contrast with Charlotte's skin and enhance its softness.

STAGE 5:

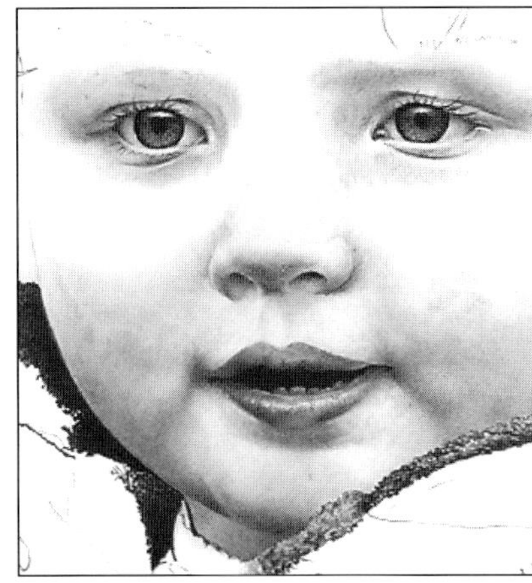

With the mouth completed and the cheeks extended upwards, the facial shaping has finally reached the nose. Establishing the nostrils first, gives me a drawing break to work from, and a local instance of the darkest tone against which I can judge all surrounding tones.

The nose, like all other areas of skin is being built up with 2H hatching, cross-hatching, and blending. As long as the shading is tight enough, and no undue pressure has indented the surface, all the blended pencil strokes completely disappear. Additional layers of graphite are then added and blended as required to build up the tones. Very light areas are left white then appropriate tone is added to these areas by blending alone. The graphite, which becomes progressively thinner as it is spread by the blender, is lightly dragged and thinned further to provide the required subtle gradation.

STAGE 6:

The nose is perhaps the most difficult human feature to draw, as the nostrils are the only elements that have hard, definable edges. Everything else is merely a collection of curves and shadows. It can be even more difficult in a young child because the bridge is broad and shallow. As I can't correctly judge the very light tones required for the bridge of Charlotte's nose, I'm first going to complete the cheeks up to the eyes then, with the bridge surrounded by tone, I can finally understand the values required to close the gap and finish the nose.

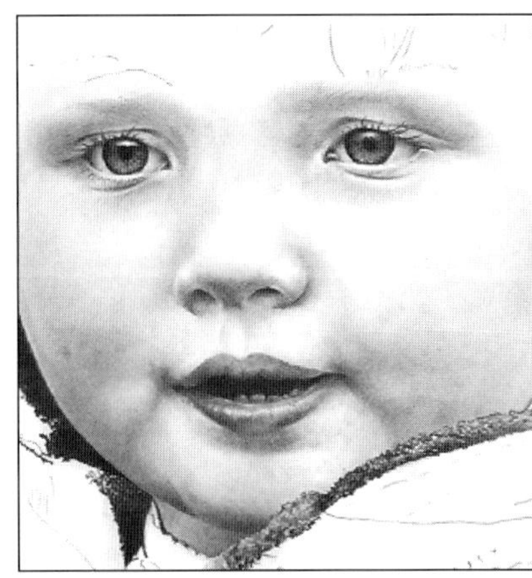

Cheeks and the shallow bridge of the nose completed.

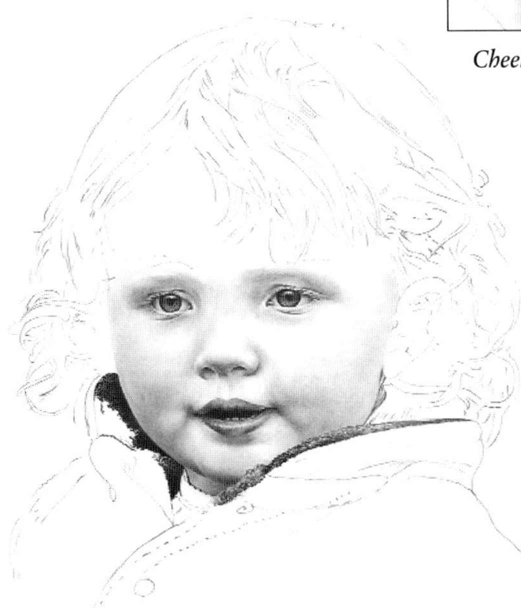

When I reached the eyes I found that the shading around them was too light. This has now been adjusted, as has the tone of the white in Charlotte's right eye. This eye, to our left, was looking in a slightly different direction to the right-hand eye. The darkening of the white has visually moved the iris to the left and corrected the fault.

TIP

Young children have shorter, wider faces than adults, especially between the eyes and mouth. Drawing a longer nose and narrower face will instantly make the child look older.
The proportions of a child need careful study and accurate drawing.

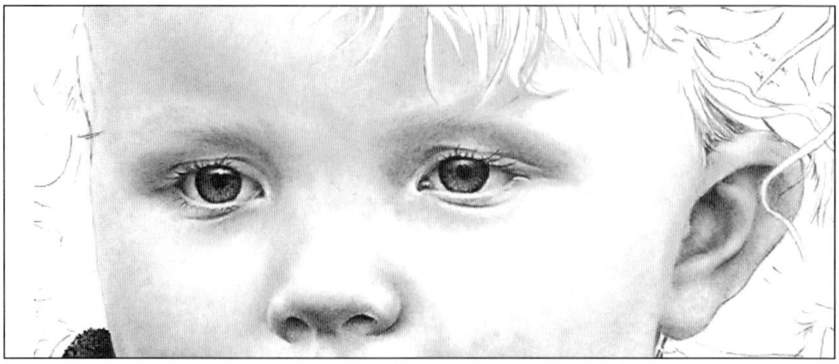

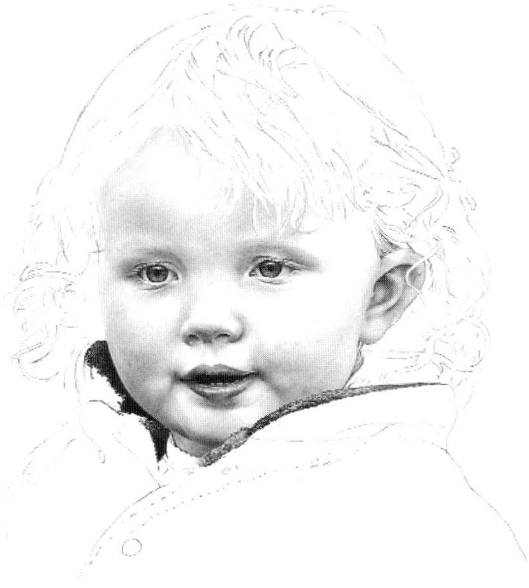

The forehead and eyebrows are finished, the shading around the eyes has been further strengthened, and the ear is nearing completion.

Stage 7:

I thought the forehead was going to be problematic. It certainly began that way, and her blonde eyebrows further complicated the area. Charlotte was lit by natural sunlight when the sun was high in the sky, so the lower half of her forehead is in partial shade. I wanted to play this shadow down to make allowances for the extra light I previously added to her eyes.

It took very careful scrutiny to detect where the brightest point of the forehead was, and even more effort to understand the very subtle shaping and changes in tonal values. After countless applications and blending of 2H above the left-hand eye I finally understood the area, and suddenly it all seemed to fall into place. Within an hour her forehead was completed and I had moved onto her ear.

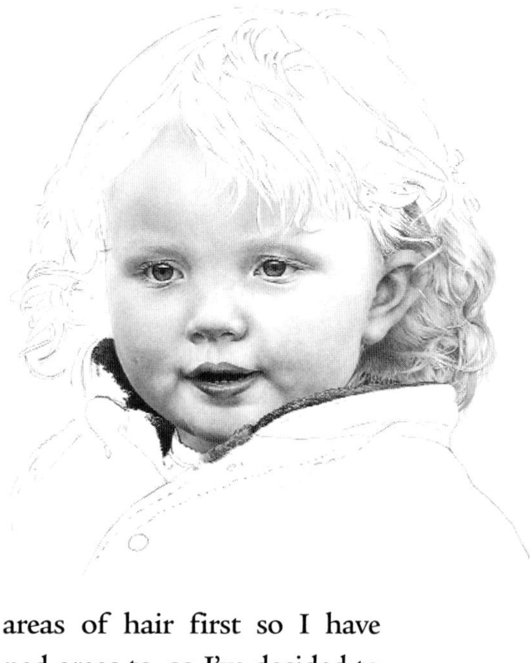

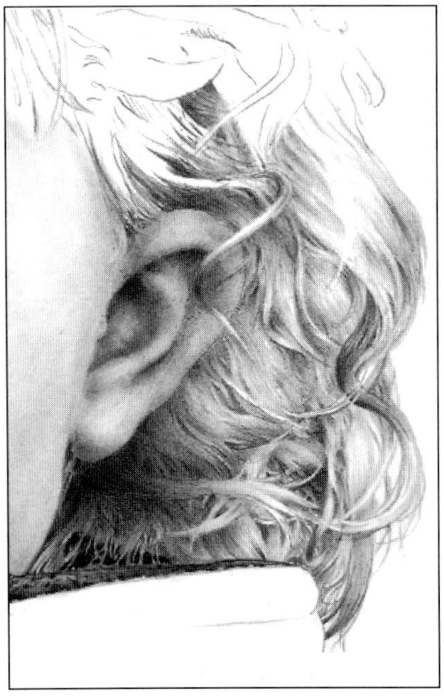

Stage 8:

The shading of Charlotte's ear has to be finalised and then it's time to move on to her hair. I need to establish some positive areas of hair first so I have something to balance the lightly toned areas to, so I've decided to concentrate tomorrow on her fringe and its cast shadows.

Well, yesterday's decision was soon overturned. The ear is still too dominant and distracting. I need to tone down the area around it in order to figure out its correct tonal values, so I've decided to complete the surrounding hair, and balance the ear to it as I draw.

I always feel uncomfortable when drawing an area such as this. A part of me wants to concentrate on detail, but I know this area needs to be almost indistinct, so it contrasts with the detail in the main body of hair and enhances it. I'm purely using negative drawing - lightly outlining a few status hairs then drawing suggestions of hair around them. I then tone down the status hair, sometimes until it almost disappears, and lightly blend the area, carefully avoiding any edges that I want to remain sharp. Most of the drawing is with 2H; I'm using 4H for very delicate shading, and F and HB for the darker tones.

When a section is complete, I stand back to get an overall impression, then adjust the strength of the shading and highlights until I achieve the correct tonal depth and three-dimensional form. My intention here is not to faithfully copy the photograph but to interpret it, depicting some existing elements and inventing others as I draw. To obtain a better compositional balance, I'm omitting some hair from the right-hand side of Charlotte's head, as her face is a little off-centre in the photograph.

STAGE 9:

The right-hand side will soon require a different technique, as it changes to long strands with strong highlights, so I've begun again at the left. The hair here is a continuation of the current technique, and the tones are similar. One thing I know before I start is that I am not going to be able to achieve the strength of the highlights in the original photograph. When I decided to omit the dark background I removed the major contrasting feature that makes Charlotte's highlights shine brightly. Instead, I'm attempting to engineer local contrasts; making the highlights appear brighter by darkening the tone around them. That I cannot engineer really strong contrasts doesn't worry me, as my aim is to use the hair as a frame, a device to concentrate the viewer's attention on Charlotte's face.

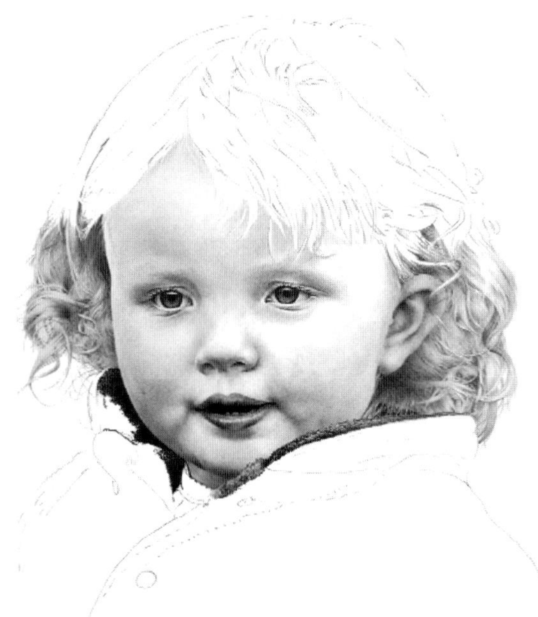

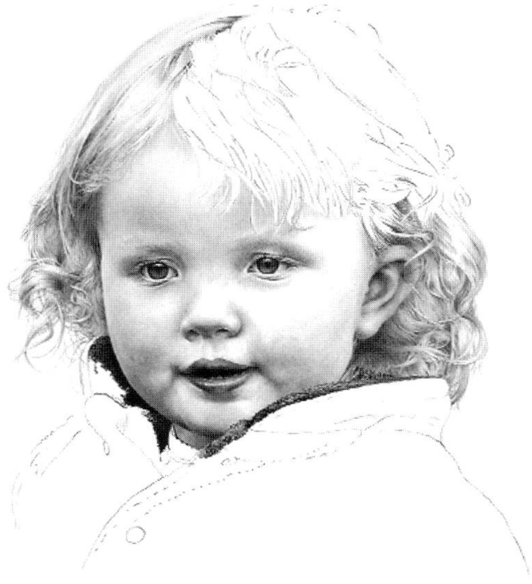

STAGE 10:

The left-hand side of the crown of Charlotte's head is considerably simpler in construction than the right, so I'm going to begin drawing the long, highlighted hair on this side. I can experiment without fear of causing major problems, and whatever I learn here can be carried across to the more complex drawing of the right-hand side.

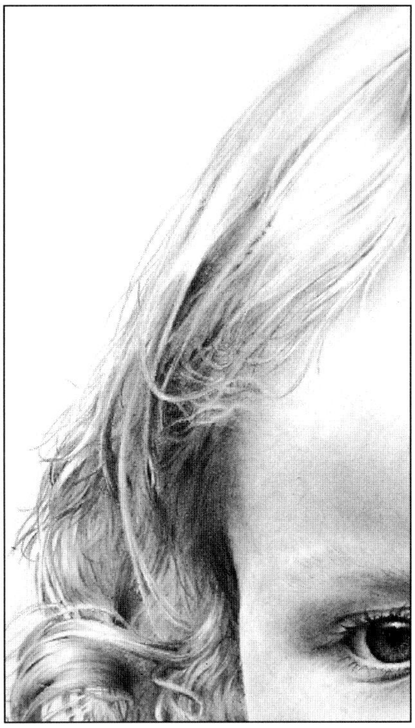

This is a deceptively difficult area to draw. The tones must be pitched precisely so that no shadow or feature predominates yet they must all be understandable. I'm using 4H here with a minimum amount of 2H for the strongest shadows. The technique involves a cycle of drawing tone and detail followed by blending, and then a partial erasure with Blu-Tack. The erasing dilutes the tones, which are then strengthened again before the process begins all over again. Each time I get a bit closer to my ideal. Finally, I'm satisfied that the area reads correctly; highlights are visible and explain the three-dimensional form, slim shadows signal the hair direction, edge shadows describe the outer boundary, and a feeling of unity exists. In short, the area can be understood without any one element standing out from the rest. The subtle difference between success and failure is very slight indeed, and delicacy of touch is of the utmost importance. The 4H is applied by virtually brushing the surface.

I've introduced stronger forehead tones where the hair overlaps it. These suggestions of cast shadows firmly connect the hair to the head, and better present the blonde hairs. The shading of the temple has also been completed. The wispy hairs above it, and all other light hairs, are the result of negative drawing. Some artists prefer to ignore these flyaway hairs until the area is finished, then they cut them in with an eraser. This is a technique that I very rarely use except in an emergency, as my personal experience leads me to believe the result is rarely as fine or realistic.

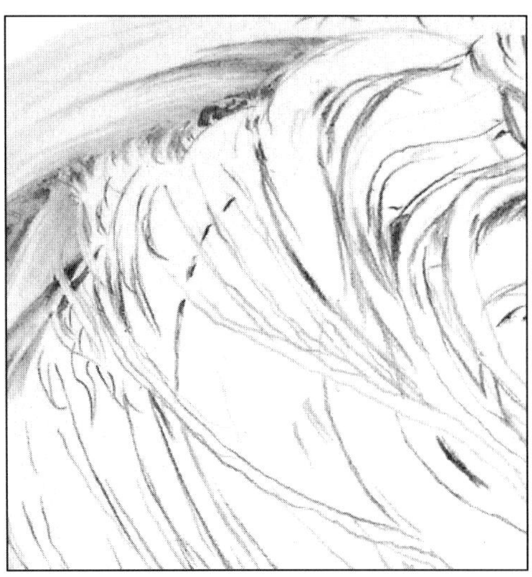

Fig 1: The position of major features is first mapped out lightly with 2B, to ensure complete erasure. Prior to drawing each section, the guidelines are erased to mere shadows.

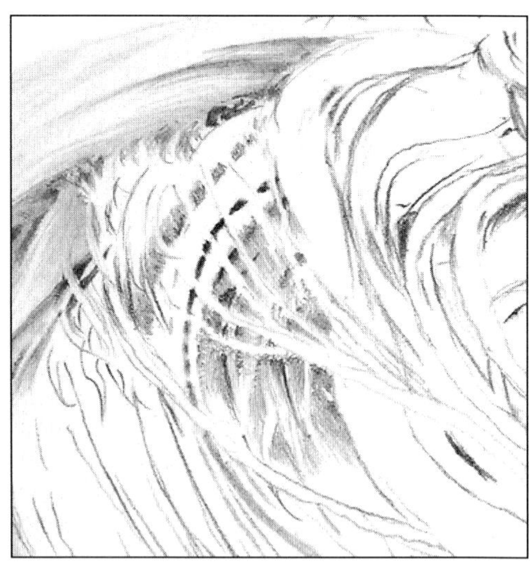

Fig 2: A strong shadow is drawn in between the stray hairs with F. Then 2H and 4H are used to begin the drawing of the locks behind them. It is easier to draw too dark and then dilute with Blu-Tack later.

The demonstration shown here employs only negative drawing. After mapping out (*fig 1*), the 2B guidelines are erased to mere shadows before each section is drawn. First the deepest shadows are established (*fig 2*) then drawing commences in the area behind the white, or light, out-of-place hairs.

It is far easier to obtain the correct relationships between tones if you draw a little darker than you feel you need then reduce the tonal strength of the whole area by dabbing with Blu-Tack or a kneadable eraser (*fig 3*). Don't worry if you fade too much. Think of it as a bonus, as it allows you to partially strengthen the area again. Repeated fading and strengthening will eventually lead you to a subtlety of tone that is very difficult to achieve in a single layer. Use your tortillon to blend smooth gradations of tone, and also use it to lightly drag graphite into areas that need only a hint of tone.

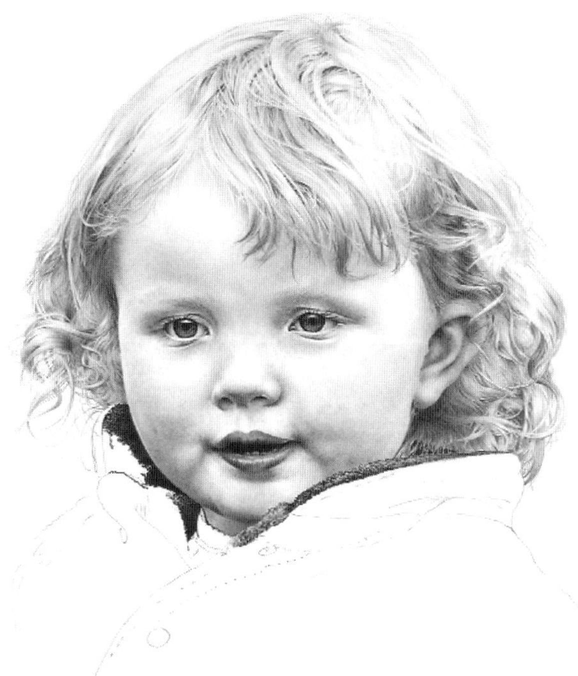

Finally (*fig 4*), stand back and view the drawn area. It has to work from a distance as well as close up. Strengthen your tones where required, fade others, and tone down the out-of-place hairs until the area reads correctly. In brief, every element should be independently understandable but none must be

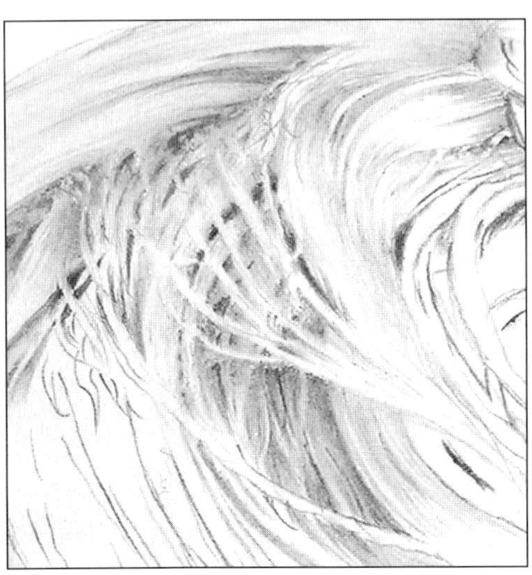

Fig 3: Areas have been repeatedly faded and strengthened, each time getting closer to the required balance. Bear in mind that this area of the original drawing measures only 1¼" (3.2cm) high.

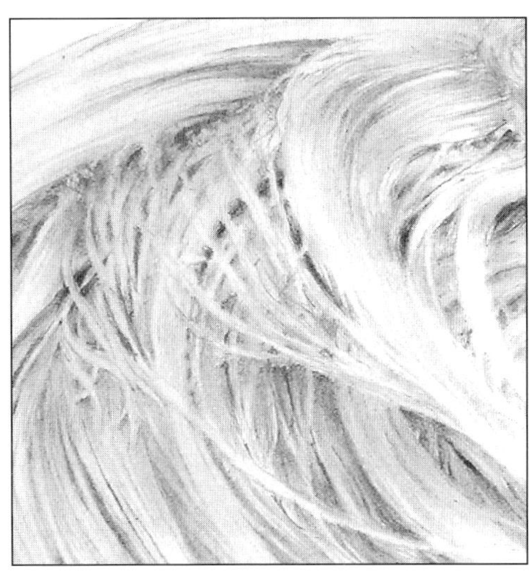

Fig 4: The completed area. Keep the layout logical at all times. Despite the roughness apparent in this enlargement, it appears quite smooth and realistic in the original drawing.

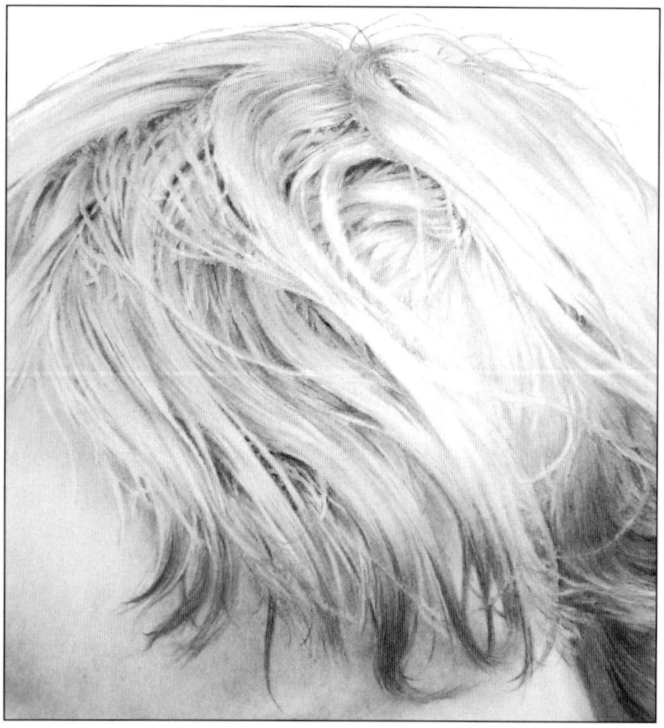

conspicuous; the area should possess a harmony that echoes reality.

STAGE 11:

Today I completed Charlotte's hair. Take your time, as your drawing will benefit greatly. The detail shown here is the result of eight hours of drawing spread over two days. Identify a recognisable shape and concentrate solely on drawing it, treating it as an independent drawing in its own right. First, establish the deepest shadow or tone in the shape and then look for the brightest highlight. Constantly refer to these values to correctly balance all the intermediate tones. Then, on completion, balance that area to the overall drawing. Do this by strengthening tone where required, or use Blu-Tack, or a kneadable eraser, to reduce contrast until the area fits comfortably into the whole drawing.

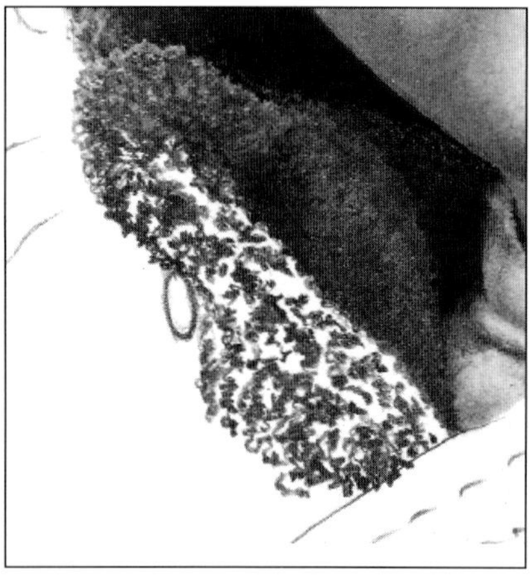

Try to split texture from tonal shaping. Establish the detail first...

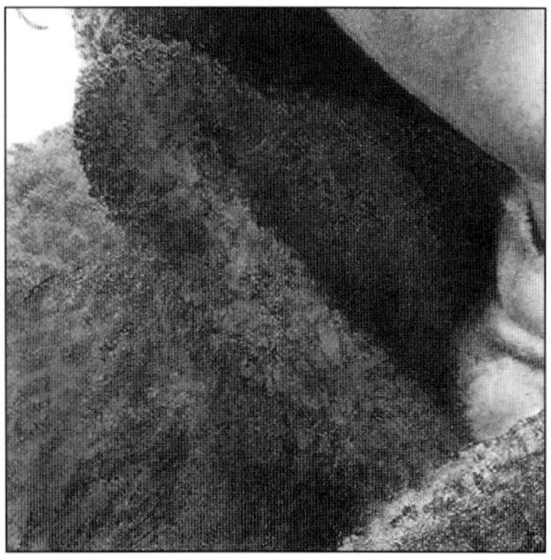

...then apply the shaping on separate layers, which allows you to adjust the tonal values without affecting the detail.

Working in this manner gives you the opportunity to fully understand each area. In fact, understanding it in three-dimensions is essential to recreating a sense of reality. You'll find that such intense concentration on one small area will permit you to see the subtlest detail, which in normal circumstances you wouldn't notice. You do not, of course, need to include such detail but it will help you to better interpret the area. In time you will become adept at working out which elements affect the way the area looks and which you can safely discard or adapt to your own plan.

STAGE 12:

Now I have a problem - one of my own making, as I failed to plan ahead. I recognised before I began that Charlotte's dark coat might overpower the lighter tones of her skin and blonde hair, and I should have found a solution. However, sometimes that isn't possible and you need to see the rest of the drawing first before making that decision.

Currently, I have two choices: to fade the coat out or to continue the coat down so that it disappears behind the mat when the drawing is framed. I suspect the latter will definitely make the drawing bottom-heavy, so I'm going to proceed with caution, complete the collar and shoulders of the coat, and then reassess the situation.

I don't want the detail of the coat's texture to become too obvious, as it may vie with Charlotte's face for attention, so I'm deliberately depicting only the 'feeling' of this fleecy surface. By first drawing the internal shadows, I can concentrate on their shapes and the direction of the fibres. This permits me to apply the shaping tones as an overlay, using a flat face on my lead so I don't indent the surface. Then I can fine-tune with Blu-Tack or a kneadable eraser, brushing the surface to lighten the shading layer, and dabbing with a point to lighten the detail layer or to form lighter spots in the surface.

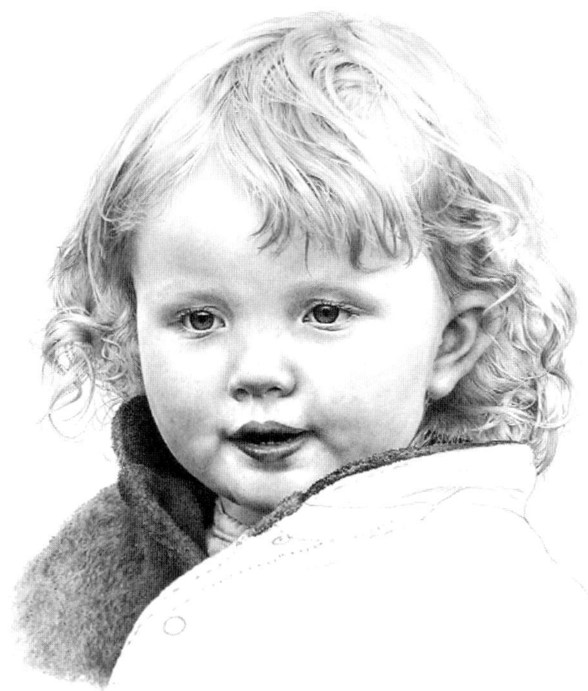

As I moved away from the collar and across and down the body, I changed to a modified way of working. Unsure of the strength required, I worked only with the flat face of an HB lead. A suggestion of an internal shadow was followed by a light application of tone. When a small area was completed, I'd apply another layer of tone, attempting to depict some shaping. Not, however, the shaping as seen in the photograph. I find that far too distracting, so I used the feeling of the shadows on the right side to rebuild the left side. At times I'd drag Blu-Tack lightly over the lower extremities to fade it out a little. Sooner or later a natural point will be reached where a complete fade out looks quite natural and adds a balance to the drawing. In conjunction with this, I strengthened some of the shadow detail higher up to increase the contrast.

Stage 13:

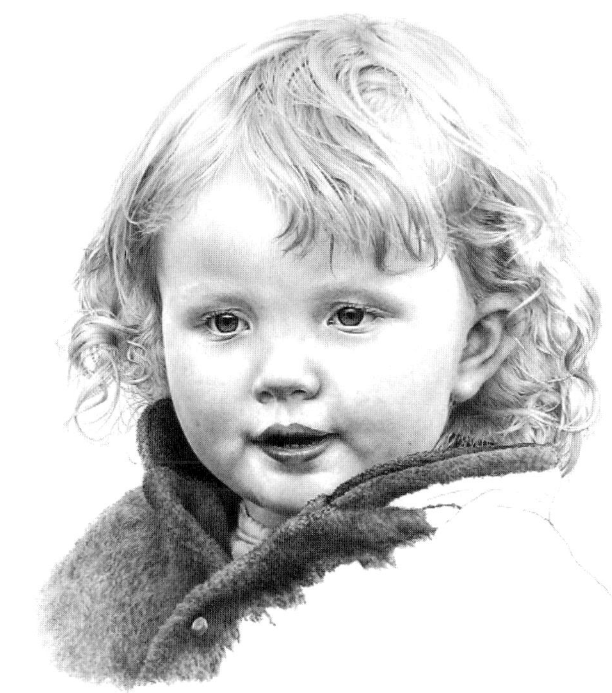

Well, the left-hand side hasn't gone too well. It looks fluffy, after a lot of work, but I'm tempted to just roll Blu-Tack over it all and take it back to white. However, it's possible that it just looks weak because the other, more positive, side has yet to be drawn. I've strengthened some detailing in the collar, and now I'll leave the area until after I've drawn the other side, where I can use the lessons learned to my advantage.

I'm relieved. Shortly after I started to draw the right-hand side, the left side began to look more appropriate. I'm working with 2B now, rather than HB, and including more suggestions of detail but still keeping it low-key. A 'fluffy' look is quite acceptable to me, and I feel no need to depict the actual fleece as it appears in reality.

Stage 14:

I've reshaped the base of the left-hand side, and taken out one or two minor, distracting elements. At the right-hand side, I've considerably dulled the potentially distracting button.

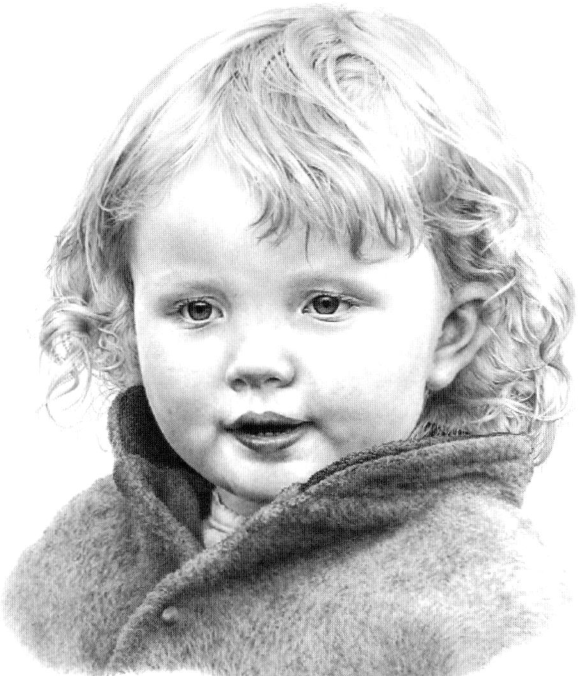

I'm continuing with the same basic technique - drawing suggestions of internal shadow with a flat, 2B point, following the line of the nap. In fact I'm using the direction of these shadows to describe the three-dimensional shape, which means I can use the minimum of tonal shaping for the curvature and gentle folds. My sole intention is to suggest a reality while not inviting the eye to linger on the body of the coat. Conversely, the sharper, more detailed drawing of the edges of the collar is designed to lead the eye upwards to Charlotte's face, as is the use of the deepest black tone that I reserved solely for her pupils.

I think it's completed, so I'll put it away for a couple of days then look at it again with fresh eyes. There always will be areas that I'm not too pleased with but there are no major faults, and any further work may destroy the clarity or even make things worse. The result is never quite what I originally envisaged but, for a first portrait, I'm reasonably pleased with the outcome.

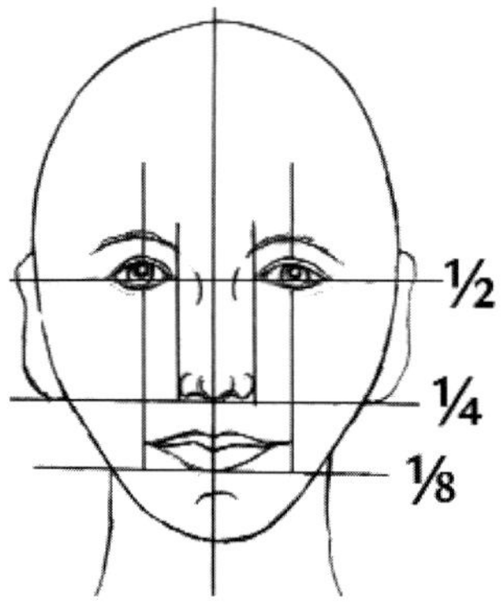

Tip

Because we focus on a person's features, we often draw them too big for the head. In general head proportions are:

- *The eyes are half way down the head.*
- *The head is 5 eye-widths wide.*
- *The base of the nose is half way between the eyes and chin.*
- *The bottom lip is half way between the nose and chin.*
- *The corners of the mouth fall directly below the pupils.*
- *The tops of the ears line up with the eyebrows.*
- *The ear lobes are on a level with the bottom of the nose.*
- *The sides of the nose fall under the inside corners of the eyes.*

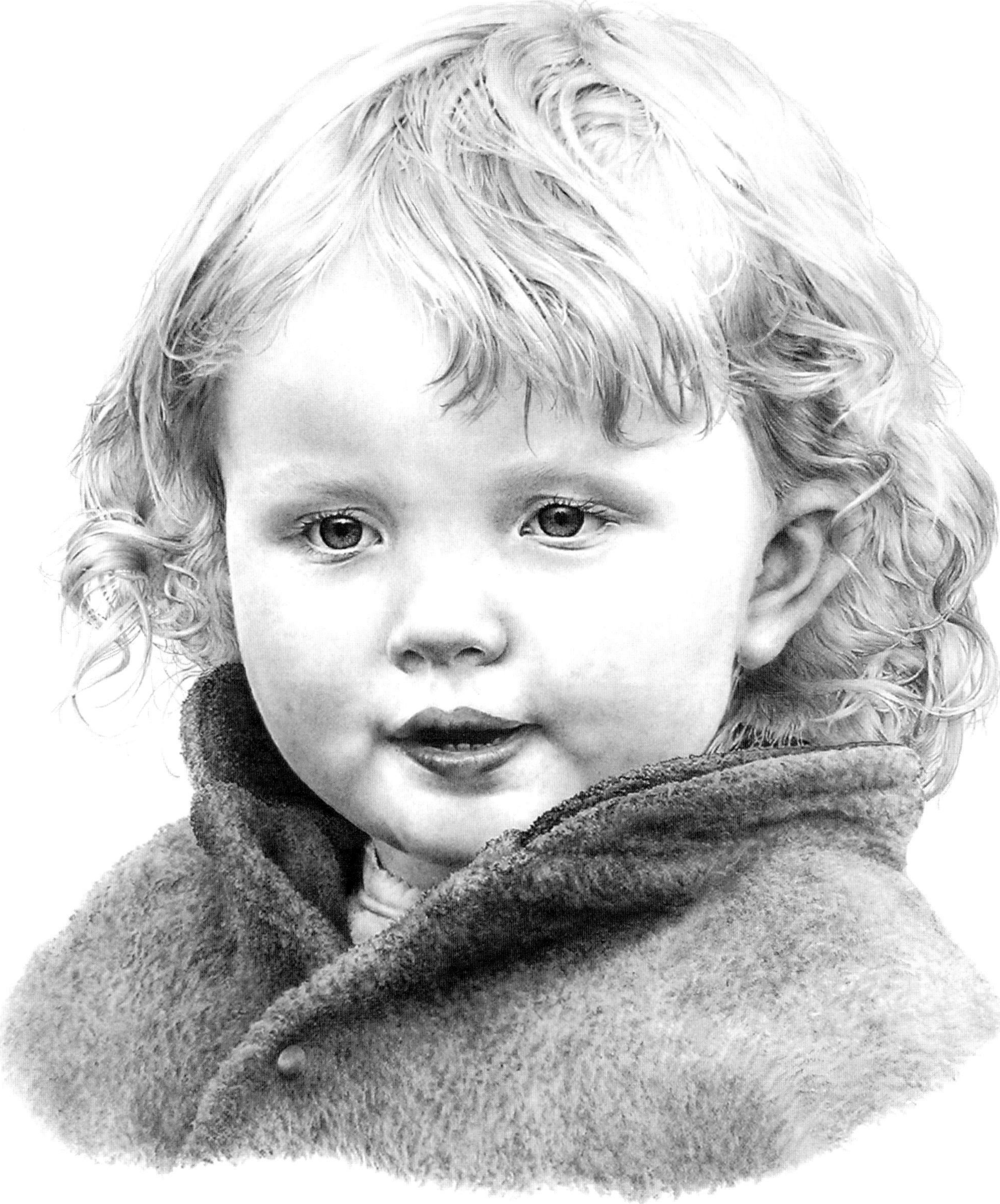

'Charlotte' by Mike Sibley ©
Image size: 6" x 7" (15 x 17.8 cm)
Total drawing time: 39 hours

Fooling the Brain

Part 1 - Fooling your own brain

'The average human looks without seeing, listens without hearing, touches without feeling, eats without tasting, moves without physical awareness, smells without awareness of odour or fragrance and talks without thinking.'

Leonardo Da Vinci

I receive many requests for assistance with drawing and this one neatly sums up the others: 'Is there a way in which you could explain step by step how to get the effect of reality in our drawings? For example, the three-dimensional effect of wood, the depth involved while drawing hair or the effect of sunlight and shadows and the reflection of water.'

Well, all these textures and forms require only one thing - the ability to analyse what you see. First you must learn to see what is really in front of you and not what you think is there. This can be a hard lesson to learn. Your brain contains a set of ready-made, shorthand shapes that it uses to recognise certain things - an eye is two facing arcs, for example, such as the eye symbol the Egyptians used. And, as in Egyptian art, the main symbols are pictured either from the front or side, not at an angle. You must learn to see the real shape - not the shape you expect it to be.

The brain is highly focussed - too focussed for our purposes. It would seem by all accounts to store memory in the form of images. These images, or symbols, are the mainstay of the brain's defence mechanism. About half of our brain is devoted to vision and continual attempts to interpret what we see - we guess on the clues available to us and our life may depend on the correct 'reality' being extracted.

Images then are of supreme importance to the brain and matches to stored, standard symbols offer very speedy classification. As the brain is programmed to make quick, sweeping evaluations most people look but do not see. They sweep their eyes across their surroundings and extract only the minimal information required for safety or to note their location. Their brains automatically overlay the image in front of them with a range of symbols. This effectively disables the ability to produce realistic drawing because the information gathered is so basic that it's suitable only for childish symbol drawing.

Because I draw dogs a question I'm often asked is 'Can you draw cats... boats... flowers... people?' These questions arise from the mistaken belief that an artist learns to draw each 'symbol' independently of the others. The enquirer sees their world as a collection of symbols and has no notion that drawing is a universal skill; that the ability to see, to understand and to reproduce textures and tones, applies equally to all subjects.

Fortunately, there are many ways of fooling the brain into letting go of the desire to 'match symbols', to classify, during the act of drawing. Most, perhaps all, of the ways available allow a great degree of spontaneity. For example, drawing at a speed that demands intuitive reaction, leaving no time for logical thought - working faster than you can think, effectively disables the argumentative side of your brain, which struggles to keep up and then loses interest.

In such ways you will either confuse or educate your brain to see correctly. First, you must learn to switch off the troublesome, analytical, symbol-loving areas of your mind. Then to become detached so you can recognise visual elements not only for their true shapes and characters but also to extract the signals that they would normally transmit to your brain. It is these elements, or 'keys', that you will learn to build into your work so you send the desired signals to the brains of your viewers. This is a subject we will return to in the next chapter.

'To look at a thing is very different from seeing it.'

Oscar Wilde

Sounds a bit heavy? Don't worry, taken a step at a time it soon begins to make sense and become second nature. Let's begin with a common fault - letting symbolism reign as you attempt a portrait.

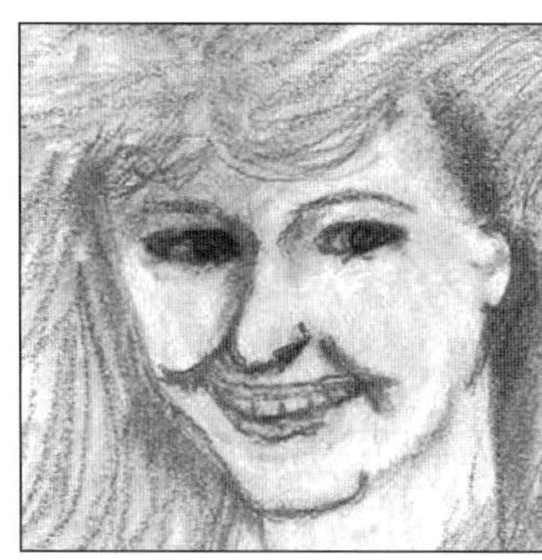

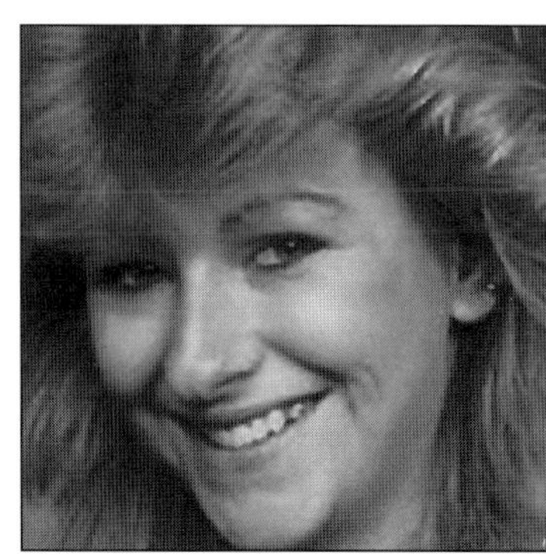

Drawing and photo by kind permission of Rosalie Ferry

What the artist has drawn here (right) is the eyes and mouth that her brain expected them to look like, not the features as they are in reality. You'll note that she has the nose correctly angled and the ear placement correct, as is the basic outline of the face. But the face has had to be distorted to accommodate the eyes as seen from the front Then the mouth, to conform to the eyes, is seen from the front also - the corners correctly placed below the mid-point of the eyes. The reference photograph shows the head naturally tilted but symbols never are, so here they are drawn 'correctly' level, migrating both eyes across the face.

Let's study the mouth. Follow the line of the top lip in the reference photo...do you see how it snakes like a shallow 'S' shape laying on its back? Place the straight edge of a piece of paper over the mouth so only the top line shows above it... now you're brain can no longer see a recognisable mouth. Previously, it just glanced down, classified the shape as 'mouth' and made the artist draw the standard mouth symbol. Now, being unable to categorise the shape, it allows exploration, unfettered by symbolism. At last we can extract more information and see, for example, that the teeth at the left hand side progressively angle away from us and narrow their viewable face. The artist, of course, drew teeth symbols - all directly facing us. Notice the ear too. An ear, our brain tells us, has a top and bottom. Despite the fact that her hair hides the top of this girl's ear, the artist's brain has demanded that her ear conforms to its known reality. Employing the artist's subconscious, her brain has forced her to produce a makeshift top to a drastically truncated ear.

To learn to see what is really there and not what you think is there you need to take your brain's automatic reaction out of the equation. Believe me, learning to see correctly really is a hard lesson to learn. In the past I've spent days trying to make a dog's eye look just right only to suddenly realise that what I had drawn was totally at variance with the photo. The best way involves fooling your brain into not recognising the troublesome feature and, fortunately, we have a heavyweight Champ waiting in the wings...

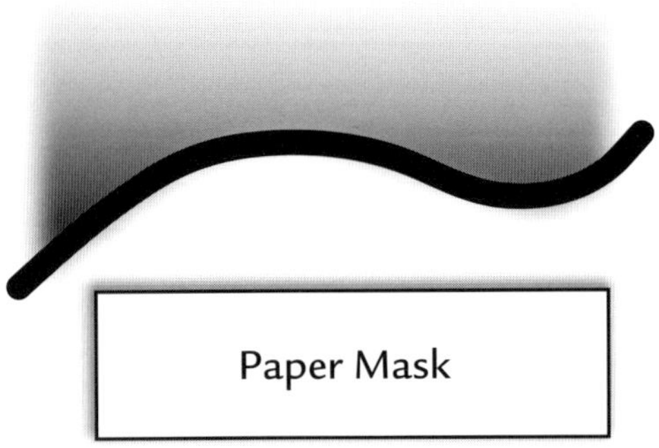

To solve the problem of accurately drawing the curve place a straight edge of paper below it...

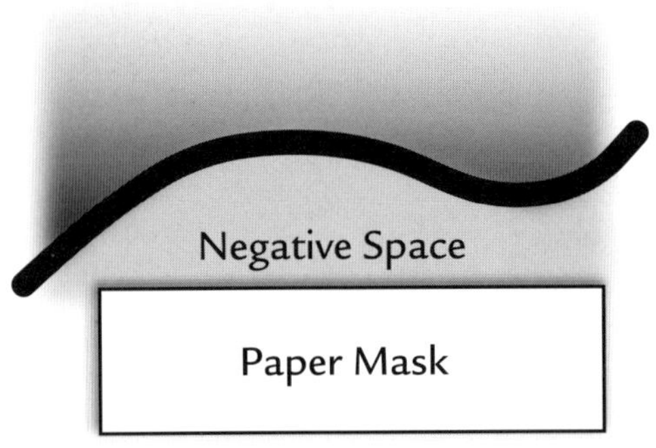

...now you are no longer drawing just a curve but a shape with a sinuous side that you can constantly refer to the straight side. Concentrate not on the line but on drawing the negative space and treating it as a shape.

Negative Space

You were using the power of negative space earlier - although you probably didn't recognise it. When we covered the mouth with a piece of paper to study the top line of the lip and destroy any recognition of the shape we did something else too - we created a straight edge against which we could gauge the sinuous route of that top lip. This is very helpful but even more useful is the empty space between the line and the edge of the paper - the negative space.

This exercise will not only help your mind to concentrate on the spaces between lines it will also help to confound your brain - your logical mind that attempts to identify everything it sees. You're going to give it a really tough time because instead of drawing an object itself, you'll be drawing the empty space around it. Take two strips of paper; say an inch by three inches (2.5 x 7.5cm). Now shade the right hand end of one strip right up to the edges...

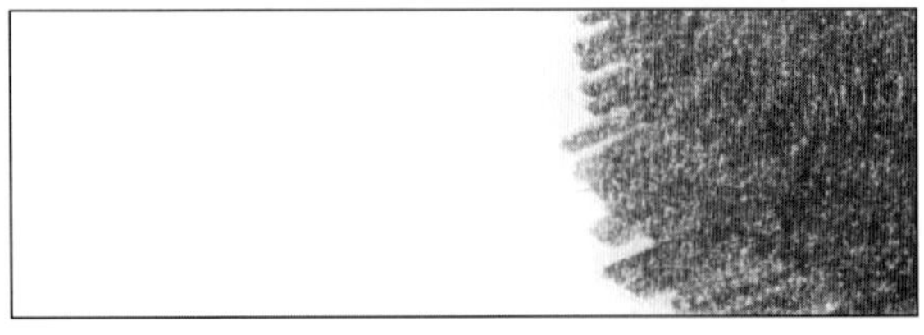

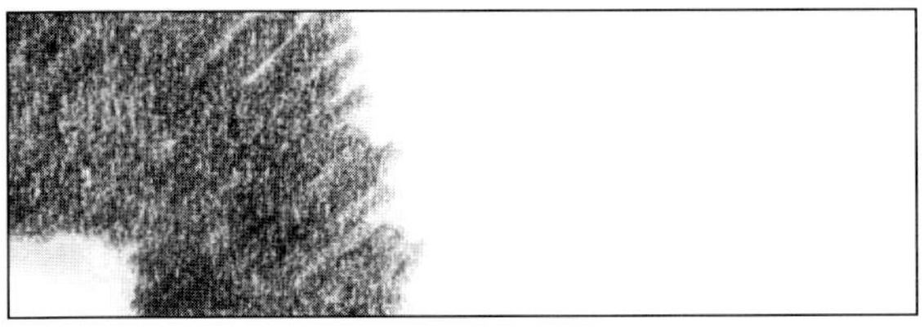

Now do the same to the left hand end of the other strip and, without drawing any lines, leave an oblong clear in the bottom corner.

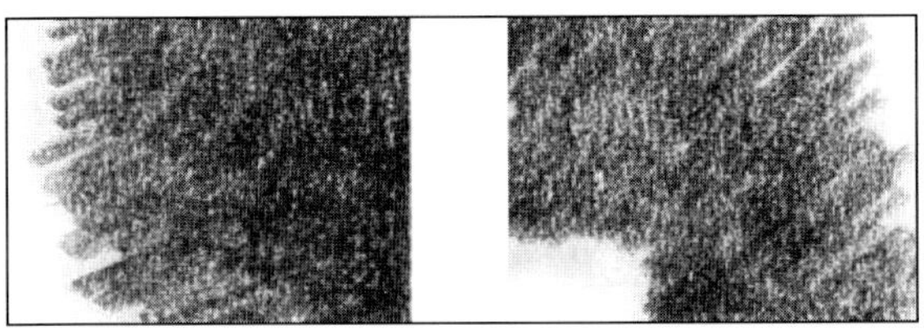

'YOU CAN EMPLOY THE DRAWING OF NEGATIVE SPACE ALMOST ANYWHERE AT ANY TIME. ALL YOU NEED TO DO IS SWITCH YOUR MIND FROM POSITIVE TO NEGATIVE DRAWING'

Now take a clean sheet of paper and lay your two strips end to end with a gap between them.

What you have drawn is the capital letter 'L'. That the letter exists is entirely due to negative space. The white of the letter is pristine, not a result of the removal of graphite. Understanding this concept is important because I'll be returning to it later when you learn to draw entire areas using this technique.

Practice drawing articles you know. Try to picture each on the page and then shade around it. Don't draw lines around them first - if you do you'll just be shading around a positive shape, not shading the negative space to cause the positive image to appear. Since these abstract shapes share a continuous border with the object, when you draw the negative shape, you'll be drawing the positive outline as well.

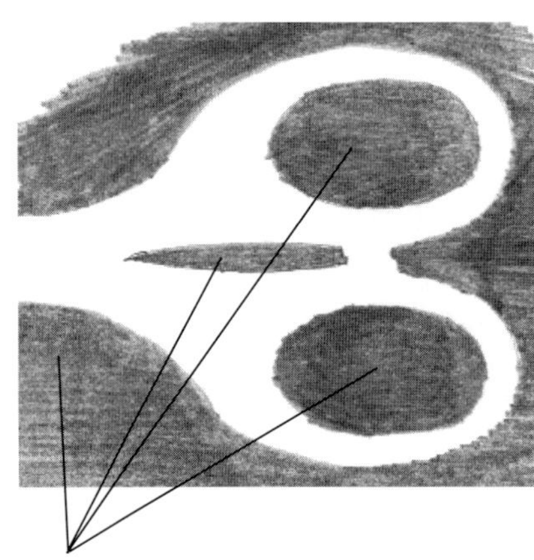

Negative spaces drawn to define scissor handles

You'll soon learn to understand that negative space is as important as positive shape. One cannot exist without the other - they share equal standing. As that is true it doesn't matter which you draw. However, drawing the negative spaces will make you really look at what you are drawing. You can't guess their shape or draw what you think is there because they have no recognisable outlines.

Use this technique whenever you are having problems with drawing something the way it really looks. You'll almost always end up with a more accurate drawing.

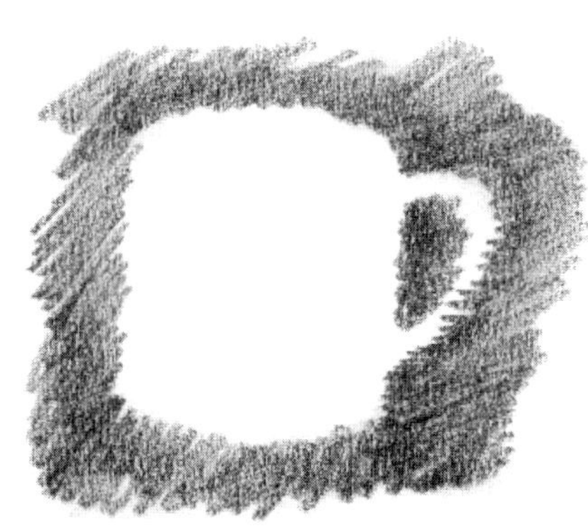

Now that you understand the concept of negative space and that it's of equal importance to the object it encloses, you will be able to use its presence in another way too. Recognising

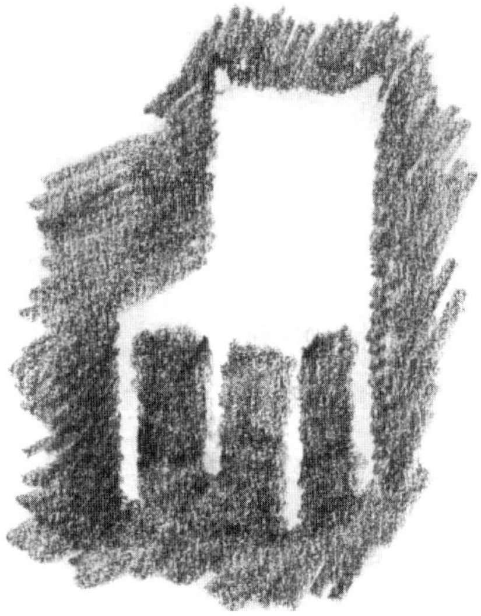

negative space and drawing around it, treating it as an object in its own right, is just as beneficial, as it allows you to completely divorce from reality the adjacent object you are trying to draw.

If, for example, discovering the correct curvatures of an eye is giving you problems, stop looking at it as one complete entity. Instead, treat it as just a contiguous collection of curves, divide it into manageable sections and look at the negative spaces that surround each one.

Making a start with the curve of the bottom eyelid (*fig 1*) you could cut an L-shaped mask from paper to give you a boundary reference (*fig 2*) and draw the negative space instead of the eye itself (*fig 3*). With experience you can dispense with the mask.

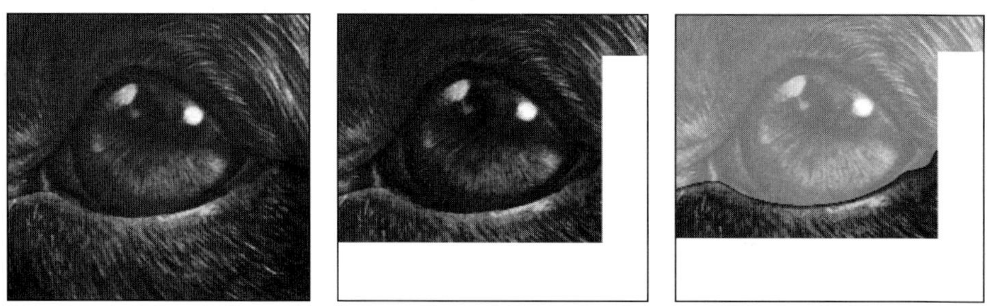

Fig 1 *Fig 2* *Fig 3*

The use of negative space offers many advantages. Not only will it assist you in determining the true shapes of elements within your drawing it will also make white available to you as a usable colour. As with watercolour painting, the only white we have as graphite artists is the paper itself. I will guard this white at any cost. There will be times when you may have to erase lines or features to create 'white' details but they will never have the clarity and brilliance of an untouched area. Learning to draw the space around those areas is a lesson well worth the effort of learning and is a subject I'll be covering in full in a later chapter.

Dividing your work

The concept of examining small positive areas and negative spaces has introduced you to another means of confounding your mental processes. In this case it's the 'I can't do that, it's too complex' belief.

It's an old problem with an equally old answer. As early as 600BC Lao Tzu stated in the Tao Te Ching, 'Prepare for the difficult while it is still easy. Deal with the big while it is still small. Difficult undertakings have always started with what's easy. Great undertakings always started with what is small. Therefore the sage never strives for the great, and thereby the great is achieved.'

By breaking down the drawing into manageable parts you achieve two advantages. First it relieves the pressure caused by that daunting task. Second, and perhaps more importantly if you want to achieve realism, it allows you to focus on just one small area at a time. This focus generates a greater understanding of the area and the way that it fits into the greater whole. It removes the desire to hurry through the drawing because each area becomes a drawing in its own right. I'm often asked how I have the patience to spend perhaps 250 hours on a single drawing. The answer is that I don't. I spend half an hour each on 500 small drawings that join up to form what others see as a single drawing.

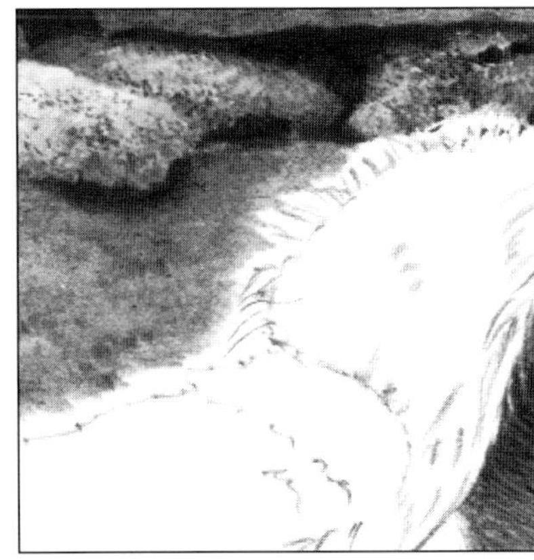

The drawing of the background has been stopped short of the hair.

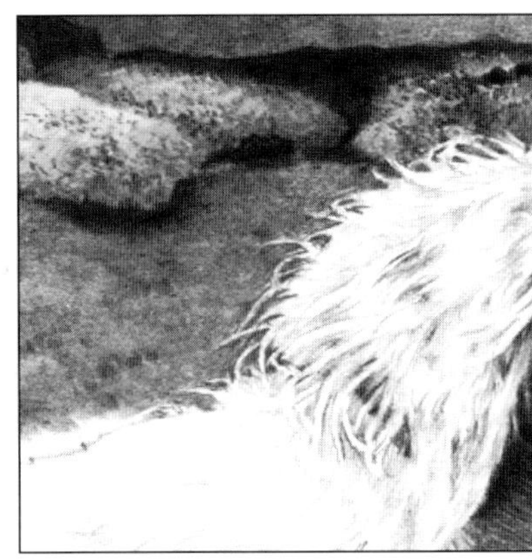

The background has been drawn back up into the existing drawing, treating it as negative space in order to expose the white hairs around the edge of the ear.

Using this strategy I'm able to concentrate solely on that single area. I can analyse its make up and three-dimensional form and I can assess its importance to the overall study - employing exaggeration or understatement as required. I'm not interested in areas that surround it, other than their affects on tone or lighting, and concentrate all my attention on a full understanding and depiction. This may then continue into an adjacent area and often a string of such areas results until I reach a point where the flow of understanding ceases. This may be the edge of the drawing, the boundary with a totally dissimilar area or simply a change in texture or visual importance. Whatever the reason, I then begin again elsewhere, often working back to where I left off. From a technical point of view this new starting point or 'drawing break' is often an area of shadow as I prefer, wherever possible, to work from dark to light - it being simpler to graft new drawing onto an area of dark tone.

The application of logic

How do you discover true understanding? How do you learn to see? There is only one way - be aware of what you're drawing and apply logic at all times. Describing my actions and reasons to myself works well for me. I don't say, 'This line goes here and I reckon it's this shape.' Instead I explain to myself, 'This is an ear, it has a thickness that I must show here so that it doesn't appear flat.' Or 'This faint highlight follows the line of a rib. I know the rib cage is rounded and I should expect to find other ribs alongside this one.'

'The world of reality has its limits, the world of imagination is boundless.'

Jean Jacques Rousseau

Trees are the darnest things to figure out. I sit and look at a reference photo and I don't have a clue what I'm seeing. I don't see the obvious branches, I don't see the lighting and I don't see the individual leaves. But logic tells me that I 'know' there is a light source, I know there are shadows and I know it's three-dimensional. As I start drawing these things start to jump out at me. I imagine myself walking under that tree.

The reference photo doesn't always give you the obvious clues. But if you remember the 'logic' and apply that as you look at the tree, that jumbled mess starts to make sense. As I go from leaf to leaf I really start feeling that empty space. I don't concentrate on the highlight or the leaf; I concentrate on drawing that dark space in between the branches and leaves - the Negative Space that Mike talks about so well.

Diane Wright, Artist

Doing this you will consciously avoid the symbol-orientated style of drawing. Instead of drawing line you are drawing real, living elements of the subject. You must apply logic to every three-dimensional form and tiny detail.

Don't just outline a muscle, for example. In fact don't think about line at all. Line is a man-made device, not a part of Nature. Think what that muscle is doing right now and what it is about to do. Draw with this in mind and you'll suggest a continuing movement. Learn to see each element for what it is - as a part of a living, moving being and not as a drawing exercise.

Your initial attempts won't be masterpieces, since you'll be too preoccupied with technique and a conscious desire to avoid symbolism. But basic techniques are quickly learned and experience is a great teacher. Your understanding, confidence and ability will grow with each drawing you attempt. You'll be surprised how soon you'll throw off your dependence on symbols and begin to understand the world around you. One, perhaps the greatest, advantage of drawing realistically will be your newfound ability to see and mentally record the tiniest details in your surroundings. How terrible that your vision was once restricted and censored by symbolism - I find that thought quite claustrophobic.

Here's a truism - 'No practice engenders no skill.' Practice doesn't just assist you in learning to handle your tools, expand your range of techniques or increase your understanding. Its chief benefit lies in its ability to make the act of drawing become second nature. In time you'll no longer give any thought to which technique is required or which grade of graphite to use. You'll find yourself lost in a world of your own creation, drawing your thoughts as they occur - direct mind-to-hand-to-art transference. Often has been the time I've 'come to' to be pleasantly shocked by the quality of the work I had just produced - only now consciously seeing it for the first time. Now you are in control and not your desk clerk, pigeonholing, symbol-loving brain.

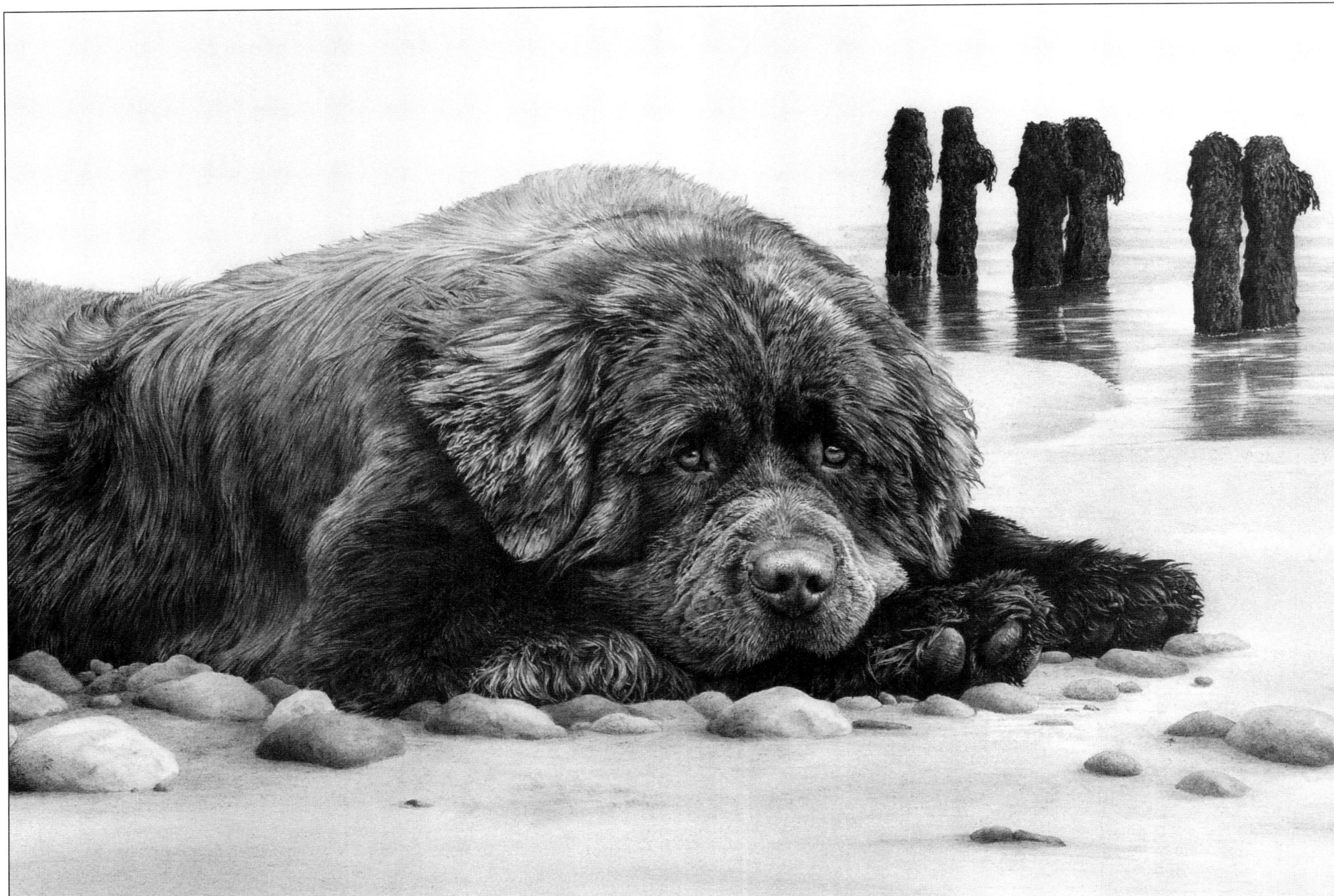

11" x 8" (28 x 20cm)

'Just Dreaming' A limited edition print of 850 plus 25 Artists Proofs. Featuring the Newfoundland.

Working with photos
The 'Why' factor...

'DRAWING INVOLVES PROBLEM SOLVING. THERE'S NO WAY AROUND IT.'

When I start a drawing I've no more idea than you have, perhaps less, as to how best to depict any one feature. But I've learned not to be afraid of attempting anything new. Each drawing is a trip into the unknown - a personal adventure during the course of which I hope to learn more about my chosen medium or Nature or both. It may be a commission, it may be to make a print but always the drawing is for me. The focus, the point of the drawing, is to say something about the animal I'm portraying - to say 'Hey! Do you see what a beautiful creature this is? Look closer! No, much closer! I want you to understand just how wonderfully Nature has worked her magic'. I want to exhibit its real appeal to me.

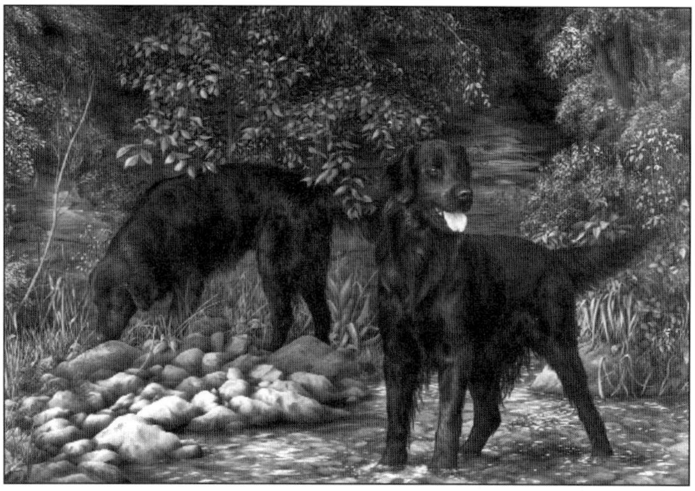

It took me five weeks to draw the foliage in *'At Gunnerside Ghyll'* (*left*) and two to draw the dogs, leaving just the flowing stream until last. I'd never drawn foreground water before and the success of the study depended on it. But, once I'd realised that the appearance of depth came from the foam being on a separate plane above the submerged rocks, two days work saw the study successfully completed.

The unknown, perhaps an element in your reference photos that you don't understand or a texture that you have to draw for the first time, can be a daunting obstacle. The solution lies in asking yourself *why* it looks the way it does. Challenge your perception - peel away the layers until you gain a full understanding.

Drawing involves problem solving. There's no way around it. No broad brush strokes to sweep over problem areas. Until someone invents the one-inch wide pencil we have only a narrow pointed stylus to work with. Each mark must count and make sense with those adjacent to it. So at every stage of your drawing, constantly question what you see. Why does that bunch of hair look the way it does? What is it about that eye that gives it that special look? Why does that surface look rusty and that one shiny?

Carry this thinking over to the way you use photos - think 'reality' and 'interpretation' not 'photograph' and 'copying'. The former may produce photo-realistic drawings, and the latter result in technically proficient drawings that are 'like a photo'. I believe there is a vast difference between the two. The brain, being gullible, readily accepts a photo as the truth so to classify a drawing as 'photo-realistic' suggests that it too is accepted as being real. Conversely if you draw 'like a photo' then you are probably treating the photograph as being sacrosanct and including everything, even the faults of photography - featureless shadows, burnt out highlights, and a restricted depth of field to name a few possibilities. You may be also drawing with a certain lack of three-dimensional understanding. When drawing from a photograph imagine you are looking at the actual scene or subject, not a flat representation, and continually question what you see. To ask is to learn.

'The faculty of creating is never given to us all by itself. It always goes hand in hand with the gift of observation.'

Igor Stravinsky

The Overview

Let's take the broadest view first - your motivation behind your drawing. Do you ever feel you will fail before you begin? Often the biggest problem is working out just what it is about something that excites you but it's an essential quest. If you can detect and extract the reason for your attraction you have something specific to incorporate into your drawing, and your personal feelings will be built in to it.

Someone once wrote about one of my drawings 'It seems as if the dogs spot me out first and are wagging and looking at me as if they know me already. I think whatever attracts the attention of an artist is what they create best, because they really love what they are creating'. So here's our first 'why' - why are you about to begin this drawing? And what are you going to say? Whatever you are about to draw, you have to have a positive, emotional reaction to the subject for it to succeed. Without that desire you will produce a copy of the photograph, not of the subject. Right now you may be asking what the difference is? But the day will dawn when the two will seem like opposing poles - another milestone in your development that will change your work forever.

'We see nothing truly until we understand it.'

John Constable

Try to work out why you were first attracted to the image - what it was that made you want to reproduce it. Imagine, for

'I have learned that what I have not drawn I have never really seen, and that when I start drawing an ordinary thing, I realize how extraordinary it is, sheer miracle.'

Frederick Franck

example, you were about to begin a drawing of a friend's baby. Is it that little upturned corner of the mouth that you love so much? The sparkle in the scrunched up eyes? Whatever it is, that is your reason for drawing that study. It is the one element you want to share and it will be the centre of attention of your drawing. It's what attracted you so strongly, so convey that to your audience and enjoy every step of the project. Remember, a copy of a photo is just a copy - but a drawing with spirit and meaning has a life of its own.

By stopping to think about what is important, why the original image grabbed you and what you want the focus of your drawing to be, you have a goal in mind all the way through the drawing. If you started without knowing where you were going you would build little, if any, of yourself into it. Discovering the power of analysis is a magical moment and your drawings will never be the same from that time.

Digging a little deeper

Now let's begin to look for more specific questions and answers. A fellow artist once told me 'All I know is that I don't ever want to work from one small photo again. I had to make so many changes'. Then she told me about her continual analysis of that photo as she worked - her constant application of why. 'The more I drew,' she wrote 'the better I got at seeing things. It was as if by magic. What eluded me at one point, suddenly came into focus.'

It's that mental breakthrough I was talking about. Analysis. How sometimes you may look at something for hour after hour then suddenly you see things for the first time that were there all the time. Try looking again at your photo alongside your drawing in a year's time and you won't believe that you ever saw all that information in it.

Now imagine how much easier it would be to have multiple photographs, the ability to see your subject from many angles. It will massively increase your understanding. Unless you have no other option, don't draw from just one photograph. There is no three-dimensional information in a single two-dimensional image. I take up to 180 photographs of each dog I draw so I can pick it up and turn it around as I work. Where does that lock of hair protruding from under the dropped ear go? Lift the ear and photograph it. You know where the lock ends but knowing where it starts is a real aid to its full understanding. I firmly believe that you cannot realistically draw what you do not fully understand.

Extracting the keys

I work from photos and nature combined but for now I suggest you work from photographs. A photo is just a frozen moment in time, which gives you the opportunity to really study why each element looks the way it is.

Imagine looking at a photograph of a tree trunk. If the bark looks rough ask yourself why you know that. What is it in that image that tells you the bark would feel harsh to your touch? You need to analyse what you see until you find the answer - the visual clue. Think of each clue as being a key that you can slot into the brain of your viewer to turn on a known response. In this case it might be that the tops of the ridges are highlighted and sharp-edged, and they contrast starkly with the deep shadows in the troughs between them. Remember, you cannot realistically draw what you do not fully understand.

When you first looked at the photo of that tree, your brain received signals from that image that told it the bark was rough. When you find the key sending that message, just build it into your drawing so it transmits the same visual signal and it will succeed realistically. The more you analyse what you see the easier it becomes to recognise the visual clues you need to include in your work.

If, for example, you draw a curving hank of hair, the keys to include should show if that hair is rough in texture or smooth and soft to the touch. The main key is simply the amount of shine you depict. If you draw the hair with an overall flat tone it will be seen as being dull and probably rough to the touch. If you draw it with a bright highlight at its most forward point then it will appear to be shiny. If you add a second key and draw thick lines between the hairs it will read as shiny and coarse - draw very fine lines instead and it will be seen as shiny and soft.

Try to find the visual keys that tell you a texture feels a particular way. Why is that flat expanse obviously water? The clues captured in those photos are the ones to incorporate into your work to relay your message. In time you will be able to extract them from Nature itself and later you can start to bend the rules but for now just believe in yourself and draw.

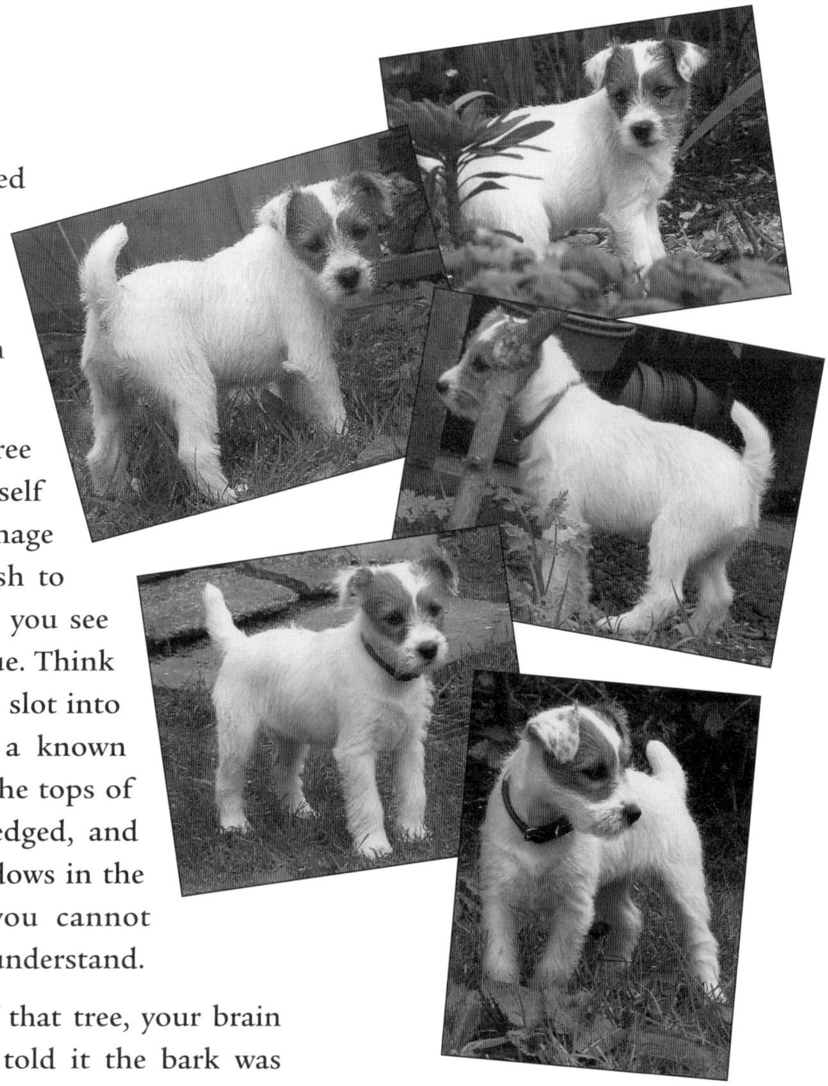

I work from photos, and may take up to 180 individual shots of any one subject. Here is a selection for a working drawing.

A Little History

In 1926 a young Al Hirschfeld sketched a caricature of an actor while at the theatre. Later he successfully submitted a copy to a newspaper and the career of one of the greatest caricaturists was born.

Hirschfeld employed a unique style of simple, flowing lines to capture a personality. His method involved finding the essential characteristics of facial features, body language and gesture. He used these 'keys' to work with as he drew by trial and error in pencil. Only when he considered it to be right did he finish in ink.

Hirschfeld recognised that the solution to a successful caricature lay in finding and exaggerating those elusive keys.

TIP

Can't make out the detail in a photograph? Stuck for that vital piece of visual information that will impart success to your drawing? Treat your photo like a transparency. Hold it up very close to a desk-lamp or other strong light source so the light shines through the paper from behind ... and be amazed at the detail that it contains!

Alternatively, scan it and open it in a program such as Photoshop. Time spent experimenting with the brightness and contrast controls will equally reveal detail in the depths of the shadows.

FINDING LESS TANGIBLE KEYS

So far I have touched only on specifics - physical details that you can analyse reasonably easily. Photographs, those frozen moments, are ideal teaching aids for this - and more.

Why can we see a white dog in the snow? Logic and analysis provide the answers. The dog will throw its own shadow onto the snow and it has a three-dimensional form so its body will possess integral shadows and highlights. Closer analysis may show that the deep shadow beneath the chest has been diluted by light reflected up from the snow. This condition may at first be unexpected by our brain but a quick scan through its memory quickly deduces a ground covering of snow as being the only logical answer. Reflected light then is the 'key'. Build that key into your drawing and you will send the same signal with the same result. But how did we see it as a dog? Or recognise its shape or outline? Nothing in life has a line around it, yet we are able to distinguish forms and planes from each other. How? By the variations and contrasts of adjacent tones and textures. Possibly by colour too, but the graphite artist works with a palette of just two 'colours' - tone and texture. And here photographs come into their own as educational tools.

A WORKING EXAMPLE

Here we have what at first appears to be a simple scene (*left*) - a dog lying on sun-dappled grass. Take a look around it - all the way around. Despite the background possessing many of the tones found in the dog, there isn't one inch of its outline that you cannot distinguish from the background. Why is that? Some areas are darker than the background, some lighter. The process of chance alone should mean that at least parts of it blend in. No part of it is outlined, the whole discernable structure is apparent only because of the effects of lighting and the tonal graduations of the edge. I'm not suggesting we copy these verbatim. Indeed we may wish to extract this dog and put it into a completely different setting. We have a valuable lesson to learn here. The analysis tells us two things. First, the tonal separation at any point between background and subject is so complex and transitory that we can almost

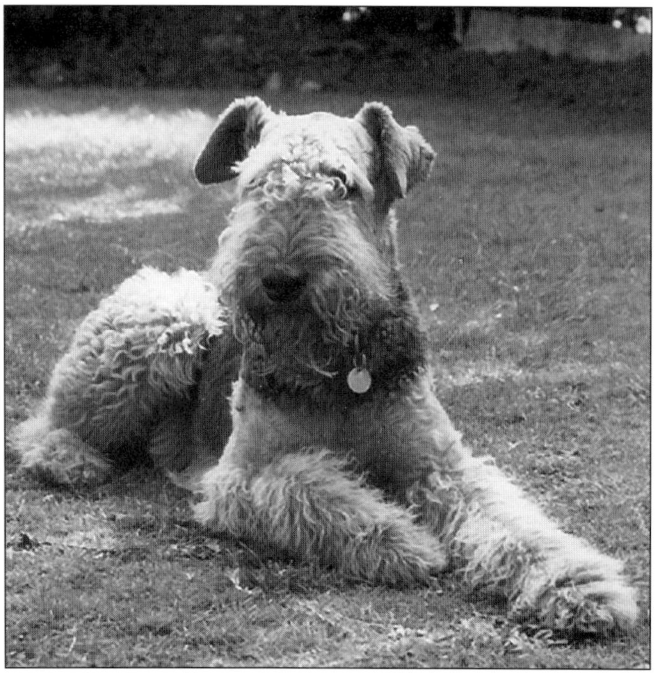

choose opposing tones at random and still fool the brain into seeing 'reality' - so we can engineer the background in the drawing to define the outline of the dog. And second, our brains read 'dog' because of the simple outline - the outline is the key. So long as that outline remains in the drawing, in whatever tonal range or lighting, the first superficial glance by a viewer will have that element categorised as a dog. From there on it's our job to draw the eye in further but the main obstacle has been overcome with ease.

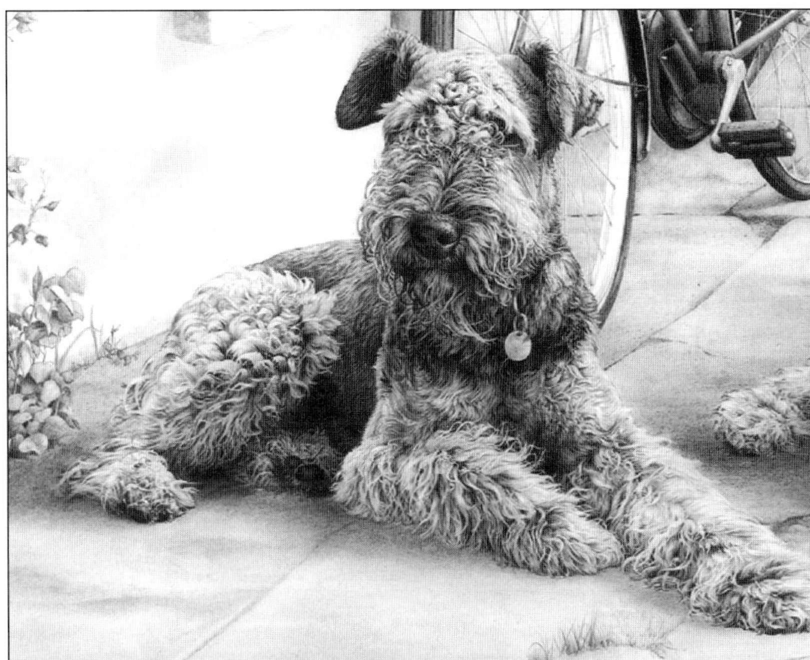

And here it is (*right* - with it's rear rebuilt from other photos) in its final setting with the background locally engineered to separate it out.

The original source photographs were in colour. I very rarely work from black and white photos. Although detail may sometimes be more discernable in a black and white photo, colour photos do not dictate tonal values and will allow you the freedom of imposing your own lighting conditions and tonal scheme. And, of course, you can follow changes of colour as they pass through areas of shadow - important information that can be lost in a monochrome photograph. Use colour photography as source material whenever you can.

Using multiple photographs

By now you may have realised why I use the expression 'Working *with* photos' and not working *from* photos. There is a world of difference between the two. Personally, I am not an admirer of art that is sourced purely from a single photograph. Celebrity portraiture, for example, holds no interest for me at all. Surely the result is a recreation of the photographer's vision and not that of the artist? There's no injection of the artist's self. No commentary. No personalisation and no message. However, they do make superb technical exercises, as any departure from reality is immediately noticeable.

If you only draw what you see in a photograph you will

Tip

When taking reference photos for the portrait of an animal, take them from its own eye- level. Lie on the ground to photograph a small animal or place it on a table.

You wouldn't stand on a box to take a photograph of a human so don't take animal photos from above either.

The framed portrait will hang at the height of the viewer's eye- level where they will not expect to be looking down on the subject. Even if the animal is looking at the viewer, the situation will be unnatural, and you will lose any direct or implied connection between the two.

'Drawing is all about 'seeing' and giving yourself the discipline to draw what you see, no matter how much your mind wants to tell you otherwise. You need to study carefully what you actually do see.

If you have been looking at Life all your life then you should have an idea of what doesn't look quite right in a photo too.'

Jim Hicks, Artist

recreate the photo. This is not the same thing at all as recreating the subject. Cameras do not 'see' in the same way that we do. They have a fixed depth of field (especially noticeable in photographs taken with a zoom or telephoto lens) so what appears to be out of focus to the camera would not appear that way in real life. Using other photos to rebuild the actual reality, as opposed to the perceived reality, is greatly beneficial - and building your own perception of the reality is the zenith.

Armed with my experience of working from multiple photos, I find that I am increasingly disinclined to believe any photo as representing the truth. I use a motor drive on a Canon SLR camera, taking photos at one-second intervals at times. Studying these photos exposes the great changes that can occur in such a short time span. I no longer feel tied to reproducing what the camera recorded. A photo will tell me the exact pose of my subject only at that split second point in time - a second later it may have changed in any number of ways. I draw with that in mind - what was my subject doing before, what was it feeling, what was it about to do? And I study balance too. Nature makes certain that every static being is balanced correctly, so the suggestion of movement can be made by subtly shifting the subject slightly off-balance.

Looking deeper and constantly asking why will soon have you thinking about an eye as an eye - a three-dimensional, fluid-filled object with reflective properties - instead of a series of lines and shapes. Because the source photo is two-dimensional it's tempting to draw that eye as being a single shape on one flat plane. In reality, of course, it transmits emotion and the curved, transparent cornea lies in front of the flat plane containing the iris and pupil.

As your three-dimensional understanding grows, you will inevitably begin to 'sculpt' the object with your pencil as you draw. Graphite pencil is the only medium I know of that allows unbroken creation - no paints to mix, no drying times and, if you work with a chisel-edge drawing tip as I do, no sharpening. When you begin to think 'reality' as you are drawing, and let the drawing process take care of itself, I think you finally begin to achieve the direct brain-to-pencil-to-art connection that graphite permits. It's what attracts me so passionately to the medium.

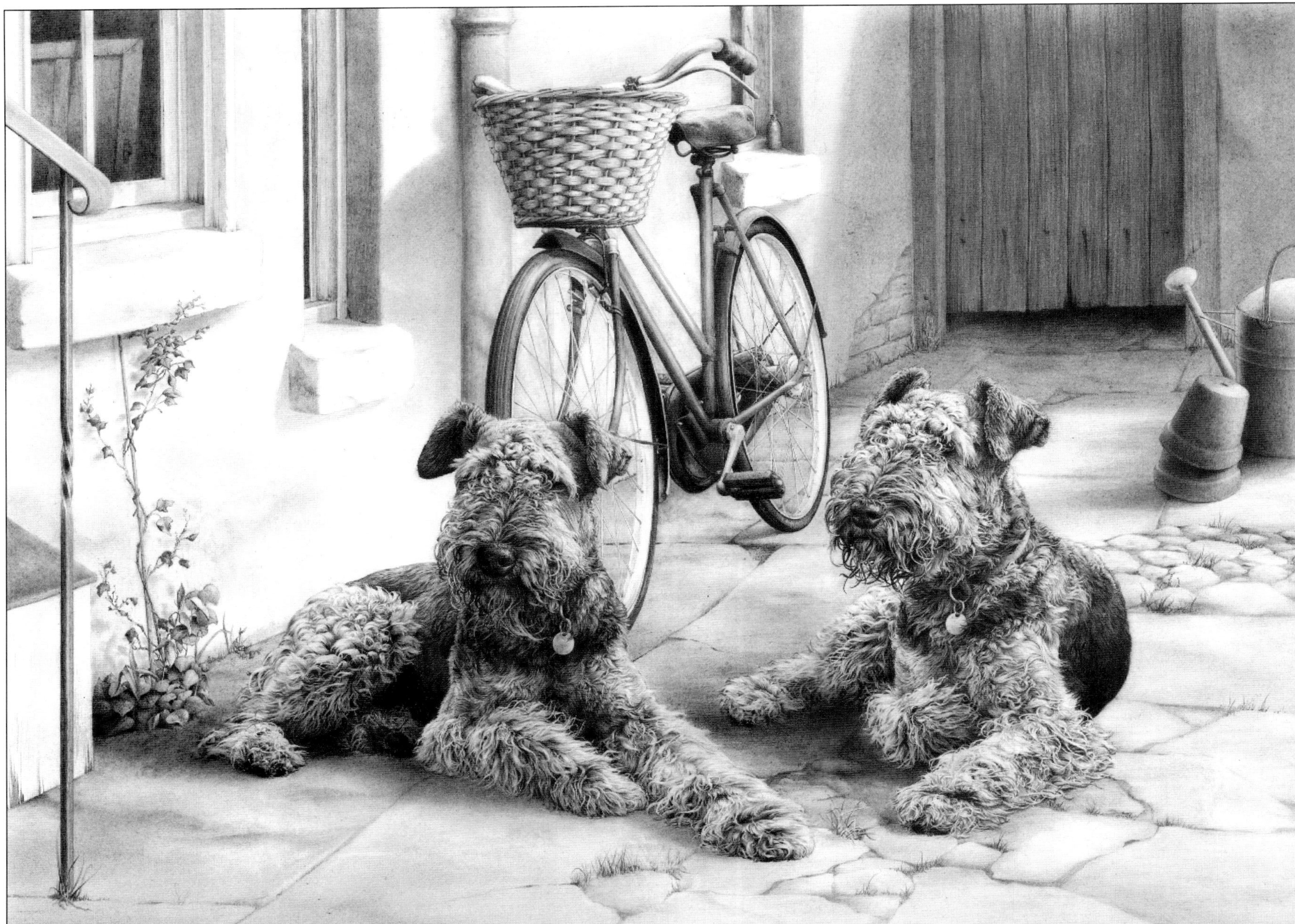

16" x 12" (41 x 31cm)

'Visiting Aunt Maud' © Mike Sibley. A sold out limited edition print of 530.

Negative drawing
Making something of nothing...

'THE UTILISATION OF NEGATIVE DRAWING INVOLVES A CONSCIOUS DECISION - IT'S A METHOD, NOT AN INTRINSIC ELEMENT OF ART.'

In *'Fooling the Brain - part 1'* you were introduced to the concept of Negative Space - the art of drawing the areas around an object to define the object itself. Negative Drawing is similar but it involves the deliberate creation of your own negative space.

There are a number of other methods that offer similar results. Erasing with the edge of a stick eraser, for example, or indenting white lines - both achieve the desired effect in certain circumstances. However, indenting is only capable of realising clearly spaced, thin lines and may be too clean-cut and unnatural in appearance. Erasing cannot easily achieve thin, sinuous lines and will inevitably smear the edges, giving an unfocused appearance.

Only negative drawing truly leaves your surface untouched, permits you to tackle the most complex of shapes, and produces a perfect clarity of edge.

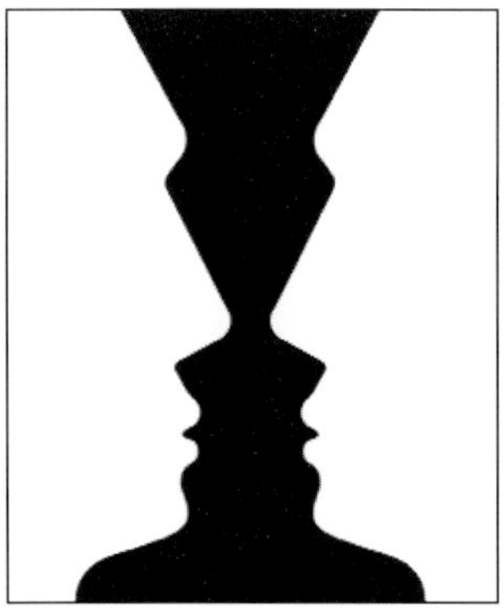

So, what exactly is 'negative' drawing? What do you see when you look at this picture on the left? Do you see an ancient black drinking cup? Maybe an ebony candlestick holder? Or do you see two white faces both looking at each other? Imagine yourself 'seeing' these two faces on a white sheet of paper and then filling in the space between so the faces are revealed. That is negative drawing.

'Negative' doesn't mean black or white, it means using the 'opposite' to create or force focus on the enclosed area. A 'negative' image then is one that is entirely created by the area surrounding it - I prefer to call it 'white space'. The uses of negative drawing extend from creating bright highlights that describe the curvature of a black object, or white shapes defined by their shadows, to the isolation of key elements that can be better drawn at a later stage. You can't draw white with a pencil so, just like a watercolour painter, you have to draw around it to define its shape.

The utilisation of negative drawing involves a conscious decision - it's a method, not an intrinsic element of art. The white space may, for example, be of greater or lesser importance than the black areas. If the drawing is of the drinking cup then the cup is a positive image - no negative drawing is involved - just draw the cup. If the drawing is of the two faces then the 'cup' is the result of the decision to employ negative drawing and exists only to define them. Teaching yourself to see white on white and drawing around it is one of the best lessons you will ever learn.

The basics

As graphite artists we can only draw blacks and greys. Pencils make positive marks - but two parallel pencil marks will contain a third white area between them. If the white area is of greater importance to the drawing then the pencil marks are just filling the negative space around it. The white area, as in the 'cup or faces' example, becomes the dominant image. Let's call it the 'positive' shape because it's defined only by the negative space around it. Now let's simplify the concept.

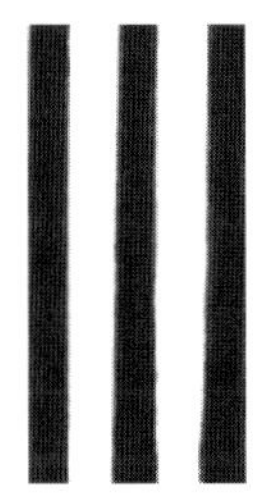

Fig 1

Fig 2

If we draw three lines (*fig 1*) how many lines have we created? The answer is five - three black and two white. Let's make that more obvious and extend and join the black lines (*fig 2*). And we'll create more and join the white ones too (*fig 3*).

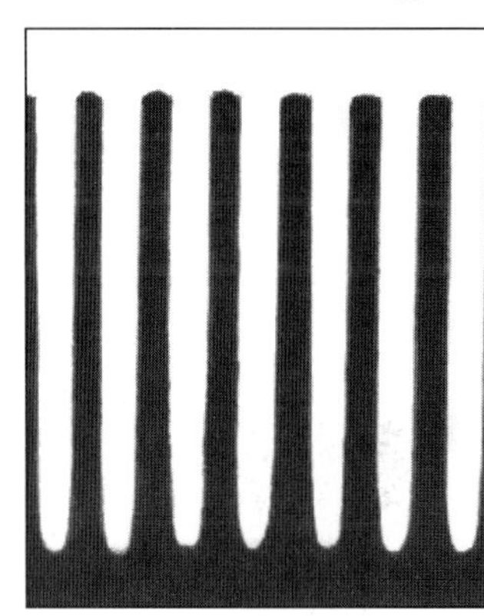

Fig 3

Which is dominant or positive? Are we using negative drawing? Right now we can't say. They share equal importance, as neither has yet been defined as an object. So let's do that - we'll zoom out until one or the other becomes a defined shape.

Now it becomes obvious that the positive shape is the white comb (*fig 4*). It existed only in my mind until I enclosed it by defining the dark negative space.

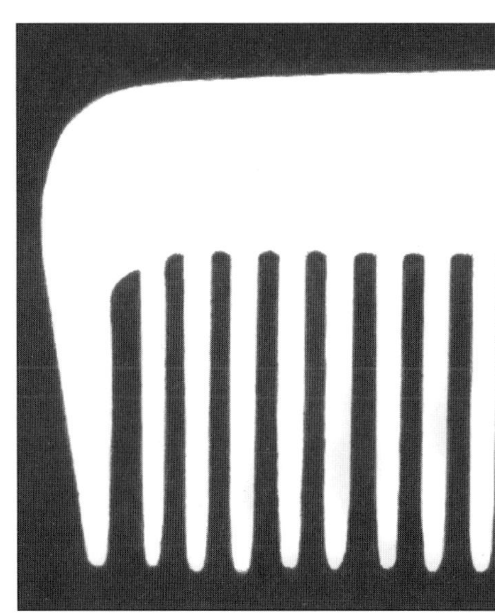

Fig 4

It's not easy to start thinking this way. However, with practice, negative drawing becomes second nature and, more importantly, you learn to switch your mind between negative and positive drawing at will and even to blend the two together.

Why use this method?

Negative drawing offers a number of important advantages that no other system can fully compete with.

• It divides a task into simple, manageable elements.

• No erasing is involved. Your whites remain pristine, and your paper's tooth is preserved.

• It permits much greater control over tonal relationships. You can draw into the white space after you have established the tones surrounding it, giving you infinite control.

• You can literally draw around potential problems and return to them later.

• You can establish the background before the foreground, giving you much greater control over the visual separation of the two.

An artist once wrote to me asking, 'I am struggling to keep a clean border between areas of varying grey through to black. I need to get this right otherwise the tyres on my bikes will look like just one mass of black, and I want to illustrate the radial lines and the writing on the tyres as well as just the tread patterns.'

This is an obvious candidate for negative drawing. You can't establish the lighter tones first because you have nothing to balance them to and it's difficult to control a complex area if you attempt to draw it in one pass.

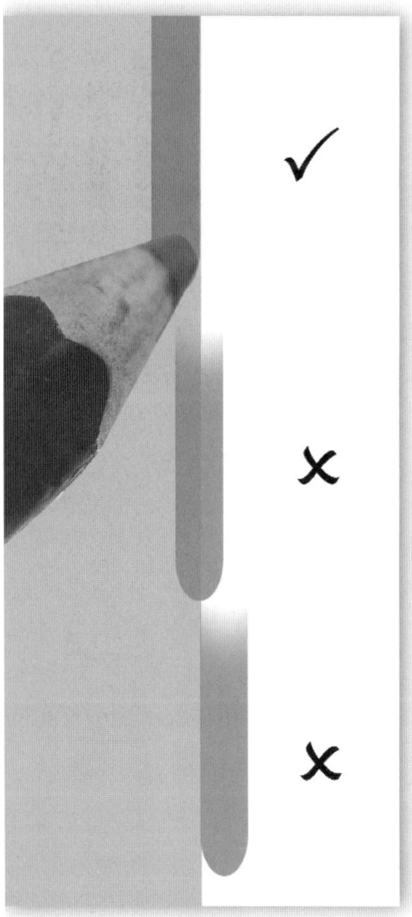

Fig 5

When defining white space, butt the edge of your line up to it - don't draw into it.

Negative drawing will allow you to concentrate on one aspect at a time. Using my way of working from dark to light, you establish the very darkest tones first. Now you know your darkest tone and your lightest (the white of your paper). The black is then extended and diluted as required to form the mid-tones and drawn around the highlights, features, and problem areas - such as the tread pattern and lettering in this case.

When the black or dark areas are completed, all your lighter tones will just be flat white spaces. Now, with the full understanding of the tones surrounding them, you can begin to draw within the spaces to give them the tonal values and shaping that they require. This is much easier to practice than explain!

As you draw be aware at all times that it's the white areas you are drawing as well as the dark. A pencil line possesses a width - watch the edges, not the line itself as you draw - it's the edge that butts up to the white (*fig 5*). Failure to observe this will result in your pencil marks being too close to each other and not leaving sufficient negative space between them or the enclosed white space being smaller than you intended. Try to concentrate on the white space - it's the space that you're drawing, not the pencil lines. With practice it becomes progressively easier to imagine white shapes and draw around them.

Types of negative drawing

Pre-planned

The art of negative drawing covers many variations and complexities. The simplest method involves pre-planned objects that already have guidelines around them. You can choose to treat these elements as 'unknowns' - drawing around areas that present a problem or features that you can only properly complete at a later stage. In both cases they result from the need for additional information that is not presently available. I used this method with all the roots and brambles that disappear into the shadows in my study of 'Overlooked!' I first drew the blacks then completed the dark localised background, leaving each root as a white shape (*fig 6*). Then I drew the roots from light into dark (*fig 7*). By doing it this way you will have already established your lightest and darkest tones so you just need to draw from one into the other. In this case I had three potential problems. I needed to maintain a sharp division between the roots and the background, I didn't know how dense to make the shadows, and I was uncertain as to how the highlights should degrade as they approached the shadowed area. Leaving them as just white space and completing the dark surroundings first, meant I could return to the roots knowing exactly the tones required to make them stand out from the rocks. And I obtained full control over the way they began to merge with the shadows, particularly with the two roots directly below the rabbit, as I now had a defined tonal target to aim for. This way of working - breaking an area up into manageable parts - often greatly simplifies the handling of different elements.

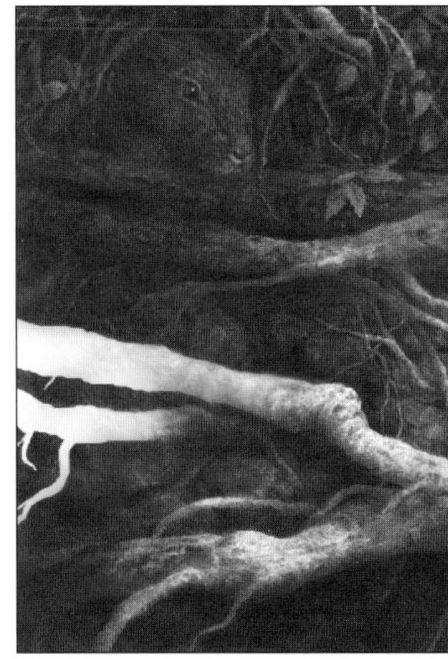

Fig 6

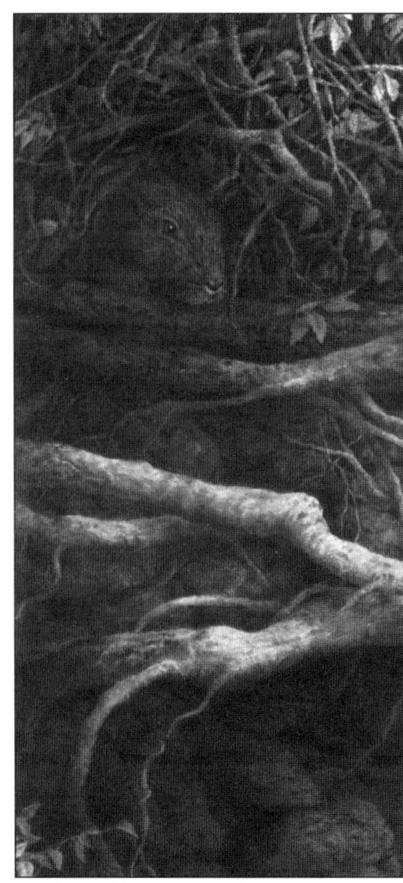

Fig 7

Spontaneous drawing

Now things begin to get a little more complex. So far I've mentioned positive drawing (the cup in *fig 1*) and negative drawing. The two can be combined in one area, one feature, or even one line. In this method a drawn line may be positive at one end and negative at the other.

First, a reminder: Pencils can draw in all directions - up, down, to either side, and all points in between. Because of the action of the wrist it often seems easier to draw down-strokes - it's a natural tendency. But lines can also be drawn on the up-stroke - if you don't regularly draw in that direction, practice it because you're removing half of the available marks from your library. Drawing a sharp, upward tapering point is far easier if

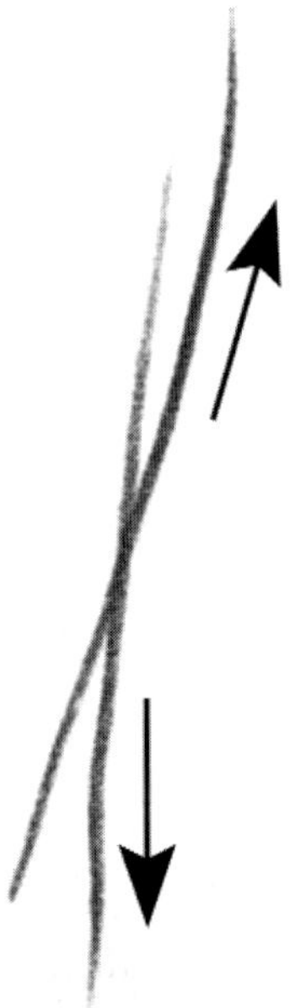

Fig 8

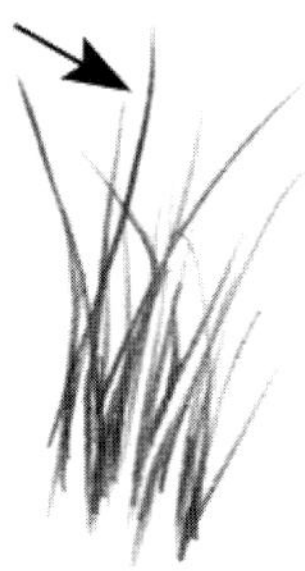

Fig 9

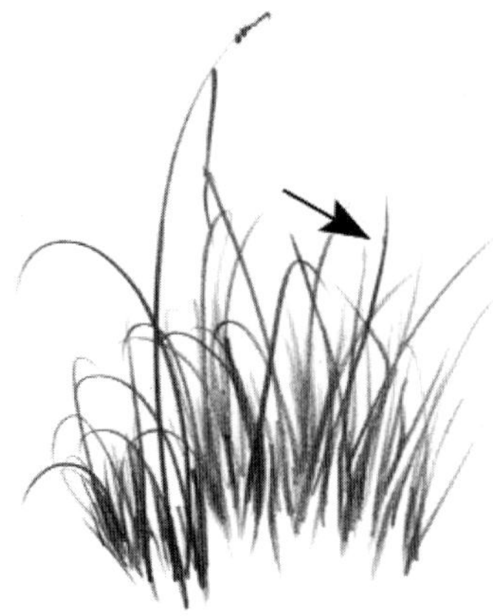

Fig 10

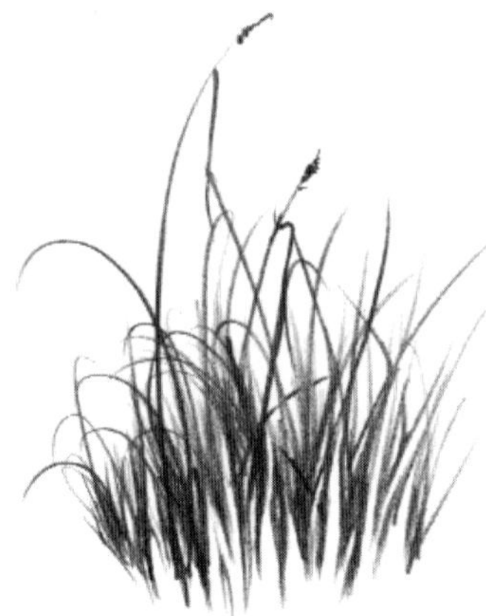

Fig 11

you use an up-stroke with decreasing pressure. Even if you don't draw upwards it's essential that you at least understand the concept for the following example to make sense. We're going to draw grass - a subject covered more fully in a later chapter - and make use of two of its visual properties: the bases of tapering blades are hidden by the blades in front of them, and less light filters down into the densely packed bases so the blades appear progressively lighter with height.

Imagine that there are only two marks that we can make: one upward and one down. I'm using the upward stroke to positively draw the stalks that spring up from the base of a clump of grass - it actually represents a blade of grass (*fig 8*). The downward stroke tapers off and defines the tops of the stalks in the clump below the one I'm drawing - it draws in negative, as it forms the shadow, the negative space, between two blades. It's also true that the same two operations may be achieved at either end of the same line. Don't worry, it gets easier!

I've added more blades (*fig 9*), the original blades are arrowed, and already a suggestion of white blades is beginning to appear below. There is no pre-planning involved at all here. All the drawing is completely spontaneous and drawn quickly - too quickly for the conscious mind to interfere.

Taken a stage further (*fig 10*) you can now clearly see the upward strokes forming grass blades at the top and the down-strokes beginning to define lighter blades below. A little extra work (*fig 11*), mainly with down-strokes, further refines the lower layer of grass.

Now the process begins again lower down (*fig 12*). This new drawing area creates two further 'layers' of grass - just as the previous one did - a positively drawn rear layer with a

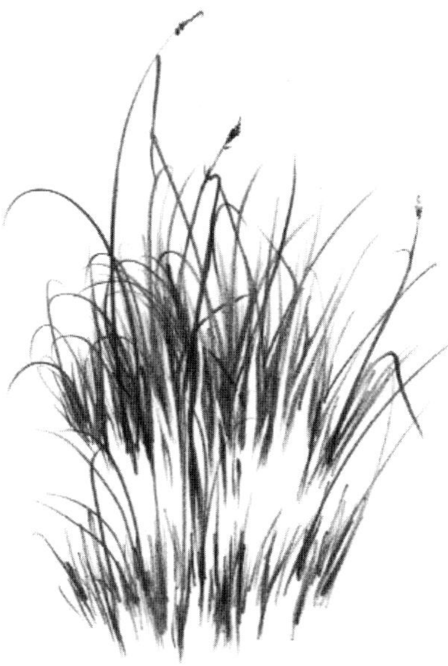

Fig 12

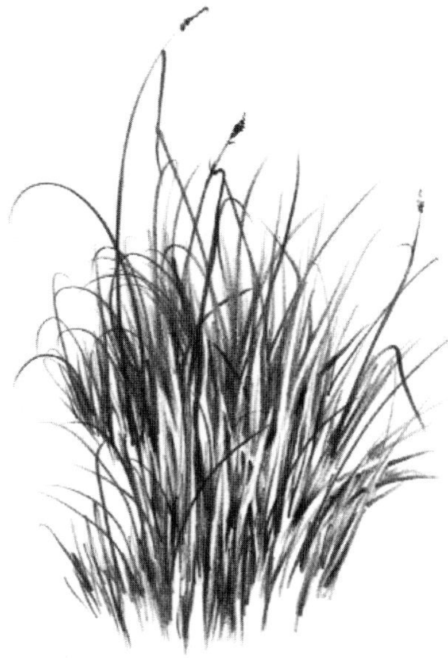

Fig 13

'HOWEVER COMPLEX A JOB MAY APPEAR TO BE, IT'S ALWAYS POSSIBLE TO BREAK IT DOWN INTO MANAGEABLE ELEMENTS OR PROCESSES.'

negatively drawn white layer in front of it. Here positive strokes at the base are drawn up into the previously-created white shapes above and begins to create new ones below, defining a new foreground layer, which we'll leave undeveloped here.

Finally (*fig 13*) a degree of localised negative drawing in the central section blends the two together and a small amount of tone has been added to give body and form to the negatively drawn grass.

COMBINATION DRAWING

Now things might appear to be getting even more complex. But, no - this is simply a combination of the two previous methods and actually makes your life simpler. I'm all for simple! However complex a job may appear to be, it's always possible to break it down into manageable elements or processes.

Here in this small 2" x 3" (5 x 8cm) drawing, I began by mapping out the main stalks (*fig 14*); lightly drawing a line either side to delineate the space that constitutes the stalk and leaf. Remember that you are defining white space so be aware that it is the inside edge of your pencil line that counts - you are drawing that line around a white shape. There is only one important consideration here - what you start you must finish. Every stalk you draw must have a beginning and an end - it must go somewhere. The eye is adept at noticing elements that it cannot understand and will be attracted by that element in passing - distracting the viewer and damaging the sense of reality you are trying to achieve.

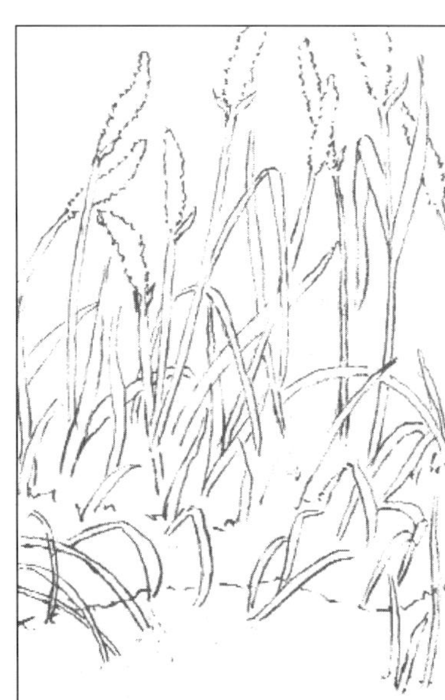

Fig 14

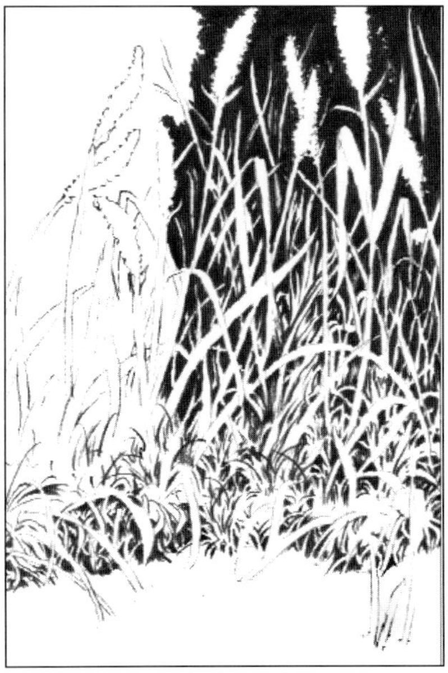

Fig 15

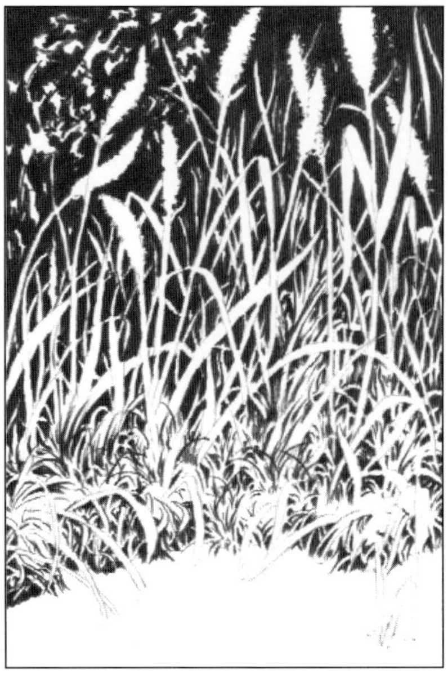

Fig 16

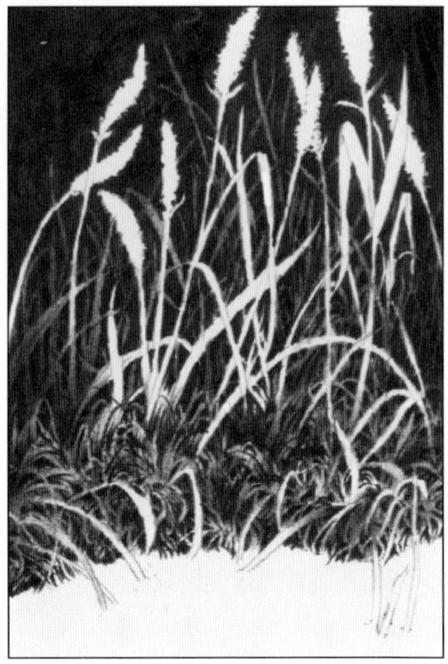

Fig 17

Having pre-planned and defined the main stalks (I call them 'status' stalks - they're food for the brain) I'll switch from my deliberate approach to a more spontaneous style of working to map out the less distinct grass on the rear-most plane (*fig 15*). I rarely outline anything in these areas but create stalks merely by drawing the negative space.

Here is where you let your imagination go free, working at a pace that prevents conscious intervention. Your aim is 'natural' so let Nature take over. Nature knows all about balance - you will find yourself introducing stalks here and there that may even surprise you with their placement. Don't be tempted to intervene, just let Nature take over. Don't try to be too accurate - inaccuracies lend an extra realism in this case. And don't touch those 'status' stalks - you cannot properly define their tonal values until you have completed the grass behind them.

As you work on this secondary area between the established white spaces that represent the status stalks of grass, introduce random shapes and lines (*fig 16*). As long as these vaguely follow the rules of natural grass and foliage, they will serve to fool the brain into seeing more detail than exists. In life you couldn't distinguish every element in such an arrangement (especially in areas of deep shadow) so you shouldn't be able to do so here either.

Now picture, really picture, yourself looking into that area and begin to add reality to the situation (*fig 17*); toning some stalks down a little and others so much that they are barely

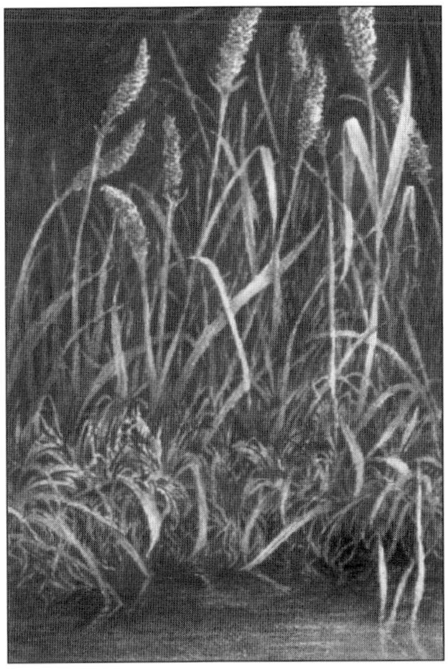

Fig 18

discernible. Just so in Nature - not everything is seen with total clarity. If you can see the reality in your mind you will achieve a sense of reality in your drawing. If you're not sure how to treat something, leave it white then go back to it once it's surrounded - as I have done here with the foreground. It's going to be water and I can't draw the reflections until I know exactly what reflections are required.

Finally (*fig 18*), the status stalks are given body, adjusting the tone of those behind them if required. The foreground grass is drawn, just as I described earlier, and the water and reflections established.

'NEGATIVE DRAWING IS A LIBERATING AND CONTROLLABLE WAY OF WORKING'

In conclusion

Negative drawing is a liberating and controllable way of working and scores above all other methods in the drawing of complex negative shapes. This is particularly true when 'negative' is meant in the photographic sense - those instances where the complexity involves a light object seen against a darker background, such as these sunlit trees against a stormy sky (*fig 19*).

Although it may take time to learn to use negative drawing I can thoroughly recommend it. It offers the means to tackle complicated tasks in manageable stages, and presents the opportunity to draw perfectly within white space and complete it without alteration or experimentation. Getting it right the first time will always give a sharply defined finish that all other methods muddy.

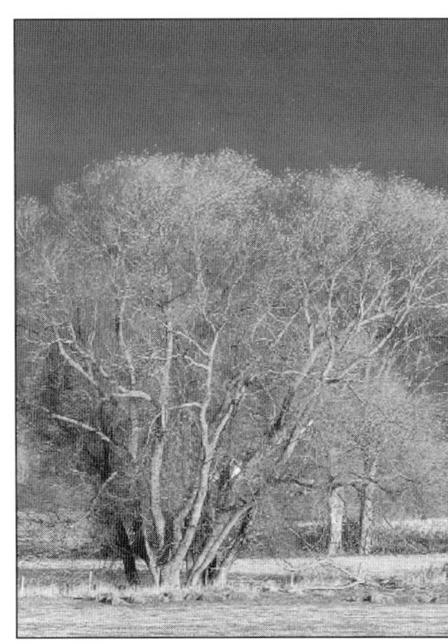

Fig 19

Perspective
The vanishing art...

'IT IS NOT HARD TO MASTER PERSPECTIVE AND ONCE YOU UNDERSTAND THE PRINCIPLES AND TECHNIQUES IT WILL BECOME SECOND NATURE.'

Take a hardback book - a big one. Hold it up vertically at arm's length so you're looking at the front cover and close one eye. Now slowly rotate it so the top tips towards you. When you reach the point that all you can see is the top of the book - stop. Now slowly rotate it back the other way - just a bit until you begin to see the bottom of the book appear. OK? Now ask yourself why the bottom of the book is not as wide as the top. *That's perspective!*

Perspective is an essential tool for all artists who are dealing with reality. It is not hard to master, and once you understand the principles and techniques it will become second nature. But first you must learn and understand the rules. A basic knowledge will allow you to begin creating believable worlds and placing your subjects into it in a credible way. A greater knowledge of the rules will greatly assist you when sketching out in the field, particularly when drawing buildings, because knowing what to expect will help you to see correctly, to make sense of the angles and orientations in front of you.

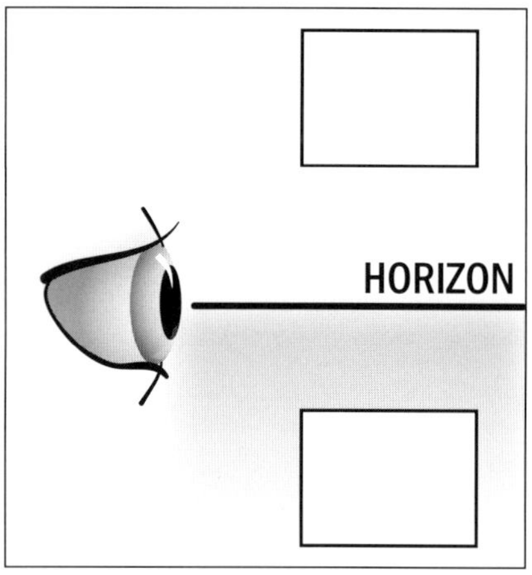

Fig 1

However, the rules are not sacrosanct and, once learned, you can begin to play games with them, moulding them to suit your composition and requirements. The brain is easily fooled in this respect as long as you adhere to the conventions that it understands. Essentially, perspective dictates that an object appears to be smaller as it moves further away from you. In fact it's not objects that shrink with distance but perceived *measurements,* and *all* measurements decrease so relationships between adjacent objects remain in proportion.

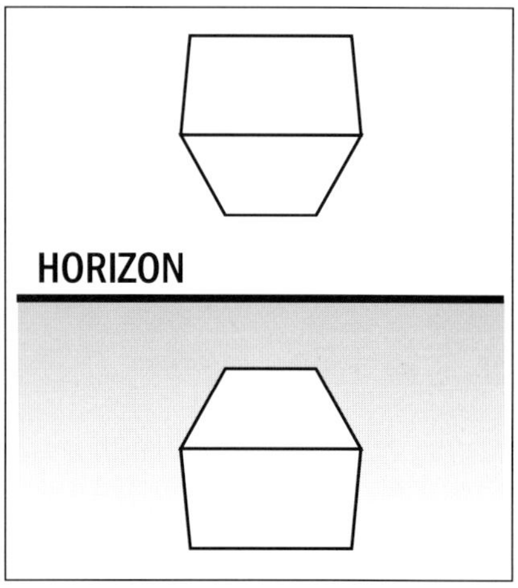

Fig 2

First there has to be a fixed constant against which the eye can judge relative sizes, altitudes and distances. This constant is the horizon or eye-level. For now, imagine this is your own eye-level. You're looking straight ahead across a huge, flat field and where the field meets the sky is the horizon (*fig 1*). You will be looking up at anything completely above that line and down at anything entirely below it (*fig 2*). If an object bisects the horizon you will be looking both up at its top and down at the bottom.

As measurements get smaller with distance they will reach a point, actually on the horizon, where they are so small that they appear to meet. This meeting point is called the vanishing point (*fig 3*). Horizontal lines are still horizontal and (when faced directly) vertical lines are vertical - but here the backs of the boxes (just like the book earlier) are further away than their fronts so their measurements will be smaller. This property is what your brain uses to detect special relationships. Without it, the next time you cross the road you'll probably be run over. To our eyes, the smaller a car appears, the further away we know it is. And the speed at which its apparent size grows tells us how fast it is moving. The system works perfectly in a three-dimensional world but we are creating a two-dimensional, static world and need to find a way of sending the same message. So let's put a window in between that flat field and ourselves. The window is our picture plane. Imagine tracing what you can see through the window onto the glass. You do exactly the same when drawing on a paper picture plane, except that you use your imagination to 'see' through the paper and into the distance (*Fig 4*).

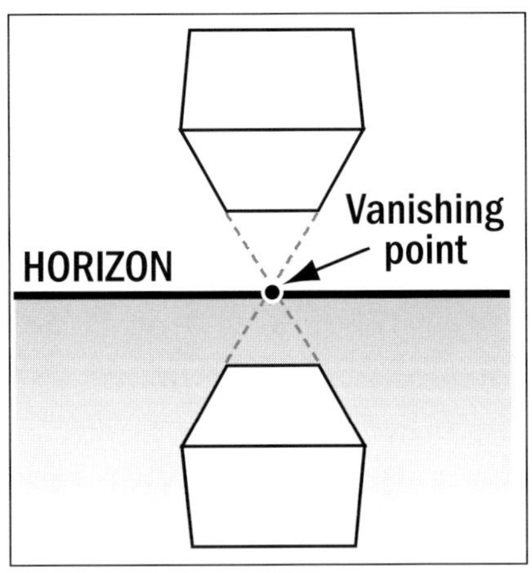

Fig 3

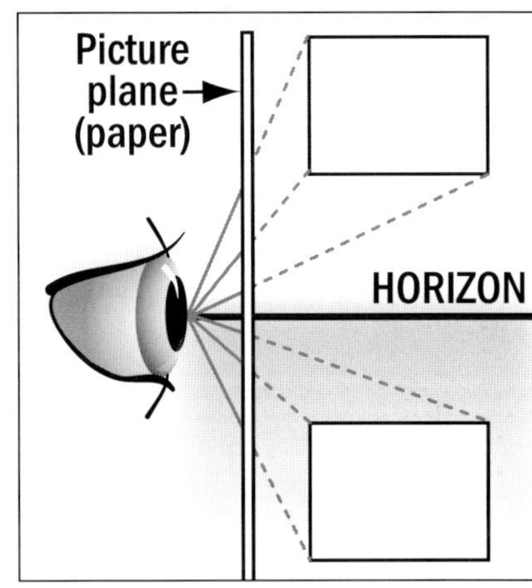

Fig 4

There are three main objectives to keep in mind: distance above or below the horizon, relativity between objects at the same distance, and logic. Of these, logic is arguably the most important.

One-point perspective

Let's take an easy image to work with - a line of tall posts. The posts are six feet (1.8m) high and let's say from your feet to your eyes you measure five feet (1.5m) so your eye-level - the horizon - will be one foot (30cm) below the top of the first post (*fig 5*). We now have a post and our horizon and, so we can see the whole line of posts, the post is slightly to our left. There will be five posts, an equal distance apart, and if they extended in a long fence into the distance, they would be too small to see and finally vanish at a point on the horizon - our vanishing point. If we mark a dot on the horizon where they will disappear we can draw a line from that dot to the bottom of our first post, because all the posts are in a straight line, and we can do the same for the tops.

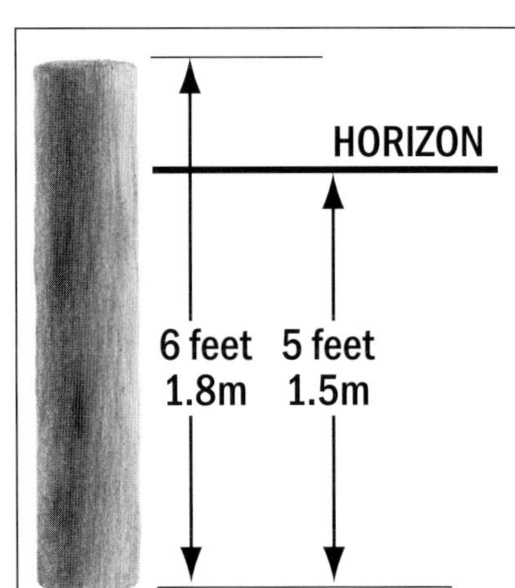

Fig 5

Now we can complete the other four posts (*fig 6*). Notice how

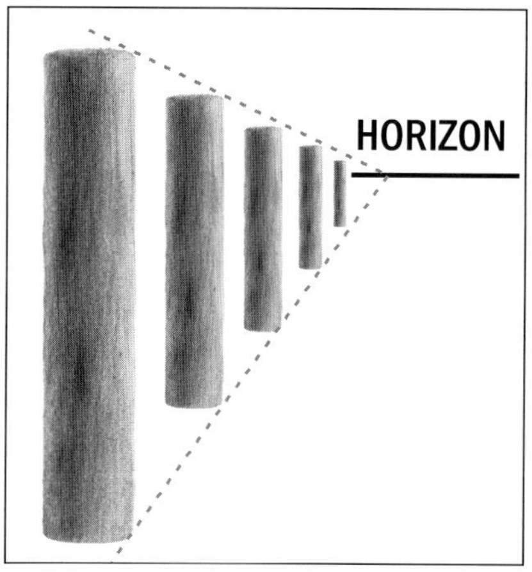

Fig 6

their heights decrease with distance - but so too do all other measurements. Let's say that the second post is 10% shorter than the first so its diameter, or width, must also be 10% less. The third post is 10% smaller again and likewise the fourth and fifth. Because all measurements decrease proportionally with distance we must take one more into consideration - the distance between the posts, which will also decrease by the same amount. In reality it's often easier to draw the first and last and then space the others between them by eye until they look right. We are, after all, artists and not mathematicians so what matters to us is visual and not academic accuracy. So, that's a relief!

Two-point perspective

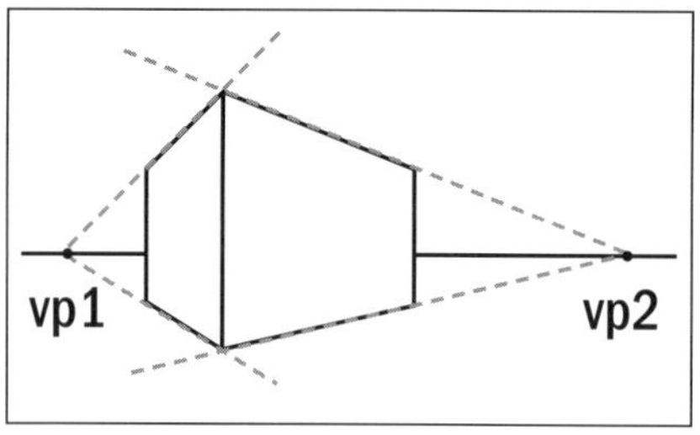

Fig 7

Let's leave the posts and go back to our boxes. So far we've only looked at them from directly in front. If we move to one side or the other then two, not one, vanishing points appear because we can now see two converging faces (*fig 7*). The position of each vanishing point (vp) will depend on the angle of the object to the viewer.

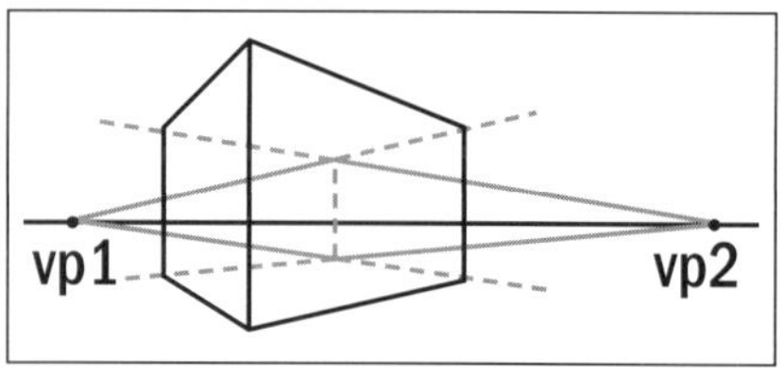

Fig 8

To aid understanding during the composition of a drawing, it's often useful to construct the unseen faces too (*fig 8*). It's the same box from the same angle so the same vanishing points apply. All you need do is extend lines through the box from both vanishing points to the furthest corners, rather than the nearest as before, and where they cross you draw your rear vertical. Try it - you'll find drawing the remaining edges is now self-evident. Practice is the key to success here. With time and practice comes an understanding that permits you to discard actual construction and to rely instead on intuition and knowledge. However, a full understanding is a necessity as the only solution to a problem may require you to physically employ the rules of perspective.

Using logic

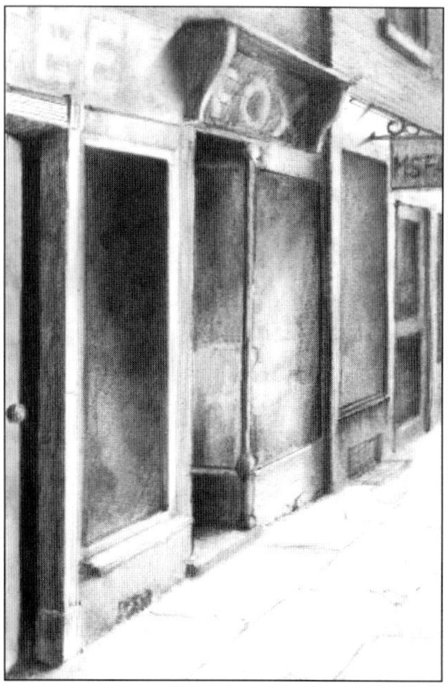

A logical street scene

Where to position your horizon in a drawing can sometimes present a problem but the application of logic usually provides the answer. Let's consider as an example a drawing of a street scene. The level street extends away from you with buildings down the left hand side and the foreground shop has an imposing doorway. A normal door is six feet six inches (2m) high and it makes sense to calculate the height of your eyes as you walk through that door. Draw a line across your drawing at that height to establish the horizon. Now you can construct all your perspective lines from vanishing points placed on that horizon. If you place your horizon lower your drawing will appear to be seen from a kneeling position. Move it higher and anyone viewing your work will think they are standing on a wall, looking down on your scene. Either viewpoint is also perfectly valid if that is your intention.

A person walking past a doorway further down the street should be in perfect proportion to that door and capable of entering it. You can use comparative measurements at any depth in your drawing to calculate the relative sizes of anything else at that depth. Logically a six-foot high man can enter through a normal door; he can see over and place his hands upon the roof of an adjacent car; his head will equal in size the head of the driver of that car. Logic is a great tool.

You can also determine the relative size of an object if you have elements, both behind and in front, of which you know the size. Two people have entered our scene - a man in the background looking into a shop window; in the foreground is a woman walking towards the man. Somewhere between the two you want to place a dog that you know to be human knee height at the shoulder. By drawing a line from the man's feet to the woman's and another connecting their knees you can now accurately size the dog anywhere in between them. Just stand it on the lower line so its shoulder touches the top line.

You can be even more abstract than that and use actual measurement. Here's a practical example. I wanted to draw a Bearded Collie and time was short so I needed a setting that was relatively quick to draw. I settled on a dilapidated trailer that belonged to my neighbour (don't laugh - I 'repaired' it for this drawing and I own it now!). With pad and pencil I walked next door and sketched it where it stood, making notes of appropriate measurements.

Back in the studio I invented a tailboard for it. Here my experience of perspective helped and the tailboard was drawn by eye. Then I needed something to hold it up and drew what I knew my neighbour would have used - a bent nail, wire and a length of old rope!

Now all I needed to do was scale and position the

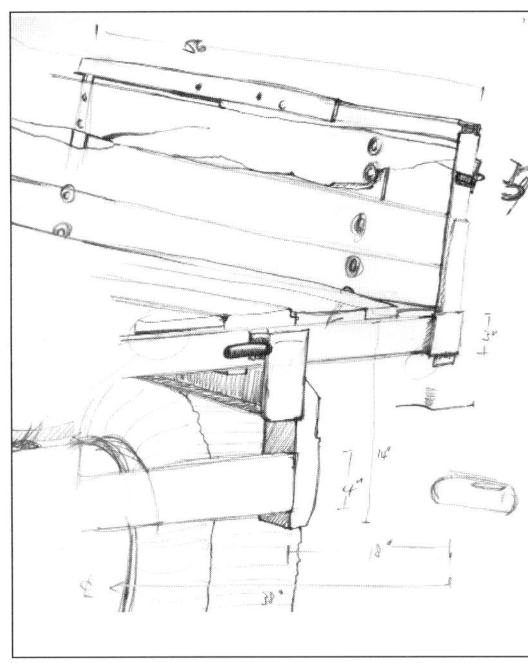

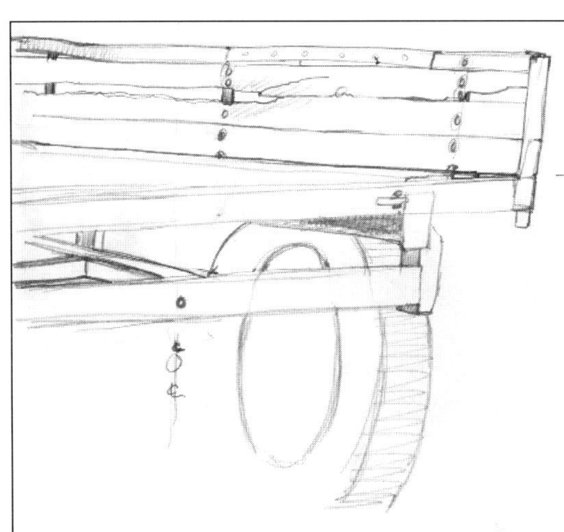

Working sketches with appropriate measurements

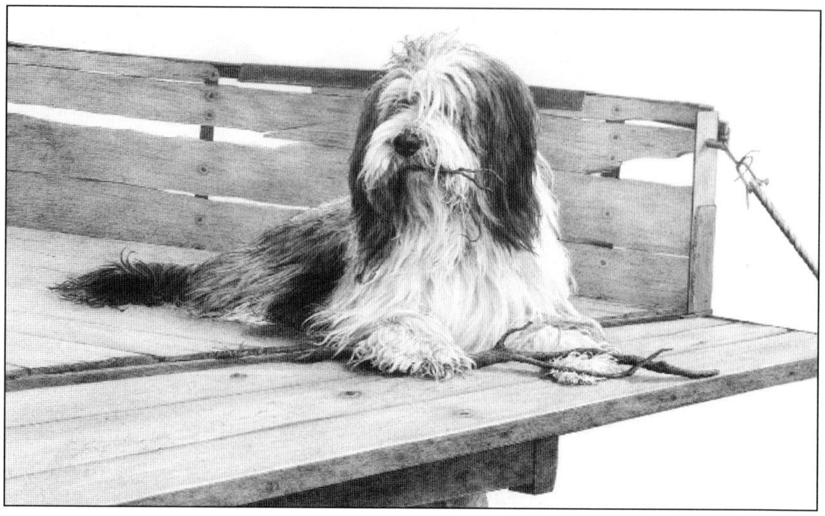

'Waiting for the first load'

dog. I have experience of Bearded Collies but don't exactly know the height of a lounging one so I imagined patting it on the head and measured the distance of my hand from the floor. Then, using the measurements I'd taken from the trailer I adjusted the size of the Collie and moved the trailer around until it suited my composition.

HORIZON VARIATIONS

The horizon need not be at your eye-level. My drawings are of dogs and depict a dog's world. When I photograph a small dog I lay on my side to take photographs of it from it's own eye-level. Consequently my drawing too must use the dog's eye-level as its horizon. There are, of course, exceptions. If I place a dog on a rock half way up my drawing, the horizon (the dog's eye-level) rises to match it. If I elevate it sufficiently its eye-level may match that of a human. In fact I have a choice with most of my drawings - I can choose the dog's eye-level or that of the human viewing the drawing. The first gives the dog prominence over the viewer; the latter suggests that the dog is just an element of the overall study. Of course you must beware of problems using the human eye-level horizon - if the dog (photographed at its own eye-level) is used below the horizon it will never be a true part of the picture. The horizon will indicate that the dog should be seen from above and set up a visual conflict. However, there are tricks you can use to get around this. One is to use only amorphous shapes in the setting - no straight lines or edges to conform to perspective - and another is to use a scale that suggests the scene can only be seen from a distance. The further away the viewer is, the greater the angle of view is restricted - like using a camera's zoom lens.

Aerial perspective

Aerial (or atmospheric) perspective concerns another form of recession. Not only do objects appear to reduce in size as they move further away they are also affected by atmospheric conditions - airborne dust, water vapour, mist, haze, fog - all serve to lighten tonal values, blur detail and, in terms of colour, become more blue. In line drawing you can suggest this by reducing the pressure of your pencil, lightening and narrowing the line. In tonal drawing we can make great use of it - exaggerating the recession to produce magical atmospheric conditions; compressing distance to achieve misty, suggestive backgrounds behind sharply drawn subjects, or subtly overstating the recession of, for example, a line of fence posts to increase the perceived depth of a scene.

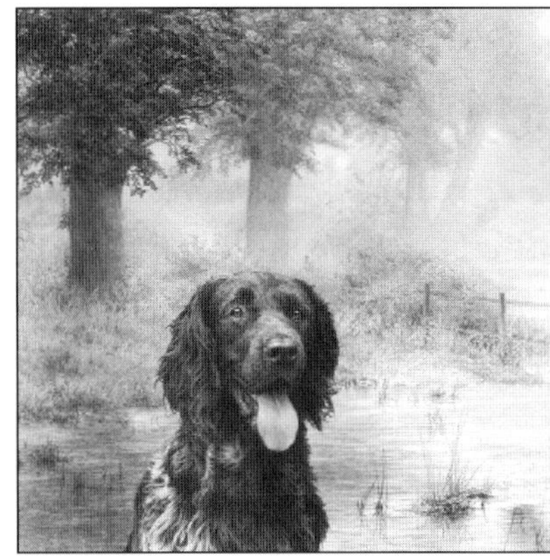

Detail from 'Early morn at Witton Marsh' showing aerial perspective

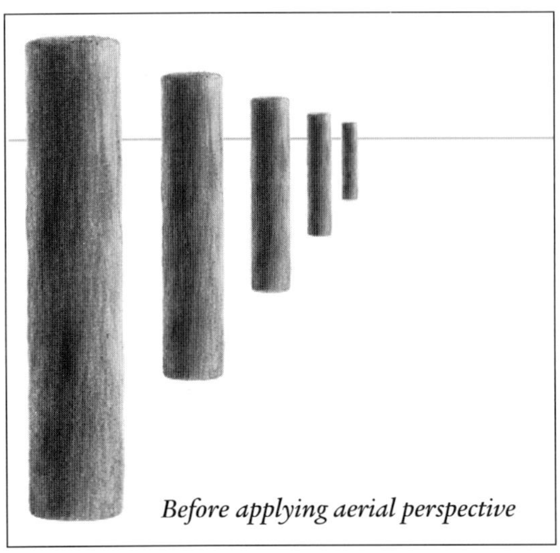

Before applying aerial perspective

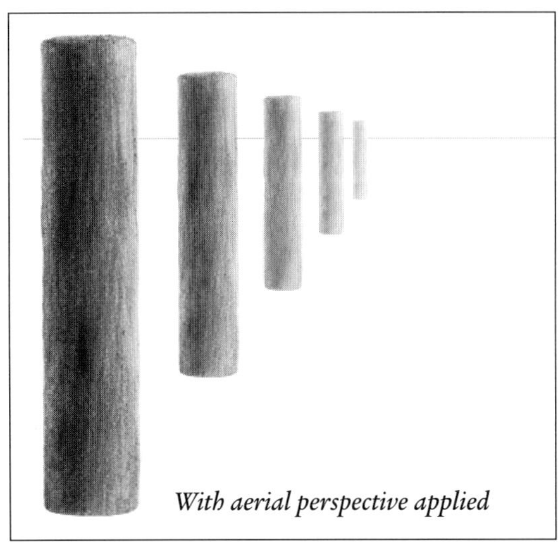

With aerial perspective applied

Ground plane perspective

If you are new to the study of perspective you'll be happy to hear that this advanced variation will probably make more sense to you once you are confidently using perspective in your drawings. Ground plane perspective concerns the grounding and scaling of elements within a composition. We used something similar in an earlier example, the fence posts and the decreasing distance between them, but here we are concerned only with their position on the ground. It's a method that can provide a solution to a vexing problem at times. When all else fails and you cannot get the various elements of your drawing to work together this presents a simple 'stage set' visualisation. A stage set comprises a number of 'flats', flat boards painted to represent three-dimensional scenes. Using these flats will greater simplify our task.

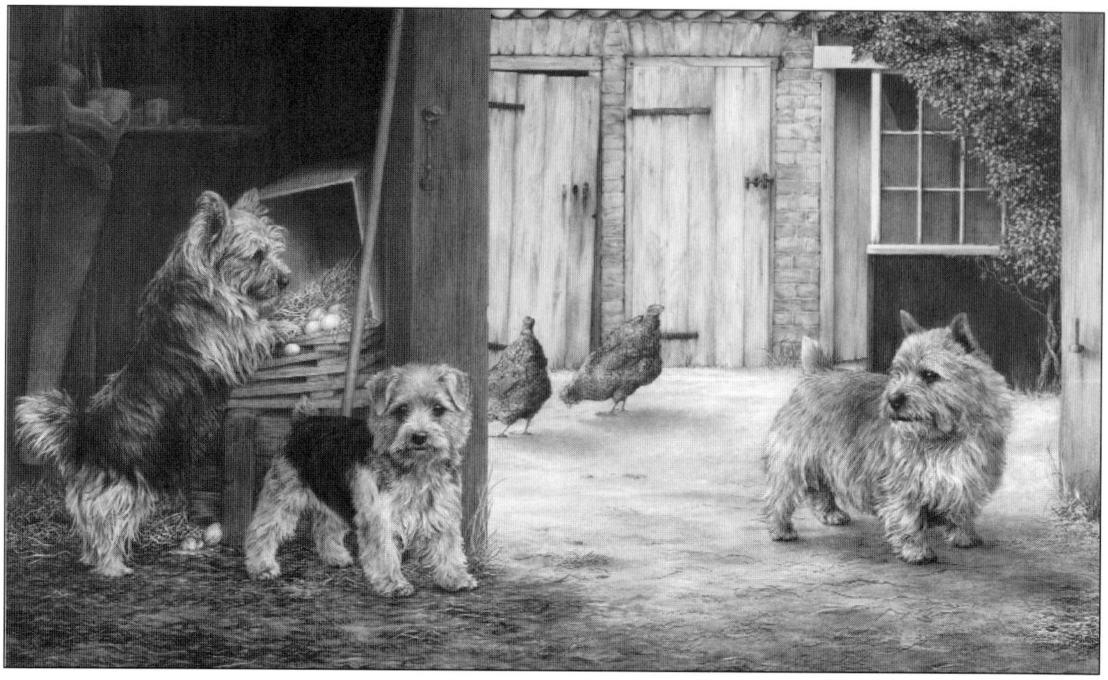

Rags, Tatters and Gentleman George

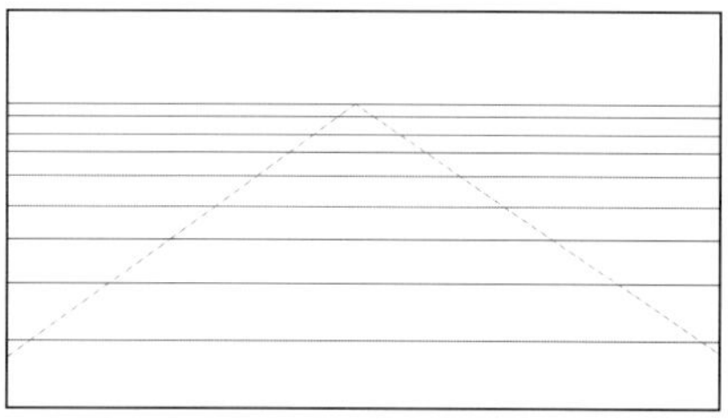

Fig 9

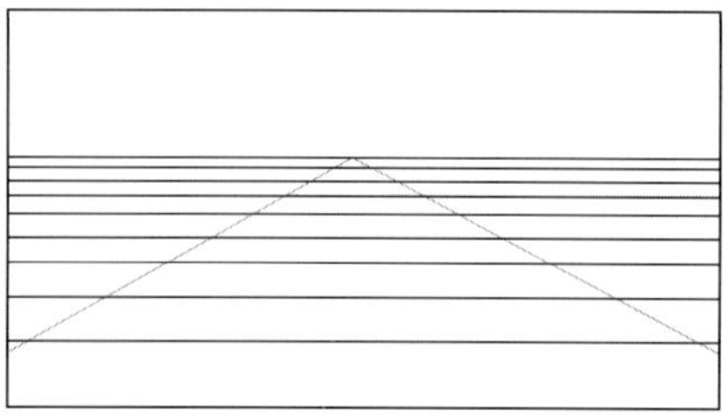

Fig 9B

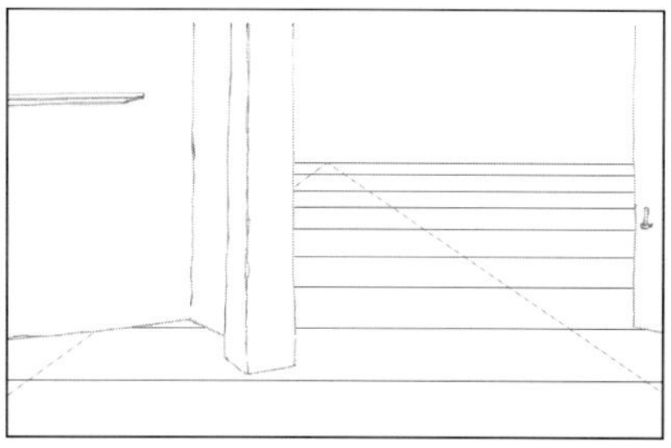

Fig 10

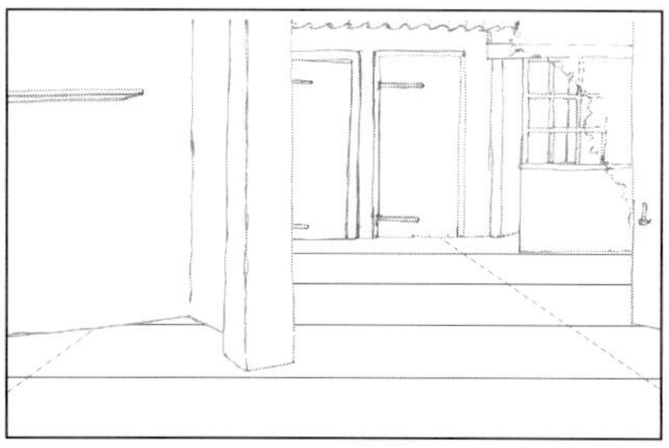

Fig 11

Let's take a practical example. '*Rags, Tatters and Gentleman George*' is a drawing that was giving me problems. I wanted to show the background outbuilding doors in their entirety but I couldn't get the scale or the angle of my ground plane correct. I constructed a series of receding lines in my computer (*fig 9*). You don't need specialised software for this and you can place the lines by eye - aiming for the same decrease in distance between succeeding lines. If you use Adobe Photoshop you have the ultimate flexibility of being able to tilt the angle of your plane by lowering or lifting the horizon once it's drawn. Flatten the image, Select All and use Edit > Transform > Scale. Then pull down the top to compress the lines, which will continuously recalculate the spatial relationships between them (*fig 9b*).

Let's begin dressing our 'stage' by introducing the barn 'flats' to our ground plane (*fig 10*), dropping in the outbuilding backdrop (*fig 11*) and finally suitably and separately arranging our dogs (*fig 12*).

So far everything has been placed by eye, as I would normally do. Here, however, the problem of correctly visualising this scene can now be resolved by physically checking placements and relationships. This uses a combination of logic and plotting.

Most objects in the scene can be of variable size but we need a known constant. Gentleman George, the right hand dog, is a show specimen and I know the breed standard dictates his height at the shoulder to be 10" (25.4cm). We can now join his shoulder to a point estimated to be 10" high on one of the 6' 6" outbuilding doors (*fig 13*) and his front feet directly to the base. Because the lines drop down towards us, this immediately tells us the horizon is higher than this dog. We're looking up at the tins on the low shelf, which we can just see beneath, so these are above the horizon. Therefore we appear to be seeing this scene from just below Rags' view - about 18"(46cm) above ground level - and the horizon can now be established with sufficient accuracy (*fig 14*). It crosses the 6'6" doors at a height of approximately 18" so they are correctly positioned and sized. Had this not been so the doors could have been moved or resized as required until our 18" high marker appeared in the correct place.

If we wish, we can also check the sizing of other elements, such as Tatters the pup (*fig 15*). We can draw a horizontal line from Tatters' feet through the base line of George. Where they cross we can extend a vertical to George's top line, a distance we know to be 10". We mark off Tatters' height of 7" on this vertical and extend a horizontal line back to him. It touches where we expect his shoulder to be and confirms his height as being proportionally correct. In practice all these elements were sized by eye, which is the natural way and my preference, but the ground plane method offers accurate corroboration when required.

Finally, in the finished drawing, I introduced the two large hens. They serve as a device to connect the foreground and background, to reinforce the scale and to tell the eye, by tucking one behind the doorpost, that space exists between the barn and the outbuilding.

In fact the final perspective of this piece is deliberately vague at the left hand end. I used dense shadow to disguise the corner, straw to cover the join between wall and floor and the timber palettes are deliberately askew, being tipped by Rags, as is the box containing the nest. All of these combine to form a believable whole yet no edges conform to any of the existing vanishing points or the horizon. Sometimes what looks right is right. As I said, when you've learned the rules you can begin to play tricks with perspective - and it's great fun!

'...WHEN YOU'VE LEARNED THE RULES YOU CAN BEGIN TO PLAY TRICKS WITH PERSPECTIVE - AND IT'S GREAT FUN!'

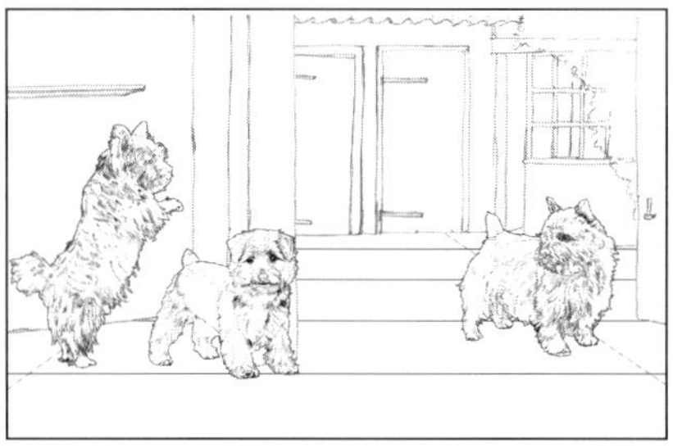

Fig 12

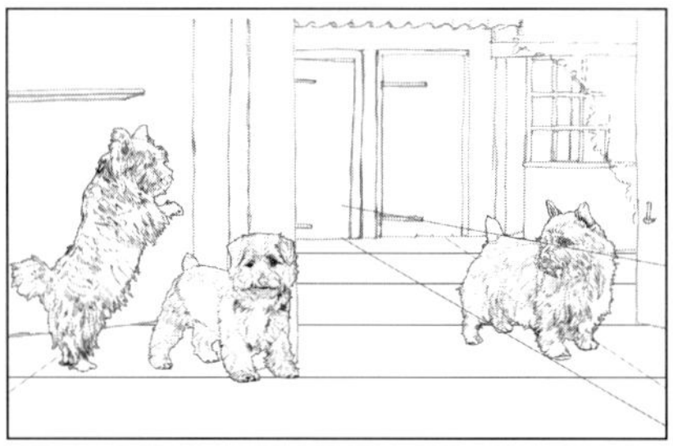

Fig 13

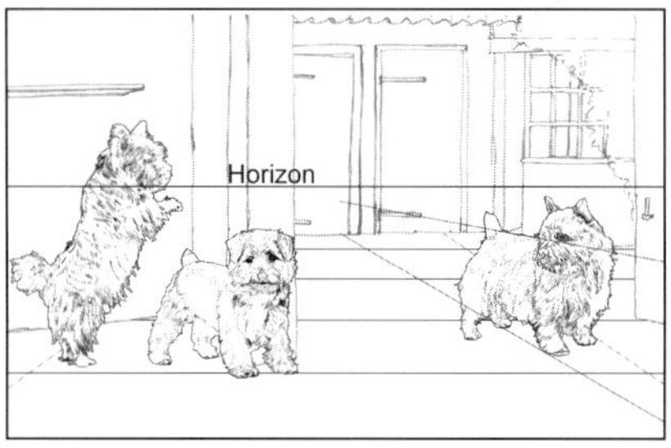

Fig 14

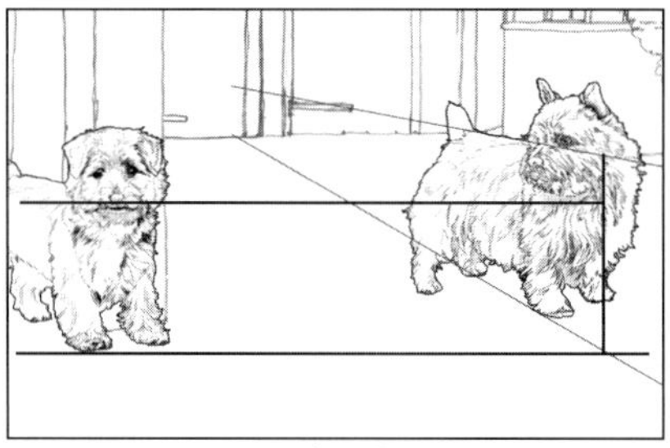

Fig 15

Light and Shade

The third dimension...

'LIGHT AND SHADOW ARE COMPLEMENTARY OPPOSITES - NEITHER CAN EXIST WITHOUT THE OTHER.'

Lighting can transform a piece of flat art into a believable, realistic drawing. It will turn mere pencil lines, that are desperately trying to represent hair, into long, silky tresses. Or give such substance and body to tight curls that you want to run your fingers through them.

Light and shadow are complementary opposites - neither can exist without the other. They're also perfectly natural - so natural that they can go unnoticed, so you need to train your eyes to look deeper than the object itself to extract the light and shade that give it form and definition.

As artists we use tonal values to translate the light and shadows we see into shading and highlights and, in doing so, we create the illusion of a third dimension. Our brains can experience the forms and textures we depict as if they existed in the real world - if we feed them clues that conform to the expected rules of Nature.

Yes, rules. Sorry, there's no getting round this one - although with experience you can lie effectively, sometimes quite blatantly. Fortunately, in essence, there exist just seven 'rules' or components of light. Take a look around you and study the first three-dimensional object you see. Now try to work out the basics of why you see it as a solid object, why it appears to be grounded and not floating, and why its texture is apparent. Look particularly for the different values created by light, reflections and shadows for it is these that hold the answers.

The seven components

LIGHT SOURCE

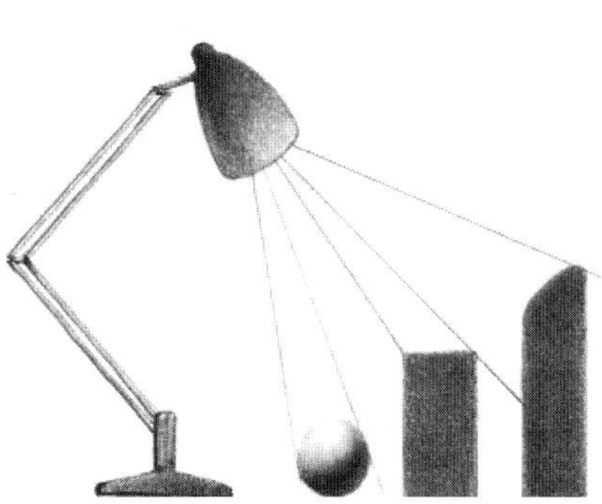

There has to be at least one light source, otherwise our subject will be in complete darkness. The direction from which the light is shining is of paramount importance to a successful drawing - identify it or decide on your own before you begin. Nothing will more disastrously destroy the sense of reality in your drawing than different elements receiving light from different directions. The same source of light applied to all elements in a drawing is the ultimate unifying factor, and a single light source is almost always the best strategy. It's often called 'Rembrandt lighting' for good reason - all the great masters habitually used a single source of light and to great effect. Use light logically and you can include a variety of objects in your composition from a variety of sources and give the impression that they naturally belong together.

Highlight

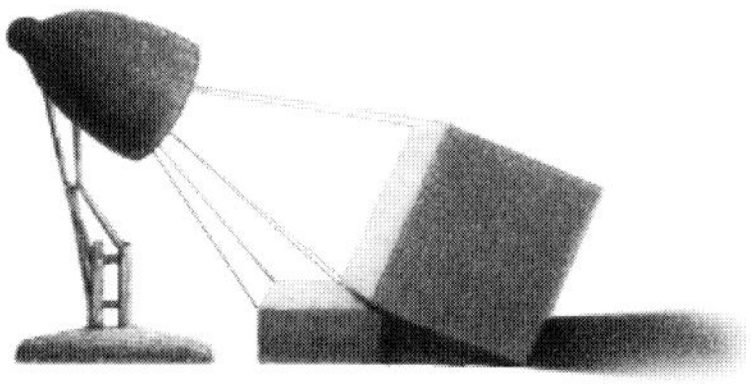

When light directly shines on any surface it will fully expose it to view. This is the highlight - the brightest surface or plane of a lit object. Fortunately, light travels in straight lines so it's relatively easy to work out which planes it will hit directly and which obliquely, or not at all. You can signal the intensity of the light by narrowing or widening the range of contrasts in your drawing. The brighter the light, the less surface texture will be apparent. Where oblique light creates shadows that display the irregularities in the surface, direct light provides little or none of this information and, as a result, flattens the perceived texture.

Shadows

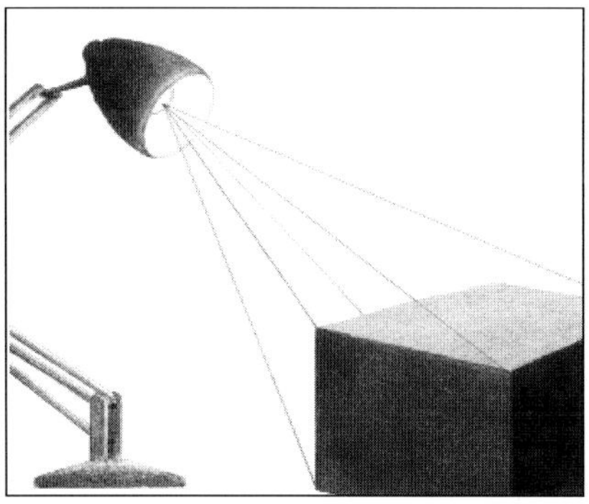

The light source creates shadows. Any areas not receiving full light will exhibit a degree of darkening or shadow and those receiving little or no light will possess strong shadow tones. You can use the difference in strength of tone between the highlights and shadows to relay the strength of the light in your drawing, and the quality of the shadows to signal the quality of the light. For example, the light will appear to be strong and harsh if the shadows possess hard edges and you create a large contrast between your highlights and darkest tones. Narrowing the tonal range and softening or blurring the edges of the shadows will signal a more diffuse or ambient light, such as occurs on an overcast day.

Cast and Contact shadows

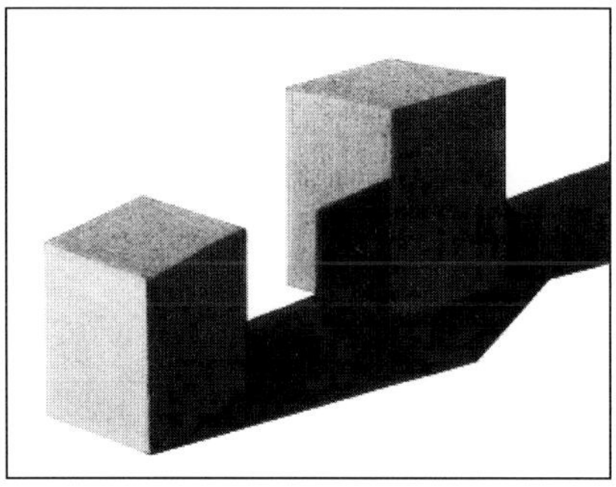

A cast shadow will appear on an adjacent surface wherever a solid object blocks the light from the light source. The positioning of the shadow will tell the viewer where the light is coming from, and its length will signal the angle of the light - left and low in the example shown here. In normal lighting conditions, cast shadows are darker than the darkest side of the object that cast them, and they always follow the contours of the surface on which they are cast. The darkest part of a cast shadow appears along the point of contact between the object and the surface it is standing on and is sometimes termed a contact shadow. Often it appears as just a thin dark line. Its omission will not be noticed but its inclusion can firmly fix an object in place.

Core shadows

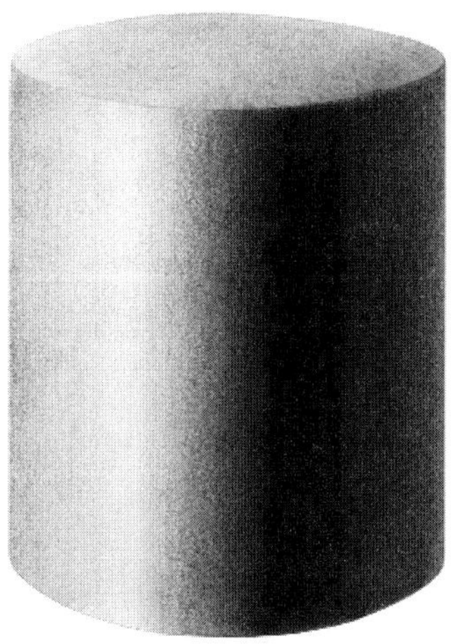

All rounded forms such as spheres, cones and cylinders possess core shadows. Unlike flat-sided forms, which have sharp edges to define different areas of tone and strengths of lighting, curved forms exhibit a single point that separates the light side from the dark side. The light side is lit directly by the light source, the dark side is partially lit by reflected light, and the boundary, the core shadow, receives virtually no light at all. Because it isn't lit in any way, the core has the darkest tone of any shadow on the object.

When drawing curved surfaces you should proceed with a confident approach and be prepared to use the widest range of tones that the situation will permit. The key word here is contrast. Be bold. Where possible establish the core shadow first. Now you have your lightest tone (your paper) and your darkest tones established. The rest should fall into place as you work. However, be careful with your choice of tones. No tone used in the light side should be repeated or equalled in the dark side. Conversely, all tones used in the dark side must be darker than the darkest tone used in the light side. And all of the tones in either side should be lighter than the core shadow. I suggest you read that again - it will eventually make sense!

Key highlight

A key highlight is created where a curved surface reflects the light directly into the viewer's eyes. The intensity of this highlight depends on the reflective properties of the surface - polished metal, for instance, will reflect almost all of the light, creating very bright key highlights. Secondary highlights can appear too, as on the top of this pencil and within the lettering, and are the result of reflected light - they will never be as bright as the key highlight, which receives and reflects direct light from the source.

Intense key highlights appear to suppress all surface texture because our eyes contract to minimise the glare. Less intense light or light falling on textured surfaces such as smooth fabrics, where it will be partially absorbed, allow a degree of discernable texture to remain. You can use key highlights to great effect by placing them near or adjacent to your darkest shadows - the greater the contrast between the two, the more they will strengthen each other.

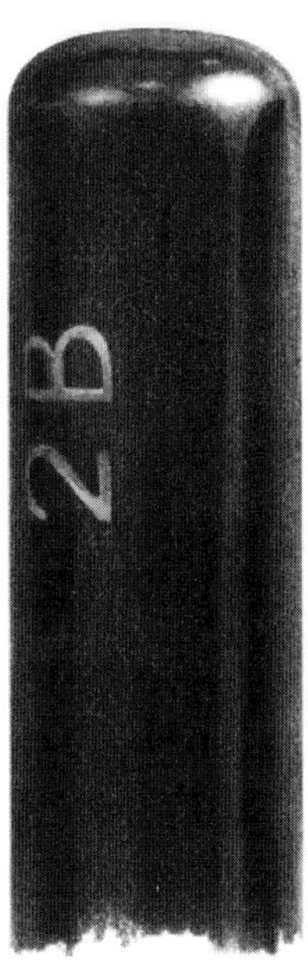

The rounded top of this pencil reflects a key highlight.

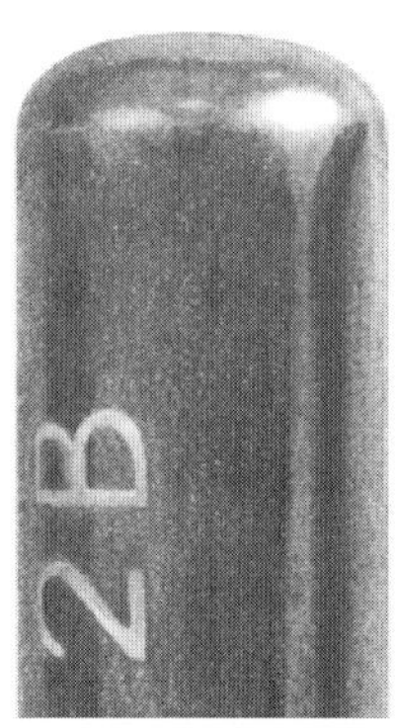

Using a restricted tonal range lowers the contrast and the impact of the key highlight.

Reflected light

The seventh component, reflected light is really a secondary property of light but for the artist it shares equal importance. This is light that bounces off one object or surface onto another, partially lighting it. Reflected light is a wonderful gift to the artist because it can be employed, even in the wrong situation, to lighten a crucial edge or surface that would otherwise be indistinguishable from its surroundings. The ever-accommodating brain will always assume that a reflective surface outside of the picture plane is responsible.

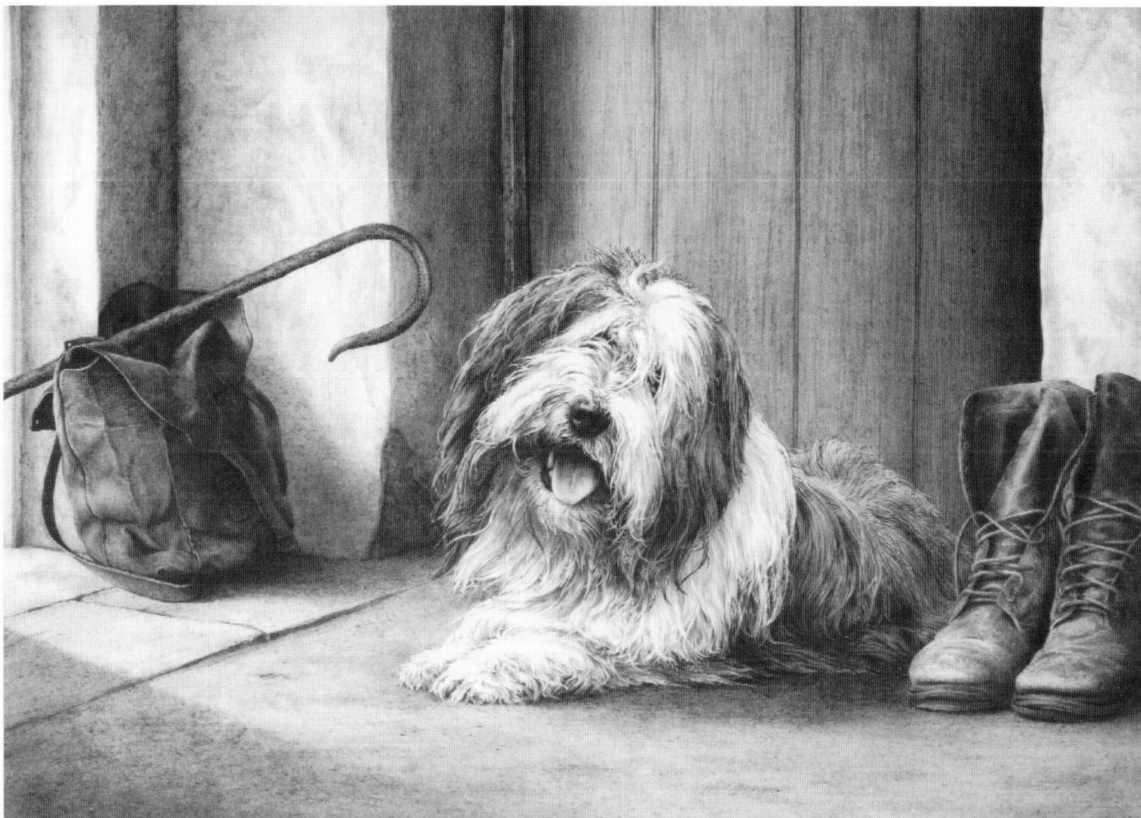

Ready and Waiting

In 'Ready and Waiting' I have three main elements receiving light coming through the open doorway to the left and all three cast a shadow to the right. The bag is correctly lit but the boots are partially lit by reflected light, the source of which is unclear. I used this as a device to allow me to considerably lighten the shadow side of the Bearded Collie. Collectors of my work buy prints of dogs, not of old boots or canvas bags - they expect to see detail in the dog and not have it in deep shade. The scene has been engineered, using reflected light to relay a sense of reality. Whenever you meet a similar problem - unnaturally pulling detail out of shade or perhaps needing to show a division between two edges in shadow that should not really be apparent - you can confidently make whatever changes you wish. The brain will always search for understanding in what it sees and will readily accept reflected light as a suitable solution. Ultimately, if it looks right, it is right.

We now know that light creates highlights, shadows where it cannot penetrate, core shadows on round objects, and that surface reflections illuminate adjacent surfaces. So, let's put it all together.

'THE FUNDAMENTAL KEY TO SUCCESSFULLY DRAWING IN THE THIRD DIMENSION IS HAVING THE ABILITY TO SEE AND EXTRACT THE TONAL INFORMATION.'

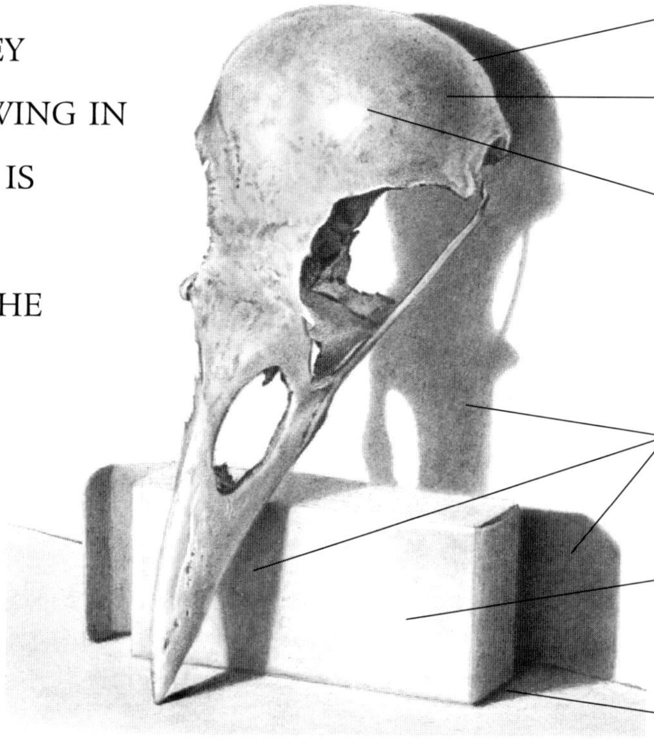

Putting light to work

The fundamental key to successfully drawing in the third dimension is having the ability to see and extract the tonal information. Now we've identified the components and can recognise them, let's see how they work together and how we can make them work for us.

We know we need to identify a light source, how that light casts shadows, and that it spreads itself by reflection, so we can begin to put our knowledge to practical use. This basic line drawing (*fig 1*) gives us a blank canvas on which to work - although I have first completed the darkest shadows, as I often do.

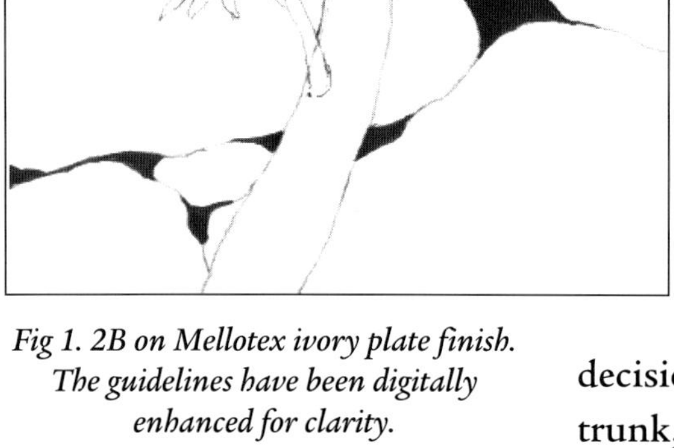

Fig 1. 2B on Mellotex ivory plate finish. The guidelines have been digitally enhanced for clarity.

Remember, it's our world so we can push some parts back, pull others forward and decide how far any part of the tree trunk is away from the rocks. Some decisions can be made at a later stage - the cast shadow of the trunk, for example. No part of the tree's shadow can be lighter than the shaded portions of the rocks so we can safely leave it. But what must be decided is the direction from which our light is shining. In this case I think the best results will come from a light shining towards the tree from below the top right corner. It may help you to draw an arrow in the margin that you can refer to at all times. From now on, every time my pencil touches the paper I will calculate whether that point can see the light or is in full or partial shade.

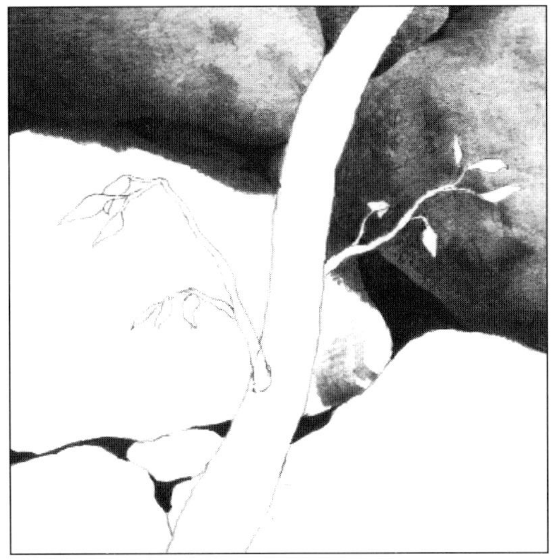

Fig 2. Drawn with 2B and HB using random circles to produce a granular structure. 'Happy accidents' have been enhanced to suggest the surface features.

Note the reflected light at the base of the right hand rock, used as a device to separate it from the deep shadow.

I'm unsure of the tonal values of the trunk until I have something to compare them to, so let's begin by working out the form and prominence of each of the rocks (*fig 2*). We use integral shadows to describe the roundness and surface features of each one, and we show which rocks are nearer to us by using the shadows they cast on those below.

Next we'll complete the rocks and then begin work on the tree (*fig 3*). Working this way, background first, means we have full control over all aspects of the edges of the tree. We can engineer

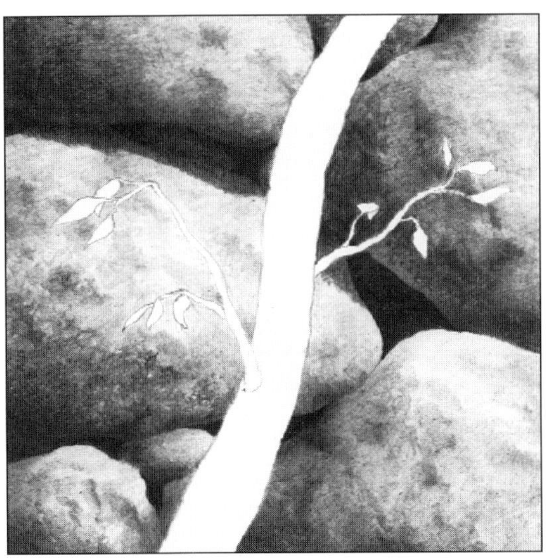

Fig 3. Completed with HB and a small amount of 2B. The HB had a chisel point with a wide, flat face for applying light tones evenly in the lighter areas, which were then lightly blended.

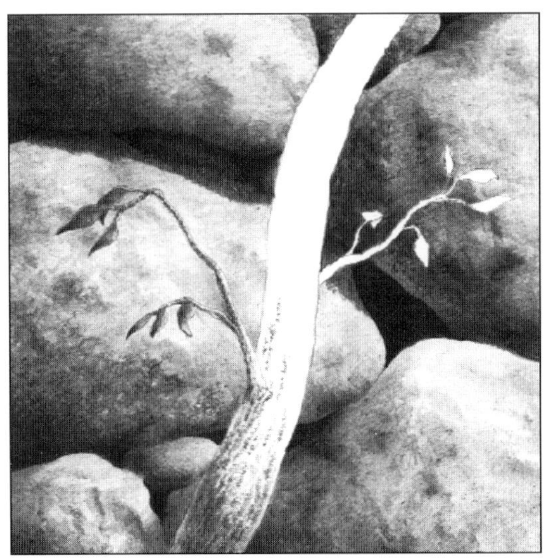

Fig 4. Drawing solely with an HB sharp-edged chisel point.Experiments at the base of the tree are now producing suitable textures. The texture is extended upwards then shaped with a top layer of appropriate shading.

the tones to separate it from the background wherever we wish. I am not advocating the prior drawing of the background in all situations. More accurately I suggest you draw the known areas first. In this case neither background nor foreground is a known element, as they exist only in my mind. However, the shading of the tree will be more complex than that of the rocks, so it's more manageable if I draw the simpler element first.

Now work begins on the tree (*fig 4*) - starting with the branch to the left, as this will not cast a shadow and the face of the leaves point away from the light source. I can be fairly certain that I can draw this section without affecting the later drawing of the tree itself. The base of the branch will, I hope, evolve naturally into drawing the texture and form of the tree.

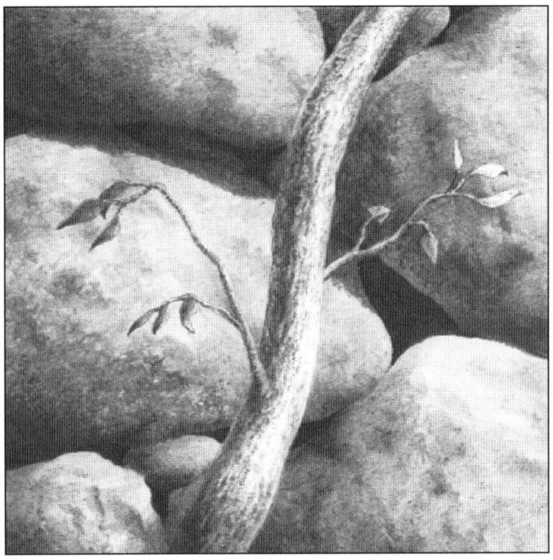

Fig 5. Drawn with an HB sharp-edged chisel point - plus a little 2B and H. The highlighted area was drawn slightly darker then faded as required with Blu-Tack.

The tree is completed (*fig 5*) - although some additional work on tonal values may be carried out later if required. Note how the core shadow and highlight serve to give a sense of solid form to the trunk, and how the three-dimensional shaping of the rocks is supplied by their surface shadows. But note also that the spatial relationship between the tree and rock face remains unknown, which gives an unreal appearance. There is no indication of depth. Just how far in front of the rocks is the tree? We have two elements with no concrete connection and both vie with each other for dominance.

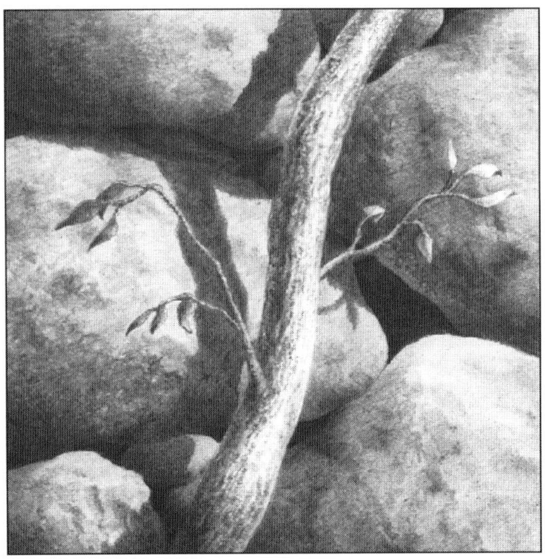

Fig 6. Cast shadow drawn with 2B. The previous HB layer has been partly removed along the track of the shadow with Blu-Tack to restore the tooth for greater adhesion.

Finally the cast shadow is drawn (*fig 6*). This shadow must equal all other cast shadows in intensity, as they are receiving the same light from the same source. Where one cast shadow meets or crosses another, their tonal values will match.

The tree's cast shadow serves three functions. It provides the eye with information about the tree's distance from the rocks at any point. It aids understanding of the three-dimensional shape of the tree. And, because the shadow must follow the contours of the surface on which it is cast, and is modified by the surface's irregularities, it tells us more about the shape and surface texture of the rocks. But above all, it unifies the elements of the drawing and pushes the tree into a more prominent position.

Types of light

Hard light

In the previous example I depicted the result of strong sunlight. The eye is informed of this by the quality of the shadows - their intensity and hard edges. The next time you're outside on a sunny summer day, study the shadows cast by you and everything else around you - all cast sharp-edged shadows by virtue of the hard light.

Soft light

Where strong light produces hard-edged shadows, soft light creates more diffuse shadows that blend into the midtones. Cast shadows, on a cloudy day, have much softer and indistinct edges because the sunlight is diffused by the clouds through which it passes. It's the equivalent of having a very large floodlight instead of the point source of a spotlight. As the light becomes ever more diffuse, so the shadows weaken in direct proportion - until their edges may not be detectable at all.

Distance of the source

The complexities of light, reflection and shade are so complex that computer Ray Tracing systems, especially in animation, require enormous amounts of processor power to operate. With this in mind I'll keep to just two simple aspects here. Think of them as a warning to always think about the effects of lighting before committing them to paper.

The distance of the light source from the object on which it shines has a profound effect on the cast shadow. The sun is so far away from us you can safely assume that all light coming from it possesses parallel rays. Because of this the width of an object's cast shadow will equal the width of the object.

However, beware if you are using a more local source. Shine a desk lamp onto an object, such as a vertical pencil, from a couple of feet (half a metre) away and study the effect it has on the cast shadow (*fig 7*). The light travels in straight lines but the rays are no longer parallel, instead the cast shadow widens with distance from the object. However, as the shadow widens it is rapidly weakened by reflected light - quite unlike shadows cast by the sun. This is especially noticeable with the use of the desk lamp with its wide reflector. The small, dense cast shadow exists only where no light falls at all. This effect is equally true of any similar light source such as the glow from a wide fire grate.

The solitary cast shadow used in our tree and rock example told the viewer that it was created by a single light source. Twin light sources, for example, create two distinct cast shadows, each opposing the direction of its source (*fig 8*). Both sources will light and substantially dilute the shadow cast by the other. An intense cast shadow is created only in the area receiving no light from either source.

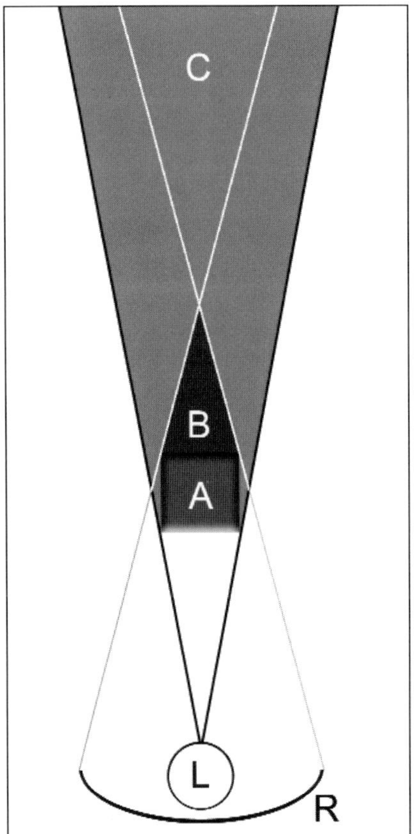

Fig 7
R - desk lamp reflector
L - desk lamp bulb
A - object
B - dense cast shadow
C - diluted cast shadow

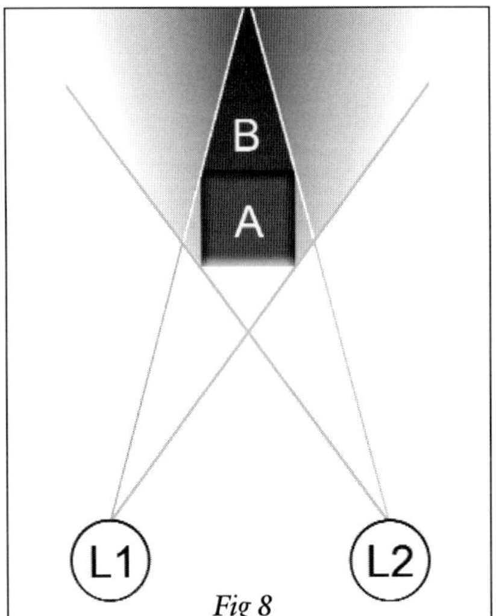

Fig 8

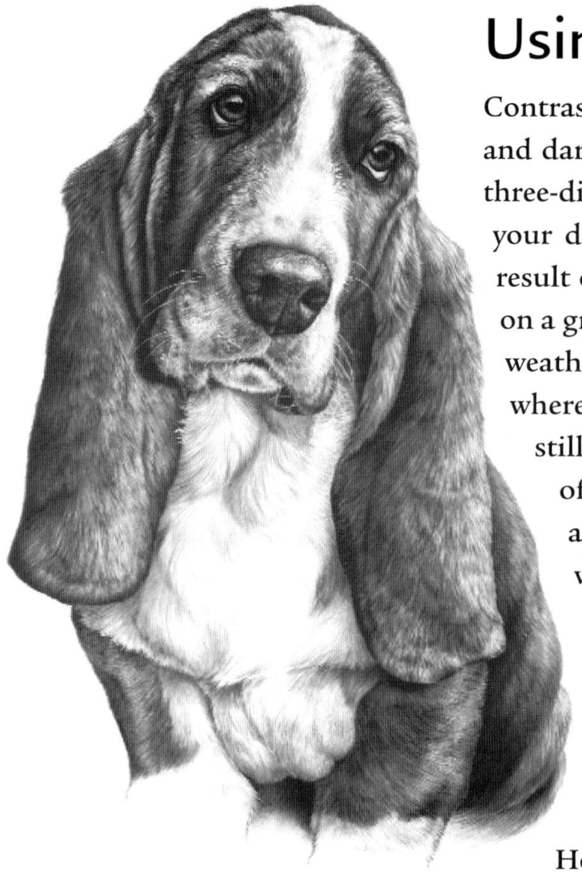

Using contrast

Contrast - the degree of tonal difference between your lightest and darkest tones - can be used to make your drawings more three-dimensional by accentuating the light and shadows. If your drawing appears flat and rather lifeless it is usually a result of using too little contrast. Look at a subject outdoors on a grey, cloudy day then directly compare it in bright sunny weather. The first is visually flattened by the lack of contrast whereas the latter is starkly evident and interesting. Worse still, depicting the cloudy appearance can invoke a feeling of melancholy in the viewer. Unless you are specifically attempting to convey a gloomy mood, always use the widest possible range of tonal values.

Employing this wide range of tonal contrasts is very effective if you decide to draw in an extreme way - to concentrate on shadows and highlights rather than midtones. Such a high contrast strategy can produce a really powerful and dynamic drawing.

However, you can use exactly the same range in a lower contrast drawing too by working mainly with midtones, and saving your white highlights and darkest areas for selected key elements. Placing the two in close proximity will serve to further boost the contrast, as shown in this Basset Hound drawing, where the whites of the eyes and their highlights gain in intensity by being adjacent to the dark irises and pupils.

In conclusion

You'll find with experience that shadows don't need to be perfectly correct at all times - sending sufficient signals to the brain will suffice. In real life, shadows are incredibly complicated structures. The art is in isolating and drawing just those elements that tell the story. If you want perfection, take a photograph. If you want to involve the viewer then make him or her have to work a little - to 'fill in the gaps'. Take away some of the elements of information, exaggerate others, and you force the viewer to pause while the message is decoded. This, surely, is exactly what we artists want - to capture attention.

The brain is very conservative, middle of the road. It drifts along noting this, categorising that - slotting its experiences into the right pigeonholes. Our job is to stop it in its tracks and cause it to re-evaluate so we can slip in and tell our story to the mind that it contains.

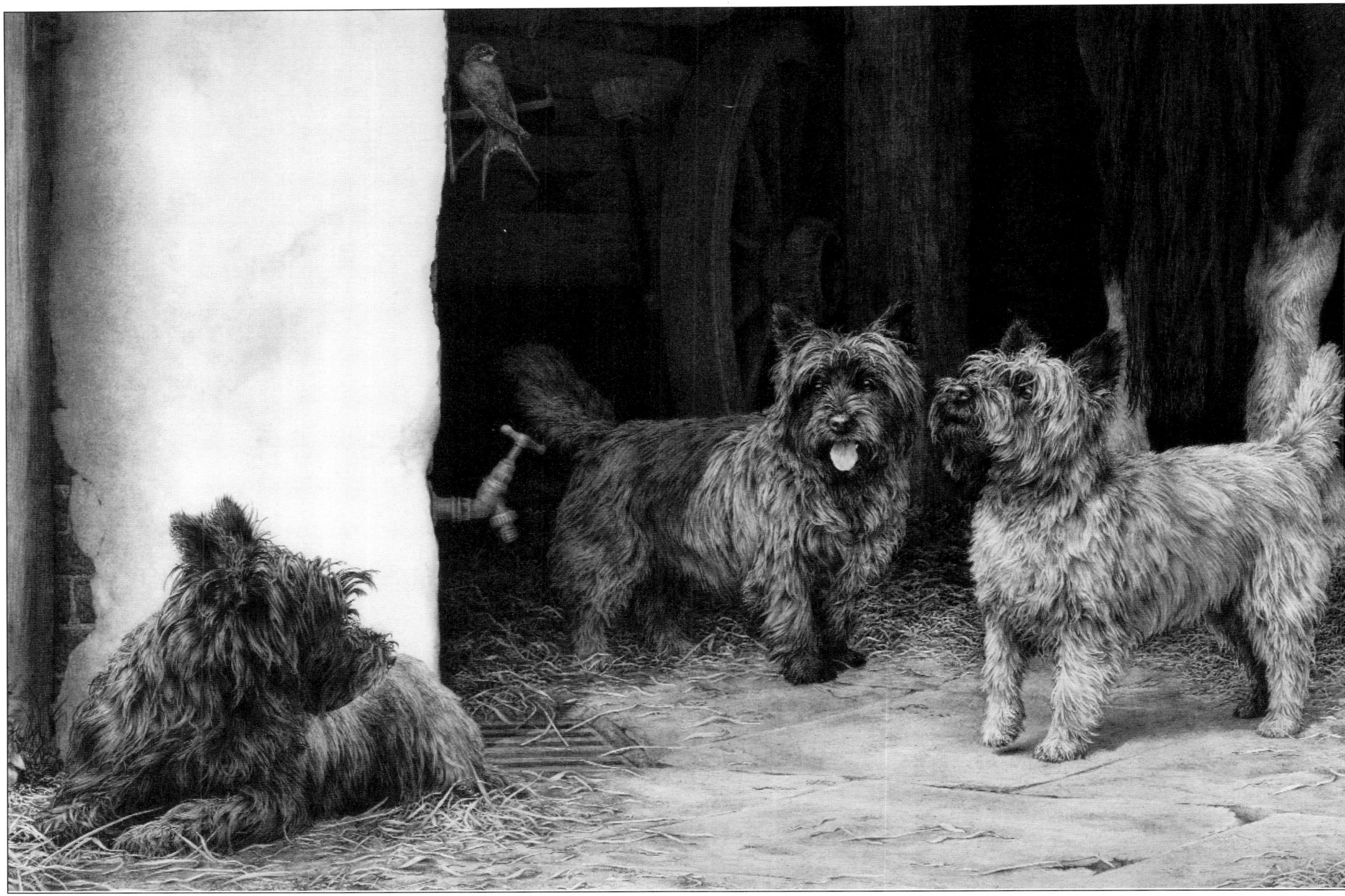

'The Barn Patrol' © *Mike Sibley. A limited edition print of 730 plus 20 Artists Proofs.*

17" x 11½" (43 x 29 cm)

Fooling the brain...
Part 2 - The viewer's brain

'Drawing is deception.'

Maurits Cornelius Escher.

The main purpose of art is to convey a message; to relay your own thoughts, feelings and emotions about the subject to your audience. Without your personal input, the message fails and the result is simply a reproduction of your subject - a lifeless copy. Drawing is a language that you use to tell your message and, like any language, there's no point at all in learning it just to say something meaningless. Every drawing you produce, no matter how minor, should contain a meaning and something of your soul in it. Whether you're working from life or reference photographs, something attracted you to that image.

If the attraction was a personal challenge of your abilities then that's perfectly acceptable, but don't expect the result to appeal to anyone else - you may feel a great sense of satisfaction and achievement but only you know that you exceeded your limitations. Others will not judge it by its application of techniques or its faithfulness to the original subject but only by its content, the way that it personally appeals to them - its message.

The key to everything

The drawings I'm discussing here are intended for general viewing and use drawing not for its own sake but as a means of conveying a love of the subject. It may be the infinite solitude and immensity of an unfolding valley at your feet or the sheer power generated by a working bulldozer. Whatever it is, you need to find the essential key that first attracted you and then to build it into your drawing. Probably you will want to modify the key, perhaps to exaggerate it, but the key as read by you will be readable too by the viewers of your work.

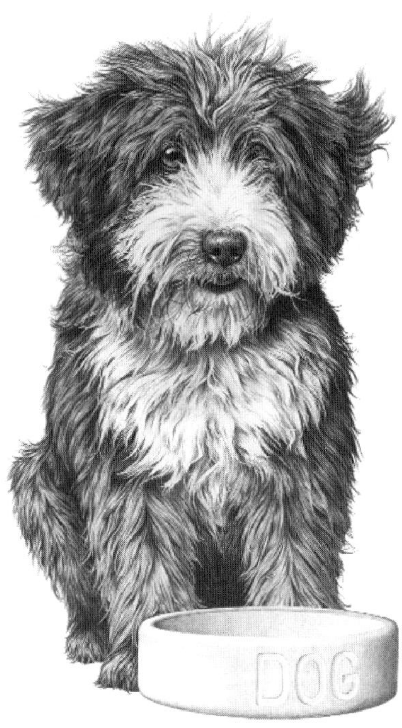

Build in your own feelings, show the viewer what attracts you to this little pup and you create a living character.

If you were attracted to the tilt of a puppy's head and its soulful expression then you concentrate on showing the angles, the drooping bottom eyelids, the sloping brows and pouting mouth. Leave out your personal interpretation of these keys and all that's left is an introspective, static animal without any connection to the world outside of itself. There is no meaning to the drawing.

If you have the vision to see and revel in the life around you and have a passion to relay what you feel to others, all you need is the technique - the physical ways of showing to others the things that you love. Extract the properties that excited you about a subject. When you can get it down to specifics you're on the home straight and heading for the tape - 'feelings' are difficult to convey but 'specifics' you can draw or incorporate.

We looked earlier at ways of fooling our own brains into allowing us to analyse what we see. Now we can begin to put that into practice. Study your subject - photographs are perfect 'frozen moments in time' for doing this as you can look at their content in depth - and search for the visual clues that tell you a texture feels that particular way or that flat expanse is water. The way velvet falls smoothly with no surface reflections, as if it soaks up light. The dull, pitted surface of an old tool that tells us it is rusty and steel. The clues before you, or captured in those photographs, are the ones that you need to incorporate into your work to relay your message. In time you can start to bend the rules but for now just keep to the raw basics and draw.

Putting the keys to use

Our aim is make the brain of the recipient, the viewer of the completed work, think it can detect a great depth of detail that it reads as 'realistic'. The deliberate inclusion of key elements - what I call 'food for the brain' - supplies the clues that tell the mind 'this is reality' when, in fact, the reality is only on the surface.

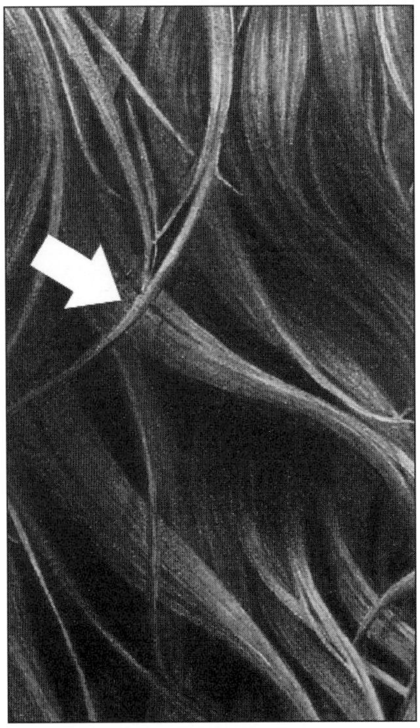

The arrowed 'status' hair in this drawing of part of a Springer Spaniel's ear signals:

3D : Yes
Element : Hair
Texture : Smooth
Type : Long, apt to bunch
Category :Realistic

The brain is an accommodating animal. If you send it the right signals (or even, with experience, the wrong ones) it will just assume that what it's seeing is correct and make excuses or find reasons to justify its decision. It seeks only confirmation of its deductions, not the truth. And it can never be wrong - if it cannot find understanding in full for what it is seeing it will label it as 'unnatural' and shift it a few rungs down the ladder until the classification 'Drawing' satisfies all criteria. The artist's job is to fool it into being satisfied with a higher rung.

Status Elements

You'll find me mentioning 'status' stalks, hairs and other features throughout this book. These are the 'brain food' elements - the ones that contain essential keys. If you give the status elements sufficient prominence the viewer's brain will see them before analysing what lies behind them. A single out-of-place hair crossing those behind it, for example, signals 'hair', 'coat-type' and 'three dimensionality'. The fact that the drawing behind may contain only a resemblance to hair

'YOU READ IT HERE.
IT'S OFFICIAL.
YOU CAN LIE!'

doesn't matter. The brain will have been satisfied and will read the entire section as we intended - hair!

There is a lesson to be learned from this - not everything in life is immediately understandable. Indeed, actual reality often demands that some elements are hazy, indistinct, blurred or otherwise beyond full comprehension. Handling omitted detail is something the brain can accommodate but adding too much detail is the road to failure. The brain, for example, uses the detectable detail of an element to judge its distance. Too much sharp detail in a midground feature will only serve to confuse; it isn't logical so your work drops down those rungs.

If you capture enough of the detail, where detail is expected, the human brain will make itself fill in the rest for you. Conversely, if you don't get the detailed parts of your picture right the brain will never be able to compensate for it.

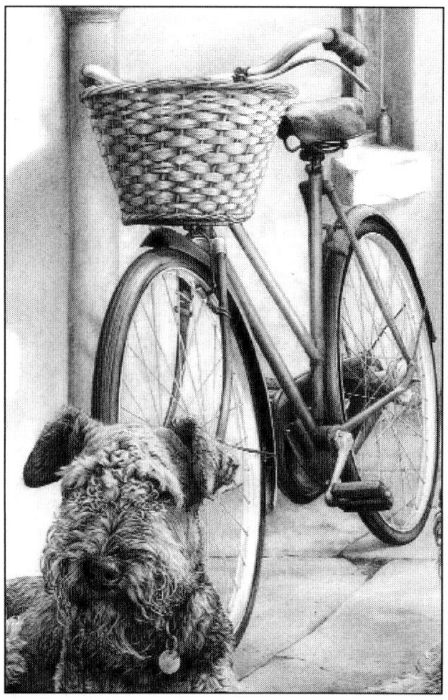

The shadow cast by the bicycle tells us it is close to wall and leaning on the pipe. The shadow cast by the back wheel fixes its position on the paving slabs.

In fact the majority of the shadow is missing. It would have been too visually distracting so I omitted it, safe in the knowledge that the viewer's brain would receive the intended signals and compensate for the omission.

I once looked closely at an original pencil drawing by an accomplished artist who had seized on the idea of a blade of grass being upright and then drooping over at the tip. He had devised a motif, which he had painstakingly applied to every blade. The result, for me, totally ruined all the wonderful work he'd put into the main feature. There was no recession, no weeds, no randomness and no reality. It was detail for the sake of detail.

I had purchased one of this artist's prints many years before and it was the quality of his trees that I set as my goal - I'd never attempted them before. I learnt a lot from his strong tones and confident approach but I quickly found that his control was far too great. I could see things in his foliage (both tree and ground cover) that would be impossible in a real situation. I still admire his print but it taught me the benefit of not letting my conscious mind overrule my gut feeling. Think 'reality' not 'drawing'.

BENDING THE RULES

You read it here. It's official. You can lie! Your drawing is your creation; it's your world and you can do with it whatever you wish. You don't need to put shadows where shadows should be or to highlight parts that you'd rather leave in shadow. Just do whatever you want to do and the viewer's brain will find its own solution as to why this should be. As long as you draw it confidently, inject a reality and send the right signals it will be believable. This is true even if the signals you send are not entirely correct for that situation. Provided that a comparison between any two elements makes logical sense, the brain accepts the result as having a believable reality, as you will see in the following example.

If you work with photographs you are probably aware of such anomalies as barrel distortion, flat shadows, false perspective, and the foreshortening caused by zoom lenses. I use a 200mm or 400mm zoom lens almost all of the time and I'm well aware of these problems. But I find they can be used to advantage. Foreshortening, for instance, can be a real blessing when it comes to composition - as long as you take pains to add logic to the composition. Admittedly, it's a false logic but if it satisfies the brain then it succeeds. A recurring problem for me involves placing dogs within a scene in such a way that they remain dominant, despite their relatively small size compared to the setting. I need to display the dogs prominently yet not make the setting itself appear too distant.

Here I wanted to include two Dalmatians, two carts, and enough of the old farm buildings to reflect the antiquity of the use of the dogs as 'carriage dogs'. They were bred to guard vacant carriages and to run beneath the axles when in motion. In America they are known as 'Fire dogs' for their similar use with horse-drawn fire engines. I also wanted my horizon to be that of the dogs - to bring the viewer down to their level. I switched lenses while filming the setting (part of my neighbour's farm) so I had a choice of view.

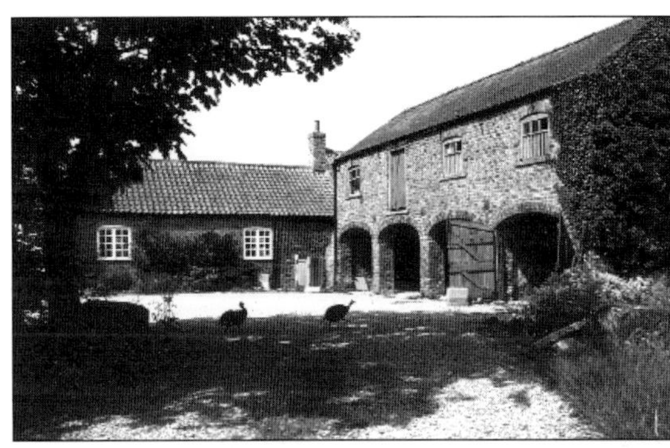

Taken with a 50mm lens - equivalent to normal vision.

You can no doubt appreciate the dire result had I chosen the 'normal vision' 50mm version of the setting. Instead I've used the photographically foreshortened setting, using the carts to suggest scale and the tree overlapping the chimney and roof to suggest recession. The foreground foliage is drawn sharply and with strength to further reinforce the 'false' depth of the piece. These elements provide the visual logic that fool the brain into accepting the scene as being believable.

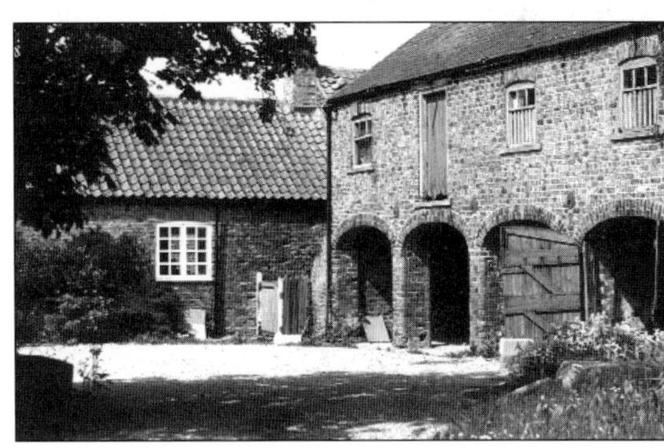

Taken with a 200mm lens showing foreshortening.

The offset base is another brain-fooling device. It's a rule-bending trick with a difference as it actually restores, albeit falsely, the adherence to another rule that I'd already broken. Without it the dog on the left would have had its eye-level half way up the drawing. This compositional trick restores the rule of thirds - the left-hand dog occupies the bottom third and the eye-level of the main dog is visually shifted downwards, the buildings appear to be taller, and recession is further enhanced. My signature and print edition number in the bottom margin restore balance to the prints.

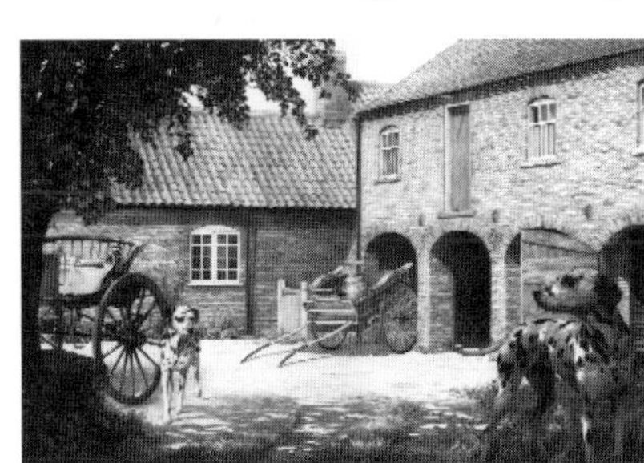

The 200mm setting as used in 'Sutton Farm Sunday'.

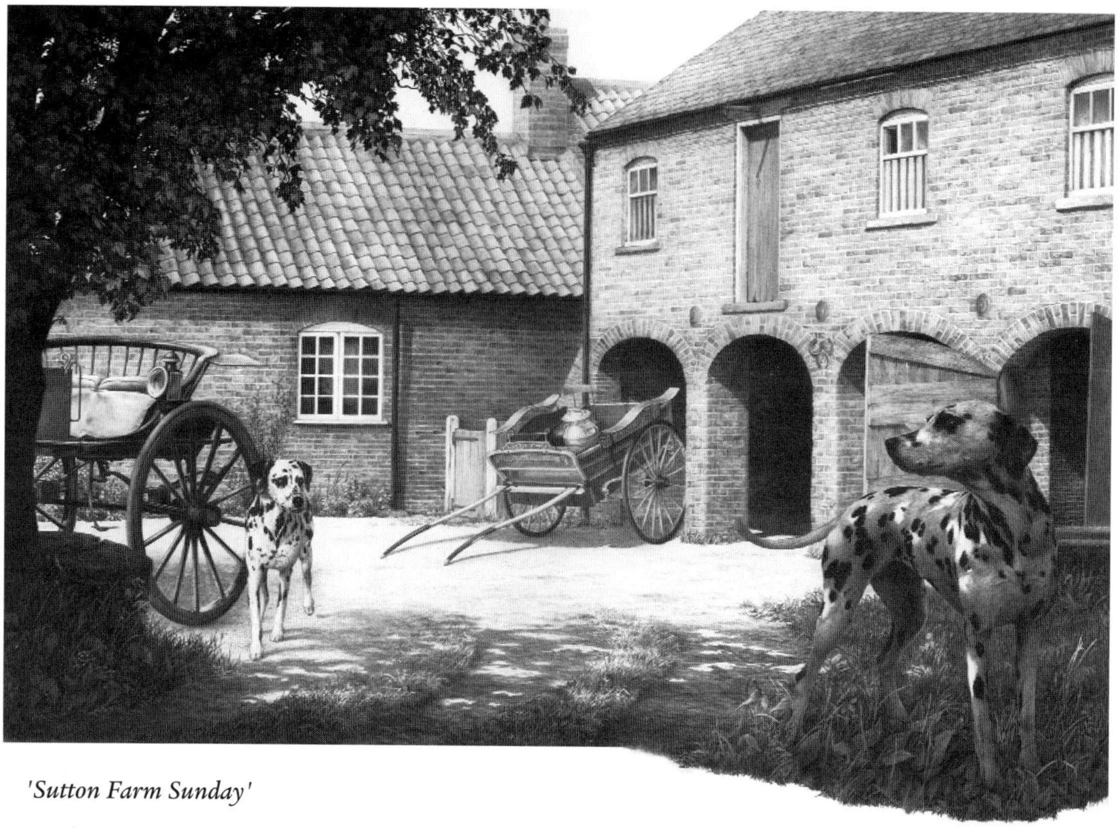

'Sutton Farm Sunday'

Presentation

Sooner or later you have to make choices concerning the display of your work. By applying a little psychology, you can fool the brain into seeing more than is apparent, and even emphasise the intended mood. Drawing involves the making of small marks with a pointed stylus and an over-ornate frame, for example, can destroy the intricacy and delicacy. Simplicity is often the best display option.

To a greater extent, matting can make or ruin a drawing. Professional framers often employ a useful strategy when matting paintings - they select a secondary colour from the body of the work and reflect that in the choice of mats - usually in the inner mat when double matting. Choosing to repeat the most dominant colour would only serve to set up competition between the mat and the work. This is an excellent plan. However, it has very unfortunate results when applied to a graphite drawing. Too often do I see drawings matted in blacks, greys or a mixture of the two. Graphite contains a clay element, which lends a warm brown colour cast to it. This is not present in black or grey matboard, which results in a disastrous coldness being imparted to the work.

A better practice, and my personal preference, is to double mat and match the inner mat to a perceived colour in the drawing.

For example, if the drawing is of a landscape, a dark green inner mat will reflect the 'greens' of the fields and trees. If it's a woodland scene, dark brown will suggest and complement the trunks of the trees. I've tried many combinations over the years, finally refining the choice to a combination of just one top mat and two inner mats. A single or top mat of ivory, or any warm off-white, will serve to increase the perceived whiteness of your drawing, boosting highlights and increasing contrasts, and leaving a 1cm margin around the print serves to accentuate this effect. Add to this a bottom or inner mat of warm dark green, dark brown or other image-connected colour, with just 4mm showing - 1mm constituting the bevel, leaving just 3mm of visible colour. This will not overpower the drawing and is sufficient to concentrate attention on the artwork and prevent the eye from straying outwards. The dark colour will emphasise the darker tones, further increasing perceived contrast, and the colour itself and its warmth will suggest colour to the brain where no colour actually exists. As a bonus this combination will also suit virtually any variety of frame.

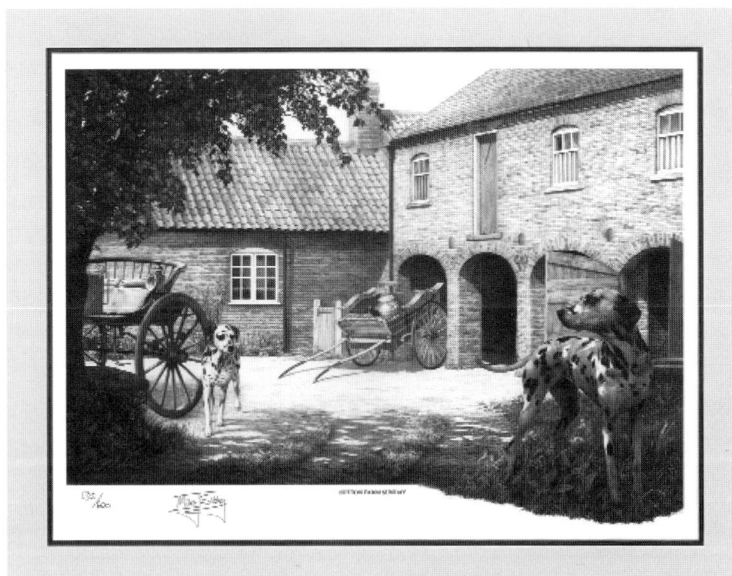

Double-matted with an Ivory top mat and Russian Green inner mat serving to increase contrast, focus the eye on the artwork and suggest a colour content.

The life-saver

So, the finished result doesn't agree with your original mental picture. Perhaps your hand slipped and the eye's highlight is not the shape you intended? Maybe you had to invent a bush in an attempt to cover that fingerprint? Possibly you set too narrow a tonal range, resulting in a weakened drawing. Whatever the reason, you are not alone - it happens to us all from time to time. Personally, I'm never satisfied with my work on completion - there's always some part I could have drawn better but to alter it would be to overwork it.

Fortunately - except for your personal grief and annoyance - nothing is lost. No need even to resort to brain-fooling stratagems to confuse the viewers of your work. Remember - the brain likes to makes sense of everything it sees. Your brain knows that what it sees is not what you intended. But everyone else's brain will seek to make perfect sense of it and not see anything wrong.

Transfer methods

The art of manipulation...

'If you can draw well, tracing won't hurt; and if you can't draw well, tracing won't help.'

Bradley Schmehl

Copying is an essential process in the creation of art. But copying needn't, and shouldn't, centre just on reproducing a specific outline or form - it involves too the transference of ideas, treatments, emotions and aims. When working from a photograph there is often a need to enlarge the image, or a selected portion of it, to a workable size. That direct copy of outline and key features may suffice in the early days of an artist's development - it's a perfectly suitable vehicle for experimentation and the refining of techniques. However, a time will arrive when you realise that there are other requirements present - the desire to show your own feelings towards the subject, to display its emotions, enhance its character, even alter its physical appearance, and perhaps to amalgamate various aspects of a number of photographs or other sources into a single study. All of these require methods of physically resizing and manipulating the available source material. The methods are many and varied - freehand, gridding, projection, to name a few - and, as with all other aspects of your art, you need to be aware of them all and employ those that best suit you.

Drawing freehand is a creditable and often lauded method. Other methods are often decried as cheating or artificial - but not by me. By using the tools available to me I can quickly produce an accurate framework in which to draw. If I draw the same outline by eye alone with the same accuracy I will have exactly the same result, gained little and lost valuable time. As a professional artist - time matters. It's only 'cheating' if it turns you into a human photocopier - it cheats you, the artist, of your creativity. In practice, the better you can draw without these tools, the better you can draw with them. In any case the ultimate goal is to reproduce the animal, person or object, not just its geometric shape and every artist needs to find their own route. The tools you use to get there are your own concern. Use what works best for you. If you disagree with the use of a particular tool, don't use it, but don't question the motives of those that do. There are no rules governing Art.

Artists through the ages have used all the tools at their disposal for producing good working drawings on which the final study is based. These tools produce guidelines and nothing else - basic line drawings that children can colour in or in which artists can work magic.

EARLY TOOLS

For centuries artists have employed tools such as drawing grids, tracing, the camera lucida and camera obscura, pantographs, mirrors and lenses, measuring guides and, more recently, photo references and projection. In the fifteenth and sixteenth centuries fresco artists, who paint directly onto wet plaster, first drew their designs on paper. Assistants then pricked through the outline, held the paper to the fresh plaster and pounced it with muslin bags of soot. This left on the wall a dotted black impression of the working drawing and that day's painting began in earnest.

Albrecht Dürer and his contemporaries revelled in their newfound 'drawing engines' as they explored perspective and foreshortening. Canaletto and Johannes Vermeer used an optical system known as the camera obscura. Jan Van Eyck almost certainly did too. Leon Battista Alberti used the Reticolato, a grid that could be placed in front of a scene to aid drawing in perspective. Artists such as the English portrait artist Joshua Reynolds employed a later development of the camera obscura - a closed box with an external translucent screen. In 2004 archaeologists discovered the first full-frontal portrait of an Egyptian pharaoh. Dating back 3500 years, it had been squared up in red chalk so a sculptor could transfer the image to stone. Artists and sculptors employ the same gridding method today as well as the use of projectors, the assistance of computers and many other modern technical aids.

Gridding

Although I no longer use the grid method it is, in my opinion, an absolute blessing to emerging artists. Why? Five reasons....

1. It divorces content from form. It rids the brain of that 'naming' habit and reduces elements to pure line - line that can be explored to gain its true course and not the pre-supposed course often imposed by the mind.

2. It removes all tone and lighting. It breaks a subject down into its constituent elements and allows you, the artist, to impose your own rules.

3. It provides accuracy of placement where accuracy is critical. At the same time it provides guidelines, not lines carved in

'I use grids for everything. Grids are great for finding out exactly how much space your drawing will take up. That way you know ahead of time exactly how the composition is going to fit on your paper.

Grids and tracing paper can help you determine the exact space between things but they won't teach someone how to draw... I wish it were that simple cause back when I had four or five people waiting for me to burn their portraits it would have been nice to just hand them some tracing paper and say 'Hey this is the secret thing I do. I've been cheating. Now you can do it yourself...' They would have just looked at me like I'm crazy.'

Jim Hicks, Pyrography artist

stone. It offers a framework that you can accept or modify at will in the full knowledge of the original form.

4. It allows you to explore, practice and learn different techniques without first having to learn to draw by eye. In my opinion this is easier once the eye has learnt to see line in its purity and the subject, which overall might appear daunting, can be disassembled element-by-element for individual attention.

5. When you copy a line passing through a square, ignoring the object it represents, you will be using and recognising Negative Space, which will increase your eye's ability to draw what you see.

THE BASIC METHOD

Gridding combines two operations; it can accurately transfer a drawing from one surface to another and, if you need to, it offers the opportunity to enlarge (or shrink) it at the same time. Its basis consists of two grids built of squares. If the squares of both grids are of equal size, the drawings will be the same size too. If the squares on your drawing paper are twice the size of those on your source image the result will be a copy twice the size of the original. And that, you'll be happy to learn, is the complicated mathematics of the system dealt with!

When sizing-up from a sketch you can lightly draw a grid of regular lines directly on to it. For photographs or anything else that you don't want to physically mark, you can use a suitable, fine pen to draw your grid on an acetate sheet. Alternatively, you can produce an accurate grid in any computer drawing program and print that directly onto acetate. The size of the squares is not critical although they must be square. The smaller you make them the more accurate your copy will be. I found that a grid of ½-inch (1cm) squares was adequate for a 6"×4" (15 x 10 cm) photograph. The acetate method is preferable as you have a permanent, ready-to-hand grid for all occasions. Let's call this the 'source' grid and the one you're going to copy your drawing into, the 'copy' grid. It will help if you identify the squares along both sides - for example, use numbers for each square up one vertical side and letters for the horizontal side. Do this to both source and copy grids to help you keep track of where you are.

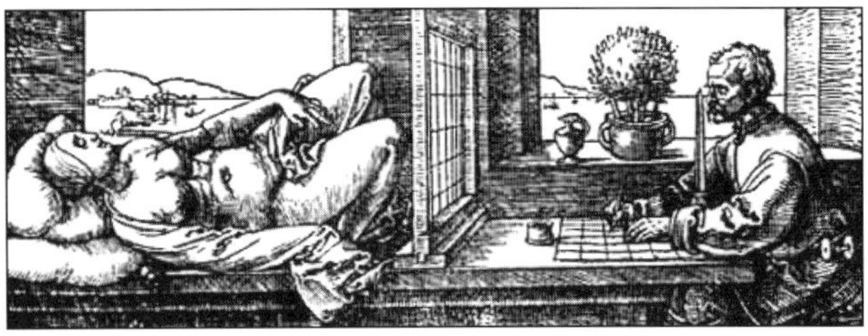

Using this foreshortening or perspective machine the artist, sighting from a fixed point, would look through a grid of strings and transfer what he saw onto his drawing surface, which carried a similar grid. If you replace the women in Dürer's drawing with a 2D sketch or photo you will see that the artist was using a precursor of the grid method.

It is, in my opinion, essential that you size-up in two stages. First translate your photograph into a larger (but manageable) line drawing then size up the line drawing to the final dimensions required. That first stage gives you the opportunity to make alterations. If drawing a dog, for example, this is the ideal time to incorporate changes of expression, open or shut the mouth or move the awkwardly lolling tongue. Often essential detail is missing in a photograph. Rather than guess what that dog's nose really looks like or just copy what you see in the photograph, now you can find other photographs, book illustrations or even a dog to help you rebuild that area. This first stage also removes all three-dimensional shading so you can dictate the lighting the way you want it to be. You might add a suggestion of the required lighting direction now - shorthand hatch marks that will carry your ideas forward to the final paper. By the time you've finished it will no longer be a copy of the photograph - it will be your creation and your understanding of your subject will have greatly increased. OK, let's get down to the 'how'...

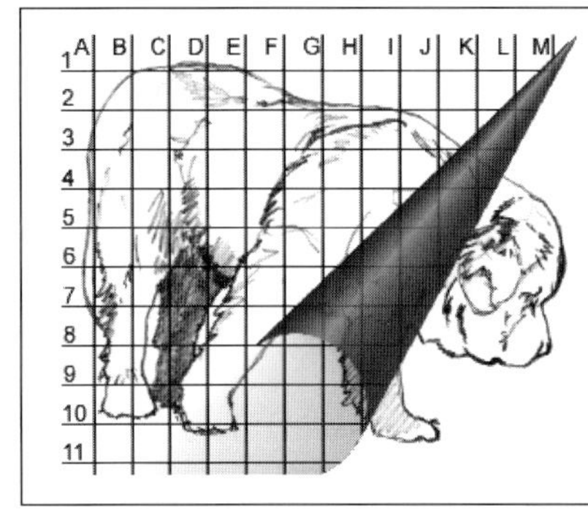

Lay your source grid over the sketch or photograph..

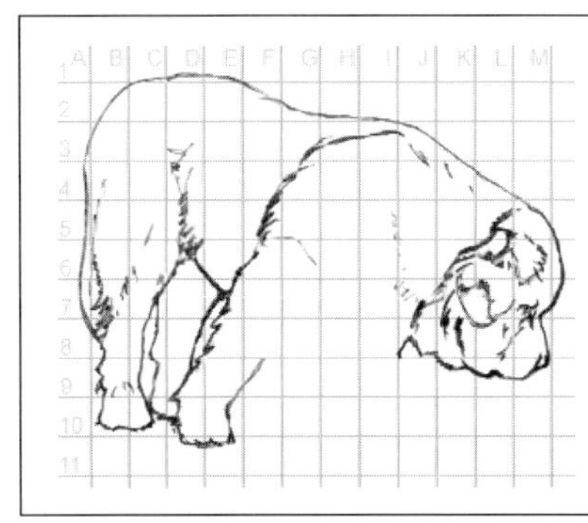

Lightly draw a similar grid on your paper then copy one square at a time.

Step 1: Lay your source grid over your sketch or photograph. If possible position it so the top left corners coincide but more important is that a major feature or potentially problematic area does not occupy a single square. If an eye, for example, fits entirely within one square, move the grid so that it's split between two or four squares. By cutting everything up with the grid you'll find you are just copying a line in a box and not the lower edge of that eye. Now count the numbers of squares across and down that cover your source sketch or photograph.

Step 2: For simplicity I'll describe the method that will enlarge your drawing by a known amount. If you want your copy to be double the size of the source image and the source grid has 1cm (½") squares, your copy will need a grid of 2cm (1") squares. Take your sheet of paper, and mark the top at 2cm intervals until you have the same number of divisions as your counted squares on your source grid, then repeat along the bottom edge. Perform the same exercise down both sides. Now lightly, so you can erase them later, connect the marks to produce your grid of squares. You will now automatically size-up your drawing or photo to the correct dimensions. This is your copy grid so number and letter the squares to match your source grid. As I mentioned earlier - if you are enlarging a photograph to a relatively large size, four times its size for example, you may find it simpler and more manageable to enlarge it in two stages - from 1cm to 2cm then again from 2 to 4 cm. Trying to enlarge a small photograph by too large a factor in one step is fraught with problems and probable inaccuracies.

'When drawing don't be a slave to your guidelines. At best they provide accurate positioning, at the worst they are simply wrong - you draw what looks right, not what the photographs or your guidelines say it should look like.'

Step 3: Now carefully copy the lines in each square of the source grid into the corresponding square on the copy grid. Do this one square at a time, concentrating on the line (or edge of a shape, if it's a photograph) without paying any attention to what the line represents. Tell yourself 'This line begins a quarter of the way down the left hand edge of this square and runs obliquely to a point almost at the bottom of the right hand side'. That line can be part of a coffee pot, an aircraft, a dog's tail, an arm - it doesn't matter, it's just a line that you are copying. This way you learn to draw and see what is really in front of you. Don't rush it - take your time.

Advanced Grid Method

This advanced variation of the method shown above has a few major advantages - no grid is drawn on the paper, guidelines are easily erased, and immediate and accurate referral to the guidelines is possible even after they've been removed.

Step 1: Calculate the size of the required squares you need for your copy grid but don't draw the grid on your drawing paper. Instead, take a sheet of white card, the same size as your drawing, and on it draw your copy grid in black ink. Save it - you can use it again.

Step 2: To the top of this card tape a sheet of drafting paper (of the type used by architects or use any tracing or strong semi-transparent paper) so it covers the grid.

Step 3: Place your previously created acetate source grid over your photograph or sketch then copy the image, square by square, onto the drafting paper, using the underlying copy grid as a guide. Be sure to keep your hand off the surface - rest it on a square of card - as moisture from your hand will quickly cause drafting paper to cockle and bend. You need to ensure that it remains flat. Alternatively, if you find cockling to be an ongoing problem, you can copy directly onto the card's copy grid then lay your drafting paper over it and quickly trace it off. Now you need to transfer the enlargement to your final drawing paper. This is the method I used for almost all of the 52 head-studies I drew for my open edition print collection.

Step 4: Fix the drawing paper to your drawing board in your usual manner then lay the drafting paper, containing your sized-up sketch, on top and carefully position it until you are satisfied.

Step 5: Tape the drafting paper in place along the top edge to the drawing paper so neither can move independently. Then take a second piece of drafting paper (about 11" × 8" suited me) and thoroughly coat its rough side with 6B or softer graphite. Don't be mean - you're making a graphite carbon paper. Keep this carbon paper in a folder and you'll have it ready for use whenever you require it - just refresh the 6B from time to time - a useful way to use up your old, short stubs.

Step 6: Now slip the carbon paper under your drafting paper and (with your hand again resting on a piece of card) re-draw over every line using just enough pressure to transfer an impression. I used my indenting tool for this but a hard-grade pencil will do the job almost as well. You can safely remove the carbon paper at any time to check your progress because the drafting paper (if you've securely taped it in place) will always accurately return to the same position.

'It's very essential to know as much as you can about the bone and muscle structure of animals and humans. Ya gotta know what's under those "traced" lines.'
Rose Baggs, Artist

This method has many advantages. Your guidelines can be removed completely with Blu-Tack or a kneadable eraser. You can lay an area of flat tone over any area safe in the knowledge that no unintentionally indented guidelines will reappear to haunt you. As the drafting paper is hinged to the top of your drawing paper it can be dropped down at any time during the drawing process to check for accuracy, which is especially useful if the removal of an error has erased your original guidelines. And when you lose your way this is the map that will get you back on course.

When working with this method my practice was to erase the guidelines by rolling Blu-Tack over them, in the local area in which I was about to work, until I had only a shadow of them remaining. If I needed the guidelines back I could just drop down the drafting paper overlay at any time.

Having reduced my guideline of an eye, for example, to a mere shadow I redraw the eye exactly as I want it to look. I use a sharp 2B pencil, which will not indent the surface of my paper and is hard enough to give a clean-edged line but sufficiently soft to be completely removed.

When drawing *don't be a slave to your guidelines.* At best they provide accurate positioning, at the worst they are simply wrong - you draw what looks right, not what the photographs or your guidelines say it should look like.

The measurement method

This method is rarely taught yet it is as useful and instructive as Sight Sizing, which is explained in chapter three. However, where Sight Sizing works for drawing from life this method applies to static sources, such as photographs. It is based around the twin principles of measurement and drawing by

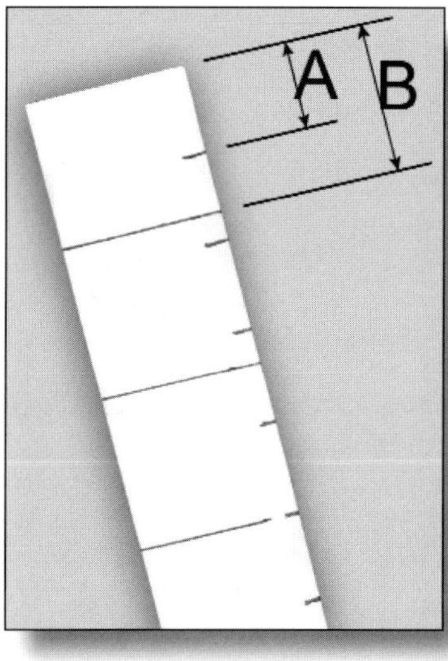

A: Source image ruler
B: Copy image ruler.
This ruler will enlarge the copy by 1¾ times.

eye, and is as accurate as a grid without sacrificing the artistic integrity of freehand drawing. I used this method extensively in the very early days of my artistic life and still use it at times to solve a problem of relative sizes or angles.

Let's take as an example the photograph of a dog's head and use the width of the dog's eye as a unit of measurement. Take a strip of paper - about 6" x 1" (15 x 2.5cm) will suffice - and lay it across the eye so it passes through both corners. Use a pencil to mark the edge of the paper at both ends of the eye. This is your '1 eye' measuring unit or 'eye-unit'. Accurately repeat the marks along the strip to form a ruler. On your drawing paper, estimate the position and final size of the eye and mark each corner with a dot. Alternatively use your eye-unit measure to set the enlargement by a known amount - two eye-unit measures wide will double the overall size. Lay the strip between the dots and mark off the distance between them and construct a second ruler. Now you should have two sets of marks on your strip - one for the photo's eye-width and one for your drawing's eye-width. The marks can form two separate rules, one down each edge, or both can be marked down a single edge. Rather than having to rotate the ruler in use, I preferred the latter and used a red pen and longer marks for the second set.

By this means you can measure the placement and size of any part or feature in the photo - the eyes might be three eye-units apart, the muzzle seven eye-units long - then transfer these measurements to your drawing paper. You can also measure and position two points relative to each other. For example, if you lay your strip exactly vertical from the centre of the eye you might measure the distance down to the top of the nose while noting that half of the nose is hidden beneath the strip. Now you can drop a similar vertical on your drawing and mark a point that you know identifies the top of the nose and its centre line too.

The strip of paper measures relationships in the same way as proportional dividers except that it also has a second and more important use. It can carry angles across from one to the other. First make certain that the photograph is square to your paper. Now you can lay your strip between two features or known points and then slide it across to your drawing, maintaining the same angle.

Triangulation

You can also triangulate as shown here (*fig 3*). Select two known points - they could be the centres of the eyes - that you know are correctly distanced on your copy. Now use these two points to accurately check (or find) the placement of any third point - the top of the nose maybe. Measure from the first point to the third then from your second point to the third. Now check the same measurements on your drawing. If both distances equal your measurements then all three points must be correctly positioned relative to each other. This is precisely how cartographers survey and draw maps where accuracy of position is essential. It helps too if you place a vertical from the most central point of the three to bisect the line between the other two. Measure either half. If your drawing's measurement doesn't agree then you have your triangle rotated. And now the good news - triangulation is much easier to use in practice than it appears to be here!

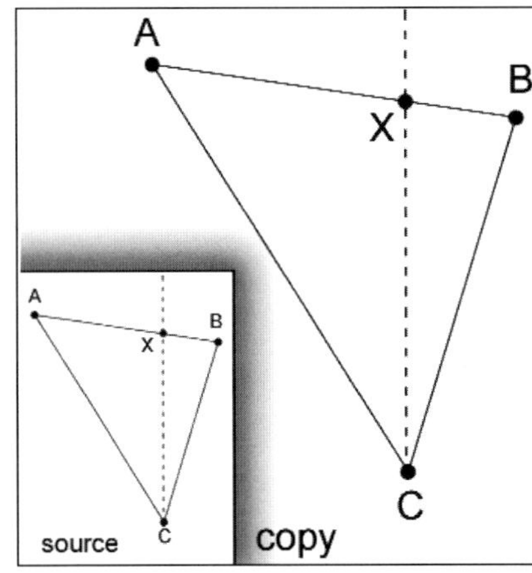

Fig 3. Triangulation

A and B are two points, known to be the correct distance apart, that can be used to check or find the position of C.

If measurements AC and BC in the source are equal to AC and BC in the copy then the position of C in the copy must be correct relative to points A and B.

To check for possible rotation, draw a vertical line through C. Length AX (or BX) must be equal in both source and copy.

Using these measurement methods teaches your eye to detect and recognise angles and relative positions. The line drawing that results has, of course, been drawn freehand but without the possible inaccuracies, as the placement of individual features and their relative angles will be known to be accurate. I found it a great way to learn how to 'see' relative positions. And the true angles between features were often surprisingly different from the angles I perceived.

Freehand drawing

If you can accurately draw freehand, entirely by eye, then you have a huge advantage over many other artists - including me. As with most skills, it requires constant practice to develop and even maintain. If, for example, you become over-reliant on gridding then your skill will degenerate with time.

Ideally freehand drawing should be the first method you concentrate your attention on. Nothing can replace the experience gained by drawing from life. No tool can make you a better artist if you don't first possess the ability to draw. My own use of tools, photographs and modern equipment serve purely to speed up the production of my work. You must learn to walk before you can run. If you cannot mentally see a two-dimensional photograph in three-dimensions then don't use them until you can. Drawing freehand, as often as you can, will teach you skills that will stay with you for the rest of your life. Eventually your use of tools will spring from necessity - but never see them as shortcuts to artistic ability.

To draw freehand effectively you look at proportions, angles and spatial relationships between different elements. In the

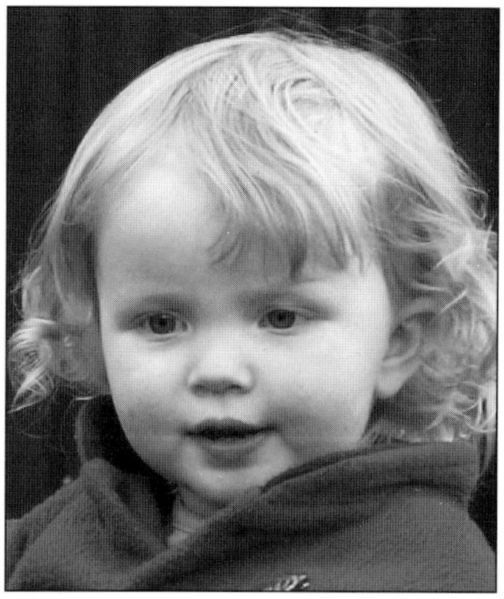

Fig 4

case of my granddaughter Charlotte (*fig 4*) you'll see that her head is slightly tilted - the right-hand eye is a little higher than the left so the same angle will apply also to her nose and mouth. The bottom of her ear is horizontally level with the base of her nose and the top lines up with the right eyebrow. The right corner of the mouth falls directly below the centre of the right pupil but the left corner, because her head is slightly turned, aligns vertically with the inside corner of the left eye. If working from life Sight Sizing will greatly assist you with proportions, angles and relative positioning. You should make use too of the negative shapes between the features. When you have drawn the nose and mouth, for example, check the shape of the space between them, the negative space, to see if you have positioned them correctly.

If you don't already possess freehand drawing skills, methods such as gridding can help you learn. As mentioned earlier, the use of small squares that divide essential features will certainly improve your ability to 'see' correctly. But if you continue to use only small squares you'll eventually cease to learn anything new. By gradually increasing the size of your squares until, let's say, an eye really does occupy a single square, you will have to reproduce it accurately as a single entity. In time you may be able to graduate to using no squares at all and dispense with the grid. You'll be drawing freehand!

You will still have the option of using the grid system for sizing up your sketches should you wish. The measurement system may prove invaluable for checking accuracy. But you won't be reliant on either. Leonardo da Vinci, and his contemporaries, used the grid system but he also knew the value of freehand drawing. It produces spontaneity and fluidity of line but, above all, it involves a total three-dimensional understanding of the subject.

Light Boxes

If your transfer of images is habitually an exact copy of a drawing in its original size, from one surface to another, then a Light Box or Light Table is probably your best choice. They usually consist of translucent Plexiglas tops lit evenly from below by fluorescent strip lights. Nothing could be simpler in use (this presupposes, of course, that you are not wishing to copy to a totally opaque surface). Lay your image or photo on top of the light box, overlay the paper onto which you wish to duplicate the image, and trace.

If you suspect your use will be infrequent (or in an emergency) you can easily improvise a suitable setup that mimics a light box. Taping your drawing to a window in sunny weather will suffice. Laying a sheet of acrylic between two chairs with a desk lamp or two underneath will work also. Or try tracing from an image displayed on a laptop computer's screen - laid flat for ease of use. All are useful ways of quickly transferring a sketch same-size and extending your drawing time.

Projection

Projectors come in three basic forms and can be invaluable time-savers. However, their use by the unwary or inexperienced, can induce a complete separation of the artist from the work. In my opinion the practice of projecting a photograph directly onto the final drawing surface is to be avoided at all cost. Let's take celebrity portraiture as an example and project a sharp studio portrait photograph. The result can produce only an accurate outline and positioning of the features - no understanding and no inclusion of preconceived ideas, treatments or aims. Even the lighting is predetermined. It's like learning a poem by rote. The completed drawing may be a technical wonder but from an artistic viewpoint it has nothing new to say. It merely repeats the vision of the photographer.

You can best avoid these and similar problems by using the same method that I outlined for gridding - by introducing an intermediate stage. First project your photograph so it's enlarged to a small but workable size. Next make the line drawing yours. Establish your lighting scheme, alter or enhance the expression, tidy loose hairs or introduce new ones to add vitality. This stage prevents the projector dictating any content, emotion or other fixed characteristic of the original photograph. As you will be working from that same photograph you can re-establish any aspect of it you wish - but now it's purely your choice.

Overhead projectors

Overhead projectors are most commonly found in teaching situations to display diagrams and text (such as sales graphs) that have been drawn onto transparent sheets and projected onto a screen. The light passes through the source and up through a lens to an angled mirror. They are relatively cheap and worth experimenting with. You may, for example, be able

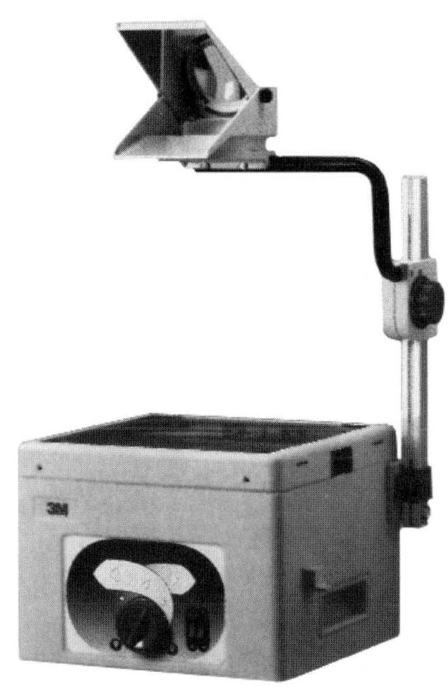

Overhead Projector

to project a line drawing on tracing paper or you can print your source material onto the transparent plastic sheets produced for use with these projectors. As a bonus, you can also use the backlit copyboard as a light box.

Slide projectors

These projectors shine a powerful light in a direct line through a mounted photographic slide and a focussing lens onto a screen. Undoubtedly, they present the ideal way of enlarging and positioning any source material held in a 35mm photographic slide format. However, if you customarily use prints you will first have to have your image converted to a slide - although you can directly project the 35mm film negative. If possible, choose a model with a remote focussing feature so you can stand close to the picture you are about to trace and more easily obtain a pin-sharp image.

If you wish to work directly from a slide there are three basic options: To project the image onto a screen, which entails working in semi-darkness; to use a hand viewer that does not allow immediate comparisons between source and drawing; or to construct a daylight viewer. The latter can be built at home with the aid of a box and a sheet of ground glass. Use a box long enough to ensure a sufficiently large projected image. Paint the inside matt-black to prevent internal reflections. Cut a hole in one end slightly bigger than the projector's lens and mount the ground glass screen into the opposite end. Building an external hood around the screen might improve legibility. Now place your projector with its lens close to, or inserted into, the hole you cut. Take your slide, reverse it and place it into your projector. You should now have a clear image displayed on your screen to which you can refer and directly compare to your work.

Opaque projectors

Unlike the previous two examples, opaque projectors (or graphics projectors) project reflected light. This makes them immensely flexible in use. Although some can also be set up to project light through transparencies if required, their strength lies in their ability to directly project photographic, sketched and drawn images. Some, mine included, can also project small three-dimensional objects.

My own twenty-year-old Artograph DB300 (*fig 5*) has been adapted to progressively fade either or both photofloods for

TIP

Some opaque projectors may display a degree of distortion, especially at the extreme edges. To check for this draw a grid of ½" (12mm) squares onto a card the same size as the copyboard then project it onto your worktable or easel. This method will display any edge distortion and show when the copyboard and receiving planes not parallel to each other - especially useful if you're projecting onto an easel or wall.

maximum flexibility, as reflected glare from photographs can occasionally obscure detail. Unfortunately the DB300 (and its more powerful 400-watt DB400 brother) is no longer manufactured but it is well worth owning and examples are occasionally available in online auctions. The nearest equivalent known to me is the Kobra K5000*.

Many currently available models of opaque projectors are simply placed over the artwork to be projected, have a relatively small copyboard area - some as small as 3" (7.5cm) square - and, like overhead and slide projectors, project horizontally. However, the copyboard of the DB300 is a useful 11" x 10.5" (28 x 26cm) and it projects vertically down onto the drawing board or worktable to which it is mounted, as does the Kobra K5000. This enables you to sit comfortably in a normal drawing position when tracing the result. Focus, through its five-element lens, is infinitely variable and resizing of up to 300% extends to both enlargement and reduction. If required, the housing can be swung over the floor to give an 800% enlargement. Turned on its side on the support column, to project horizontally on to a wall, it can give a maximum enlargement of 1800%, which is a massive 16 feet (5m) square.

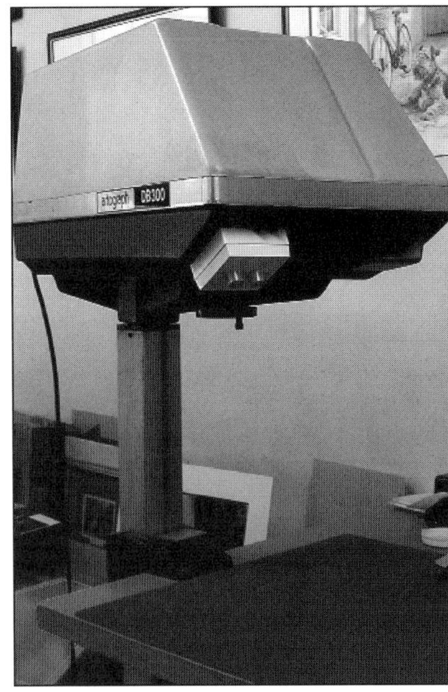

Fig 5
Above: Artograph DB300.
Below: Copyboard being loaded.

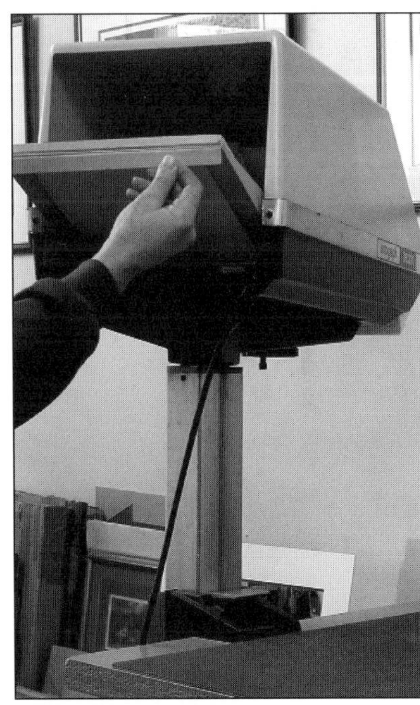

When selecting an opaque projector to purchase, look for a high quality multi-element lens, a front-silvered mirror (rear-silvered mirrors cause double-imaging), a light output sufficient for your purposes and an internal fan - three hundred watts of heat from nearby photofloods can easily scorch your source material on the copyboard. Remember too that an opaque projector works best in a dark or dimly lit room. You must either work at night or be able to black out your studio. Some (including the DB300 but not my old model) are fitted with a low-wattage light that enables you to view what you have drawn - I manage with a nearby desk lamp.

The ability to project opaque material is invaluable. I can, for example, project one photograph of a dog on top of another to see if the head of one works better with the other's body. When composing, I can quickly produce a workable line drawing by enlarging a photograph and tracing it. At this stage there is no point in producing a time-consuming, accurate line drawing of an element that I may later discard. I can also project a line drawing of a dog onto a sketch of the setting to check its viability or find the most natural position while resizing it at will. In fact a variant of this procedure is now my main use for my Artograph - as you will read in the next chapter.

**The Kobra K5000 is available from: KOPYKAKE, 3699 West 240th Street, Torrance, California 90505, U.S.A. www.kopykake.com*

Preparation
Plotting and planning...

'Vermeer achieves uncannily photographic effects while painting in a way that is often locally imprecise and where focus is sometimes lost. Stillness, reticence, hesitancy and psychological ambiguity are qualities not unrelated to his use of the camera obscura.'

Philip Steadman

Whatever method you use to prepare your drawing, comprehensive preparation is a necessity. Just preventing damage to your paper's surface from erased errors is sufficient enough reason. Unlike painters, who can experiment directly on their canvases and start afresh with a single scrape of a palette knife, we graphite artists are not permitted that luxury. Errors, experiments, alterations all combine to damage the available tooth of the paper and can irrevocably mar the finished result. Better therefore to plan and compose elsewhere, then to transfer the finalised set of guidelines to the drawing paper in one operation.

In his later years, the English artist Walter Sickert (1860-1942) based much of his work on photographs and even produced self-portraits from them. His answer to critics was that the only test of any artist was the finished product, no matter what preparatory steps had gone into its making. Sickert's use of photographs introduces another aspect of preparation - sourcing material for the drawing.

Sourcing content

This is a subject I intend to leave to your own preferences. However, to illustrate the range of possibilities open to you, I'll describe my own approach. I agree with Sickert - the means are unimportant; the result is paramount - so I use all the tools at my disposal and regularly mix sourcing methods. I never throw away a magazine without trawling it for suitable inspiration and tear out anything of interest - including artwork. I'm not suggesting you indulge in plagiarism or copyright infringement but these images may trigger ideas in your own mind that add or lead to a successful composition. If you have time to stop on your travels, take a sketchbook and make a note of anything that interests you; you never know when it might become important to you. I keep a cheap camera in my car and clip my digital camera to my belt when I walk the dog every morning. Sometimes the photographs directly result in compositions; at others they provide additional substance or just a different viewpoint that adds to my understanding. My

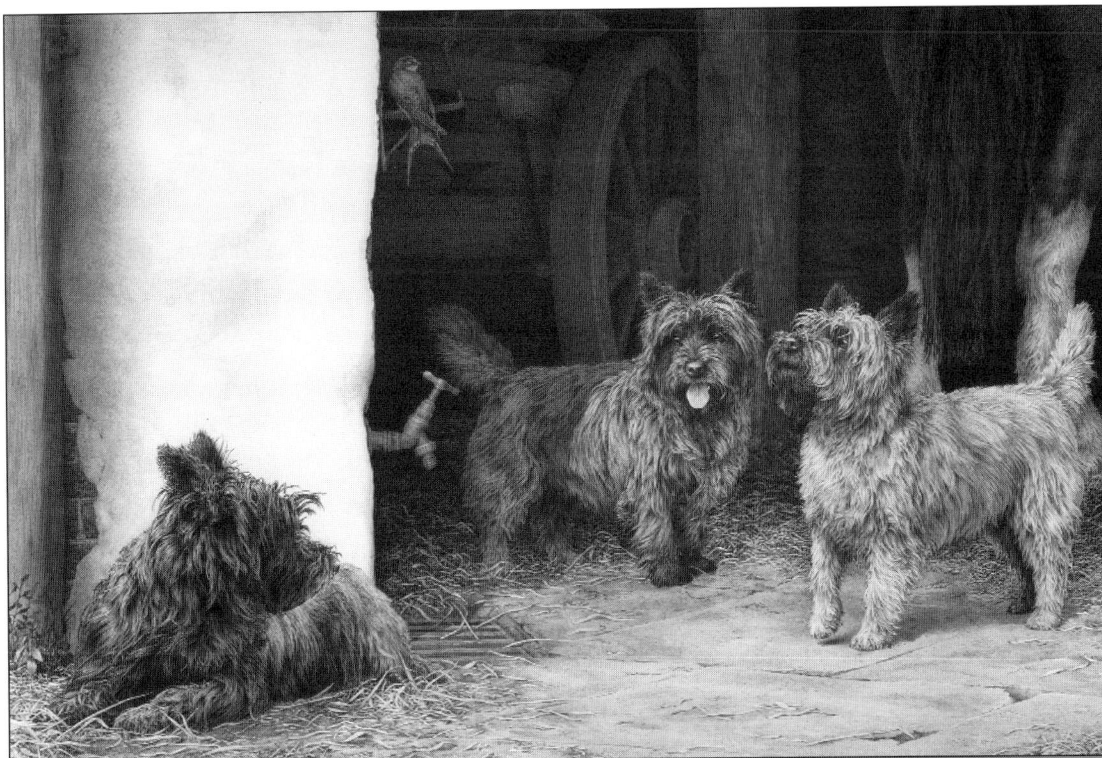

The Barn Patrol

drawing 'The Barn Patrol' contains a diverse collection of elements drawn from a variety of sources. I visited and studied the dogs and took more than 150 photographs from which I worked. I ran my hands through their hair to feel the texture, noted their dark inquisitive eyes, characteristic movements and poses, followed them on a ratting expedition, and studied the way they worked together.

The dogs were drawn with the aid of the photographs and the line drawings were reworked to incorporate the characteristics that I wanted to display. In the drawing, the right-hand dog has its own head, the body of another, the colouring of a third and its rear feet have been repositioned to correct its balance. The cart was standing derelict in a farmer's field when I photographed it some years earlier. I reconstructed it by eye for this composition.

The rear of the horse, seen in the right-hand shadowed area, is our own Badger, and was based on photographs and personal knowledge. The swallow on the bracket was photographed near its nest under the eaves of our goat house and the pose constructed and drawn freehand from the photographic detail. Finally, the brass tap was drawn from life as I held it in my hand. The setting and everything else in it is imaginary - drawn from memory and experience. The trick is to make you believe they all belong to each other.

Planning ahead

THE CONCEPTUAL STUDY

It's always preferable to refine your ideas during the earlier stages rather than ruin your drawing later on. Better to produce a dozen small concept drawings than to redraw your final study many times. I begin with small, manageable line drawings - thumbnail sketches - that may be just an inch or two high. They are quickly drawn as a means of visualising and sorting out my mental ideas although, being in my personal shorthand style, they are virtually meaningless to anyone else. As my ideas crystallise I begin to draw a little bigger for clarity but they are still only about 3" x 5" (7.5 x 12.5 cm) so I can see the whole drawing without having to move my eyes around to take it all in (*fig 1*). These sketches contain only the setting and occasionally a rough indication of where the dogs will be placed. Later a concept drawing is often directly enlarged and transferred to the final drawing surface where it forms the basis of the setting - a method that permits and encourages spontaneous drawing and invention.

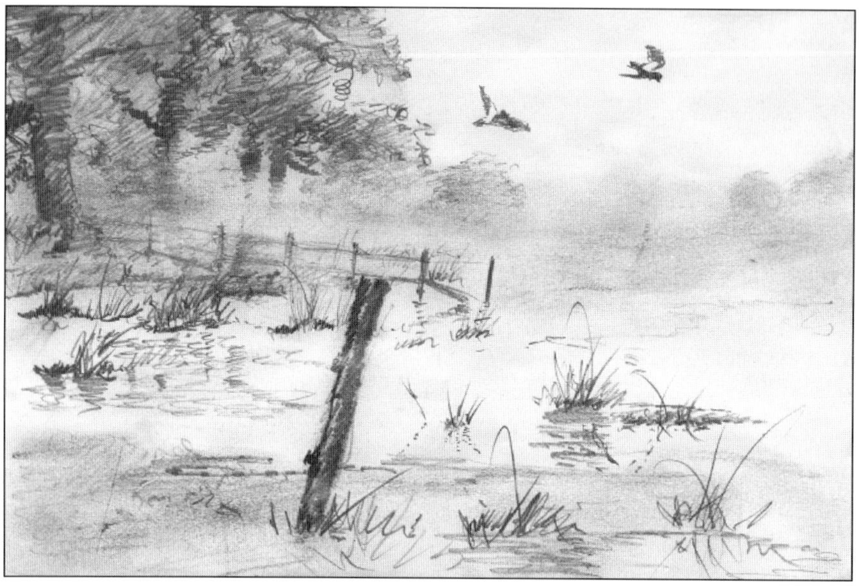

Fig 1. 'Early morn at Witton Marsh' concept drawing. Size: 3½" x 5½" (9x14cm).

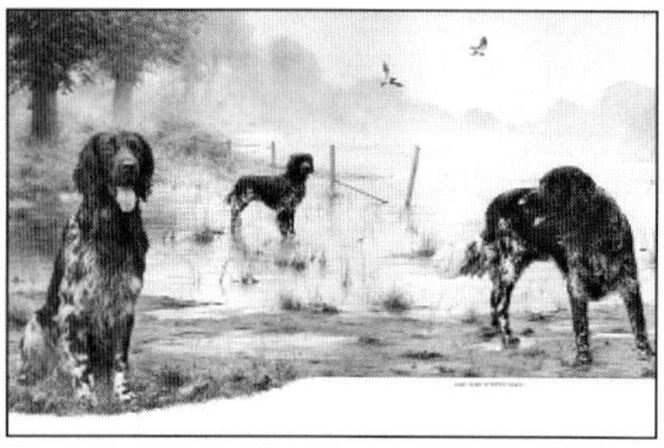

'Early morn at Witton Marsh'

Drawing thumbnail sketches will allow you to quickly experiment with format and composition. At this stage, don't concern yourself with detail but only with placing the major features. When your ideas begin to refine, increase the size and include more detail. Make a note of the horizon if it assists you; add shadows to indicate lighting direction and the atmospheric conditions, and include shorthand notes to yourself - as I have done here with the reflections of the grass in the water.

The working study

The next stage, or the first if you know your goal with certainty from the outset, is to produce a working drawing. This is the master copy from which you will produce your final study.

A working drawing is usually fairly large but still manageable. Mine are never bigger than 10" x 8" (25 x 20 cm). Draw this study on the same paper that you will be using for the final drawing - if you don't you may find that what works now won't work later on. This is the stage that major changes and decisions are made, the composition finalised, problematic areas sought out and resolved, and you might also add trial tonal values to get a flavour of the actual drawing. Essentially, the overall concept is fine-tuned before you embark on the finished drawing. It's your last chance to make certain that everything is balanced, in proportion and achievable. In short - it will work - and occasionally it won't! Better to backtrack now and find a solution - after all, that's what this preparatory stage is all about.

If the problem is one of composition you may find it difficult and time-consuming to resolve. If time is of the essence, use shortcuts. Today I compose on the computer using Photoshop but I have in the past photocopied my working drawing multiple times, cut out the main subjects with a scalpel and physically rearranged them. And I have cut out offending areas and drawn in alternatives. Most of this preparatory drawing for my 'Overlooked!' study (*fig 2*) is a photocopy of a previous version but the right hand third has been cut away and redrawn with graphite. I was trying to solve a problem. The drawing, as seen in this preparatory stage, is split vertically and I tried in many ways to relate the two sides to each other but they never looked right.... until I realised that I had the scale wrong.

In reality the dogs are about 18" (0.5m) high so the 'cliff' behind the dogs, with the rabbit poking its nose out (top left in the briars), is at most just six feet (2m) high. It suddenly made sense that if I squat down and look up at a point six feet above me there's no way I could see that steep bank and the trees on the right hand side. When I drew the area correctly to scale, it worked and the drawing succeeded (*fig 3*).

Persevere! I would never have learned that lesson if I'd thrown my working drawing away or abandoned the idea. It may help to put your drawing away for a while until your mental picture of it has faded. Then, without

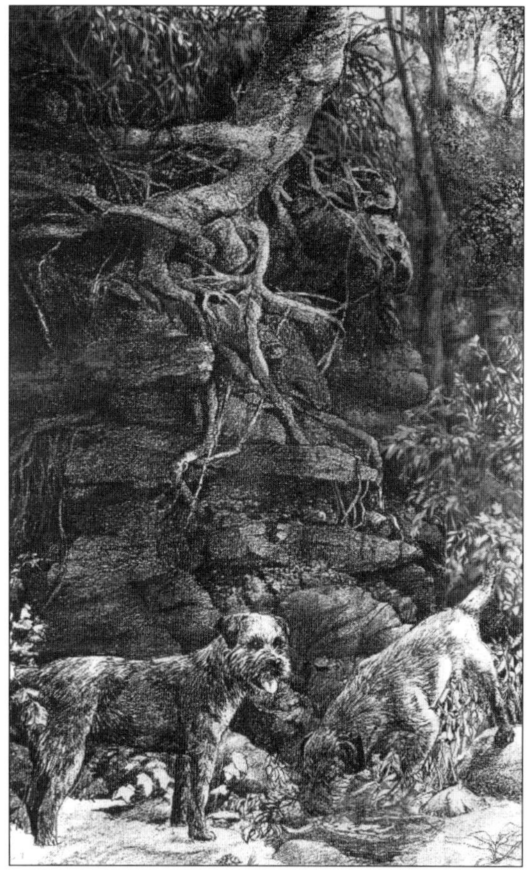

Fig 2. Photocopy of working drawing showing graphite areas top left and down right-hand side.

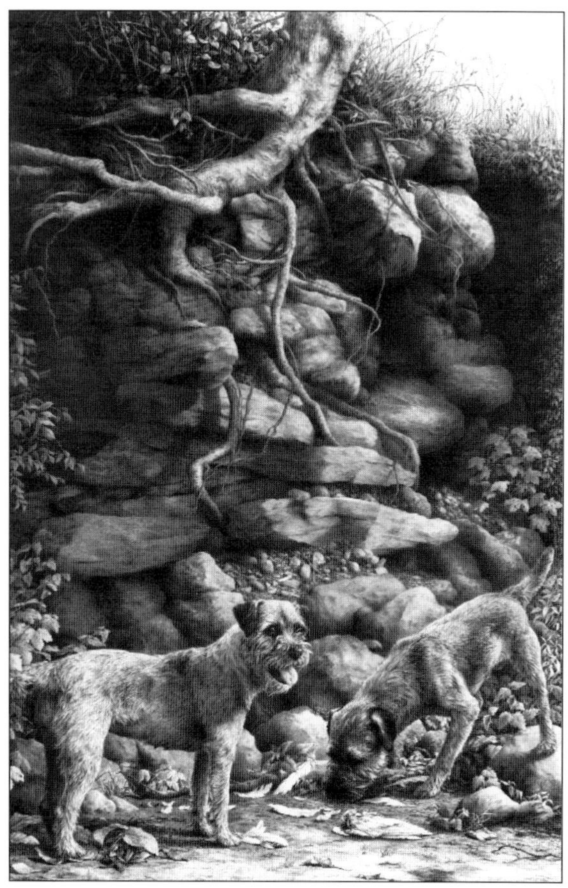

Fig 3. The completed drawing showing the solution.

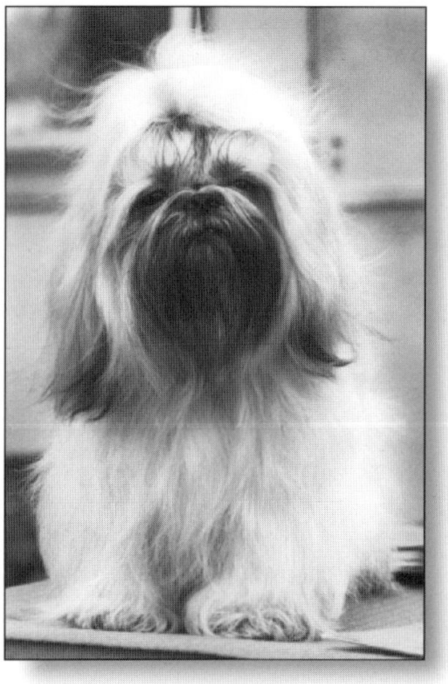

Source photo

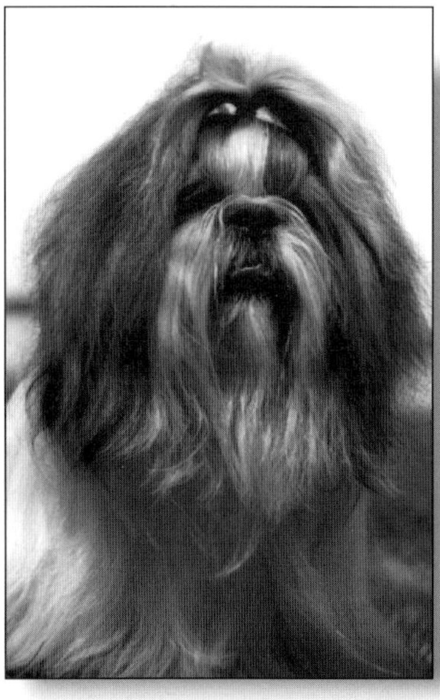

Colouration source

looking at it, take it out and pin it up, step away, turn round and you should see it with fresh eyes. It often provides the solution.

A preparatory drawing can solve many problems and allow manipulation of an image, free of the constraints imposed by your final drawing surface. Here, for example, I've drawn a Shih Tzu with the more usual colouring of another dog - being a print it had to appeal to the greater audience. The preparatory line drawing removed all colour and tone so it was not too difficult a job to transpose the colouring. In this case I drew it without first drawing a trial study to sort out the tone structure, but I wouldn't recommend that procedure. I was lucky!

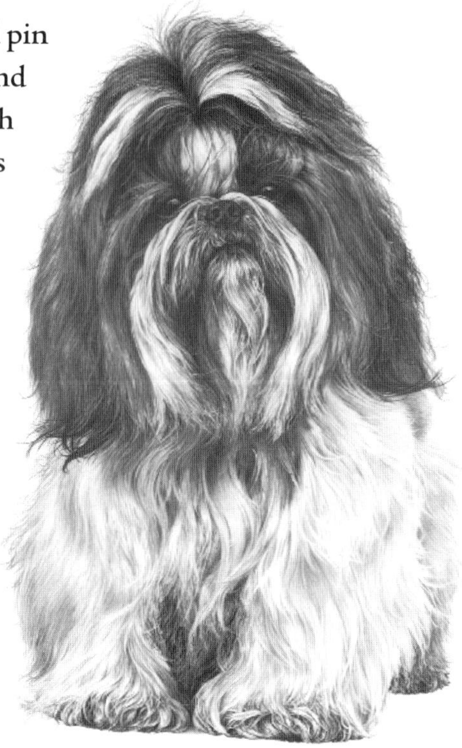

Completed study

The isolated subject

If your drawing involves a single subject without a background, like the Shih Tzu or a child's portrait perhaps, and you are basing your drawing on a photograph, you may be tempted to size-up and transfer your photo to your working surface in one step. I would emphatically council against this method - but you knew I'd say that! And here's why...

First, you will also be transferring potential problems that occur naturally in the photograph but may destroy or unsettle your finished drawing. The removal of the background may, for example, show up distracting natural lines that run through your drawing. It may upset its tonal balance, emphasise camera-induced distortion, or make nonsense of the lighting conditions. Using the intermediate step I outlined above will allow you to fix optical errors and create a new man-made 'natural' balance that adds harmony and pleasure.

However, an arguably more important reason is that you are directly copying the vision of the photographer. I never directly transfer a photograph to my final drawing surface. If I'm planning an 11" x 16" (28 x 40 cm) drawing, for example, I will enlarge the photograph to about 8" x 10" (20 x 25 cm) then make any changes that I consider necessary. Only then will I enlarge my drawing to the final size. Using this method allows you to stamp your authority on the image, make it yours and customise it in any way you wish. In doing so you gain an understanding of your subject that will undoubtedly be reflected in your drawing. It's no longer a two-dimensional collection of textures and tones but a living, three-dimensional being. In this Great Dane example you'll notice that I've used the head much as I photographed it but I've completely remodelled the neck, and introduced reflected lighting to enhance the detail of the nose and eyes. All these changes were worked out and established at the line drawing stage.

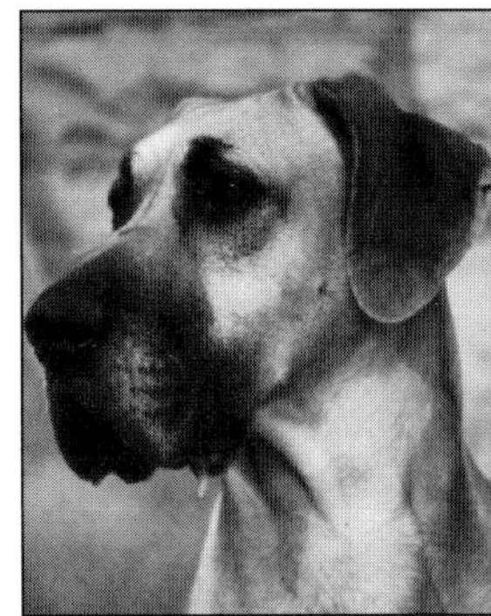

Source photo.
Head: 9 x 8cm.

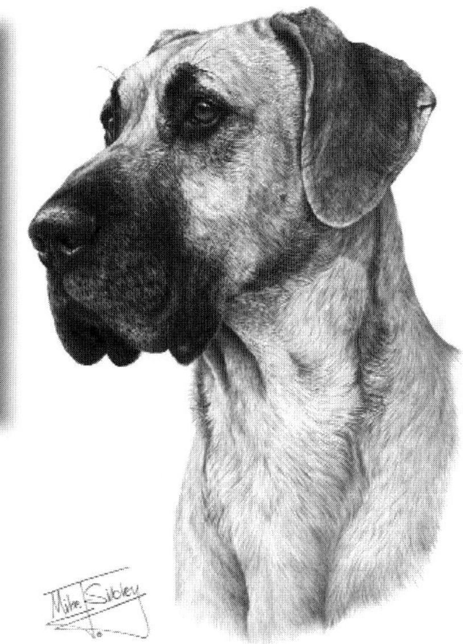

Completed study. Image area: 23 x 33cm.

In this example from 1983 the reverse is true. I didn't give enough thought to what I was drawing and concentrated instead on the actual structure. The source photograph (*fig 4*) shows that the dog was backlit to some degree resulting in a shadow cast by the right ear that extends over the eye. Having removed the background and adjusted the lighting a little I faithfully reproduced the shadow as though it was a part of the dog's markings (*fig 5*). Some years later I replaced this print and didn't make the same mistake! This time everything was studied and suitably organised in the preparatory line drawing and the lighting firmly established (*fig 6*). Where I had previously copied a photograph now I was interpreting what I saw.

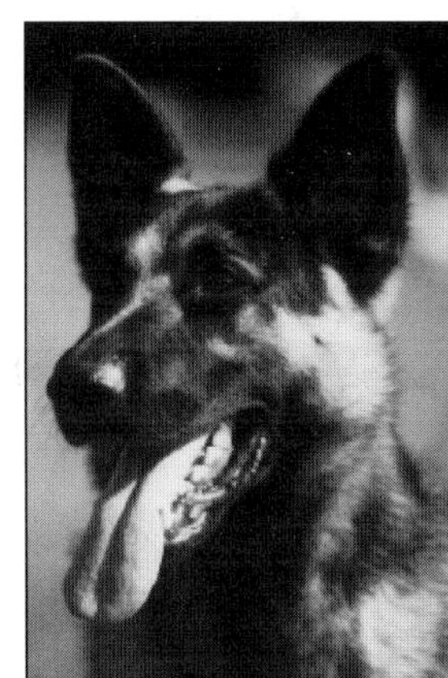

Fig 4

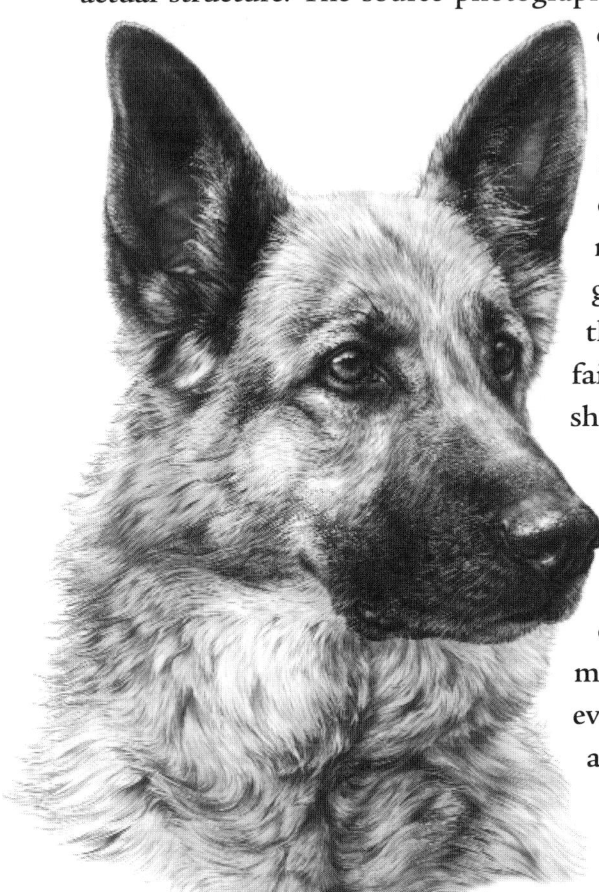

Fig 6

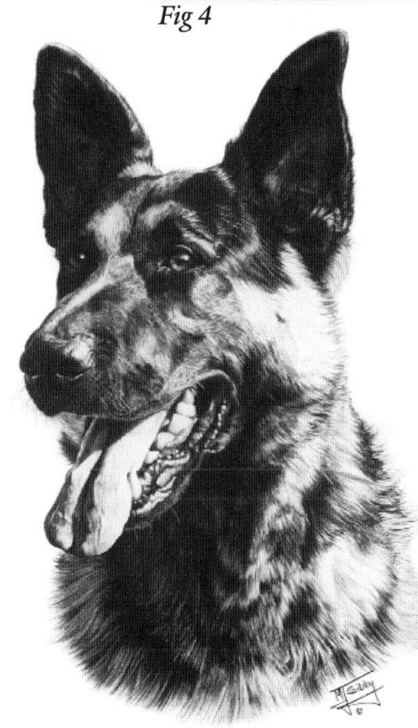

Fig 5

You may wonder why I suggest you should make time to produce this extensive preparatory work? No doubt you would rather be getting on with the drawing itself. Well if, like me, you know you are going to be spending at least 75 hours drawing a head study you'll want to remove as many potential problems as you can. I'm a professional - I can't afford a failure. Time spent now will save you time later on and more probably ensure the success of your study. Changes made at this stage are simple to make, easy to reverse, and they won't affect the quality of your drawing paper. Maybe my system seems very mechanical to you? It doesn't involve any actual 'drawing'. But that's yet to come - the icing on the cake! The end-result of all this work is just a line drawing - nothing more than a simple but accurate set of guidelines. There is plenty of room left for spontaneity and invention in the final drawing. Despite my seemingly clinical approach, this is not 'drawing by numbers'.

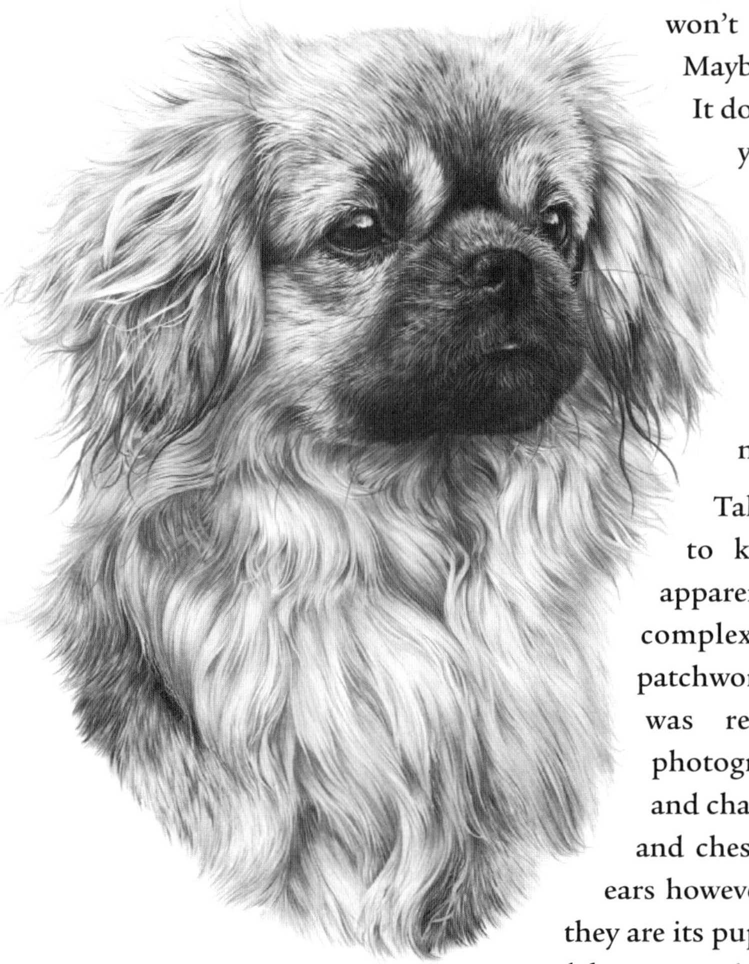

Fig 7

Taking a step-by-step approach will allow you to keep control of the composition. Some apparently simple drawings can contain hours of complex preparation, as in this ultimate in patchwork construction! This Tibetan Spaniel (*fig 7*) was reconstructed from five major source photographs - with many others supplying detail and character. The head does not belong to the neck and chest, which are based on a different dog. The ears however do belong to the owner of the head, but they are its puppy ears, suitably aged. And, as my principal model was a parti-colour, I used the more general colouring of yet another dog. Only the use of a preparatory drawing could allow me the necessary freedom to experiment. The final working drawing gave me the confidence to know that the end result would succeed - an important consideration when the drawing time of 78 hours is taken into account.

The multiple-subject composition

At first compositions such as the Tibetan Spaniel and 'The Barn Patrol' shown earlier may appear daunting but they easily break down into more manageable elements - indeed they greatly benefit from division, as individual attention can be focussed on each element.

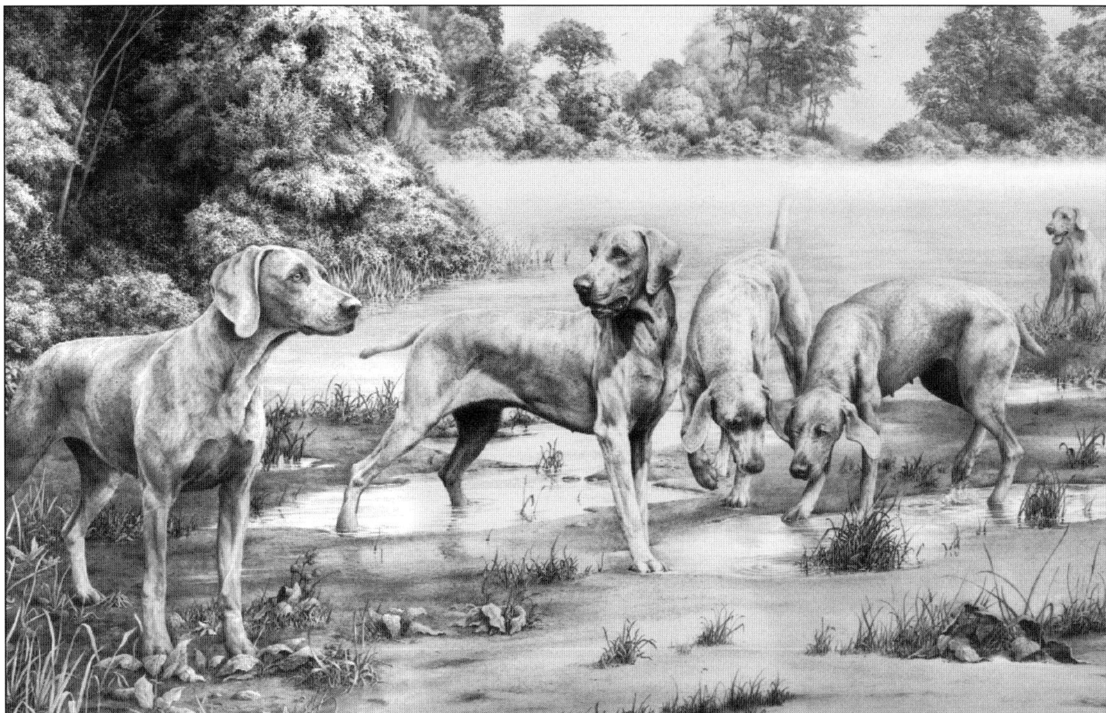

Vanished!

Step 1: The first step in my own approach, as applied to my study 'Vanished!' was to establish the basic content. This was achieved by looking through the mass of photographs of the dogs until a story began to emerge, one that I could develop between a few selected images. Don't rush this stage - it can take me a week or more. A concept drawing of the setting in which to stage the story has been produced and the selection of the characters has been made so now let's see what we can do with them.

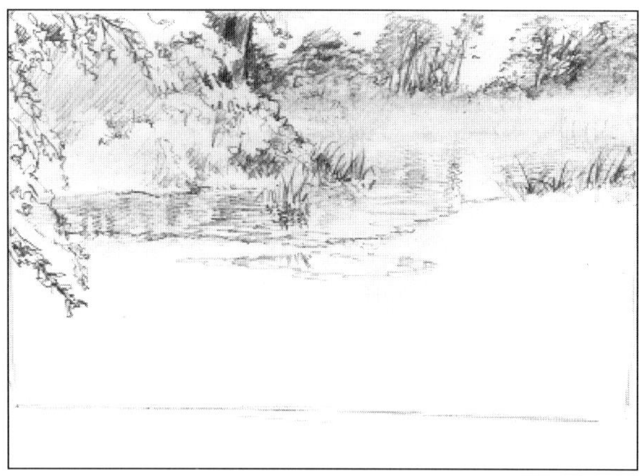

Concept drawing for setting.

Step 2: For speed, as I don't waste time on accuracy at this stage, I simply project the images and trace them off to produce rough line drawings. One (*fig 8*) needs constructing to fit my

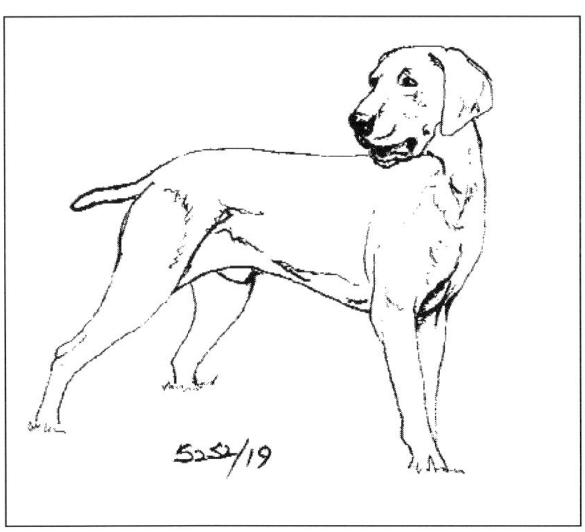

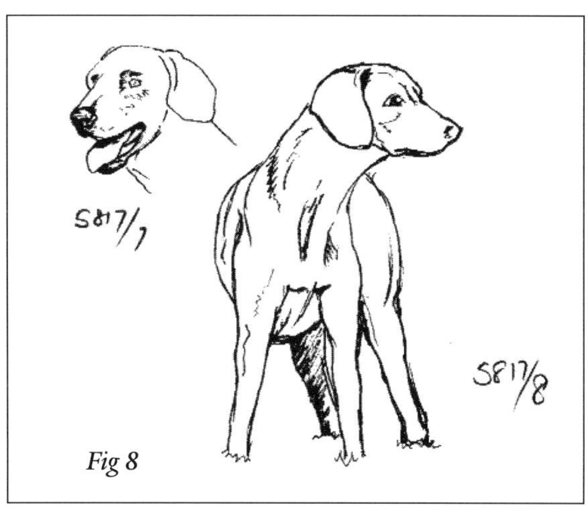

Fig 8

initial composition. I'm going to use the body from one photograph, reverse it and add the head of another dog. I used to do this with my Artograph, now I use Photoshop on my computer. I need this dog to turn the viewer's attention back into the drawing.

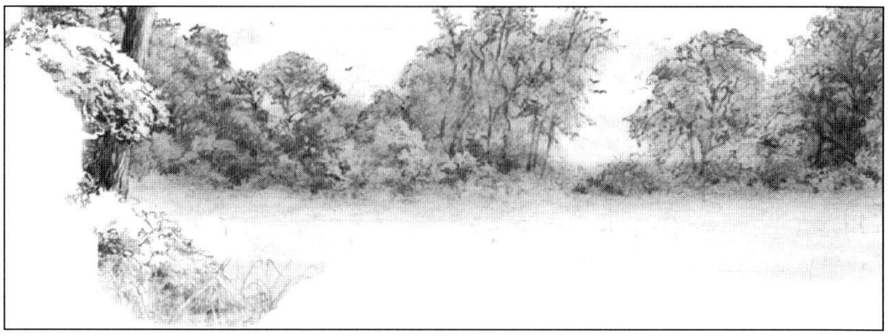

Redefined and redrawn background.

Step 3: From these line drawings I produce transparent-background images with Photoshop. Using the concept drawing of the setting as a background, I individually overlay the images of the dogs and move them around until I'm satisfied with the composition. In this case the concept stops short of including the foreground, which was drawn later once the position of the dogs had been established and the background too was refined and redrawn.

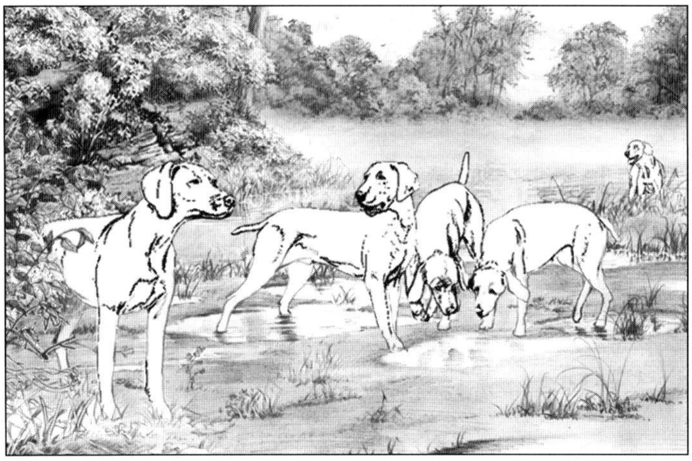

Fig 9 Composition #4

Step 4: Now we can put it all together and gradually refine the composition. The differences between composition #4 (*Fig 9*) and composition #6 (*fig 10*) are slight but very important. The central dog has moved left, the bitch at the left has moved back a little and I've decided to redesign the left-hand midground. It's beginning to take shape.

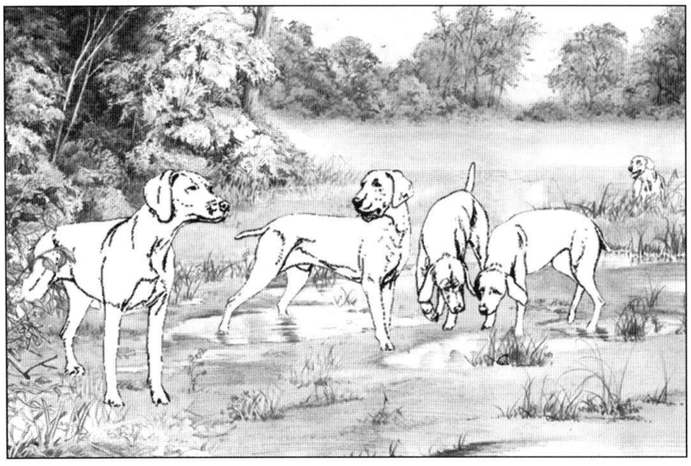

Fig 10 Composition #6

By composition #9 the dogs have moved again and I'm happy with the result (*fig 11*) so now the work begins in earnest. Unusually, I've worked the setting up into a tone drawing at an early stage.

Step 5: First the dogs are individually and accurately redrawn. Paws are invented where none existed, as the dogs were photographed in a grass paddock, individual characteristics are finalised and poses fine-tuned. I now have a collection of five accurate line drawings and the less-defined drawing of the setting. At this stage I often work a printout of the composition into a tonal study. This tone-map may help me relate tones in the final drawing. It's important that I get everything right at this stage, as I'm going to be spending over 140 hours drawing the final study.

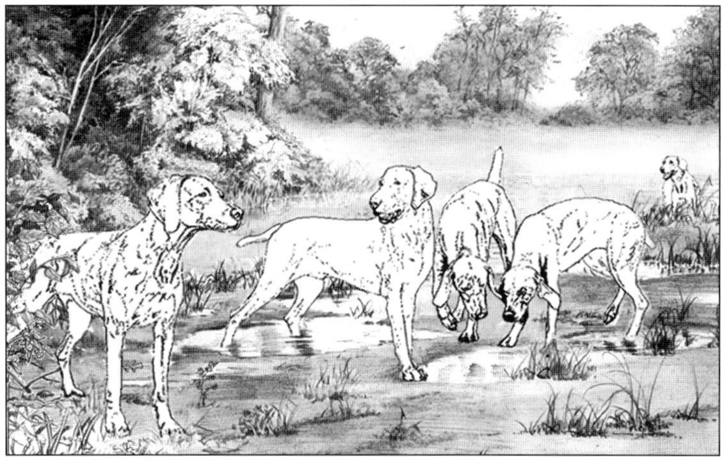

Fig 11 The final composition with the dogs redrawn.

Step 6: The whole thing is taken apart and reassembled, element-by-element, onto my actual drawing surface. An accurate outside border is drawn then a printout of the composition is projected and sized to fit. Using a 6B Progresso pencil the position of each element, a placeholder, is lightly marked and the printout discarded. The background is then projected and the principal elements carefully marked. No detail is included, just the bare bones. The detail will be invented during the actual drawing, aided by the tone drawing used for the setting. All the other elements - the dogs and their 'vanished' entertainment - are individually projected into their placeholders and lightly drawn in with a 2B pencil. This method removes the potential problem of distortion towards the outer edges exhibited by graphics projectors. The result (*fig 12*) shows the inclusion of

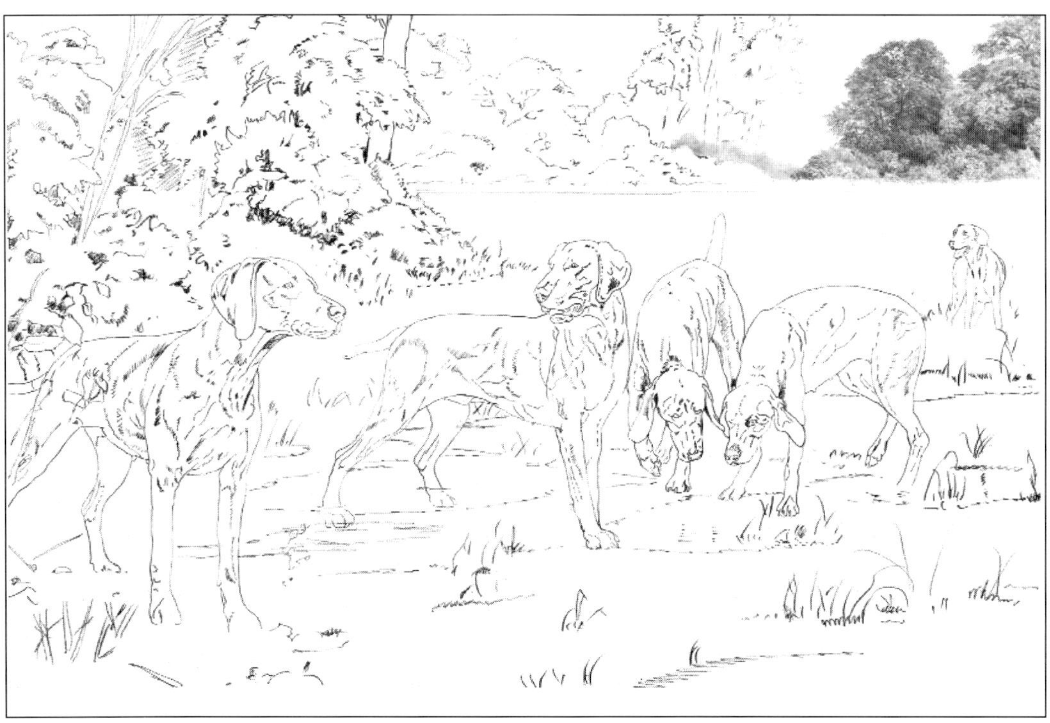

Fig 12 Work has begun on the actual drawing.

six hours drawing in the background. (The line drawing has been digitally enhanced to make it more legible.)

Although the preparatory work, composition, and line drawing used up valuable time I was able to use productive time when drawing. The finished 'Vanished!' drawing tells the story that I wanted to tell. Drawing is about saying something, portraying and transmitting your thoughts to the viewer. It is not about 'colouring in' or technical prowess.

We all have different ways of working. For me the line drawing is just the armature around which I sculpt. And I really don't mind if the armature was machine-made or hand crafted so long as I get to tell my story.

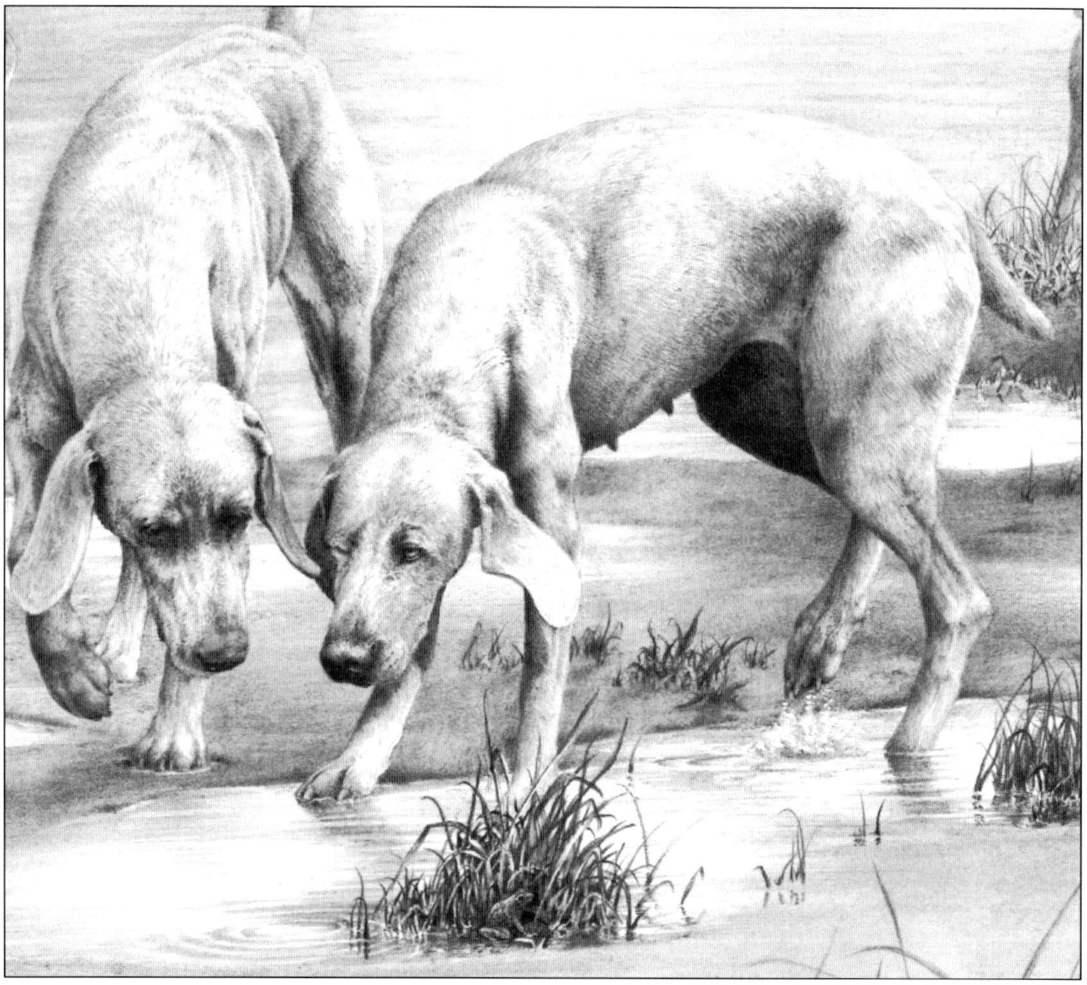

And finally, the dog's entertainment just leapt into the grass... and Vanished!

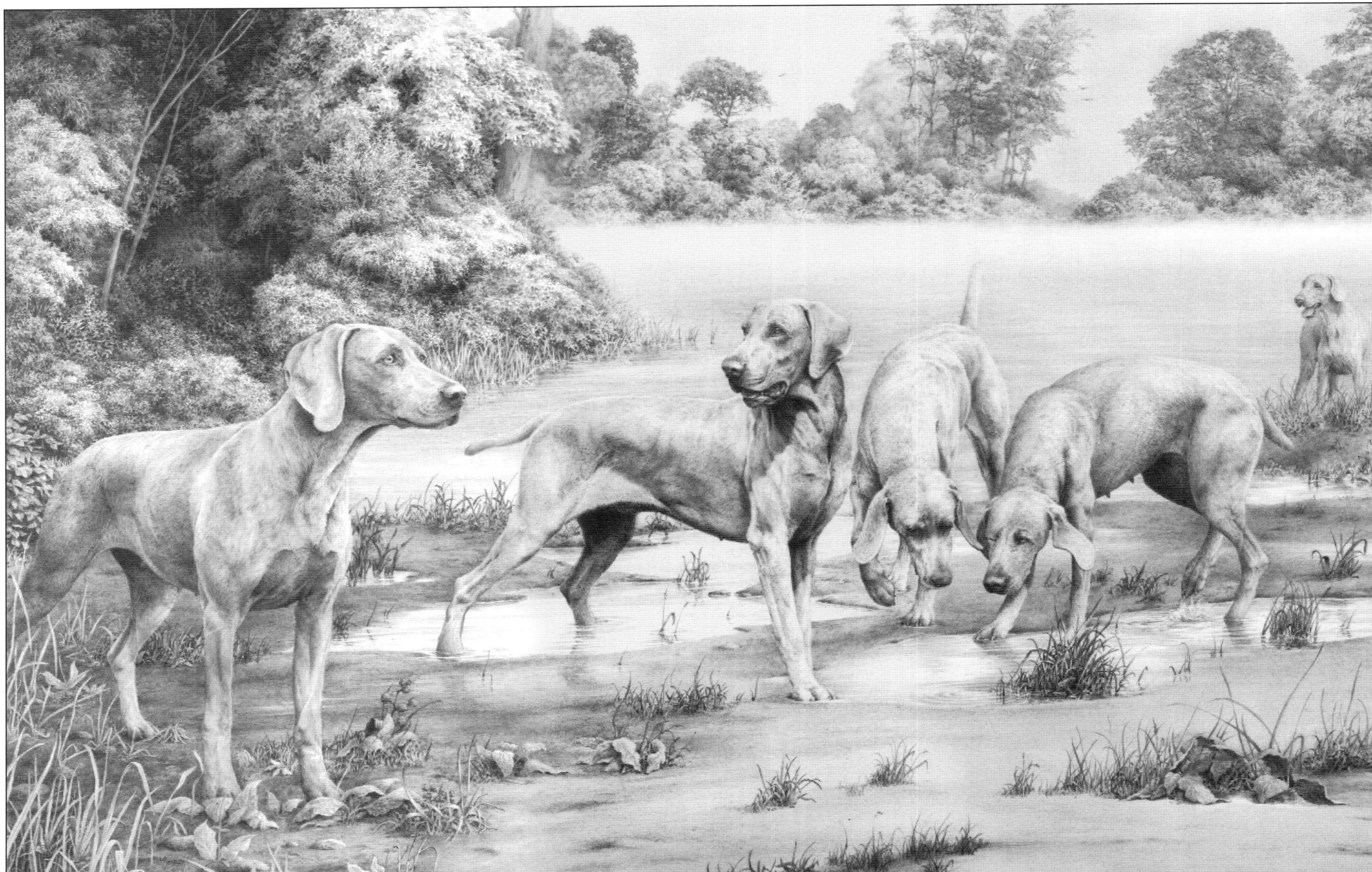

'Vanished!' © Mike Sibley. A limited edition print of 630 copies featuring the Weimaraner.

17¾" x 11½" (45 x 29 cm)

Live demonstration
Clarrie, my Tortoiseshell cat...

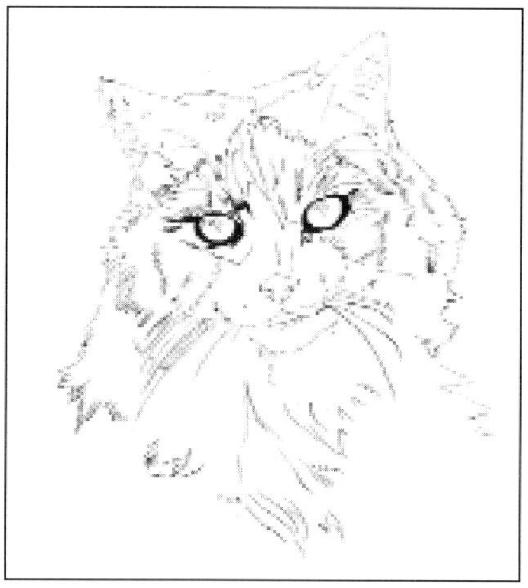

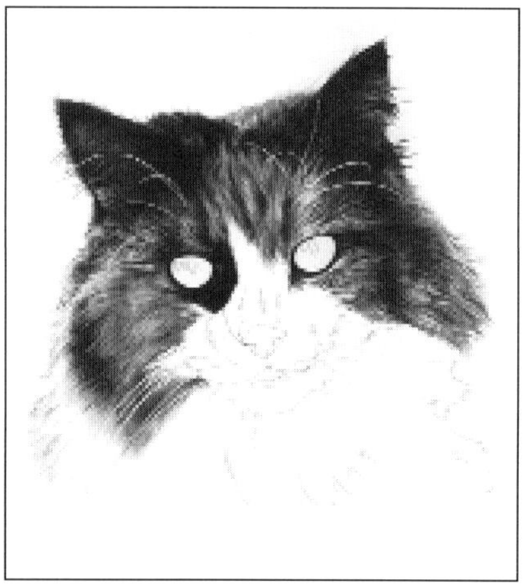

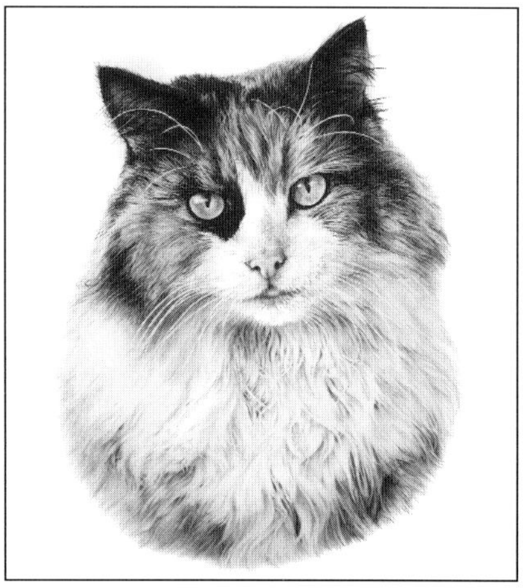

I originally drew this as a commission to be printed onto cat food bags. Taking the printing system into consideration and the semi-absorbent surface of the paper, I left the detail fairly course and used no blending at all. Blending would have produced very subtle areas of gradated tone that would have been lost in the final printing. My plan was to attempt to keep everything sharp with good, delineated edges and boundaries between 'colours'. Clarrie is, of course, a true Tortoiseshell cat with markings of black, white and shades of orange.

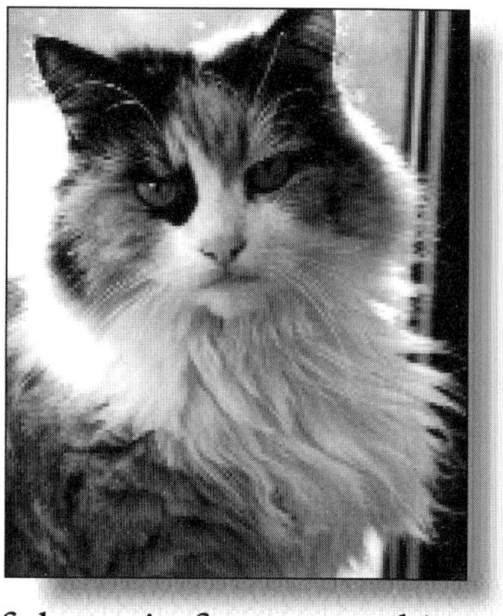

At the time of the commission my client chose an existing drawing of a kitten then decided it needed a 'mother'. A quick look around my eight cats alighted on Clarrie. No contest! She perfectly fitted the bill.

For speed, the original photograph was projected and traced off to produce the guide line drawing. I was only interested in fixing the positions of the main features at this stage, knowing that I would later be adapting the line drawing to emphasise two main features - her eyes and bottom lip.

When I first began drawing animals I used to start by drawing the eyes. This is where the character and soul are reflected and any error at this stage can render a drawing unusable. But as my confidence increased I began to leave the eyes until later - in this case almost until the end. As experience grows it becomes more apparent that there are right and wrong times to draw particular features or areas. The tonal quality of each depends largely on the drawing around it. Once you've lost the habit of trying to draw the whole project as one huge drawing and concentrate instead on the full understanding of each area in turn you, like me, will know when it feels right to complete a major feature.

The following notes were made at the time of drawing.

Stage 1:

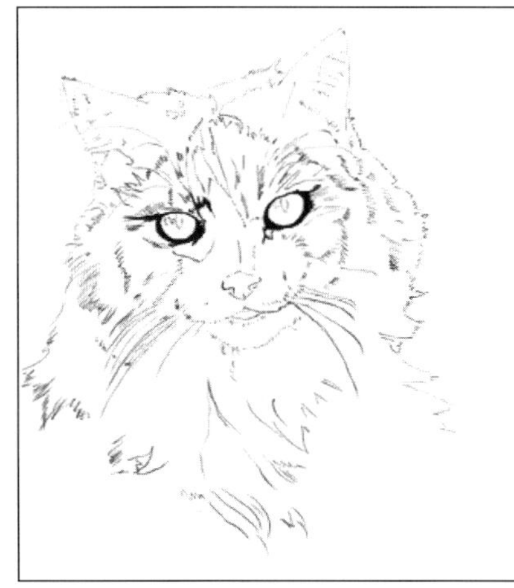

The line drawing has been digitally enhanced throughout these stages. In reality they are very lightly drawn with 6B for easy erasing.

The position and shape of both eyes has been established, with particular care being taken over the smoothness of the curvature, using a sharp 2B. Often an HB line around the eye before 2B is applied works best, as the edge of the line is sharper. The human eye is adept at spotting irregularities it does not expect.

I'm about to define the right side of the black area adjacent to the left eye - creating the outer edge of this line first, ignoring the inner edge, which will be completed later. As usual I'm working dark into light.

Stage 2:

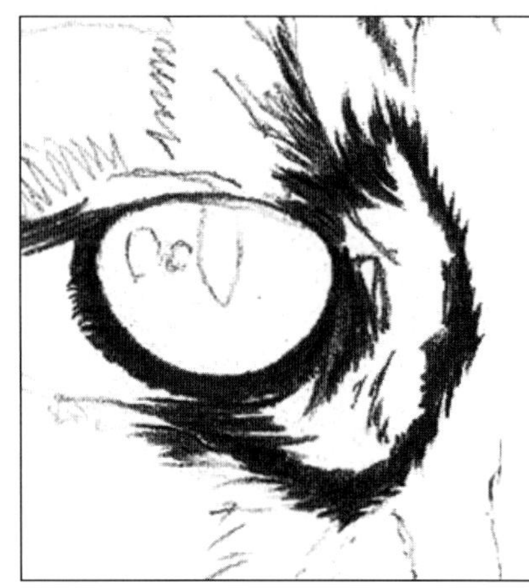

I've been concentrating on the outside edge only of this area, ignoring the centre. The edge has been completed using 2B, working outwards so that black hairs diminish into white, and white 'hairs' are negatively drawn and defined in such a way that they appear to cut into the black. The central area will be worked next.

Surrounding areas are constantly being mapped out more completely as more information becomes apparent. This is a continuing process and a reminder to myself of what I was seeing at the time.

Stage 3:

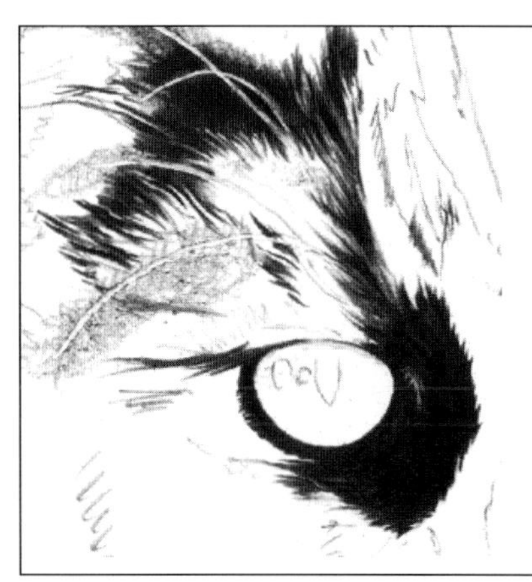

The enclosed area has been completed. Above the eye a near-vertical, hard edge has been identified and is being used as a 'drawing break' - a natural edge that can be drawn away from then returned to and worked away from in the other direction. White hairs have been indented and their positions displayed - achieved by a light application of soft graphite obliquely across the lines with a 6B Progresso pencil, which can be easily and completely erased if required.

The dark area arching above the eye has been drawn down into the white below and left faded out above so new drawing can be grafted onto it later. As this brow area is almost completely enclosed it will now be completed.

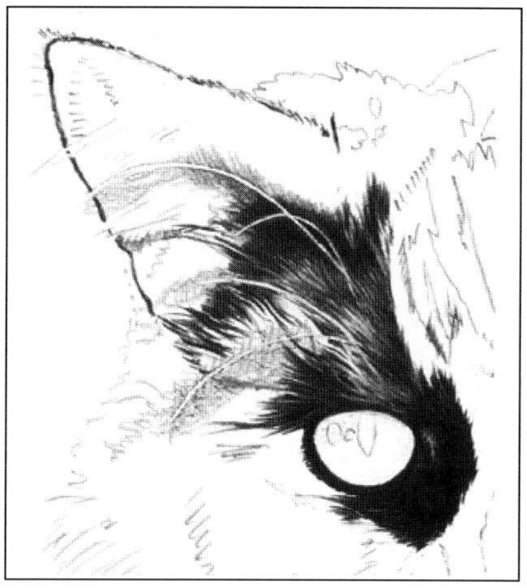

Stage 4:

Well, it didn't quite happen did it? I lost concentration so, instead of completing the area, I moved to the outline of the ear.

This is always a good decision. If I'd tried to regain my concentration while working on the brow area I could have done a lot of damage, maybe irreparably. By moving to a completely different area, I've given my brain something else to think about and a rest from drawing hairs spontaneously as the pencil moved.

Maybe I'll go back and complete the area or maybe I won't. It matters little as sooner or later I'll find myself back in there completing the job - easier now that most of the groundwork is already in place and tones established.

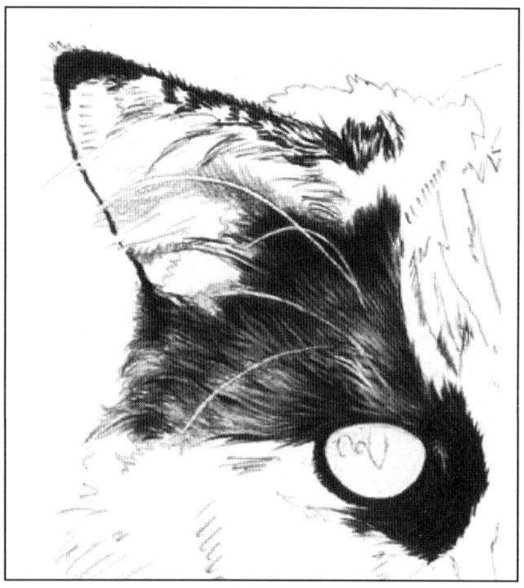

Stage 5:

It seems I was in the mood to complete it! And now I'm moving into the ear - if it feels like a natural progression just go with the flow.

The completed area shows a lot of use of negative drawing followed by a layer of 2H to provide three-dimensional shaping. Rather than trying to achieve shaping and structure at the same time I often concentrate solely on the structure, leaving all light and highlight tones as white. Then I can properly concentrate on lighting conditions and tone down the white as required to form true highlights that recede into shadow.

Here I've identified the feature directly above the eye as being the most prominent highlighted area and have based all surrounding lighting tones on it.

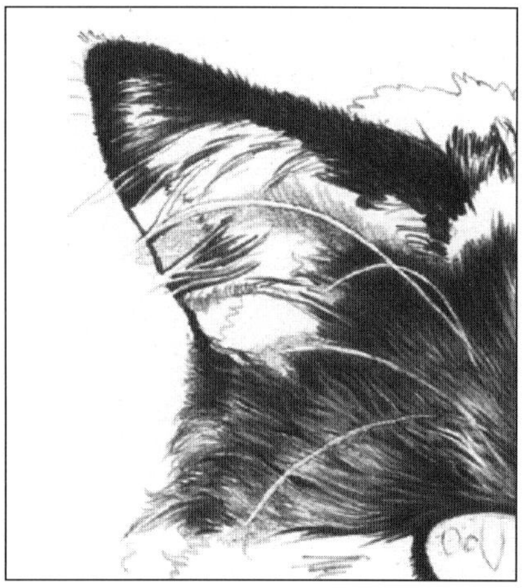

Stage 6:

I've completed the top edge of the ear. The thickness of the ear appears almost completely black on the photographs but I resisted the temptation to just block it in. Instead I drew and defined the lower edge in almost pure black tone then quickly filled in the central section, a quarter-inch length at a time, with short marks. Each of these marks pointed in the direction of growth of the hairs and I allowed the tone to lighten slightly towards the top edge. The idea was to allow random, lighter marks to appear that would represent hairs. What you see is achieved by random chance, not by careful planning. As hair and chance are both provided by Nature it seems quite natural to allow one to produce the other. Studied 'randomness' can often appear stilted so better to give randomness free reign.

You will note that I have begun to define the position of a few stray light hairs down the lower left hand side. Next will be a continuation of this area leading to the final drawing of the central section. All that then remains is a degree of tidying-up and an overall adjustment of tonal values to integrate all the areas into one believable whole.

Stage 7:

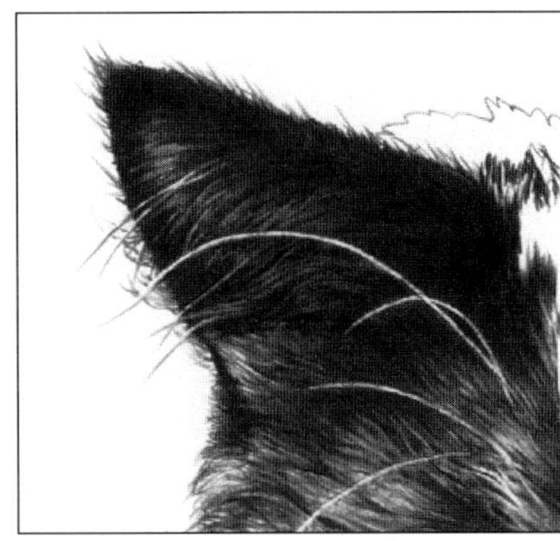

The ear is complete. In different circumstances I might have blended the hairs in the ears a little. As this drawing is primarily destined to be printed onto relatively coarse paper cat food bags I'm leaving the area unblended. The increased definition and clarity will assist in the printing process. Where to work next? I'm not sure. I'll just see what I have a feeling for and proceed from there.

Stage 8:

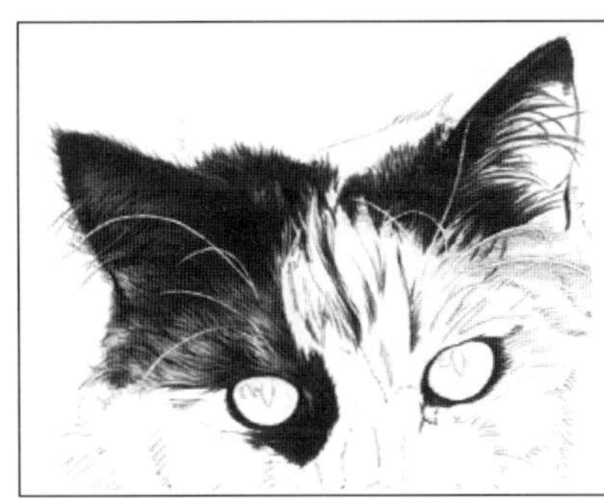

The work has been extended across the top of the head to the opposite ear. Areas of lighter tone that I'm unsure of have been left undrawn. All the time I'm looking for an area of dark tone from which to work outwards. The area chosen should be almost devoid of detail to make it as easy as possible to seamlessly graft later drawing to it.

Here the ear has had its dominant shadow areas completed and these are now being extended into the lighter areas.

Stage 9:

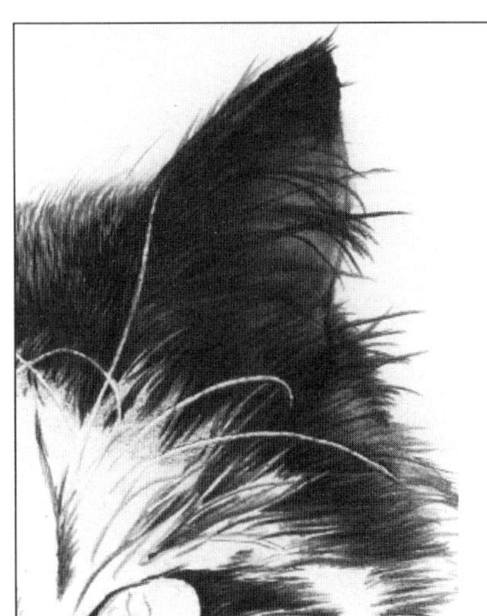

I'm still working from dark to light, following the arcing line of darker hair down the right side of the face.

This area has been drawn into the central lighter section (negative drawing) to define the position of that area's outermost hairs. As yet I feel unable to correctly determine the tonal values of the central area so I'll keep drawing around it until the tones become apparent.

So far the tools used have been few and simple; a blunt needle to indent the white hairs, Blu-tack to adjust tones and just three grades of graphite - 2B for the medium to dark areas, HB for the mid to light tones and 2H for the lightest tones and to lightly work across the other grades to tone down any areas left white in order to maintain a balance of tone across the drawing.

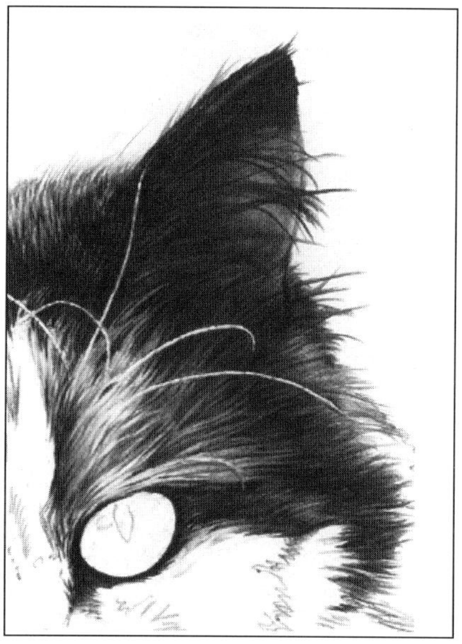

Stage 10:

OK, so I lied! The time is not yet right to complete the central vertical section but I felt I could set the tonal values for the hair above the eye. Because I'm after a look of happiness (OK, cats don't do 'happy' but bear with me...), my main intention, while maintaining a degree of hair-direction accuracy, was to emphasise lines that curve up then down. This is to mimic human traits - the arch of the amused eyebrow, eyelashes and forehead furrow. Why? Well, the viewers I'm aiming to please are not cats but humans and they will inevitably be looking (subconsciously, at least) for recognisable signs of emotion. As we human beings know human emotions best, those are the ones we're looking for. This is a simple trick to learn - just look in the mirror, make faces and study the changes. I learned this technique from Walt Disney - not personally, I hasten to add. I read of his directive to his animators that they should study their own actions and movements and transfer them to the animals they were drawing. If carried out with subtlety, it is a good lesson to learn and practice.

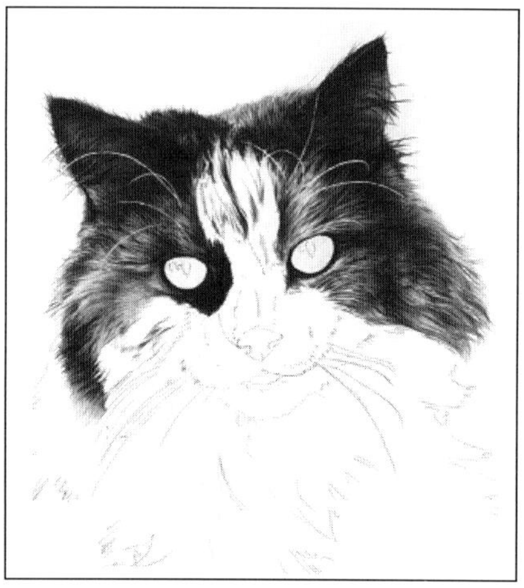

Stage 11:

More of the same - working wherever possible from dark to light, both cheeks are nearing completion. Evidence can be seen of the use of 'status' hairs - hairs growing in contra-direction and deliberately emphasised.

By defining the position of these brain-food hairs and then drawing positive lines 'beneath' them (as described in Fooling the Brain - part 2), you create two important elements at one time. A true sense of depth is created and the eye of the viewer is directed to the out-of-place hair, fooling it into believing that all other marks surrounding it must also be hairs. Send the right signal and you'll generate the desired response.

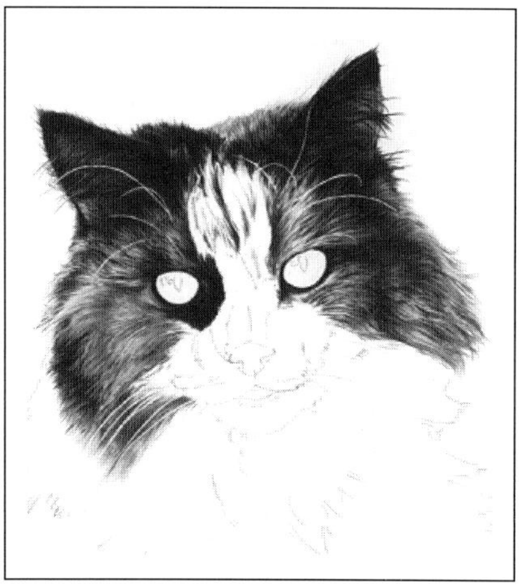

Stage 12:

I've decided to complete the side of the face as the resulting relationship between the tan and white will help me to decide on the tonal values for the central, undrawn section.

It's also about time I began to fix the position of the mouth so I can monitor the appearance. It's essential that this cat looks contented or even pleased and the mouth plays a major part in this. From now on I will be constantly checking the area being worked on to ensure that it is not adversely altering the look that I'm after.

STAGE 13:

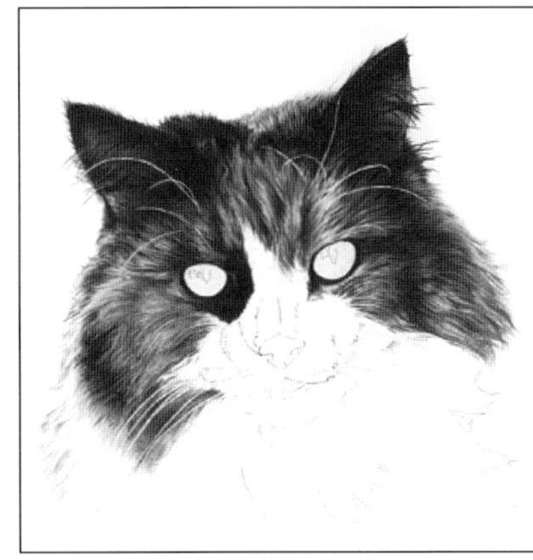

I finally felt I had the information I needed to determine the look of the central brow area. My model has a lighter tan than I'm portraying here but I've decided to keep the tan dark. This should emphasise the mouth, which is surrounded by white hair. I only have the shadows below the mouth to give it form, shape and position - by darkening all other tones I can now use stronger shadows around the mouth without losing the appearance of the hair being white.

I've tried hard in this area to divert any apparently vertical hairs. I want curves reminiscent of human eyebrow arches and not vertical lines echoing the human emotions of anger or worry. I still need the vertical bunches to maintain feline characteristics but my aim was to subtly emphasise the curves - deliberately misleading the viewer's eye.

STAGE 14:

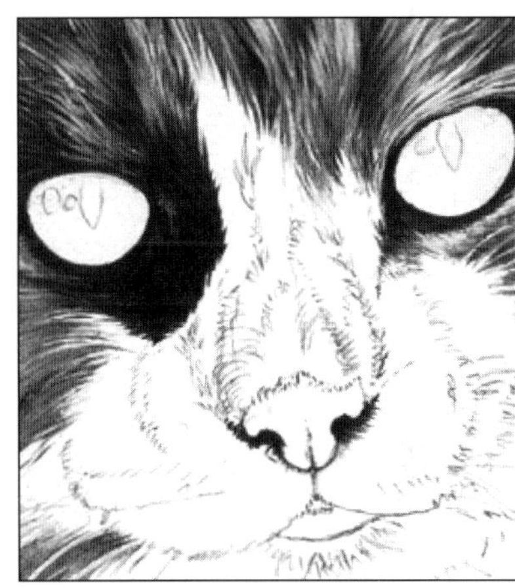

Work is beginning on the nose. It seems to be the next logical step as, by fixing the tonal values above and below the undrawn muzzle area, the drawing of it should be far more easily accomplished.

As I'm drawing, tonal values are constantly being checked against surrounding areas in order to maintain a feeling of 'wholeness'. As usual I'm looking for deep shadows and drawing-breaks from which to start. Here I've defined the shadows within the nostrils, which themselves give me the break I require. I've also sketched in some structure and hair direction guides to the nasal passage area above the nose. These 'notes' are lightly drawn with a 2B lead so they can be completely removed if required.

STAGE 15:

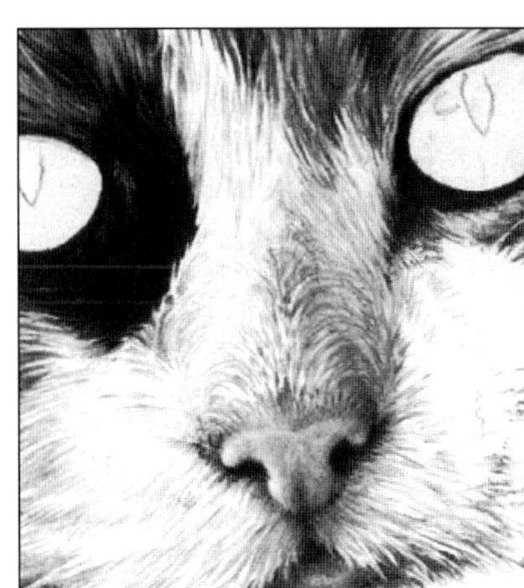

Work has now commenced on the nose and it has been worked up into the brow area. With no obvious stopping point, the drawing has inevitably continued around the nose and down to the top lips. This is real negative-drawing country! Every pencil line represents a shadow cast by a hair. The shadows have defined the position and form of the hairs, which, in reality, exist only as negative spaces.

I need to add tone to the bottom lip and the curves of the top lip to check that the expression is continuing as planned. The shadow cast by the top lip has been drawn upward into the descending 'hairs' - the spaces between the shadows forming the hairs themselves. Later drawing can be easily grafted onto this shadow area to extend it downwards into new drawing.

STAGE 16:

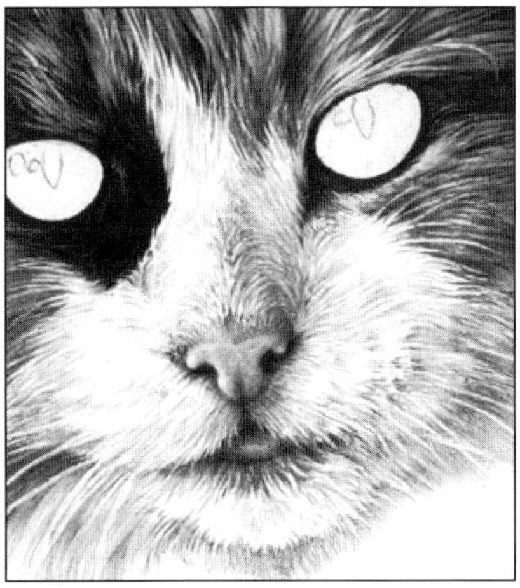

The work didn't go so easily in this area - in the main due to a lack of definition. The whole section is made up of gently gradated areas of tone, each flowing into the other, with no hard edges to work to. Trial and error is usually the only way to tackle such problems. With pencil in one hand and Blu-Tack in the other, tone is laid down between hairs (and even over or into them where required). The area is then progressively lightened before being strengthened over and over again - each attempt bringing the drawing a little closer to reality. At one stage I was forced to define the outline of the lower jaw in order to check for correct expression. As a result I've attempted to manufacture an upward curve extending from the corner of the mouth by emphasising the roots of certain whiskers. My intention is to suggest the curve of a human smile without losing the natural look of a cat.

STAGE 17:

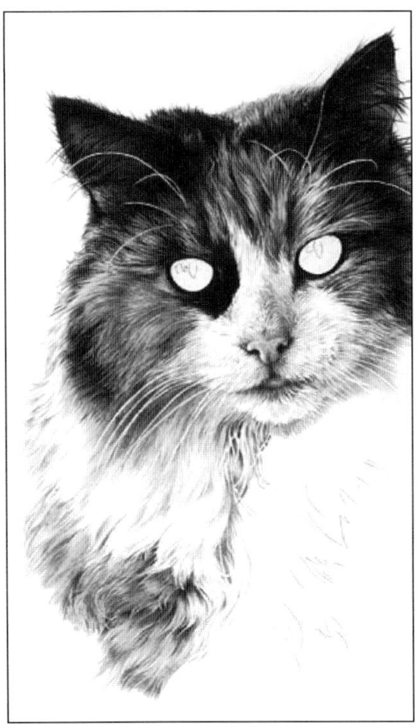

I've sufficient tonal information now to complete the eyes but I've decided to concentrate on the body for this session.

Although I started with no clear idea of what the body of the cat was going to be, ideas are now suggesting themselves. The actual cat has a completely white front that tapers off into tortoiseshell markings around the bottom of the breastbone. I've decided to make the orientation of the body something of a mystery and let the viewer's mind find it's own solution. This allows me to introduce darker tone and markings wherever I want them.

I've incorporated a small number of deep shadows containing carefully worked detail. These will give enough information to the viewer's eye to suggest greater detail than actually exists and, as long as the shadows don't form directional lines, they will enhance the look of reality. Too many lines travelling in one direction are to be avoided, as the body orientation must remain unclear. Similarly the outside edge must apparently fade out making the viewer uncertain as to its form - is it just fluffy hair that appears to be receding or has the artist simply faded the hair into the background?

Notice also the strong negative-drawn areas. The one below the chin has been newly mapped out. The drawing of the positive shapes between the 'hairs' is crude at this stage but the white hairs are defined and ready to receive tonal shaping and to be incorporated into the adjacent drawing to come.

Stage 18:

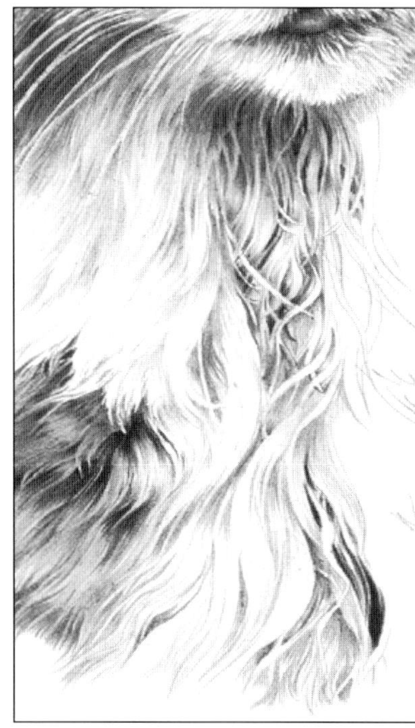

Sometimes the local tone of an area is not clearly apparent. The natural response is to tread lightly, to add just a little tone to see its effect. But the best way is the reverse - always add too much tone. Keep building an area up; introduce shadows, valleys, crests and highlights. You needn't be too precise; the chances are that you're going to remove most of it. But only in this way can you properly adjust tone to the 'correct' values. It is always easier (but only if you use Blu-Tack or a kneadable eraser) to progressively reduce tonal strength than it is to add it. Learn to 'draw' highlights with your eraser, drag it lightly over an area to gradually reduce the tone - back to white if necessary.

Here I've extended the central, detailed area too low. It appears almost as a column and I need to blend it into the white hair below, which itself is too dark. These areas have been principally built up with 2H - if used lightly it will erase with ease. Never be afraid of erasing work, no matter how long it may have taken. It won't take long to restore it to its former state if you decide you've erased in error. So let's take the Blu-Tack to the area I've just drawn.

Stage 19:

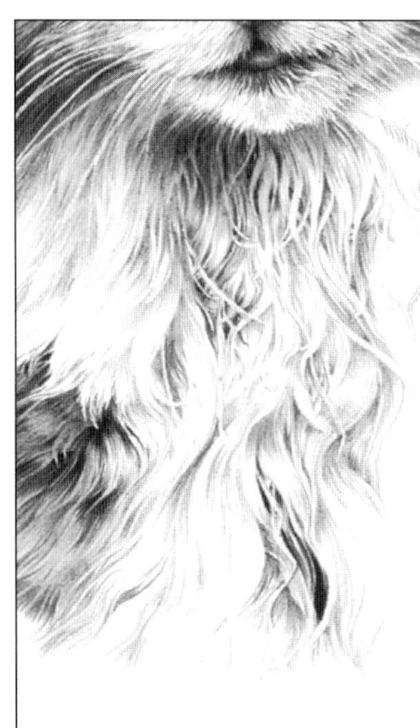

Half close yours eyes and compare the two drawings. Do you see a dark shadow line running down the neck, extending top left to lower right? Unfortunate, isn't it? I need to break this 'line' and make the eye read it differently.

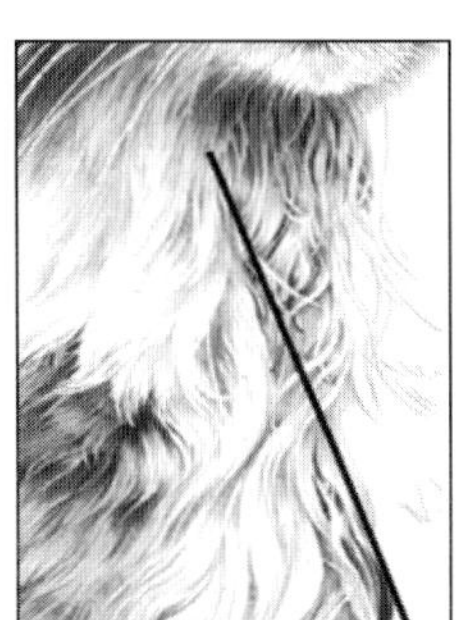

Squint now at the second version. Do you see how the distracting line has been split and replaced by a sinuous curve of white? The original line was leading the eye down and out of the drawing. Now the eye is gently directed to circle and settle elsewhere in the study.

Note that the erased areas have not been completely obliterated. Instead a shadow of the previous drawing has been allowed to remain, adding to the sense of reality, which can rarely be read perfectly. This is what I'm doing here - producing delicate forms, that cannot be understood completely, and providing occasional detailed depths and crests to satisfy the eye and allow the brain to classify the area.

The brain, as I've explained, is a great 'classifier', never happier than when it can pigeonhole something and put a name to it. Learn to use this to your advantage. Supply 'labels' in specific areas of less detailed work and the brain will accept what you have drawn as perfect reality.

STAGE 20:

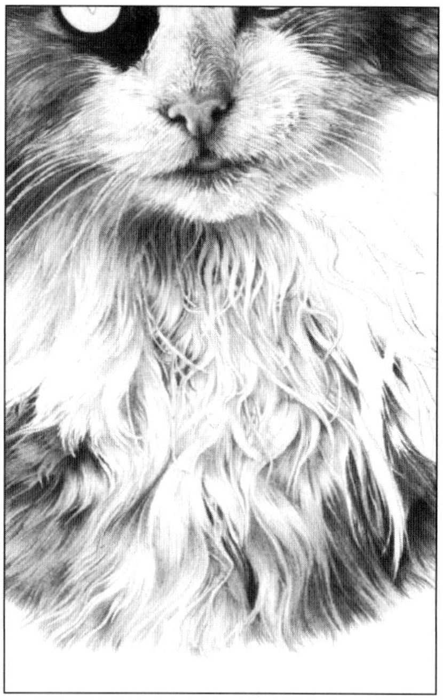

Well, I made a complete mess of it today. I was not in the mood to draw at all but, despite knowing better, I decided to continue and completely lost the plot. These things happen. So the first job today is to stand back and re-evaluate what it is I'm trying to achieve - then take out an eraser and start removing most (or all!) of today's drawing. It is far too complex and overworked!

When I was working on the central section (below the chin and on down) I had a mental picture of what I wanted to the right of it. This was smooth, almost unbroken hair with very little detail. Keeping this in mind I was attempting to bridge the gap but I didn't succeed in gradually simplifying the section I was working on. This 'bridging' technique is one I often use, but this time to little avail. However, I won't touch the offending area until tomorrow. When I uncover the drawing it will be seen afresh and solutions may suggest themselves.

This morning, it doesn't look as bad as I had feared. In fact a lot can remain although I need to formulate a plan of action to regain an overall feeling of reality. The problem is that I've been indecisive about where the white finishes and the tan begins and, as a result, the white does not presently follow any proper rules of nature. The expectation is that the white front should be smoother and less complex and distracting to the eye. And it should either join the tan area in a low sweeping curve or the tan should be lifted to underlie the white, whereas the two now meet in a disjointed, untidy and unnatural way.

STAGE 21:

Very strange! I was expecting to work the eraser on the right-hand half but instead attacked the left. I think I knew all along that the white edge had to be lowered but I was protecting my previous drawing. This is never a good idea - if it has to go then go it must. Besides, erasing can be made to leave a faint shadow, which can be worked back up again if you decide you've erased in error.

I'm a little happier now. The boundary between tan and white now has a softer look but I need to emphasise the overall shaping more. The emphasis has to be extremely subtle but I can use it, I think, to curve the ends of the white hairs into the body so they are toned down to blend more comfortably into the tan, which I can also lighten if required.

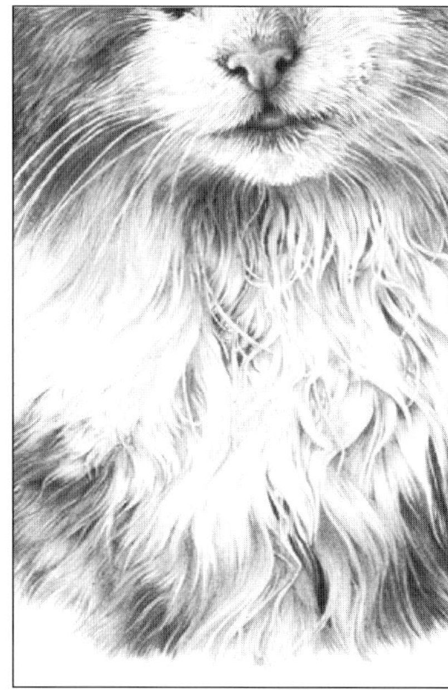

But, for now, I'm going to concentrate on the right side of the face and work my way down the body. Finally I plan to correct any unnecessary imbalance between the two sides.

STAGE 22:

An hour's work and suddenly an improvement is evident. As soon as the shadowed side of the body was established it defined the strength of the highlights on the other side. What this drawing is going through is the 'ugly duckling' stage. This common and dispiriting occurrence is the point at which the likely outlook is a failed drawing. Often the drawing looks flat and lifeless, the tones can appear to be muddied and no amount of highlight treatment will lift the study into the realms of three-dimensions. With experience, this stage can be identified early on in its development and passed through without causing much harm. The less experienced should be warned to expect this troublesome stage and to not despair or even abandon the drawing. Instead a policy of forging ahead should be adopted. Accept the apparent faults for now and keep drawing because something further on in the development of the drawing may set it alight. It might be a simple shadow or a single sharply drawn feature. Whatever it is, its creation is suddenly going to cause everything else to fall into place.

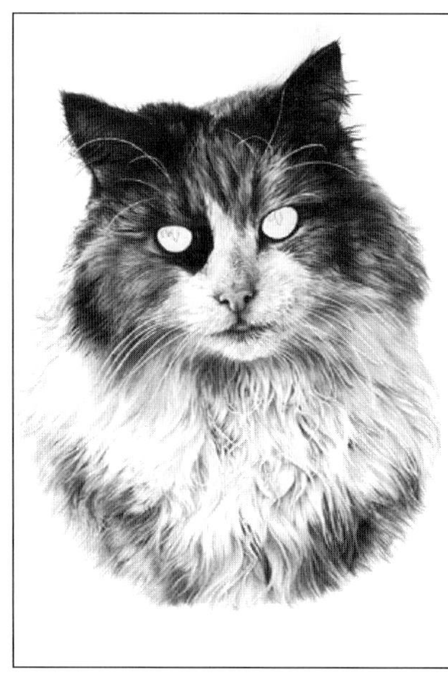

Occasionally the occurrence is so magical as to be memorable, as with my drawing "Early morn at Witton Marsh". I drew the misty background first and worked forward over the next 115 hours. I was reasonably pleased but always a little regretful that a certain 'spark' seemed to be missing. Then, in the last half hour of the drawing, I drew the two circling Lapwings and suddenly the background receded at great speed before my eyes. The whole composition gained an incredible depth and a life I could never have planned for. It doesn't happen often but it's a great feeling when it does!

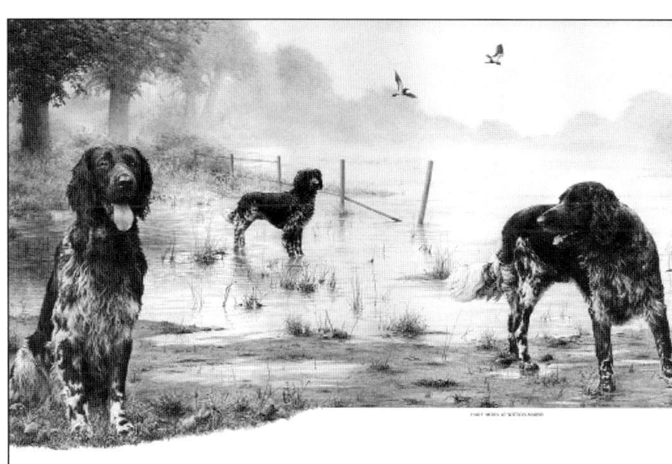

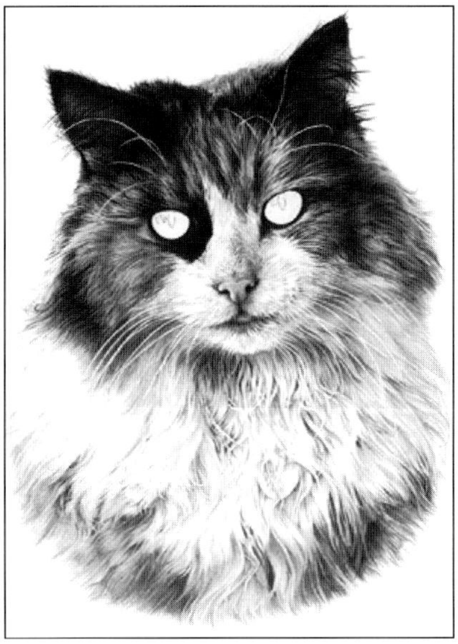

Stage 23:

I've decided to visually widen the face. I've done this by extending the dark marking below the cheek out to the left. And... well, it had to be done... I've once again taken the eraser to the lower left area to extend the white further down and sought to soften the tan/white boundary even more.

To compensate for this increased visual width I've restored the balance by extending the depth of the drawing. The tan of the body, at the base of the drawing, has been generally lowered.

Well, I've been putting off drawing the eyes for no good reason so I reckon it's finally 'eyes' time.

Step 24:

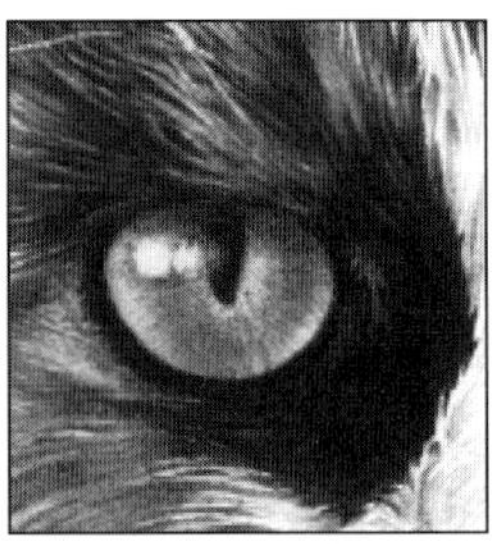

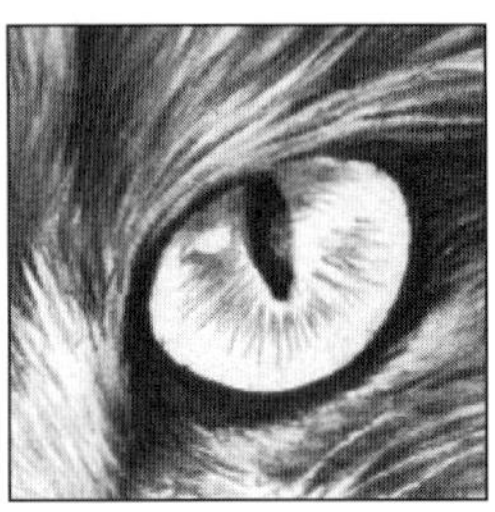

I've drawn cat's eyes on a few occasions before so I understand their make-up and peculiarities but I am going to take a little artistic licence. I'm going to draw the eyes light - lighter than they are in reality - in order to prevent the shadows of the brows being so dark that the top of the eyes get lost under them. The idea from the start was to give the top of her eyes a good rounded 'friendly' curve so this must be readily apparent in the finished drawing. What I want to avoid is the human flat-topped eye that signals 'scowl'.

Points to bear in mind when drawing a cat's eyes include the angles of the pupils - these are not parallel but angle inwards towards each other at the top. Also the irises lighten very slightly as they approach the centre and often have a thin, subtle highlight at the very edge as they curve slightly into the pupil. The subject of drawing eyes in general is covered in a later chapter.

The drawing of the second eye has just commenced. An initial suggestion of the striations has been drawn in (using 4H indenting) and the striations themselves have been used to mark the lightening of tone around the pupil. The shadow of the brow has been noted and the positioning of the highlight.

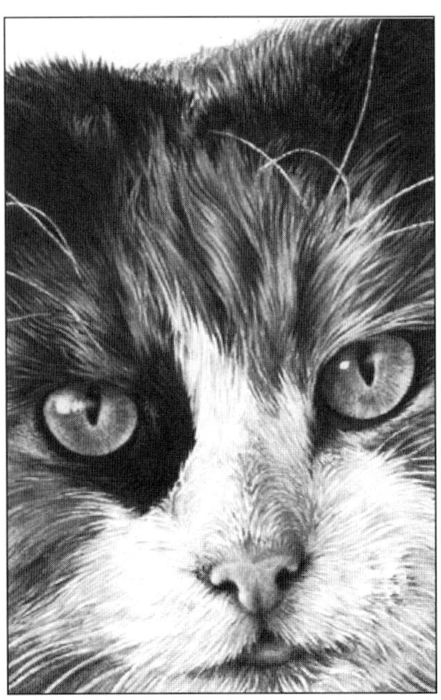

Step 25:

The second eye is complete and the first eye adjusted slightly. Also a little work has been carried out to the crown of the head to soften the black to tan junction and to round off the valley between them.

I'm pleased with this and it's time to stop. There are, and always will be, areas that I wish I'd tackled differently but there

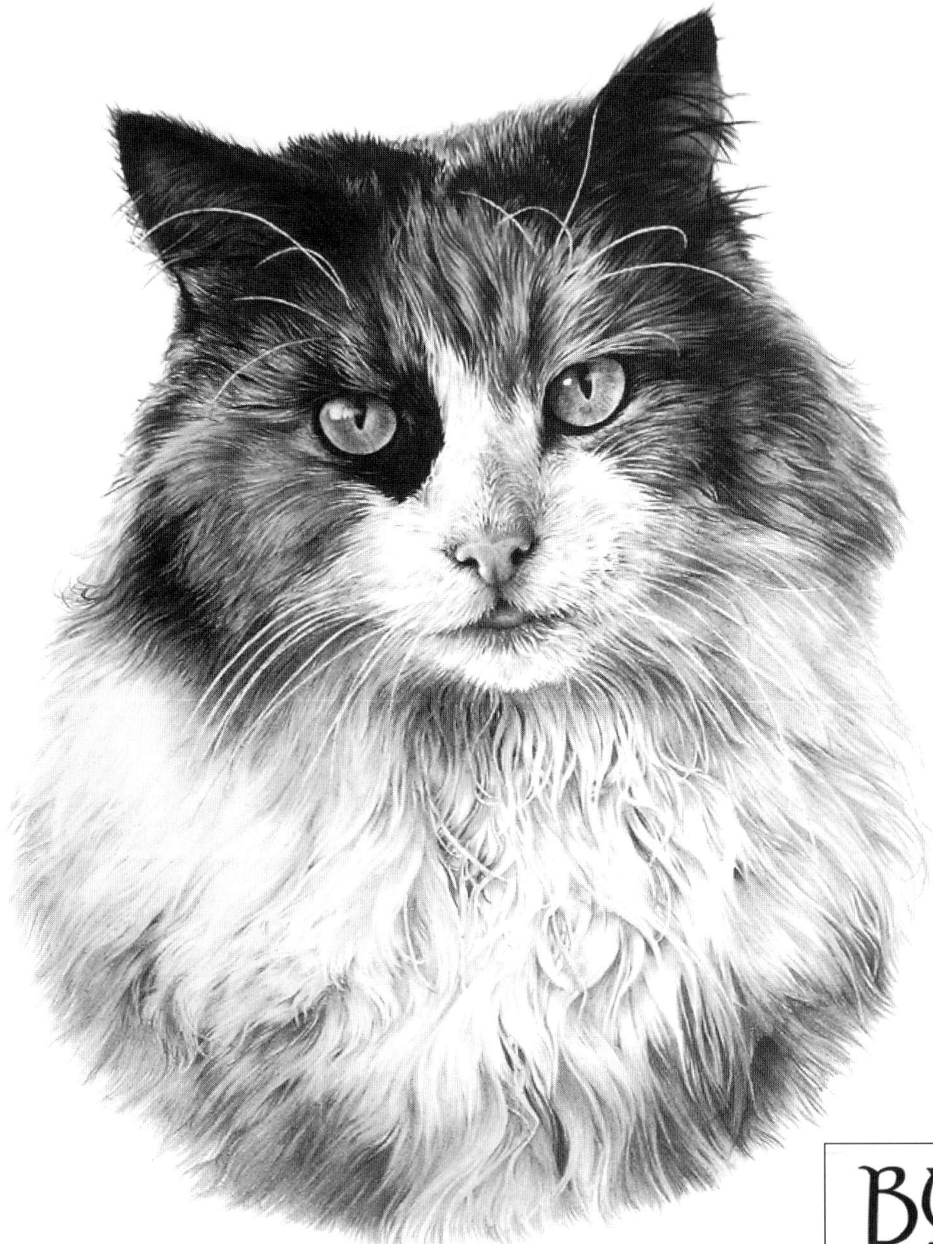

Image size: 5" x 7" (12.5 x 17.8 cm)   Total drawing time: 47 hours
Tortoiseshell Cat by Mike Sibley ©

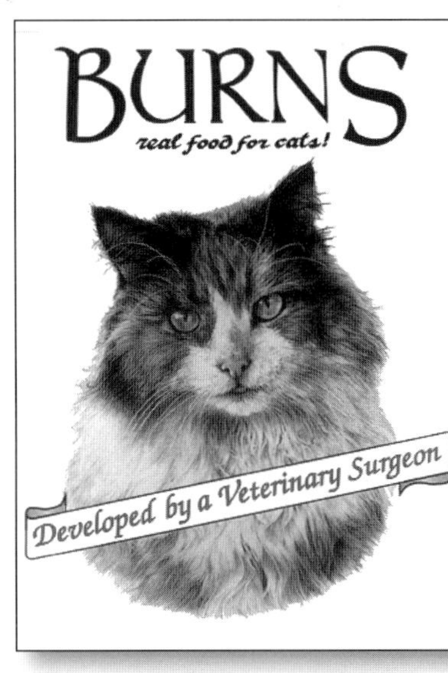

...and here is how Burns Pet Nutrition used Clarrie on their packaging!

are no major changes to be made and any further work will probably only serve to muddy the detail. I've achieved what I set out to do, even if the result was not quite what I expected.

The decision has been made so I'll underline my decision by fixing the drawing. I used Winsor & Newton's Artists' Fixative for Pastel, Charcoal and Pencil, which allows a measure of reworking if required. It also dries with a matt finish that removes the majority of the sheen from the graphite. It's quite a magical moment as, with the sheen banished from the darks, I get to see the drawing with the full tonal range for the first time.

Drawing Ellipses

A sideways look at circles...

'AN ELLIPSE IS SIMPLY A CIRCLE SEEN IN PERSPECTIVE AND THEREFORE CONFORMS TO THE CIRCLE'S RULES.'

Drawing ellipses freehand can appear quite daunting at first but, like most problems you will encounter, they can be broken down into more manageable forms.

Let's get the bad news out of the way right now - to be believable, an ellipse must be drawn very accurately. The eye can readily detect any irregularity in a shape that it fully understands. A square that does not have sides of equal length, a circle that is not circular, and an ellipse that deviates from perfection is immediately noted as being not what it claims to be. More precisely, it is not what the eye expects to see in that situation and is detected as being 'foreign' or unnatural. Any attempt you were making at depicting reality will have been lost - no matter how accurate or technically perfect the rest of your drawing is. In short, a circular circle is accepted in passing and the overall reality of the scene is maintained. The same is true of the ellipse.

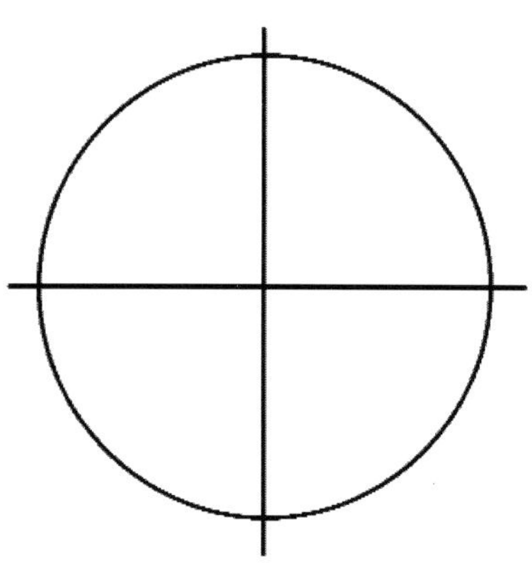

All segments are identical

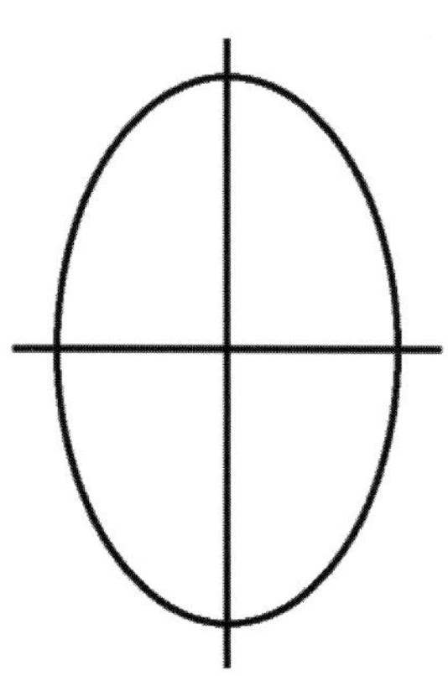

Dividing the ellipse into quarters

What is an Ellipse?

An ellipse is simply a circle seen in perspective and therefore conforms to the circle's rules. This is an important concept to keep in mind. Fortunately the rules of a circle are quite simple:

- It consists of arcs.
- It contains no straight lines.
- It contains identical segments when divided into quarters.

BREAKING THE PROBLEM DOWN

As the ellipse and circle share the same rules, an ellipse always contains four identical segments. To study this, draw an ellipse using an ellipse template. Or use the circle/ellipse tool of a computer graphics programme to draw one and then print it out. Draw a line vertically through the ellipse to divide it equally in half then draw another across it. It becomes immediately apparent that each quarter is identical to the others - just the orientation is different. The top left segment is a mirror image of the top right, which is a vertical mirror image of the bottom right segment below it. We've just reduced the problem by three-quarters and it's getting easier by the minute!

Study the geometry

Now let's draw a box around our ellipse so we can properly study the geometry of one of those segments. The box will enable you to use negative space to better understand the route of the arc. If you're right-handed I suggest you concentrate on the top left segment - using the natural movement of your wrist, this is probably the first arc you will want to draw. Notice that both ends are 'flat' to the sides of the box - an ellipse never comes to a point. Notice also how the arc, as it travels from top to bottom, gently unwinds from a tight to a gentle curve. It does this smoothly with no hint of a straight section - this is, remember, a circle seen in perspective so only curves are involved.

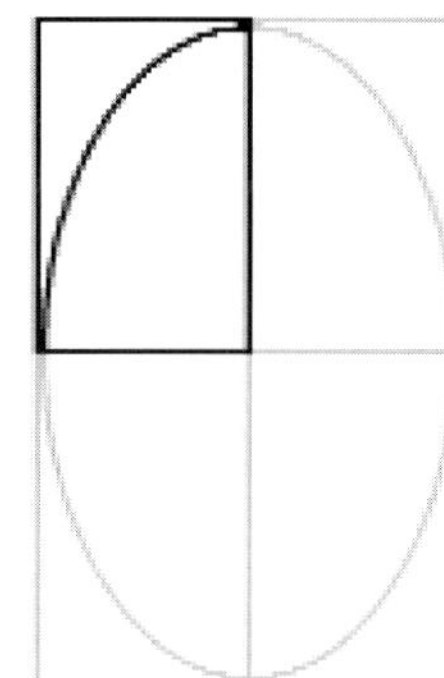

Study the top-left segment

Drawing an ellipse

Keep your template or computer-drawn examples handy. In time you'll be able to discard them and draw with understanding but they'll help you to draw the right curves in the following exercises. We'll start by repeating what we've learned so far but in reverse.

Draw a square in perspective

First, draw a square in perspective on a vertical plane. A square about 8cm high by 4cm (3"×1½") will be about right. By keeping it small you don't need to move your arm during the exercise and you can see the result without moving your eyes. Now divide it vertically in half - but you have to allow for the perspective foreshortening. Simply draw two diagonal lines to connect the opposite corners, and where they cross is the correct centre. Now divide it in half horizontally to form the horizon.

Let's get started. We'll begin in the top left segment but, if you're left-handed, you might prefer to start top right. Study again the curve that your template produced then try to repeat the geometry in your top left segment. Starting almost flat to the top line of the square begin to curve down towards the side's halfway point, gently reducing the curvature as you go (*fig 1*). Aim to meet the side in the same 'flat' manner that you started. It's more important to know where you're going than where you are so, as you draw your curve, look at the spot you are aiming for rather than the line you are drawing - look ahead of your pencil point to its destination. Getting this first curve right is important - everything that follows is just going to be a repeat of it.

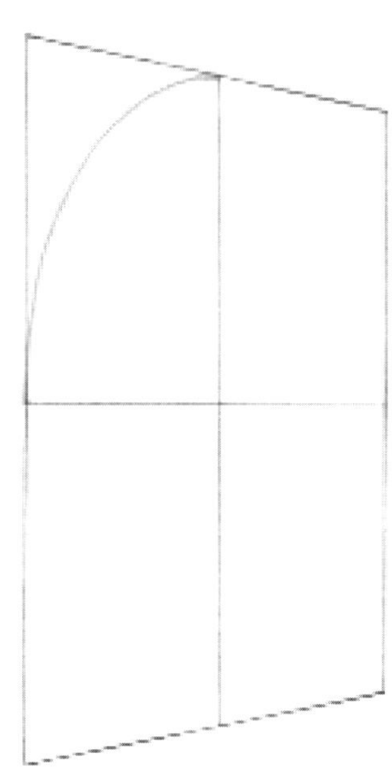

Fig 1

Now we have our first curve all we need do is copy it. I admit this is easier said than done but it gets easier with practice.

'If you are having trouble working out why it looks wrong, try viewing your ellipse in a mirror or turning it upside down to give your eye a fresh way of looking at it.'

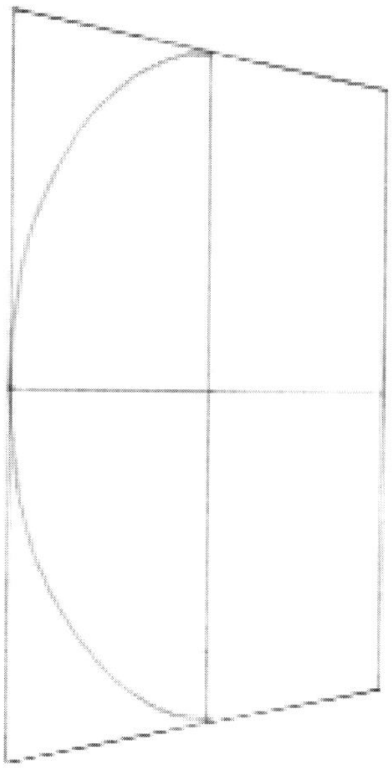

Fig 2

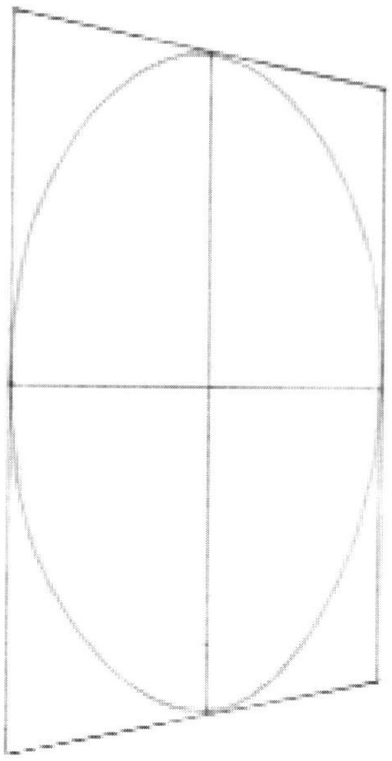

Fig 3

Begin by copying the curve you just drew into the segment below - but in reverse (*fig 2*). You will probably find it easier to do this if you turn your paper around.

Finally complete the last two segments. Turn your paper around again to help make use of the natural movement of your wrist and hand then copy the curves you just drew as mirror images (*fig 3*).

Does your ellipse look right? Are there any flat sections? Do your lines meet smoothly as they pass from segment to segment? If you are having trouble working out why it looks wrong, try viewing your ellipse in a mirror or turning it upside down to give your eye a fresh way of looking at it. If your paper is thin enough to see through when you hold it up to a light, fold it in half along the horizontal dividing line - the two halves should match exactly so it will be easy to spot any errors. Having found the problem, erase the lines in that area leaving just a shadow to guide you. Now redraw to correct the flaw. Remember, the eye can always spot a fault with an ellipse so when it looks right, it is right!

The more you practice drawing ellipses, the easier it becomes. I doubt that's it's possible to draw a perfect ellipse first time but your first attempts will get closer and closer to the finished shape.

The Horizon factor

As an ellipse is a circle in perspective it follows that it must conform to the rules of perspective too. This is easier to handle if you treat an ellipse as a circle distorted within a square conforming to perspective - just as we've been doing - and you

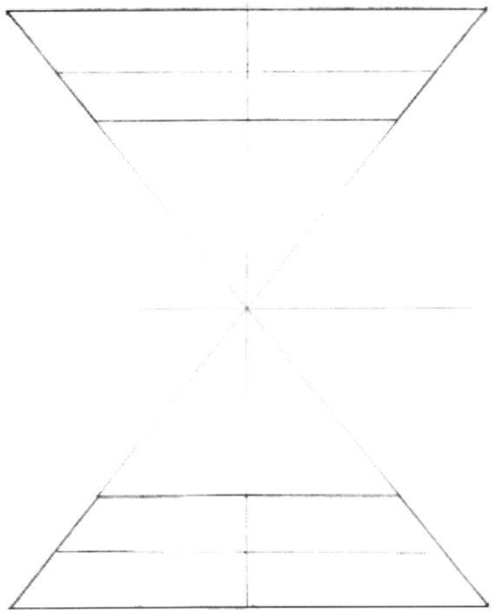

1 - Draw the horizon, mark your vanishing point, draw two squares of identical width in perspective, and divide the squares into quarters.

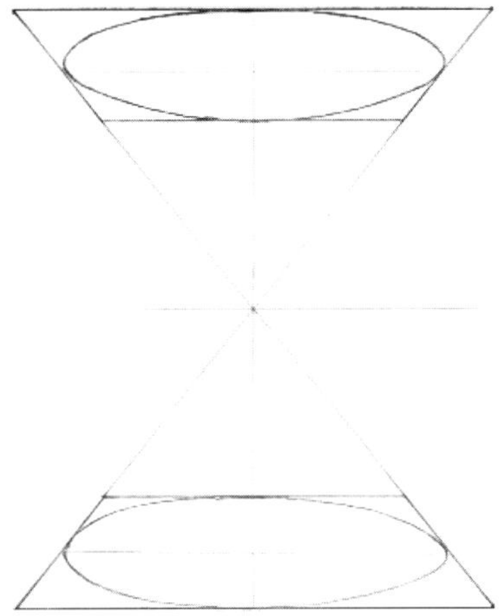

2 - Construct ellipses within both squares - turning the paper if it helps you to draw them.

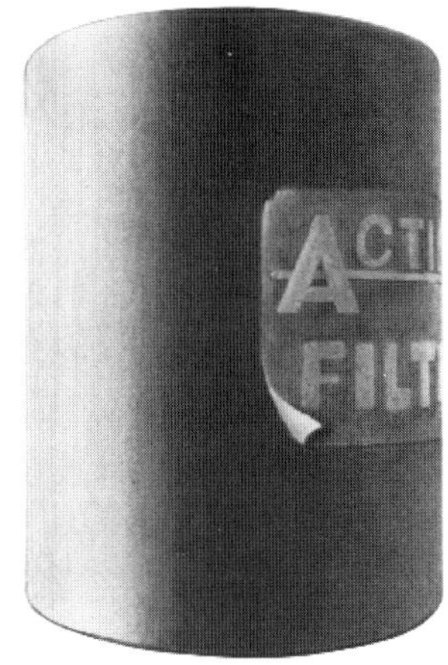

3 - Connect the outside edges and add shading to form a three-dimensional cylinder.

must also take its distance above or below the horizon into account. If you hold up a tin can in front of you and lift it above your eye-level (the horizon) you will be looking up at the bottom of the can; below your eye-level and you will see it from above. Hold it straight in front of you and you will see the top half of the can from below and the bottom half from above.

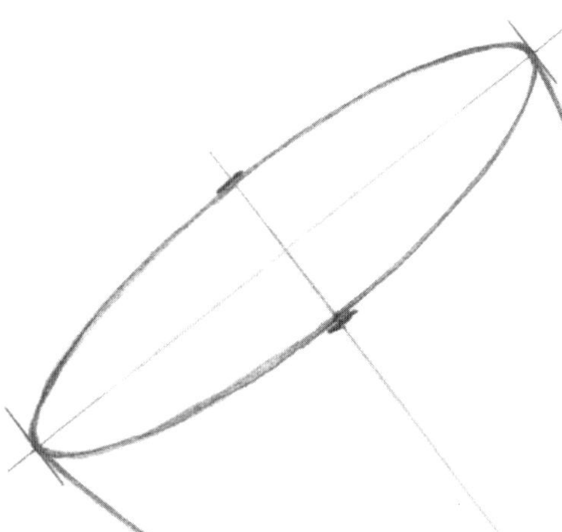

Once you understand the basic geometry of the curves involved you will probably find it sufficient to only lightly draw length and width guidelines with points marking the required dimensions.

If you need to draw a large ellipse, drawing a smaller version first will often assist you - small enough so you can see the whole ellipse without having to move your eyes. You can then enlarge this onto your final drawing surface (using any means

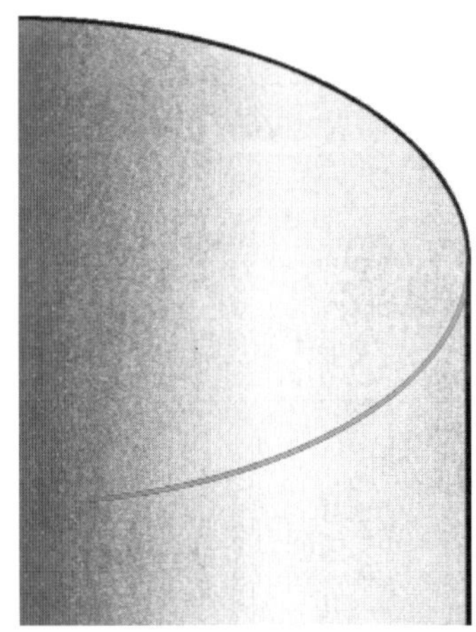

Note how the elliptical top of a cylinder 'flows' seamlessly into the side.

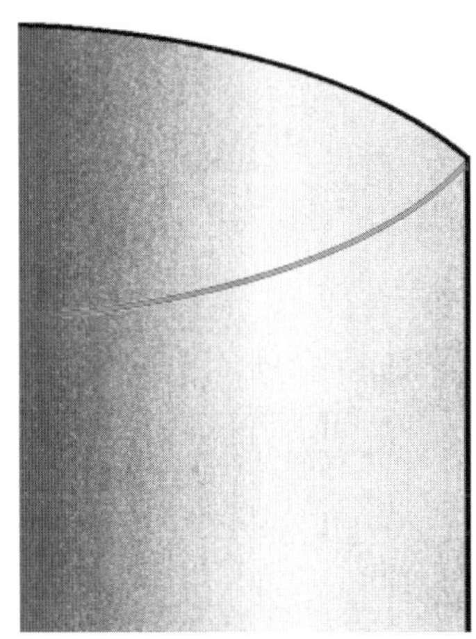

There is never a sharp join.

you prefer from projection to mechanical resizing) or use it as a visual template to guide you when you draw it full size.

Ellipse within ellipse

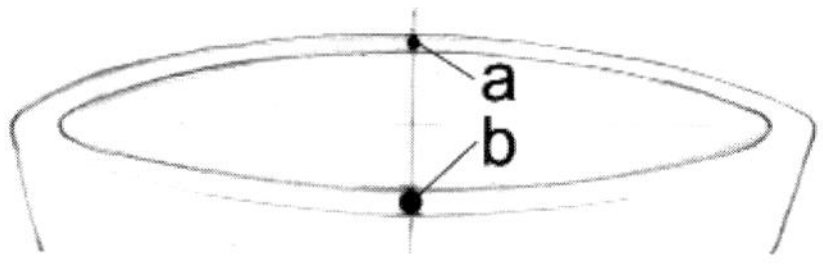

The rear wall is further away than the front so a is narrower than b.

There will be times when you need to draw one ellipse (or more) inside another. For example, when drawing a round, hollow object with substantially thick walls, such as a terracotta flowerpot. In this particular case you need to draw just the top half of the outer ellipse and to shift the inner ellipse slightly higher to account for perspective (*shown left*). The lower half of the outer ellipse needs to exist only in your mind as it's solely defined by the lighting and shadow of the front face. If you attempt to draw this line first, however lightly, you stand a good chance of it remaining to haunt you - even after you've erased it, the slight indentation may attract extra graphite from your shading and be forever present!

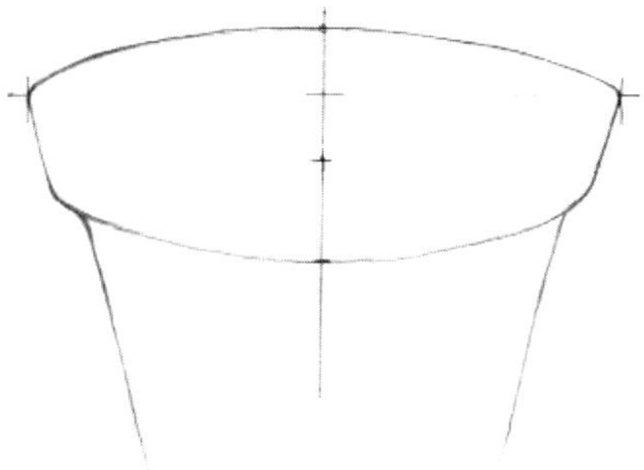

Mark but omit the lower half of the top ellipse.

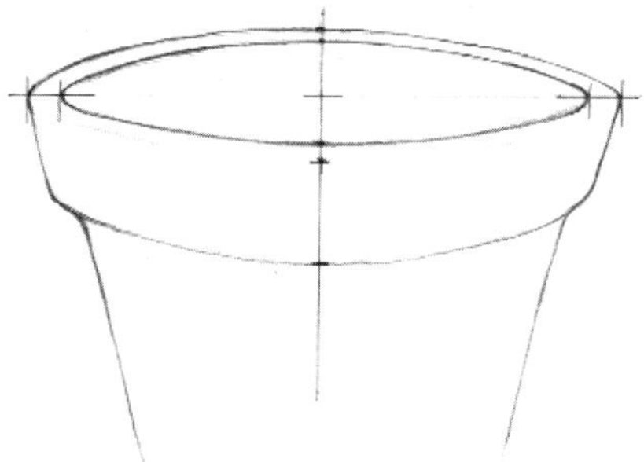

Mark the position of the inner ellipse and draw it.

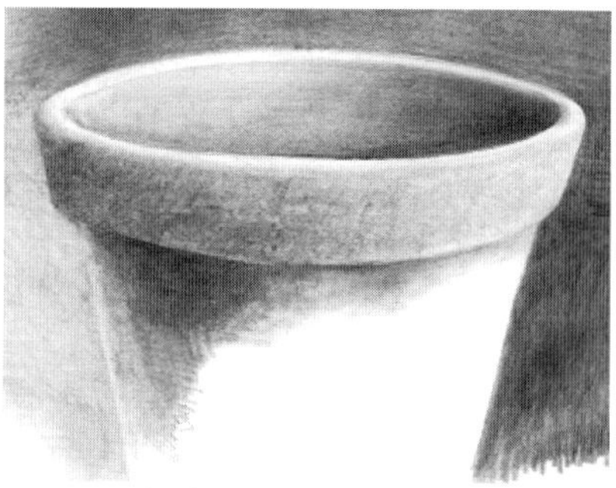

Use shading to complete the lower edge of the top ellipse.

Is this flowerpot perfectly elliptical? Not quite - but I decided to leave it. Little in life is perfect and pots from kilns often show flaws. In this case I decided that the slight distortion

The wheels and lamp housing of this stick-back gig are as perfectly elliptical as I can draw them. Any deviation would ruin the attempted reality.

The old tins on the shelf however gain a feeling of age and use from being a little inaccurate.

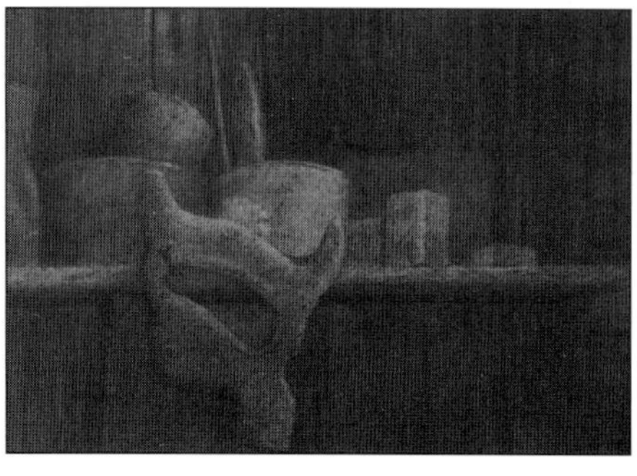

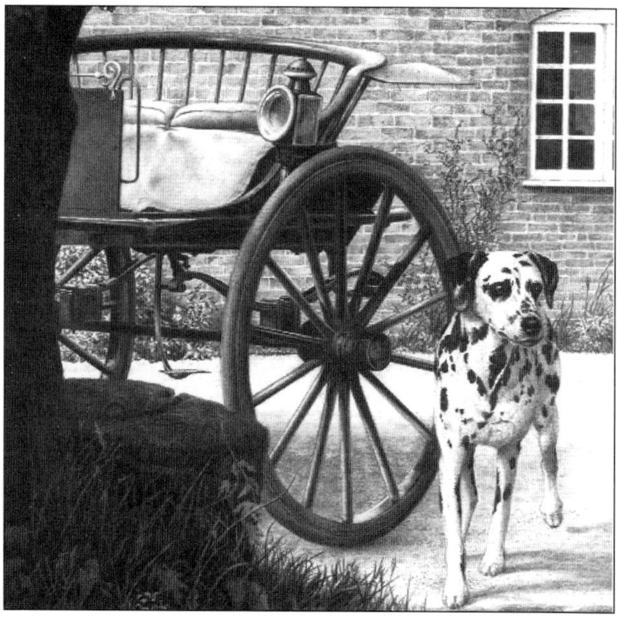

added to, rather than detracted from, the reality. But often ellipses have to be perfect to be believable and time spent perfecting their appearance is greatly rewarded.

The ellipse and its benefits

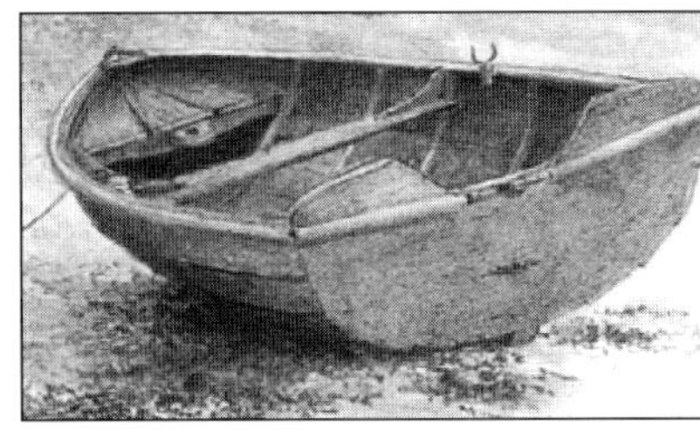

You may feel that ellipses are not something that you will often draw. But being able to construct them aids you in many other ways too. The drawing of the back of the carriage shown below left, the curve of its step support bar, and the semi-elliptical spring beneath the rear all involve ellipses or portions of them. Even non-elliptical but sinuous curves are simpler to understand and draw with the experience gained from drawing ellipses. Boats, for example, often possess quite complex curves and even partial ellipses, such as the internal ribs, rowlocks and the transom (the 'blunt end' for landlubbers).

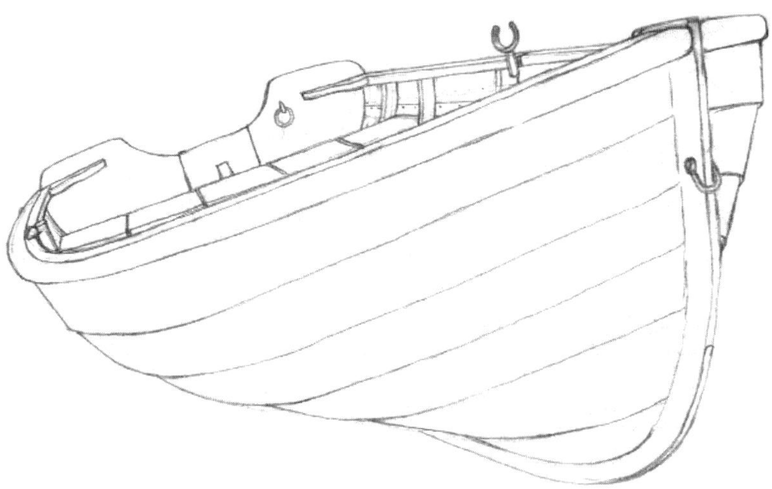

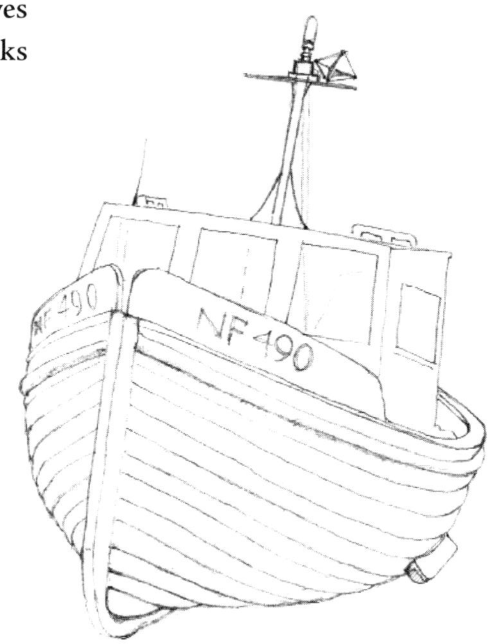

Drawing huge ellipses

As a graphite artist, working with tools that make small marks, you are perhaps unlikely to want to draw enormous ellipses. But maybe you'll want to create a gallery display involving an ellipse, realise a mural or sculpture - or just create an archway through your kitchen wall. Fortunately there is a well-tried system, often known as the Pin & String method, which offers a practical and accurate solution. You could use this system for almost any size of ellipse but let's assume that our goal is one that measures 122cm (48") wide by 61cm (24") high.

All you need is two drawing pins or nails, a pencil, and a piece of string. Choose string that doesn't stretch, or you could use fishing line or picture-hanging wire. The size of the ellipse determines the placement of the pins and the length of the string.

Draw a horizontal line the length of the required ellipse then mark the centre point and draw a vertical line through it, the same as the height of the ellipse (*fig 1*).

Next, you need to know where to push in the pins. Divide the width AB by two (122/2=61cm in this case). Measure that distance out from point C and where it meets line AB, mark

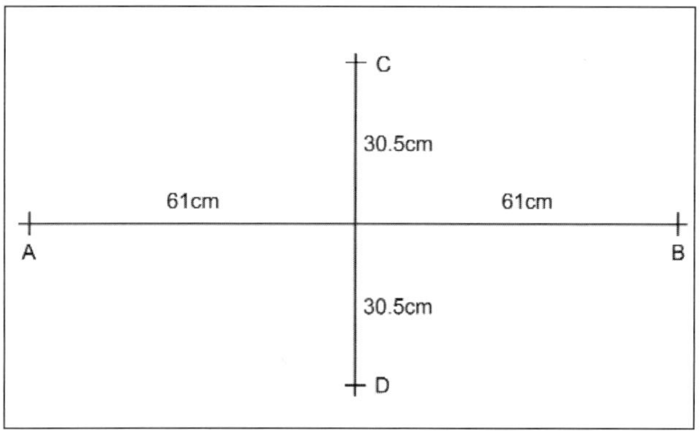

Fig 1. Width of ellipse AB = 122cm (48")
Height of ellipse CD = 61cm (24")

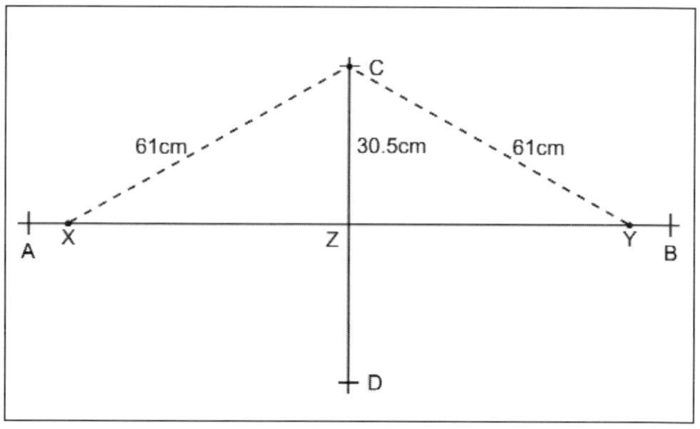

Fig 2. If you're mathematically-minded XZ=52.83cm using Pythagoras' theorem.

that point (X), then repeat on the other side (Y). Push pins into marks X and Y and a third at point C (*fig 2*).

Now pass the string around all three pins to form a loop, pull it taut and tie the ends together.

That's all there is to it. Just pull out the pin at C, place your pencil point in the same position inside the string and use it to control the path of the pencil. Remember to keep the string taut at all times and you can draw a perfect ellipse!

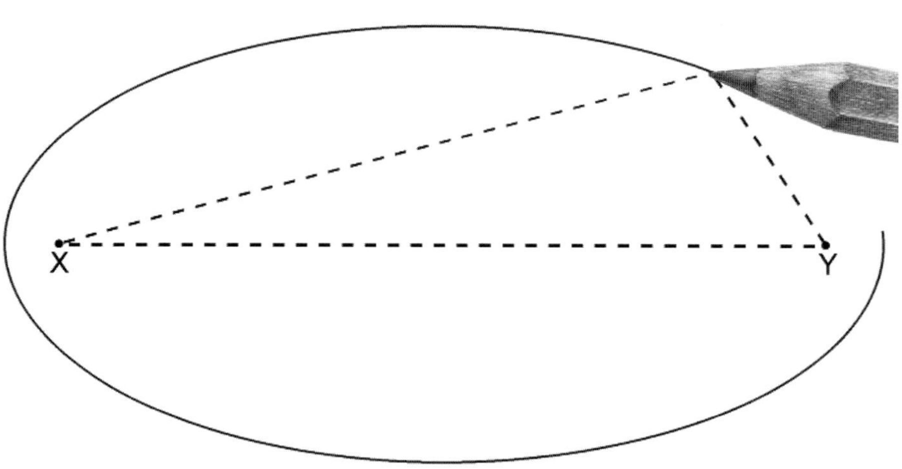

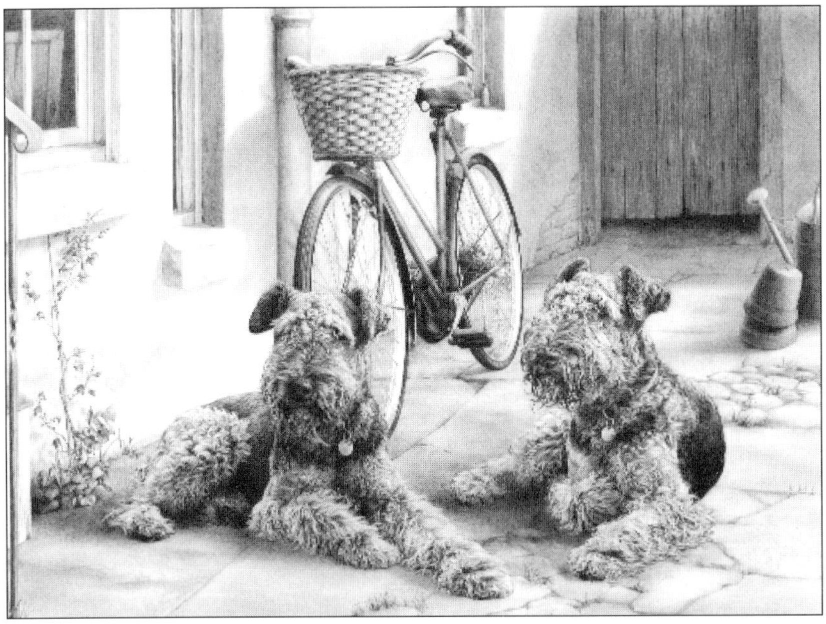

Ellipses are a invaluble tool in an artist's range of skills. Here is a range of work showing how and where ellipses are used in portraying everyday objects.

Visiting Aunt Maud: Ellipses galore in this work! From the scroll work on the hand rail of the steps, the bicycle tyres, the dog tags, the upturned pots and watering can, even to the arc of the bicycles basket - ellipses are integeral to this drawing.

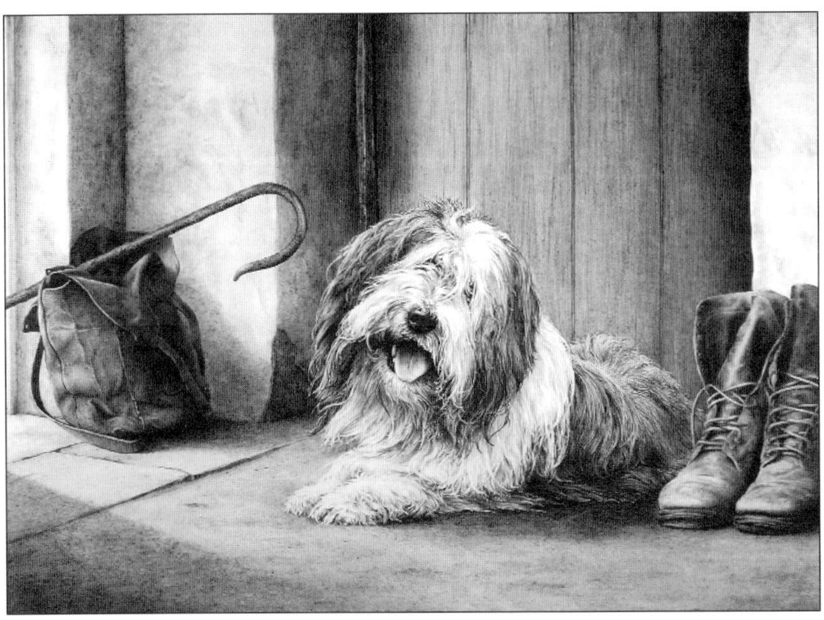

Ready and Waiting: A more unusual use of an ellipse - the 'hook' of the shepherd's crook is a modified ellipse.

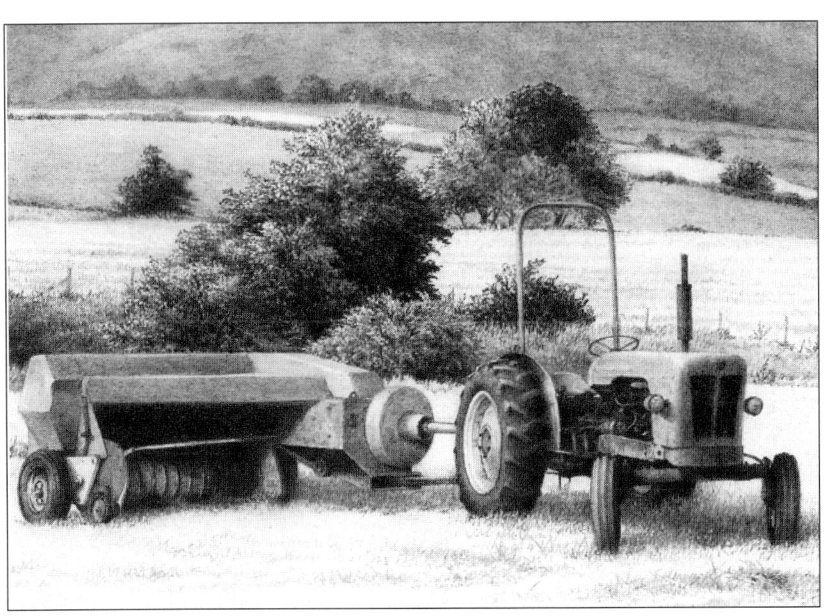

A detail from Done Balin':
More ellipses! The tractor's steering wheel, headlights, and rollbar, and the baler's flywheel cover. And ellipses within ellipses, make up the tractor's wheels.

Drawing Textures
The Rough with the Smooth...

'DRAWING TEXTURES CONVINCINGLY IS AIDED BY A SOUND UNDERSTANDING OF THE NATURE OF THE SUBJECT YOU WISH TO PORTRAY.'

Drawing textures is about the art of illusion. A successful drawing should make you believe that what you are seeing possesses a sense of reality. Even though you know it is an illusion, the signals contained within the image trigger the same reactions in your brain as its real life equivalent.

At the core of drawing any texture is the ability to mentally experience it, to 'feel' the texture as you work. If you're drawing from life, touch it, run your fingers over the surface. If it's imaginary, mentally do the same; imagine it under your fingertips, study the surface and describe it to yourself. Does it reflect light and, if it does, how much? Is it solid and smooth, or soft and decaying? Does it drape over the article beneath or is it stiff and unyielding? With this knowledge comes the ability to extract the visual clues or keys that make the surface look the way it does, and to draw the experience rather than attempting to painstakingly recreate the actual texture.

Drawing textures convincingly is aided by a sound understanding of the nature of the subject you wish to portray. The more personal the knowledge, the more effective the result, and the easier the task. For example, creating a believable composition involving a grassy bank with protruding rocks is greatly simplified if you possess knowledge of the way rocks are formed. Similarly, personal experience of different woods helps you create believable wood textures, whether they are polished, sawn, planed or even decaying.

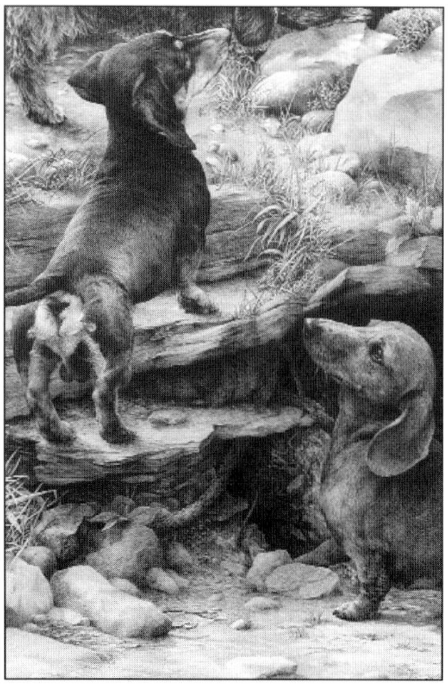

Sedimentary rocks, such as this sandstone, can provide useful steps and stages in a composition.

Fortunately for me, I studied geology at school and once managed a timber yard. But even the simple experience of polishing the dining-room table will teach you a lot if you take the time to actually study the surface beneath your duster. Wood is not just wood; all rocks are not smooth and grey. You must ask and answer questions of what you see and touch. The more you do so, the greater will be your store of available tactile and textural information.

Understanding the structure of your subject permits you to extract the key visual elements, and draw it convincingly without resorting to slavish copying. On seeing a picture of a hand, for example, your brain will analyse the image and search its memory for matching classifications. In an instant it will deduce that it is of human origin, whether the person is male or female, the age of that person, and possibly their position in society. To draw realistically you must first consciously ask yourself why you deduced that information and what keys triggered those deductions. Then look deeper, ignoring the hand as a known object, and extract the physical information. What is it about the skin that tells you this is the hand of a manual labourer or a society hostess? What is the principal key?

Now look deeper still and explore the shapes, the way they interact with each other, the highlights and shadows, the proportions of each element. Break it down to its essentials in the way that a cartoonist does, and you will discover why it looks like a hand to you - even though it's a two-dimensional pictorial representation. When you possess both the technical and conceptual knowledge, the actual physical techniques of drawing are greatly simplified. You can now reconstruct the hand in almost any form you choose but the keys you include or emphasise will send the desired signals. However abstract your drawing, it will be correctly read as having the same properties as your source.

Tip

Occasionally, when first beginning a texture that's new to you, a 'happy accident' may occur that correctly defines the texture. Be on the lookout for such occurrences, immediately extend the area and make a mental note of what you are doing. Now use the newfound technique as a basis for the remainder of your subject.

Pattern as a tool

Many surface textures contain repetitive elements. You need to detect and observe patterns when drawing or studying an object for drawing. Some patterns may be very repetitive, such as the spiralling twists in rope or the weave of cloth. Others will be more abstract, less repetitive in terms of exact replication, as exhibited by woodgrain around knots, where the pattern is a repeating growth habit. As an exercise, try drawing a flat area of woodgrain. The distance between the light spring and darker summer bands of grain is one repetitive element. Once you have the bands spaced convincingly, or any similar repetitive element of any texture, you need only repeat the pattern with local variations. This frees your mind to concentrate on form, lighting, and other considerations.

Tip

Look for adjacent, contrasting textures. By applying emphasis to one, you can increase the perceived visual intensity of both surfaces.

Contrast smooth with rough and both will increase in effectiveness.

Starting out

Don't be nervous of beginning a texture that is new to you. Analyse first then break the area down into manageable parts. Instead of worrying about creating the overall look, search instead for the area that you most feel comfortable with. Just

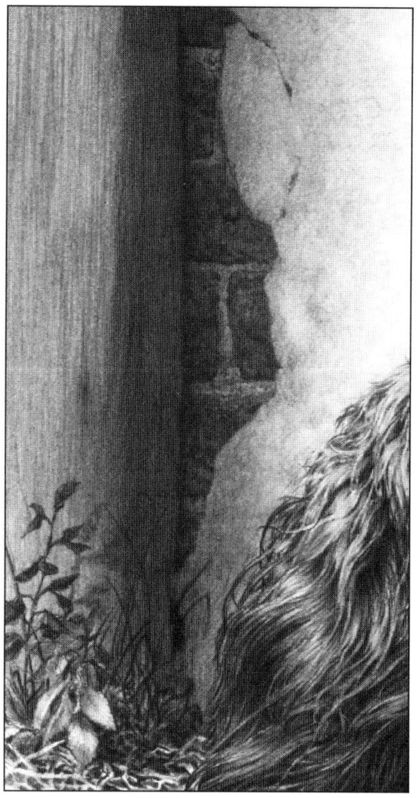

This incidental use of bricks employs just highlights and shadows to describe form and texture, and the contrast between brick and mortar to send the 'this is brick' signal.

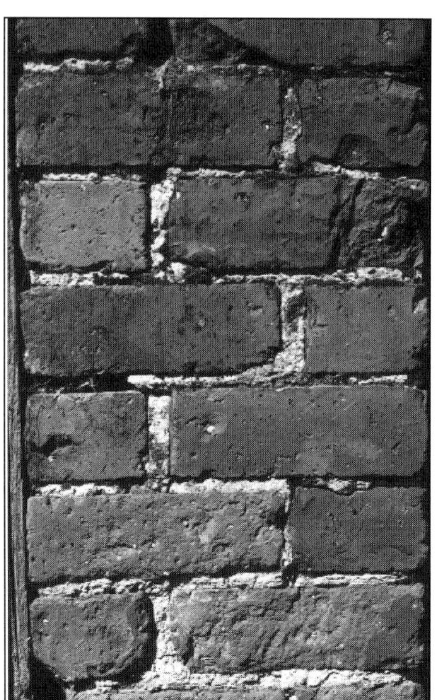

Weathered machine-made bricks and lime mortar.

concentrate on drawing that one small area. If your initial attempts at reproducing the texture fail then erase and try again, or experiment on a scrap of similar paper. When that first area succeeds, complete it and extend it into the next section. The drawing of this new area is now made simpler in light of your previous experience, which can be used as a guide or starting point. Master simple areas before you deal with the more complex ones.

As your discovery of how to create realistic looking textures increases, you're on your way to creating realistic looking drawings. The emphasis here is on the word 'looking'. Carbon copying of reference material is not required, just your interpretation with the inclusion of the visual keys. Let's study a few examples...

Drawing Bricks

Analysis: Bricks may be smooth or rough to the touch, or a combination of both. Machine-made bricks measure 3" x 9" (7.5 x 23cm), a length three times that of their height. Modern bricks, from gas-fired kilns, possess a uniformity of surface texture. Older bricks, from coal or coke fired kilns, markedly exhibit surface variations, both visual and textural. Hand-made bricks, at least the ones I dig up in my garden, measure 2½" x 9½" and have a unique structure. Because they are made by clay being layered and compressed into simple wooden moulds, they have a distinct folded structure, often clearly seen on the outer faces. Other bricks, such as adobe, ash-composites and concrete, will each have their own unique textures. I will concentrate here on those that most interest me - the early twentieth century common house brick.

Clay bricks inevitably require mortar - usually in half-inch (1cm) thick bands. Again each type possesses its own characteristics so acquaint yourself with your local variations and choose the one that best suits your drawing. Modern cement-based mortar can be soulless so I have a personal preference for lime mortar, which my own house predominantly uses.

Technique: When you begin a drawing, find, or picture in your mind, a typical and suitable brick, then use that as a basis for the invention of others. To increase your store of information, study or sketch bricks at every opportunity, as they possess a fascinating variety of surfaces and features. Study the surface irregularities of older, and arguably more interesting, bricks that impart character. Note too the way that frosts often split the outer surface away from the body (known as spalding), which expose a host of interesting textures.

Oblique lighting is probably the most favourable when drawing bricks, or any texture. Direct light flattens surface details but any light hitting a brick at an angle will display surface blemishes, and enhance high spots and holes by imparting both a highlight and a starkly contrasting shadow.

Using different techniques for the bricks and mortar can be helpful. I tend to explore the surface textures of bricks with small circular or angular marks, depending on the smoothness of the surface, and often reserve a stippling technique for the mortar to reflect its granular nature.

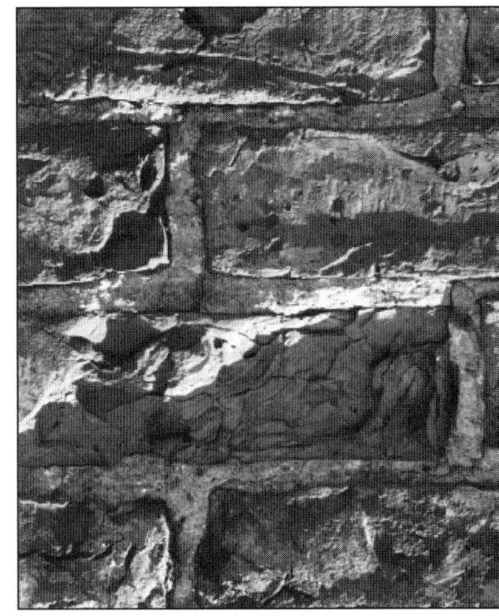

Hand-made bricks showing spalding, the folded structure, and oblique lighting enhancing the surface features.

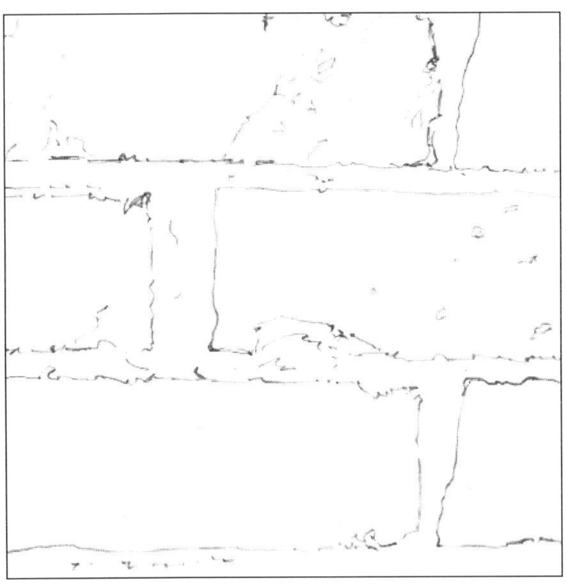

Fig 1

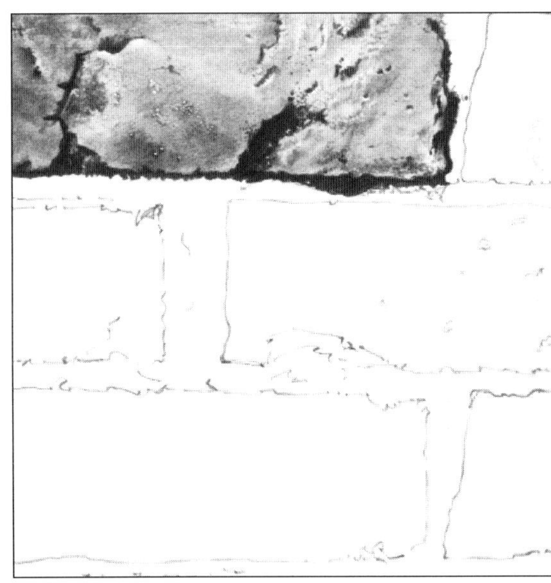

Fig 2

The initial guidelines have been drawn (*fig 1*), with indications of the principal features to remind me of what I was mentally picturing as I designed them. Even so, most features will be included as they suggest themselves - either as 'happy accidents' or to restore balance to the composition.

I can elect to begin with the mortar, bricks or both. I'll start with a brick and take it from there.

I'm enjoying this! I never know what shape or feature is going to emerge next (*fig 2*). The only known constant is the light shining down from the top left corner.

The keys I'm using are the small indentions with their internal shadow and highlighted edge, the deep fissures, and contrasts between rough and smooth areas. Final light layers of H smooth and blend the otherwise too obtrusive detail.

Tip

The more technical information you can gather about a texture, the better will be your understanding and powers of invention. However, merely drawing what you see will produce very credible results, so don't worry if the technical aspects hold no interest for you.

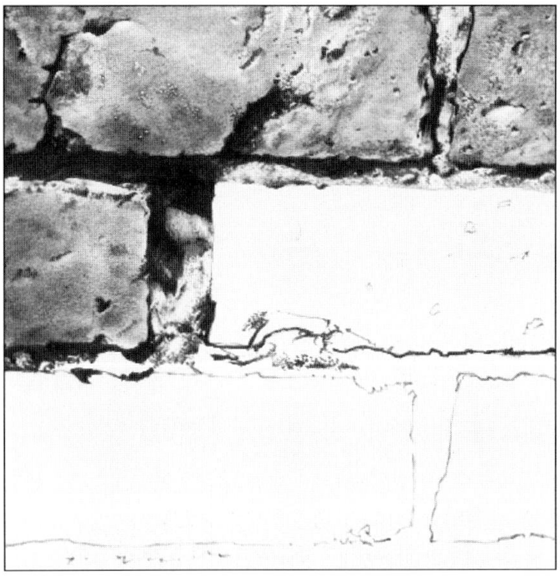

Fig 3

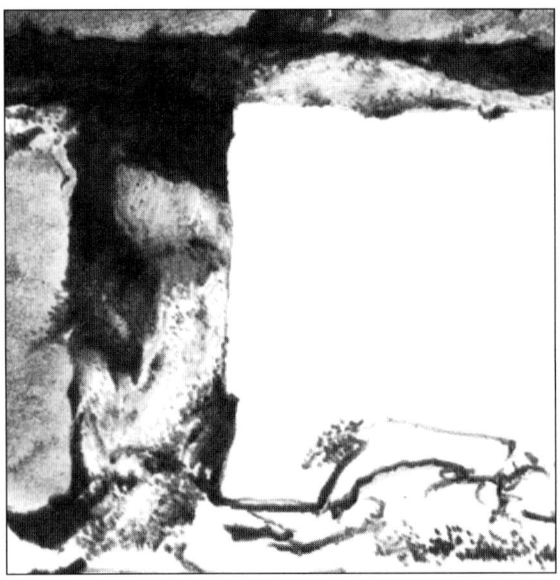

Fig 4 (2½ x enlargement)

I've begun work on the mortar using a stippling technique to build up the three-dimensional form (*fig 3*). To simplify the work I'm drawing darker than is required then finally applying Blu-Tack to reduce the strength of the tones and overall contrast. The granular structure and folded forms are the two keys that I'm using. I'm attempting a look of age coupled with a rough application.

The mortar (*fig 4*) shows the use of stippling to build up the tones and impart a granular appearance. Blu-Tack has been used to brighten the highlights and blend them into the surrounding areas.

The bottom left brick is under construction (*fig 5*). The drawing is loose and spontaneous, and features are introduced as they occur to me and to maintain balance. There is very little, if any, pre-planning.

Note the highlights along the edges of the deep surface depressions, which are simply drawn around. Try to not let distracting pencil lines show in the shading. Much of this is formed with a broad, flat HB pencil point, and circular exploratory marks where changes of weight create the surface textures. Light hatching creates the smoother areas, which are later lightly blended with a tortillon.

The study is complete (*fig 6*). The first brick has a complex structure so I've simplified the others, as an overabundance of detail can distract the eye.

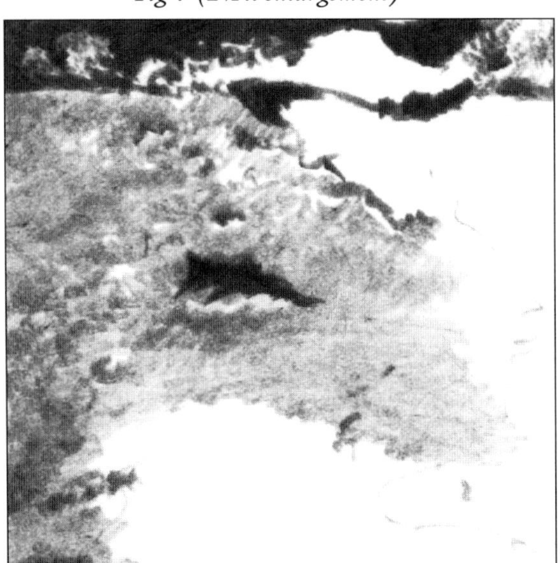

Fig 5 (3 x enlargement)

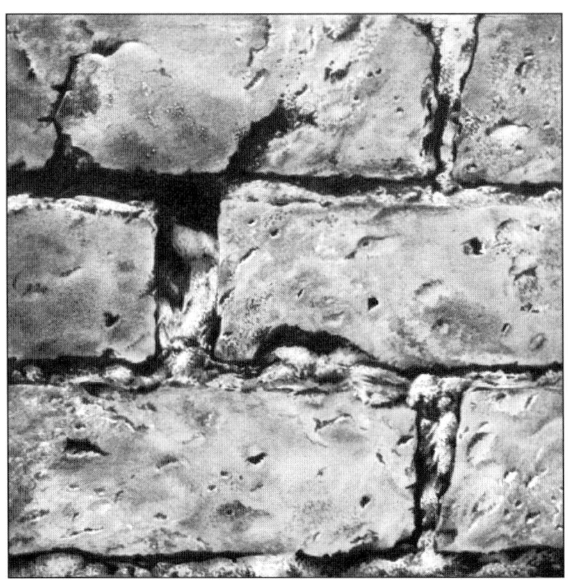

Pencils: HB with some 2B and tortillon blending in smooth areas. Shadows: 2B. Blending layers: H and 2H. Size: 3" (7.5cm) square as illustrated. Time: about 4 hours

Fig 6

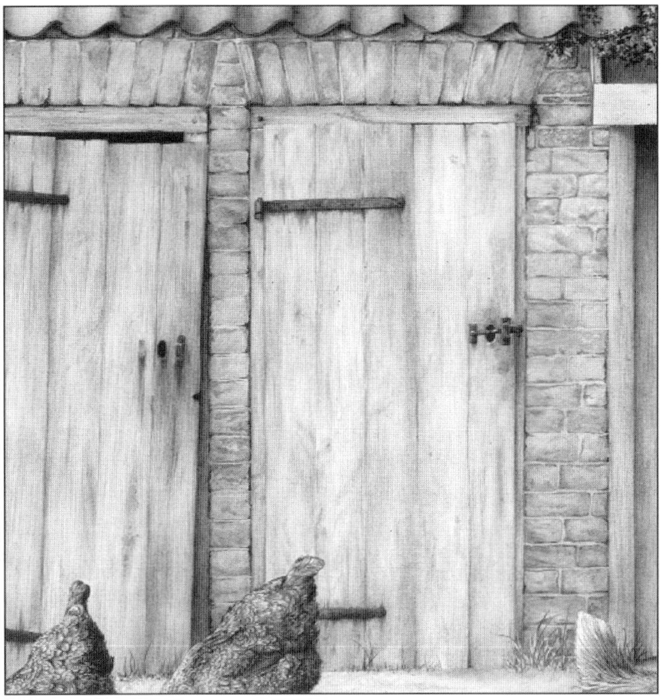

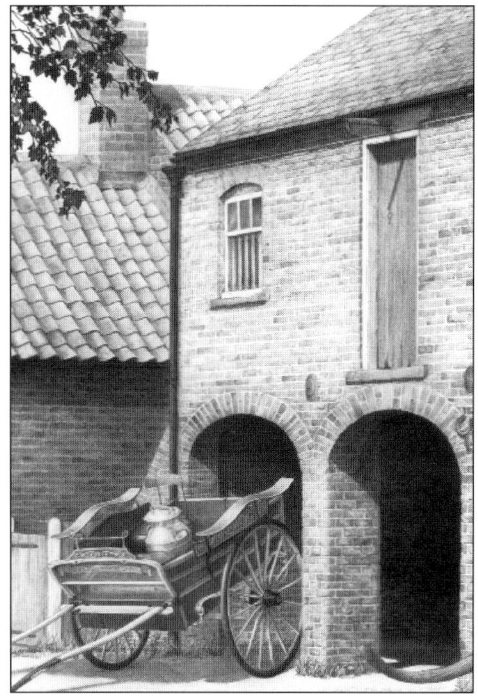

Midground and background bricks

Drawing Wood

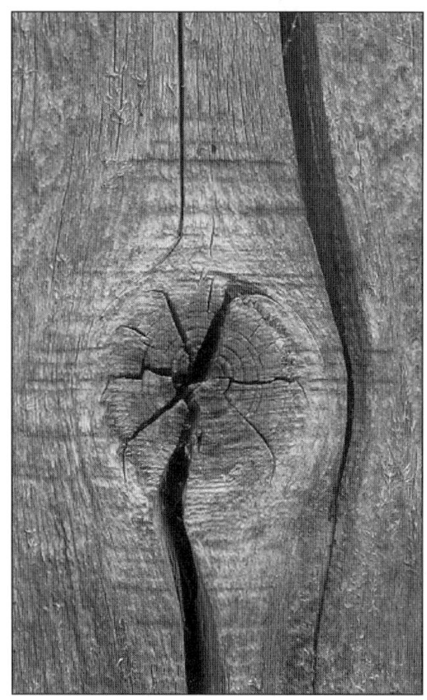

Weathered wood showing longitudinal cracks, or 'shakes', horizontal marks left by a band saw, and a knot with typical radial splits.

Analysis: Wood can be roughly sawn, axed or adzed to a dimpled finish, planed smooth or varnished to a high gloss - the surfaces are numerous. Depending on its internal structure, it can be a hardwood or softwood (neither of which terms have anything to do with hardness - Balsa wood, the softest of woods, is a hardwood). Within these two types, different varieties possess differing characteristics, such as the silver-grain of Oak, the swirling patterns of Burr Walnut, or the wonderful red and cream streaks and bands within Parana Pine.

External, untreated wood weathers to a silver finish. Knots, where branches originally sprung from the tree, dry and contract. Some will fall out and others may have radial cracks. Timber shrinks across its width, often causing long cracks (known as 'shakes'). Some boards may possess a 'wany edge' where bark still adheres.

The principal features, the keys that we require, are the pronounced grain, knots and the way the grain parts to surround them, and, on rough timber, the small slivers of wood that stand proud of the surface. However simple or complex we draw the surface, inclusion of one or more of these keys will ensure that it is seen correctly as wood.

Technique: My own depictions of wood are usually confined to incidental surfaces, so I concentrate only on the suggestion of grain, surface imperfections, and signs of end-grain decay.

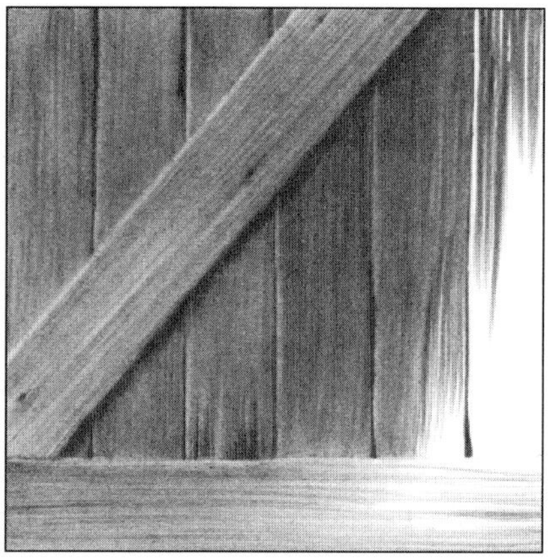

Fig 7. Midground wood - HB with an H blending layer.

Showing at right, the initial strokes being laid down. Note how they stop short of the groove to form the highlighted edge.

This incidental use, often confined to the midground or background, depends mainly on a technique of laying down parallel lines and leaving thin, lighter bands between them (*fig 7*). The lines themselves follow the expected route of woodgrain - slightly meandering, parting to accept a nail hole, a dark line sometimes describing a split, and the lower end of a vertical board may show signs of damp and decay. Sharp detail is not required, nor expected by the eye, so the aim is to echo a generic woodgrain effect.

This small drawing shows the evidence of rot at the base of the third board from the left, three nail holes in the angled board with rust-staining following the line of the grain, and warped (hand-drawn) grooves between the boarding. These features suffice to send the appropriate message to the viewer's brain.

Foreground wood demands much closer inspection, understanding, and careful drawing. Now pencil lines can no longer describe the grain. Indeed grain is not a line drawn onto a 'woody' background. Woodgrain, as seen in a sawn plank, possesses its own characteristics. In a standing tree, wood consists of upright fibres and it's these fibres that describe the grain, which is cut obliquely by the sawmill.

Trees grow quickly in spring, making a depth of soft wood beneath the bark. In summer the rate of growth slows and the new wood is harder and darker. The two combine to form the familiar rings seen in a felled tree. Growth stops during the dormant winter season then restarts in spring. This break forms the sharp edge of the summer ring. Its other edge is less defined, as it marks the gradual growth transition from spring to summer (*fig 8*).

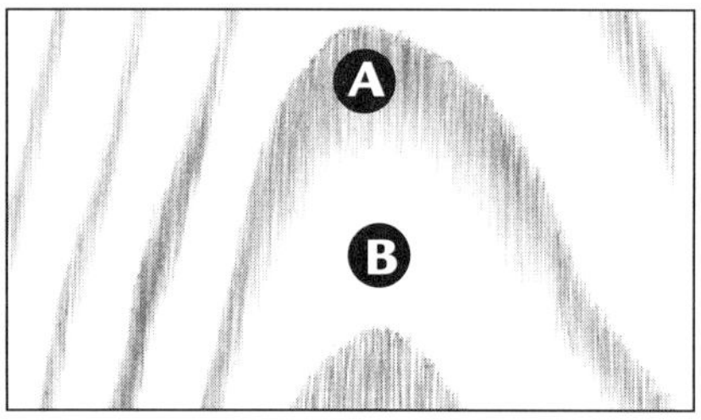

Fig 8. Vertical HB marks begin the grain. An abrupt start forms the hard edge of the summer ring. By decreasing the weight, each line then merges into the spring wood below.

A - Summer ring
B - Spring wood

To give the summer ring a hard edge, begin by very lightly outlining its shape. Then place your HB pencil on the line and draw downwards with decreasing pressure. The abrupt start will define the edge for you. Keep all the lines approximately the same length, and leave narrow gaps between them. As you work down the near-vertical edges the line length will automatically narrow the ring for you. Using a sharp point, introduce cracks for added interest, choosing points where you left abnormally wide gaps between the lines of HB.

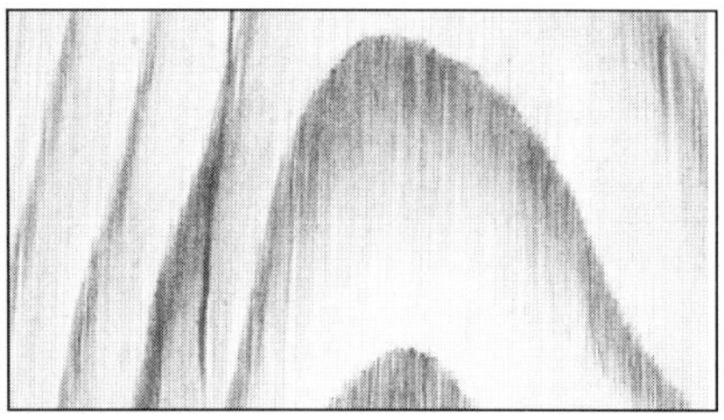

Fig 9. After layering with grade H and blending with a tortillon.

When all the summer rings are complete draw over the same areas again (fig 9), this time with an H grade, and extend the length of the lines. This will diffuse the gaps between the HB lines and soften the blend into the spring area. Draw around any cracks leaving an untouched white line adjacent to your dark HB line. This will form the highlight. Add more blending layers until there are no coarse, distracting lines left in the HB layer. Then lightly blend with a tortillon, avoiding any highlights and working always in the direction of the grain.

To finish, apply layers of 2H to further blend the previous layers (*fig 10*). Once again begin at the summer ring's hard edge, but extend your lines, lightly drawn, almost down to the summer ring below it. Aim to leave just enough sense of the vertical fibre structure without it being dominant. Now blend with a tortillon again. This time extend the blending right down to the next ring to tone down the remaining white band. Where you have cracks, slightly darken the other side of the highlight, which suggest the highlight is raised and casting a shadow. This subtle shadow will contrast with the highlight and increase its effectiveness. With a sharp H point, add short vertical lines in the lighter areas to reinforce the sense of vertical grain. Blend and layer as necessary until you have achieved the desired result.

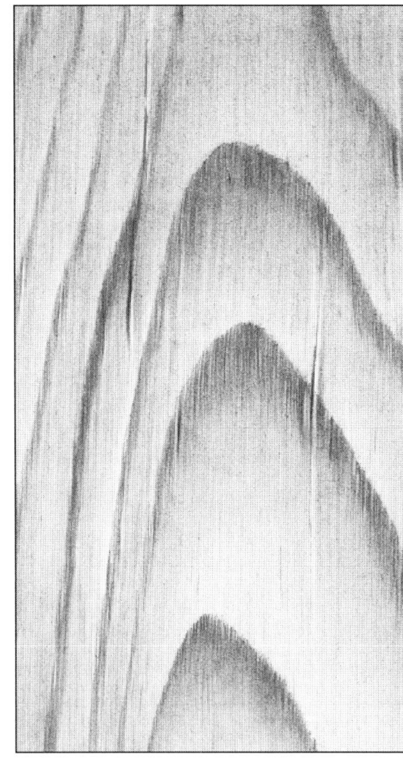

Fig 10. The completed section with obtrusive detail diminished with 2H blending layers.

Drawing Old Paintwork

Analysis: Possibly the lazy man's way to draw wood! Paintwork can be a boring surface unless it's enhanced, perhaps by reflections of nearby objects or those standing on it. Old, flaking paintwork, however, possesses character and interest. As with bricks, oblique lighting is required to bring out the surface detail.

Paint gets harder and less plastic with age so it exhibits sharp and angular edges wherever it cracks and flakes off. Where it parts company with the surface and lifts, it will possess a shadow beneath its edge. These cast shadows will visually lift loose and peeling paint clear of the drawing surface, turning a fundamentally two-dimensional surface into an exciting three-dimensional one. Even just one or two such flakes can enliven a surface and provide the essential 'this is old paint' key without overpowering adjacent objects and surfaces.

Bear in mind that wood exposed by flaking paint will often not possess the breadth of tonal values seen in unpainted wood. Vestiges of undercoat and primer will usually fill the grain and soften the surface features.

Technique: Contrast the smooth, intact paint with the exposed woodgrain or rusty metal beneath it. Paint possesses a thickness so even adhering paint will cast a narrow shadow along its margin. You may think I'm stating the obvious but going through this exercise before starting your drawing helps to fix the characteristics in your mind - especially those that you can use to your advantage. By describing the surface to yourself, and its possible variances, you build up a mental picture before committing anything to paper. When that time comes you will have concrete characteristics to depict, not just a vague notion of the surface.

Using the analysis we've just made, I'll attempt to draw an old painted wooden surface directly from my imagination. Let's try thickly painted white paint over an older, slightly darker layer on a pine surface, and light it from top left. I'll begin with a rough plan (*fig 11*) and then see what evolves from there. I'll also establish some of the darkest shadows first so I have something to judge the other tones against.

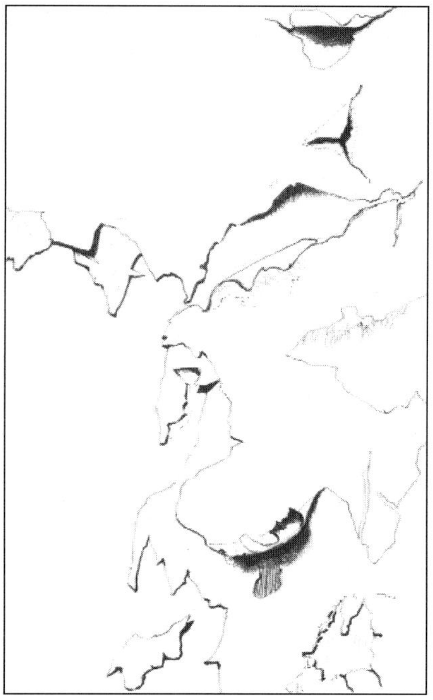

Fig 11. The rough plan with the principal shadows noted to remind myself of what I had in mind.

The woodgrain has almost been completed (*fig 12*). Some parts may be too visually obtrusive but I'll return to it later when I have other elements to compare it to. I began by using HB but quickly changed to the harder H to reduce the overall tonal strength. The area was blended with a tortillon, following the line of the grain, before two blending layers of 2H were applied to reduce contrast. I want the woodgrain to possess a reality without it being the dominant feature.

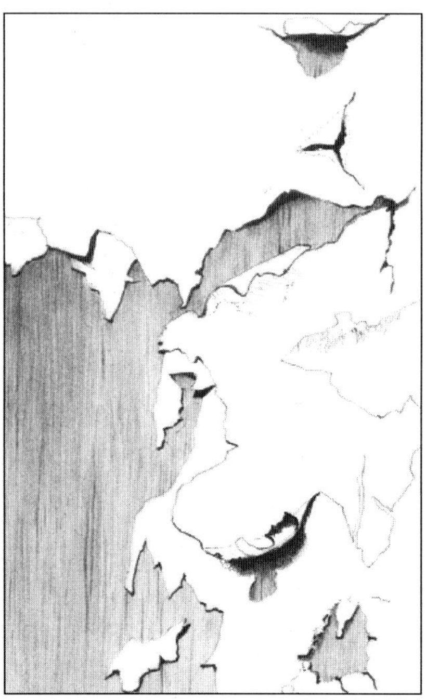

Fig 12. The woodgrain is almost complete.

Now the drawing of the peeling paint begins (*fig 13*). Starting at the left side, the darker undercoat of paint is gradually and gently toned down. Layers of H and 2H follow the initial light layer of blended HB.

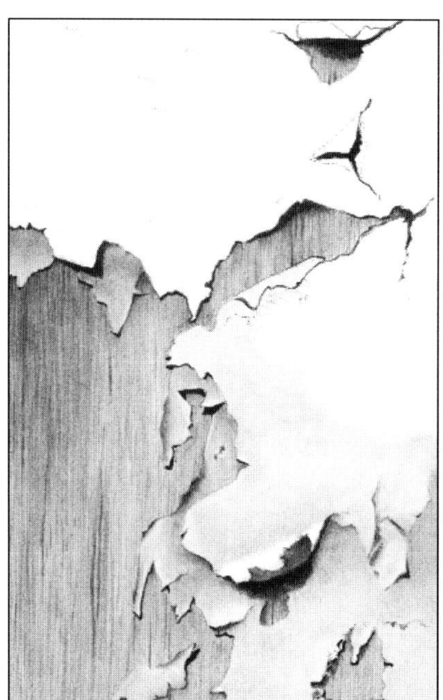

Fig 13. Lower half almost completed.

At all times I'm mentally describing to myself the forms that are under my pencil. Will it receive full light? Will it cast a shadow? Will reflected light dilute the strength of tone on its shady side? Is this edge raised slightly so it will receive more direct light than a flat surface?

Finally work begins on the top layer (*fig 14*). Although this is white paint I've decided that age will have yellowed it. This allows me to add a little more tone, which will increase the brightness of the pure white highlights. If I feel a highlight will benefit from a further boost, I engineer areas of adjoining darker tone. Looked at with this knowledge, these areas may appear to be slightly artificial, but the unapprised viewer will see only the brighter highlight and gain a fuller and speedier understanding of form.

I've included more features here than I would usually countenance. The two major curving forms vie with each other for attention and don't sit too happily together but, as this is a demonstration, I felt it gained by having one shape facing the light and the other curving away from it.

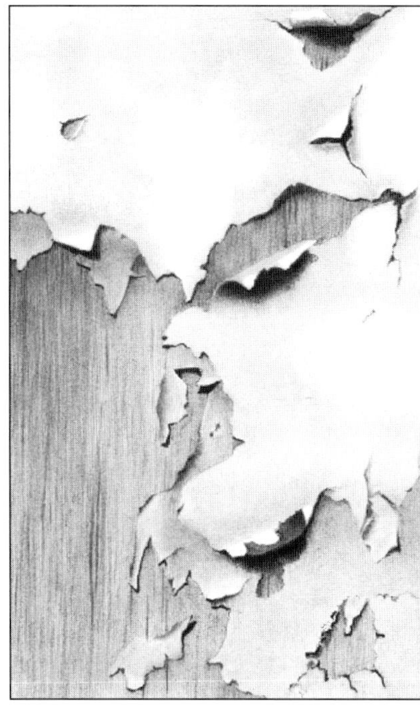

Fig 14. The completed drawing.

Drawing Rusty Metal

Analysis: A useful surface for contrasting with soft textures. Lacking strong reflections, it makes an ideal background feature against which tonally weaker textures, such as the hair of a white dog, can be shown to advantage. It possesses character, and suggests age, tradition, history, and bygone times.

Technique: My basic approach involves drawing with a flat-faced lead in a circular motion. Think 'rust' and 'pits'. Each pit has an internal shadow and one highlighted edge. I introduce tonal and surface variations too because rust patterning is often not uniformly distributed. The technique employs a mix of negative and positive drawing. Just as in the brick and paint examples, highlights are merely drawn around and shadows are simply created by applying more pressure to the pencil. Essentially one grade of lead can achieve all the required tones. This is ideal because complete areas can be spontaneously created using a direct chain from thought to hand to paper with no interruption. This truly is sculpting with a pencil.

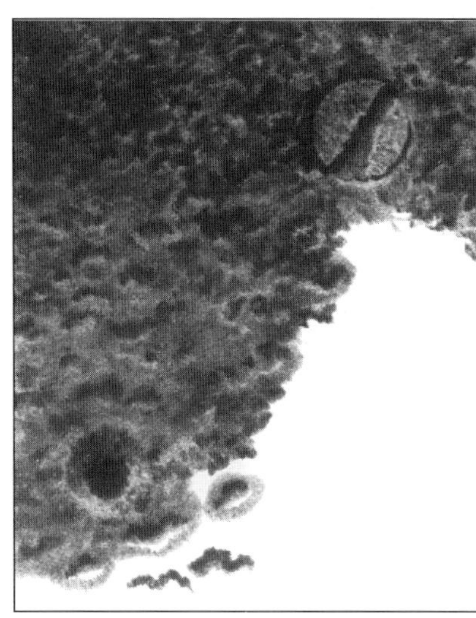

Fig 15. Rust under construction with a flat 2B lead and an H blending layer.

Showing at the bottom, an initial internal shadow, a shadow softened at the base, and a surround of midtone creating the highlighted edge of the pit.

This demonstration (*fig 15*), shown here full size, was drawn slightly larger than I would normally recommend for this method but it more clearly shows the steps taken. There are three basic tones - black for the deepest shadows, a slightly lighter tone that blends the shadows into the highlight, and a midtone that I reserved for the unpitted surface of the metal. I used the same 2B point on Mellotex ivory plate finish board throughout, including the very light blending layer that tones down the highlights. However, a final blending layer of H was applied to smooth the coarse 2B granules and unify the whole area.

At the bottom you can see the first three stages. The initial

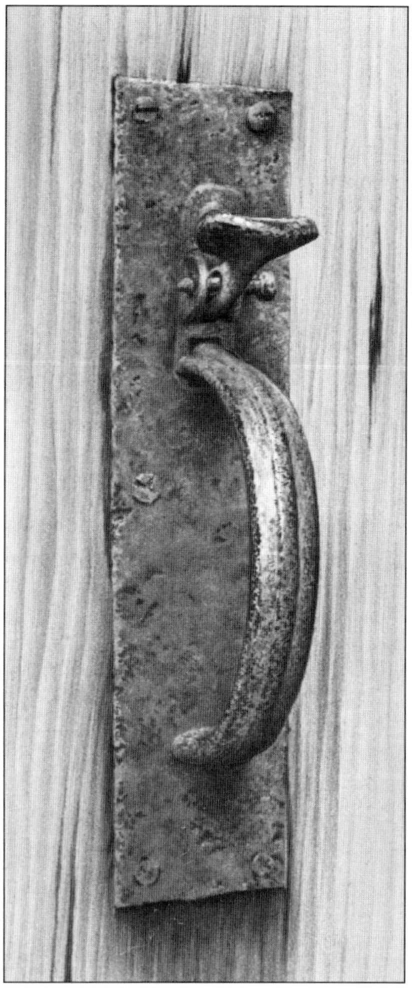

Fig 16B. Shown actual size

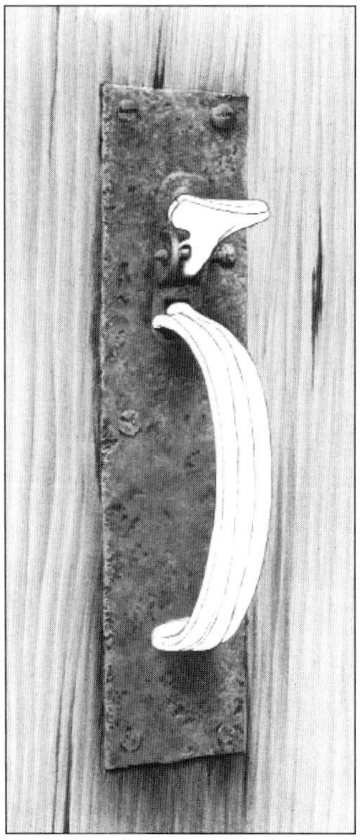

Fig 17

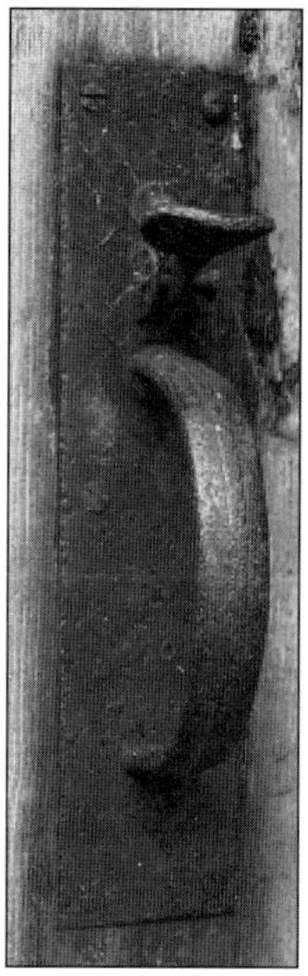

Fig 16A. Photo Reference

shadow shape, the shadow softened at the base, and then, still working in small circles, a ring of midtone drawn to create the highlight. This demonstration was drawn spontaneously over a period of thirty minutes without prior planning - including the screw head and empty screw hole, which I included as a means of intensifying the 'this is rusty metal' signal.

So let's draw an actual object. I photographed this old latch (*fig 16A*) as a reference source but my drawing (*fig 16B*) will be my interpretation of it, not a faithful copy. The reference photo will supply only the basic shape, the 'feel' of rust, and the lighting direction. Studying the real latch I can see that years of use have smoothed parts of the handle and thumb latch. I will incorporate this wear but in my own way.

First I establish the deep shadows at the base of the thumb latch with 2B so I have something against which I can gauge my lighter tones. Using a flat-faced HB lead, I begin by feeling my way around the top left corner of the backplate, working in a series of small circles and sometimes making small angular marks. The highlighted edges of the backplate will be drawn later and are left as narrow white margins. As soon as I feel comfortable with the texture that my pencil is producing I move on, gradually extending the drawn area. At this stage a few highlights are left white while most are lightly shaded with the same HB pencil that I'm drawing with. Later, when I've completed the top half, I'll return and add an H blending layer to gradually diffuse the detail and dull the highlights until none are dominant.

The wood is complete, as is the rust staining, the backplate, and the edge detail now I have the tones established to either side. The drawing has reached its 'ugly duckling' stage (*fig 17*). Without its major features and deepest tones, the drawing looks flat and lifeless. To restore my confidence in the study I next draw the latch (*fig 18*), aiming for maximum contrast between shadow and highlight, bearing in mind that only the well-thumbed surface will possess a key highlight. Now I feel much better about the outcome and move on to the handle.

The handle involves negative drawing. There are other methods for creating the pitted surface, such as dot indenting, but I prefer the more intuitive and direct method of drawing around the highlights.

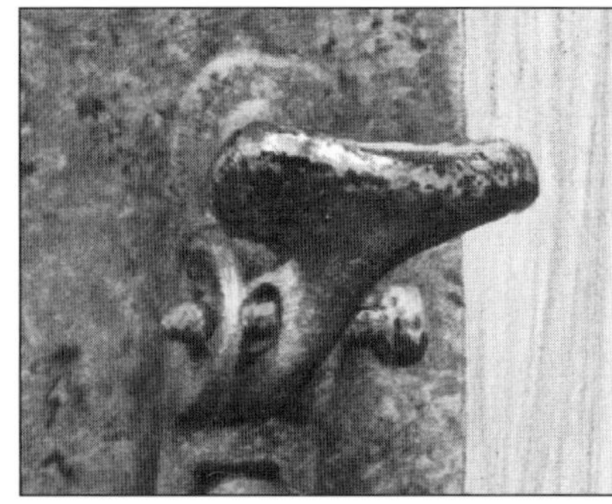

Fig 18

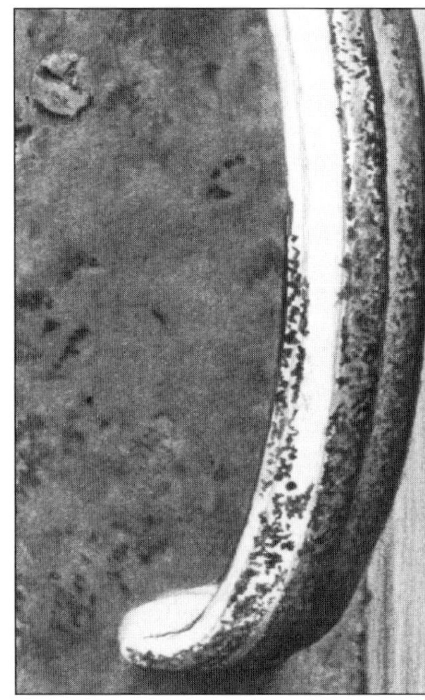

Fig 19

Running up the handle are four parallel bands - the left hand edge, the central rib and the two areas to either side of it. I begin by carefully drawing the narrow shadows of the right hand edges with 2B then, beginning at the bottom and switching back to HB, I work my way up the right hand area. All the time I'm calculating which parts will receive light, and visualising the shape as a double curve - both vertically and horizontally. I let the pencil create the highlights around the edges of the pits; at times imagining a white shape and letting my pencil draw around it, and at others seeing a pit and drawing its shadow - switching constantly between negative and positive drawing.

Now the right-hand side and central rib have been completed and blended with grade H, you can see this process in use in the final two bands (*fig 19*). A broken dark line of shadow begins to delineate the edge between the front and side faces. Drawing to either side of this edge exposes white patches and highlights. Later these will be considerably dulled so the patches become flat, unpitted steel, but they're easier to handle as pure white marks at this stage. Notice how drawing stops short of the central band, so forming its highlighted edge.

Drawing of the right hand face is continued up to the well-polished highlight and faded out. Next the side face is completed, establishing the broken dark edge that will contrast with and boost the major highlight. Working now from the top of the handle, dark into light, the left hand face is drawn back down to its highlighted area. Finally, light detail is drawn within the highlight itself then reduced to subtle hints with Blu-Tack, and the drawing is finished.

Drawing Fabrics

Analysis: Although this subject covers a very wide range of textures, the analysis is made in a similar manner to the other textures previously covered. Here that initial analysis should centre on the three major properties; folds, edges, and surface texture. Also, where appropriate, transparency too should be considered.

An analysis of canvas, for example, will show that it is relatively thick and stiff. Folds are usually broadly rounded, and converging folds meet in a very rounded manner. Seams and hemmed edges multiply the thickness of the material and form

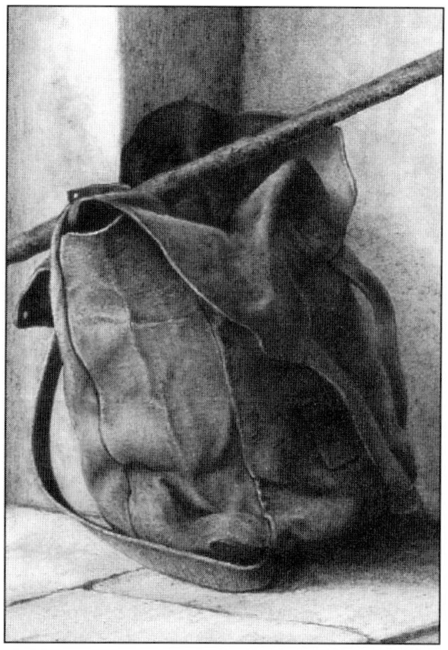

A strong canvas ex-army bag showing the typical folds of stiff fabric.

Narrowly spaced cross-hatching on the side of the bag, following the directions of the weave, supplies a subtle indication of the nature of the material.

ribs that stiffen it. The texture is relatively harsh to the touch and has a coarse appearance. The result of these aggregated properties is a fabric whose own form often dominates and hides the form beneath it. This concealment is further compounded by the light absorbency of the coarse weave resulting in very little reflected light.

At the other extreme, silks, satins, and varieties of diaphanous materials are so thin and pliable that they can cling like a skin to the underlying form. The tight, fine weaves form smooth and often highly reflective surfaces that aid a better three-dimensional understanding of the structure beneath. Secondary surface reflections are very likely to be found in these materials.

Any thick or stiff fabric resists folding. The folds themselves will be widely spaced and exhibit gently curved troughs and ridges. The general travel of the ridges will be straight, as a heavy fabric will tend to curve in one direction only. When it is compelled to bend in two directions it will inevitably do so in a very sharp and angular manner. To test this out, bend a length of paper lengthwise into an inverted 'U', now attempt to slowly bend it towards you. The nearest wall will collapse inwards, meet the outer wall and form a sharp crease. The heavier the paper, or fabric, the more pronounced will be the crease.

Thin, light fabric may exhibit similar creasing but will more often distort to accommodate the double curve. Its greater pliability results in the folds being thinner and more closely spaced. Silks, satins and their nylon equivalents fold easily, and will often faithfully display the contours of the shape they cover.

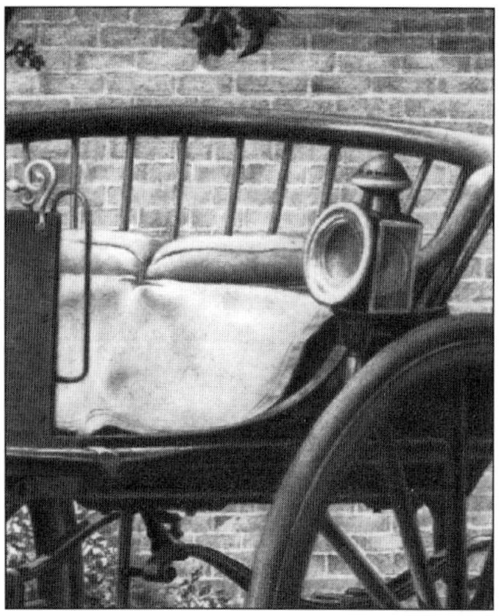

The heavy seat cover of this stick-back gig possesses a stiffness that is signalled by the angular edge seam, and the scarcity and shallow nature of the folds.

Technique: Depicting the surface textural detail, with the possible exception of crocheted or coarsely knitted items, need not be your principal aim. Indeed, in most real situations surface texture is difficult to discern, even when closely studied. Instead, complete an analysis along the lines suggested above, and extract the major visual keys.

Once you have a firm mental grasp of how a particular fabric behaves, and the inherent forms that signal its type, you secure a very valuable freedom. Now you can arrange or compose the fabric in a way that suits your aesthetic sense - one that adds balance and harmony to your composition while displaying or hinting at the form beneath it. This ability to engineer form allows you to use it as a major visual tool. In its position as a secondary element in your composition, it can be used to

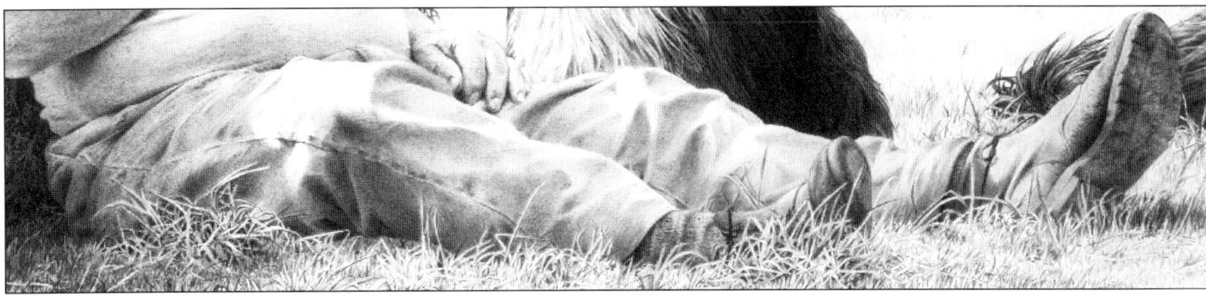

Fig. 20

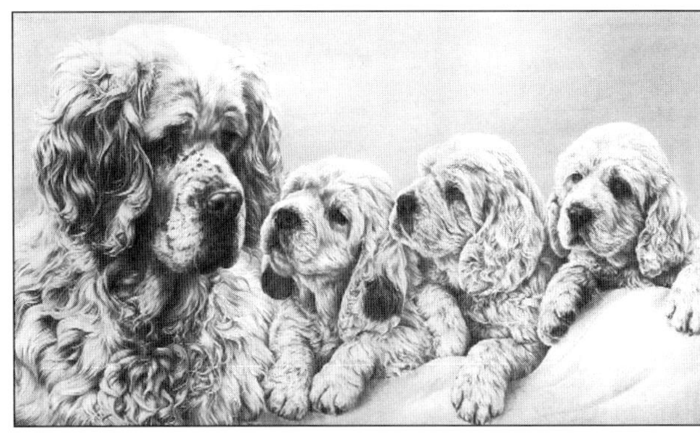

Fabric folds (bottom right) are used to steer the eye around the composition.

covertly steer the eye of the viewer to areas of importance, to take it on a circular tour of the piece, or to stop it from straying outside of the boundaries of the study by gently shepherding it back in. Remember, the brain is lazy and easily fooled. Serve it with relevant and logical keys and it will always seek the simplest and most obvious understanding of what it sees. You can see in this detail (*fig 20*) that the rendering of surface texture is minimal but I've included major keys that tell us, for example, that the material of the trousers is denim. The widely spaced folds tell us that the material is heavy but the gentle curves rule out thick fabrics, such as canvas, that tend to form straighter folds. Fortunately, due to the method of manufacture, jeans possess two distinctive keys not found elsewhere. The external side seam has both a cast shadow and edge highlight, and unique undulating indentations between the twin lines of stitching that accommodate the four thicknesses of material. Note too that the woollen sock is contrasted with the smoother jeans by displaying its main key of longitudinal ribs.

Drawing it all together

Whatever the texture, first closely analyse what you see and determine the fundamental keys - the unique combination that makes the surface appear as it does. Then look for properties peculiar to that surface or material - the way it hangs, the amount of light it reflects, how its transparency affects the visibility of the underlying surface, its pliability, the depth of its polished sheen... Armed with this information, you can draw free of control by reference sources. Coupled with your knowledge of the use of light and shade, you now have sufficient information to draw spontaneously, creating the surface that best suits your composition while maintaining the intrinsic textural properties of the surface.

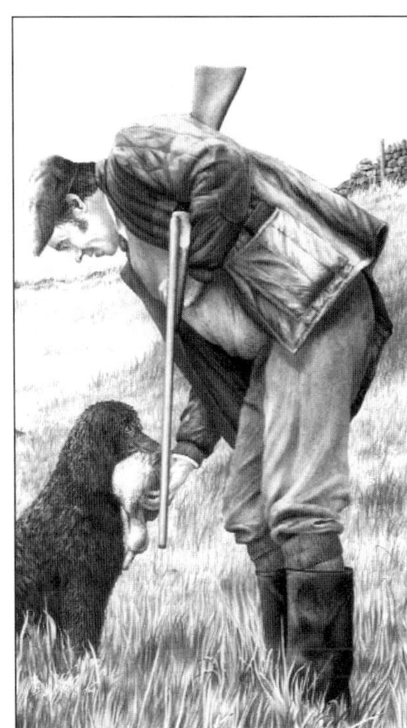

Strong surface reflections are used to show that this waterproof jacket is of nylon origin. Conversely, the lack of reflections is used to contrast the suede shoulder and elbow patches.

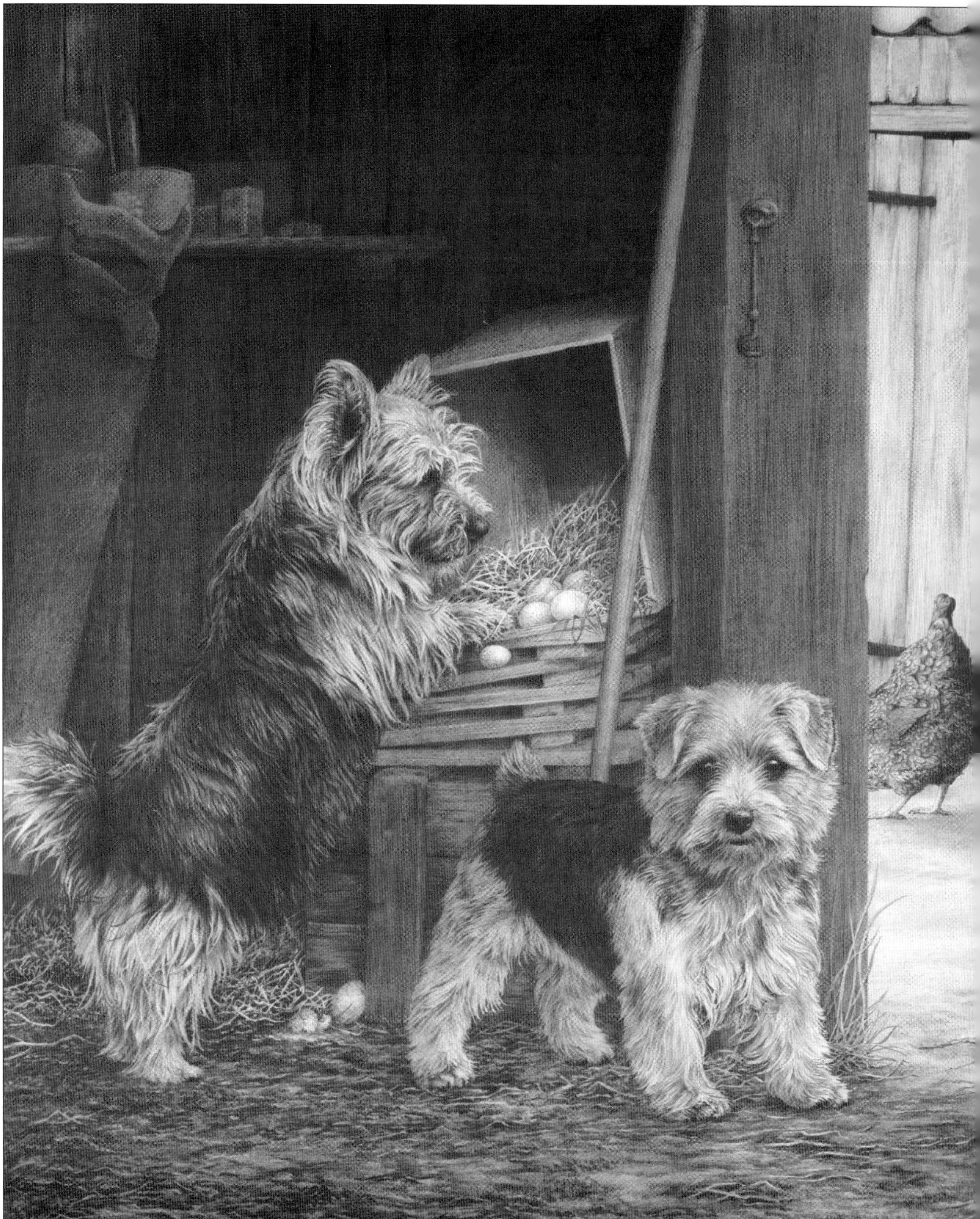

'Rags, Tatters and Gentleman George' by Mike Sibley ©

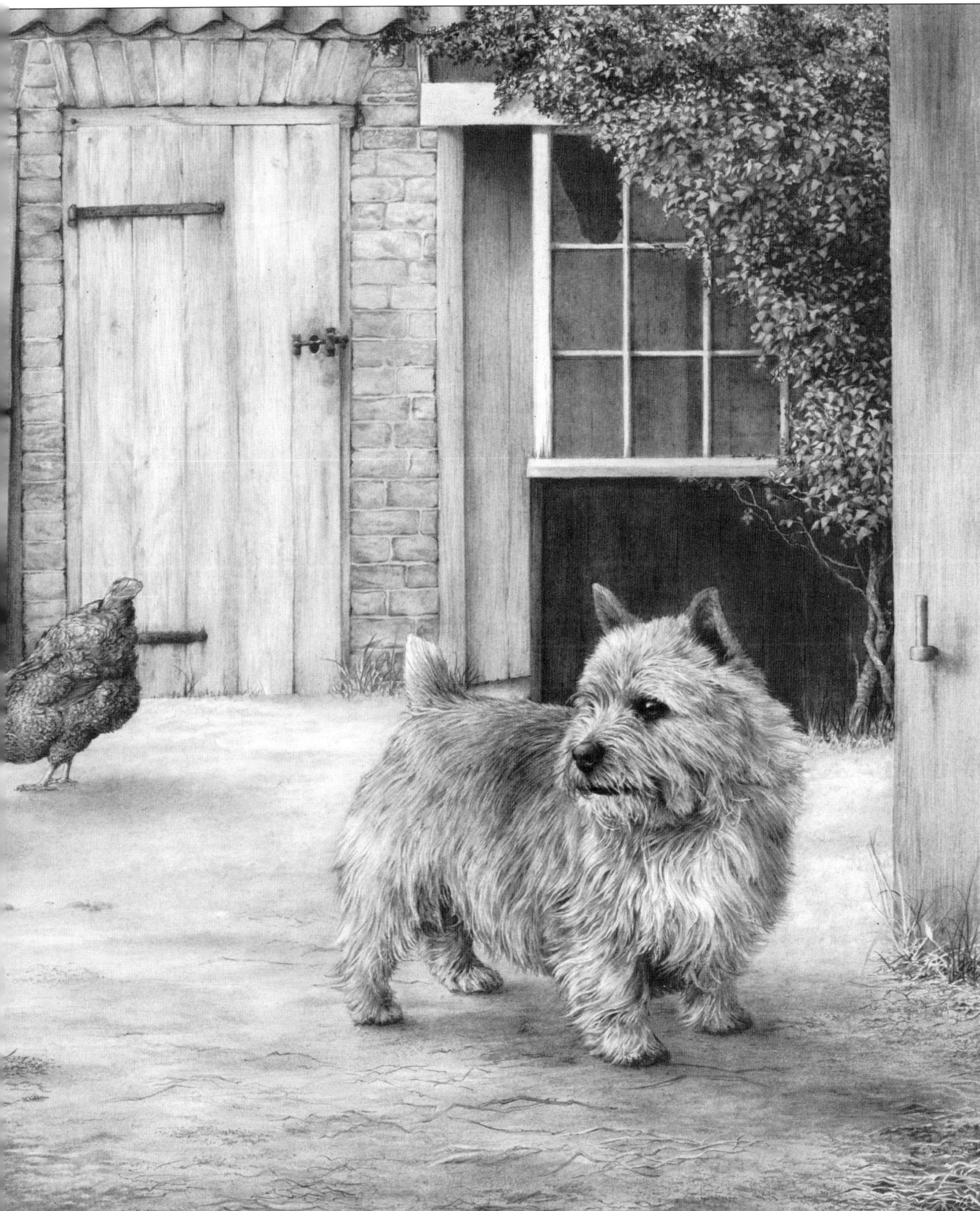

18½" x 11½" (47 x 29 cm)

Limited Edition print of 630 worldwide plus 10 Artists Proofs

Drawing Reflections

Double Trouble...

'The faculty of creating is never given to us all by itself. It always goes hand in hand with the gift of observation.'

Igor Stravinsky

If drawing textures is about the art of illusion then reflections are sheer magic. No matter how faithfully you reproduce a texture, making it live depends on the way that it reflects the world around it. A mirror and a calm expanse of water share many reflective similarities but something exists that allows our eyes to differentiate between the two. Of course, we don't expect to find a boat floating on glass nor water hanging vertically, so context plays a part, but even in isolation we can still detect the difference. Finding that essential key information is paramount to the success of your drawing.

To produce believable reflections, you must have an understanding of surface properties, a sound grasp of perspective, and knowledge of reflection and refraction. Of course, you can just copy everything you see in a photograph, but nothing beats personal invention for achieving a sense of reality, and this is one instance when copying often just doesn't work.

Reflections can become so complex that faithfully reproducing them may only serve to confuse. By exercising your artistic control to include only the simple key elements, you will send clear, easily understood signals so your viewers can instantly grasp and react to the intended message.

To simplify matters we'll tackle reflections on flat and curved planes of solid surfaces, and then surface reflections on water. But first we need to understand how reflections occur.

The basic rules

'Don't show me that what you are doing is difficult.'

Pierre Parisien

Reflections are totally dependent on the degree of light absorbency of the reflecting surface. A mirror reflects all the light that falls on it; a chrome-plated surface will reflect almost as much; and highly polished or varnished wood will reflect considerably less, because much of the light will travel through the transparent layer of varnish and be absorbed by the wood beneath. As surfaces become less smooth and shiny they reflect less light until coarse surfaces, such as canvas, reflect very little light at all. And here we must distinguish between reflected light and reflection.

The laws of reflected light were discussed in chapter 13 (Light and Shade). There we found that a ray of light hitting a surface (*fig 1*) will reflect at exactly the same angle, and if it reflects directly into our eyes, we see it as a key highlight. Our line of sight, of course, follows the reverse path - looking directly at the highlight, an imaginary 'ray' from our eye will trace right back to the light source.

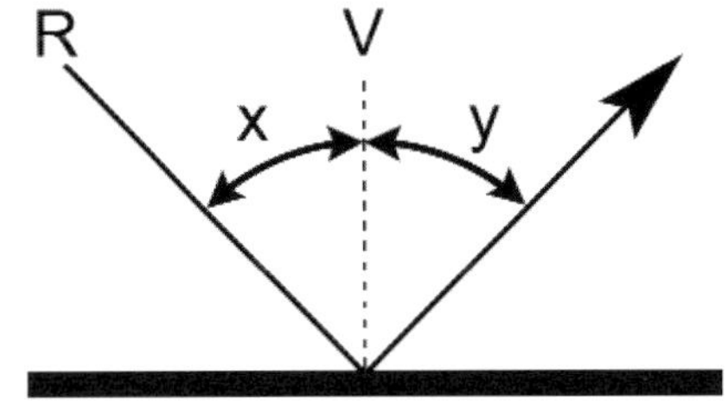

Fig 1. Reflected light
R - ray of light
V - vertical line
Light rays illuminate and reflect at the same angle so x and y are always equal.

A reflection, however, is the result of light illuminating surrounding objects (*fig 2*) from which reflected light travels to the surface that we're looking at, where it is again reflected into our eyes.

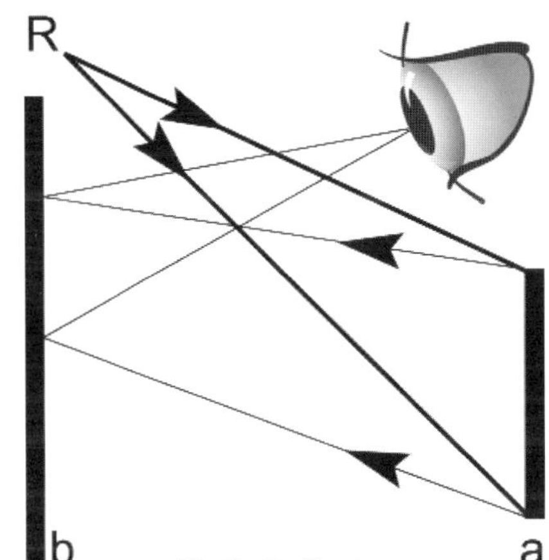

Fig 2. Reflection
R - rays of light
a - illuminated object
b - reflective surface

Both reflected light and reflections can occur at the same time. You can see on the side of this vintage car (*fig 3*) how the bottom of the rear wing, or fender, reflects the skyline and the sky above, and displays a key highlight from a direct reflection of the sun. But notice too that the wing and running board are themselves reflected in the paintwork of the side of the car, as is the key highlight. This second highlight is weaker because it is a copy of the first, a secondary light reflection, and not a direct reflection of the sun.

Other factors too can affect the strength of a reflection. Ask yourself why the running board appears light yet its reflection is almost black. The rubber-covered surface has longitudinal ribs; we see the sunlit side of each rib but the unlit side faces the car. A reflection is a copy of what a surface 'sees', not necessarily what we see.

Higher up the door you can plainly see that the sunlight has illuminated a seated group of people. The light has reflected from them to the car where it has again been reflected into our eyes. It has, in effect, been projected onto the car as though it was a movie screen, and, just like a movie screen, we are seeing the light being bounced back towards us. The reason these people can be seen has to do with your line of sight and the

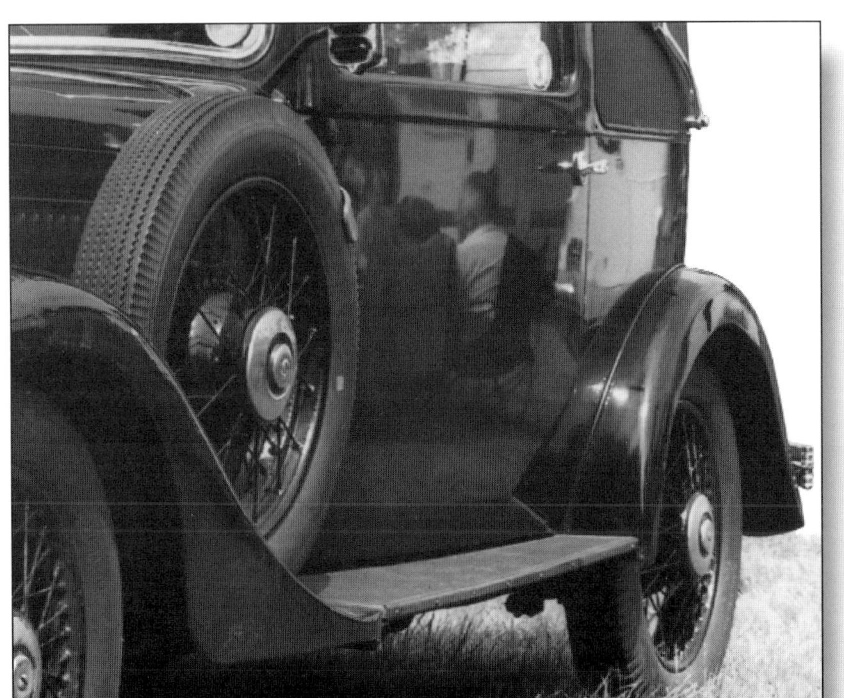

Fig 3

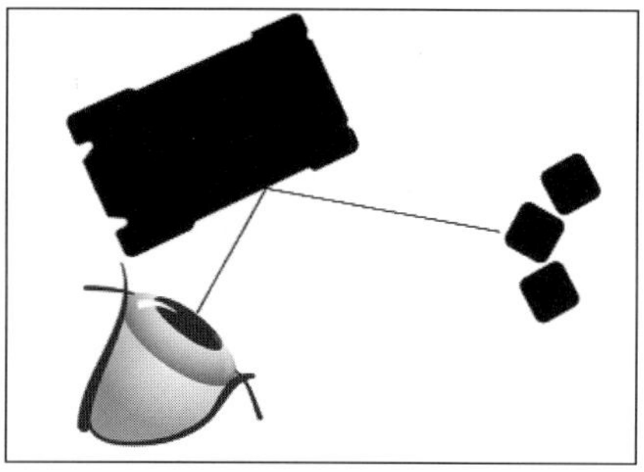

Fig 4: Our line of sight travels to and reflects from the car at equal angles to the seated people.

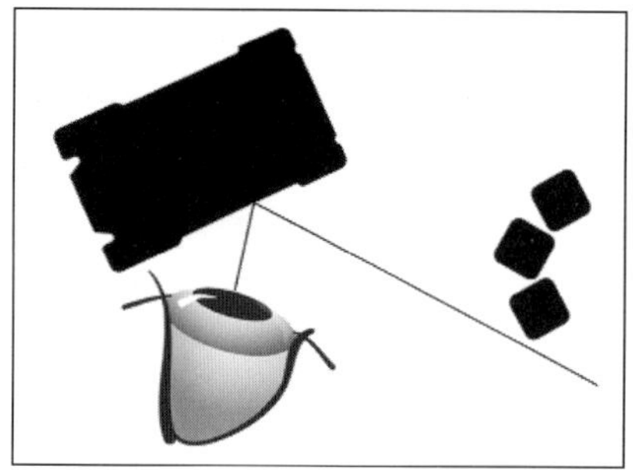

Fig 5

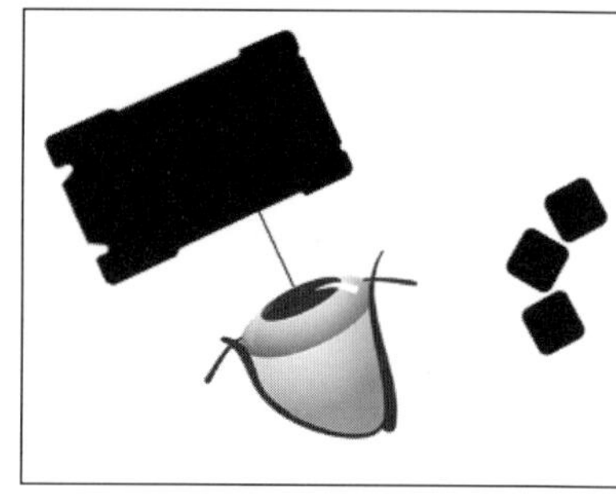

Fig 6

angles involved (*fig 4*). If you move round (*fig 5*) you lose sight of the people until (*fig 6*) you see yourself instead. Reflections are always darker than the directly lighted source because of their relatively complex path, and the light absorbency of both the reflected object and the reflector.

Reflections from shiny surfaces

The flat surface

It is important that you are aware of many aspects of reflections, as knowledge will better train your eye to see. For example, which surface is actually the reflector? In the case of the car door, it is the paint. A coat of polish or lacquer may increase the degree of shine but that coat is transparent, so light will travel through it and still reflect from the surface of the paintwork. Of course, this particular transparent coat is so thin that it makes no visible difference, but you should consider its possible effects because a thick transparent layer may markedly affect reflection, as I will explain later.

Stand an object on a solid reflective surface and you will see a reflected mirror image (*fig 7*). Tip the object at an angle and the reflection will always mirror your action. Lift it up a little and the mirror image is maintained but the perceived gap between the object and its reflection will appear to be doubled, as the gap too will be reflected.

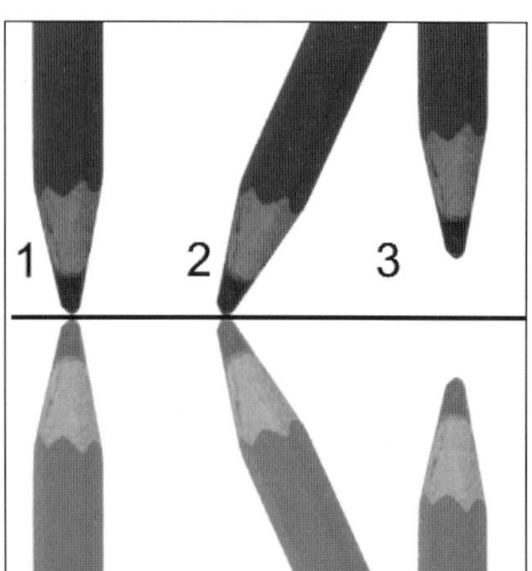

Fig 7
1.Pencil in contact with a reflective surface.
2.Changes in angle are mirrored in reflection.
3.Gap reflected to seemingly double its size.

You can safely assume that any shiny object will reflect directly from its surface. But there is one exception - glass and, in particular, mirrored glass. A mirror will reflect from the quicksilver coating on the back of the glass. The thickness of the glass prevents an object in contact with it from touching the actual reflector. So there will be a visible gap between the object and its reflection. The same effect, although muted, applies to glass that is darker behind than in front, such as a plate glass shop window. Draw something leaning against such a window and you may wish to leave that important gap.

This is also where science and art depart. Touch your pencil to a mirror then look at the mirror obliquely (*fig 8*). You will see two reflections - one from the silvered back and a weaker reflection from the shiny front face of the glass. This instance is an example of when the artist should take control. Do not overcomplicate your reflections. Consider omitting trivial reflections, like the weaker reflection from the glass itself, because they can dilute the intended signal. In this case you want the brain to recognise a mirror in your drawing, so send only the strongest signal to ensure that your message succeeds. As long as the reflection sends the right signals the brain will understand your meaning and accept its reality, even if it is scientifically incorrect.

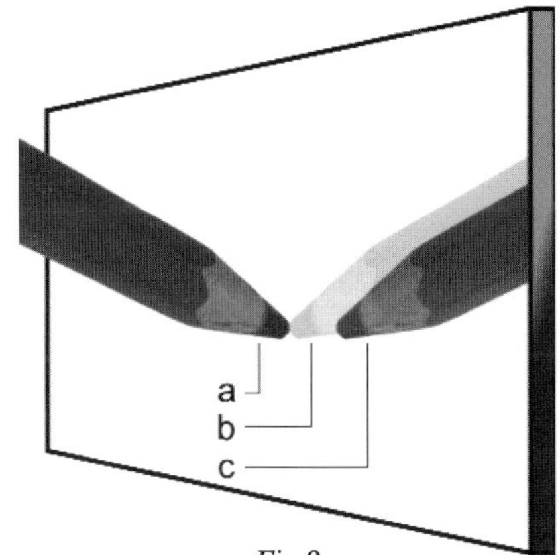

Fig 8
a - pencil touching mirror
b - front face reflection
c - true mirror reflection

Do you need all of this knowledge to construct credible reflections? No, but you do need the desire to enquire and analyse, and the more you analyse the better your eye becomes at detecting the subtleties within reflections. As your understanding increases so too will the success of the logic you apply to their construction. All reflections are logical; a flat surface facing up, for example, reflects only what is above it, such as the sky, but never the ground. Imagine each reflector can see; it can't reflect what it cannot see.

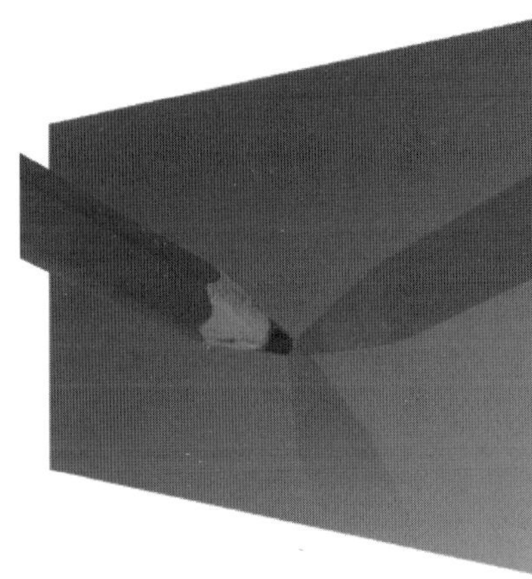

Fig 9. A dark reflective surface, a pencil, and its reflection and cast shadow.

As an exercise, walk around your home and place the point of your pencil against a variety of surfaces. Look closely at the reflections and try to find explanations for their behaviour. Maybe darker shiny surfaces reflect more clearly than light coloured ones? Perhaps surface imperfections, such as brush marks in varnish, affect the shape of the reflection? This is all valuable information.

Look too for cast shadows. Any object close to, or in contact with, a reflective surface will cast a shadow (*fig 9*). As a rule, given sufficient light, the weaker the reflection the stronger will be the cast shadow. This is because a light, highly reflective surface reflects so much light back through a cast shadow that it effectively destroys it, but you should be aware of its possible existence. Its inclusion might be just what you need to send a clear signal of the surface type.

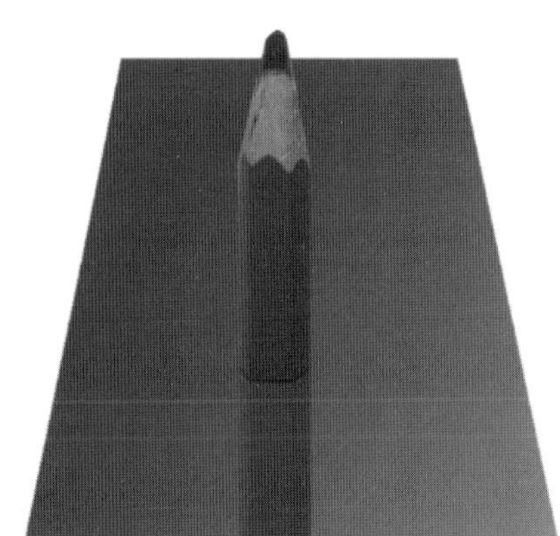

Fig 10. A contact shadow suggests depth to the surface coating and forcefully defines the junction between the object and its reflection.

Contact shadows can also be present (*fig 10*). The reflection of an object standing on a shiny surface will extend immediately from its base. However, if that surface has, for example, a thick coating of transparent lacquer, a narrow gap may exist between the object and its reflection. Within this gap, depending on the lighting direction, the object might cast a contact shadow. This

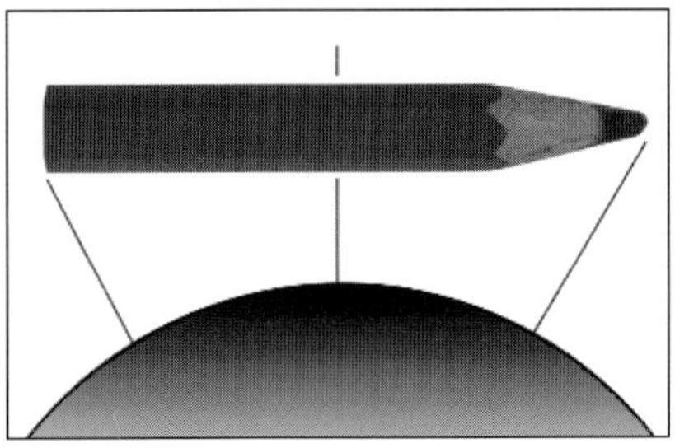

Fig 11. How a curved surface 'sees' an object it reflects - as demonstrated in fig 12.

can be a useful device, even in a scientifically inappropriate situation, if you need to show a visible division between the object and its reflection.

THE CURVED SURFACE

Let's look at a flat, outward-curving surface. The first thing you notice is that something reflected in such a surface appears to be not only curved but shorter too. Any point on a curved surface behaves exactly like a tiny flat mirror; it reflects only what it can directly see straight ahead so the result (*fig 11*) is an optically shortened reflection.

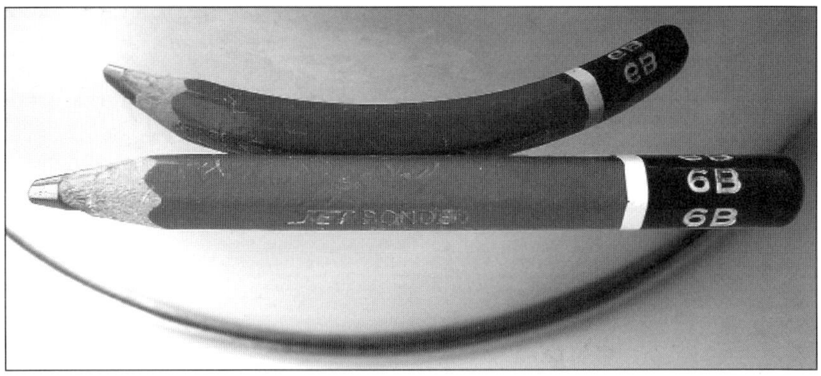

Fig 12. A no-expense-spared, scientific demonstration of figure 11 - how reflections distort on a convex surface. My battered 6B pencil Blu-Tacked to our kettle.

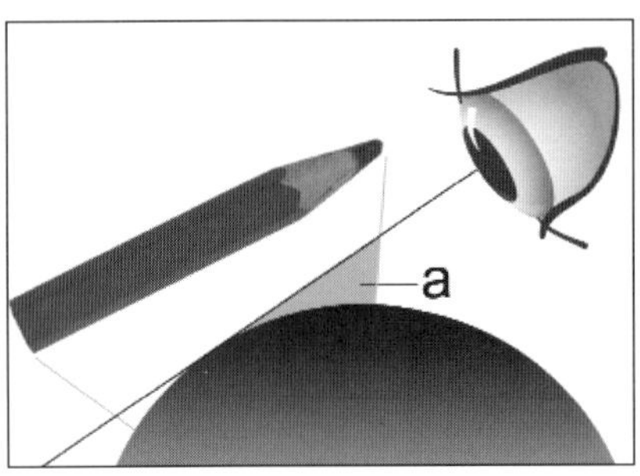

Fig 13. Viewed obliquely, only area 'a' of the reflection is visible.

Think of the curved surface as a pincushion full of pins. Find the pin that's pointing directly at one end of your object, the pencil in this case; do the same for the other end, and now you know where on that surface to construct your reflection.

In addition to these basics you must also allow for the effects of perspective and your chosen line of sight. Depending on your position, you may not see all of the reflection in figure 11. Viewing at an acute angle for example (*fig 13*), will remove the furthest part of the curving reflection from view. Imagine turning the kettle in figure 12 - while all of the pencil remains visible, its reflection will begin to curve out of view.

An inward curving, concave surface works on exactly the same

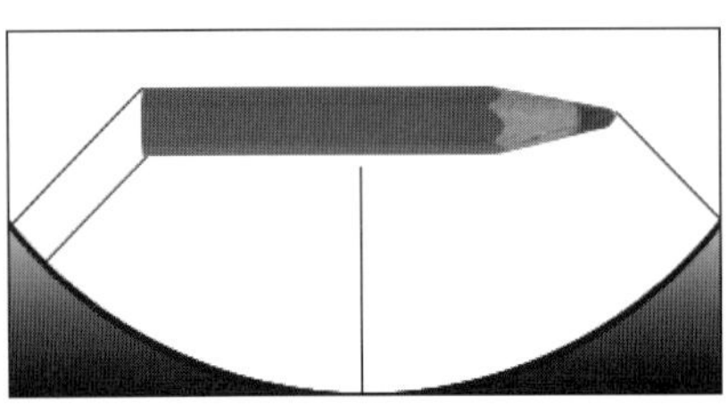

Fig 14. A concave surface can stretch the reflected image. Notice that the reflection will display the end face to view - see fig 15.

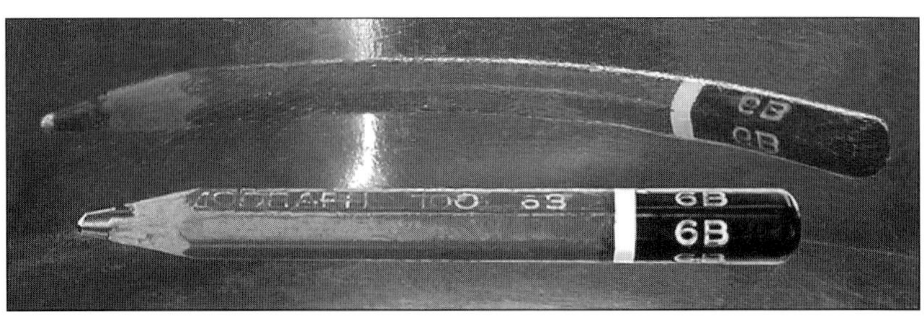

Fig 15. Another hi-tech demonstration showing how reflections distort on a concave surface (the inside of our dog's bowl).

principle but it can stretch the reflected image (*fig 14*). Note too that the ends of the pencil's reflection will be curving towards the viewer so both the point and the face at the other end will be fully visible.

Be aware also that a concave surface can, and often will, reverse the reflection. If you slowly lift the pencil in figure 14 its reflection will gradually lengthen. Lift it above point 'x' (*fig 16*), where the 'lines of sight' from the reflector converge, and its reflection will be overlaid by a reversed one. Keep lifting and this reflection will gradually shorten to reveal that the point on the right hand end of the pencil now appears on the left hand end of its reflection.

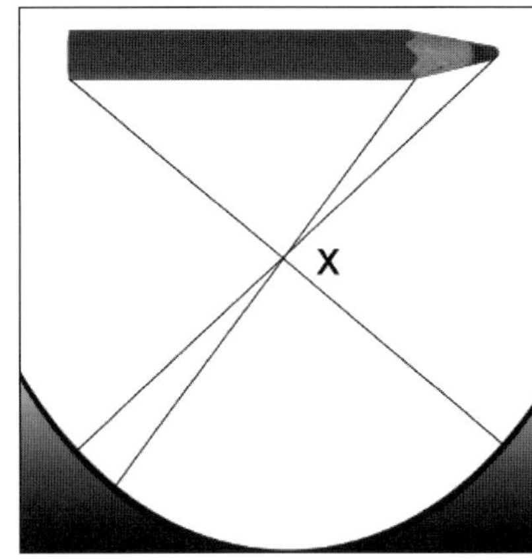

Fig 16. A concave surface can also reverse the reflection.

We've seen how flat, curved surfaces distort in one dimension, just like fairground mirrors (*fig 17*). But dished, or hemispherical, convex and concave surfaces distort in two dimensions. Achieving a high level of realism in these situations requires a highly trained eye, and often the only solution is to set up and study real-life examples. Begin to collect polished metal and chrome-plated objects - tankards, jugs, pipes, polished balls, and anything else you can use as references for your studies - even kettles and dog bowls. It's only when you study that you begin to appreciate the complexity involved in constructing true reflections on rounded surfaces.

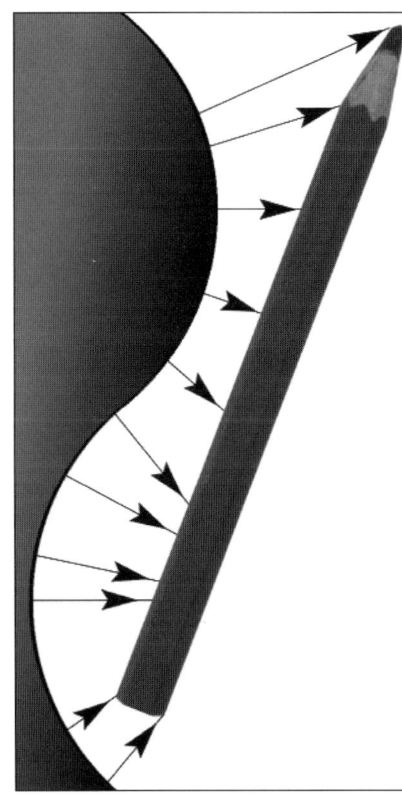

Fig 17. How a flat curved surface 'sees' the pencil and distorts its reflection like a fairground mirror.

My personal experiments have led to the conclusion, however scientifically erroneous, that the brain possesses no built-in recognition of reflections. It reacts to them in an analytical way, resolving only the major features to determine the basic shape of the reflector. That is why I advocate simplicity. The brain may be completely baffled by over-complication. Or the complexity may force it to progressively ignore minor detail until it filters out all but the major keys. In short, over-complication delays the resolution, and included trivial detail is ultimately discarded. Experiment, think logically, and keep it simple.

Reflections on water

Objects not in direct contact

We apply the same basic rules when drawing reflections on water. Remember, an imaginary ray from our eye will meet the surface of still water at the same angle as it is reflected. This constant allows us to work out what will reflect and where the

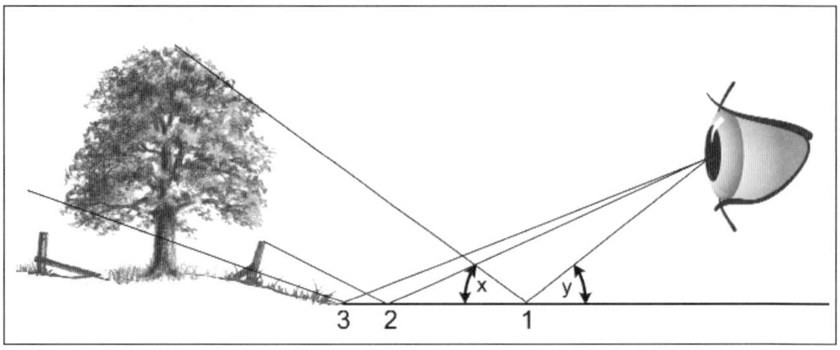

Fig 18. Viewed from a high vantage point reflections are shortened. Note that angle 'x' always equals angle 'y'.

reflection will appear (*fig 18*). Here, from this high viewpoint, you can trace the lines of sight and see:

1. where the top of the tree will reflect
2. where the top of the post will reflect and
3. that the bottom of the tree trunk will not reflect and neither will the furthest fence post.

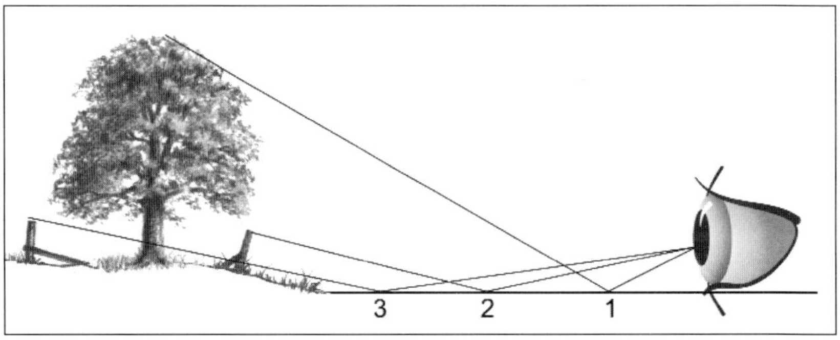

Fig 19. Reflections are lengthened when viewed from a low vantage point. Note the increased spacing of points 3, 2 and 1.

As you begin to explore the world of reflections you will discover that all objects are reflected as mirror images, and when your eyelevel is near to the water's surface (*fig 19*) the reflections are longer than when you have a high viewpoint. We now see more of the tree's trunk reflected but still just miss seeing the far post.

The same rules apply to an ocean swell and waves, and ripples on a pond or puddle. As mentioned earlier, a curved surface only reflects what it can see. Take the case of a rolling wave between you and a boat, and think of the wave as having two sloping sides and a top surface. You cannot see the furthest side of the wave so it reflects nothing (*fig 20*). The side facing you cannot see the boat so it will reflect only sky, as will the trough between that wave and the next. The top surface however, being curved, is bound to offer the perfect angle for your line of site to see a reflection of the boat.

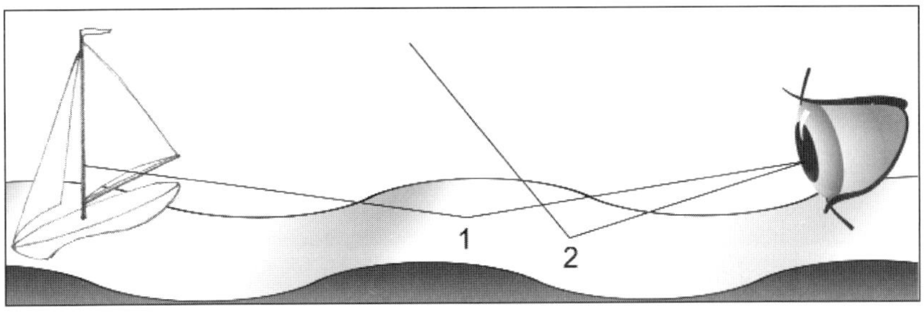

Fig 20. Point 1 reflects the boat. Point 2 reflects the sky.

If there were multiple ripples in figure 20 instead of a heavy swell, each ripple would still reflect a portion of the boat and an area of sky, as the same rules apply to each. The overall reflection would appear to be separated into bands with the sky reflected in between them. In choppy water, the reflection will be fragmented and largely unrecognisable, so choose to emphasise strong vertical elements, such as a mast, to assist the eye.

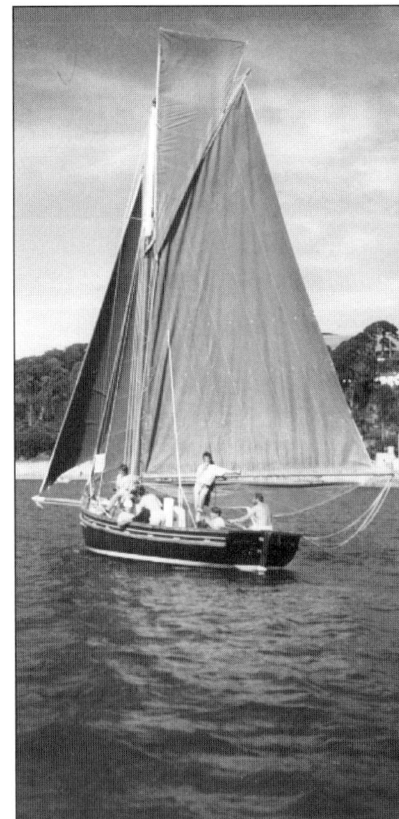

Waves break up the reflection of these sails but the long reflection of the jib sail's deep shadow allows the eye to make sense of what is occurring.

In practice you only need to include the basic keys for a reflection to work. A key I often use is a horizontal band of light cutting through a mirror image reflection (*fig 21*). Here, there is also a second key being used - one that visually separates the posts from their reflections. At the base of each post is a broken white line that represents surface tension.

Surface Tension

I could go to great lengths explaining the science of the surface tension of water. However, as artists we need only be aware that it exists, and that it provides a very useful tool. Basically, water particles cling together really tightly; so tightly that water insects can walk on the surface 'skin' that this tension creates. Fill a glass tumbler full of water, then carefully add more, and you will see the water level rise above the rim of the tumbler. Note the rounded edges of this extra water, which is entirely contained by surface tension. If you insert a pencil into the tumbler (*fig 22*), the surface tension will cause the water to rise up its body and form a convex reflector around it. It is this reflector that we can put to good use.

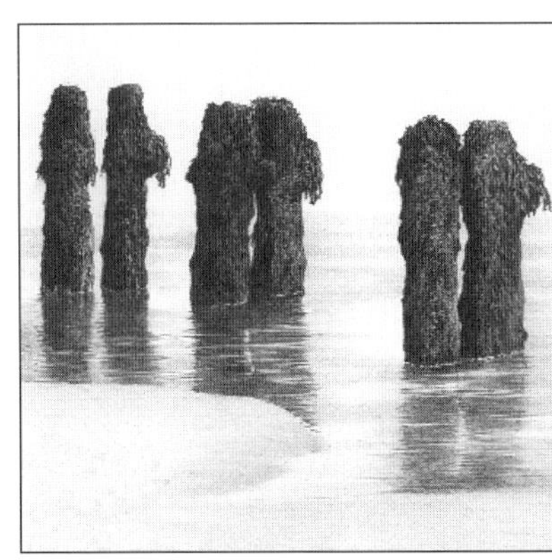

Fig 21. The key to these reflections is the horizontal bands of light cutting through suggestions of mirror images.

Including the surface tension ring around objects standing in water sends the eye a definite signal of where the object stops and its reflection begins. It also indicates the surface of the

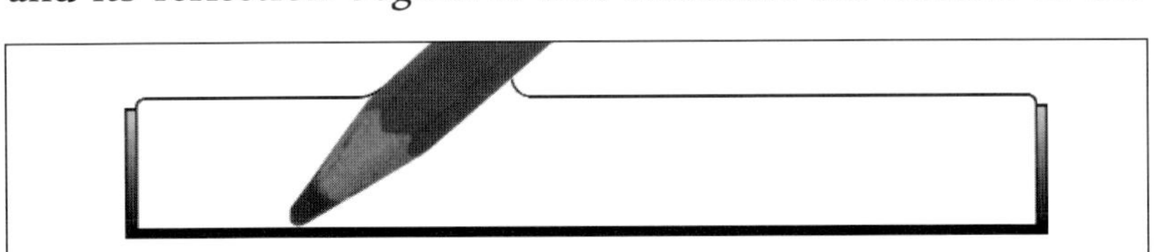

Fig 22. Surface tension supports water at the edges and causes it to climb up anything inserted into it.

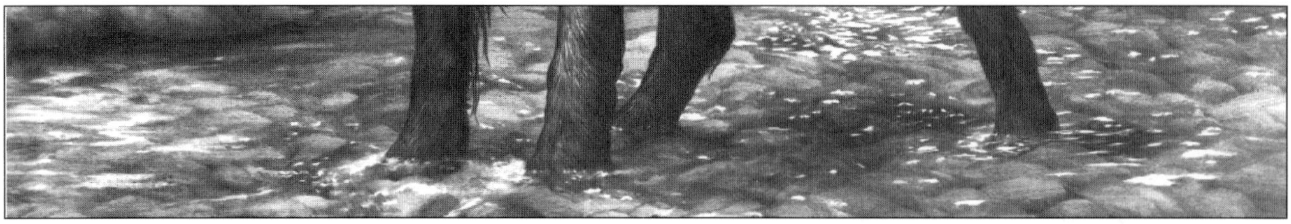

Fig 23. Surface foam and highlights completely ignore the form of the stones on the bed of this stream, and visually establish a plane above them. Surface tension and water droplets around each leg give further clues to the existence and position of this plane.

water. If you have a number of objects in water, their combined surface tension reflections will precisely describe its surface plane. Such devices are very valuable tools, as you cannot draw water itself - it's transparent. Other tools you can use are floating leaves, water weed that bends flat onto the surface, and foam in a running stream (*fig 23*).

'If in doubt, leave it out.'

In shallow, clear water a shadow will fall on the bed of the stream. I've included a cast shadow between the legs of the dog in figure 23 - just enough to help boost the contrast of the foam, and to have the dog interact with the water. If in doubt, leave it out. Include the shadow only if it offers a positive advantage.

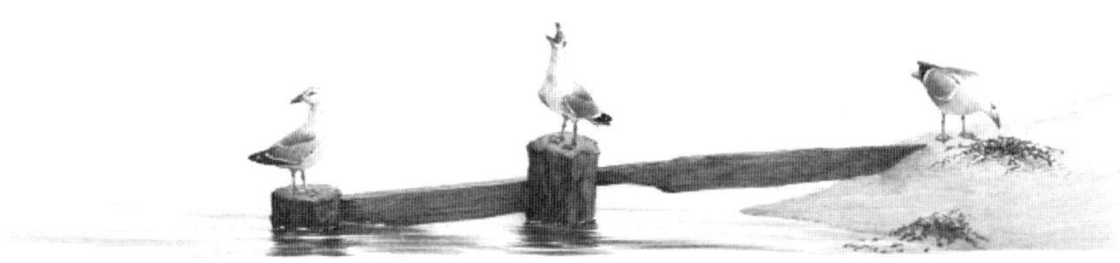

Part of a remarque. This 1½ " (38mm) high drawing contains only major keys. Bands of light signal water, and surface tension rings separate the posts from their reflections.

Drawing water droplets

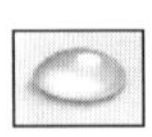

Actual size

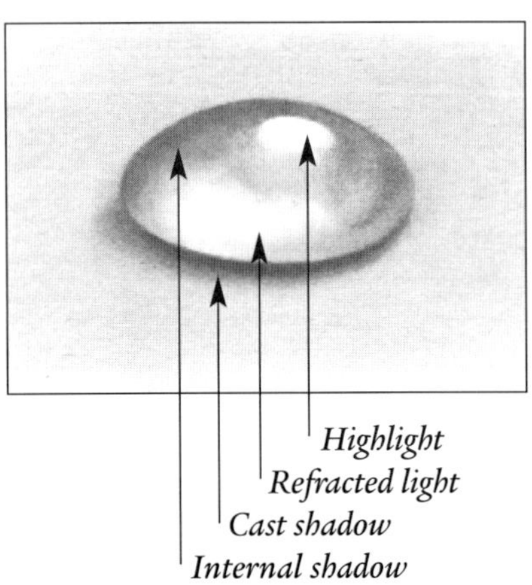

When Nature invented water droplets, the result of surface tension, she had the artist in mind; where we need a highlight to shine, she has provided a dark background; and where we want a shadow, she has provided internal illumination to increase the contrast.

A water droplet casts a shadow, and has a key highlight facing the light source. Internally the light entering through the highlight is conveniently bent, so the area behind the highlight is in shade and the redirected light illuminates the opposite face. If you are working in colour, don't forget that water is transparent and colourless so, except for the white highlight, it will take up the colour of whatever surface it is on.

Refraction

I'm told that early settlers in America nearly starved until they learned to spear fish by watching the local Native Americans. The settlers could see the fish but they couldn't understand why their spears kept missing them. Refraction was the problem. The fish were not where they appeared to be.

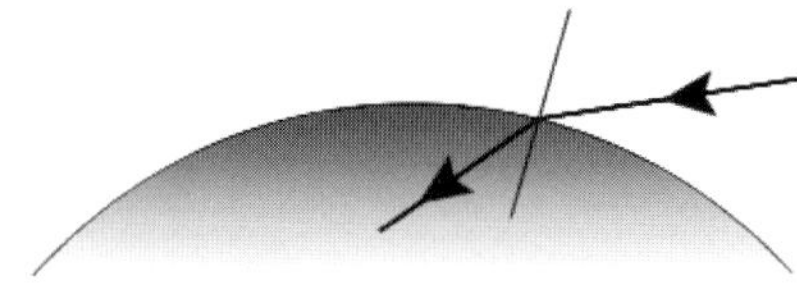

Fig 24. Light passing obliquely through the surface of a fluid-filled body is bent towards an imaginary perpendicular line.

Light passing obliquely through the surface of a fluid-filled body is bent, or refracted, towards an imaginary perpendicular line (*fig 24*).

The reverse effect is true of reflected light because the light rays from the object are bent away from the perpendicular as they move from water to air. The reflected light leaving point 'a' (*fig 25*) is bent before reaching the eye, giving the impression that the water is shallower than it really is, and that the pencil's tip is at point 'b'. As a result of refraction, any object partially in water will visually alter direction - but note that its reflection will still be a mirror image, because this occurs on the surface of the water.

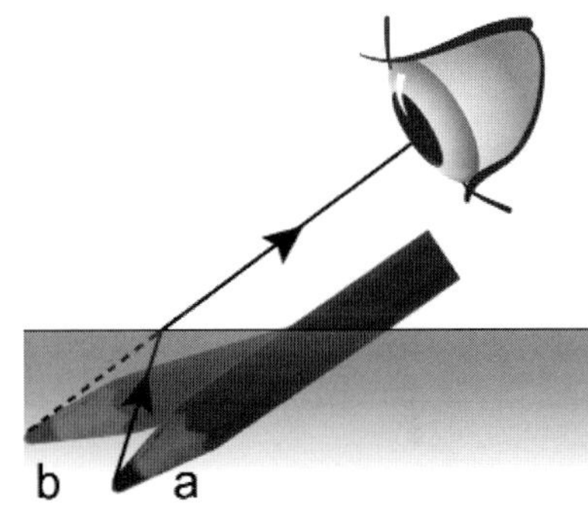

Fig 25. The reverse is true of reflected light shining up from the water.
a - the pencil's true position.
b - the perceived position due to refraction.

Each material, such as water, has its own scientifically calculated, ray-bending factor. But we're artists so just bend it to suit your purpose - including no bend at all.

Water and depth

The more you look directly down into water, the more transparent it is. Look at it at more of an angle and your gaze simply reflects off the surface, and you see nothing below it. If you draw reeds emerging through the water close to your feet you will need to include the underwater part of the stem, its change of direction due to refraction, and the bed of the pond too. The underwater part will be darker simply because there is more available light above water than below. But if you draw those same reeds further away, only the parts above water will be visible and, of course, they will reflect on the surface. There is one exception; where a cast shadow, perhaps from overhanging trees, prevents light reaching the surface. This will extend the distance that you can see into the water. But the shadow itself, by cutting out light, will quickly result in very dark water, which will then have neither a visible bed nor surface reflections. It may assist the eye in this region to include the occasional reed, grasses, flecks of foam, or floating leaves to describe the surface plane.

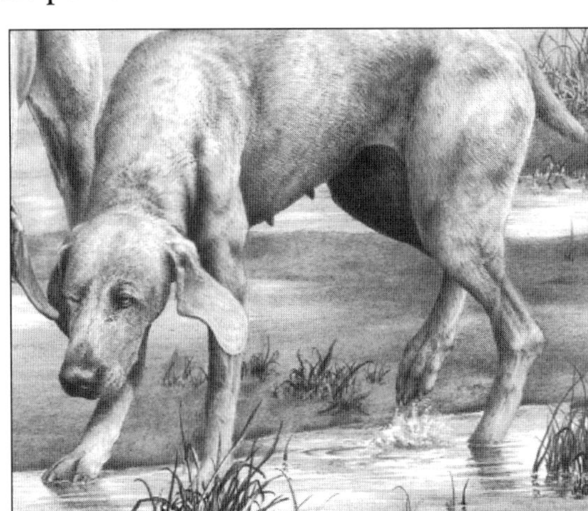

Deliberately simple key reflections connect this dog to the water, and bands of light signal ripples. Simplicity avoids visual confusion.

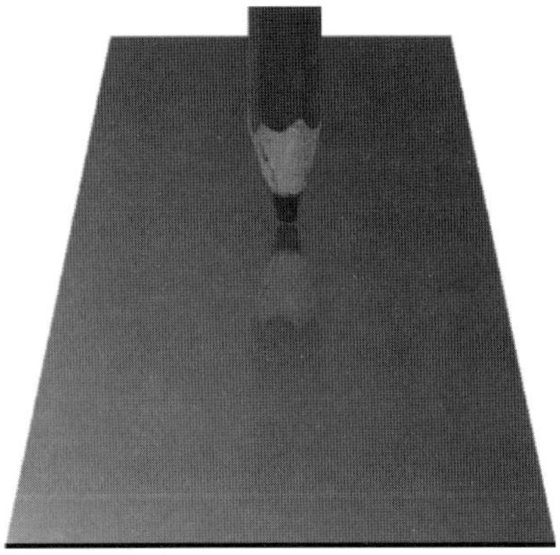

Fig 24. At some point the light absorbency of the reflective surface will equal the strength of the reflected light and the reflection will cease.

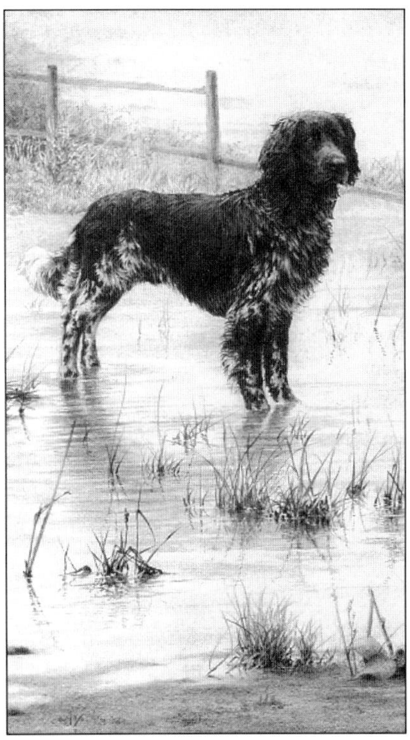

You decide when a reflection fades out, not scientific calculation or your reference photos.

Does accuracy matter?

Frankly, in most situations, accuracy is not important. Don't include elements that should not reflect, don't overdo refraction, and when possible adhere to the rules. But if your overriding artistic aim requires, for example, a longer or shorter reflection than is natural, it will still send the same basic signals. The lazy brain will be grateful for an easily decipherable clue, classify the surface as water and move on. Unless your drawing calls for a greater understanding, you needn't calculate your water reflections with scientific accuracy.

REFLECTION DEPTH

Reflections from solid surfaces, however, do need to more rigidly conform to the rules. Viewing from great distances is rarely involved, and the brain more clearly understands the way foreground reflections work. If you stand a vase on a varnished surface and are unsure of the correct depth, or length, of the reflection, you can use illusion to overcome the problem. The base of the vase will reflect clearly, as it is in contact with the surface. A point half way up may reflect, and a point at the top may not. As light is reflected from points ever higher up the vase it has further to travel down to the surface, and the light itself is more likely to have become scattered and weakened. At some point (*fig 24*) the light absorbency of the reflective surface will equal the strength of the reflected light and the reflection will cease. There are no visual rules to determine where this will happen so we, as artists, can engineer that point to suit our own purposes.

Reflections really are magic. Calm, transparent, and colourless water is defined purely by the reflections on its surface; remove the reflections and Hey Presto! - the water simply disappears.

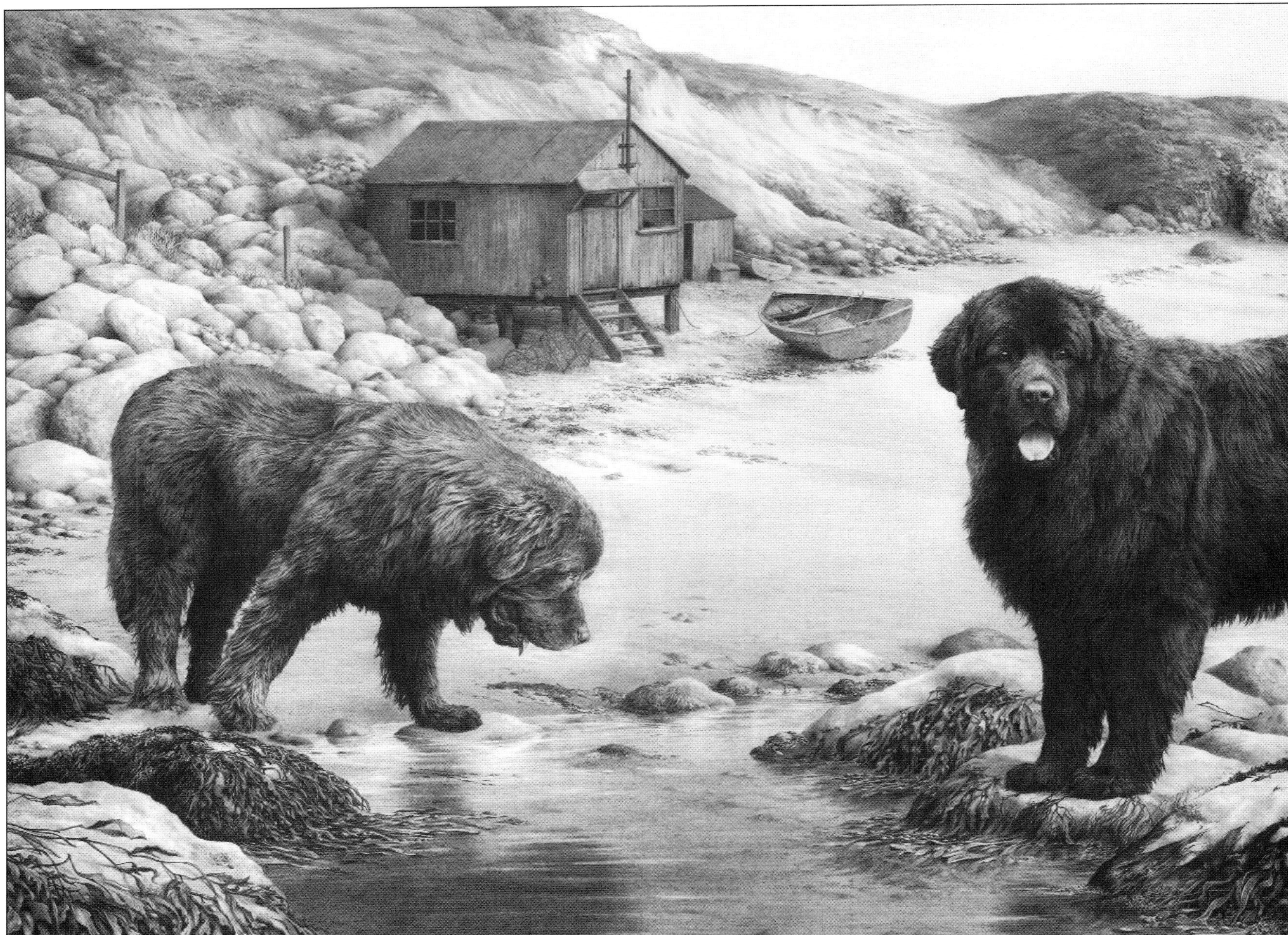

'Whistlers Cove' featuring the Newfoundland. A limited edition print of 650 plus 25 Artists Proofs *16½" x 13" (41.5 x 32 cm)*

Drawing Foliage
Leafing through the methods...

'IN PRACTICE EVERY TYPE OF FOLIAGE, BE IT TREE, WEED OR GRASS, REQUIRES THREE DISTINCT DRAWING METHODS'

This is where country walks pay dividends, or even a stroll around your garden or local park. Nothing beats personal observation. When I'm drawing ground-cover foliage I often collect samples during a walk along our lane. Back in the studio I draw with the samples in my hand, turning them around to study the leaves from different angles. Fortunately I live on a two-mile long farm track, so I have plenty of natural inspiration. If I want to draw a particular weed, such as stinging nettles, I find a patch in one of our fields and draw them from life. Simple line drawings usually suffice as memory aids for when I return to the studio.

Initially, drawing any form of foliage, with the profusion of leaves and their apparent complexity, might seem difficult. However, grasses, weeds, bushes, and trees all becomes much simpler to draw if you first observe the overall form and ignore the details. If you are new to drawing trees, ignore the leaf shapes and concentrate instead on the way they are grouped - fan-shaped sprays or rounded clumps for example. It often helps if you squint at foliage, which reduces the detail and displays only the shapes or groupings. Draw your tree with the aim of displaying its overall shaping rather than getting fixated on detail. This is a useful exercise because, with the sole exception of foreground trees, most foliage is not readily seen as individual leaves.

When you first begin drawing weeds and grasses you cannot, of course, adopt the same strategy, as most consist of nothing but leaves. Instead, identify the principal leaf shape - spiky, sinuous, slender, wide and flat - and incorporate the general shape into your drawing, which will allow you to concentrate on the arrangement instead of the detail.

Later you may wish to be more type-specific with your foliage. With your earlier experience of drawing generalised leaf shapes you will find you notice and retain more information whenever you have the opportunity to observe foliage. I often use known leaf shapes such as Sycamore or Oak but I also invent many as I draw. As long as you are consistent with your shapes and growth habits, the eye readily accepts such manufactured foliage as possessing a reality.

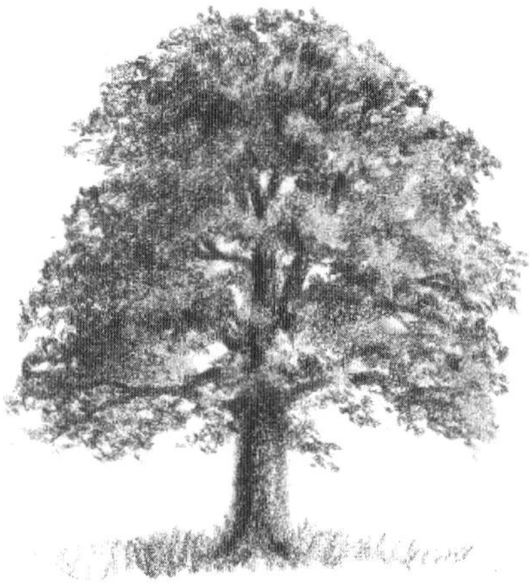

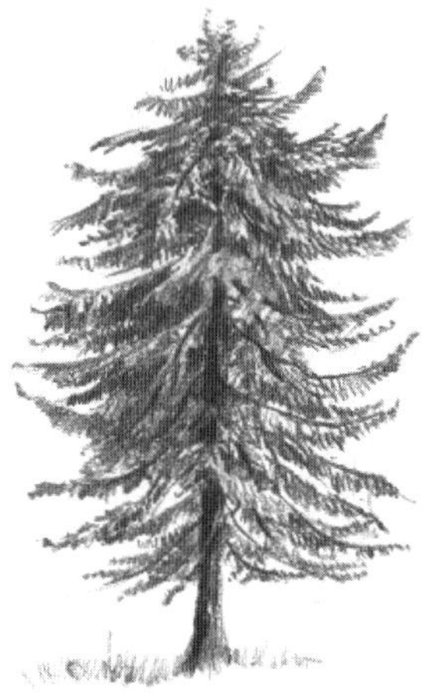

Initially, draw the tree with the aim of displaying its overall shaping rather than getting fixated on detail.

In practice every type of foliage, be it tree, weed or grass, requires three distinct drawing methods:

- *Background*: Hazy, only the overall form is apparent, not individual leaf shapes.
- *Midground*: A combination of overall form with a suggestion of individual leaves.
- *Foreground*: The closest leaves are clearly seen but diminish in clarity with depth.

For simplicity we'll concentrate on foreground foliage and return to the other two later in the tree section. For now bear in mind that the later techniques apply equally to grasses and weeds.

Drawing ground-cover foliage

I covered the basics of drawing grass in Chapter 10 (Negative Drawing) so refer to it now if you haven't already done so. It's worth refreshing your understanding, as the majority of my foliage, plant and tree drawing techniques employ negative drawing. In essence, a pencil does not draw grass; it defines its edges by drawing around it.

The inclusion of weeds in grass is an omission I often see; yet they add a greater sense of reality. They are especially useful for suggesting depth. This is easy to accomplish (*fig 1*). First, establish the grass using negative drawing - lightly outlining each status stalk, drawing the less-defined grasses behind, and then shading them to add form and suggest which stalks are behind others. Then, at any future time you choose, add positive-drawn weeds (*fig 2*). I tend to favour twigs or a make-believe form of Dock with seed heads, both of which I've used here. These dark, woody stalks can be woven between the grasses, drawing behind some and over others to establish a true sense of recession. They also serve to fool the brain into seeing far more than is actually present. They attract the eye because of their tonal prominence, and allow the brain to accept the grass as a profusion that doesn't require further understanding. I often employ this device, using a prominent, or status, leaf, twig or even plant, to suggest that everything surrounding it possesses the same reality. In actual reality the surrounding drawing is quite basic, as you can see in figure 2.

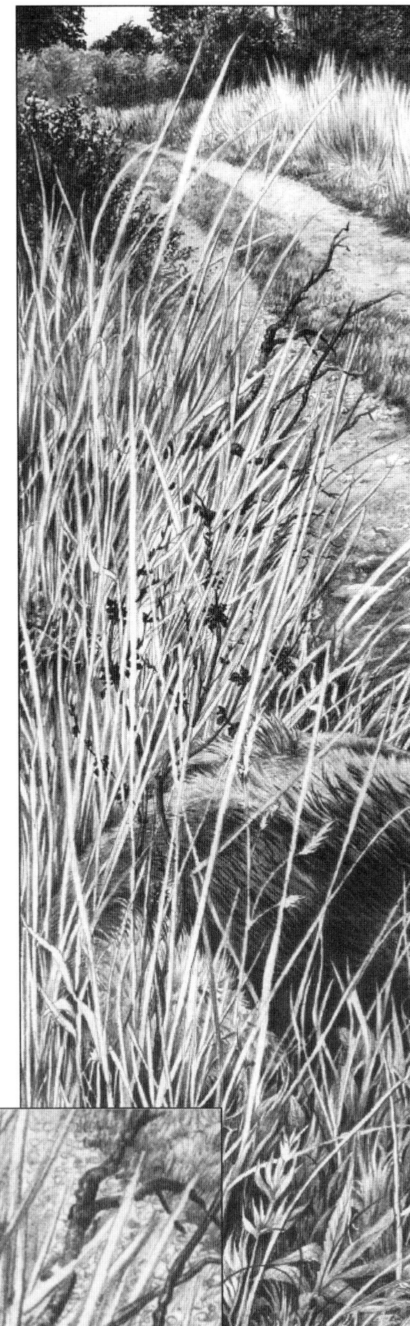

Fig 1. (above) The inclusion of positive-drawn weeds adds depth to negative-drawn wild grasses.

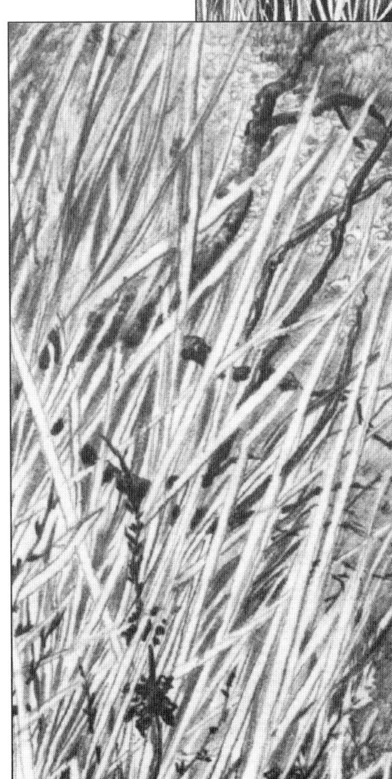

Fig 2. (left) Detail from figure 1. Actual width: ¾" (18mm).

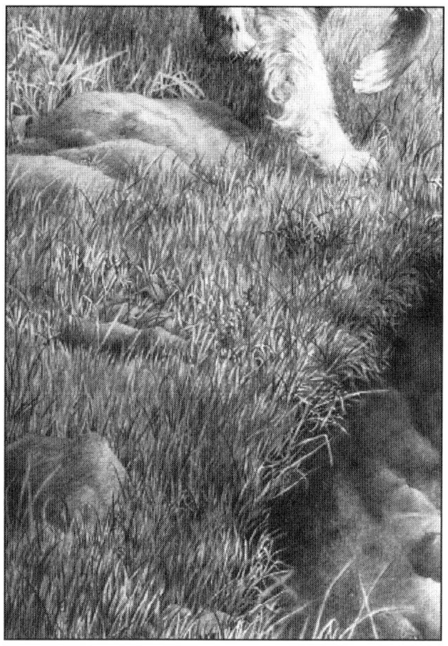

Detail from 'Pyrenean Pals'

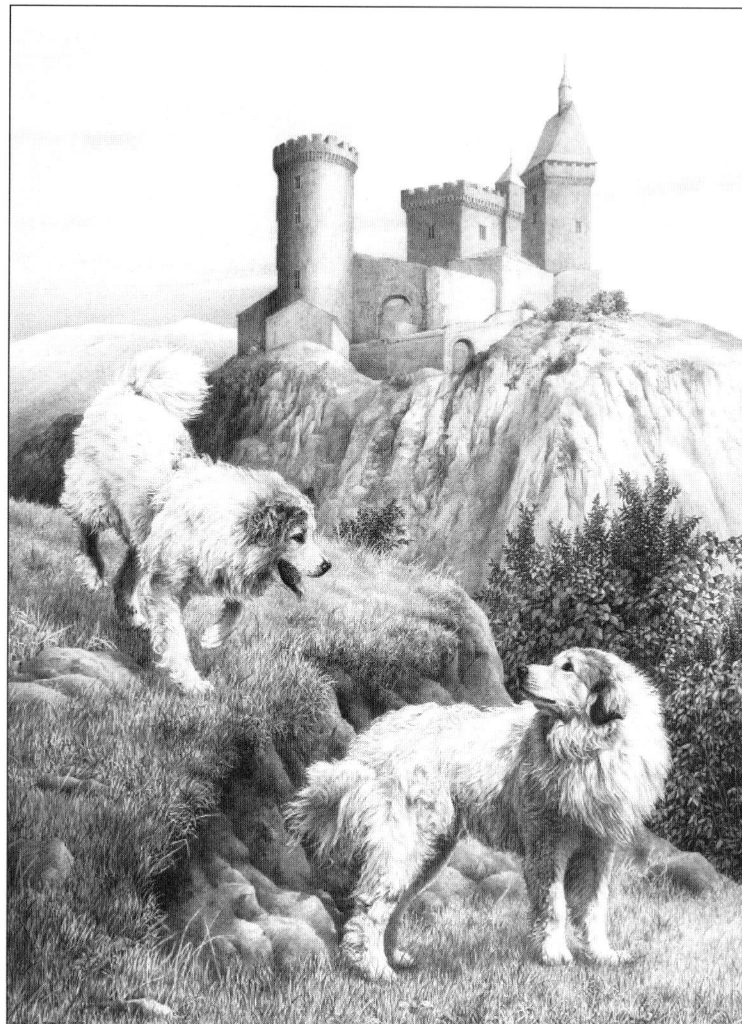

'Pyrenean Pals' featuring Great Pyrenees or Pyrenean Mountain Dogs.

'TRAIN YOURSELF TO 'SEE' THE GRASS AS YOU DRAW AROUND IT, USING ONLY NEGATIVE DRAWING'

Drawing short grass

The technique used for drawing short grass once again involves negative drawing. In the area in which you're working, establish a few key foreground status blades then draw a spontaneous resemblance of grass around them. Occasionally you may get positive-drawn grass to work but, as a rule, pencil lines do not form believable foreground grass.

Work quickly so your brain is forced to work intuitively; too much forethought can lead to regimented or stilted drawing. With practice the drawing of the status leaves can be incorporated into the drawing as you work. If you work quickly and intuitively, and concentrate on drawing the shadows and not the actual blades, you will find blades suggesting themselves. Slow down a little to develop these serendipitous accidents then move on. Ring the changes; introduce a subtle variety, and occasionally include a positive element to add

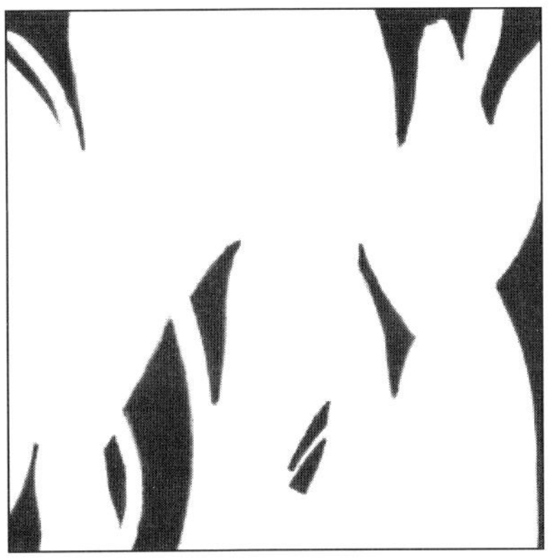

Fig 4: Think about shapes

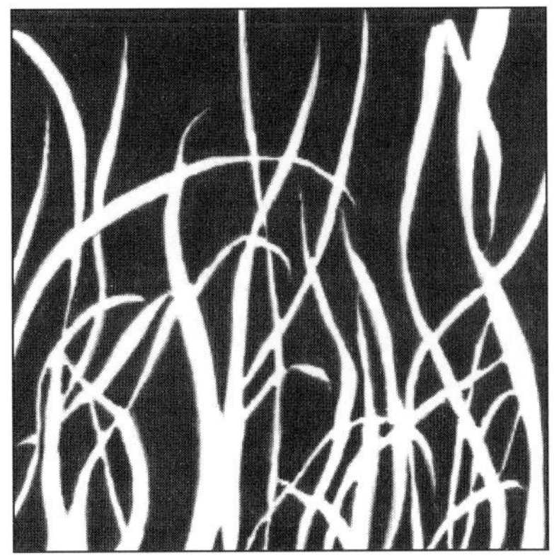

Fig 5: Complete the design

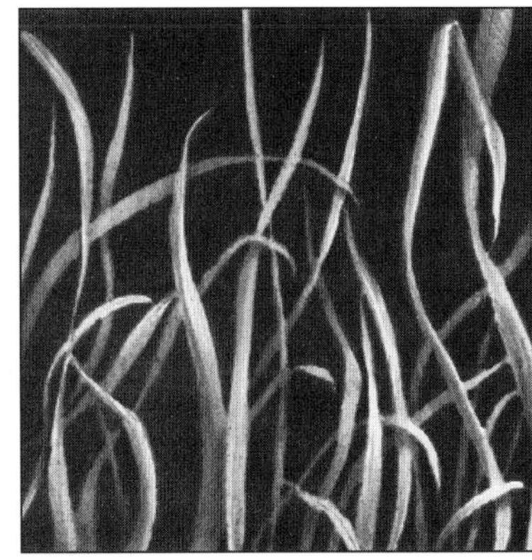

Fig 6: Add tone

depth to the grass. I favour twigs and low-growing weeds. But don't overdo it. Grass almost always constitutes a minor element in a drawing; it should enhance and not compete with the main subject. It should however, look realistic and one common error often negates this. Grass does not grow from the baseline of your drawing; it extends below the baseline and right under the feet of the viewer. Also note that grass recedes quickly into bands of broken tone and finally into variegated tone only. (*fig 3*)

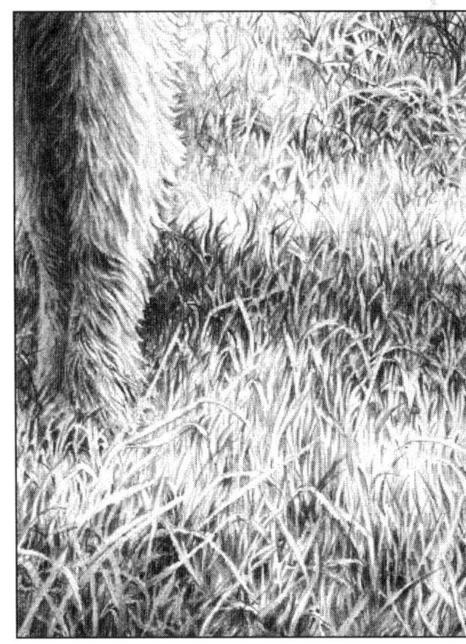

Fig 3: Draw grass emerging from below the baseline, not rooted in it. Note how it quickly degrades in clarity as it recedes. This detail is from the drawing shown at the end of this chapter.

Train yourself to 'see' the grass as you draw around it, using only negative drawing. A useful and entertaining exercise to is to draw the background in black without first outlining any stalks. Accuracy is unimportant; just have fun. Think about the shapes; the great majority, like blades of grass, will involve curves (*fig 4*). Do not draw outlines around blades of grass at any stage. Look for accidental blade shapes that suggest their own route then carry them through to a completion, and introduce blades emerging from below the baseline. Complete the design (*fig 5*), keeping it logical throughout; what begins must end convincingly. Now add tone (*fig 6*) to push some blades back into the shadow, weave others through the design, and bring some to the front.

My drawing of the grass in figure 3 uses almost the same technique except that the black areas are suggestions of grass. This technique applies also to the drawing of hay bales, loose straw, and even snakes in a pit!

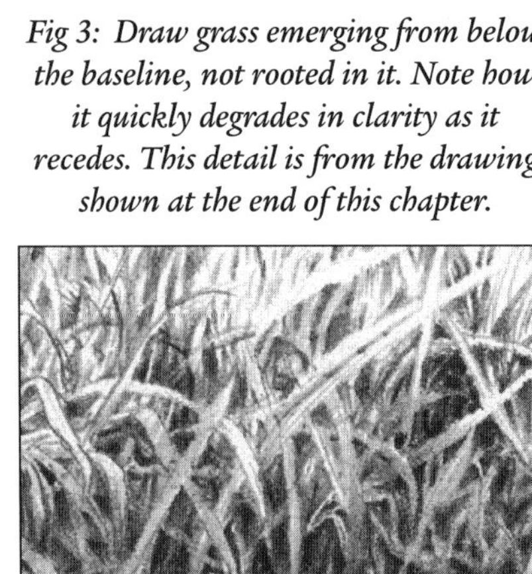

Close-up of fig 3: Most blades were not pre-planned. The spaces between them were first spontaneously drawn then the blades shaded to give them body.

Researching foliage sources

Sooner or later you come across a major problem - how to vary your leaf shapes to maintain a natural random appearance. Observation of Nature will provide the answers you need and sketching from Nature will provide ready reference material. It

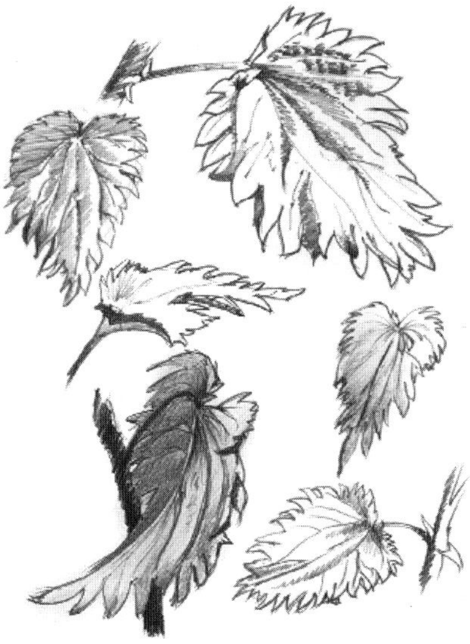

Fig 7: A sketch of nettles. Source material the safe way!

will also increase your understanding of growth habits. I prefer to draw simple line sketches with perhaps a suggestion of form (*fig 7*), which help me to invent a succession of differing leaf shapes. Sketching also gets me around a personal problem - I like to use Stinging Nettles, because of their distinctive leaf shape, but don't enjoy holding a bunch in my hand as live models!

The basic technique explained

The following technique, which forms the basis for all other techniques, is one I use in areas of deep shade where detail isn't important.

Step 1: With no particular plan in mind, I begin by defining the major elements - the status leaves and stalks - letting each one suggest the next. Just keeping an overall balance to the composition is sufficient to create a pleasing arrangement.

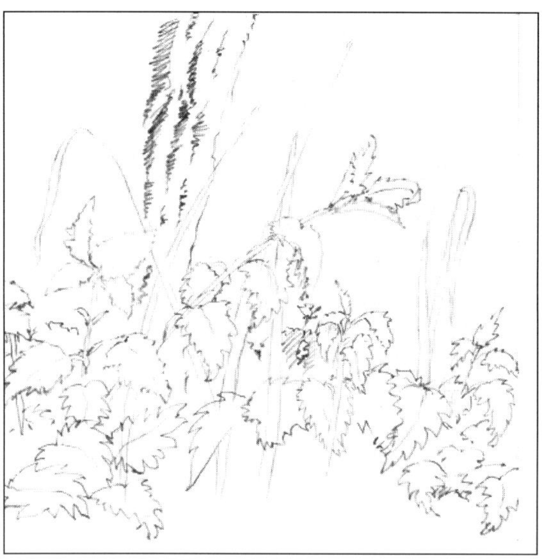

Step 1

By creating the foliage as I draw I find I get a more instinctive and natural appearance.

Step 2: I've begun to create the nettle-like background. This is negative drawing so I pay attention to the inside edge of my line as I draw around the status leaves.

I'm using the points around the perimeter of each leaf as the visual key, so I'm making sure they are well defined. I'm also leaving small random shapes to break up and add interest to large black areas.

Step 3: I've applied the first layer of tone to describe the rounded form of most of the leaves, and highlighted the status ones. Many other leaves and shapes have been forced into the shadows. Imagine

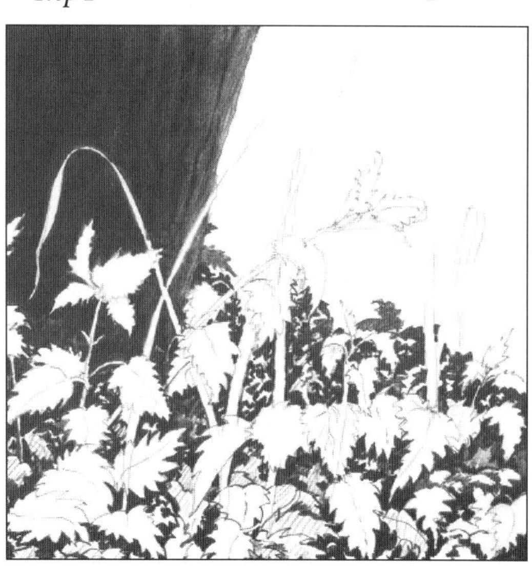

Step 2

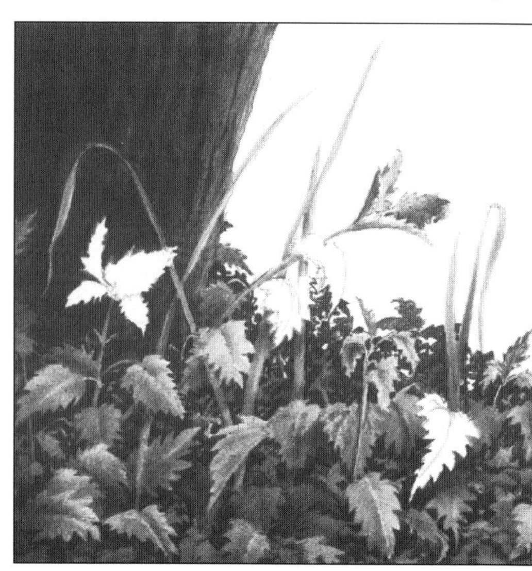

Step 3

pushing your pencil into the nettles themselves as you draw. Truly picturing the leaves as being real.

Some areas are being left white until I decide how shady they are to be.

Step 4: One leaf is reshaped before being shaded and a final layer of tone adjusts others.

To keep this simple I used the same chisel-pointed 2B lead throughout. The only attempt at detail, apart from the saw tooth edges, was the occasional leaf's central rib and the suggestion of tree bark - both solely produced by the shading.

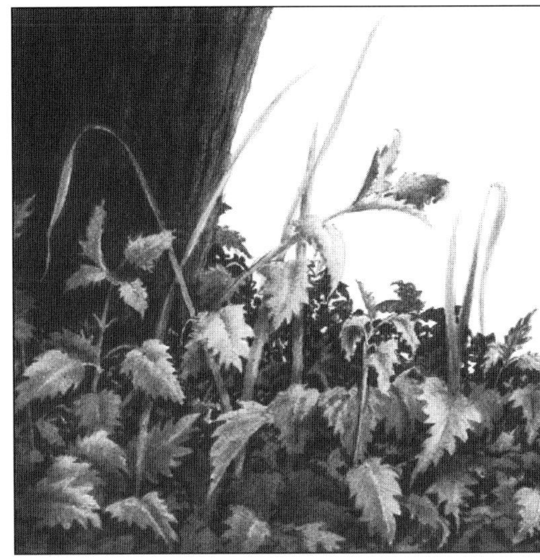

Step 4
Size: 2 3/4" (7cm) square Time: 2 hours

Notice how your eye is attracted to the status leaves, which provide the visual keys to shape and texture, and how your brain readily accepts the less-distinct shapes as being leaves too. Working in this way will allow you to concentrate on one element of the drawing at a time - deep shade, partial shade, or highlight - and greatly simplifies the complexity.

Detailed, foreground foliage

Where the inclusion of detail is essential I use a modified version of the previous method. I still outline the status elements but far more lightly. Then I design the less important leaves, often completing each one as I plot its position. Finally the status leaves, which hold the visual keys, are completed. As I mentioned before, I have a liking for big Dock leaves. They're very good for filling an area without over-complicating it - or making too much work!

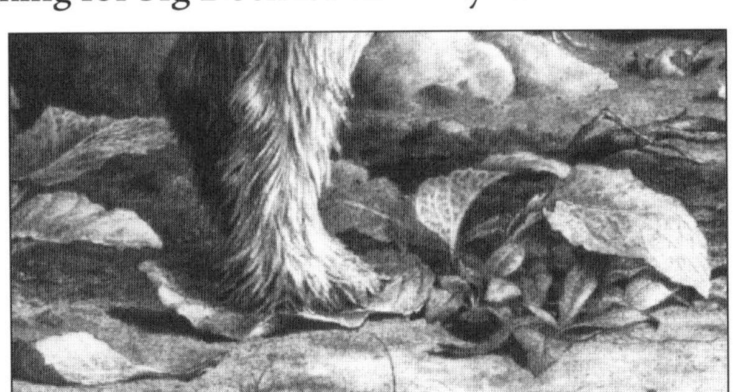

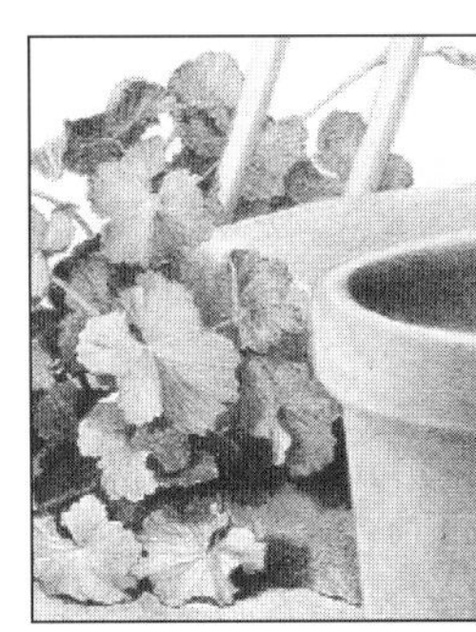

Being observant and storing visual information about plant types and habits is certainly beneficial. However, unless the drawing demands species accuracy, I usually invent the foliage while basing it on actual plants I am familiar with. If you adopt this approach you must be aware that certain rules of Nature must be applied.

Some leaves spring straight from a plant's stem and others have stalks. Also the growth habit can be either opposite or, most often, alternate (*fig 8*). To draw believable foliage the basic rules must be followed. Even if your drawing style involves an interpretation of leaves, rather than actual leaves, the growth habit

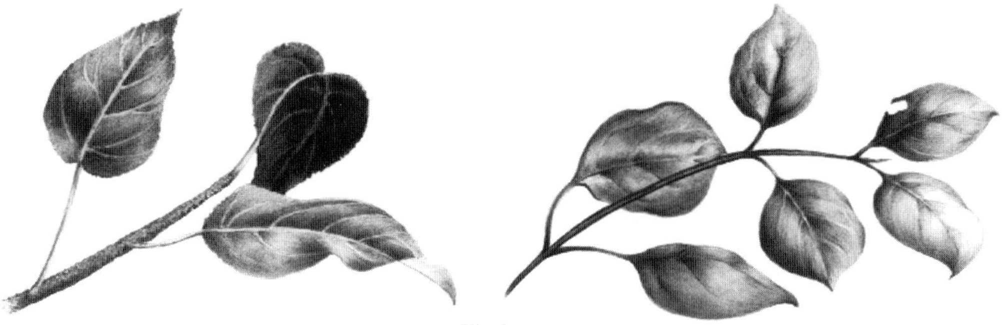

Fig 8

Alternate leaves *Opposite leaves*

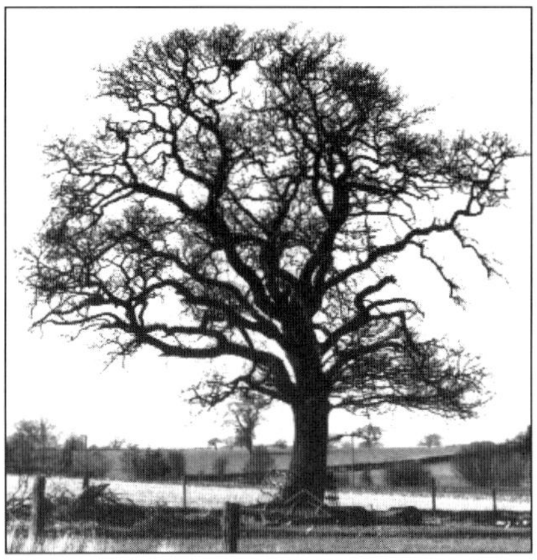

Photograph or sketch trees in winter to gain an understanding of their structure.

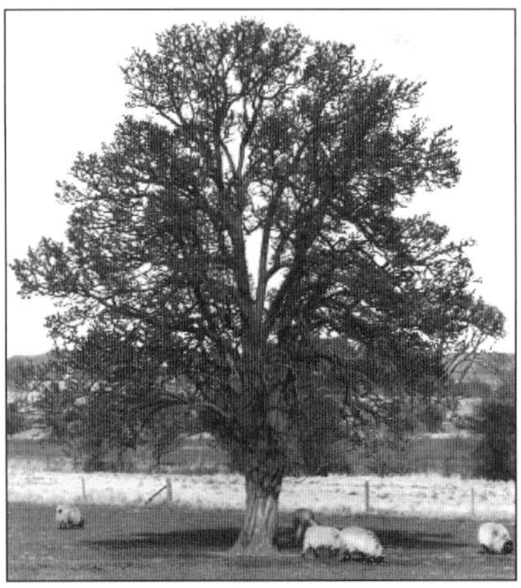

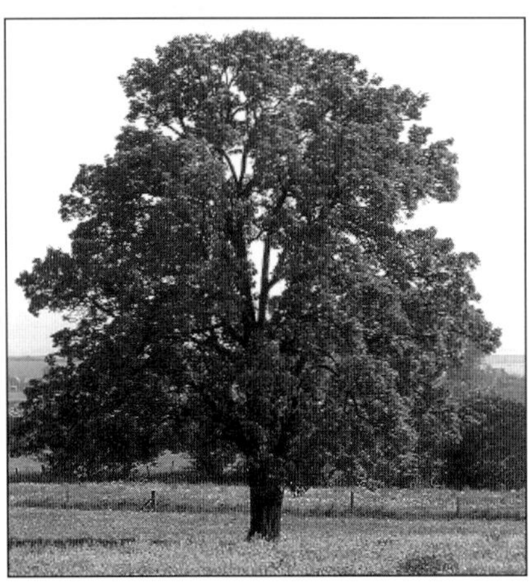

Photograph the same tree from the same viewpoint at different times of year.

must be both natural and consistent throughout the drawing.

Notice the variety in these two drawings; some leaves have been turned so they are in full or partial shadow, others are in full light. This arrangement gives not only visual interest but also the chance to broaden the tonal range, which boosts the perceived contrast.

Drawing trees

First find your tree. This is not as easy as it might appear - trees have a habit of looking unbalanced or just plain awkward. Despite Nature's best endeavours, not all trees make good subjects. Finding or designing one with the appearance of good balance can take some time. Unless a leaning or grossly unsymmetrical tree is going to be of some advantage to your drawing, you would benefit from first studying and sketching trees. Note the way they are firmly rooted in the ground, and how the branches spring from the trunk.

Personally, I often use photographs as a base from which to work, amalgamating elements from two or more trees into one. Whatever your approach, one aspect remains constant - trees posses three-dimensional form. For simplicity I will concentrate on common deciduous trees but the same rules and techniques will apply to evergreens.

Overall Form and Structure...

Trees are not flat structures of entwining branches. Nor are they composed of fully visible trunks with branches and foliage only at the sides. Of course, some branches will extend to each side but others will recede beyond the trunk or will be pointing straight at you. A country walk in winter offers a good opportunity to study this. Later, when the trees are clothed in leaves, you can study the same ones again with a full knowledge of their internal skeleton.

Brought right down to basics, a tree in leaf is like a distorted and truncated cone on a stick. As that three-dimensional conical shape conforms to normal lighting rules, so must a tree. It will possess a shady side, a highlighted side, and a shadow beneath. The trunk, being cylindrical, will have a highlighted side that curves round to a core shadow, and the shady side will be partially lit by reflected light, which may help you to better show its edge.

Keep this basic shape in mind as you work, coupled with the chosen direction of light, and the tree that you produce will possess an overall reality of form.

Analysing what you see

There are three major aspects of a tree that are important to its appearance - surface texture and shape, internal bough structure, and gaps through which you can see through to the other side. A tree is not an amorphous collection of leaf-shaped items or random marks that, you hope, will fool the viewer's brain into reading as 'tree'. A tree is an ordered, layered object with an outer covering around an inner armature or core. It's only by analysing what you see that you will gain the full understanding that allows you to draw realistically.

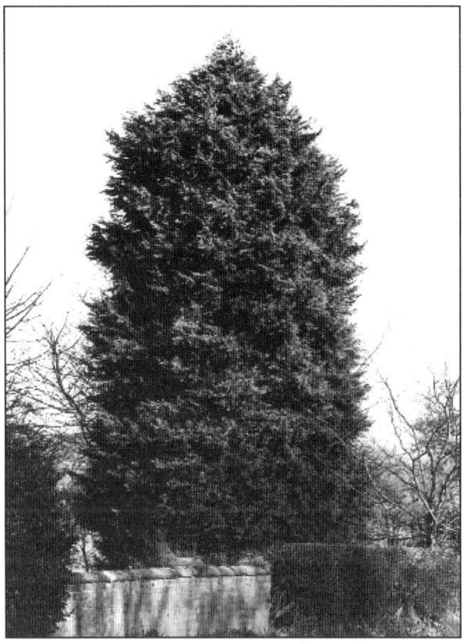

Texture and shaping

Texture and Shaping

Your tree must look as though it is clothed in believable leaves. It is these leaves, combined with the prevailing lighting direction, that are used to describe the internal shapes that make up the tree.

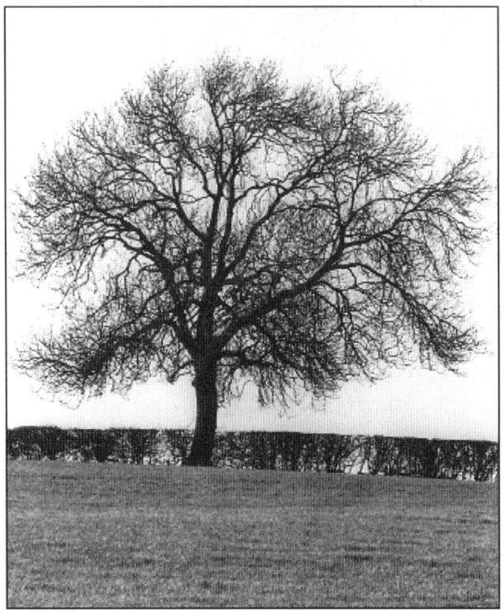

Internal structure

Internal structure

Whether you are drawing hair, grass or a bough of a tree, one important point extends to them all - what you start you must finish. Nothing looks more false to the eye than a bough that springs from nowhere or one that simply disappears. When designing the structure of a tree, imagine you're building a wire frame for a sculpture - every wire must be attached at some point to another. The trunk forms the major armature and it has to be sufficiently sturdy and well grounded to support the entire structure. From this radiate thick 'wires' that form the major limbs. A common mistake is to draw limbs that are too straight. Many trees possess wildly contorted shapes, and it's these shapes that partly define the species of tree. Notice too how lower limbs may grow horizontally or even down towards the ground, and that the higher up the tree a limb emerges, the more the angle between it and trunk decreases, until the topmost limbs grow almost vertically.

'Most trees will flair out just as they meet the ground. Emphasizing this flare and avoiding drawing the tree trunk straight will give the tree a good base.'

Diane Wright, Artist

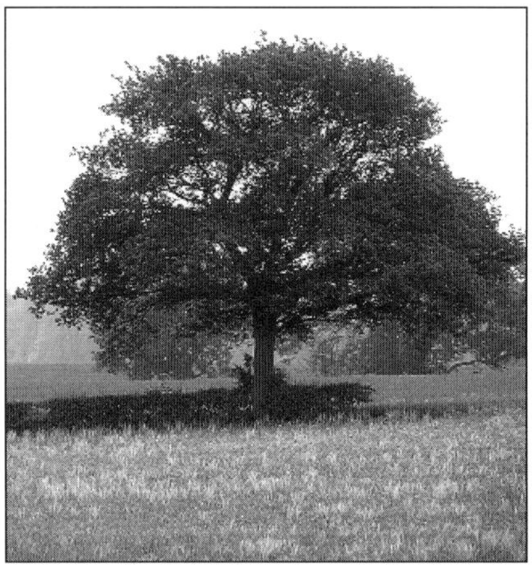

Holes and gaps give clues to the internal structure of a tree in leaf.

From the limbs spring a greater number of branches. Study the way these emerge from the limbs. Often the limb will be seen to thicken at the joint, like a knuckle. Identify the irregularities, the bends, kinks, and thickenings that give the tree its reality. You can often see these more easily by studying the negative space between the branches rather than looking at the branches directly.

Finally the branches themselves subdivide a number of times into more, progressively thinner, branches until they eventually fountain out into a mass of thin, leaf-bearing, twigs. If you make your internal structure believable, the eye will accept what you draw as reality.

HOLES AND GAPS

Holes through the foliage are a great boon as they enable you to show the far side of the tree and add reality to your drawing. These holes and gaps often expose the hard edges of the limbs and boughs, which you can use to your advantage in two ways. Drawing the boughs in stark silhouette (they rarely receive direct light) will allow the eye to more easily follow their route and gain an understanding of the tree's structure. And the dark boughs will contrast well with the foliage, imparting a softer, more enigmatic look to the leaves.

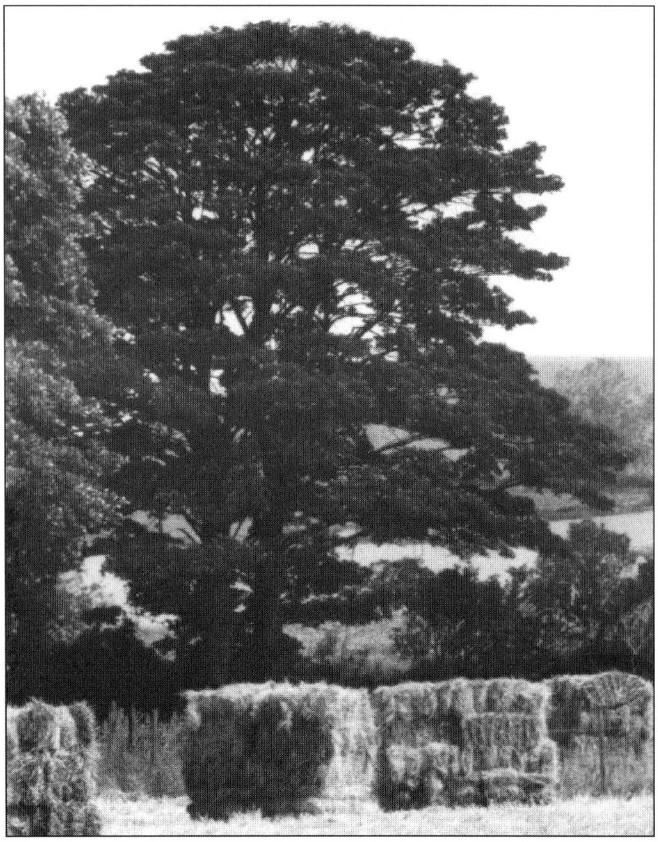

Fig 9

The drawing technique you choose is largely determined by the position of the tree or bush in your composition - foreground (where each leaf shape is discernable), background (where the leaves form a mottled pattern that merely describe the overall three-dimensionality), or midground (somewhere in between the two). Let's begin with a midground scenario.

The midground tree

Let's assume that a suitable tree has been found and photographed. First the armature is created then indications made of where the major masses of foliage, redesigned to suit our requirements, will be appear.

This tree (*fig 9*) was photographed with a 200mm zoom lens at a distance of about 250 metres for incorporating into a specific composition. The lack of detail and sharp focus is not important - indeed it is a bonus, as it concentrates attention on the forms within the tree. The internal structure is nicely silhouetted, allowing the eye to follow the route of the major limbs.

The internal structure has been mapped out (*fig 10*) and the main areas of shadow noted. Note that the tree originally had two trunks. One has been removed and the emphasis placed on the centre and right of the tree, as the composition requires other trees to overlap the left side.

This preparatory stage is not drawn on the final working surface but separately for later transferral. Use of this method allows unlimited exploration of the form with no fear of damage to the eventual drawing paper. Examination established, in this case, that the masses of foliage have rounded tops when viewed straight on, and those to the side sweep downwards. We can put this understanding to good use when the drawing commences.

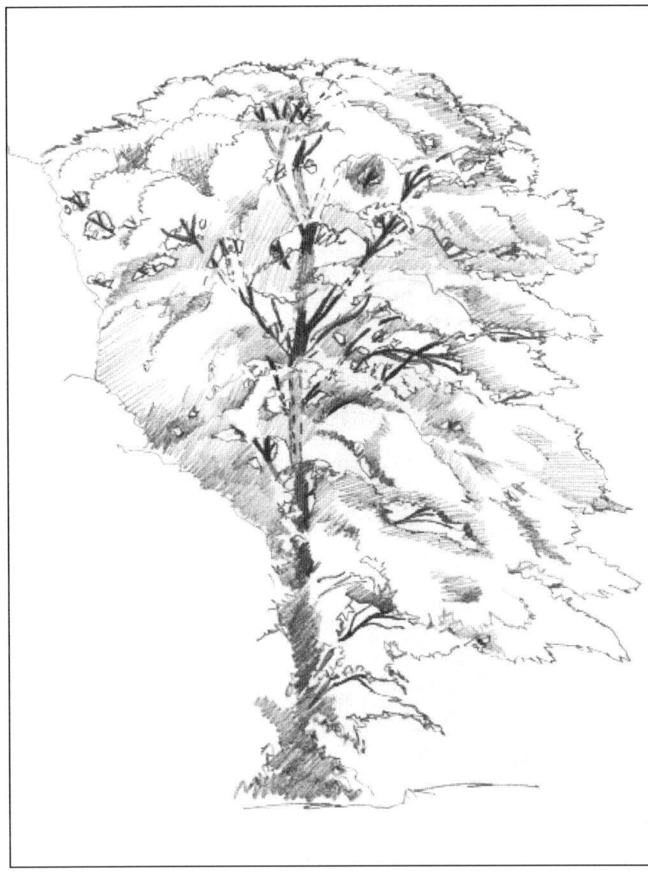

Fig 10

Note in my completed drawing (*fig 11*) that the left-hand side of the tree is pure invention, the right hand side conforms only to the photograph's outline, and some of the holes through the foliage have been closed and others opened.

Only the spirit of the tree has been used; the actual foliage masses have been altered to better suit my requirements. Photographs can provide detail but they are better used as compendiums of overall information; they give a feel for form and texture, which can add a sense of realism to invention.

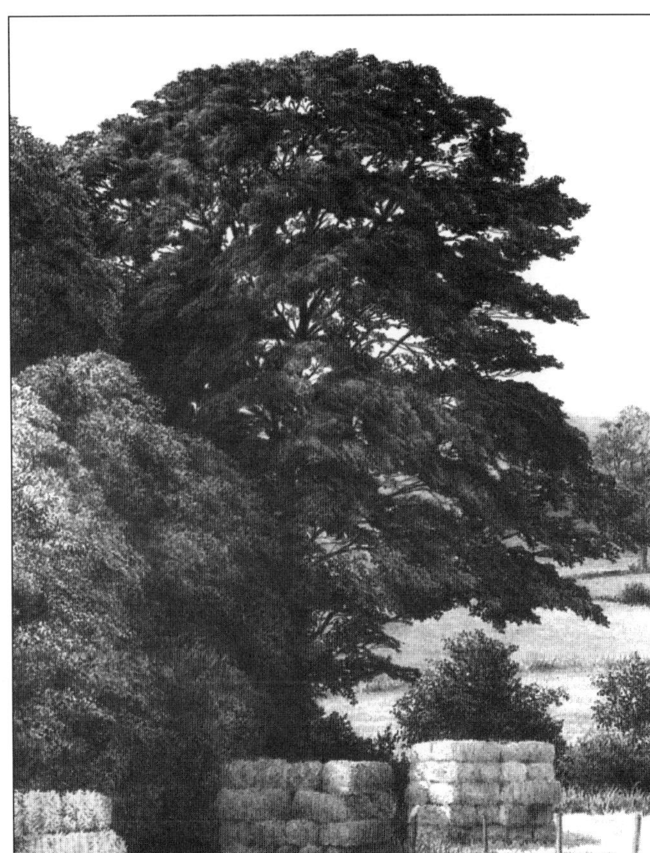

Fig 11. Detail from Done Balin'

Degrees of detail

To make life easy the 'clothing' of a tree can be broken down into a collection of similar elements.

Just experiment with small sections until

Tip

Initially, try making very small drawings of trees so you are forced to concentrate on the major features and not the detail.

Gradually increase the size and imagine them getting nearer to you. You'll find a need for the detail at the right time and in the right quantity.

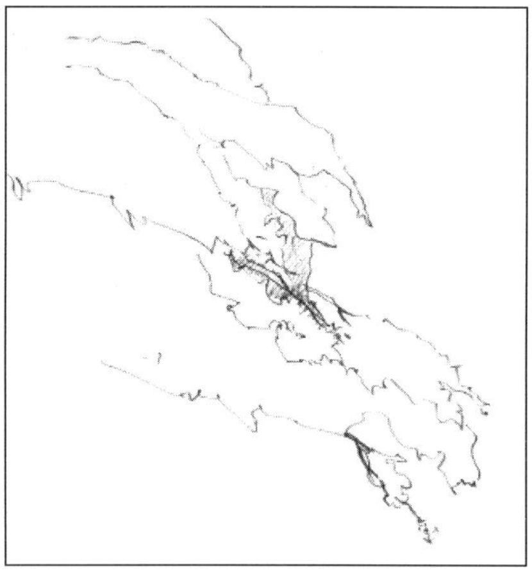

Fig 12

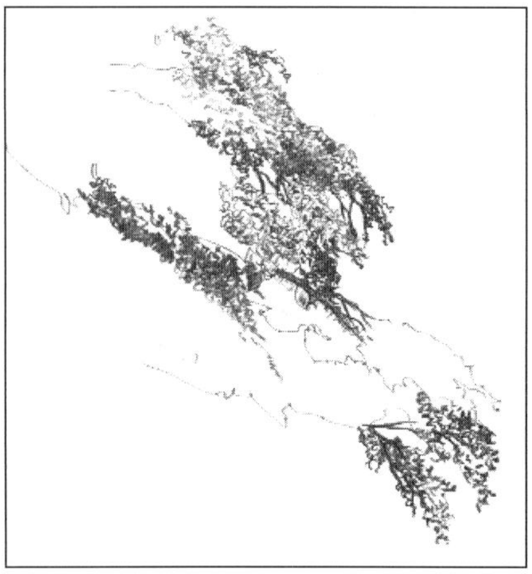

Fig 13

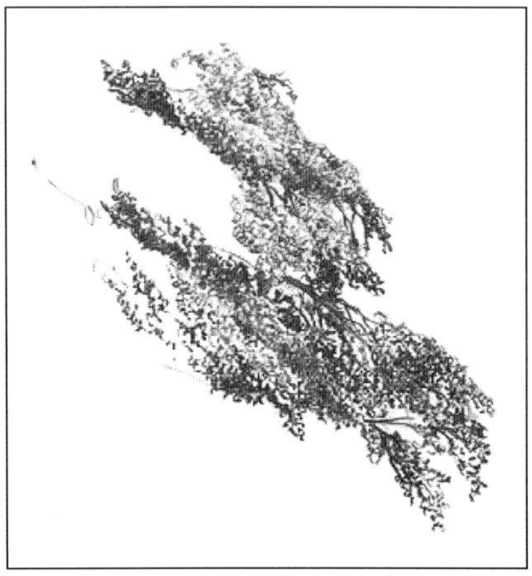

Fig 14

you arrive at a texture most resembling the effect you wish to attain, and then repeat it. In the case of the previous example (*fig 11*), the tree is in the midground so the leaves only need to appear as highlighted points where light reflects from their variously angled surfaces. Foreground trees will display almost every leaf, and background trees merely a mottled pattern at most. Far distant trees will simply exhibit their outline with no apparent detail at all. All these require differing techniques, although in practice each technique is often a modification of the one preceding it, with a modified mindset to suit.

To draw the foliage of the tree in the previous example and, more pertinently, the trees to its left, I employed a scheme of small random shapes. At all times I was concentrating on the negative spaces, leaving larger or more frequent spaces in areas that I intended to be the highlights. Shady areas simply possess fewer and smaller negative spaces.

Midground detail

This exercise measures 2"×2½" (5 x 6cm) and was completed in just over one hour. Picture a tree in your mind then establish the basic guidelines, marking out the principal masses of foliage (*fig 12*). Consider the angle of the view of each mass. Are you looking directly at it or is it extending to either side? Here I'm drawing just a part of one side but I'll extend it later.

Next establish the darkest and lightest tones (*fig 13*) and begin to get a feel for the form. Don't add tone to the white, negative spaces. Instead, when you've properly defined the shadow and highlighted areas, add a later overall tone layer to provide light and shade that conforms to your chosen lighting direction.

Working in random patterns, begin to build up the texture (*fig 14*). Vary the weight of your pencil marks, graduating from dark to light, leaving more negative space between the marks as you progress. The shadows rely on the positive, weighty pencil marks and drawing around the white 'leaves' produces the highlighted areas. More leaf, more highlight. Less leaf, more shadow. Work quickly. Speed fools the brain, so tap into your creative side by working too quickly for your logical side to keep up. Work loosely and spontaneously. There is nothing pre-planned or precise about this method.

Whenever you feel the need, reinforce your deepest shadows (*fig 15*) and add an overall layer of tone to adjust each area of foliage so it possesses a roundness that conforms to your chosen direction of lighting - as we did earlier with the weeds.

Adjustments can easily be made with Blu-Tack or a kneadable eraser, which is why I advocate laying the final shaping tone on top. Blu-Tack can lift this off so gently that the detail below is left undisturbed. The layer can be continually adjusted and re-adjusted with little harm to the underdrawing.

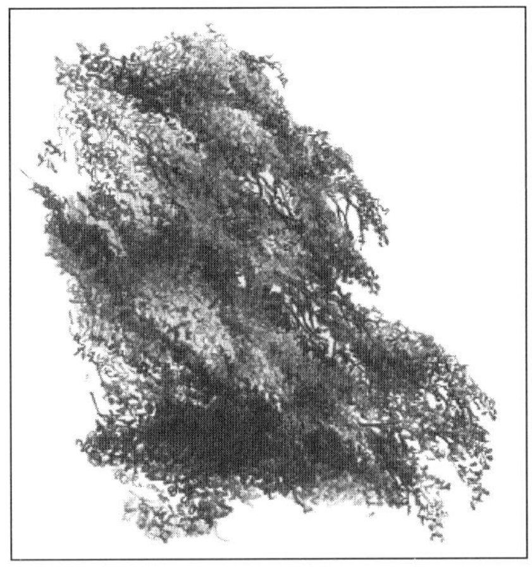

Fig 15

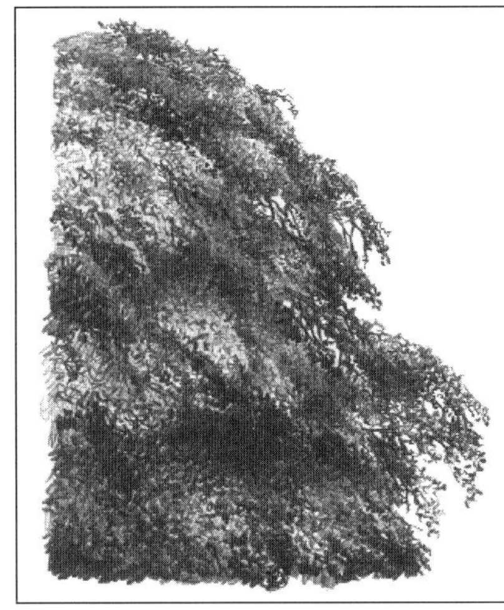

Fig 16

Satisfied that this is looking sufficiently tree-like, I couldn't resist extending it (*fig 16*) to better display the overall rounded form and the internal features.

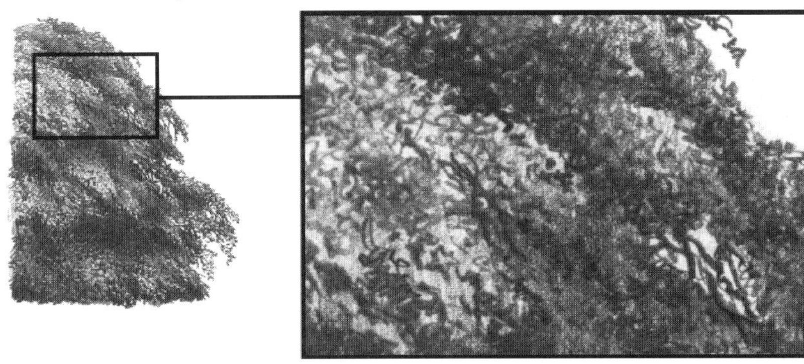

Work loosely and spontaneously. There is nothing pre-planned or precise about this method.

With practice, some of the early stages can be dispensed with. For example, the trees to the left of our example tree (*see fig 11*) merely had their positions marked in my line drawing. The trees themselves grew organically as I worked. I had only to decide where the sun would catch their tops before starting out.

Background detail

The methods employed here should reflect the hazy, indistinct look of distant trees. Depending on the prevailing light they may be pale, misty forms, or dark silhouettes. In the latter case, aerial perspective will decree that the darkest tones never equal those of the foreground, or even midground. Leaf and bark detail is non-existent, the only discernable features are holes in the foliage, through which trunks and branches may be seen against the sky. There may also be a vague suggestion of three-dimensional form.

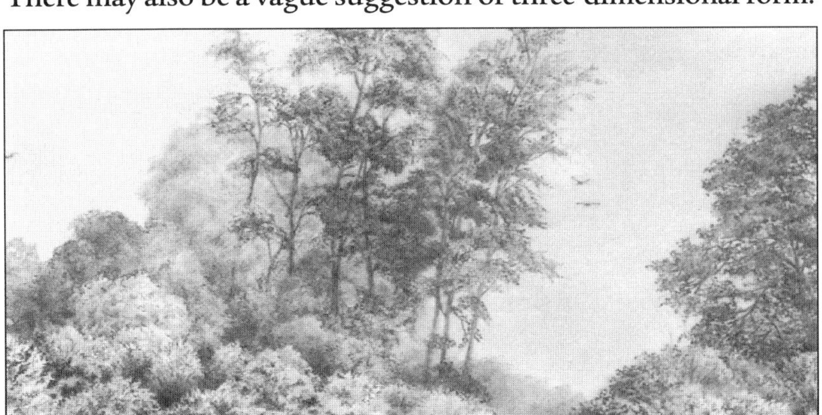

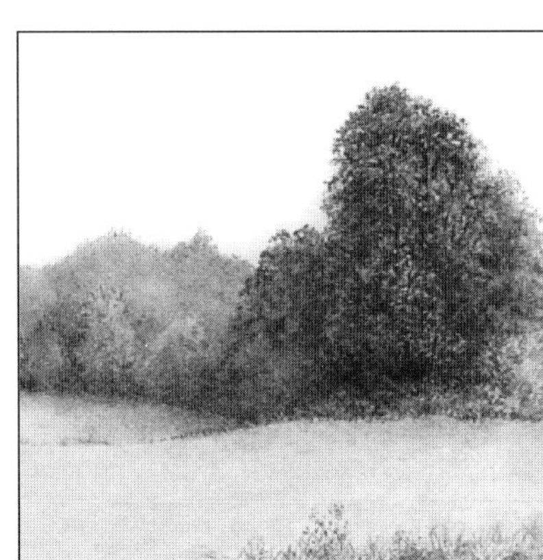

Tip

Don't get obsessive about the time taken to complete a drawing. Taking longer doesn't necessarily mean 'better'. If the drawing took three weeks to complete then that's what it required - it wouldn't be any better for a month spent on it. In fact it may have resulted in the drawing being overworked.

When you begin a drawing don't have any preconceived ideas about how long it will take.
It will take as long as it requires.

The techniques are very similar to the midground method but employs a lighter touch, and less contrast and negative space. Blending with a tortillon or colour shaper may assist in blurring your pencil marks, although I prefer a combination of layering and minimal blending.

Foreground detail

As I mentioned at the beginning, you have no need to attempt to draw every leaf. Nor should you do so, as little in the real world is ever clearly seen at all times. While it's true that individual leaves will be seen, in reality you need only draw in detail the status leaves - usually those that are foremost and highlighted. Secondary leaves, in shade or behind the status foliage, need only contain the main visual keys to be read as companions. The most prominent key is usually the outline, so choosing an interesting leaf shape helps in this respect. This is one reason why I often employ Sycamores. I confess the other reason is that I can walk out of my upstairs studio and into the bathroom to study our Sycamore's leaves at very close quarters!

As you will have realised from my description, we can use the basics of the midground method for the drawing of foreground trees. We need only add an overlay of status leaves; the random shapes are largely exchanged for correct leaf shapes; and, as clarity is the major requirement, no blending is used at all.

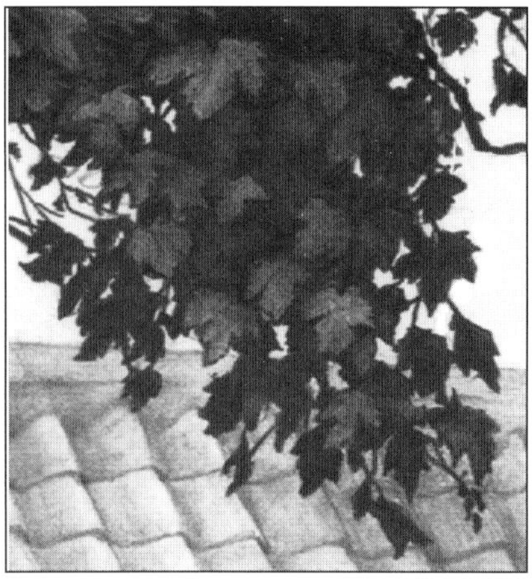

Fig 17

There are several keys used in this detail (*fig 17*) that steer the brain towards making the deduction I require. Highlighted, status leaves signal the leaf shape and surface texture. Holes through the foliage, that silhouette twigs and leaf edges against the sky, tell us that the foliage contains areas of dense shade. The brain's logical conclusion, hopefully, is that the

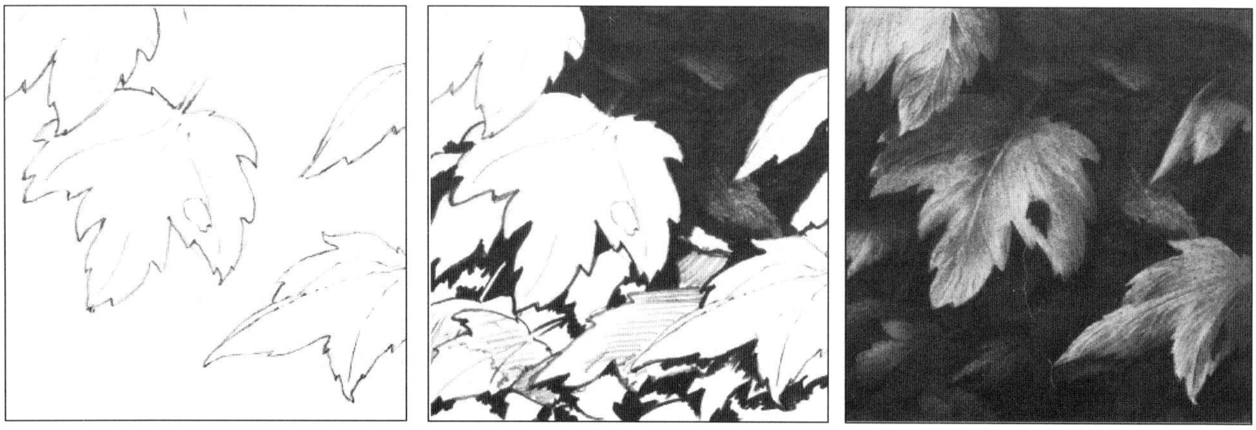

Left: Line drawing of status leaves. Centre: Background partly drawn. It contains no actual leaves, just motifs that contain the principal key - the deeply cut edge. Right: the completed drawing.

vague shapes in shadow are actually leaves. Of course, they're not - they are merely portions of shapes that use the deep-cut part of a Sycamore leaf as a motif.

Drawing Tree Bark

Now we have techniques to draw leaves, and the scaffolding to support them, there is another subject that also needs to be considered - tree bark. Where midground trees merely exhibit a suggestion of bark, foreground trees demand it

Personally, because my uses of bark are most often incidental to the study, I rarely attempt to recreate varieties of actual tree bark. I prefer instead to use a number of shorthand motifs. Each of these depends on the inclusion of the principal key found in that particular generic bark texture. For example,

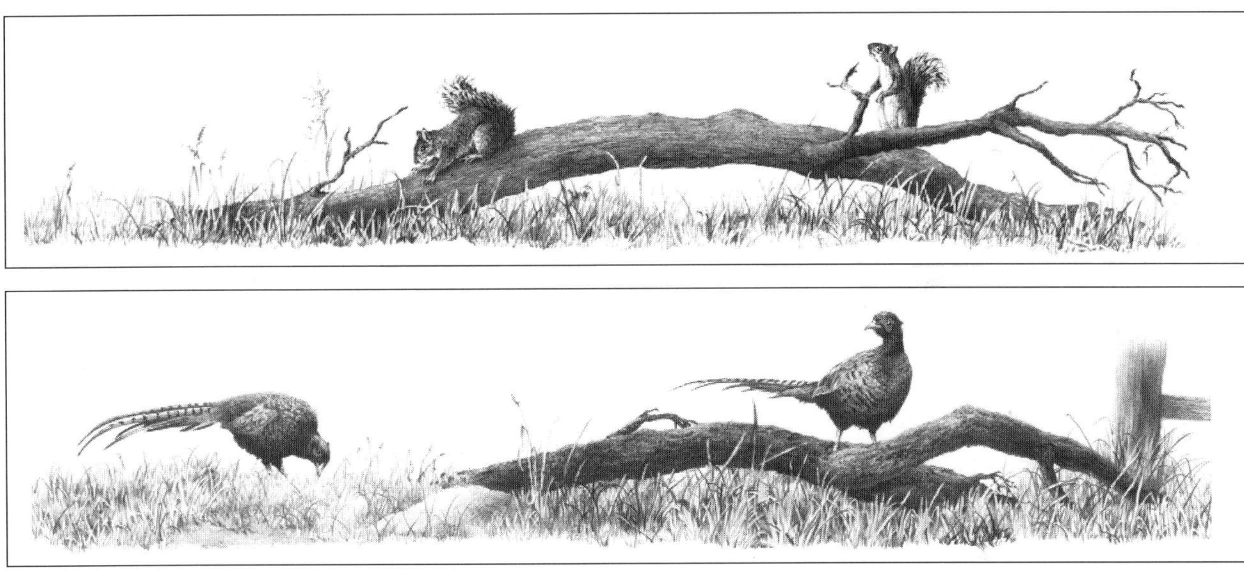

Both remarques are shown actual size. Working at this scale compels you to concentrate on finding and drawing only the most essential visual keys.

rough bark usually has vertical ridges. The keys are the uneven ridge-top highlights coupled with the dense trough-bottom shadows. This is an excellent texture for small drawings, such as remarques, as the keys are particularly conspicuous.

Whatever type of bark you choose to draw the usual strategy applies. Seek out the keys, those essential elements that make it look the way it does, and choose the most suitable method to reproduce them. Remember also to treat the trunk as a true cylinder. In particular, smooth bark, which usually reflects light, will exhibit the full range of light and shade from highlight through the core shadow to reflected light. Conversely, the surface texture of rough bark tends to absorb light so has a darker and more even appearance.

Drawing Shrubs and Bushes

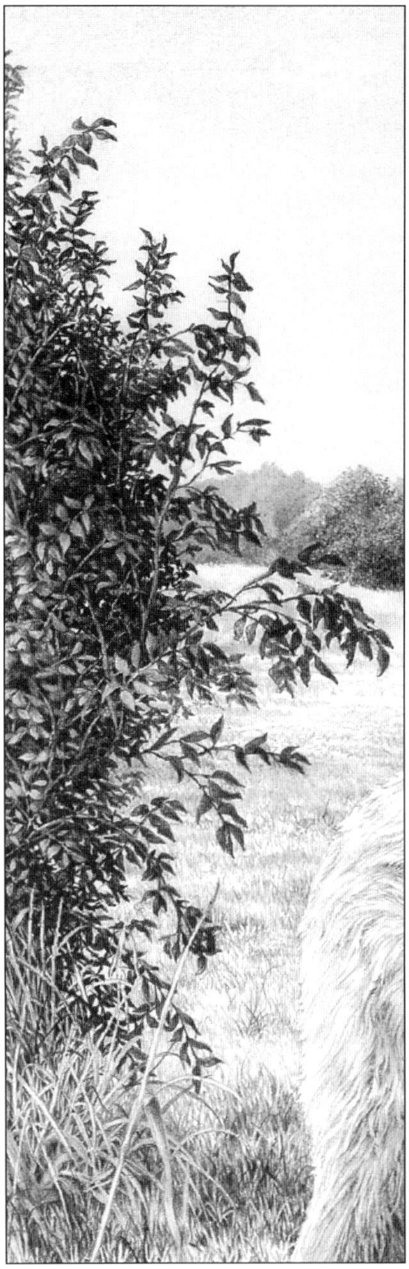

The growth of bushes is often predominantly upward

Essentially, shrubs are small bushes, and bushes are just miniature trees with multiple, slim trunks. However, both exhibit certain properties not common to trees.

- The growth is often predominantly upward.
- There is no twig mass - foliage grows directly from the branching stems.
- Leaves are smaller and more compact.
- Very few display individual foliage masses.

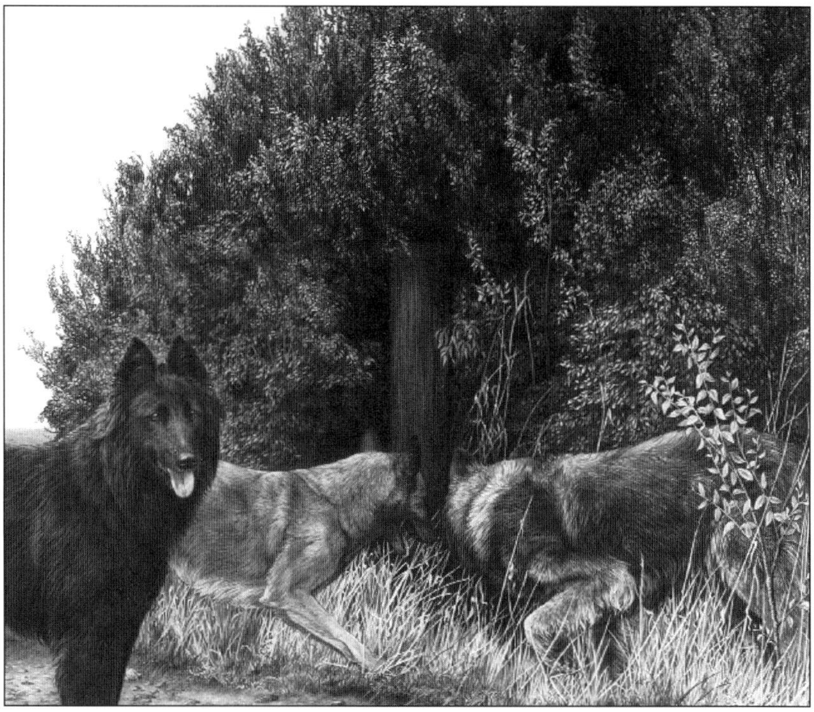

Large Blackthorn bushes as they appear in 'Taking Five'

The technique employs the same methods as mentioned in drawing foreground tree foliage. The principal status leaves and stems are first outlined then the secondary foliage is drawn 'behind' them. Finally the status elements are completed. Keep in mind the rounded nature and depth of the bush as you draw, and leave strategic and logical holes through the foliage - more towards the outer edges; less or none towards the centre, as foliage around the back of the bush will block them.

Choose the most suitable method for the position and recession of your foliage; don't include detail where it wouldn't be naturally visible; and always apply consistent lighting. Make life easy; tackle every bush and tree in logical layers - full shade, partial shade, and highlighted status foliage - and you can't go far wrong. And a bit of patience helps too - if a job's worth doing it's worth doing well!

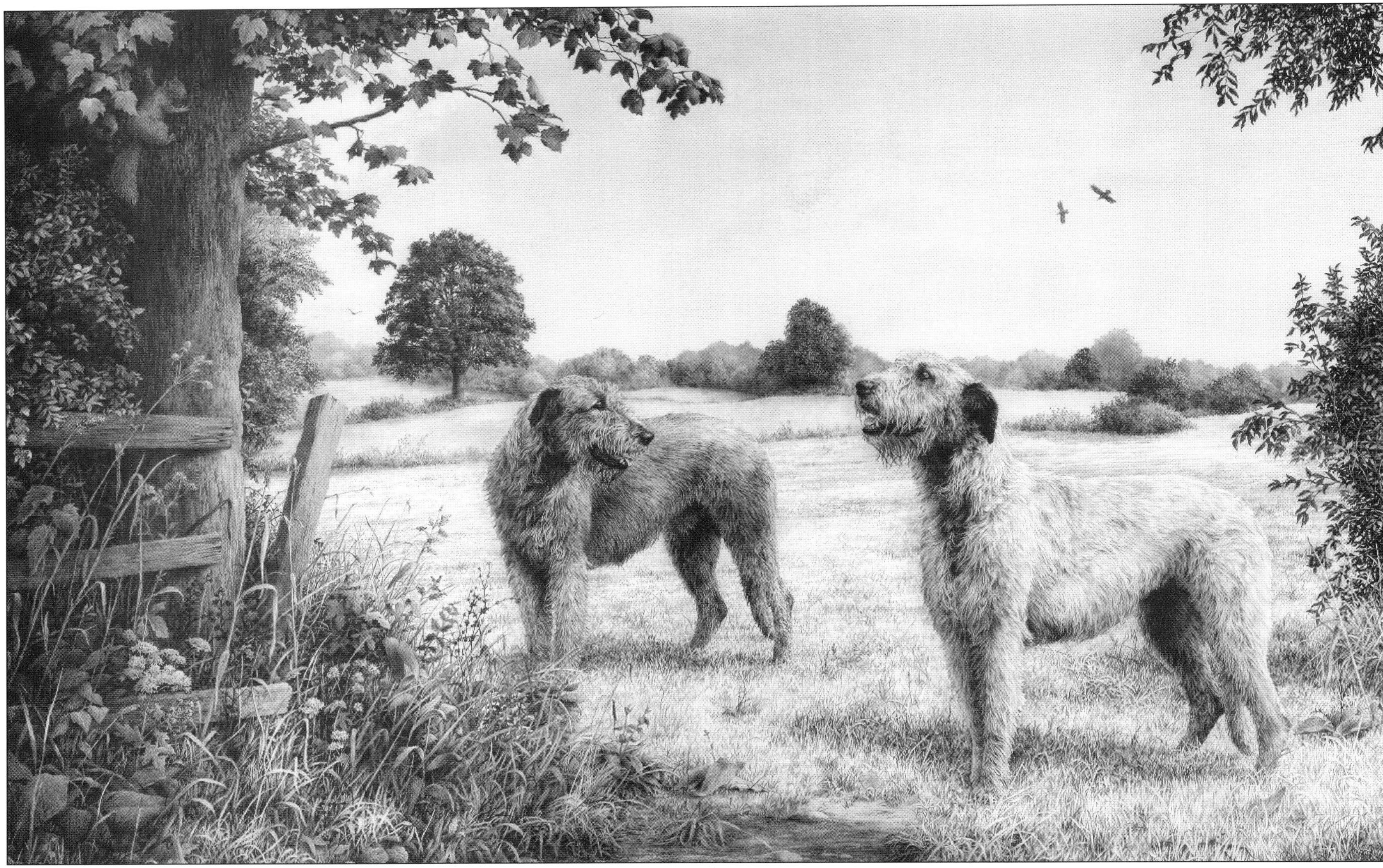

18" x 11½" (45 x 29 cm)

'Spinney Lane End' featuring Irish Wolfhounds - Limited edition print of 550 worldwide

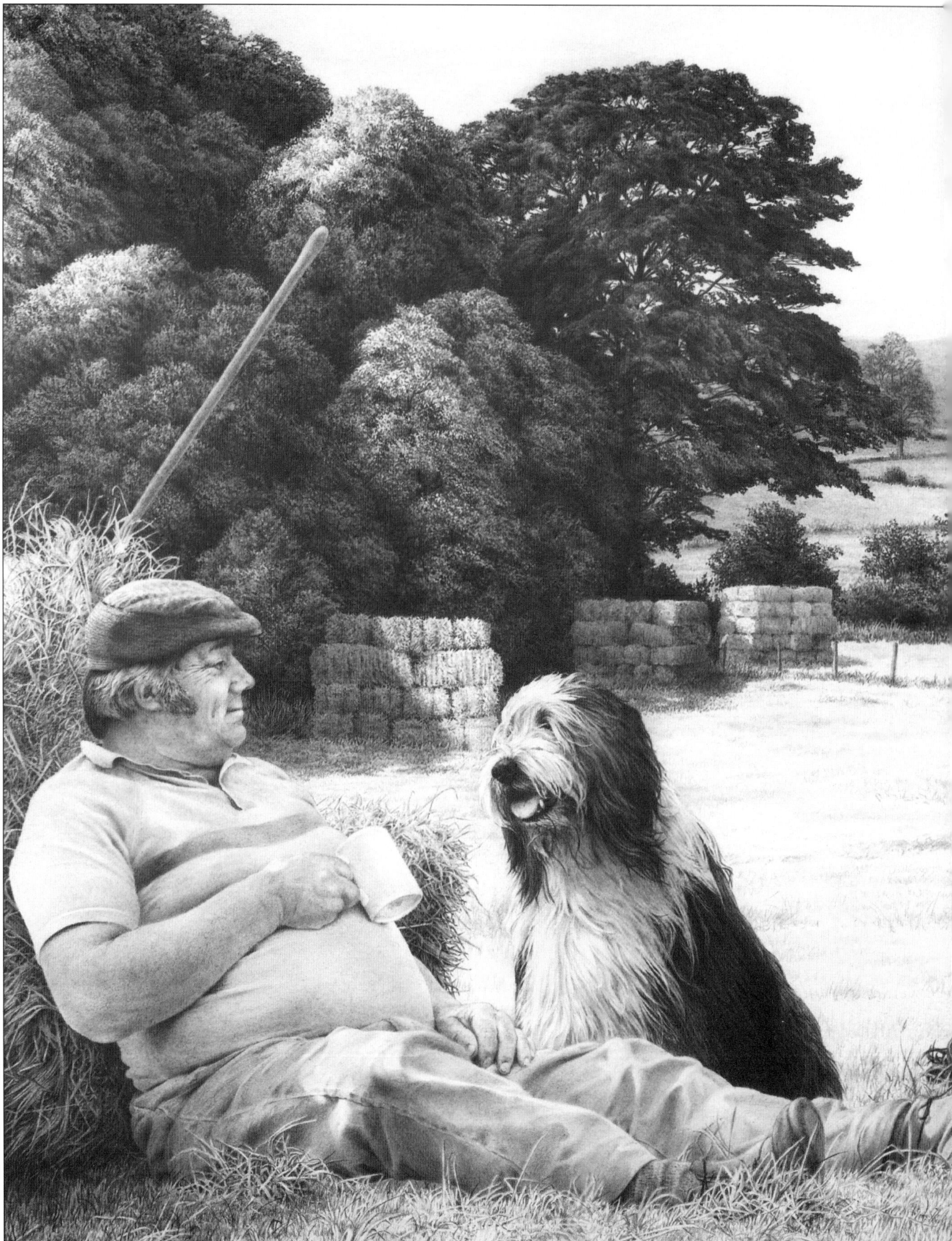

Done Balin' by Mike Sibley ©

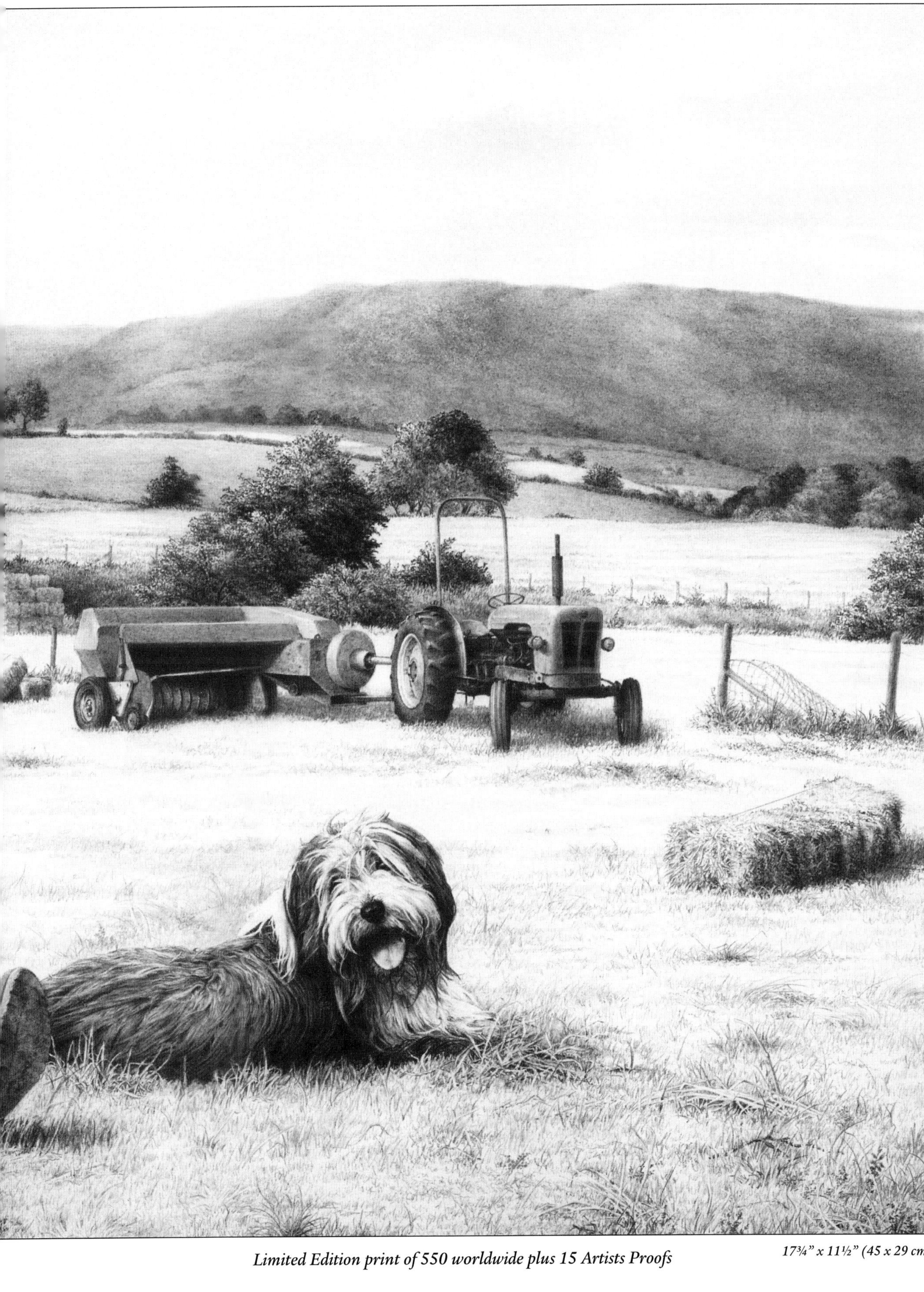

Limited Edition print of 550 worldwide plus 15 Artists Proofs

17¾" x 11½" (45 x 29 cm)

Drawing Hair
The well-dressed dog...

'YOU NEITHER NEED, NOR SHOULD ATTEMPT, TO DRAW EVERY HAIR TO MAKE THE OVERALL LOOK BELIEVABLE.'

Although this chapter is predominantly about drawing the hair of animals, there are plenty of women who would die for long, silky hair like an Afghan Hound! In fact, animal hair is more complex to draw than the hair of humans because of the diverse variety of underlying forms. The drawing of human hair shares the same techniques but, in the main, is easier to accomplish.

Comprehensively describing the many ways of drawing hair, a seemingly simple exercise, is actually an almost impossible task. Not only do artists' styles differ widely but so too do their aims. I can at least present you with my way of drawing hair; the techniques that suit my style and ambitions, and offer that as a grounding on which you can build or adapt to your own way of working.

SEEING IS BELIEVING

You neither need, nor should attempt, to draw every hair to make the overall look believable. Adopting a technique that suggests more detail than is actually present easily produces a sense of reality. In that respect, however, some methods produce better results than others. There are a number of approaches that you might choose to take:

- Concentrate solely on the three-dimensional underlying form.
- Partially overlay the solidly shaded form with the resemblance of hair and texture.
- Use the way the light hits the hair, and the hair itself, to create the appearance of the underlying form.

Any of those approaches is as valid as any other but my personal preference is for the last, as the results most resemble reality. It is better suited to the drawing of animals, which do not have the same, simple cranial dome beneath their hair but complex, full-body structures.

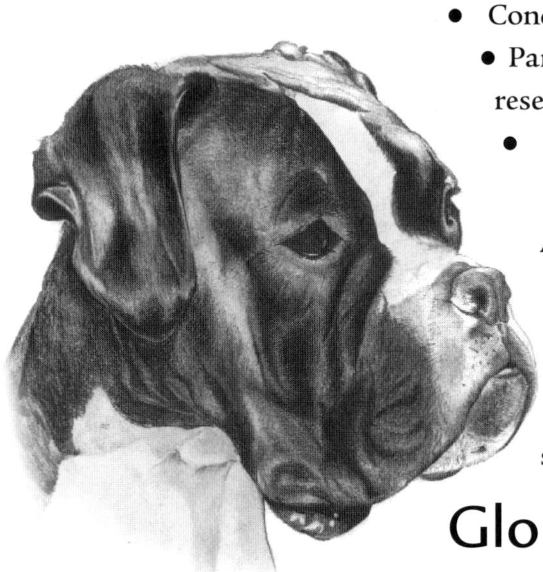

Global shading concentrating purely on the underlying three-dimensional form.

Global and Local methods

The Boxer illustration (*left*) shows the use of global shading - treating the subject as a single three-dimensional object without surface texture, and applying just tonal blending and shaping. In giving visual priority to the underlying, solid form, the presence of hair is left almost entirely to the viewer's imagination. The lighting is based on the overall perception and does not take localised variances into account. Shape is paramount.

In drawing the Basset Hound (*right*) I have used local shading - sculpting with light and shade - calculating the lighting of each lock of hair as it is drawn and applying the required tones. No global shading exists but all local shading is calculated with reference to its position within the overall subject. Priority has been given to the outward appearance - only the hair, its texture, and surface highlighting describe the underlying three-dimensional form. This system takes into account such localised variations as reflected lighting between adjacent locks of hair, which increases the perceived reality.

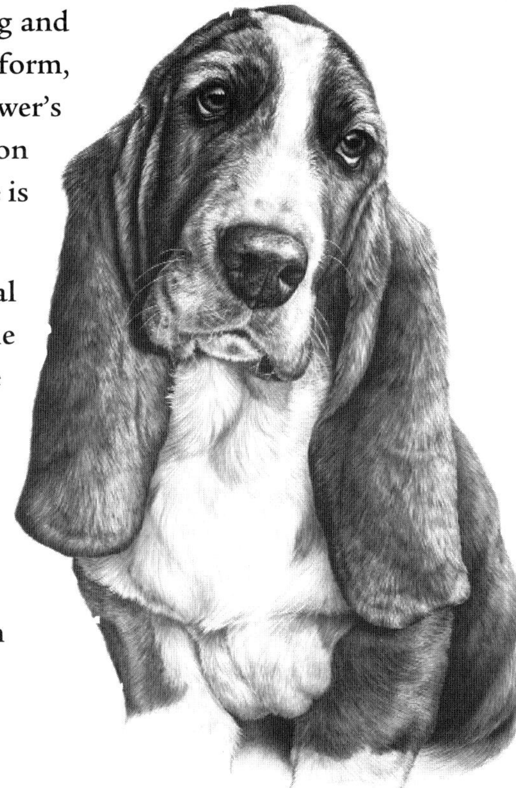

Local shading

It's not all black and white

Before you learn techniques and begin drawing hair you must first understand the way our brains see and understand hair, so you can extract and use the visual keys. If everything 'black' was really black and everything 'white' was pure white we would see nothing except flat, featureless shapes with sharp outlines. But nothing in life is so simple - in reality reflections and absorbance of light play a full part in what we see. It's the highlights and shadows of a Black Labrador's glossy coat that tell us what shape the dog is - the underlying structure is never overtly seen. The hair, only the hair, defines its three-dimensional form. The same is true of a white Bull Terrier except that the emphasis is reversed - the shadows play a greater part than the highlights. But there is also one other aspect that is as true for each in the drawing process...

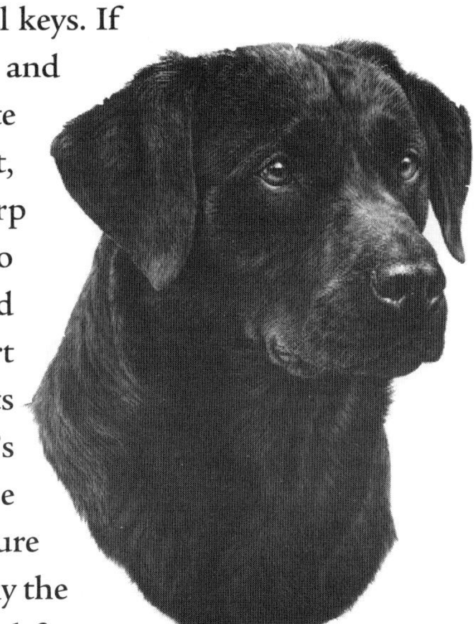

The highlights define the hairs of a black dog.

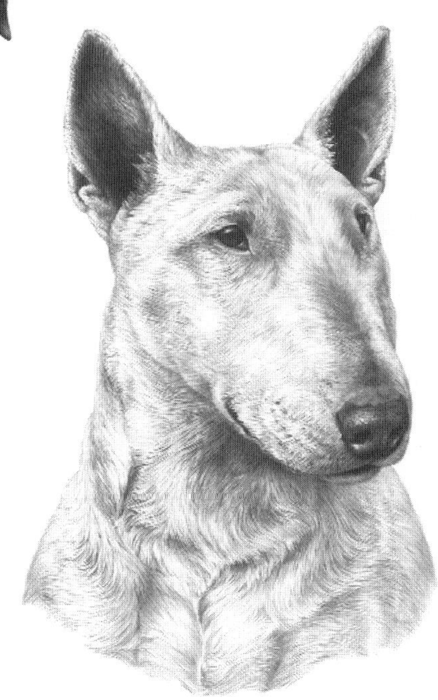

The cast shadows define the hairs of a white dog.

A PENCIL MARK IS **NOT** A HAIR

I cannot stress this too much or too often - pencils do not draw hairs - they only define the edges, position and shape of hairs. Now we have set the rule there are exceptions that prove rules are made to be broken. For example, a positive pencil stroke can be used where dark hair overlays a patch of white hair. Generally however, the pencil line does not mark the hair itself - it forms the boundary between hairs.

Negative and Positive

Drawing hair is about positive and negative drawing, and combining the two to reproduce hair with a sense of reality. As I stated above, we see black hairs because of their highlights; white hairs are outlined by their shadows. The hairs are visible because of their 'opposite' properties. In practice you create not the hair but the shadow or highlight. For black hair the highlight will range from bright white through a series of darkening greys but not, however, to black - the darkest tones available must be reserved for the shadows that define the edges of the black hairs not for hairs themselves.

The key to negative drawing is to focus your full attention not on the actual lines you are drawing but on the spaces in between them. The line you are drawing has no importance in itself - it is the space between the lines that is paramount (*fig 1*). Having defined that white space it can later have tone layered over it to produce the correct three-dimensional appearance (*fig 2*). Breaking the exercise up greatly simplifies the operation and allows you to keep control of it.

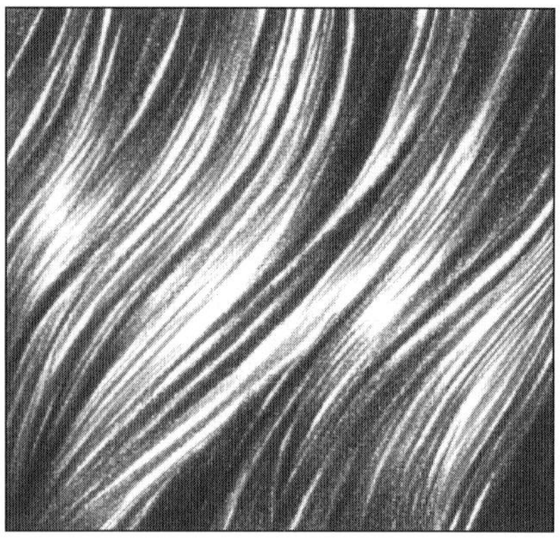

Fig 1. Draw the shadows first and leave the 'hairs' white.

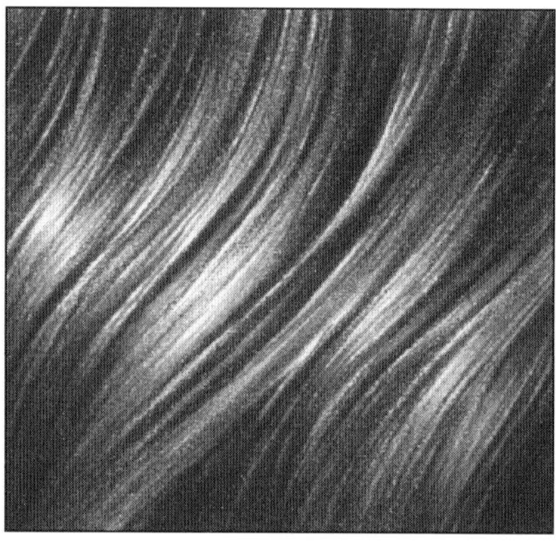

Fig 2. Layer appropriate tones to form three-dimensional shaping.

- Treat the locks of hair as three-dimensional shapes, not as individual hairs.
- Draw from dark to light.
- Define the edges, leaving the 'hair' white.
- Shade as required, when surrounding tones assist you in choosing the tonal values.

From a practical point of view, suppose that there are only four layers required. First is the negative drawing layer that produces the cast shadows of each hair or lock of hairs. A second layer more sharply defines the first and adds finer detail. Third is the shading layer that gives the locks their three-dimensional shape. If a lock of hair emerges from shadow and passes into highlight then it's at this stage that the lock receives the gradated tonal values that it requires. If you've drawn the negative layers tightly enough this tonal layer can be drawn over the top without any regard to detail, as all the detail resides in the layers below. The tone layer really determines how much of the detail layers show through. Heavy shading can produce really remarkable results as the detail layers almost, but not quite, disappear. The result can be very subtle.

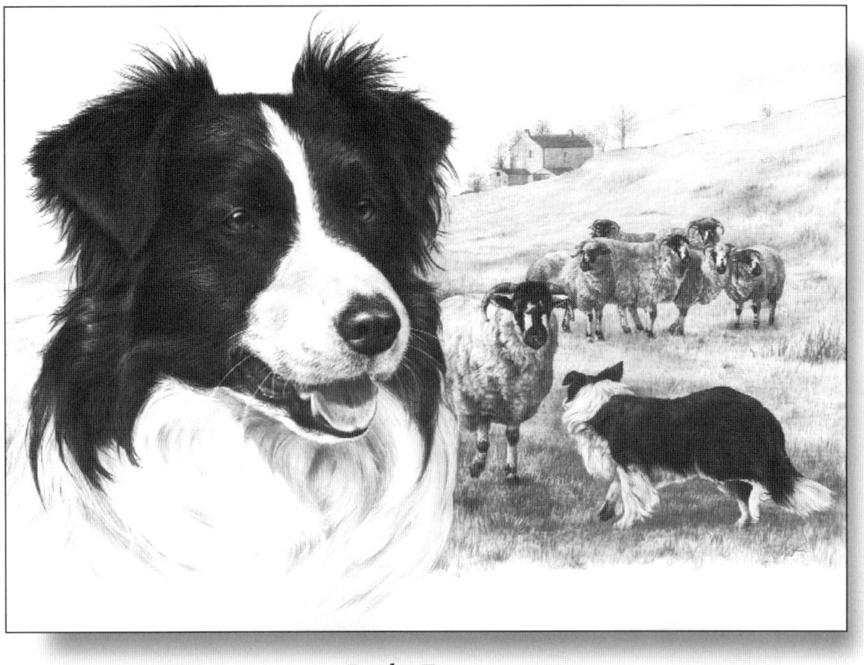

Border Encounter

Finally, when you have a sufficiently large area completed, the more widespread shadows and highlights that give overall shaping to the head's structure can be layered on top. With experience, you can eventually combine the last three stages.

Establishing a Drawing Break

Wherever possible, as in the previous example, I work from dark into light. From a purely practical point of view it is far easier to graft later drawing onto a dark area of tone - what I term a drawing break. This enables me to draw away from the centre of the dark area in one direction then return to the break and seamlessly continue in the opposite direction.

To demonstrate, let's take the left hand ear of this delightful Border Collie. (*top right - Border Encounter*)

I would work this area in four distinct stages.

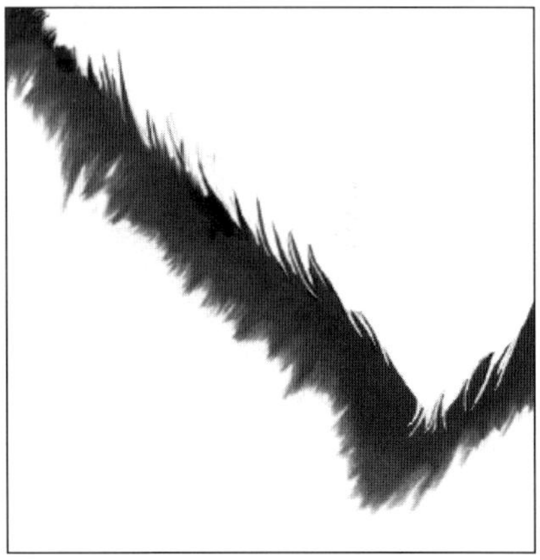

Step 1

Step 1: I've identified and established the black shadow area, the drawing break, from which I can work outwards. The top edge of the shadow has been carefully drawn up into the area above to define the lighter hairs. Remember, I'm drawing the shadows between the hairs here. The white 'hairs' are left white until the next stage.

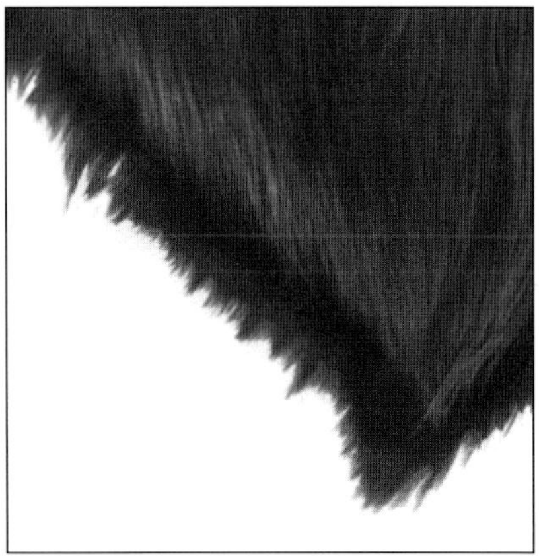

Step 2

Step 2: Working from dark into light, the ear is drawn down into the shadow. This is negative drawing, as in all cases I have drawn the shadows between the hairs and not the hairs themselves. Once these hairs are defined, a layer of tone is applied to give them their correct three-dimensional shaping.

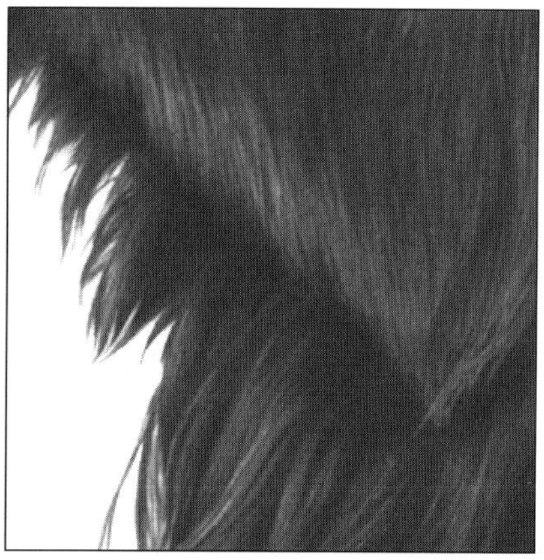

Step3

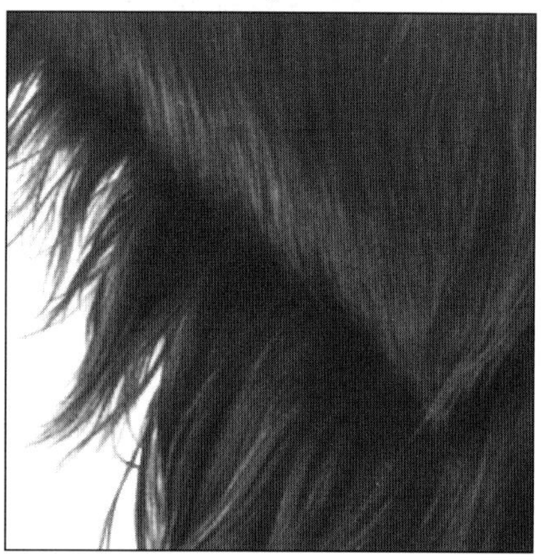

Step 4

Step 3: New drawing is grafted onto the dark shadow and extended down into the area below. If some of the new light hairs need to go back up into the shadow this can be achieved with Blu-Tack or a kneadable eraser - a line of graphite is removed from the shadow then defined and shaded to merge the two areas correctly. All that remains is for the ends of the locks of hair to be completed.

Step 4: Switching from negative to positive drawing, the two outside boundary lines that define each negative-drawn highlight are brought together to form one positive line. This is drawn to a point to complete the end of each lock of hair. A few additional stray hairs are introduced to add an 'untidy' reality to the area. The ear and its surrounding area are finished.

Black hair, white hair

We've just seen how a black dog's highlights define the direction and shape of its locks of hair, and how the very deepest tones are reserved for the darkest shadows. The cast shadow beneath the Border Collie's ear has to be the darkest in the drawing in order to make the ear stand forward of the hair behind it.

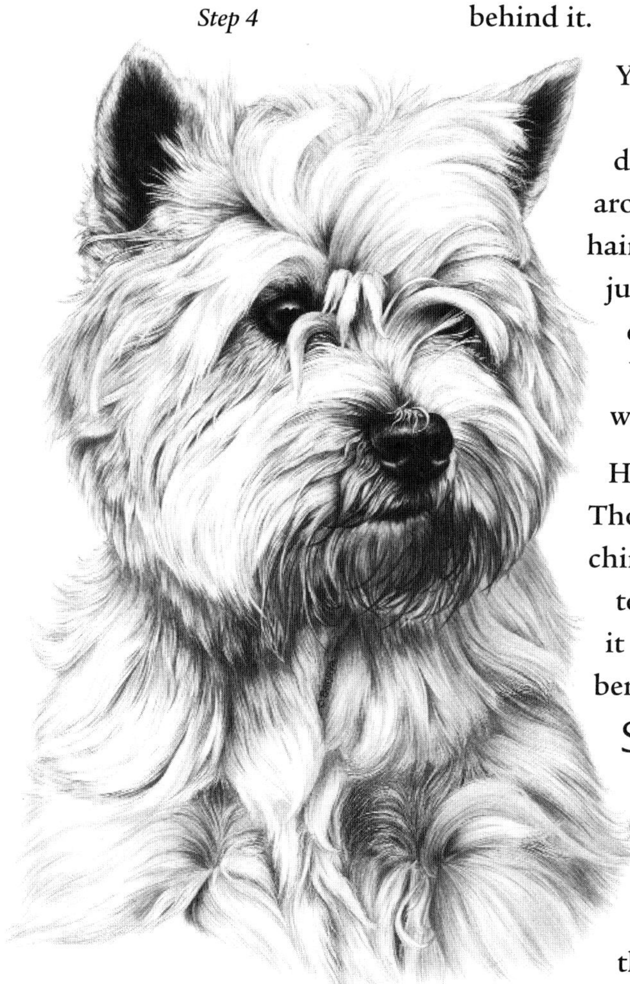

You can plainly see in this West Highland White Terrier study that not one of the white hairs was drawn - just the shadows. Drawing the nose around the hairs, for example, produced the white hairs that rest on top of it - the hairs themselves are just plain paper. After the white locks of hair were defined by their shadows, they were shaded, area-by-area as I worked, according to their position within the chosen lighting regime.

However, positive-drawn, dark areas also exist. Those between the nose and mouth, and under the chin, are wet hairs that clump together and tail off to a point. By using positive drawing for these it can be clearly shown that they lie above the hairs beneath them.

Staying in control

Working one small area at a time will make your overall project far easier to handle both mentally and physically and will keep you firmly in control. Don't be tempted to work on the whole drawing at once; and nor should you attempt to fill whole areas with tone. It's true that your drawing will look more complete far more quickly, and you may feel that it's helping you establish form. But the bright highlights you may later wish to create will no longer be achievable, resulting in a distinct loss of life and tonal depth, and the previously applied tone will muddy your efforts to produce believable hair textures. You will never achieve the clarity and freshness of line that working on a virgin surface produces.

Decide on the light direction, consider the position of every lock of hair you define and then apply the illumination accordingly. Defining your hairs and then calculating and adding specific local tone will give them an enhanced reality - don't use global shading and hope it will work locally.

TIP

Photograph your subject outdoors in natural daylight for best results.

When photographing a white dog, aim to underexpose the film - you want strong shadows, not bright highlights that 'burn' the film.

With a black dog, aim to overexpose your film - you want to encourage the dim highlights to burn into the emulsion. You are not trying to achieve the perfect photograph but an awful, washed out photo that shows all the detail.

Drawing Hair

THE SPECIFICS

Try not to get too involved with details. In time you will develop an instinct for knowing how much is too much. If you feel the detail is overwhelming you, that's a sign that you should stop. Getting the right tonal values and shaping in an area is visually more important. However, having created the detail, a word of warning - don't blend hair! You need to preserve the sharpness and clarity of your drawing for it to resemble reality. If you need to blur an area to suggest recession, use layering to diminish contrast and Blu-Tack or a kneadable eraser to reduce detail. With that said, let's make a start.

'TRY NOT TO GET TOO INVOLVED WITH DETAILS. . . IF YOU FEEL THE DETAIL IS OVERWHELMING YOU, THAT'S A SIGN THAT YOU SHOULD STOP.'

Drawing long, straight hair

Analysis: Straight hair on a human head tends to cling to the shape of the skull due to gravity and the weight of the hair. The same is true of dogs or any other animal and is the easiest to draw, as it hides the underlying structure. There will be few, if any, deep shadows occurring, as individual locks don't readily form. Hair from blonde to black exhibits bands of highlight that conform to the shape of the skull and any other underlying structure that it curves around, such as the shoulder.

Technique: If the colour of the hair is blonde or light you might consider making the background darker to better display it. If you choose that design, draw the background first so you can judge the tones of the hair against it.

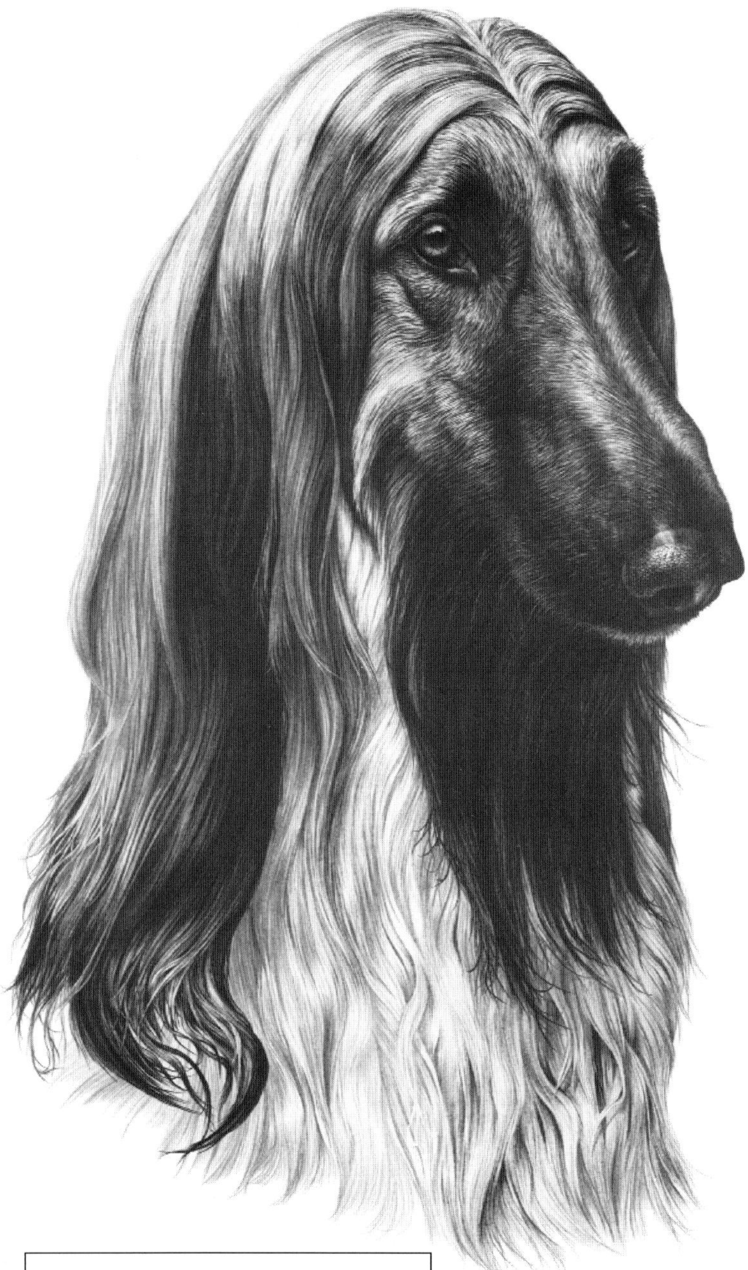

First, find and establish the darkest tone at or near the top of the head, perhaps in the parting if there is one, and work outwards from it. You are not drawing individual hairs but shading by linear hatching, letting variations in your pencil strokes give the appearance of hair. Use a sharp line for greasy, gelled or shiny hair, and a less-defined line for soft hair. Soft pencils can draw very grainy lines when applied lightly so choose the hardest grade suitable for the required tone. Work down towards the brightest highlights. Let your lines of shading follow the direction of the hair at all times. Whether blonde or black, dog or human, there will be a band of highlight that appears as the hair curves over the skull. As you approach this band, reduce the pressure on your pencil or change to a harder grade so your drawing fades just short of it. Then establish the darkest tones below the highlight and work back up in the same manner.

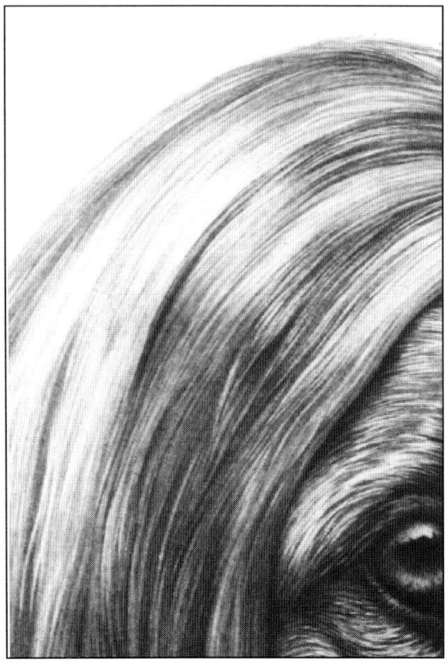

Now that you can properly judge the highlight tones, draw into it lightly to suggest faint detail. Simply emphasising the occasional line will be sufficient for the eye to follow the direction of the hair and send the 'this is hair' signal. Leave the highlights white and, if possible, invent at least one slim shadow running through it - this will increase the perceived contrast and brighten the reflection of the highlight.

When drawing the rear of the head, don't make the edge of the hair sharp. Slightly blurring it with a harder grade will suggest recession. Adding the occasional, lightly drawn, stray hair will further soften the outline and give a better sense of reality - but don't overdo it!

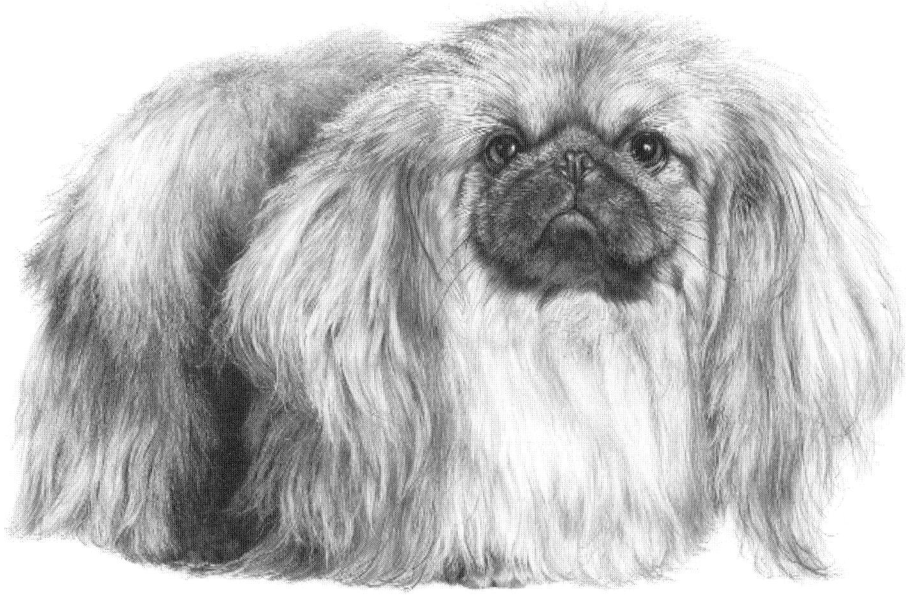

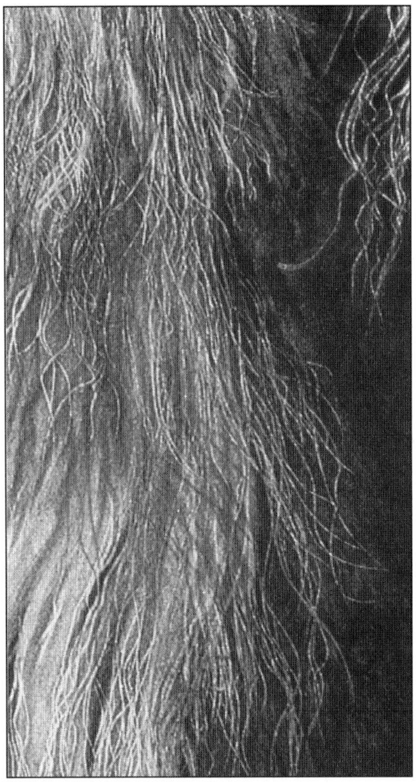

Prior indenting produces the crinkly, flyaway ends seen in the Pekingese.

Drawing fine hair

Analysis: Almost devoid of deep shadows as the hair doesn't part cleanly. Long, fine hair tends to be flyaway and so has many hairs not following the general direction of growth. The crimped tips of many variations of fine hair form the most notable feature. Light reflection is scattered and minimised by the, sometimes profuse, stray hairs.

Technique: Extract and concentrate on drawing the most prominent visual key or keys. Here in this Pekingese (*above*), the keys are the softly defined hair, and the flyaway, crinkly ends, which are produced by prior indenting. Drawing this type of hair is not an easy task, as there are no apparent hard edges within which you can work. As a result, this 15" x 10" (38 x 25 cm) drawing took approximately 80 hours to complete.

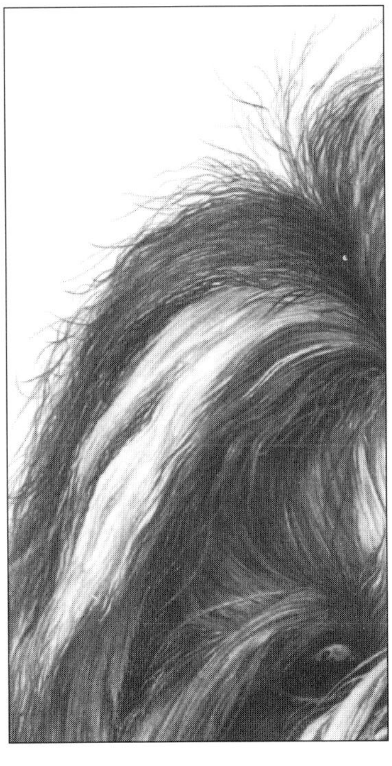

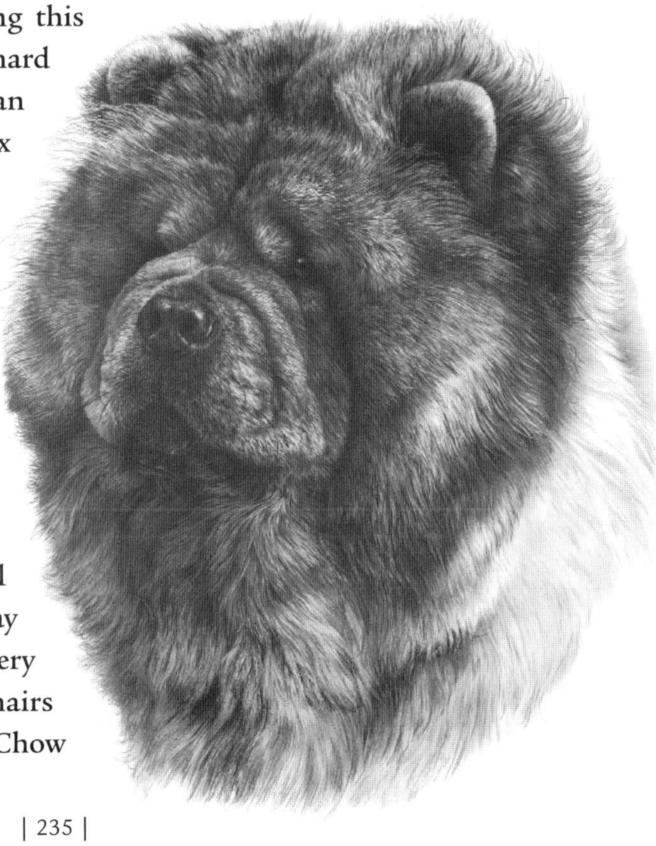

The Shih Tzu (*left*) and Chow Chow (*right*) exhibit slightly thicker hair. Here very little indenting, if any, has been carried out. Instead, the Shih Tzu relies on visual signals sent by the flyaway hairs around the periphery and crinkled, random hairs within the topknot. The Chow

Chow's hair-type is defined by the almost complete absence of partings and edges, and the way the hair curves smoothly into and out of the depths of the facial creases.

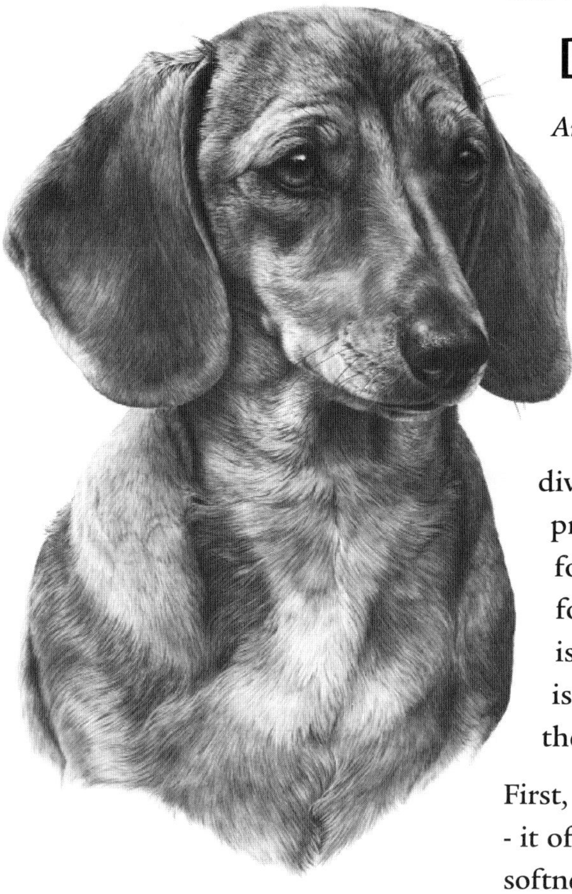

Drawing smooth, short hair

Analysis: This ranks among the most time-consuming and difficult as the hair both follows and defines the bone structure beneath. The reflective properties depend on the quality of the hair but are similar in most respects to smooth, long hair. There will be few deep shadows occurring, as the hair has insufficient length to form locks.

Technique: This is the coat-type where I see the greatest divergence in treatment by artists. At first glance, the most prominent property appears to be the three-dimensional form so this is often drawn first, as semi-solid tone, followed by an attempt to portray hair. My own approach is the reverse. Here, the body structure of this Dachshund is entirely suggested by the highlights and shadows within the hair.

First, look closely at the quality of the hair you are about to draw - it often subtly varies from area to area. I was attracted by the softness of the hair on this Dachshund's ears and sought to contrast it to the hair on the head and body.

Decide on the direction of the light source. In this case it's high up on the left hand side and slightly behind the dog - but I've also introduced some reflective lighting too to soften the shadows. When drawing any area (working only in one small

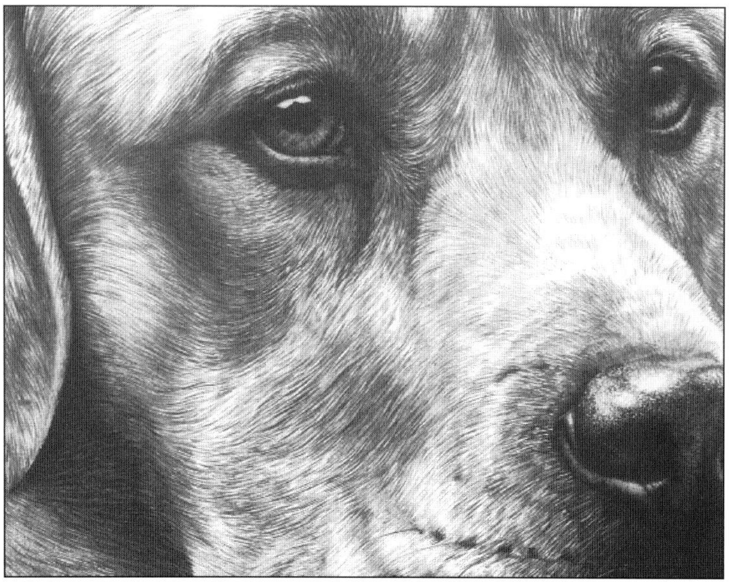

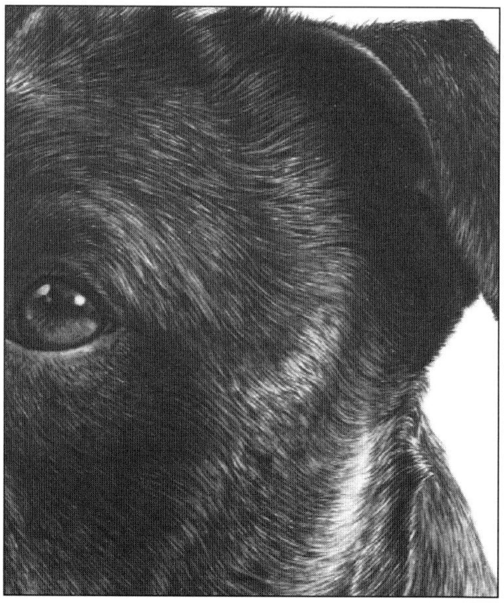

Only the highlights and shadows within the hair describe the underlying bone structure.

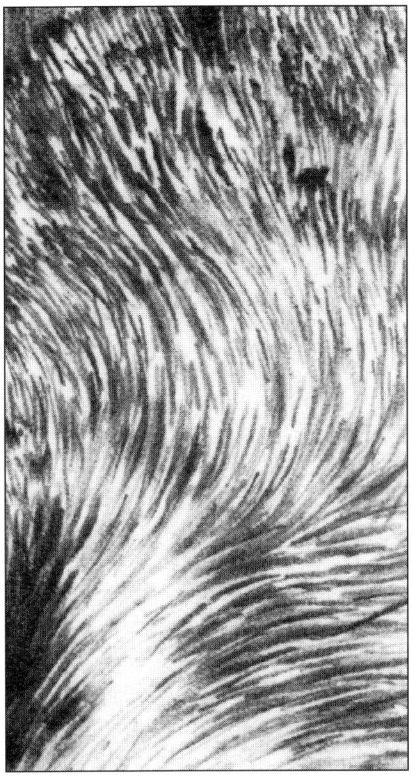

Detail of Lynx-point Siamese enlarged 300% of original.

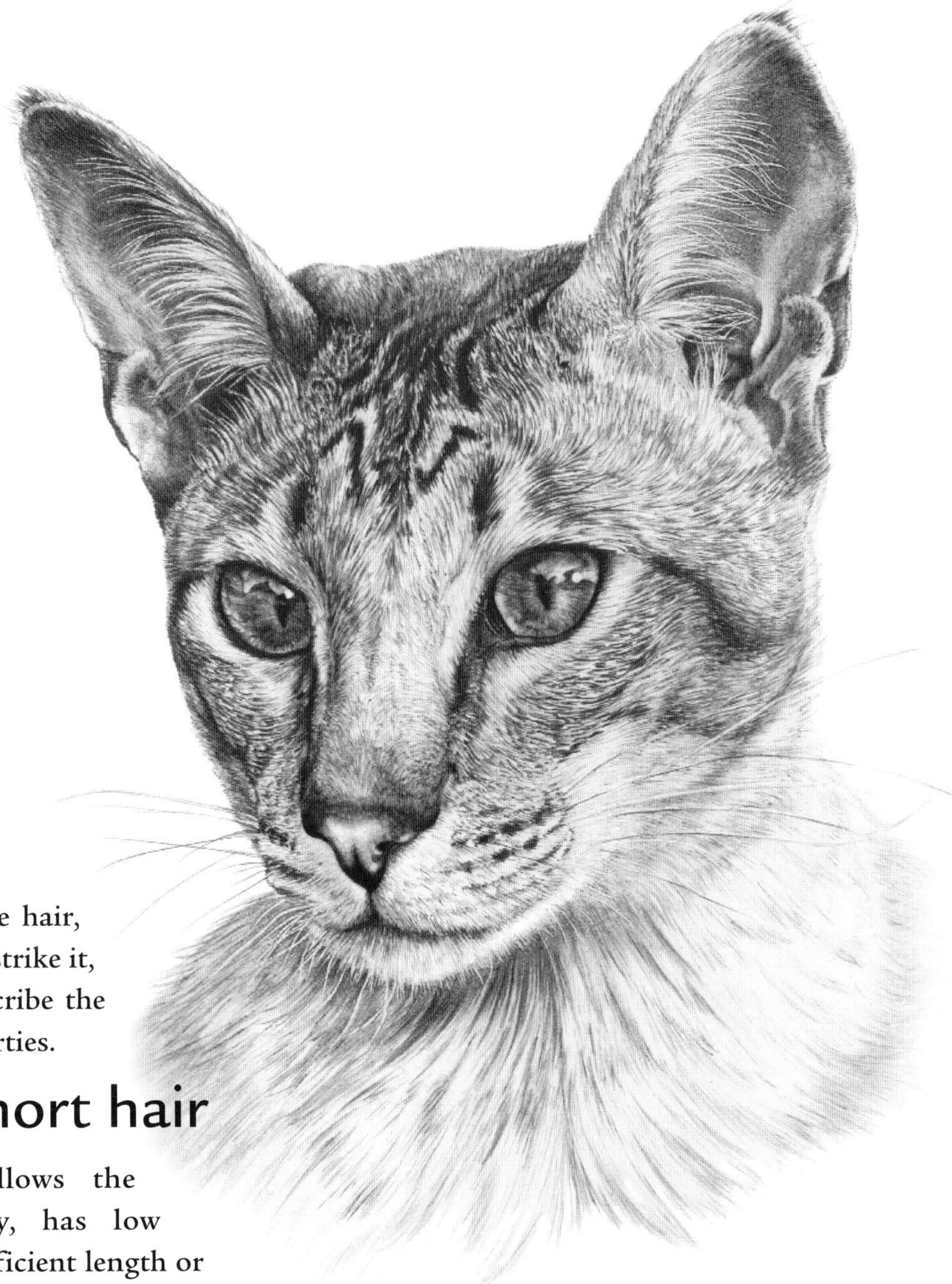

area at a time), first define the hair, take note of how the light will strike it, then use layers of tone to describe the area's three-dimensional properties.

Drawing very short hair

Analysis: This hair-type follows the underlying structure exactly, has low reflective properties, and insufficient length or substance to form locks. Highlights can appear as mere flecks but their inclusion is essential.

Technique: It's when the hair becomes really short that the fun begins. Now every facet of the skull and body-shape are evident and you have only the hair, with low reflective properties, to portray it. This type of hair can further compound the problems by being brush-like with short bristles emerging vertically or at an angle. In some cases this can actually be a benefit, such as with the pig and mole. The pig has such short, sparse hair that you hardly need give it more than a passing mention. Conversely the mole has such a profusion of short, erect hairs that they visually blend into a velvety smooth surface, seemingly solid and best treated as such.

When drawing this Lynx-point Siamese, as much importance was paid to the white space between lines as the lines themselves.

Note how the hair at the back of the skull is less defined, giving a sense of recession.

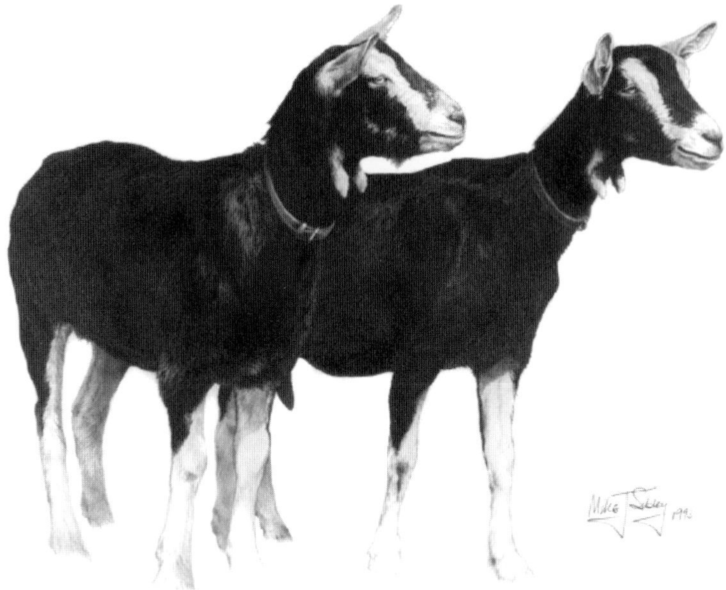

Our goats Willow and Araminta (Minty).
The drawing uses mainly 2H indenting in the dark areas of their bodies.

Unfortunately, most animals fall between these two extremes and make our task more difficult.

The major requirements when drawing this type of hair are sharpness and clarity of line, and well-defined highlights. Any relaxation may result in a muddied appearance that fails to achieve a sense of near-reality. Note that animals with very

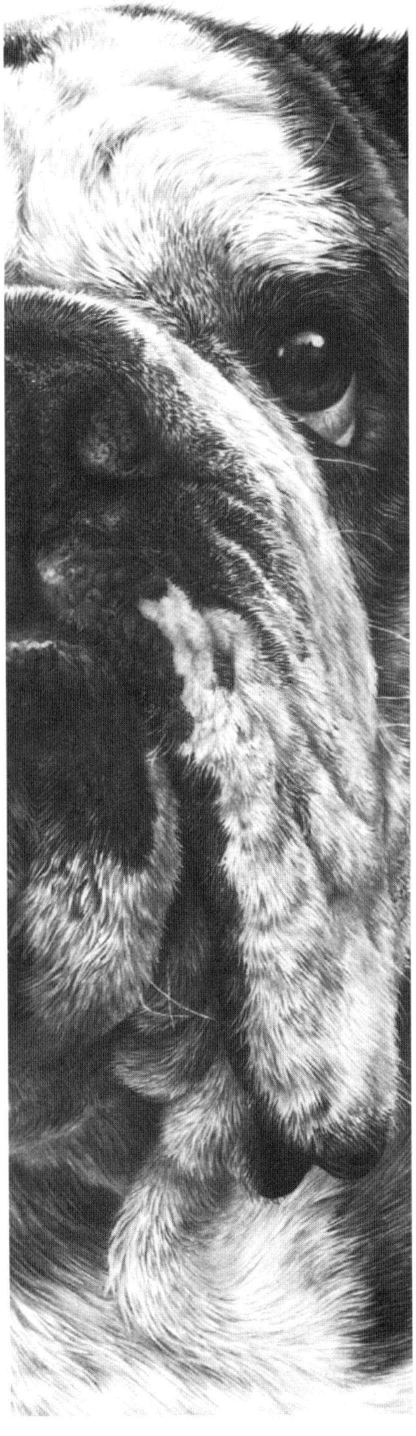

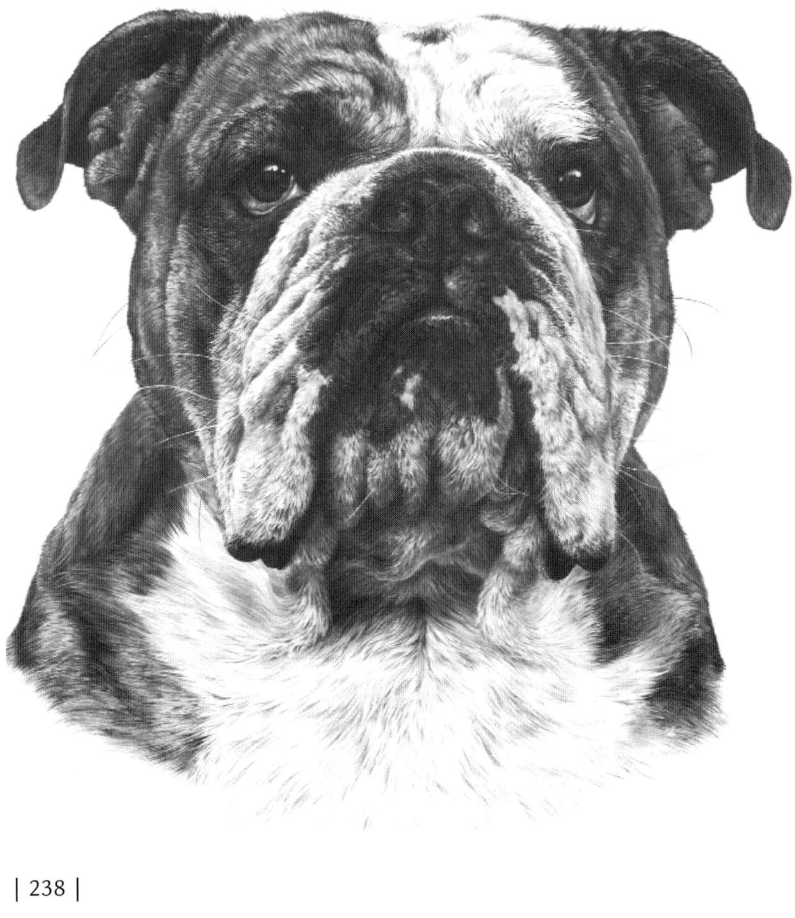

Sharpness, clarity of line, and well-defined highlights are of utmost importance when drawing very short hair.

short hair often expose areas of the skin to view. The Bulldog (*below left*) and Pug (*right*) both exhibit bare skin on both the top and bottom lips beneath the nose. It is important that you find a way of showing the different surface textures as clearly as possible. Here the lack of bright reflection from the short hair has been used to advantage, as highlights have been incorporated into the more shiny skin.

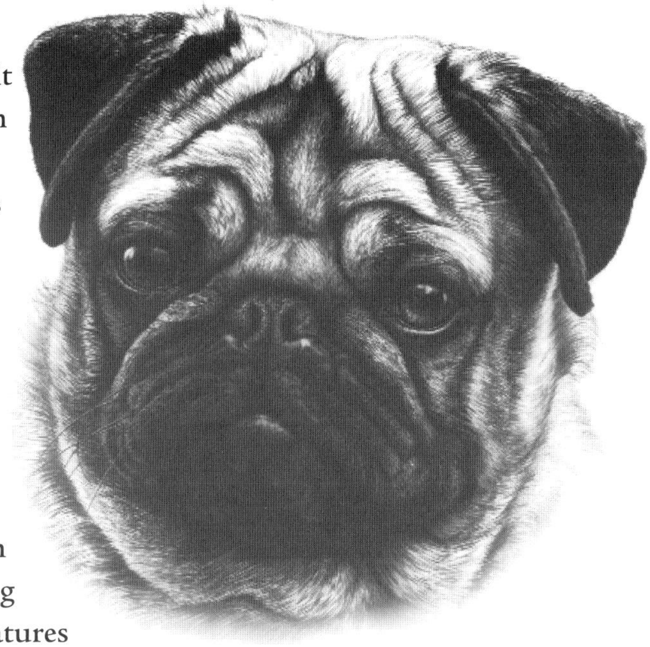

Drawing coarse, wiry hair

Analysis: There are no shortcuts available for drawing wiry hair if a sense of reality is the aim. In common with short hair, it displays the underlying bone structure but to a lesser extent. The main features of the hair are the multiple, deep shadows between narrow locks, the many minor divergences from the general direction of growth, and the seemingly blunt-ended appearance of individual locks. The coarse surface of the hair does not reflect light well so no bright key highlights are present.

Technique: This hair texture requires clear, sharp drawing of detail coupled with severe, positive shadows and highlights. Much use can be made of status hairs. These overlay less detailed suggestions of hair that describe the general direction of growth. There is little sinuous or silky about this variety of hair. 'Spiky' might best describe it - sharp V-shaped shadows predominate, and harsh contrasts between shadows and highlights combine to reinforce the coarseness of its texture. This coarseness can be used to great advantage as it offers ideal conditions for contrasting dissimilar textures. In this case the relatively silky ears work

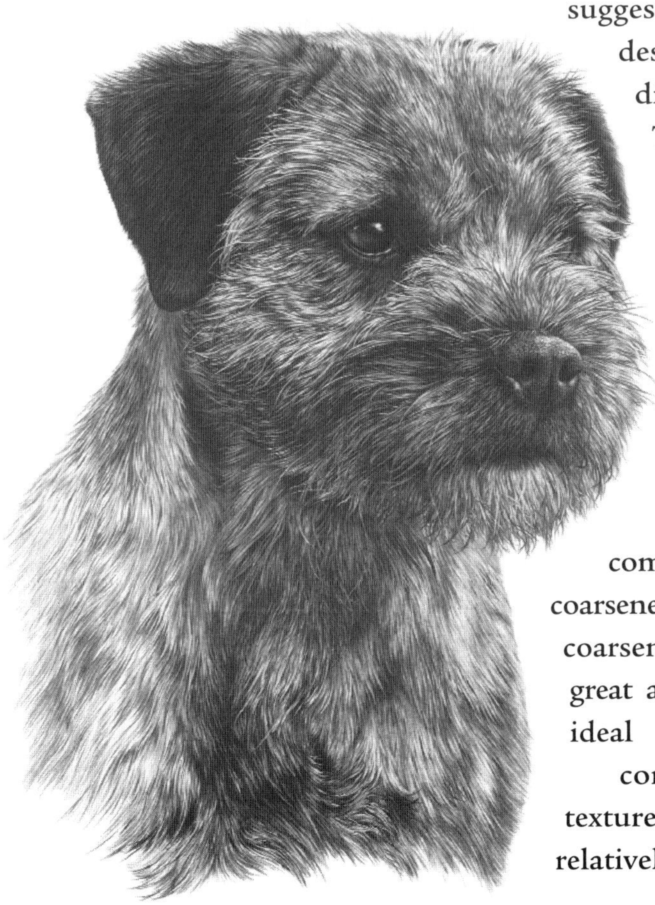

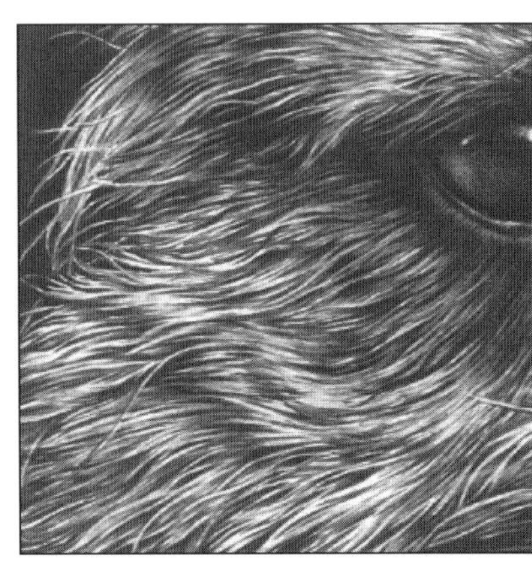

Eye-catching status hairs overlay more general drawing that describes the predominant hair direction.

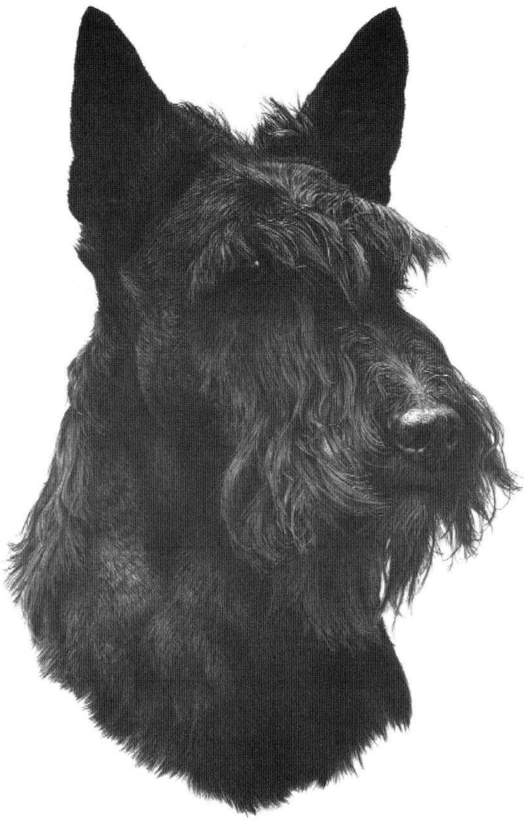

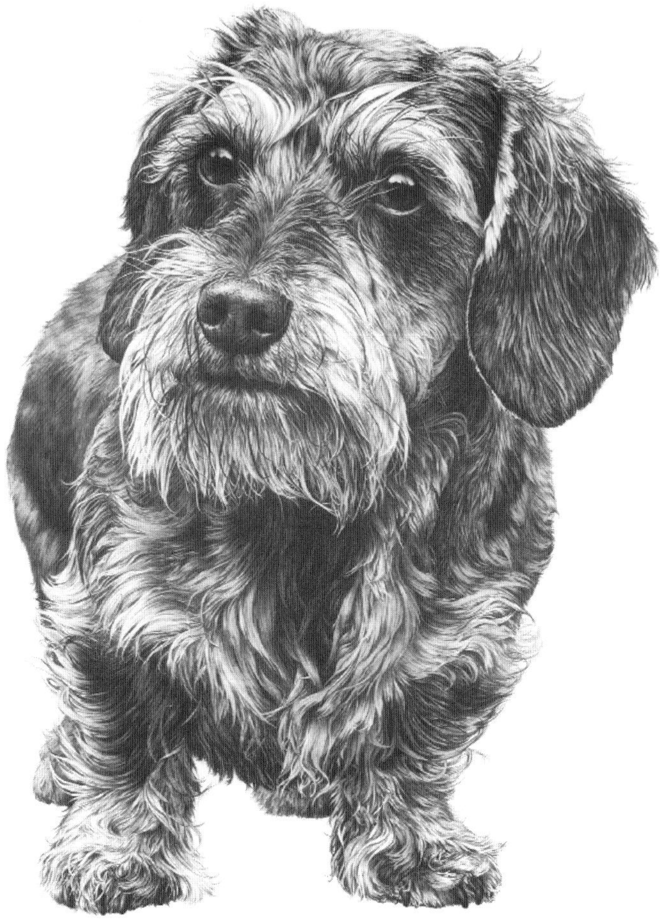

Wire-haired dogs are complex subjects to draw, require close observation, and a full understanding of each element that is about to be drawn.

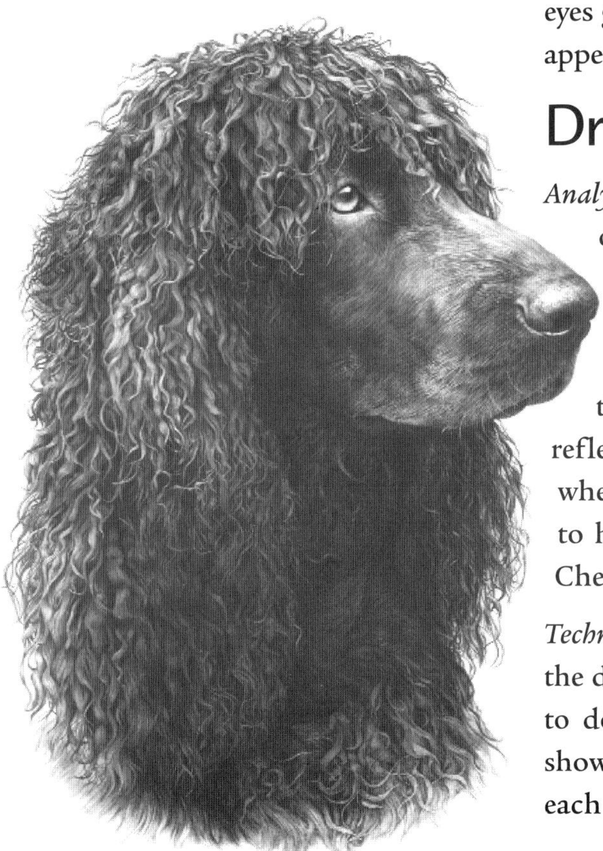

against the coarse facial hair to the greater benefit of both. The eyes gain also, as the hair texture accentuates the smooth, glassy appearance of their surfaces.

Drawing curly hair and ringlets

Analysis: Curls are circular, spiral when they form ringlets, or a distortion of either. They exhibit deep shadows between each other, and possess the usual highlights expected of curved surfaces. The degree of reflection depends on the smoothness of the hair. However, no matter how coarse the texture, an exception is the bright key highlights reflected by wet hair. This is an important consideration where dogs are concerned, as curly coats belong in the main to hunting dogs bred to work in water, such as the Poodle, Chesapeake Bay Retriever and Irish Water Spaniel.

Technique: Like many of the other hair types mentioned so far, the drawing of curly hair relates as much to humans as it does to dogs and other animals. The most important points are shown here in this Irish Water Spaniel's head-study (*left*). Treat each lock or curl as a solid three-dimensional object.

Layer tone to comply with the local lighting conditions and give the correct shaping. Then, if required, layer additional tone so it conforms to the overall lighting.

The Irish Water Spaniel has hair that naturally forms locks and these tail off into spiky ends, which point in random directions. The presence of single hairs is uncommon. Compare that to the Poodle below, which has softer hair. Here the curls on the body have the appearance of almost fusing, as the stray wispy ends and loose hairs diffuse the shadows. This is even more markedly apparent on the looser curls on top of the head. In both

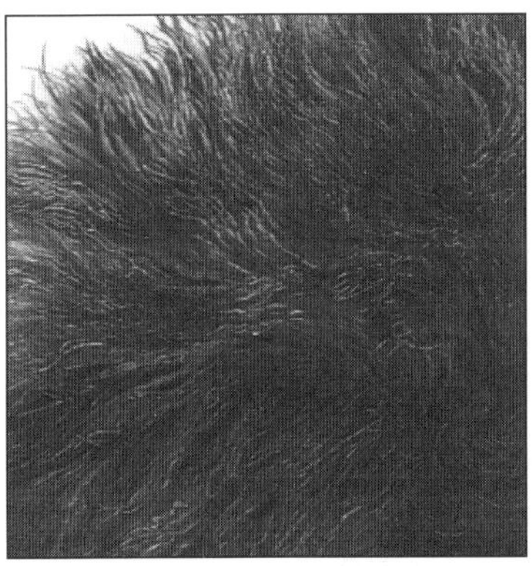

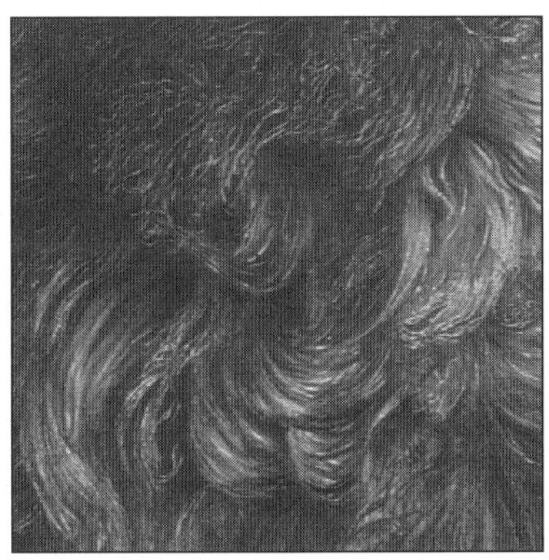

Poodle's head curls and body showing the use of fine indenting.

cases a controlled amount of fine indenting has produced the wispy look. That the indenting looks like fine hairs is less important than sending the right visual signal. The key must be transmitted even if this involves a little exaggeration.

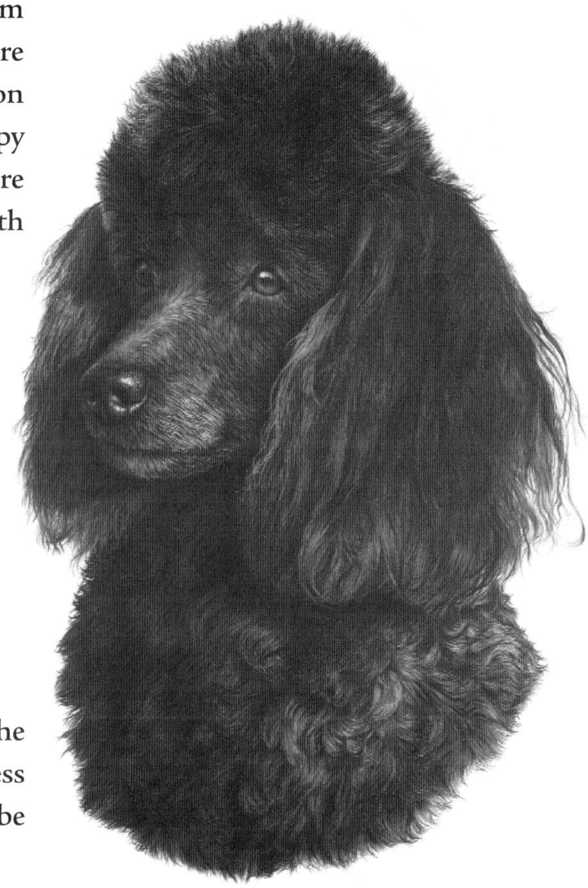

Drawing wavy hair

Analysis: Deep shadows are usually present between the locks, from which the waves are formed. The waves themselves conform to the lighting rules of curved surfaces. Hair that clumps together easily often doesn't possess stray hairs or wispy ends. Because of their absence the resulting smooth surface has a high reflectivity.

Technique: The same techniques and objectives apply to the hair of both humans and dogs. However, human wavy hair is often finer, so expect to find more stray hairs and adopt a softer approach. As with drawing all hair, first imagine running your fingers through it and keep that texture in mind as you draw.

Personally, I enjoy drawing this type of hair because of its tonal opportunities and simplicity of execution. The deep shadows and bright highlights can be engineered to work against each other to exaggerate the overall contrast, and the profusion of hard edges easily breaks any area down into manageable elements - I like to

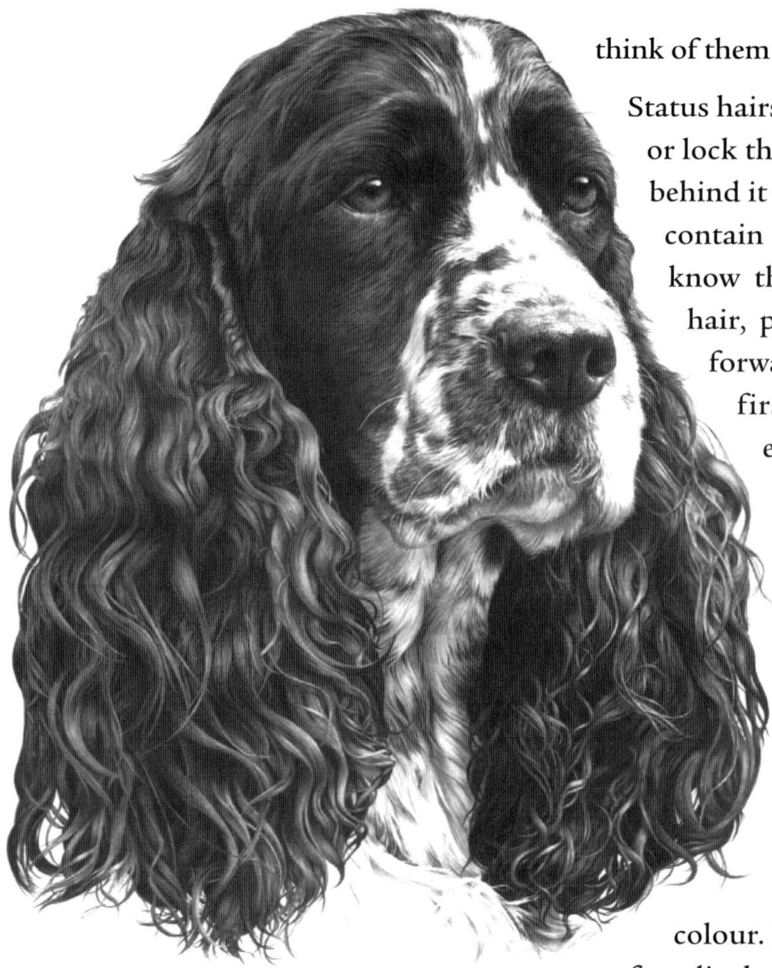

Springer Spaniel

think of them as built-in coffee breaks.

Status hairs figure strongly here. Pick a foreground hair or lock that you want to emphasise then draw the hair behind it - it needn't be too detailed, although it must contain some semblance of reality. Now that you know the surrounding tones, complete the status hair, perhaps drawing a cast shadow to throw it forward. It's this hair, or lock, that the eye will see first before making the assumption that everything behind it must be hair also.

As I demonstrated at the beginning of this chapter, draw from dark into light, fading your pencil lines as you approach the highlight. This will best preserve the virgin highlight for you.

Drawing colours

Apart from bleached or grey highlights, representing the colour in human hair is relatively simple, as we each have a single colour. However, dogs, cats, cows and other animals often display multi-coloured coats, which complicate the drawing process. Experience is the best teacher but you do need to decide before you begin how you are best going to tackle the problem. This is where slavishly copying a source photograph will get you into trouble. You need to engineer your tones for the colour differentiation to succeed. If, for example, you're drawing a black and tan dog, your tones must be pitched so the eye can distinguish between a highlight in the black and

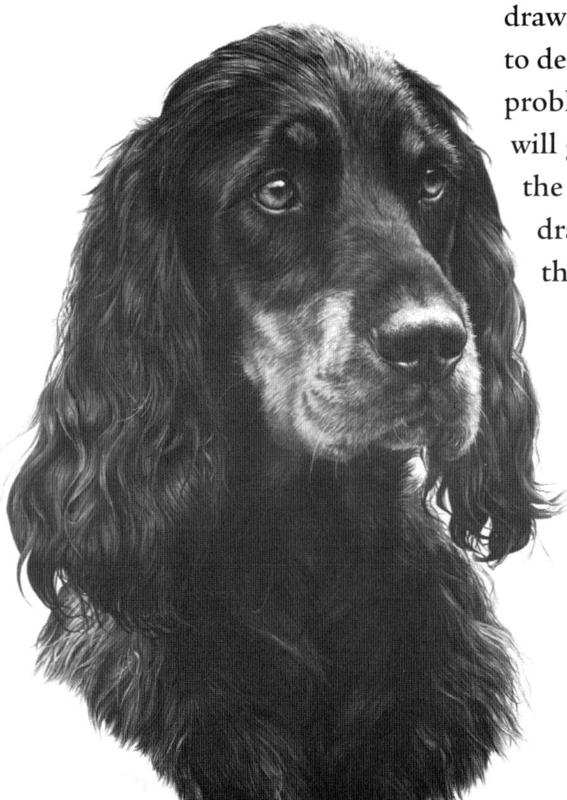

Black and Tan Gordon Setter

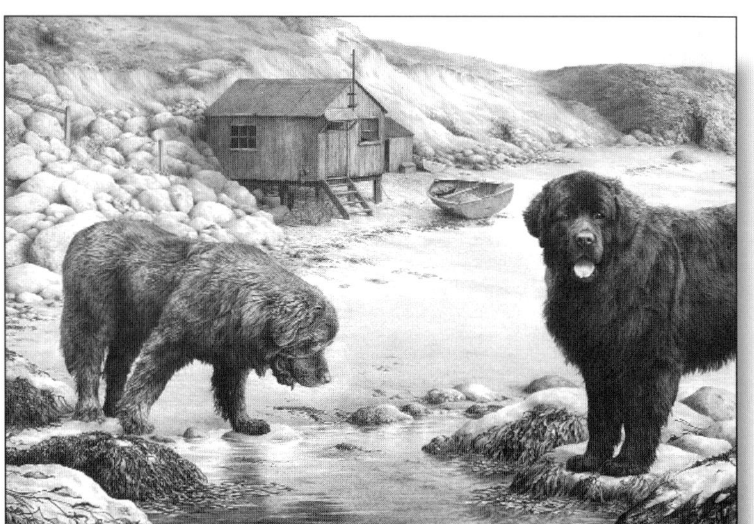

'Whistlers Cove' Showing both brown and black Newfoundland dogs.

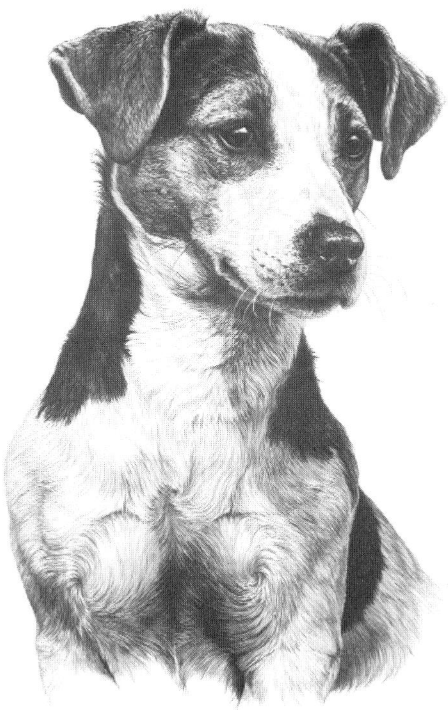

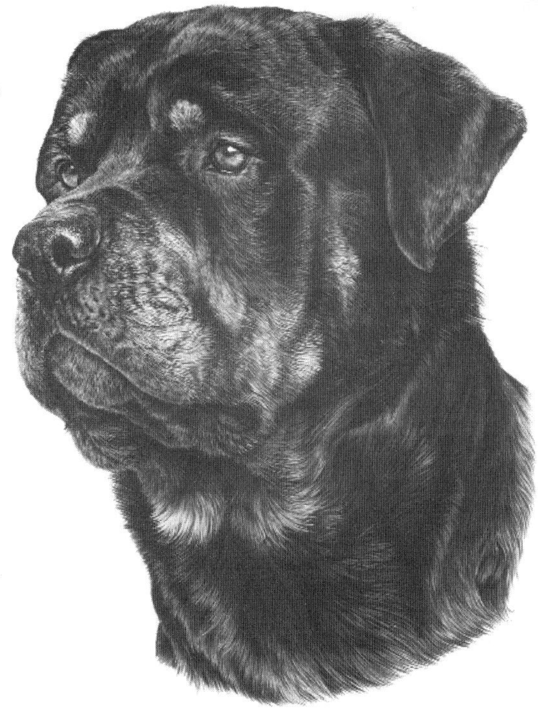

Far left: Black, white and tan Jack Russell terrier.

Left: Black and tan Rottweiler

Your tones must be pitched so the eye can distinguish between a highlight in the black and the body colour of the tan.

the body colour of the tan.

To the eye, a brown dog will appear lighter than a black one, and a fawn or wheaten one lighter than a brown - even if the other colour isn't present for comparison. If the perceived colour is important to your drawing, you need to carefully consider and decide on your tonal range before you begin.

Finally

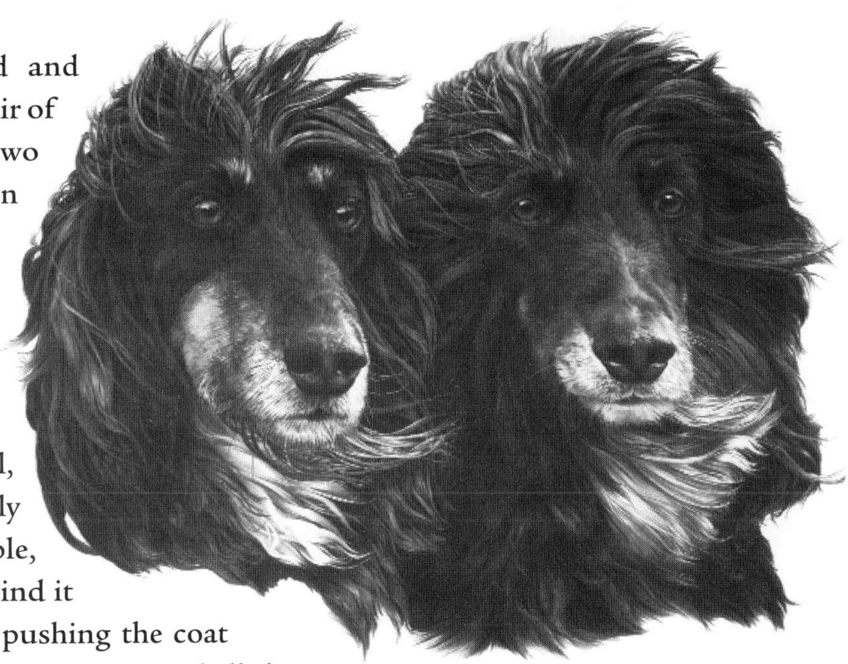

The possibilities are endless. Wild and windy, for instance - the windblown hair of these Afghan Hounds serves two purposes. It formed a direct connection between the two dogs, unifying the arrangement, and it allowed me to display their entire faces - rarely visible or in full light with a coat this long and profuse.

Hair, whether it is human or animal, has more uses for the artist than merely clothing the subject. Little, for example, better connects a dog to the bush behind it than the interaction of a leaf or two pushing the coat out of place. If you stand a dog in water and draw wet belly hair you immediately relay the story that it has been wading but not swimming.

'THE LESSONS TAUGHT IN THIS CHAPTER APPLY EQUALLY TO FEATHERS, FLEECE AND OTHER SKIN COVERING.'

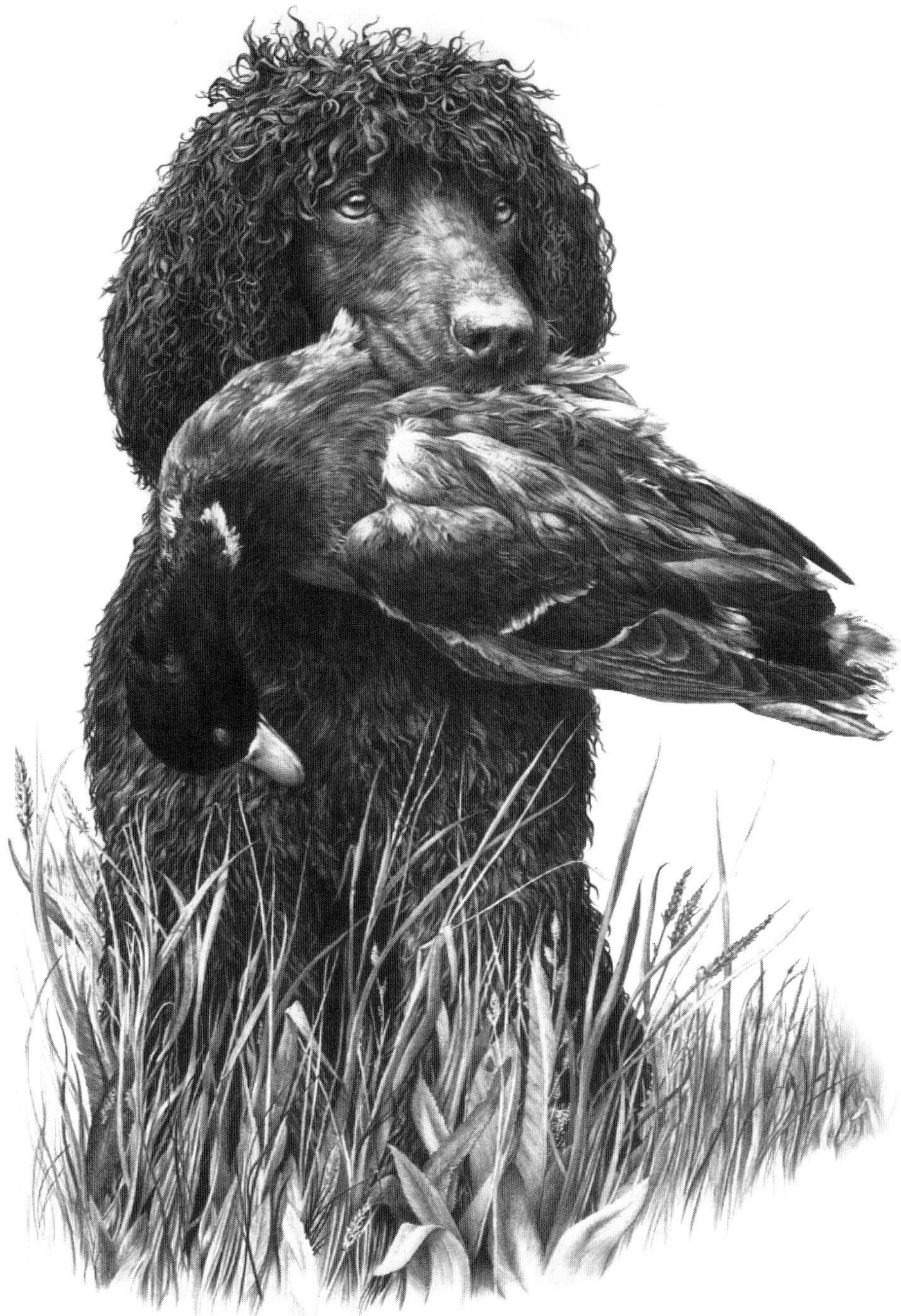

Keep environmental influences firmly in mind. As you draw hair you have to take into consideration what movements your subjects are making, how they are interacting with their surroundings, and how their hair will react to these factors. Try to picture the motion of the hair in your mind and it will become an ally in your endeavours; often the smallest interaction between hair and situation will greatly increase the sense of reality.

The Irish Water Spaniel shown above originally held a pheasant in its mouth. In substituting the much bulkier duck I had to work out how the top lips would stretch and bunch up to accommodate it. Notice too how the mouth has affected the lie of the feathers. They are now pushed out of place by the lips; firmly connecting the two into one believable whole.

The lessons taught in this chapter apply equally to feathers, fleece and other skin covering. Analyse why it looks the way it does, extract the visual keys, then incorporate your findings into your drawing. Mentally run your hands over and through the surface, determine its texture and, with your newfound knowledge, picture each in your mind as you work. Talk to yourself as you draw; explain how the fleece of the ewe you are drawing is laying flat to the sides here and now curving around a shoulder - so, surely, at this point the wool should part, creating a veritable abyss of a shadow? Indeed it should. Don't draw a resemblance of hair, or fleece or feathers; observe, research then draw what you see in your mind as living, mobile, three-dimensional shapes and forms.

'A very important thing I've learned in drawing is that the only way to do something well is to know it well. In fact, if you can't draw something completely from your mind, it means you don't know that something well enough.

Can you draw hair completely from your mind? If you can't, that just means you don't really know what hair looks like. There's a simple solution. Study it.'

Rebekah Lynn, artist

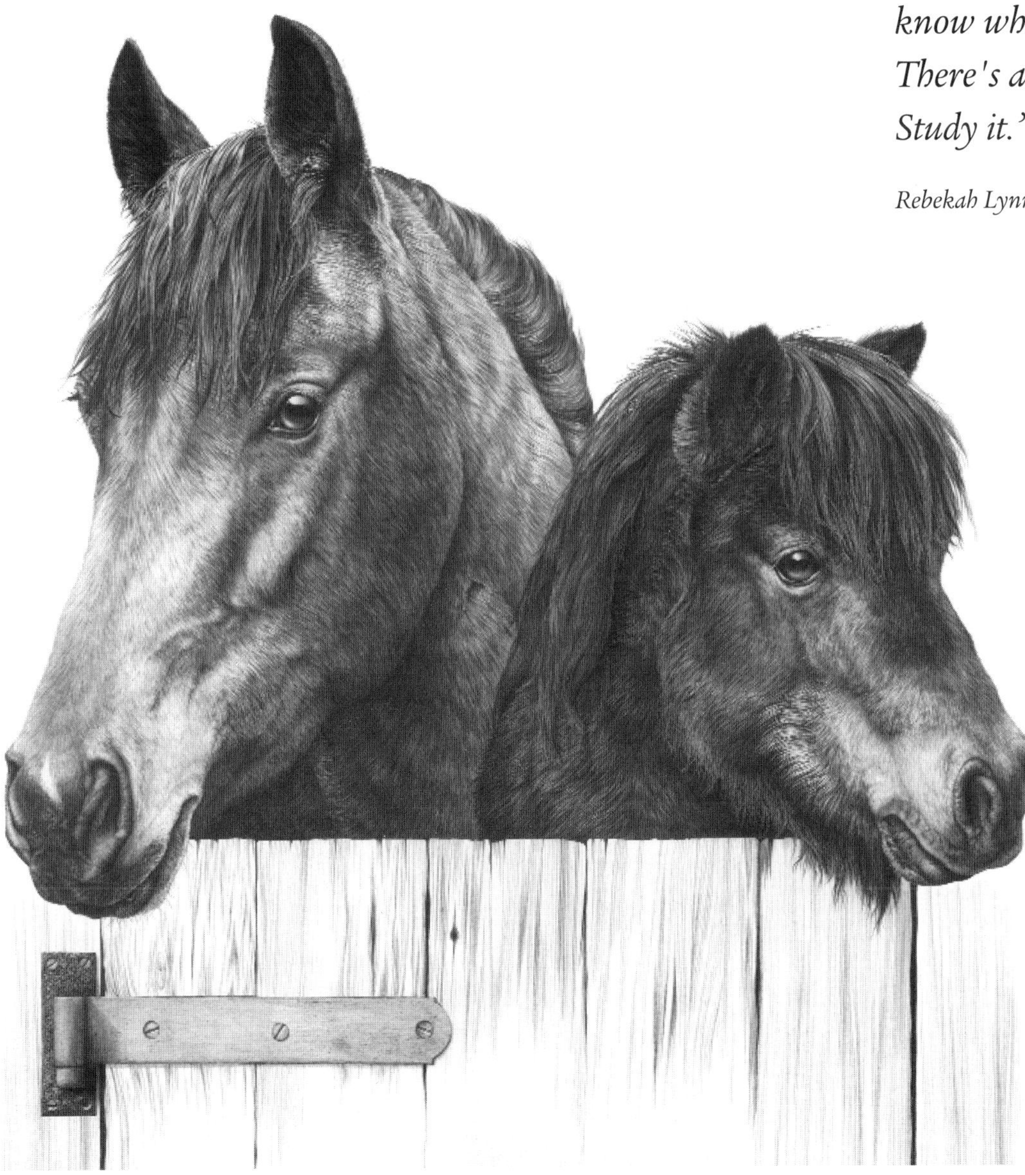

Drawing Features

Being nosey about eyes...

'Being 'the window to the soul', eyes are inevitably the main attraction in any portrait'

Many, possibly most, of the techniques mentioned in this chapter are equally attributable to both humans and animals. Eyes, in particular, share many visible similarities, and an identical means of operation. Being 'the window to the soul', eyes are inevitably the main attraction in any portrait, human or animal, so they will be covered in depth. However, as humans exhibit more of the eyeball than do most animals, the demonstration will concentrate on the human eye. And, to redress the balance, the canine nose will be featured, due to its more complex nature.

Drawing Eyes

There are two main points to consider when drawing eyes - draw what you see and understand, not just what you think you see.

In order to draw eyes realistically, you need to at least understand both the basics of their operation and the internal structure that dictates the outward appearance. An eye is not a glassy bulbous shape with a coloured iris attached and a central black spot. In fact an eye is a complex instrument akin to a digital camera.

The eyeball is spherical in shape (*fig 1*) with only a portion partly visible between the upper and lower eyelids. Just like a camera, it possesses a lens and a 'film' to produce an image. A protective and transparent membrane, the cornea, is situated in front of the coloured iris, and bulges forward from the surface of the sphere. It serves to pass light rays through the pupil and internal lens onto the eye's retina, the photosensitive array or 'film', at the back of the eye. Here the image is captured; the light is converted into electrical signals, and then sent to the brain to be 'developed'. The cornea also reflects light, just like any other curved and glossy surface.

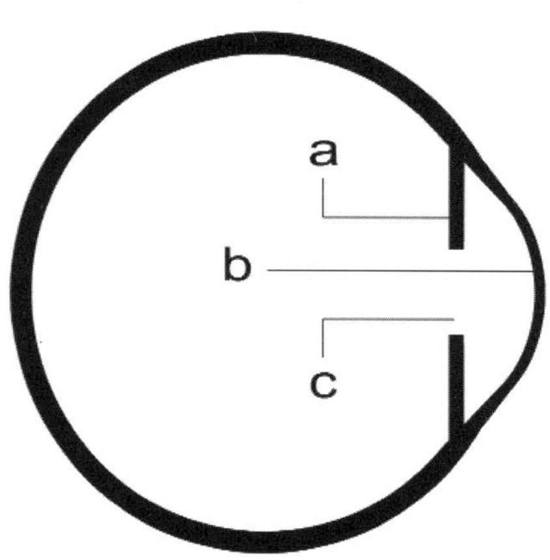

Fig 1
a: Iris
b: Cornea
c: Pupil

What has this got to do with drawing an eye? Simply that without this knowledge, two common errors can occur. The first is treating the eye as a shiny opaque object. The second is depicting the iris as being a part of the exterior curved surface.

It isn't. It's a flat plate lying behind the curved cornea. This is not readily apparent in the human eye but is markedly present in the eye of a cat, which possesses a much more rounded cornea. Look at any cat's eye from the side (*fig 2*) and you will immediately appreciate the separation of the curved cornea and the flat iris. In reality the iris is slightly curved but it's easier to work with if thought of as being flat. At its centre is a hole, the pupil, which the iris (just like a camera's iris) can vary in size depending on the intensity of the light.

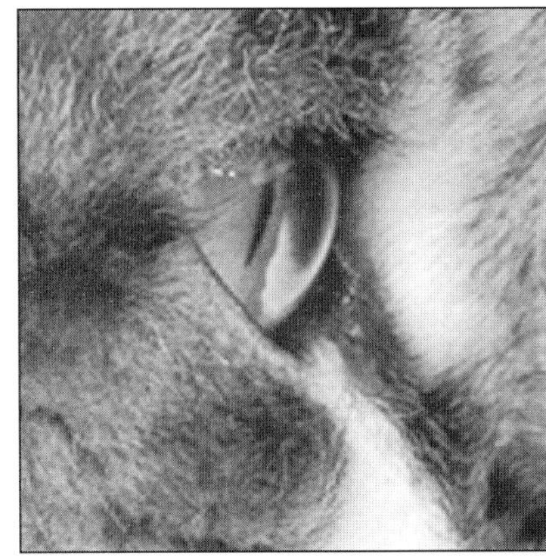

Fig 2. Cat's eye showing the noticeable separation between the curved cornea and the flatter iris.

Little of this understanding is of apparent importance when the eye is viewed from the front (*fig 3*). However, as soon as the head turns (*fig 4*), this understanding immediately becomes very important indeed. When viewed at an angle, we have two planes to consider - the curvature of the cornea, and the flat plane of the iris behind it. Perspective will dictate that the circular iris, and the pupil at its centre, become ellipses, and neither conform in any way to the completely independent curve of the cornea.

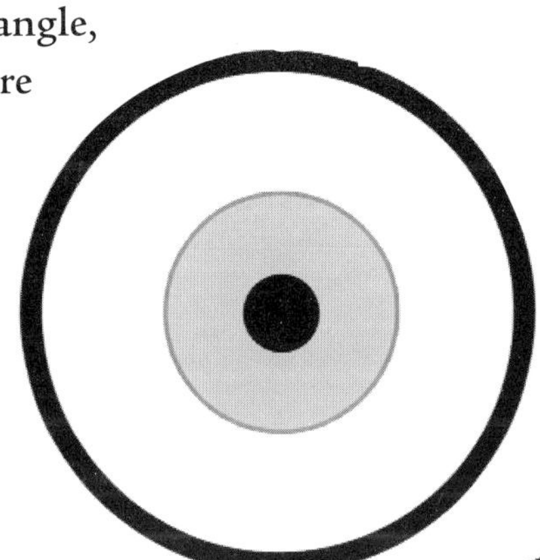

Fig 3. Eyeball viewed from the front.

Points to consider

Before you begin drawing there are a number of attributes and properties of eyes to consider. First and foremost, as the eyes are almost certainly going to be the main focus of your portrait, consider giving them the extra clarity that will visually promote them above the other elements. One way to do this is to slightly blend all other areas, leaving the eyes as the sharpest features. Another is to ensure that you reserve the darkest and lightest tones for the eyes. The pupils will certainly be the darkest value and the key highlights (sometimes called 'catchlights') will be the brightest. Their close juxtaposition will add both sparkle and depth, and enliven your portrait.

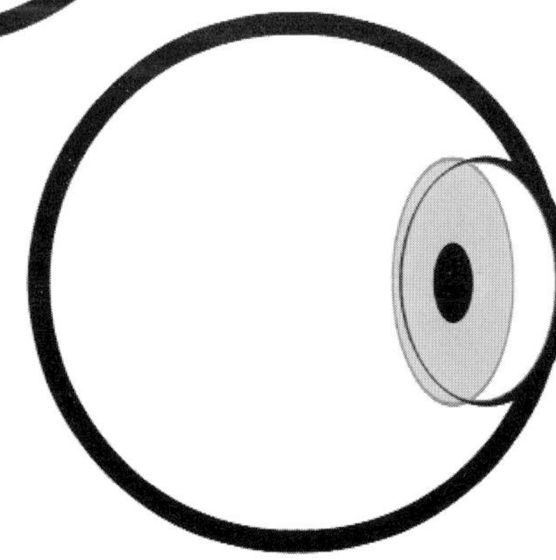

Fig 4. Three-quarter angle showing how the flat iris conforms to perspective independently of the curved cornea.

From a practical point of view, pay particular attention to ensuring that the eyeball truly conforms to the lighting rules of a globe, and that the highlights are correctly fashioned. We'll return to the highlights later as their apparent simplicity conceals a surprisingly complex arrangement.

The eyes of humans and animals are fundamentally similar. However, one major difference is that few animals show any white of the eye unless they are looking to either side. Also the pupil of the human eye is round but in animals, depending on

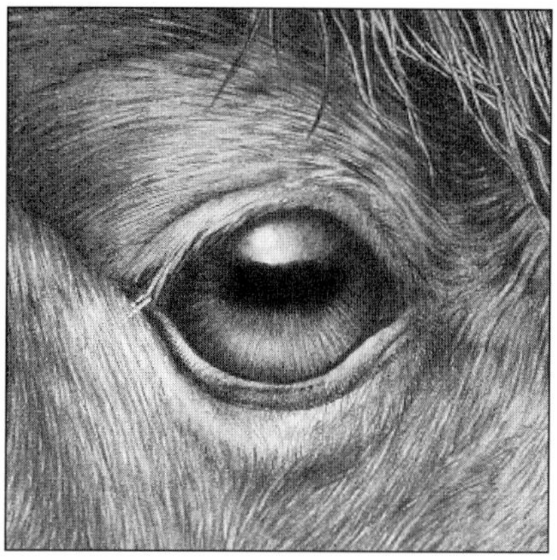

Fig 5. Drawing of a Shetland Pony's eye showing the typical oblong shape of a horse's pupil.

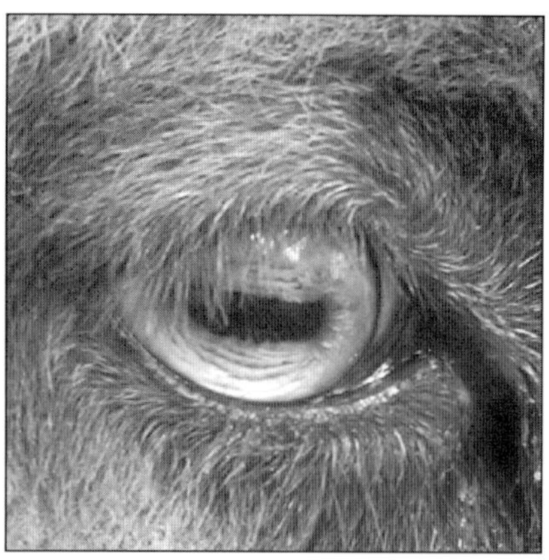

Fig 6. Oblong pupil of the eye of one of our Manx Loughtan sheep.

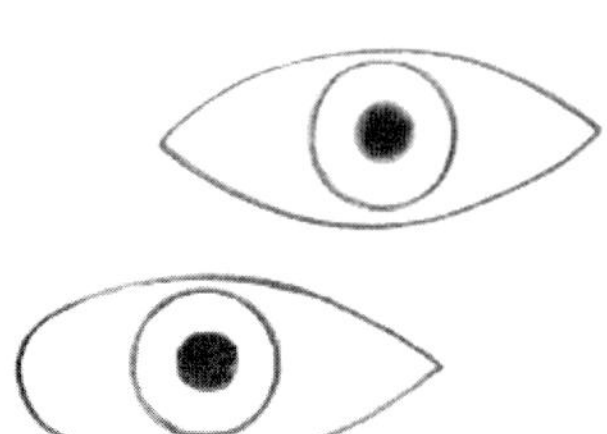

*An eye is **not** symmetrical nor is it almond shaped.*

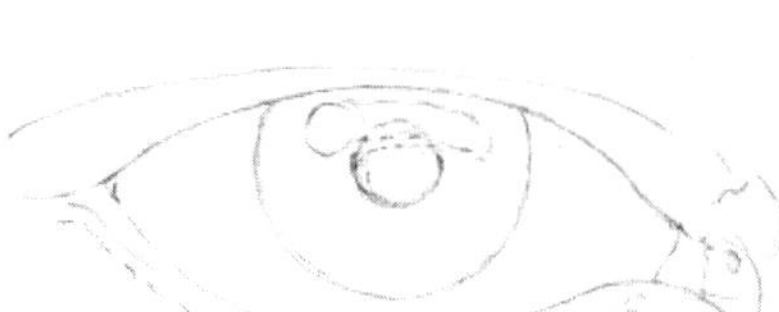

Fig 7. Initial 2B line drawing showing only major features. Simplicity at this stage will later allow you a greater artistic freedom.

the species, it can be a variety of other shapes too. For example, the eyes of horses (*fig 5*), and goats and sheep (*fig 6*) have oblong pupils running horizontally across the iris. Cats have large, round pupils in low light situations but they close to vertical slits in bright light.

I'll mention when other differences need your attention. The following examples concentrate on the human eye but everything is equally applicable to the eyes of animals.

The initial line drawing

By now you should be aware of falling foul of symbol drawing. An eye is not symmetrical nor is it almond shaped. Indeed, eyes contain unique variations that alone can often identify a person. So, carefully observe the eyes of your model, and look for the fundamental characteristics - the keys that you must incorporate. If you're new to drawing eyes, first try drawing full-face portraits. Then, when you progress to drawing faces at a three-quarter angle, you'll already have an understanding of the basic mechanics and three-dimensional form.

Make full use of negative space, as discussed in chapter 9, to help you better understand the complex curves involved. Gridding (see chapter 15) helps in this respect too. In this initial guideline stage (*fig 7*), include any significant boundaries that you think will help you later. These include the main contours of the lids, and the position of the iris and pupil. You can use these as reference points when you are drawing - a map to help you keep track of where you are.

Unless you are using the grid method, begin by marking the principal facial features and check their positions for accuracy, either by measurement or triangulation. Now is the time to make necessary changes - to reshape, for example, a cat's pupils if flash photography has artificially widened them. Don't outline minor features at this stage; simplicity is the key. You need a town map rather than a street plan, so concentrate on the position and shape of major elements. If you're drawing an animal, include the edges of markings and changes in hair direction. When you're satisfied, include helpful secondary elements, such as the eye's key and secondary highlights.

Drawing the Pupil...

Once you are satisfied that everything is positioned correctly and the shapes are as they should be, I suggest you begin by establishing the pupil (*fig 8*). This is one of the rare times that I use 6B, although I finally blend the grains with 2B. The pupil will always be the darkest point of your drawing. It's a hole that leads into the dark interior of the eye and, with the single exception of 'red eye', caused by flash photography, light will enter through it but not reflect back out again. It's the original 'black hole'. Complete the pupil and you will have your darkest and lightest tones to refer to. Now all your intermediate tones will more easily fall into place.

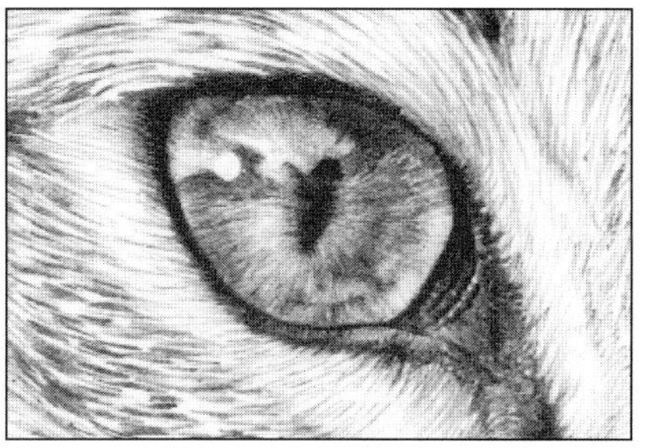

In normal light a cat's pupil closes to a slit. Study the shape carefully - it is more complex than it looks - and note that the edge facing the light source is highlighted.

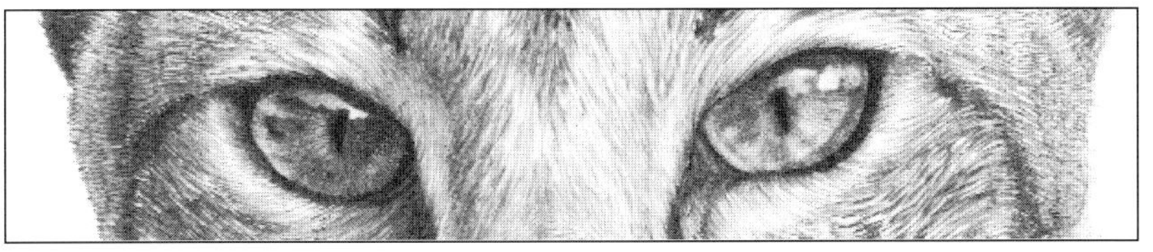

As this drawing shows, a cat's pupils are not vertical - the tops lean inwards towards each other.

Drawing the Iris

As drawing a perfect circle or ellipse is not easy, some artists use templates. Personally, I never have and don't recommend their use, especially if the head is angled, as both the iris and pupil will form ellipses. You may find the perfect ellipse on a template but you might also be confused by an array of slightly different ellipses and be fooled into thinking the nearest to perfection will suffice. It won't. Your brain knows when an ellipse is correct for a given situation, so allow it to help you draw one freehand. If you feel the need to use a template, draw your circle lightly then draw a darker freehand line over it. Don't make this line too hard edged (*fig 9*), as a slightly ragged edge, or light blending into the eyeball, will assist in depicting reality.

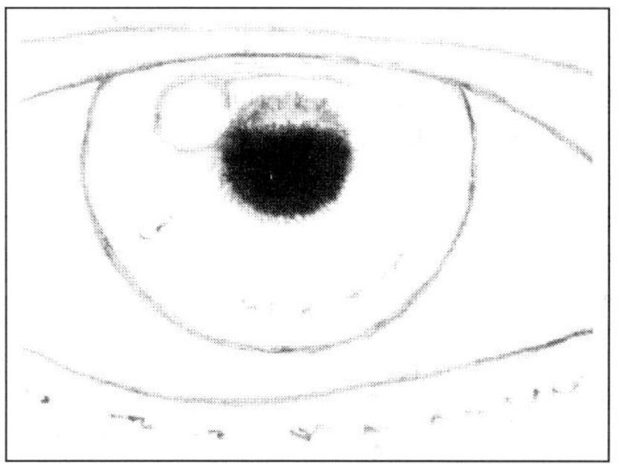

Fig 8. Iris guideline redefined with greater accuracy, and the pupil established as the darkest tone. Don't draw a circle around the pupil and fill it in - a hard edge is not natural, especially in dogs.

The iris is not a solid tone. It is darker around the outer edge and lightens towards the centre. It also contains flecks and striations that radiate from the centre, which are of a random nature and not spoke-like bars. We'll begin work on them here then break for a while.

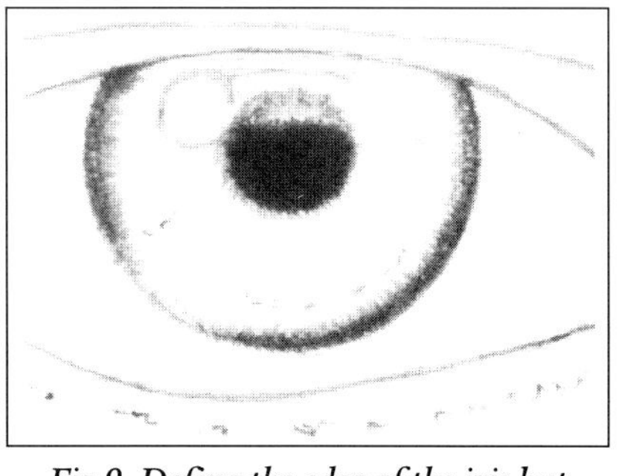

Fig 9. Define the edge of the iris but don't draw it too hard-edged. I prefer to draw short radiating lines.

There are various methods available for producing realistic iris striations and flecks, such as indenting and erasing. Experimentation will help you find the method that best suits you. Personally, I use 2H and 6H indenting (*fig 10*) when working on Mellotex or smooth Bristol board.

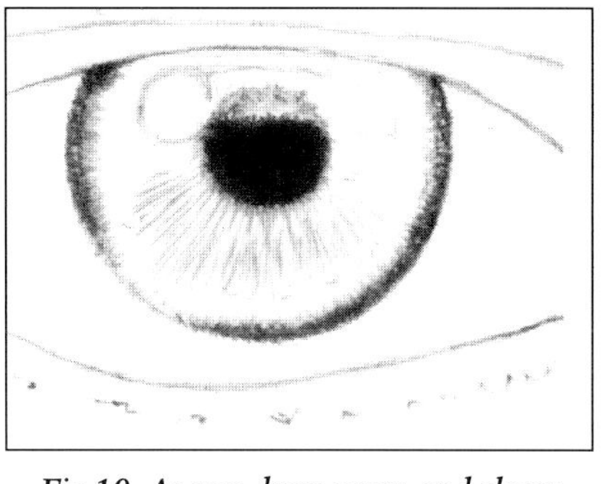

Fig 10. As you draw more and closer radiating lines, the lighter that area will eventually become. Crowd the lines nearer to the centre to ensure it contrasts with the darker rim. The finer 6H indenting is barely visible.

Keep in mind when using this method that the marks you are making are going to be highlights that represent light flecks and lines in the darker iris. The 2H will act as a 'resist', preventing softer graphite from adhering to the paper so, as you draw more and closer radiating lines, the lighter that area

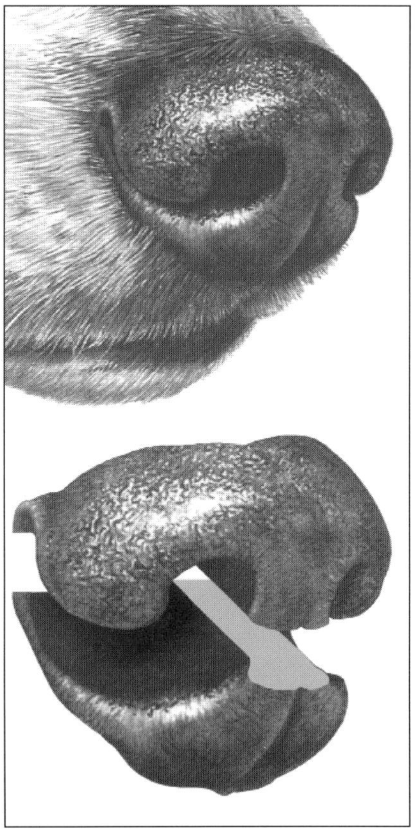

Fig 17. Exploded view of a dog's nose.

Drawing noses

I am often asked for assistance with the drawing of dogs' noses, as they are quite complex and very different from our own. Other noses, such as those of cats, horses, and humans, are simpler in construction and often more easily understood on examination.

THE BASIC SHAPE

Despite the many different breeds of dog, including wolves and foxes, the structure of the nose remains the same. The simplest way to picture a dog's nose is to see it as being two halves (*fig 17*) a top and bottom connected by the central septum, the vertical section between the nostrils.

The top half has a leathery appearance, almost smooth in some breeds and coarse textured in others. These textural variations often account for one looking dull and dry and another shiny and wet, and it's important that you look for these variations as they considerably affect the reflected highlights. At the front are the two nostrils flanked by bulbous corners. The dividing septum usually has a central groove, to a greater or lesser extent.

To each side of the nose are flared curves, which catch the light and cast a dark shadow beneath. The leather on top of the nose, and the nose itself, finishes at a line drawn between the ends of these two flared curves. Beyond that, some breeds grow hair and others possess a bald area of smooth skin, the same colour as the nose. Don't confuse this area with the nose - look carefully and you can usually detect the change in texture. The two parallel nasal passages travel through this area along the top of the muzzle, which gives it a flat appearance due to the slight central dip.

The simpler bottom half of the nose contains only the floors of the nostrils. The front edges almost always catch the light. If your drawing is very small (*fig 18*), these highlights are of the utmost importance as they read easily from a distance and mark both the position of the nostrils and the curvature of the nose. And if the two nostril highlights differ in brightness they also signal the angle of the head to the light source.

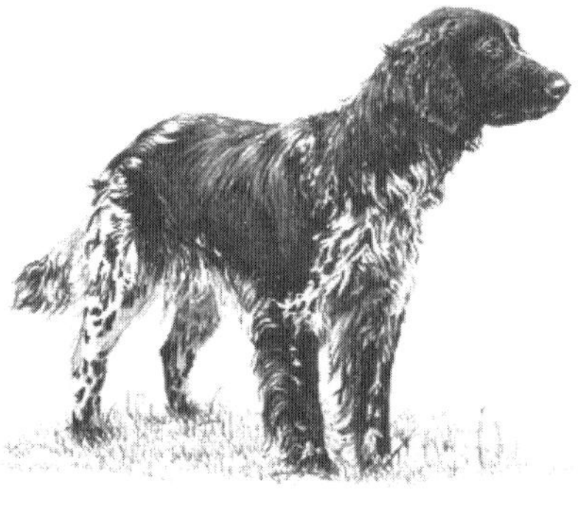

Fig 18. In this 1½" high drawing only the top and nostril highlights mark the position and direction of the Munsterlander's nose.

Pay particular attention to the texture of the leather on top of the nose, which is very variable. An interpretation of the texture is perfectly acceptable but do first take time to analyse its reflective qualities. A lightly textured, shiny nose will possess very strong blacks, and a dry, more heavily textured nose will usually appear to be lighter in tone. A brown nose requires an overall diminution of tone to contrast with the black nostril shadows.

will always be the darkest point of your drawing. It's a hole that leads into the dark interior of the eye and, with the single exception of 'red eye', caused by flash photography, light will enter through it but not reflect back out again. It's the original 'black hole'. Complete the pupil and you will have your darkest and lightest tones to refer to. Now all your intermediate tones will more easily fall into place.

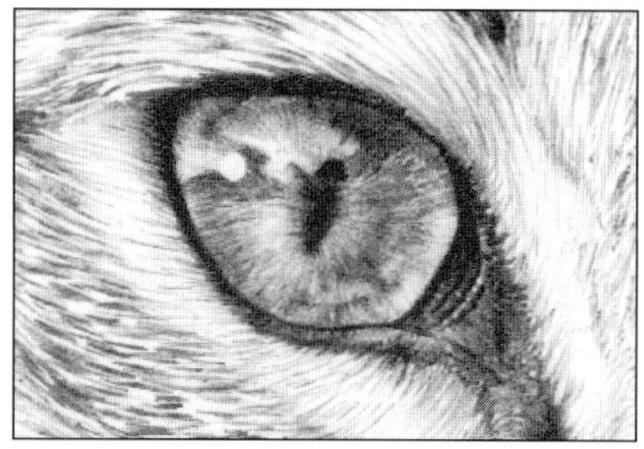

In normal light a cat's pupil closes to a slit. Study the shape carefully - it is more complex than it looks - and note that the edge facing the light source is highlighted.

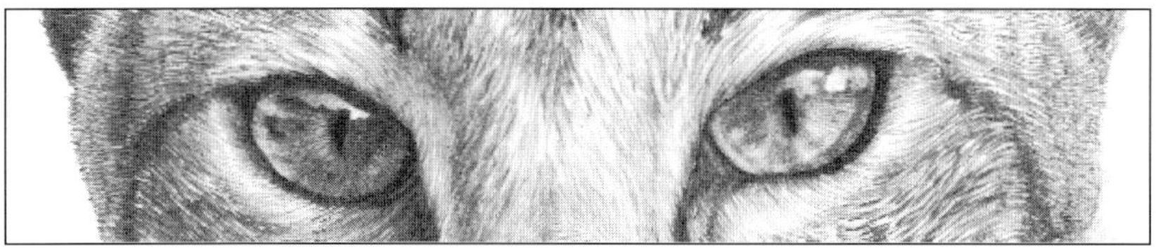

As this drawing shows, a cat's pupils are not vertical - the tops lean inwards towards each other.

Drawing the Iris

As drawing a perfect circle or ellipse is not easy, some artists use templates. Personally, I never have and don't recommend their use, especially if the head is angled, as both the iris and pupil will form ellipses. You may find the perfect ellipse on a template but you might also be confused by an array of slightly different ellipses and be fooled into thinking the nearest to perfection will suffice. It won't. Your brain knows when an ellipse is correct for a given situation, so allow it to help you draw one freehand. If you feel the need to use a template, draw your circle lightly then draw a darker freehand line over it. Don't make this line too hard edged (*fig 9*), as a slightly ragged edge, or light blending into the eyeball, will assist in depicting reality.

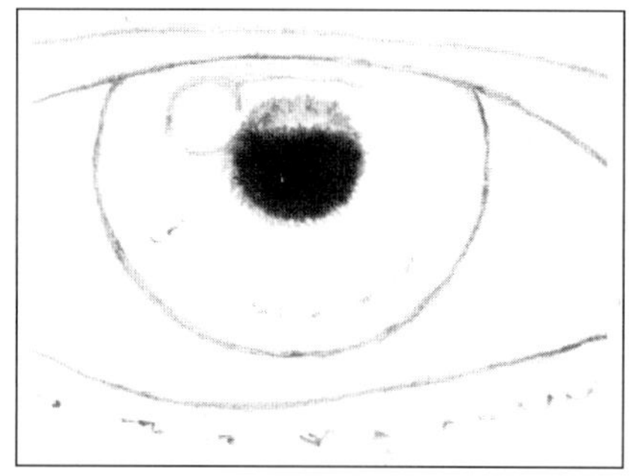

Fig 8. Iris guideline redefined with greater accuracy, and the pupil established as the darkest tone. Don't draw a circle around the pupil and fill it in - a hard edge is not natural, especially in dogs.

The iris is not a solid tone. It is darker around the outer edge and lightens towards the centre. It also contains flecks and striations that radiate from the centre, which are of a random nature and not spoke-like bars. We'll begin work on them here then break for a while.

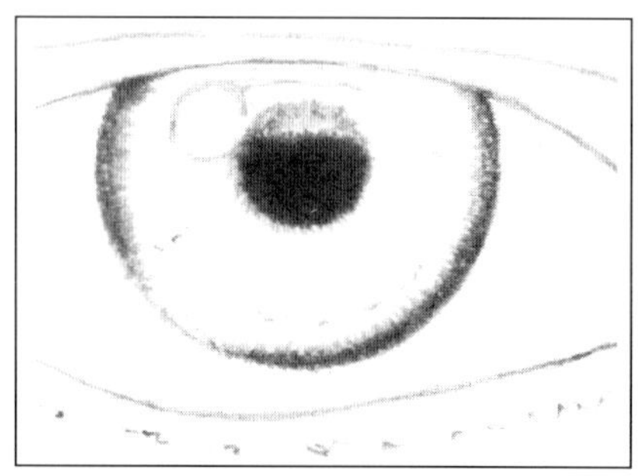

Fig 9. Define the edge of the iris but don't draw it too hard-edged. I prefer to draw short radiating lines.

There are various methods available for producing realistic iris striations and flecks, such as indenting and erasing. Experimentation will help you find the method that best suits you. Personally, I use 2H and 6H indenting (*fig 10*) when working on Mellotex or smooth Bristol board.

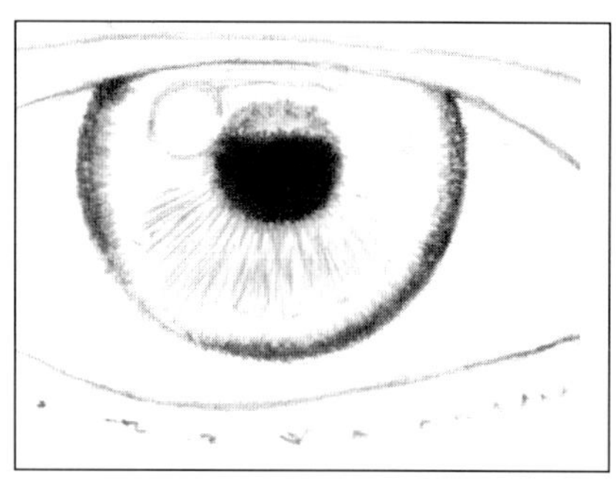

Fig 10. As you draw more and closer radiating lines, the lighter that area will eventually become. Crowd the lines nearer to the centre to ensure it contrasts with the darker rim. The finer 6H indenting is barely visible.

Keep in mind when using this method that the marks you are making are going to be highlights that represent light flecks and lines in the darker iris. The 2H will act as a 'resist', preventing softer graphite from adhering to the paper so, as you draw more and closer radiating lines, the lighter that area

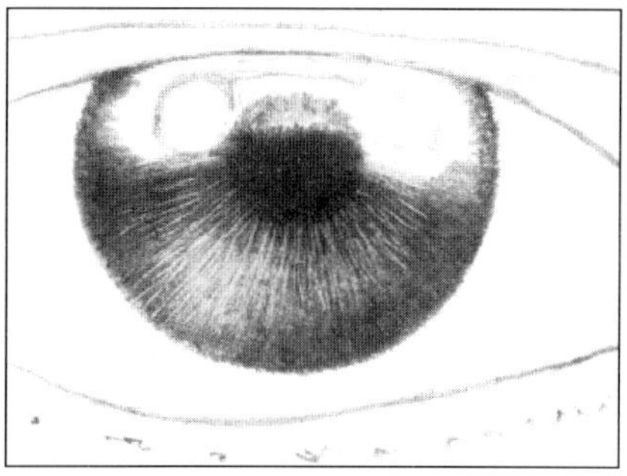

Fig 11. Iris with initial radial applications of 6B and 2B, built up in multiple layers.

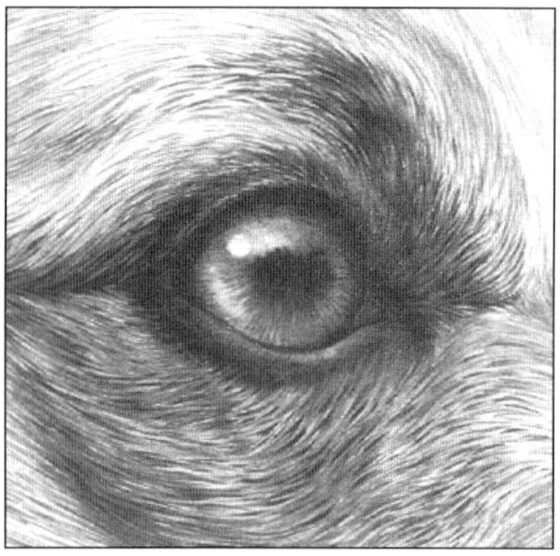

Fig 12. This Whippet's simple curved highlight, reflecting from the surface of the cornea, incorporates the key highlight.

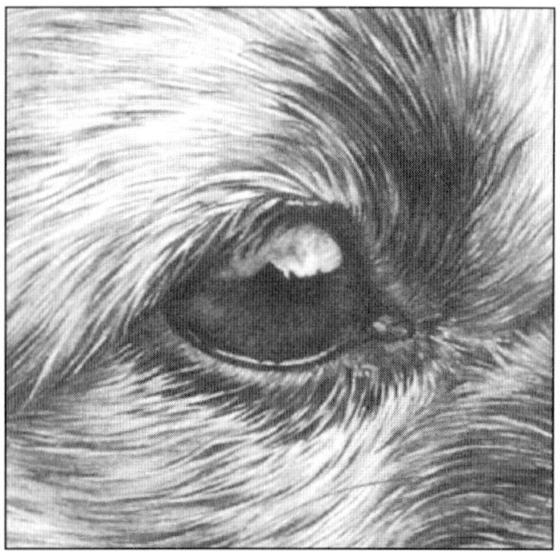

Fig 13. Drawing of a dog's eye with the highlight reflecting the skyline of the location.

will eventually become. Use this to your advantage by crowding the lines nearer the centre to ensure it contrasts with the darker rim. Eyes, especially in dogs, sometimes possess dark spots within the iris, so I draw them at this stage to avoid indenting through them. When the 6H indenting is complete, the next step is to add tone. However, I'll just make a start (*fig 11*) then we'll break to consider the highlight, before completing the iris. The 6H striations will resist a softer grade so I'm using 2B, with a flat face, to build up the tone until the striations and flecks achieve sufficient prominence. I'll refine the area later.

Incorporating the Key Highlight

If you've already sketched in guidelines for your highlights, you might like to reconsider their number and placement before proceeding. No matter how many key highlights your source photograph or model's eyes display, I recommend you draw only one. Multiple key highlights are most often the result of studio lighting. A single highlight infers a more natural, single light source.

A key highlight attracts attention and brings life, emotion and character to the eye, so add one if there isn't one in the photograph. Very lightly outline a single key highlight that directly faces the light source, then incorporate it into a wider curved highlight. This secondary highlight (*fig 12*), which may cut across both the iris and pupil, is reflected by the curved outer surface of the cornea and will effectively signal that the iris lies on a plane behind it. It will never be as bright as the key highlight.

An exception to the simple curved highlight, which I sometimes encounter in animals, is when the eye reflects an image of its surroundings (*fig 13*). These are often very complex but can add a wonderful feeling of reality.

Before we can complete the iris, which incorporates most of the highlight, we need to consider a more complex aspect of the highlight - a very important aspect and, for the artist, a highly beneficial one.

The highlight and key highlight behave differently from each other. The curving highlight is a result of reflection from the eye's moist and glossy surface. The hard-edged key highlight however, not only reflects light from the source directly into the viewer's eye, it also passes a beam of light directly through the interior of the eye via the transparent cornea on which it is situated. The eyeball itself is fluid-filled and this causes strange, but extremely useful, anomalies.

As we saw in chapter 20, the fluid interior causes refraction; the light bends. This results in two bonuses (*fig 14*). First, the bend steers light away from the area behind the key highlight, giving it a dark background and thereby greatly increasing its apparent strength. And second, the refracted light travels to the other side of the eye (following the direction of the light source) and lightens it, as it obliquely hits the iris, and secondary reflections light the cornea. This effect is far more pronounced in an animal's large dark eye than in the human eye. As a result the side opposite to the highlight, often in shadow, is helpfully illuminated internally, adding life to an otherwise dead area.

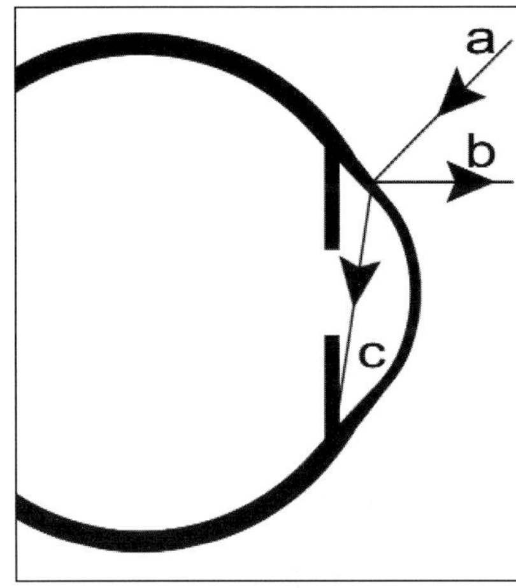

Fig 14. Light from the source (a) reflects from the key highlight to the viewer (b) and passes into the eye. Here it is bent and hits the opposite side of the iris (c), lighting up that portion of the cornea.

Bear in mind that we are creating our own world so our rules apply. It is quite possible, indeed most often desirable when drawing animals, to deliberately incorporate this effect. By simply changing the position of the highlight, or introducing one, we can transform a lifeless, dull eye into a living one with real sparkle.

I often add muted highlights where they are not scientifically possible - in deep shade, for example, or other situations where the eye receives no direct light. The accommodating brain of the viewer merely assumes the presence of some form of reflected light outside of the picture plane, and takes note of the life the eye now contains.

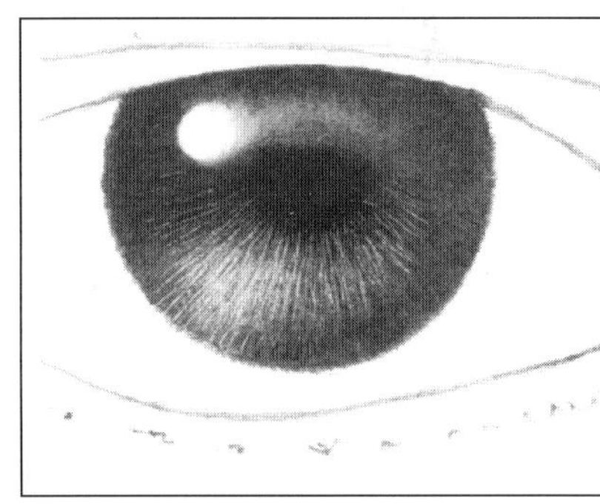

Fig 15. Using 2B to build up the tone until the striations and flecks achieve sufficient prominence. Delicate touches of Blu-Tack may be used to fine-tune key areas.

We can now complete the drawing of the iris (*fig 15*). At this stage I often over-darken the iris and then use delicate touches and strokes of Blu-Tack to lighten key areas. I repeat this until I feel that the correct appearance has been achieved. Finally, having spent time on producing the sharp detail within the iris - don't blend!

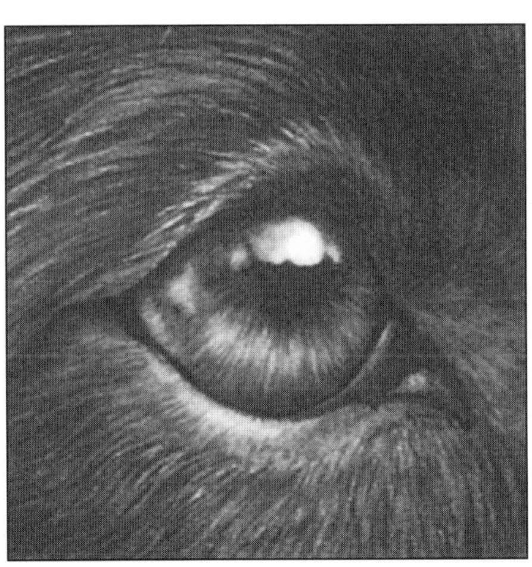

Having created sharp striations, don't blend them. Note that the pupil of a dog's dark eye rarely shows a sharp edge.

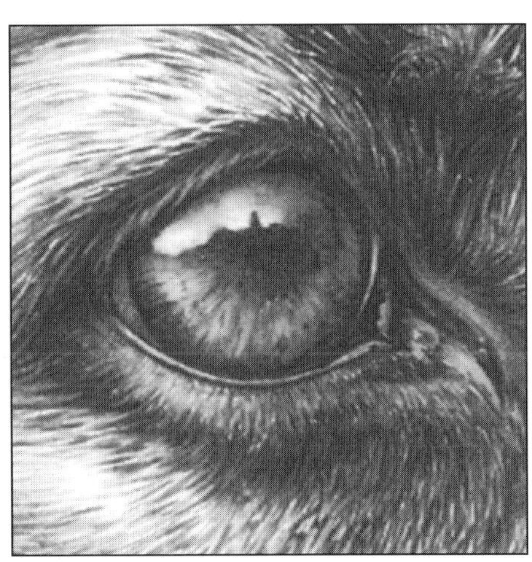

Some dog's top lashes descend to show against the dark eye.

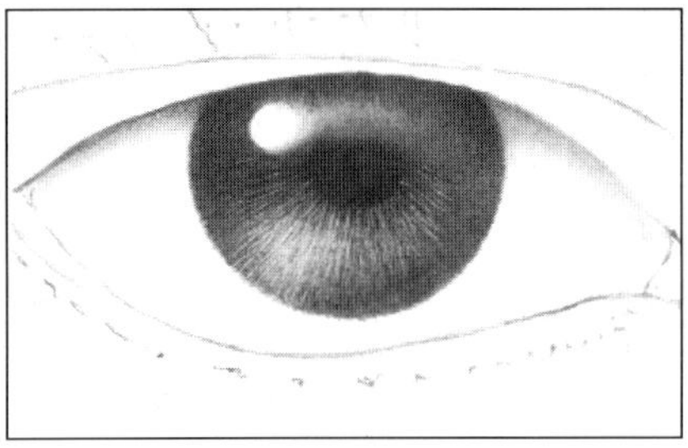

Fig 16. Establishing the shadow cast by the top eyelid.

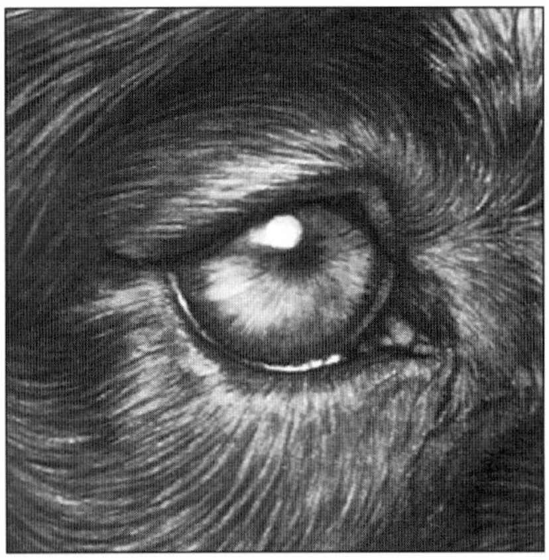

Fig 17. Some breeds of dog show a highlighted watery line at the base of the eye.

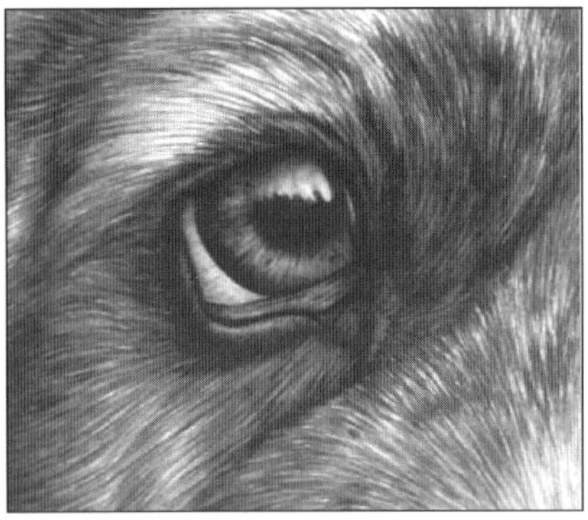

Fig 18. Few animals show any white of the eye. As this Basset shows, its inclusion can make the eye immediately grab attention.

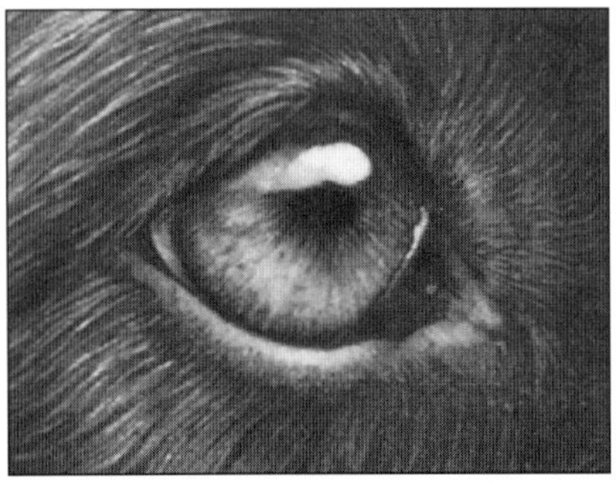

A few breeds of dog show a portion of their third eyelid, which possess a highlight, as shown in this drawing of a Gordon Setter.

Drawing the top of the eye

This is one of the areas where the drawing of human and animal eyes often diverges. Where humans have upward-sweeping top eyelashes, dogs in particular have hairy eyelids and top lashes that sometimes descend to overlay the eyeball. However, they both cast a shadow on the exposed upper part of the eyeball. In the human eye, this shadow forms a dark curve across the top of the eye that gradually softens into the shaded areas at each corner (*fig 16*). It is less noticeable, but just as strong, in an animal that rarely exposes the white of the eye. In both cases, this shadow can be used to advantage because it throws the eyelid forwards, and also deepens the tone around the eye's highlight, further increasing its intensity.

Bear in mind that this cast shadow rarely has a sharp edge. The lashes or hair will diffuse the light and feather the edge, so establish the shadow then draw a little of the edge down with a tortillon or, alternatively, gently fade it by stroking the edge with a point of Blu-Tack or kneadable eraser.

Drawing the bottom of the eye

This is another area where the eyes of humans and animals differ. Although both tend to show the rim of the lower eyelid, which catches the light, some breeds of dog also show a highlighted thin watery line at the base of the eye (*fig 17*). This presents another opportunity to use high contrast to boost the perceived intensity of the eye's highlights, and to visually separate a dark eye from surrounding dark hair.

Drawing the white of the eye

Few animals show any white of the eye unless they are looking to either side - a feature you can use to advantage (*fig 18*), as inclusion of white immediately grabs attention. For this reason I usually only incorporate a minimum of tone in the corners of this area - sufficient to denote it as a curved surface while maintaining the pristine white of the majority of the area.

In drawing the human eye, however, it is necessary to tone the eye correctly. The 'whites' aren't really white, as they possess slight colour changes and often minor blood vessels. The top, as mentioned earlier, displays the upper eyelid's cast shadow, which extends in a diluted strength into the corners. This tone in the corners will boost the white and give a more pronounced orb-like curvature to the eyeball. Delicacy and observing the subtle changes in tone are essential when shading the eyeball. Pure white should be reserved for your highlights, as it will preserve their intensity.

A small highlight is often reflected from the moist tear duct in the inner corner of the human eye, as shown in the completed eye (*fig 19*). Its inclusion can heighten the reality of your drawing, but over-emphasis may distract the viewer's eye. Getting it right can be a fine balancing act.

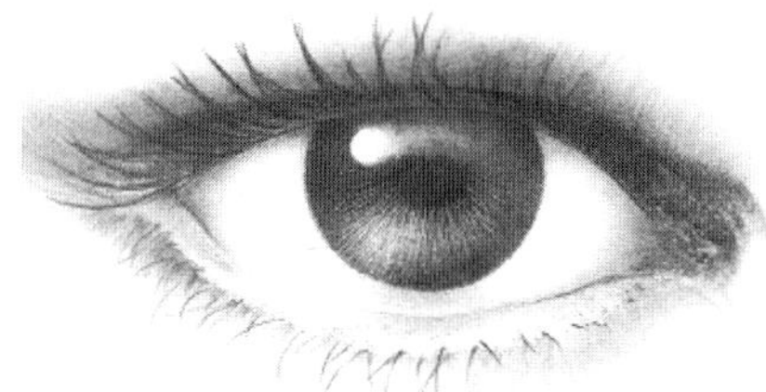

Fig 19. The eye completed with the top and bottom lids and lashes in place.

There are a variety of methods you can choose from to add tonal shaping to the white. I prefer light, close hatching with H to 2H followed by gentle blending with a tortillon or colour-shaper. I then fine tune with Blu-Tack or a kneaded eraser. If required, tone is replaced and the process repeated until the desired result is obtained. Some artists prefer to pull tone from the surrounding drawing with a tortillon. Others flood the area with tone then lightly erase as required with the point of a kneaded eraser. The best method is found only by experimentation, and is often dependent on the physical size of the eye.

Achieving Expressions...

Study expressions, and the way they alter the shape of the eye, and you'll learn how to engineer them to suit your needs. You are your best model. Pull faces in front of a mirror and watch the way your eyes change shape. Smile and notice how they crinkle at the outer corners; look pensive and feel the muscles tauten beneath your eyes to lift the lower edges. If you can work out which muscles do what for a given emotion, and the way they change the shape of your eyes and brows, you can reproduce the same emotions in your portraits. This applies to animals too, but not to birds. With only a few exceptions, birds close their eyes by lifting the bottom eyelid and not by lowering the top one.

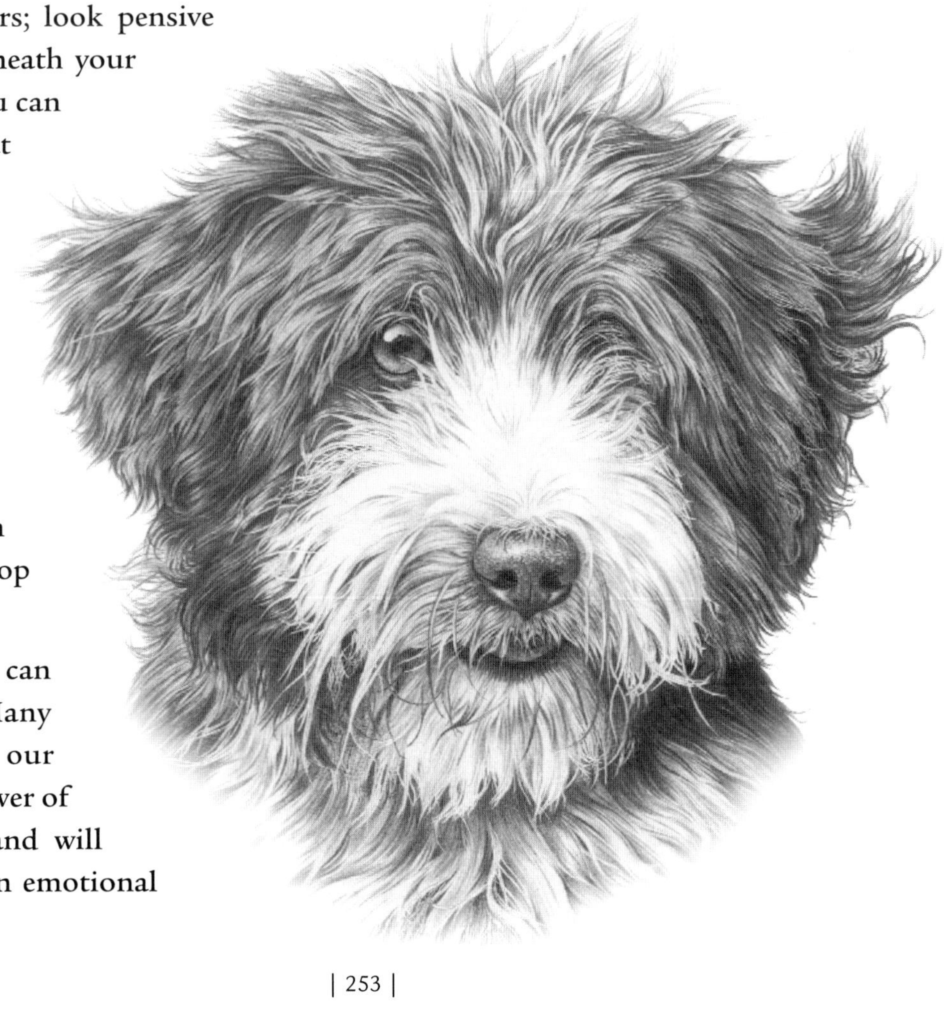

Subtle changes to the eye shape can send powerful signals. Many animals may not share our particular emotions, but the viewer of your portrait will be human and will respond to the perceived human emotional content that you inject.

Drawing noses

I am often asked for assistance with the drawing of dogs' noses, as they are quite complex and very different from our own. Other noses, such as those of cats, horses, and humans, are simpler in construction and often more easily understood on examination.

The basic shape

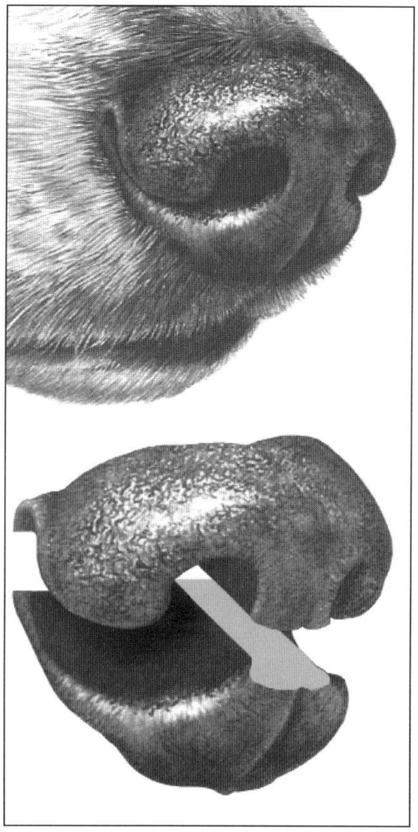

Fig 17. Exploded view of a dog's nose.

Despite the many different breeds of dog, including wolves and foxes, the structure of the nose remains the same. The simplest way to picture a dog's nose is to see it as being two halves (*fig 17*) a top and bottom connected by the central septum, the vertical section between the nostrils.

The top half has a leathery appearance, almost smooth in some breeds and coarse textured in others. These textural variations often account for one looking dull and dry and another shiny and wet, and it's important that you look for these variations as they considerably affect the reflected highlights. At the front are the two nostrils flanked by bulbous corners. The dividing septum usually has a central groove, to a greater or lesser extent.

To each side of the nose are flared curves, which catch the light and cast a dark shadow beneath. The leather on top of the nose, and the nose itself, finishes at a line drawn between the ends of these two flared curves. Beyond that, some breeds grow hair and others possess a bald area of smooth skin, the same colour as the nose. Don't confuse this area with the nose - look carefully and you can usually detect the change in texture. The two parallel nasal passages travel through this area along the top of the muzzle, which gives it a flat appearance due to the slight central dip.

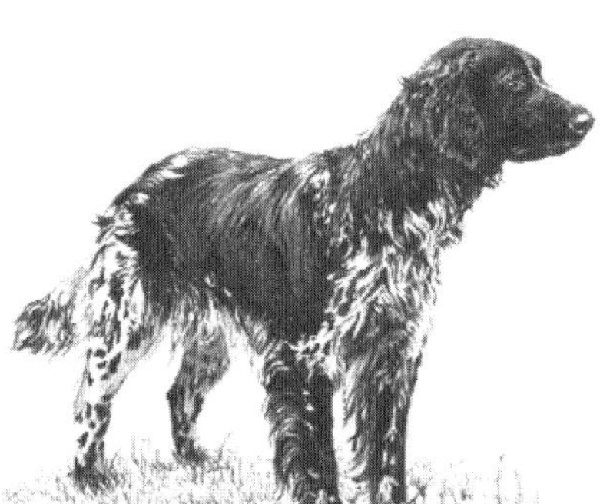

Fig 18. In this 1½" high drawing only the top and nostril highlights mark the position and direction of the Munsterlander's nose.

The simpler bottom half of the nose contains only the floors of the nostrils. The front edges almost always catch the light. If your drawing is very small (*fig 18*), these highlights are of the utmost importance as they read easily from a distance and mark both the position of the nostrils and the curvature of the nose. And if the two nostril highlights differ in brightness they also signal the angle of the head to the light source.

Pay particular attention to the texture of the leather on top of the nose, which is very variable. An interpretation of the texture is perfectly acceptable but do first take time to analyse its reflective qualities. A lightly textured, shiny nose will possess very strong blacks, and a dry, more heavily textured nose will usually appear to be lighter in tone. A brown nose requires an overall diminution of tone to contrast with the black nostril shadows.

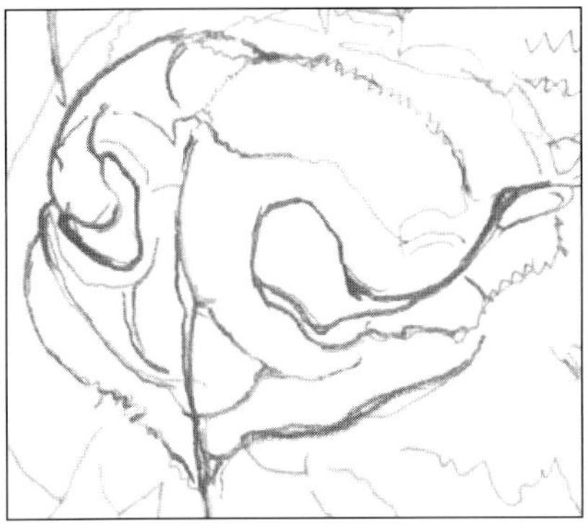

Guideline drawing of a Staffordshire Bull Terrier's nose.

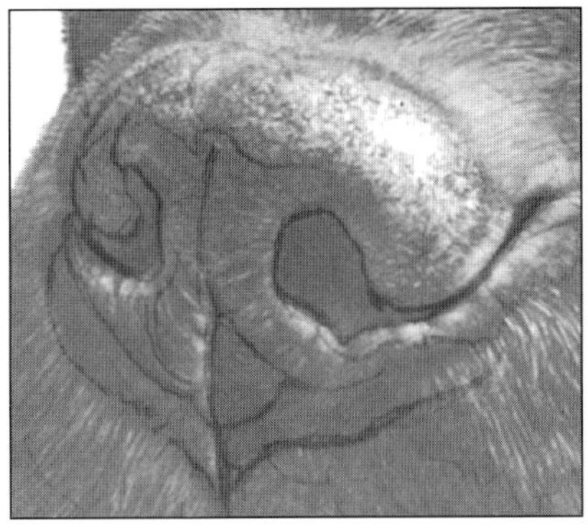

Guidelines superimposed on the drawing. Adjustments have been made to the left side. Guidelines are guides, not fixed boundaries.

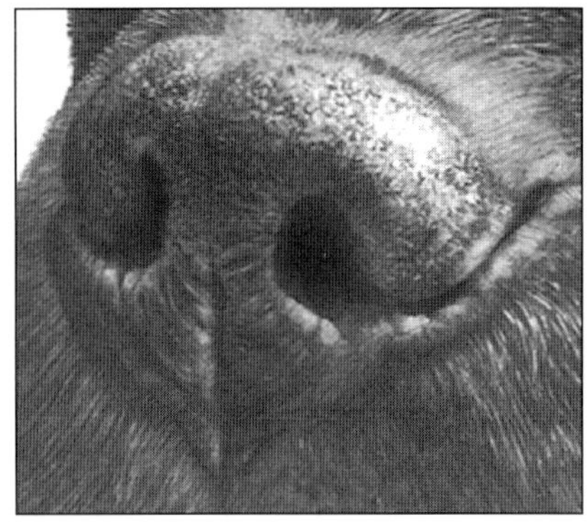

Completed drawing of the Staffie's nose.

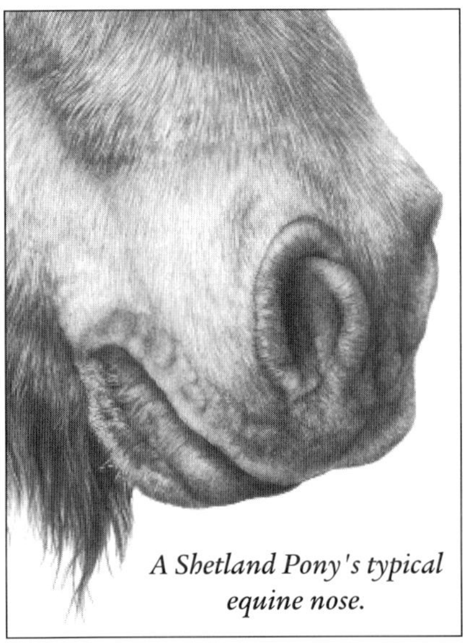

A Shetland Pony's typical equine nose.

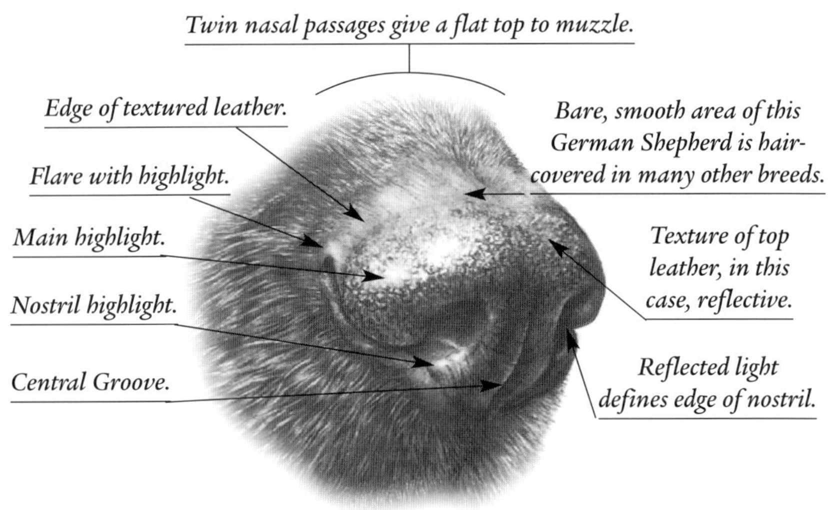

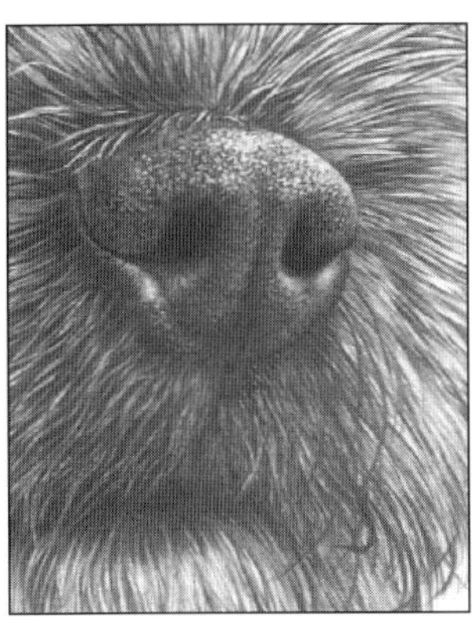

The dry, black nose of a Border Terrier.

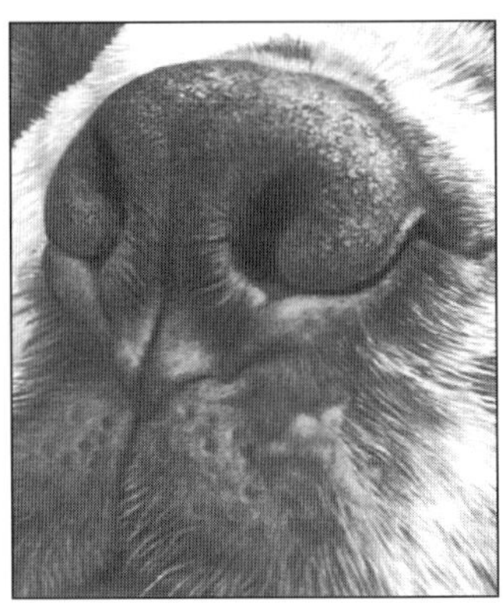

A Boxer's nose. Note the bare skin beneath.

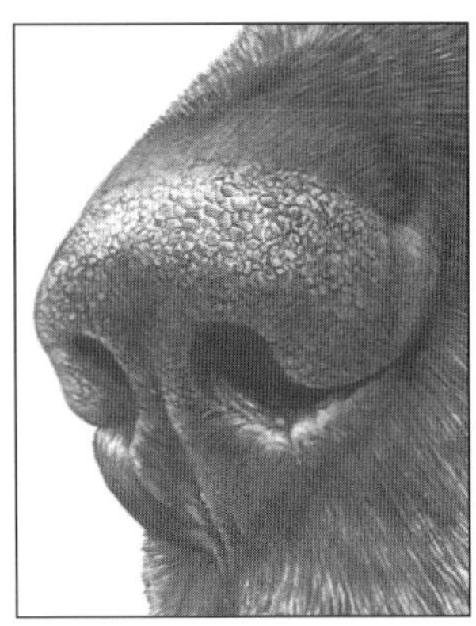

The textured nose of a Great Dane.

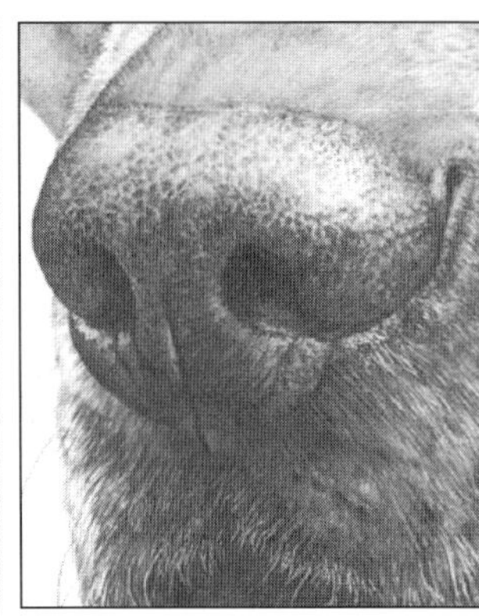

Weimaraner's textured, brown nose.

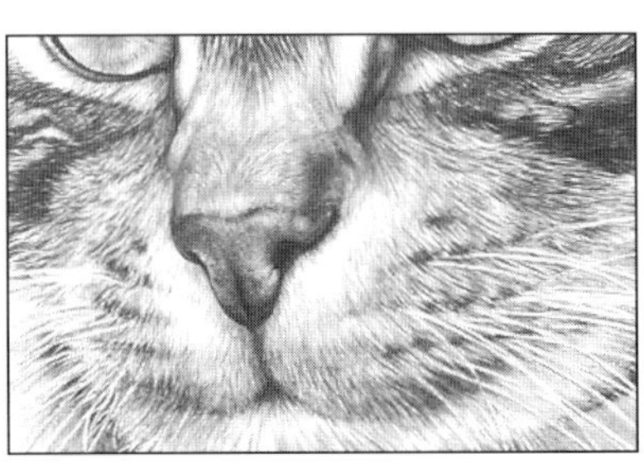

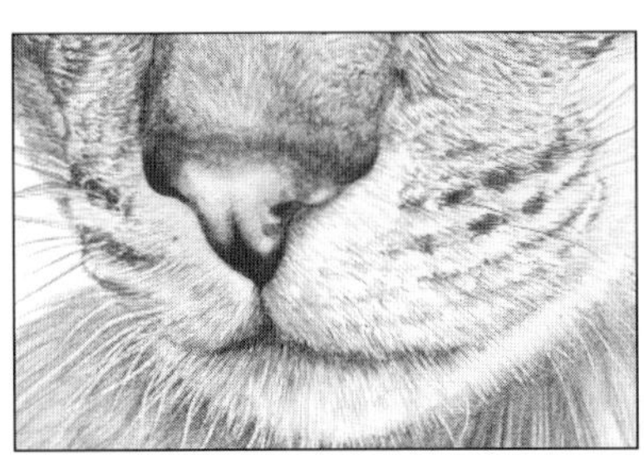

Shorthair Tabby and Siamese. Cats' noses vary little with breed.

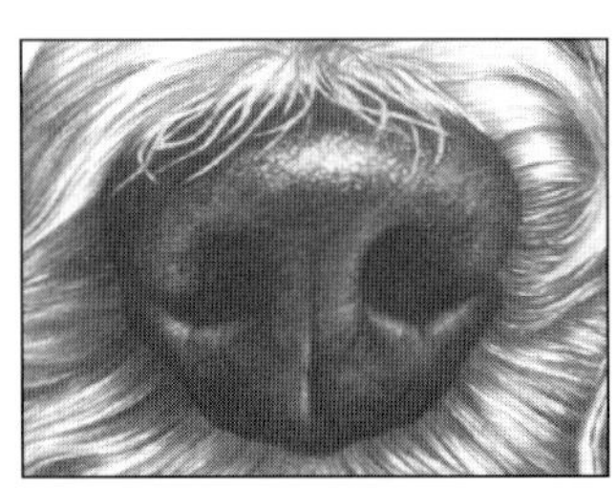

An Old English Sheepdog's shiny, black nose.

Drawing Ears

As with drawing all features, an understanding of three-dimensional shape is an absolute necessity before drawing commences. A folded, drooping ear is perhaps the simplest to understand (*fig 19*) but careful study is still required. The 'rose' ear (*fig 20*) may be the most geometrically complex and the least easy to understand without a thorough examination. However, I'll concentrate here on drawing the pricked, or erect, ear (*fig 21*), as it applies to many different animals - from domestic dogs and cats to horses, big cats, bears and cows.

The features of this German Shepherd's ear (*below*) are typical of the ear type and all can be turned to our advantage, whatever the animal.

Curvature and thickness

Hair doesn't just lay flat and stop at the edges; it has form and curvature, and light and shade are your principal allies in depicting them. Look at the edge of an ear and you'll see that it is softened by the fringe of hairs, some of which are the ends of hairs on the reverse surface. As the hairs progress from the inside of the ear to the edge, they conform to the expected reflection of a curved surface and reflect highlights. It's these that tell the eye how rounded the curvature is, and at what angle it is to the light. Even a thin ear, such as in figure 20, displays highlights and shadows that describe the thickness of edges and the overall curvature.

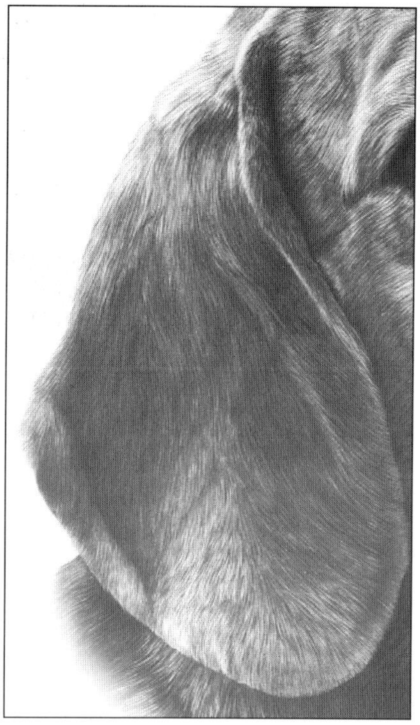

Fig 19. A typical folded ear.

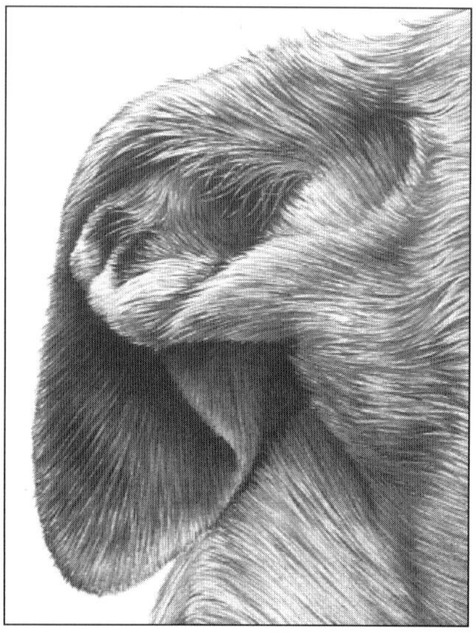

Fig 20. A complex rose ear.

This German Shepherd's ear has a wrap-around curvature and:

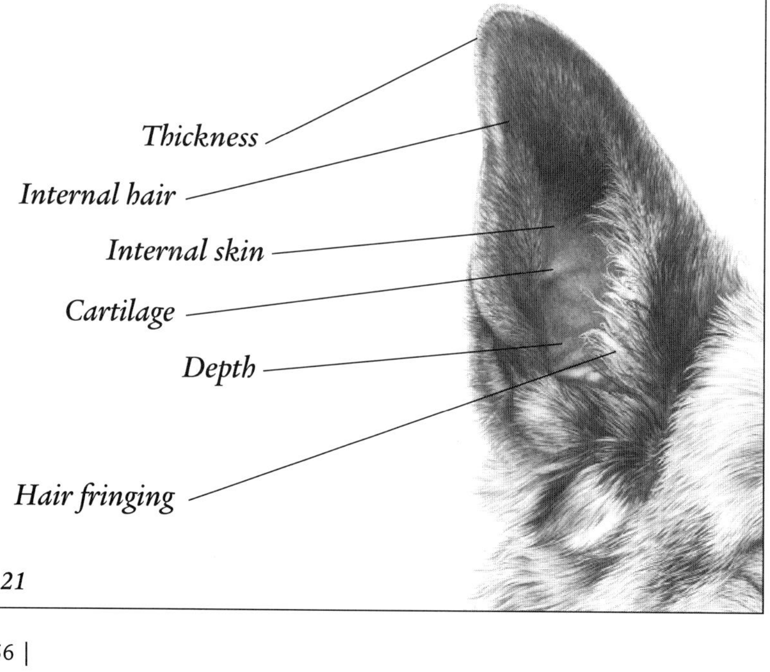

Fig 21

INTERNAL FEATURES

Ears possess depth that you can push your finger into, and this must be brought out in your drawing. What we need are internal features that we can overlay with foreground elements to send our message. Here (*fig 22*) I emphasised the disappearance behind the internal hair of the curving cartilage, that internal hair's crisp, sharp edge, and the sharply defined foreground fringing that overlays the internal skin. These combine to visually push back the interior of the ear, and reinforce the appearance of depth.

Negative drawing is an essential tool when describing the short hair typically found inside an animal's ear. To achieve a feeling of depth and form, it must be made clear that closer hairs overlay those that are further around the curve. This is greatly simplified by the two-stage approach of negative drawing. The first layer details the layering of the hair; and the second adds the tone that gives it form.

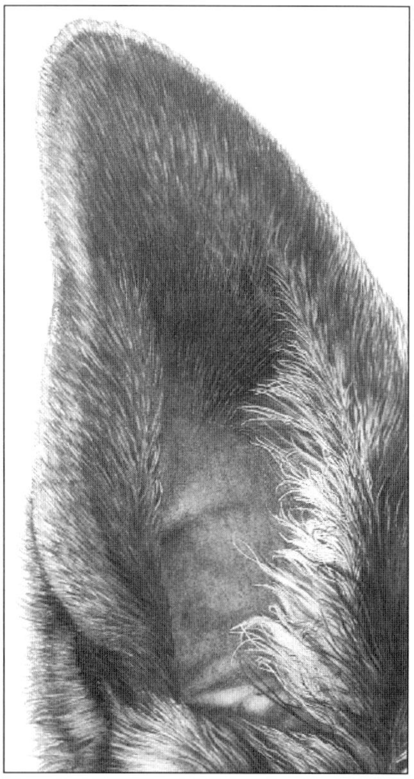

Fig 22

USING CONTRAST

Contrast plays a vital role and can withstand a great deal of engineering, while still possessing a sense of reality. Try to incorporate blacks internally, maybe in the deepest depths, and reserve your lightest tones for foreground detail. Where possible, place the two adjacent to each other for maximum contrast and visual separation of the two planes. Clarity too plays a part. Retaining the sharpest detail for foreground use and softening internal detail will further emphasise the depth of the ear.

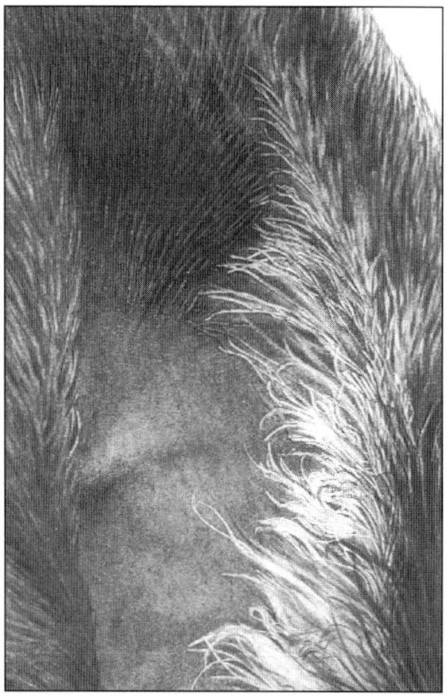

Note the use of internal 4H indenting, and external stylus indenting to create crisp fringing.

Drawing with understanding

Whatever feature you are drawing, one aspect remains paramount: you can only draw realistically what you fully understand. Once you have an understanding of the structure you can begin to be selective and choose the signals that best describe what you are attempting to say about it. You can edit your message. Unfortunately, copying a two-dimensional source photo often sends the same signals that you are receiving - incomprehension. You cannot expect a viewer of your work to understand more than you did when you created it.

Live demonstration
Maisie, bringing it all together...

'I HAVE A MENTAL PICTURE OF A FORGOTTEN CORNER OF A FARMYARD - OLD BRICKS, WEEDS, DECAY AND DERELICTION - AND AN INQUISITIVE PUP.'

This featured drawing brings together many of the previously described methods and tutorials. However, it's more than just a test-bed for techniques. It has also to have a believable scenario, possess a sense of reality, and be suitable for reproduction as a saleable print. So let's follow it from conception to completion.

The concept

I have a mental picture of a forgotten corner of a farmyard - old bricks, weeds, decay and dereliction - and an inquisitive pup. In the midst, our eleven week-old Parson Jack Russell puppy Maisie will feature centre-stage. Maisie was with us for just three fun-filled weeks until she escaped into a field and was tragically kicked by one of our horses. So this is also a personal tribute to a little soul who filled our lives with pure love and joy.

As I live on a farm, with an abundance of scrap and derelict machinery, I'm not short of raw materials. My initial collection of suitable props for the drawing includes cast-iron wheels from an old henhouse, a spare ring from my tractor's Cambridge roller, and a length of wood known to have once been a part of a sailing ship. As a result, the drawing will include wood, rusty cast iron, and ellipses as well as bricks, hair, weeds, and grass.

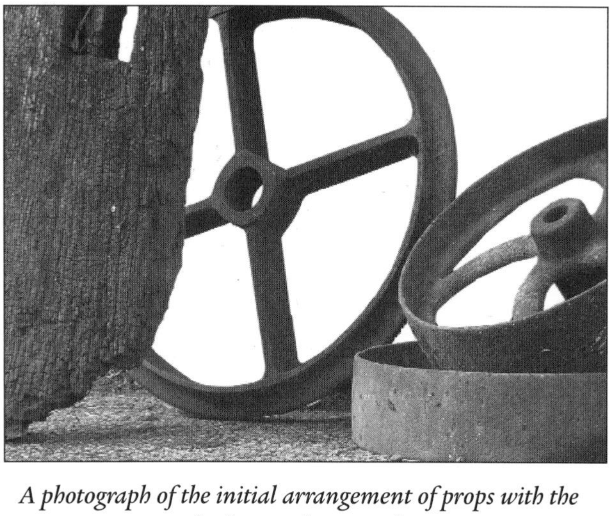

A photograph of the initial arrangement of props with the background removed.

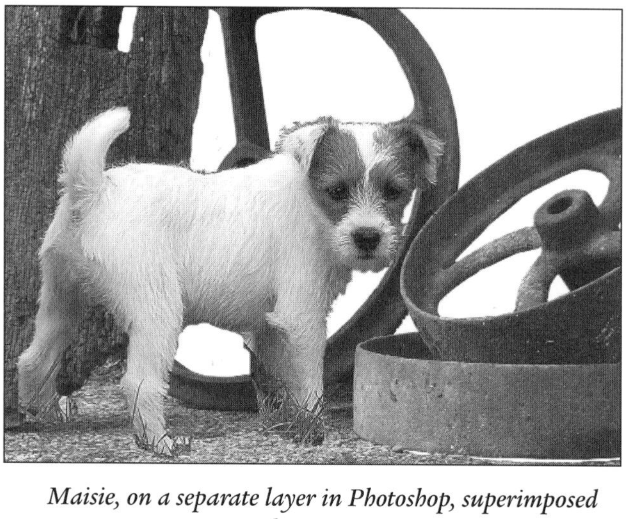

Maisie, on a separate layer in Photoshop, superimposed onto the arrangement.

The composition

Sometimes I begin with concept drawings, and at other times I compose directly in Photoshop. No one method is preferable, as long as the chosen method gives me a 'feel' for the subject and, as in this case, helps to build a story. I need to connect Maisie to the setting and what suggests itself is a length of rope that she is pulling from inside the wheels. I can either alter her balance, so she's actively pulling it, or I can draw her as photographed - stationary and slightly annoyed by the viewer's interruption. The latter appeals to me, because I'm drawn to her typical, solid terrier stance. This will also overcome the problem of her features being unsuitable for much emotional manipulation.

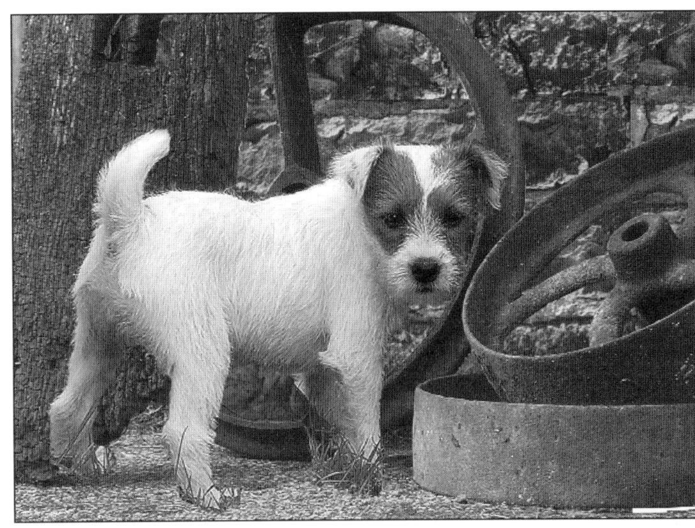

I've now separated all the elements so each occupies its own Photoshop layer. This allows me to independently move and resize each one, and I can hide any layer with a single click.

With a brick wall now positioned behind Maisie, the composition is definitely too complex. The wood looks out of scale and is too prominent - it has to go - but I may need another prop to prevent the eye travelling out of the picture to the left. Also the brick wall, taken from my store of photos, is so heavily textured that it's distracting. I've made a mental note to correct this problem when I'm drawing.

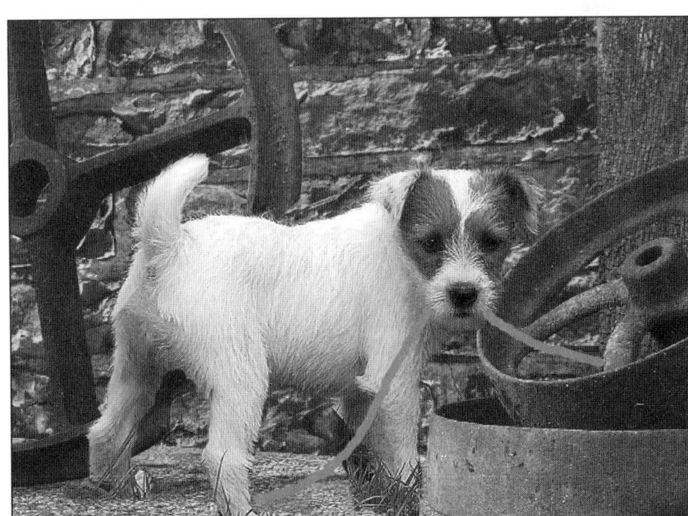

Rather than discard the wood, it's been moved to the right to become a doorpost that prevents the horizontal lines of mortar directing the eye out of the picture. The Cambridge roller ring has been repositioned, and also enlarged to make Maisie appear smaller. And Maisie is now holding a quickly painted suggestion of a rope.

What's missing, except in my mind, are the weeds. I can use them to steer the eye around the composition, and to further connect Maisie to the scene. It's time to transfer this to paper and begin work on a more spontaneous version.

Tip

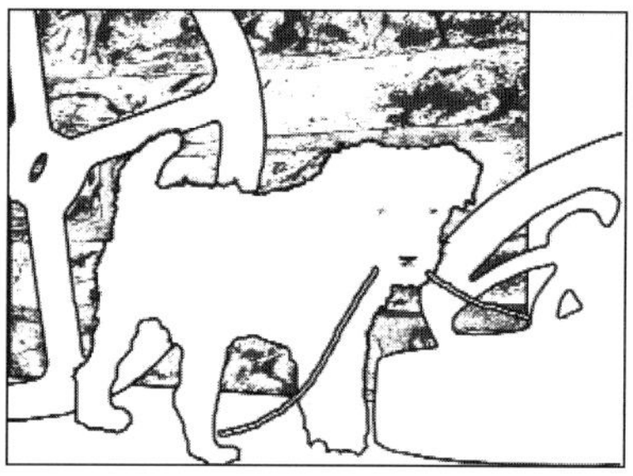

To quickly reduce layers to outlines in Photoshop:

- *Duplicate the image for safety then click a layer in the Layers palette.*
- *Click 'add a layer style' and choose 'stroke'.*
- *Set width to 2, position to 'inside', and click OK.*
- *Press CTRL key and click on the layer in the Layers palette to select the object.*
- *Make white the foreground colour, select the fill tool, and click within the selected area.*
- *Some detail may remain (see brick wall above). Click each remnant to delete if required.*
- *Press CTRL key + 'd' to deselect.*
- *You now have an outline of that element.*
- *Repeat with remaining layers.*

I'm going to project a printout of the composition onto a piece of Mellotex, reduce it to a manageable 5" x 7" (13 x 18 cm), and trace it. By using the same paper that I will use for the final drawing, I ensure that what works now will also work later. In its present state, the tonal uniformity of this image will make tracing of the printout difficult, so I'll greatly simplify it by reducing each element, which is on its own Photoshop layer, to pure outline. Refer to the margin for the method I use.

Now that the printout has been traced, I'll complete the design by adding the weeds, and finalising the layout of the bricks. Working in this manner allows me to quickly formulate a composition, gets me fully in touch with the story and subject matter, and the drawing stage injects spontaneity.

The working drawing

This may look unfinished but it does its job. Any further development will now take place during the final drawing phase, when I can best judge what is required. The ground, for example, may eventually be grass, dust, gravel, or a mixture of any of these. I may also place a weed or two growing through the wheels at the right to give the impression that they have been there for some considerable time. I'm also aware that the weeds at the left-hand side, lacking any continuation to the right, look unreal. This will be corrected at the time of drawing.

I'm happy with this; I think it works, and I can see it in my mind as a finished drawing. It's time to take it apart and reassemble it.

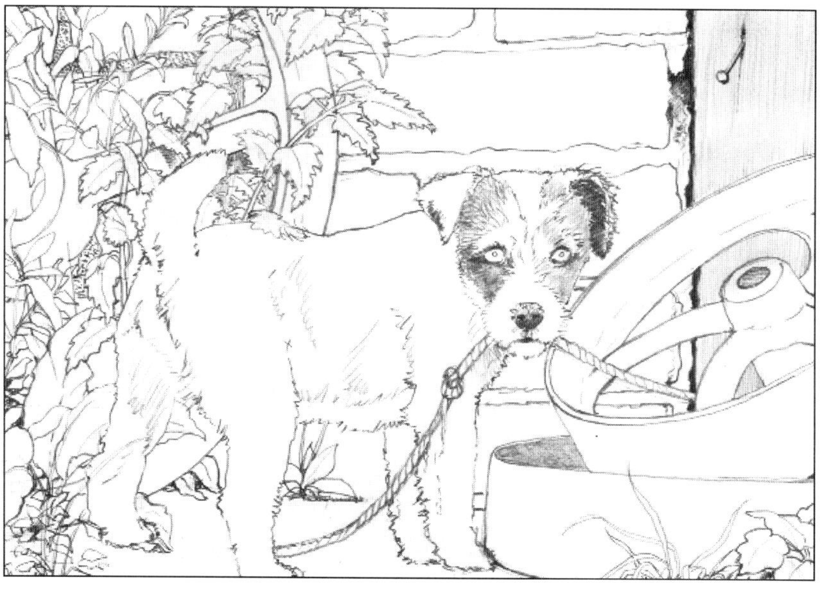

The working drawing.

The reworking

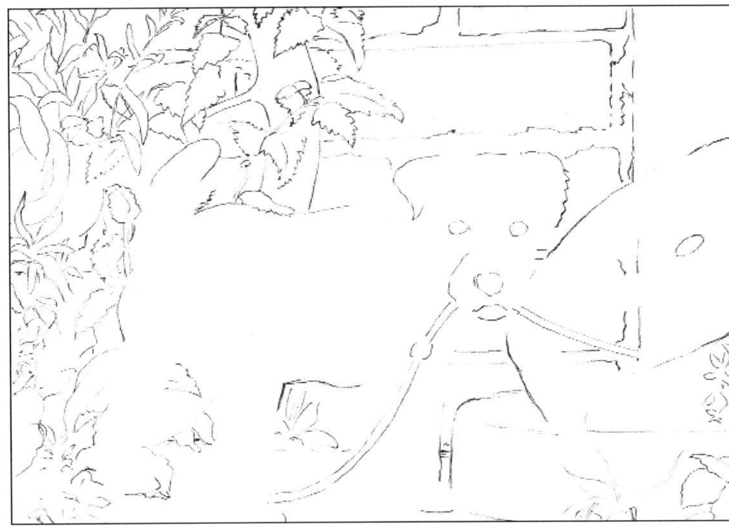

Up to this point I've been using quickly produced outlines to work out the composition. There was little point in producing accurate, time-consuming versions, as any element might be discarded or switched for another at any time. Now, however, accuracy is required. Although I need only concentrate on redrawing Maisie, as I consider all the other elements to be sufficiently accurate, I'll rework them all to show the process. The weeds, bricks and other secondary components are never reworked, as they rely on spontaneity at the time of drawing for their reality.

Before I begin redrawing anything, an accurate border measuring 11" x 8" (28 x 20 cm) is lightly drawn in the centre of my final Mellotex drawing surface, which itself measures 24" x 20" (61 x 51 cm) so I can expand the area if required. The working drawing is now projected down and sized to fit the drawn border. Then simple placeholders are marked with a soft 6B lead. Here (*above*) you can see the positioning marks for the wheels, Maisie, and the roller ring - just enough clues to allow me to position the redrawn elements correctly.

Switching to 2B, the weeds and bricks are copied, but not with any real accuracy. The approximate positions are sufficient for me to transfer my thinking across from the working drawing, to which I can refer as I work.

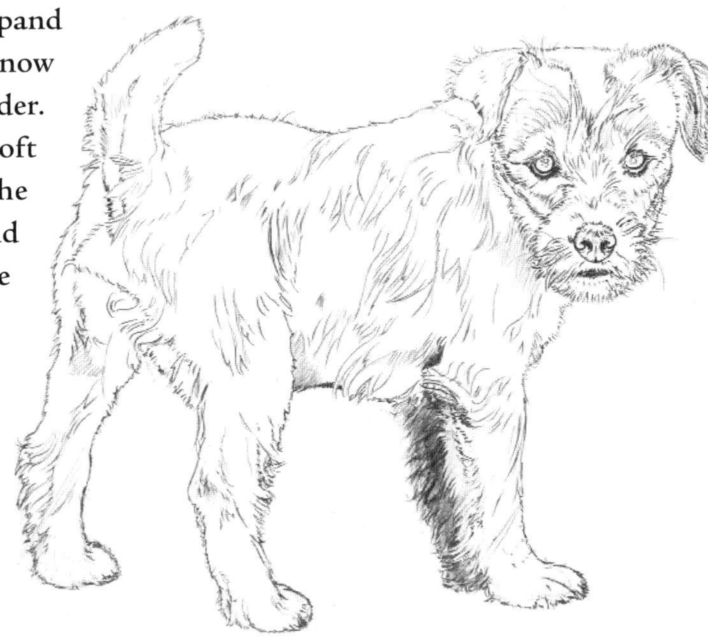

Now I'll spend time separately redrawing the wheels and Maisie. The time spent will save me much time later, as corrections and amendments made while I'm drawing will be minimised. At this point I would usually construct accurate ellipses for the wheels and the roller ring but I have photographs that I can project and trace to save time. However, once traced I will still rework them by eye to smooth out any irregularities. This hand finishing, and the redrawing of Maisie, teaches me a lot about the way they are actually formed - information that will be invaluable later. It is at this stage that

The new and more accurate line drawing of Maisie. The photo was first projected and traced to fix the position of the major features, and then constructed by eye.
This 8" x 6" (20 x 15cm) drawing is larger than required, so the final reduction in size will minimise rather than exacerbate any inaccuracies.

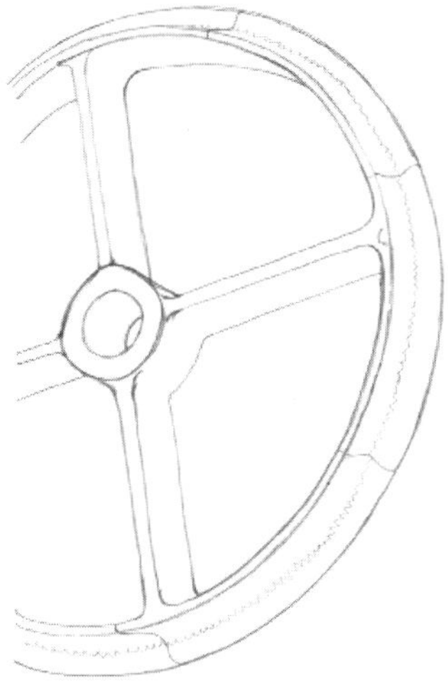

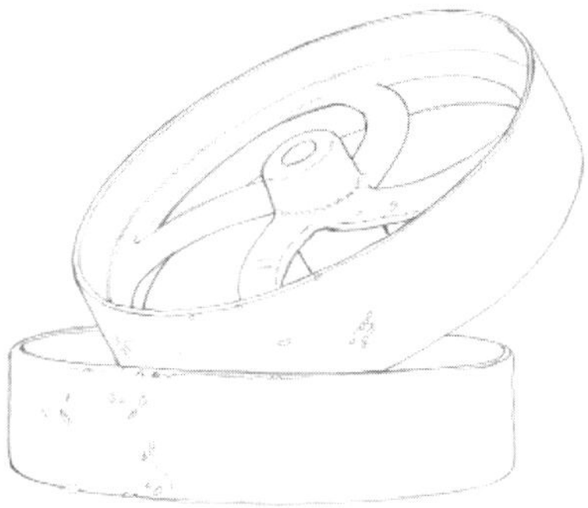

the direct connection between the photos and the images is broken. They cease to be copies and are now the way I want them to be; altered and moulded to suit my own purposes. Paws have been fabricated for Maisie and, hopefully, all potential problem areas have been resolved.

We've now reached the final stage in the preparation. The line drawings are checked, and any errors corrected. The final drawing surface, containing the lightly drawn placeholders, is positioned beneath my Artograph projector, in which I have mounted the first of the line drawings. The Artograph is carefully adjusted and focussed until the line drawing exactly fits within its placeholder, the placeholder's lines are now completely erased, and the line drawing is lightly traced with a sharp 2B point. I'm using a hand-guard at all times to protect the surface of my paper.

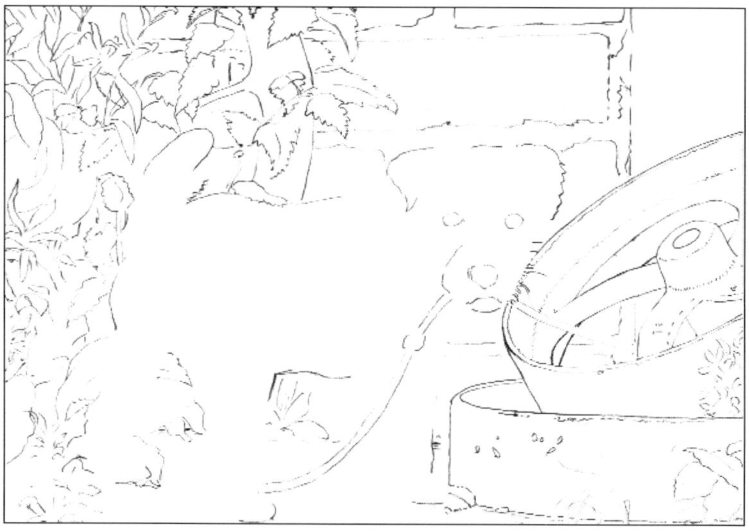

The line drawing of the wheels has been transferred and moved slightly to the right.

'...THE DIRECT CONNECTION BETWEEN THE PHOTOS AND THE IMAGES IS BROKEN. THEY CEASE TO BE COPIES AND ARE NOW THE WAY I WANT THEM TO BE; ALTERED AND MOULDED TO SUIT MY OWN PURPOSES.'

Some adjustments may be made at this time too. For example, I know that Maisie will not fit into her placeholder, as her front paws are longer than I had anticipated. Either the wheels must be moved to the right or Maisie to the left to accommodate them. Whichever choice I make, I have to be certain that that the adjustment won't unsettle the balance of the drawing in any way.

All elements are now in place and drawing can begin. You may think that this preparation is unnecessary or too time-consuming. Without it, I would be drawing with no overall plan, and no idea of the relationships between the different elements. I wouldn't even know if the composition was balanced, or that the telling of the story might succeed.

More crucially, I've gained a much deeper understanding and a fuller knowledge of the reality of each feature during the preparation. I estimate that this drawing will take me about sixty hours to complete, so the five hours I've spent in preparing it are well worth while if they ensure that the sixty hours won't be wasted.

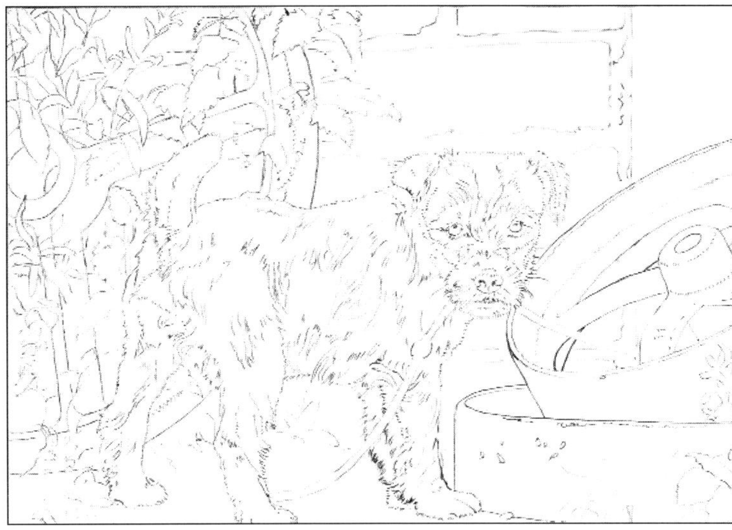

The drawing surface with all line drawings transferred, and ready for work to begin.

Finally, I sometimes work up the discarded working drawing into a tone drawing. As the drawing is on Mellotex, all tones I apply here can be reproduced exactly within the final study. It will provide me with a starting point for the various textures, and a central reference of values and contrasts that I can accept or modify as I work. It can also reveal potential future problems. I now know, for example, that the tones I use for the roller ring will need careful attention in order to separate it from the wall. I rarely pay any attention to the foliage, as I know I can engineer the tones to suit any situation as it arises.

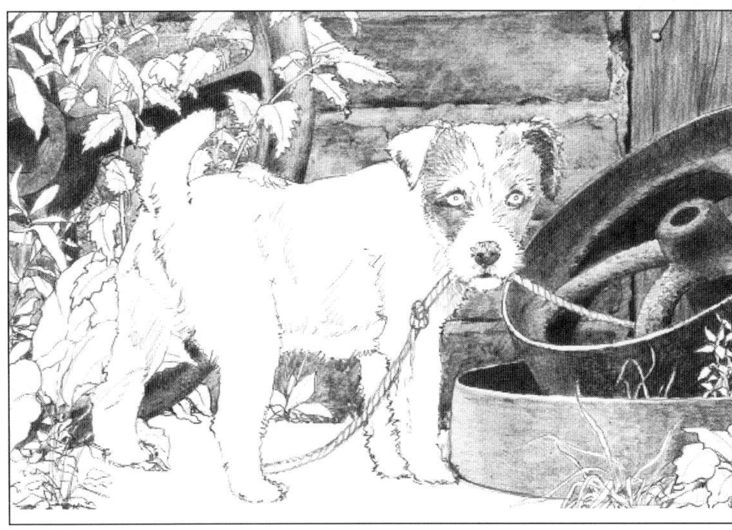

Exploratory tones and textures applied to the discarded line drawing.

The final study

Where to begin

As I'm right handed I usually begin in the top-left corner. However, I cannot yet determine the tones required for that area. It involves brick, foliage, and rusty cast iron, so any errors made now will be carried throughout the drawing. Instead I'll begin in a similar area but one that contains a known tonal value - the roller ring's spoke just above Maisie's tail. Whatever the direction of light, the underside of this spoke will always be in deep shade and, being rusty, it is not at all reflective. I'm also aware that it needs to be one of the darkest tones in the drawing, so it balances the equally dark shadows inside the wheels at the right. It's beneficial if either of those areas attract the eye, because looking from one to the other will always pass through Maisie's head.

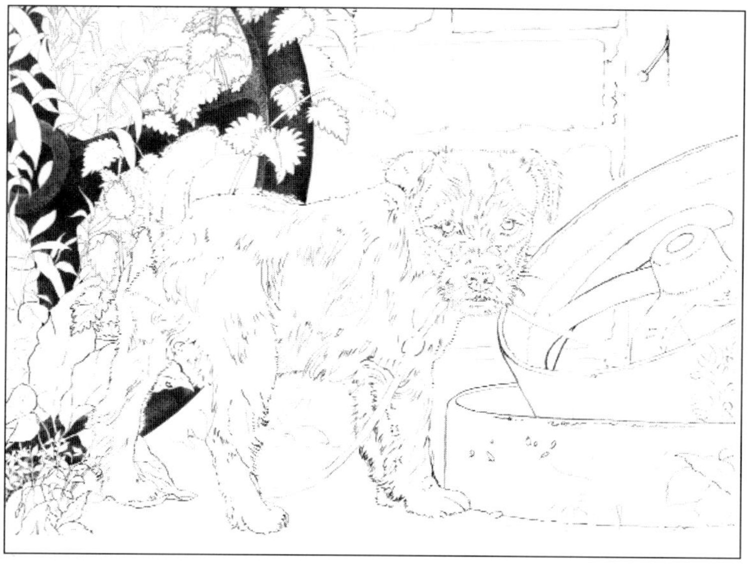

Stage 1

Well, I got off to a good start. It's possible that the roller ring might need to be lightened at a later stage, but it's always easier, when using Blu-Tack as the eraser, to lighten than darken.

I have been drawing only the ring, as I find concentrating on just one texture and object focuses my mind. All the leaves were redrawn as I reached them, and new ones were introduced where I felt they were necessary. I'm using the foliage to maintain a balance between the ring having an identifiable presence, and its overall prominence. Whenever I feel that the ring is becoming dominant, I hide it behind more foliage.

I often save a little design work for the end of the day. This time I've been working on the foliage in the bottom left-hand corner. Leaving an unfinished area at the close of work means I have somewhere to immediately begin the next day.

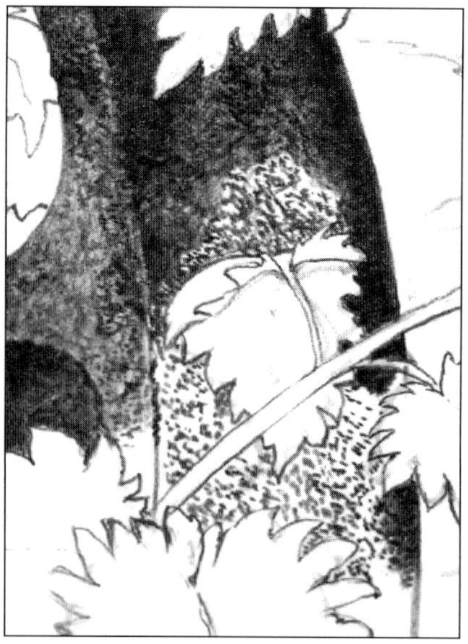

Stippled texture...

I want to suggest the texture of lightly pitted cast iron for the rim of the roller ring, but not so blatantly that it becomes distracting. The technique that suggests itself is stippling, followed by toning layers. This whole section is being drawn with a chisel-pointed 2B lead, which allows me to produce a sharp edge where required, or to lay a light layer of tone with just a turn of my pencil.

The stippling is applied with some force, and I occasionally allow the dots to merge so they form dark, randomised marks that give the appearance of deep pits or surface rust. A tone layer is then applied in random lines or circles, leaving spots of white where they seem to be appropriate. Then a final layer of 2H dulls the spots and unifies the area. There is yet more work to do on this but, from a distance of a foot (30cm) away, it looks quite promising.

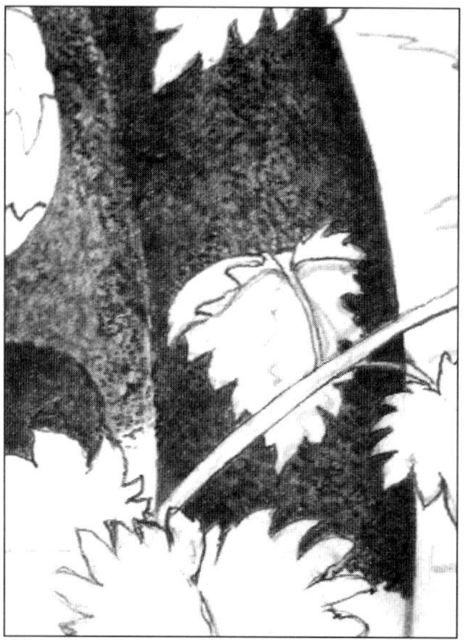

...with 2B shaping and 2H unifying layers.

The use of 2B to outline the leaves provides a number of benefits: it achieves a sharply defined inner edge, it's capable of complete erasure, and the lines will not indent the surface. As long as the lines are never darker than the surrounding tone, the use of strong outlines is perfectly acceptable. They may later be substantially erased, before the drawing of the enclosed area commences, as the presence of any visible lines is to be avoided at all times.

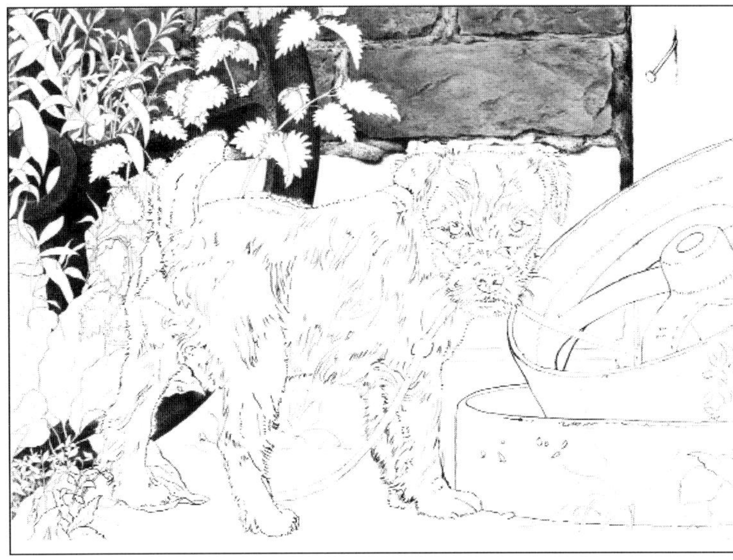

STAGE 2

Today, I decided to begin work on the brick wall. Once completed, I'll know whether or not I have chosen the correct values for the ring. This is important, because those same values will also be used for the wheels. I'm hoping that the ring will maintain a visible presence while not being too eye-catching.

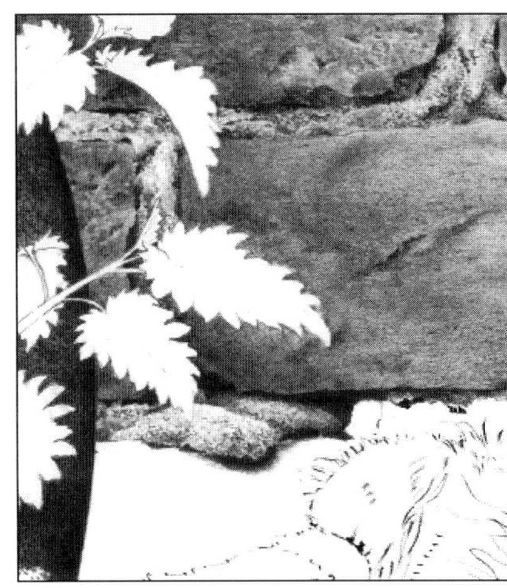

The bricks that I used for the original Photoshop mock-up had surface textures that were far too complex, so I'm creating my own bricks and mortar. I'm aiming at an understandable texture that is not conspicuous, and I can engineer the textures and tones to suit whatever is in front of them.

I've chosen to use old and relatively smooth bricks, and weathered lime mortar. The bricks should form a backdrop that contains interesting but controllable features. If any flaws or shadows catch the eye, I fade or even remove them. I have two close-up photographs of brickwork to assist me. These are not for direct copying but for extracting ideas, the occasional small feature, and the overall feeling of the textures. It's been a good day but it's a quarter to midnight and I've had enough. Tomorrow, I'll complete the brickwork.

STAGE 3

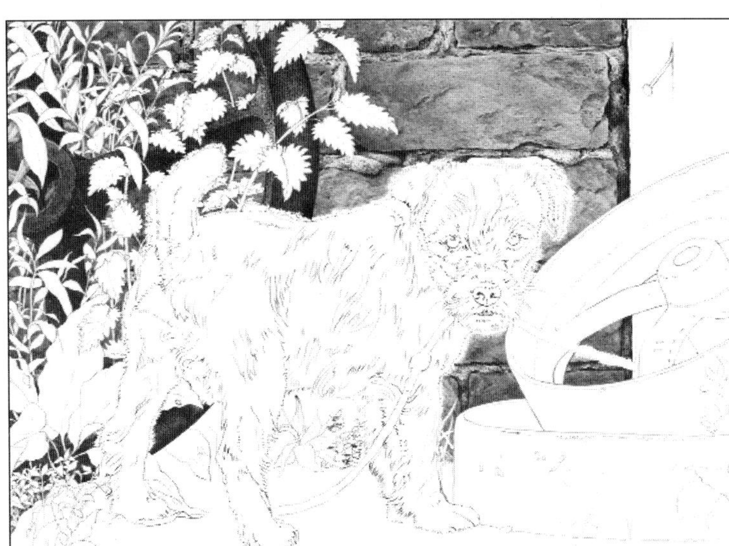

You may think these bricks look planned and involve laborious work. In fact, they're the result of working quickly and spontaneously with a chisel-pointed HB lead. A lead with a polished flat face never leaves a hard edge, and HB is a good medium grade, capable of achieving many tones. As my Mellotex paper has a smooth plate finish, and I have a hard surface beneath it, I can press surprisingly hard without producing a really dark tone.

The initial layer often consists of random marks and white

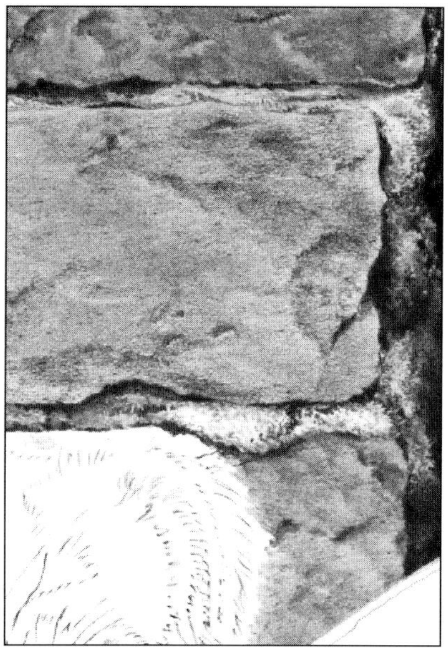

holes. Zigzag shading plays its part too, despite my warnings in chapter four. Although I vary the widths of the zigzag lines, some visible edges occur to suggest texture and surface flaws. A tone layer then unifies the area I'm working on - often immediately after drawing the initial layer, and without lifting my pencil from the surface.

Further layers, each applied at a different angle, then build up the tone, and blend the initial detail layer until it appears to match my ideal. Once the tooth is partially filled, no matter how much pressure I apply to the HB, it will not produce a really dark tone, which allows me the freedom to work spontaneously. The few corrections are carried out with Blu-Tack. Moulded to a blunt point, and applied by dabbing the surface, it creates broken areas of tone while lightening an area. A tone layer of 2H then blends and narrows the range of contrasts of the eraser marks, leaving an interesting, subtly textured surface.

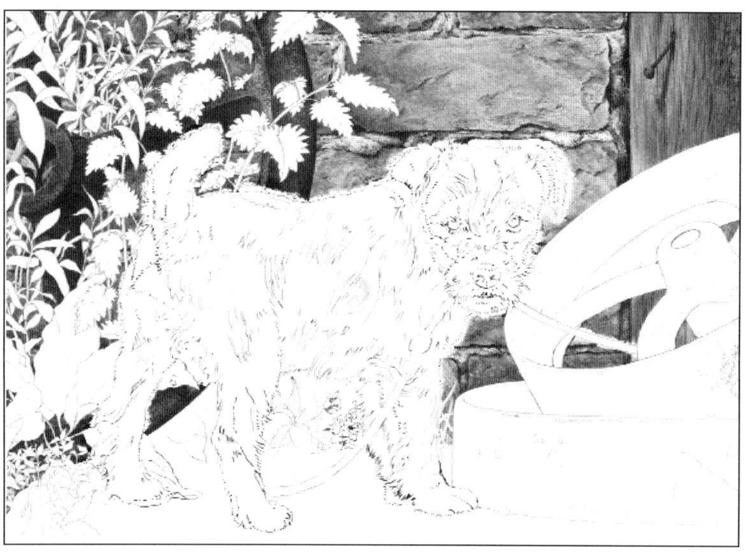

STAGE 4

No matter what overall tonal value I apply to the wood, I know the hen-house wheels will stand out from it, as the rims are highlighted. So I plan to draw the wood next, making sure that I do not use the very darkest tone that I have reserved for the wheels. That tone is required to balance the dark tones of

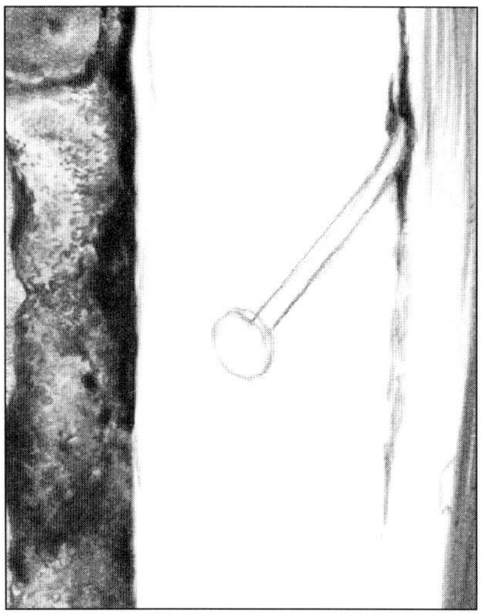

The position of the nail has been mapped out lightly with 2B, to ensure complete erasure and no possibility of surface indentation.

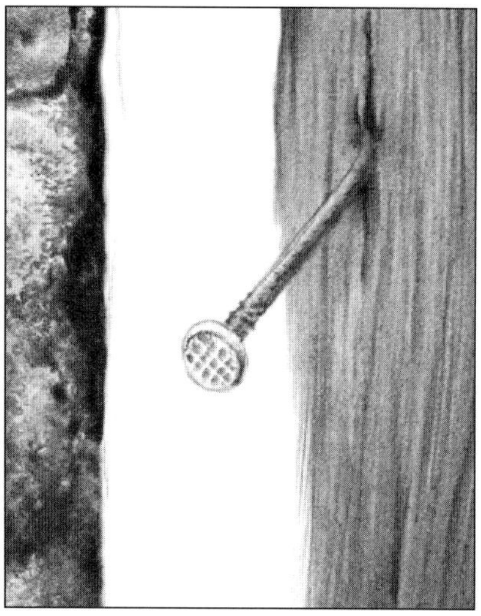

The angle of the head has been altered, and its non-slip surface suggested. This detail may not show later but even a trace may add a sense of reality.

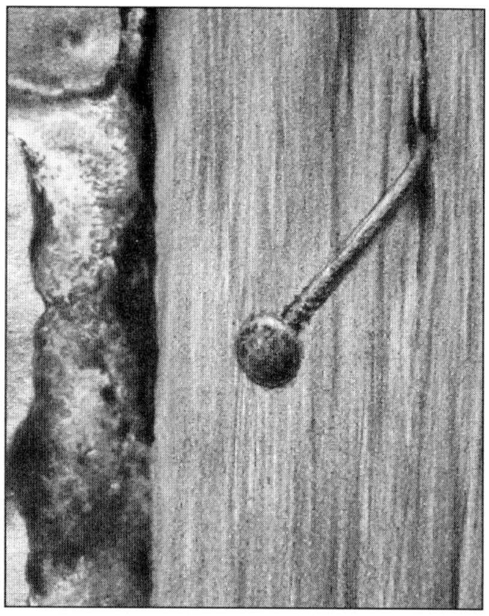

The highlights approximately conform to the direction of the light, and are positioned so they don't appear at the edges, allowing dark outlines to be used.

the roller ring, and I don't want the wood to attract the viewer's eye.

Well, it hasn't begun very well but it's salvageable. I started in the top-right corner, referring to a single photograph of a part of the wood. Originally it was an old ship's timber but was more recently used as a fence post. I was attracted by the decay, which had split the surface into rectangular blocks, and I began to incorporate it into the drawing. I really should know better! I should have considered the consequences, as it caused three errors. I finally realised that the decay was caused by wet rot, and I had the photograph upside down; the horizontal splits were very distracting; and the texture was far too complex for what should be a simple secondary element in the composition.

To salvage the work, I've decided to make the decay look more like raised and torn fibres. The contrasts have been reduced, the horizontal splits cut vertically with an eraser; and I've applied a tone layer to blend the area.

Changing to a much quicker and spontaneous way of working, I'm now drawing only a suggestion of weathered wood grain. As I work towards the left edge, I'm lightening the timber to exaggerate its junction with the brickwork - a positive statement to draw a wandering eye back into the drawing. The original error now seems to be of benefit, as the darker, more textured area defines the corner of the study, stopping the eye from straying out of the frame. The nail helps too in that respect. It was purposely angled to point directly at Maisie's head, a device to steer the viewer back towards her. Without it, I think that relatively empty corner would have been an unwanted distraction.

'I REALLY SHOULD KNOW BETTER! I SHOULD HAVE CONSIDERED THE CONSEQUENCES...'

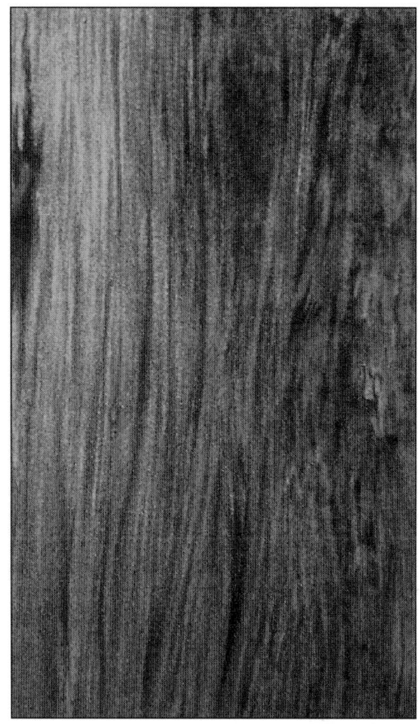

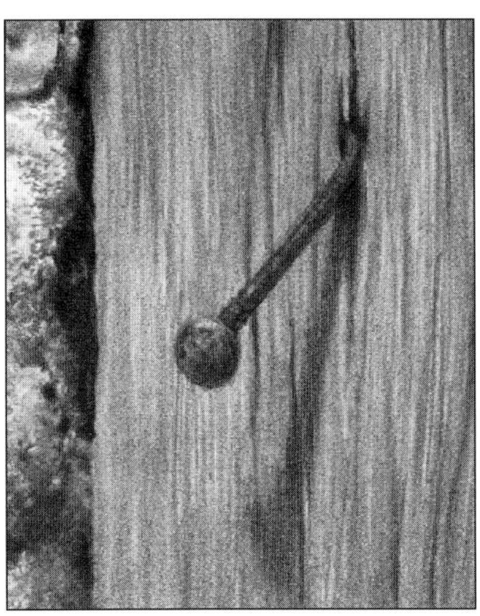

The shadow has been drawn, but the nail has had to be made rustier and less reflective. It must only steer the viewer's eye to Maisie, and not attract attention to itself.

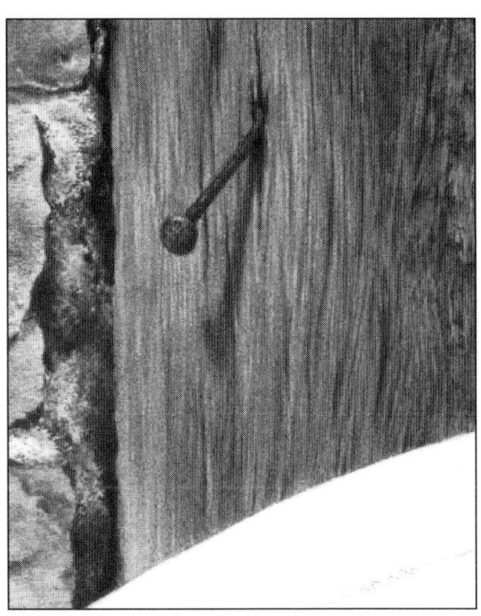

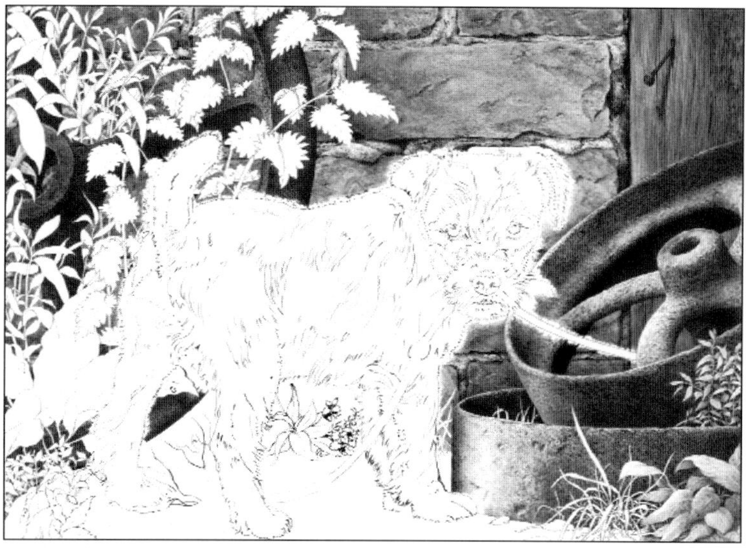

Stage 5

I can draw either the wheels or the rope at this stage. The rope passes through a midtone section of one of the spokes, so I have to decide which element is the controlling one. I could draw the rope, and let it dictate the tones used for the spoke, but I've decided to let the wheel be the controlling factor. I will draw close to the rope but leave a gap to accommodate any stray fibres. I've used the same strategy for the junction between the bricks and Maisie.

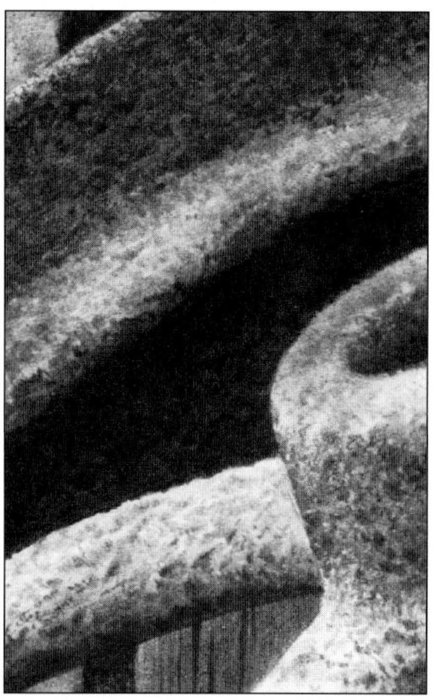

Yesterday evening I began drawing the inside surface around the top of the upper wheel. This morning I can see that the work hasn't gone too well; a result of working late at night under artificial lighting. If I begin drawing an area in daylight, I can match the tones later under artificial light. But, if I begin under that light, my tones are inevitably too dark, and the detail too coarse. Fortunately, lightly dabbing with Blu-Tack removes the excess graphite, and I can successfully rebuild the section around the remains of the previous detail.

I'm tempted to include the sharp detailing of the rust pitting, but I'm certain that doing so will cause the wheels to vie with Maisie for attention. As the wheels are in the foreground, I need a way of suggesting the rust sufficiently well for it to have a semblance of realism while not being sharply detailed.

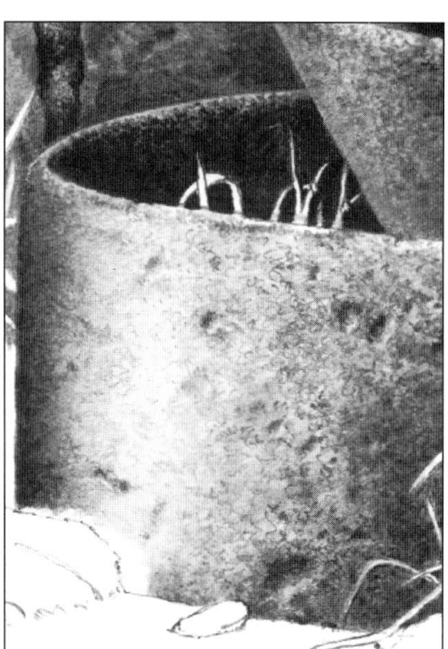

To render the top wheel, I'm using three, flat-point techniques with either 2B or HB. The darkest areas involve random, sinuous scribbles that leave white shapes as the dominant features. The area is then immediately toned down until the white shapes become barely discernable.

The midtone areas depend on the opposite treatment; a series of dark shapes are drawn to resemble pits, some are merged, and then a similar layer of tone blends them into the white that surrounds them. Finally, the lightest areas receive lightly drawn, random scribbles, overlaid with a unifying 2H tone layer. Each section is then repeatedly fine-tuned with Blu-Tack and refinished. Each time I get a little closer to my ideal until I feel that the section reads correctly.

I've redrawn the ellipse for the bottom wheel, as it was looking too flattened. Although it was traced directly from the photograph, real life sometimes doesn't translate well to the eye.

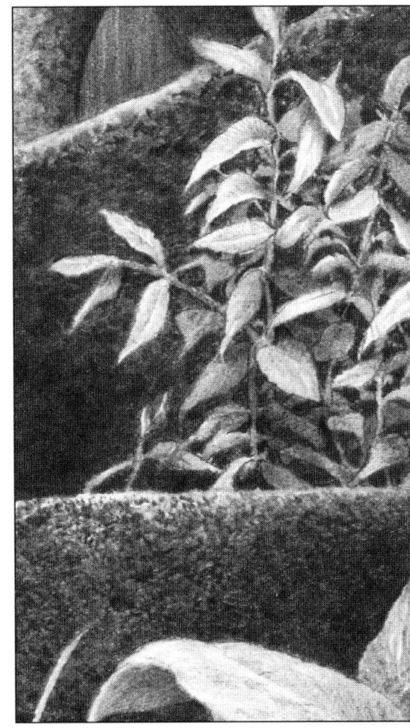

To draw its surface, I'm using techniques similar to those used for the top wheel, except for the grades used. Working right to left, dark to light, the darkest tone is produced with 2B, and then I'm using progressively harder grades; HB, F and finally 2H. Beginning again at the left-hand end, the process is repeated until a very light application of blended 2H closes the gap. Any overly conspicuous detail is reduced with Blu-Tack. And the wheels are complete.

Stage 6

I feel it's time to complete the right-hand foliage. You may have noticed that I had begun the work last night, at the end of stage 5. If I can get this small area of foliage to work successfully then it will greatly assist me when I draw the mass at the left-hand side. Last night's work was far too light and timid but, at least the detail and shaping have been established.

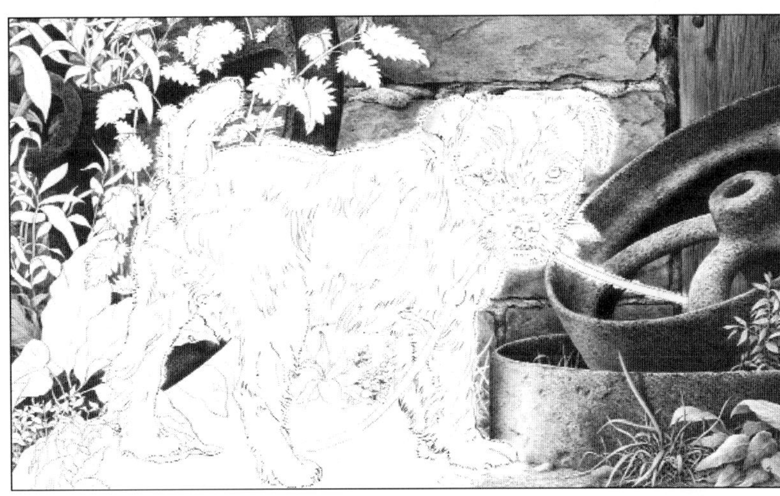

Tackling one leaf at a time, I first decide on its three-dimensional shape, and then establish the position of the central rib. Finally, I imagine how the result should look when lit from my upper left light source, and where its shadow, if any, will fall.

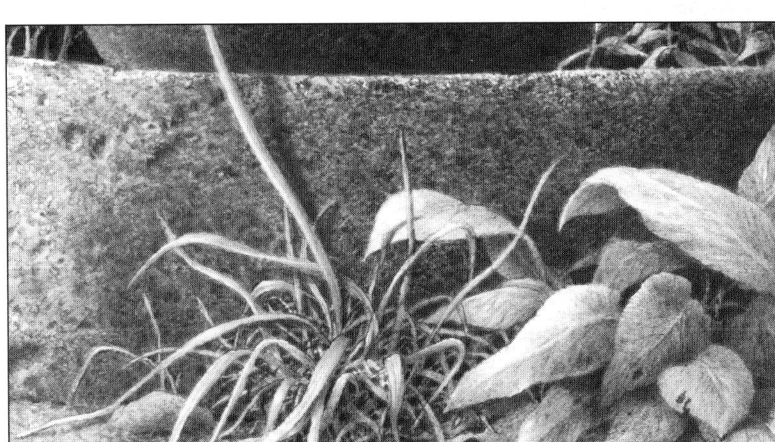

As the foliage is a secondary element, I'm not seeking to produce detailed realism, just an impression of reality that will withstand a fairly close scrutiny. Devices, such as holes in leaves, are included to add a degree of reality, when viewed from a distance.

The lighting direction is borne in mind at all times, as I begin to add tone and detail to each leaf. The central rib and veins are negatively drawn; left white until the leaf shaping is completed. Then an overall layer of tone darkens the ribs so they are subtly suggested, in a way that would be far more difficult to achieve had I attempted to physically draw them first.

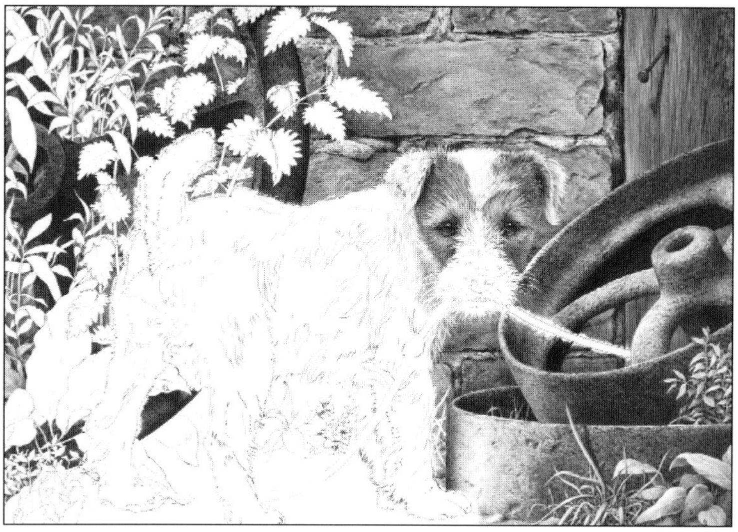

STAGE 7

Now that I have a feel for drawing the foliage, and something I can later refer to, I've decided to move on to the drawing of Maisie. As she is predominately white, and the setting is relatively dark, I can afterwards use the main mass of foliage to provide just the right amount of midtone to connect and balance the two components.

I'm beginning with her eyes, because it's important that I get close to the required emotion as soon as I can. I can amend it later if I need to. In the meantime, her eyes will contain the darkest tones, and provide fixed references for both the darkest and lightest.

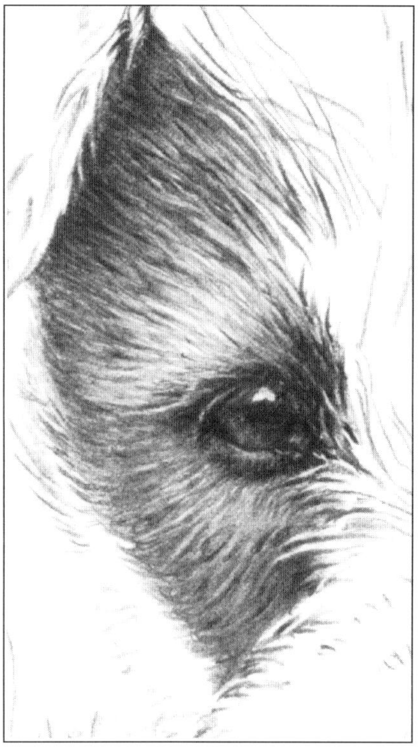

Fig 1. Actual height: 2" (5cm).

You may think that indenting, particularly with 2H, might suit the drawing of this rough coat. In fact, when drawing hair, I rarely use indenting in any form, except for single status hairs, such as whiskers. Indenting produces clean-edged lines, but what I want here is merely a suggestion of slightly wayward, wiry hairs that follow a general direction. My preferred technique is spontaneous negative drawing (*fig 1*).

I'm looking for a natural line that runs through the hair, across the direction of growth; a raised edge that tells me a line of hairs stops at that point, and which I can use as a drawing break. From there I can draw back down into the hairs, establishing the shadows between them, and then return to that same point to draw up into the hair above, as described in chapter 11. In some places, a swinging action of my pencil point draws lines that taper at both the ends of the stroke, and which quickly form random shadows between hairs. Then shaping is applied as a separate layer.

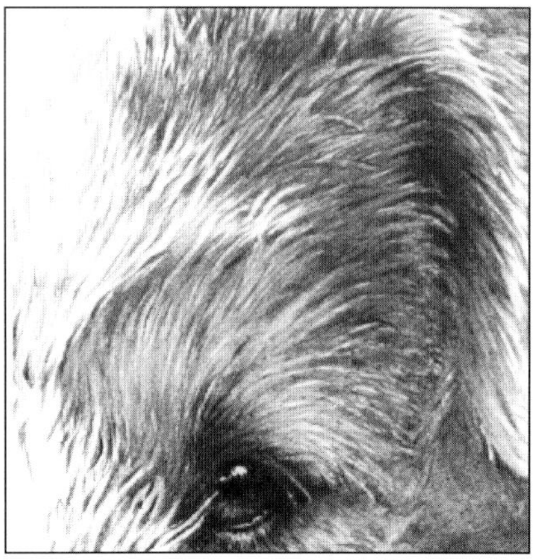

Fig 2

Another possible candidate for indenting is the drawing of the stray white hairs within the brown hair above the left eye (*fig 2*). Once again, however, I've opted to use only negative drawing. This becomes a much simpler task when split it into manageable stages, of which there are two in this case: the drawing of the shadows between the hairs, and the combined 'colour' and shaping of each hair. The initial layer uses negative drawing of all the hairs, regardless of their actual colour. Then a tone layer is added to the brown areas so that it avoids white hairs wherever they are required.

Negative drawing plays another important role too in this study - the hairy outline of the head, ears, and body (*fig 3*). You will have noticed that I stopped the positively drawn background short of the dog, so I could concentrate solely on drawing that one particular texture without any distraction. Later, that background becomes the medium for producing the negative drawing of the dog's outline.

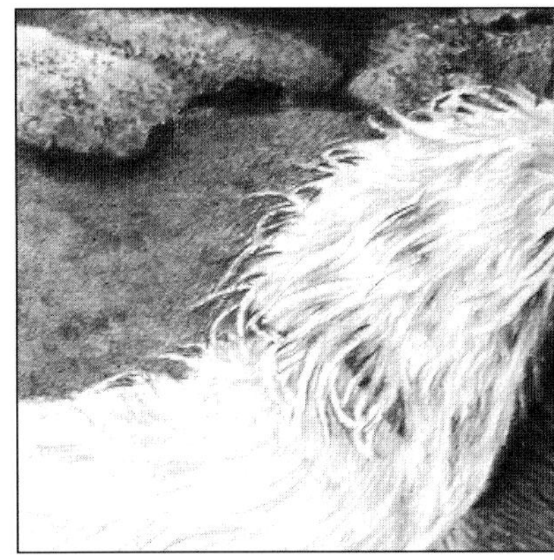

Fig 3

The hairs are first individually drawn around so the outline forms a safety zone, a width of graphite that I can join additional drawing to. Then the gap between the hair and the unfinished background is closed. With a little practice, it's easy to exactly match tones.

Stage 8

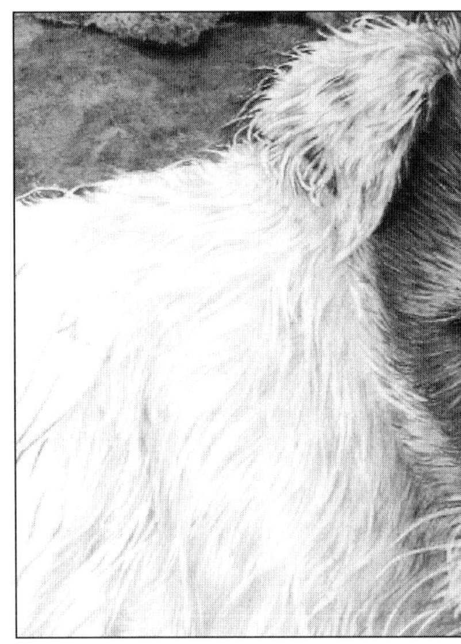

After drawing the left ear I decided to move into the body, just to get an idea of what is required. It will later provide a reference of the lightest tones to help me determine those needed for the muzzle.

I'm using only lightly applied 4H so, by design, I am prevented from making really dark marks. This white hair needs to contain very subtle detail; just a suggestion of shadows between locks of hair, while still presenting the appearance of a white coat. I'm drawing just one small area at a time, establishing shadows, and shadowy shapes, just sufficiently strong for me to see the tonal variations within them, then I lightly dab with Blu-Tack to fade the area until only ghosts of the original drawing remain. This greatly diminishes contrast and strength. However, the tonal variations will be preserved but in a form so subtle that I cannot physically draw them.

'Act as if it were impossible to fail.'
Dorothy Broude

As the completed area grows, I add a toning layer to better describe the overall shaping, keeping in mind the prevailing lighting direction. As I'm not using the lighting evident in the photograph, I can only use that source as a means of understanding the shaping, which I must then translate to comply with the direction of the light in my drawing. Now I know what tones are required for the body, and I have a reference established, I'll go back to the head and complete the muzzle.

Stage 9

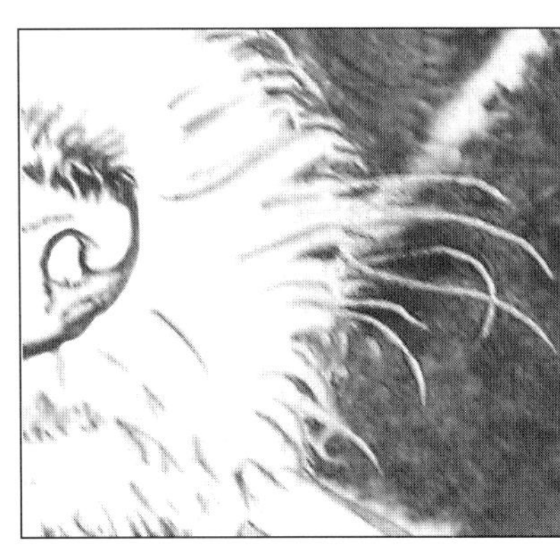

First I need to establish the position of the whiskers, and this is probably the only time in this drawing that I will use indenting. I'm using my fine indenting stylus, and applying it directly to the surface of the paper. I erase any temporary guidelines that may exist, decide on the start and end points of

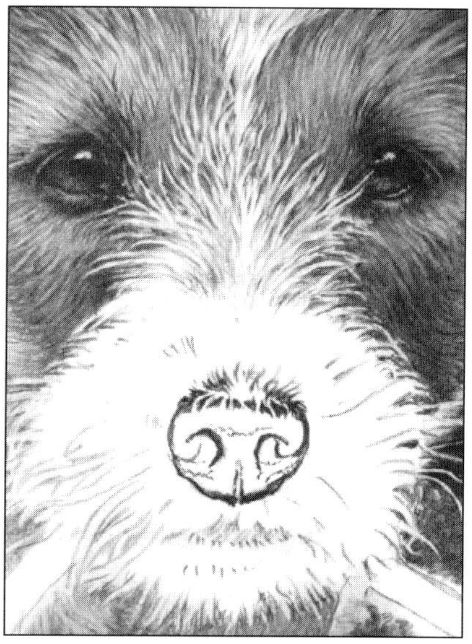

Hairs negatively drawn on top of nose.

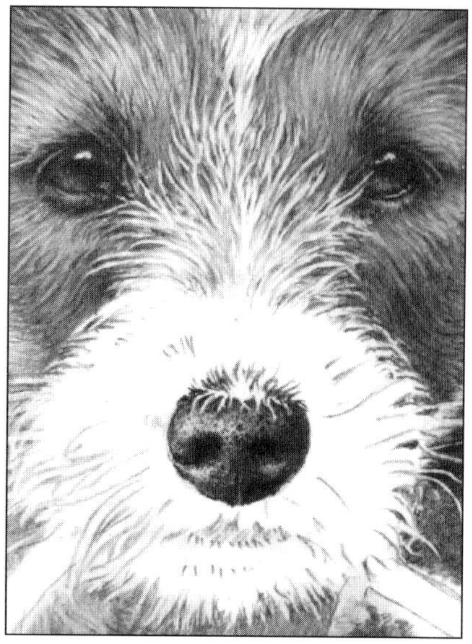

The nose completed.

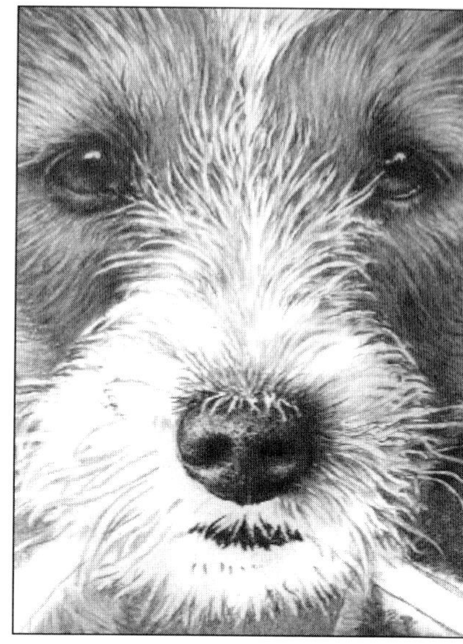

Work begins on the muzzle.

my whisker, take a couple of 'practice swings' with the tip of the stylus just above the surface, and then finally commit the line to paper. I start the line somewhere within the muzzle, because I can disguise that end later if I need to, and end the line in a fine taper.

I can now begin to complete the muzzle, starting with the nose. Although my guidelines are reasonably accurate, I'm redrawing it (*above left*); reminding myself that Maisie has her head slightly lowered, so we are not looking directly at her nose. Incorporated into this revised line drawing are the positions of the white hairs that lie on top of the nose. There is no indenting involved, only negative drawing.

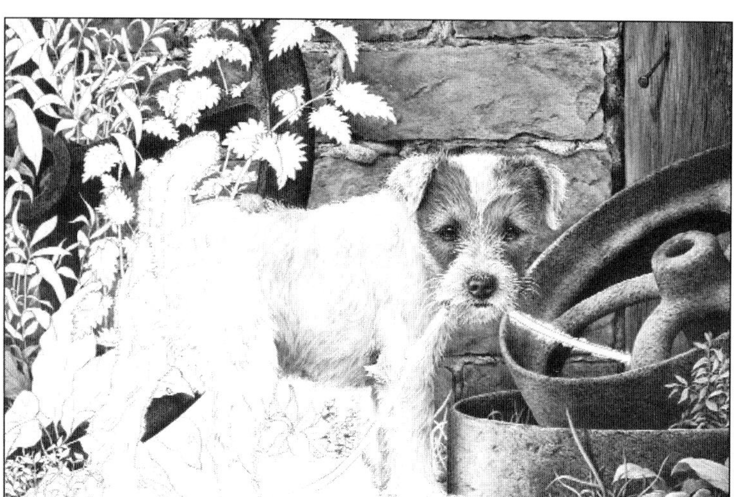

Stage10

I've completed Maisie's muzzle and now I'm returning to the body. My aim is to present a suggestion of the coat's texture without an abundance of detail. Unfortunately, I know from experience that this can go in one of two ways: the work can proceed quite quickly with the minimum of detail; or it may need much of the detail to be established and then progressively erased until only the suggestion I desire remains.

Well, the latter has proved to be the case and I can foresee four days' work ahead of me. The drawing of the body is complicated by the constant need for reshaping, as I'm dictating my own lighting conditions. As I draw each group of hairs, I have to consider how they are affected by the lighting direction, and how that group relates to all the others. Much of the time I'm drawing the detail with darker tones than are needed, and then adjusting them with Blu-Tack.

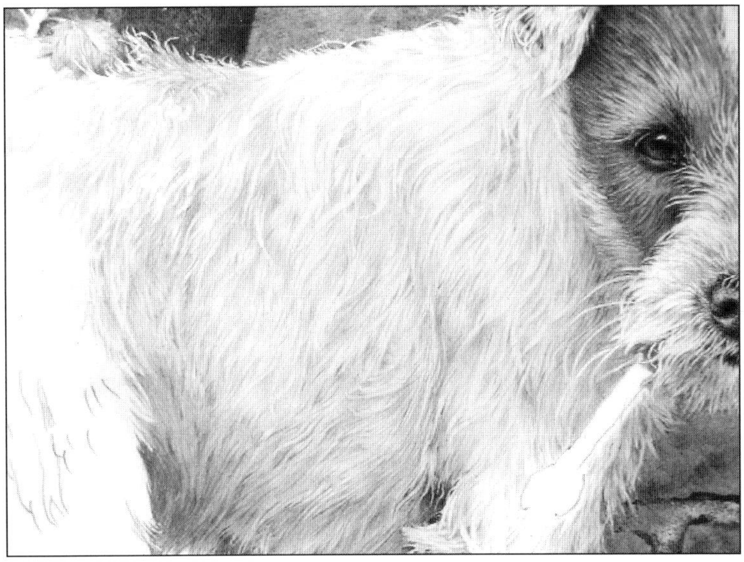

The drawing has just reached the 'ugly duckling' stage. Everything I'm drawing today looks wrong, overworked, coarse, and it's very depressing. But I know it will all come together later. Even if it doesn't succeed completely, I can still salvage something from it, and the structure will have been worked out, so any rebuilding will be accomplished relatively quickly.

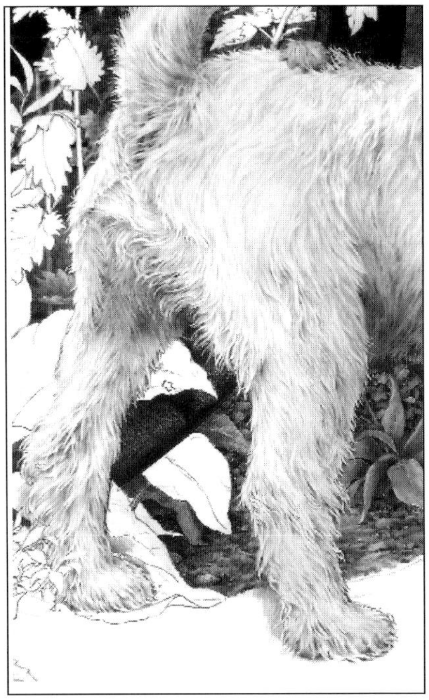

STAGE 11

I've completed Maisie's body, except for her front paw, which I've decided to draw after I've established the ground. Its foreground prominence demands special attention and, as it's evening, I'm working by artificial light, which is not ideal for drawing light detail.

It's been a long four days of work, mainly because of the amount of detail involved, and the need to constantly translate the lighting from the source photographs. The absence of all but a couple of strong shadows has meant that I've been working with a very narrow range of contrasts, and, as I explained earlier, much of the detail has ultimately been faded to provide only a delicate suggestion. But that detail must first be established, as attempts at taking short cuts rarely succeed in providing the required reality.

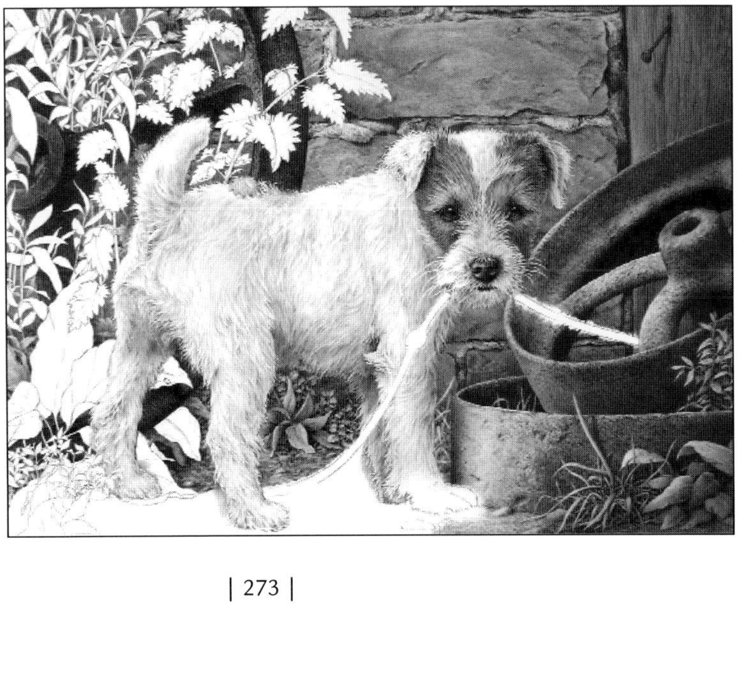

Working out the three-dimensional form of parts of Maisie's body proved to be a problem. Although I took sixty-nine photos of her before her demise, I have only five that contain relatively close detail. In places I've had to resort to drawing no more than my interpretation. No, I'm not going to point them out to you. But I find that if an area that is not fully understood, is drawn with confidence, the viewer never seeks to question its validity - especially if a little prominent detail is included as a distraction. Even if such an area fails at first, it provides a positive step towards success. It's easier to alter and refine a drawn area than it is to worry about its initial rendering.

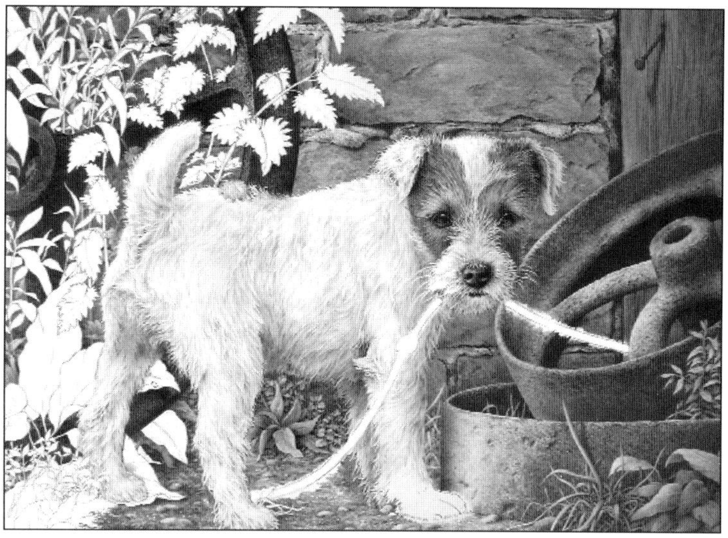

STAGE 12

I've decided to draw the ground next - an area that I prefer to complete in one sitting. I have no ideas in mind at all, and plan to draw spontaneously to see what results.

I established two small sections while I was completing Maisie. They look promising, and suggest three main elements: broken dusty ground, small pebbles and stones, and loose blades of dried grass or straw. I thoroughly enjoy the freedom of drawing these areas, as I have no idea of what they're going to look like until the drawing unfolds beneath my pencil.

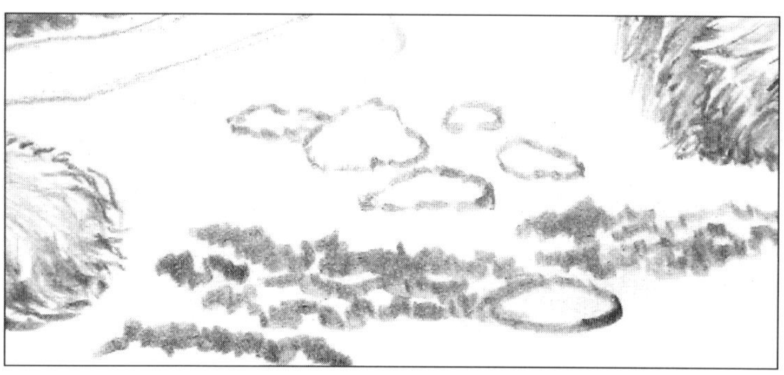

Fig 4

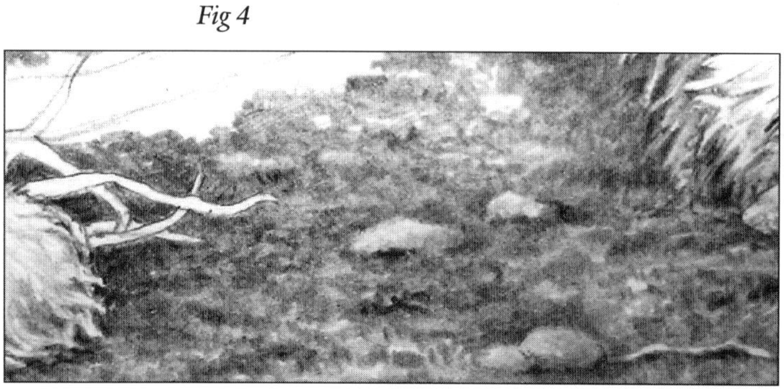

Fig 5

I'm using the flat face of a chisel-pointed HB pencil to make a series of random marks (*fig 4*), varying the weight and direction, and imagining the white spaces created between them as surface highlights. Simply rotating the pencil, and using the edge of the chisel point's face, produces any dark shadows or sharp marks I require. Stones, pebbles, and bits of grass (*fig 5*) are drawn quickly, without breaking the flow, and appear simply because they suggest themselves - to add balance, or additional interest to an area that is beginning to look too uniform. Tonal, unifying layers are added as the drawing progresses, and without pausing for thought.

STAGE 13

Now that I've completed the ground, it's time to begin work on the rope. If I can pitch the tones correctly, it should make

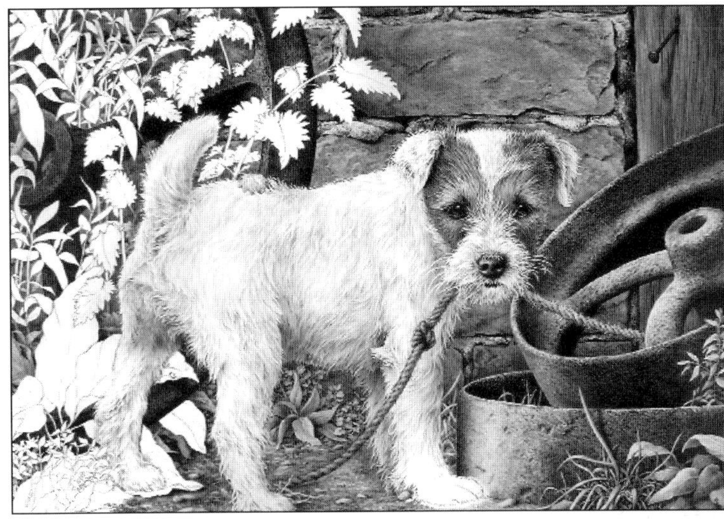

Maisie look whiter, and, by drawing the rope with sharp detail and edges, the contrast with Maisie's coat should make her look softer. Although she is 'broken coated', her puppy hair is still soft to the touch.

The first step is to make sure the fall of the rope forms a natural arc. Then the positions of the twists in the rope are marked, keeping the widths constant. I have a length of old rope in the studio, which I've hung over my drawing board so I can refer to it as I work.

Each twist is individually drawn, incorporating the visual keys that I've extracted from my rope. These include the rounded outlines of each twist, and the longitudinal strands that form them; the shadows between the twists, which are often broken by stray strands; and the random fibres that protrude from each side. Before any of this is actually realised, the guidelines in the immediate work area are faded (*fig 6*), the width of the rope is checked for constancy and, if required, a more accurate guideline is lightly drawn.

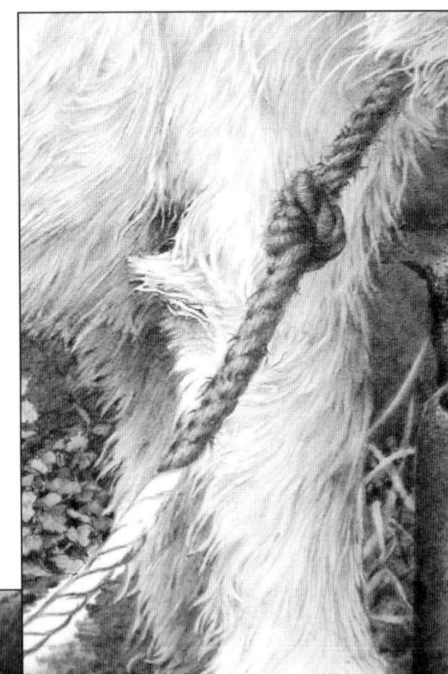

Fig 6

Where the rope crosses Maisie's legs, it is positively drawn but, to her right where it crosses the top wheel (*fig 7*), a mixture of both positive and negative drawing is used. You may recall that I stopped the drawing of the wheel and brickwork short of the rope. This allows me to draw the body of the rope in a positive manner, and then use negative drawing to establish the stray fibres along its edge. Having outlined the fibres, the surrounding background is then completed. I've only lightly toned the fibres on this side of Maisie to assist the eye in detecting the rope at a normal viewing distance.

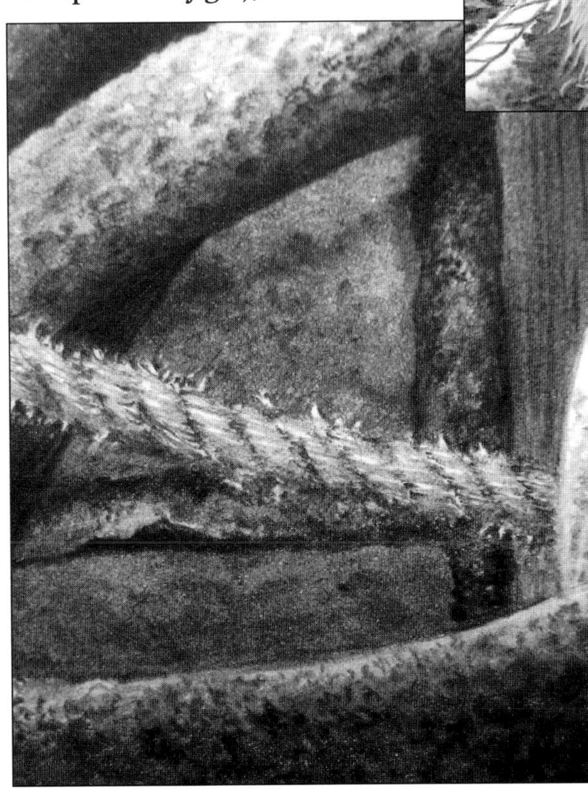

Fig 7

Finally, I'm gradually darkening the rope as it nears the ground. I originally intended the end to be hidden by Maisie's rear paw but it looked contrived. It still disappears at the same point but, as the rope now almost merges with the general tonal value of the ground, its termination no longer attracts any interest.

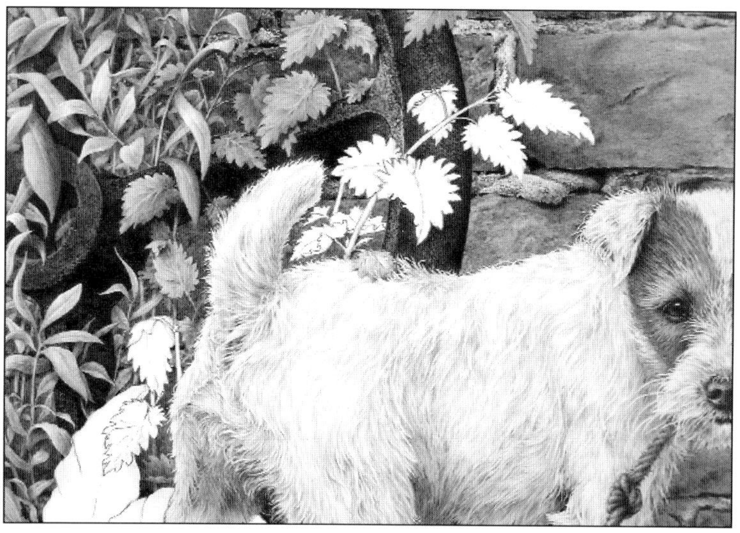

Stage 14

Today, I'm making a start on the main block of foliage. It is my custom in these areas to work everything out as I draw, rather than plan ahead. Each leaf is drawn individually, and, before I begin, thought is given to its three-dimensional shaping and shadows, especially its cast shadows. Often I accept my previous guidelines but, if the shadow of one leaf falls at an unfortunate place on another, I simply reverse the spatial order, by drawing the first leaf beneath, rather than over, the second.

I am not aiming at species accuracy. Indeed, the leaves themselves, at best, only loosely conform to their natural counterparts. Many are simply my own creation. So I'm quite content to draw a rib down the centre of a 'nettle' leaf, even though the rib of a natural leaf divides before reaching the tip. In this case, I want the leaves to appear to be detailed, yet remain as slightly indistinct secondary elements.

When drawing prominent foreground leaves, the vein structure can take a considerable time to accomplish. So, over the years, I've developed a shortcut method. This is a three-stage process, which I will apply to the large Dock leaves behind Maisie. To assist me, I have an actual Dock leaf laid alongside my drawing, from which I can freely interpret the structure. Be aware that this method works with Blu-Tack, and probably not with kneadable or other erasers.

First I very lightly mark the position of the central rib and the main side ribs. Then (*fig 8*) I use a flat-tipped 2B pencil to negatively draw the appearance of a vein structure, completely disregarding the required tonal values of the area, and drawing darker than is required. You must use a soft grade of graphite, and avoid indenting the surface of the paper.

Now, I take my Blu-Tack, pull a pencil-width piece out from the

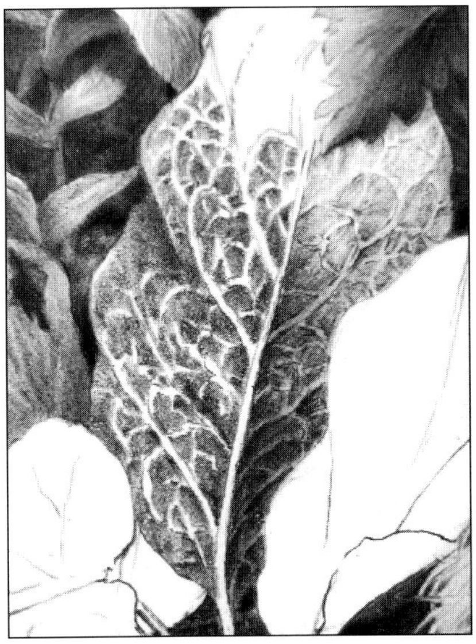

Fig 8

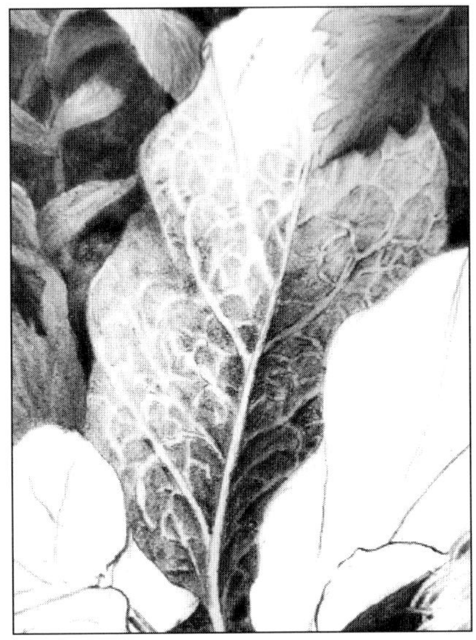

Fig 9

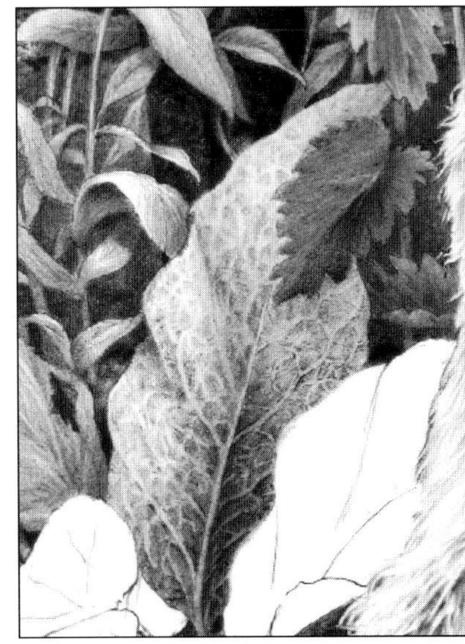

Fig 10

ball, slightly flatten it and then (*fig 9*) dab it over my leaf to remove the 2B until the desired shaping and tones are achieved.

Finally (*fig 10*), after making any adjustments, the whole area is toned down, unified, and shaped further by a layer of 2H, applied with a flat tip.

I've now completed all of the leaves, refined some, and tonally strengthened or weakened others. Where necessary, for increased clarity, I've also adjusted the background tones. In this case portions of the wall have been darkened, as have the shaded areas of the roller ring.

STAGE 15

Only three jobs now remain. First, I complete Maisie's front paw. Although this appeared to be correct in the detailed line drawing, her paw now looks too long, so I've shortened it and added a small pebble to break up the lower arc of the bottom wheel.

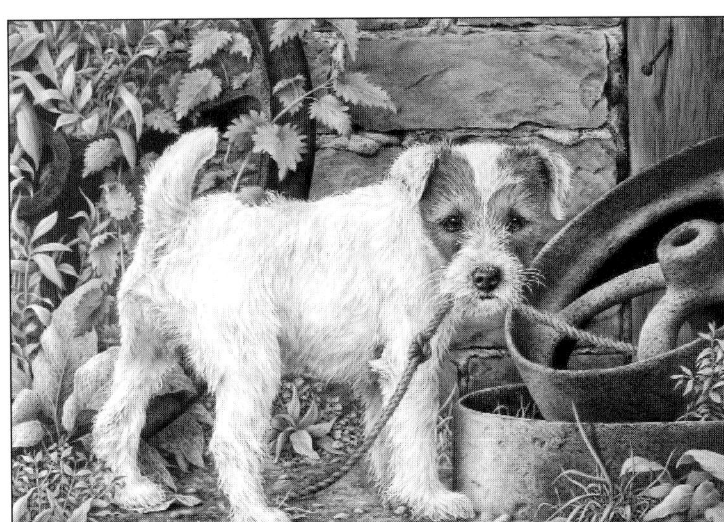

Size: 11" x 8" (28 x 23 cm)
Drawing time: 72 hours 43 minutes

The drawing itself is complete, but I have now to strengthen the darkest tones throughout the drawing. These inevitably suffer some degradation beneath my hand-guard. The missing graphite must be replaced to restore the intended range of contrasts, which also serves to boost the highlights.

Finally a wide margin around the drawing is thoroughly cleaned, first with Blu-tack and then a soft art eraser. I may make a few adjustments in a few days but, for now, the drawing is finished.

I hope you found the process interesting and instructive, and that it might have added to your personal arsenal of methods and techniques. Or leads you to develop your own. I do not, of course, produce every drawing using these same techniques. I still experiment and find new ways of working. To this end, I participate in online drawing groups and forums, where I can learn from others. I thoroughly recommend that you do the same. As an artist, you will always be ceaselessly learning - about techniques, about Nature, and about yourself. The search for knowledge is endless.

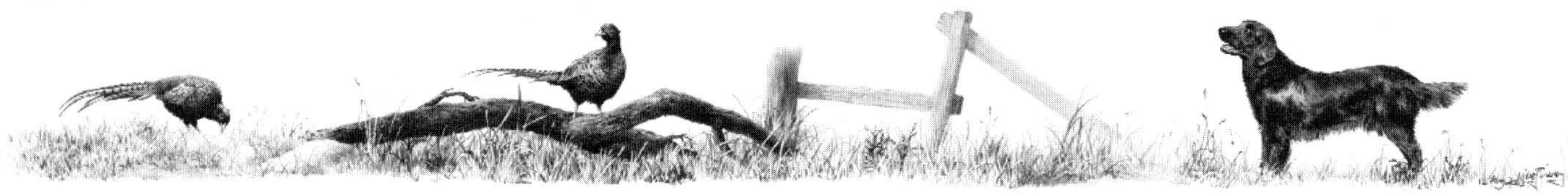

And finally...

This book has been an incredible journey for me. What started off as a vague concept almost 20 years ago has evolved and grown into this book that you hold in your hands.

I progressed from answering queries sent by letter and, more recently, email, to the writing of my online tutorials, which themselves elicited many requests for a more fully-fledged instructional book. With over 25 years of professional knowledge of drawing in graphite pencil stored in my head, this was a book I had to write.

I was astonished by how much I actually knew, and perhaps not as surprised by how much I have still to learn. To remedy the latter, I read, discuss, and just listen - especially to my fellow forum members at ArtPapa.com. There I host my own forum in the company of my fellow moderators; the gifted trompe l'oiel artist J.D. Hillberry, and the site's owner Alexei Antonov, the premier exponent today of oil painting in the old Dutch masters tradition.

I have thoroughly enjoyed every minute of the year that it taken me to write this book, and I have learned so much along the way that my work will never be the same again. I have new horizons to explore. I sincerely hope that your own work will equally benefit. Thank you for sharing this journey with me. Happy drawing!

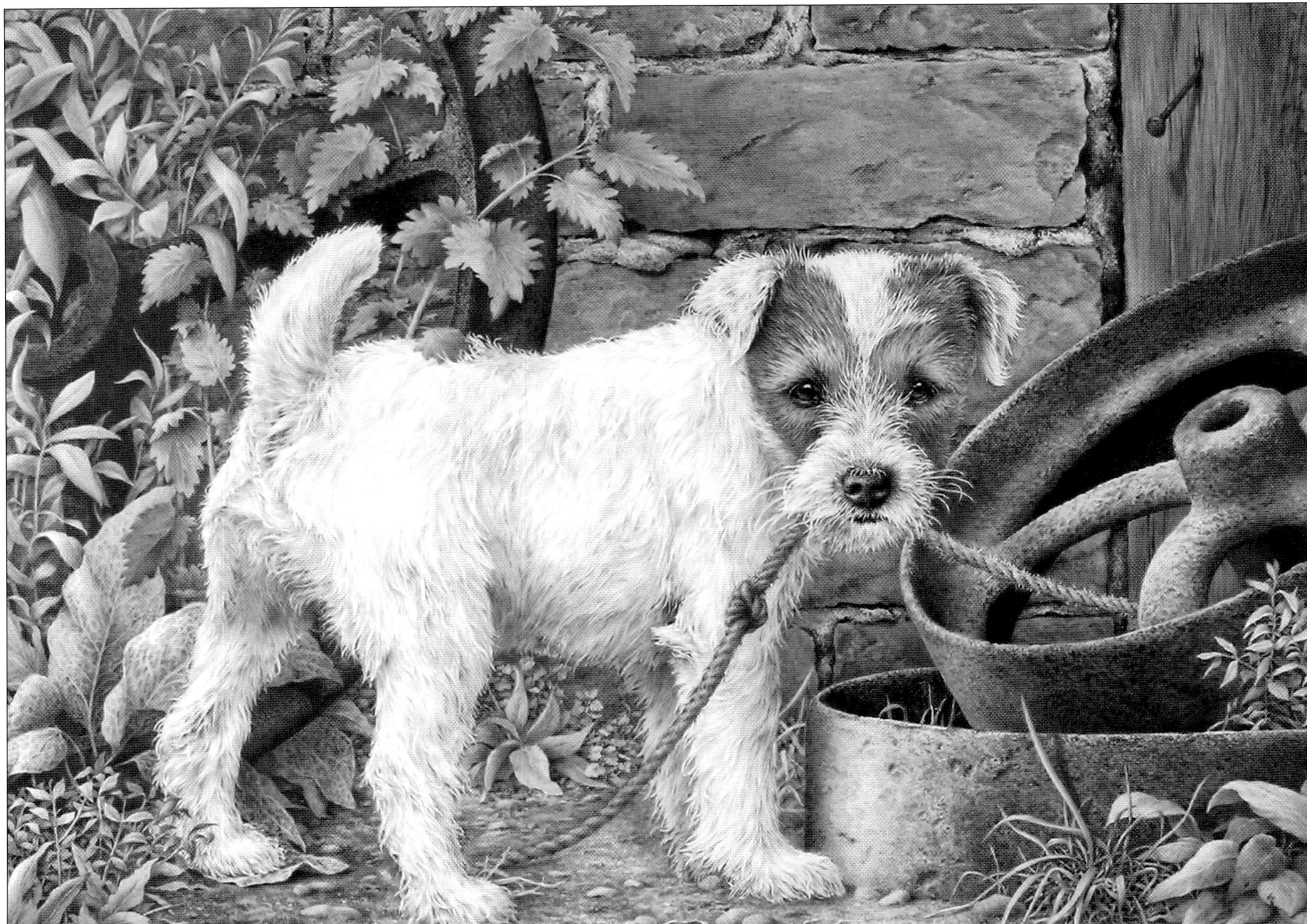

11" x 8" (28 x 20 cm)

'What?'
Limited Edition print of 850 plus 50 Artists Proofs. © Mike Sibley 2005

Index

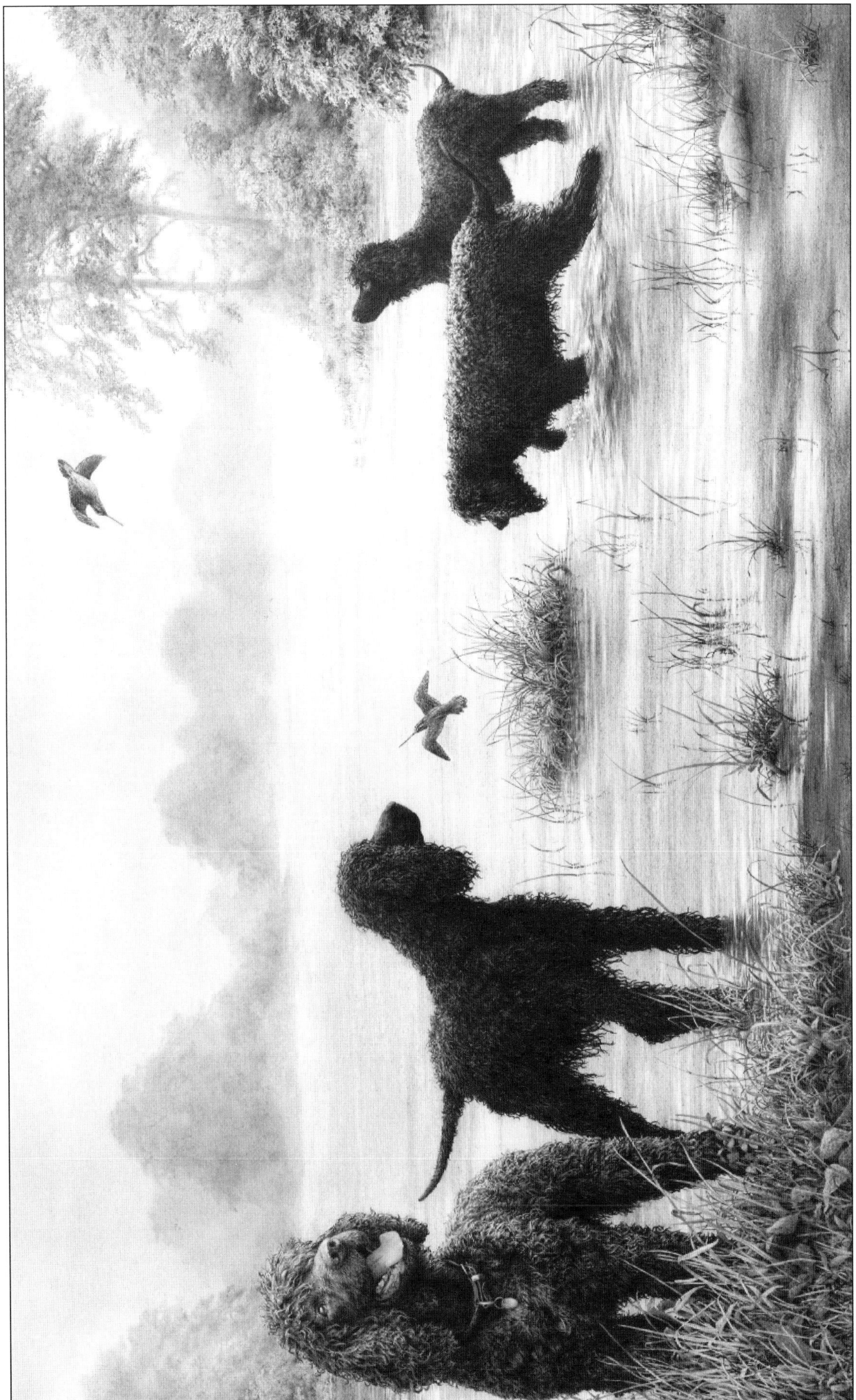

17½" x 11" (45.5 x 28 cm)

'Connemara Encounter' © Mike Sibley, featuring Irish Water Spaniels. A sold out limited edition print of 250.

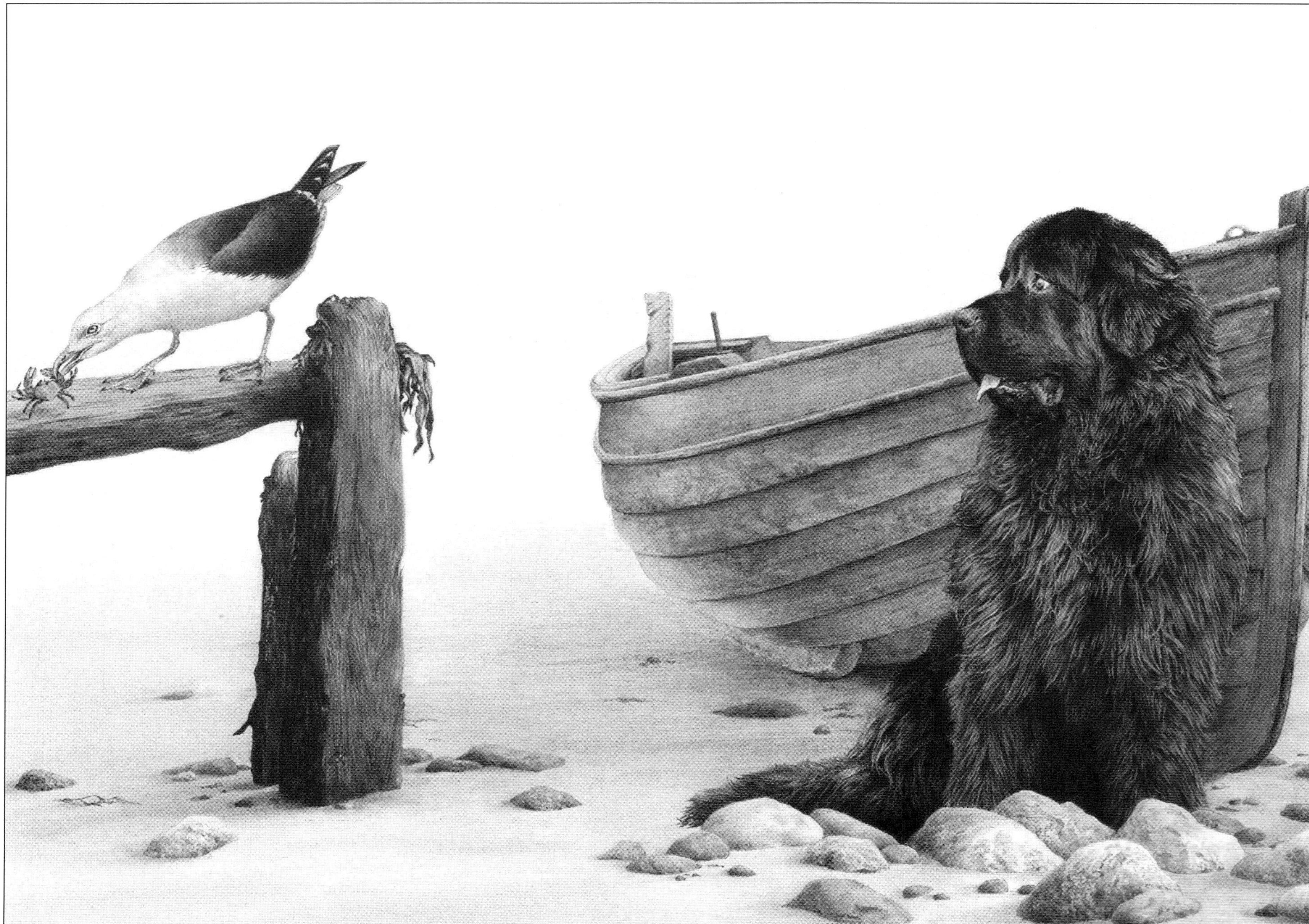

'Just Thinking' © *Mike Sibley. featuring the Newfoundland. A limited edition print of 850 plus 25 artists proofs.*

11" x 8" (28 x 20 cm)

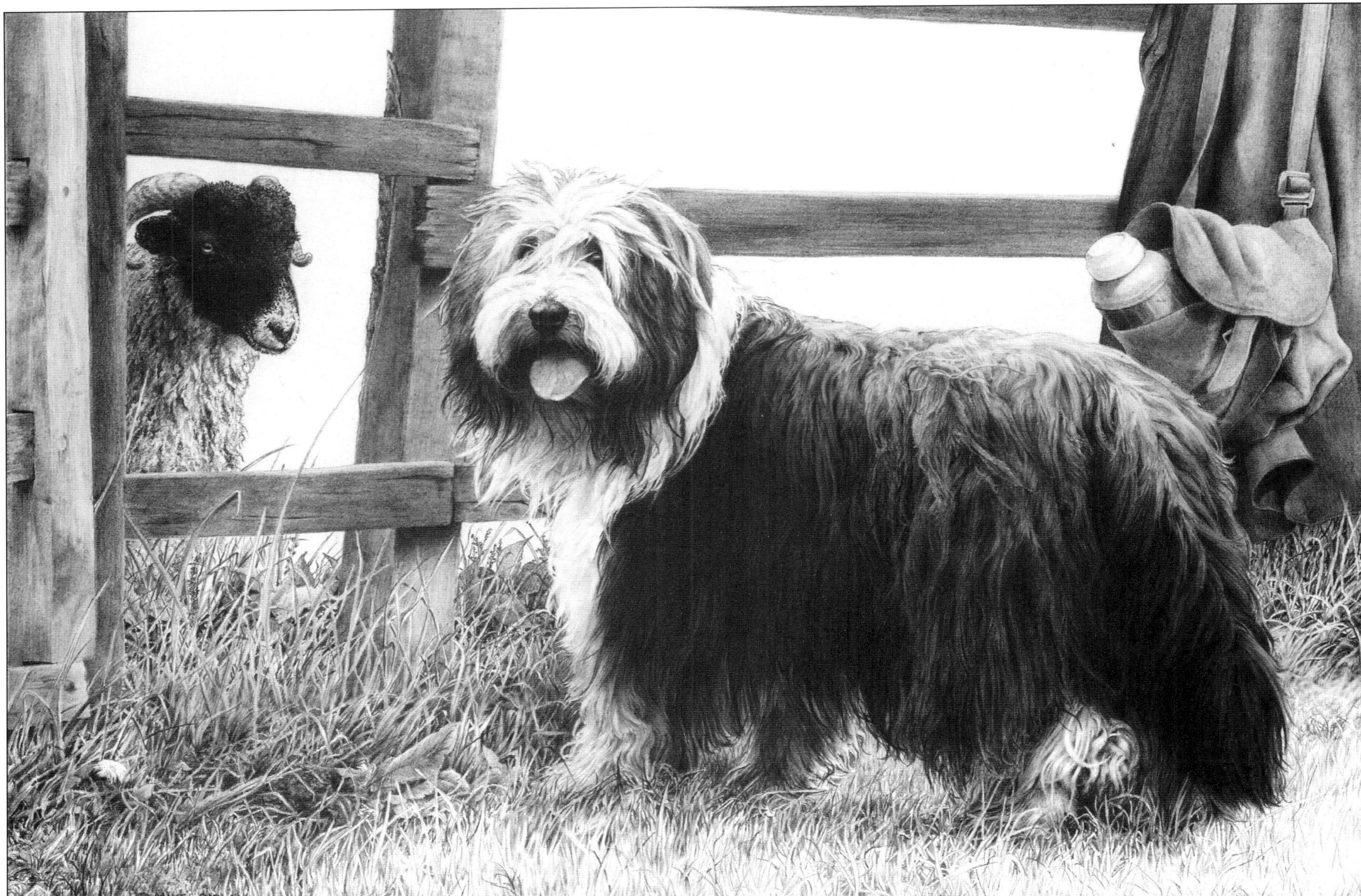

11" x 8" (28 x 20.3 cm)

'I see the sheep are out again.' © *Mike Sibley. featuring the Bearded Collie. A sold out limited edition print of 700 plus 15 artists proofs.*